THE LIBRARY, BOOKS 16–20

DIODORUS SICULUS (Diodorus of Sicily) lived and worked in the first century BCE, spending much of his life in Rome. He entitled his historical work *The Library* because he intended it to be a 'one-stop shop' for historical information, from mythological times until 60 BCE, stopping just short of the Gallic campaigns of Julius Caesar. *The Library* was divided into forty books, of which fifteen survive: 1–5, and 11–20. All that remains of the rest are fragments and summaries. Books 11–20 contain the only continuous narrative from a Greek historian that covers all of the Classical and Early Hellenistic periods, from 480 until 302. The work is divided by years, and for each year that he covered, Diodorus tried to include information from every part of the known world; in fact, however, his focus is particularly on the Greeks.

ROBIN WATERFIELD is a writer, living in Greece. His previous translations for Oxford World's Classics include Plato's *Republic* and five other editions of Plato's dialogues, Aristotle's *Physics* and *The Art of Rhetoric*, Demosthenes' *Selected Speeches*, Herodotus' *Histories*, three volumes of Plutarch's Lives, two editions of Euripides' plays, Xenophon's *The Expedition of Cyrus*, and *The First Philosophers: The Presocratics and the Sophists*.

T0043739

OXFORD WORLD'S CLASSICS

*For over 100 years Oxford World's Classics have brought
readers closer to the world's great literature. Now with over
700 titles—from the 4,000-year-old myths of Mesopotamia to the
twentieth century's greatest novels—the series makes available
lesser-known as well as celebrated writing.*

*The pocket-sized hardbacks of the early years contained
introductions by Virginia Woolf, T. S. Eliot, Graham Greene,
and other literary figures which enriched the experience of reading.
Today the series is recognized for its fine scholarship and
reliability in texts that span world literature, drama and poetry,
religion, philosophy and politics. Each edition includes perceptive
commentary and essential background information to meet the
changing needs of readers.*

OXFORD WORLD'S CLASSICS

═══

DIODORUS OF SICILY

The Library, **Books 16–20**

Philip II, Alexander the Great, and the Successors

═══

Translated, with Introduction and Notes by
ROBIN WATERFIELD

OXFORD
UNIVERSITY PRESS

OXFORD

UNIVERSITY PRESS

Great Clarendon Street, Oxford, OX2 6DP,
United Kingdom

Oxford University Press is a department of the University of Oxford.
It furthers the University's objective of excellence in research, scholarship,
and education by publishing worldwide. Oxford is a registered trade mark of
Oxford University Press in the UK and in certain other countries

© Robin Waterfield 2019

The moral rights of the author have been asserted

First published as an Oxford World's Classics paperback 2019

Impression: 5

Published in the United States of America by Oxford University Press
198 Madison Avenue, New York, NY 10016, United States of America

British Library Cataloguing in Publication Data

Data available

Library of Congress Control Number: 2018968362

ISBN 978-0-19-875988-1

Printed and bound in Great Britain by
Clays Ltd, Elcograf S.p.A.

To the memory of Peter Bruce Waterfield (1924–2018)
and Janice Hope Boyles (1939–2018)

CONTENTS

THE LIBRARY

CONTENTS

PREFACE

THE Greek text taken as the basis for this translation is the Teubner edition: *Diodorus: Bibliotheca Historica*, vols 4 and 5 (both published in 1906), edited by C. Fischer on the basis of original recensions by I. Bekker and L. Dindorf. The relevant volumes of the Loeb Diodorus are also useful: *Diodorus Siculus, Library of History, Books 15.20–16.65* (ed. and trans. C. Sherman, 1952); *Diodorus Siculus, Library of History, Books 16.66–17* (ed. and trans. C. Welles, 1963); *Diodorus Siculus, Library of History, Books 18–19.65* (ed. and trans. R. Geer, 1947); and *Diodorus Siculus, Library of History, Books 19.66–20* (ed. and trans. R. Geer, 1954). Books 16–19, but unfortunately not yet Book 20, have also been published in the Budé series, with facing French translation and excellent introductions and notes: *Diodore de Sicile, Bibliothèque Historique, Livre XVI* (ed. and trans. D. Gaillard-Goukowsky and P. Goukowsky, 2016); *Diodore de Sicile, Bibliothèque Historique, Livre XVII* (ed. and trans. P. Goukowsky, 1976); *Diodore de Sicile, Bibliothèque Historique, Livre XVIII* (ed. and trans. P. Goukowsky, 1978); *Diodore de Sicile, Bibliothèque Historique, Livre XIX* (ed. and trans. F. Bizière, 1975).

All deviations from the Teubner text have been marked in the translation with an obelus, which refers the interested reader to a note in the Textual Notes section at the back of the book (pp. 529–33). An asterisk in the text means that there is a note on that passage in the Explanatory Notes (pp. 425–528).

I would like to thank Richard Berthold, Dexter Hoyos, and Bill Murray for answering questions of detail, and especially Lisa Hau for improving the Introduction. Diodorus is a critical source for much ancient Greek history, and I am very grateful to Oxford University Press, in the person of Luciana O'Flaherty, for allowing a degree of annotation that will help to make this translation more useful to readers both lay and professional. Nevertheless, the notes fall well short of a complete historical commentary. I have restricted them to points that required immediate elucidation, and have listed in the bibliography enough works for an interested reader to gain a sense of the complete history of the period.

INTRODUCTION

A HUGE amount of ancient history can be recovered only with the help of Diodorus of Sicily, who wrote in the first century BCE. He is our main source not just for less mainstream events that other historians ignored, but for central aspects of ancient Greek history: the history of Sicily, the career of Philip II of Macedon, and the struggles of the Successors following the death of Alexander the Great. And he is always to be consulted on every other period as well; he is, for instance, the earliest surviving historian by over a hundred years to cover the career of Alexander the Great. He importantly supplements Thucydides on the fifty years preceding the outbreak of the Peloponnesian War in 431, and often gives different versions of Roman history from the usual historians, such as Livy. Every page of *The Library* contains information that we would not otherwise know, and the loss of much of it is lamentable.

Almost all we know about Diodorus' life is what can be gleaned from *The Library* itself. He was born in Agyrium in Sicily (1.4.4), a prosperous town at the time of his birth, and one of the older Greek settlements in the interior of Sicily, rather than on the coastline. By coincidence, of only two inscriptions that are known to have survived from this town, one is a tomb marker for a 'Diodorus, the son of Apollonius'.[1] Diodorus is not an uncommon name, so we cannot be certain that this (undated) inscription refers to our Diodorus, but it is a curious coincidence.[2]

We cannot be sure of the years of his birth and death, but there are clues in his work that allow us to home in on them. At 16.7.1 he says: 'But eventually, after Caesar had expelled the people of Tauromenium from their homeland, it was made the site of a Roman colony. This happened in my own lifetime.' This colonization probably took place in 36 BCE. Octavian (the 'Caesar' referred to here) held a grudge against Tauromenium, which had refused to surrender to him earlier that year, in the course of his war against Sextus Pompey, and the historian Cassius Dio says that Octavian punished a number of

---

[1] *Inscriptiones Graecae* XIV.588.
[2] The modern town, Agira, boasts a statue of Diodorus in the main square.

Sicilian cities at the end of this campaign (*Roman History* 49.12.5).
That is the latest event mentioned by Diodorus. At 12.26.1 he refers
to the Rostra (public speaker's platform) which stood 'in those days'
in front of the Senate-house in Rome. Since it was removed by Julius
Caesar in 45 BCE, that bit of Book 12 was written after then. Book
37.27 refers to Caesar's refoundation of Corinth in 44, and at 16.70.6
Diodorus refers to the blanket conferral of Roman citizenship on the
Sicilian Greeks, which also happened in that year. He several times
alludes to Julius Caesar's deification, an honour that was first granted
in 48 BCE (1.4.7; 4.19.2–3; 5.21.2; 5.25.4; 32.27.1).

He cannot have started writing earlier than the mid-40s,[3] because
(see below) his original intention was to take the work down to 46 BCE,
choosing this end-point perhaps because Julius Caesar had by then
conquered his internal enemies and pacified Rome's external enemies,
so that for the first time for decades the world seemed to be at peace.
Nevertheless, he began his research much earlier. He was on a research
trip to Egypt during the 180th Olympiad, 60/59–57/6 BCE (1.44.1;
1.83.9; 3.11.3; 3.38.1; 17.52.6). He mentions at 1.83.5–9 that in the
course of this trip he witnessed an Egyptian mob force the death
penalty on a Roman official for his accidental killing of a sacred cat,
despite their fear of Rome and despite the fact that 'King Ptolemy
had not yet been officially recognized as a friend of Rome'. The king
at the time was Ptolemy XI, and his reign was recognized by the
Romans in 59 BCE. At the time of Diodorus' visit, Macedonian rule of
Egypt had lasted for 276 years (1.44.4). Since he dated the Macedonian
takeover of Egypt to 331 (17.49), he is talking about 55—a minor, but
not untypical, lapse in his arithmetic (see e.g. 17.17.4, 19.27.1, 20.2.3).
Presumably, he spent at least some of his time working in the famous
library of Alexandria,[4] or as much of it as an outsider was allowed
into; at any rate, at 3.38.1 he refers to 'royal records' that he consulted
in Alexandria.

---

[3] I place little value on St Jerome's statement in his *Chronology* that Diodorus became
well known in 49 BCE (Abrahamic year 1968). It is late (written around 380 CE), copies an
earlier *Chronology* by Eusebius, and reproduces all Eusebius' errors. Even later is the
tenth-century encyclopedia known as the *Suda*, which states that Diodorus lived 'at the
time of Augustus Caesar and earlier'. Augustus (as Octavian) began to be influential in
the late 40s, so this assertion is vague enough to be reasonably accurate.

[4] The library was badly damaged by fire a few years later, in 48, in the course of one of
Julius Caesar's campaigns on behalf of Cleopatra.

The sentence in 1.44.4 suggests also that at the time of writing, Diodorus was unaware of the end of the Ptolemaic dynasty of Egypt. As far as he was concerned, Macedonian rule of Egypt was still ongoing; if he had known about the fall of the regime in Egypt, he would have mentioned it. Its end came in 30 BCE, when the last Ptolemy, Cleopatra VII (the famous Cleopatra), committed suicide. So he was either unaware of this fact, or did not bother to go back and revise this statement in his first book. Assuming the former option, and given the reference to the colonization of Tauromenium in 36, we can say that the work was published some time between 35 and 30 BCE.

As was commonly the way in the ancient world, however, a certain amount of 'publication' had already taken place. At the beginning of the whole work, as part of the general preface that was written after he had completed the entire work, he mentions the possibility that some of the books that make it up might be 'mutilated' by being pirated or privately copied (1.5.2), and at the very end (40.8) he complains that, indeed, some of his work had got into circulation before the work as a whole had been completed and properly published.[5] In fact, at 1.4.6 he says, oddly, that although the work is complete, it has not yet been published, which raises the possibility that Diodorus himself never published the work, and never got around to revising it before his death; otherwise, he would presumably have removed this statement from the published book. There are a lot of easily correctible mistakes in *The Library*, as we shall see, and the idea that it remained unrevised is an attractive one.[6] Be that as it may, we can say, with some assurance, that Diodorus was researching and writing from the mid-60s to the mid-30s BCE, and this chimes with his own statement (1.4.1) that the work took him thirty years.[7] As a result of all this we might guess that he was born *c*.95 and died *c*.30 BCE.

---

[5] What counted as 'publication' was often a matter of an interested reader arranging for the copying of the work. See e.g. Cicero, *Letters to Atticus* 2.1.2 and 4.13.2. Unauthorized copying was not uncommon: Cicero, *Letters to Atticus* 3.12.2.

[6] See especially Muntz, *Diodorus Siculus*.

[7] To judge by the working methods described by another Greek historian (Cassius Dio, at *Roman History* 72.23.5), Diodorus would have spent about half this time on research (i.e. reading widely in order to narrow down the sources he wanted to use, taking copious notes, and planning the structure of his work), and half on writing it up, an immensely complex process. This fits in with what I have already said, that he cannot have started writing until the mid-40s.

Despite the impoverishment of Agyrium during his lifetime, as chronicled by Cicero in his speeches against Verres, Diodorus must have had sufficient wealth to choose a lengthy career as a writer, and to have undertaken his research trips. He was upper-class enough to mingle in Egypt with high society—priests and ambassadors. It is perhaps not surprising, then, that he not infrequently displays an anti-democratic bias, typical of the wealthy elite of the Greek and Roman worlds (see e.g. 1.74.7; 18.18.8; 18.67.6; 19.1.5; 20.79.3).[8] Some time after these trips, he settled in Rome (as did many other intellectuals at the time), where there were good libraries (1.4.2), and focused on library research.[9]

At 1.4.1 he claims to have visited much of Europe and Asia, but this seems to be an exaggeration. He shows familiarity with places in Sicily, naturally, but seems less certain about even southern Italy, and the trip to Egypt is the only one he mentions. It makes sense to think of him working primarily in the libraries of Sicily and Rome, where he stayed 'for a long time' (1.4.3). But if Rome was important for his research phase, it was less so when he began to put all of his notes into order and write them up; perhaps he left Rome and returned to his native Sicily.

We can infer a few other personal characteristics. His religious morality was conventional, but he believed that the gods were originally culturally important mortals who later became deified (e.g. 1.17.1–2; 1.22.2; 5.67.1).[10] He had a magpie-like attraction for the exotic and unusual. He was a misogynist, as is most clearly revealed by the statement at 12.14.2 that it is better to expose oneself to the perils of sea-travel than to those of a woman, and that therefore for a man to marry twice is sheer lunacy. His praise of the constitutional kingship of ancient Egypt in Book 1 suggests that he might have been a monarchist.

[8] See also 20.93.6–7, where Diodorus seems to express surprise that a democracy could arrive at a good decision.

[9] There were good libraries of Greek texts in Rome because the Romans had systematically plundered Greece during their imperialist takeover. At 1.4.4 Diodorus says that he also had good knowledge of Latin.

[10] Arguably, it is this belief that justifies Diodorus' inclusion of mythological time in his history. If the gods were originally humans, they become part of human history. And Diodorus did not confine the transformation of men into gods only to mythological time; the divinization in Diodorus' own lifetime of Julius Caesar, of which he approved, was, in his view, a contemporary case of the same phenomenon—a great benefactor of mankind becoming a god. In a sense, then, Diodorus was encouraging the future leaders and benefactors among his audience to aspire to immortality.

And, finally, we can safely say that he was hard-working and determined, otherwise he would not have begun or completed his great project.

Diodorus and Rome

The chances are that Diodorus' attitude towards Rome was ambivalent. His sojourn in Rome coincided with a period of unprecedented political turmoil and violence, including the first and second triumvirates, proscriptions, rioting and murder on the streets, and two civil wars. Rome achieves no prominence in his account until well into the third century. At 37.3, he describes the Romans of his time as decadent, corrupted by imperial wealth,[11] and at 32.4–5 and 32.26.2 he contrasts the decency of earlier Romans, which had gained them an empire, with the terror tactics currently employed to maintain the empire.[12] His remarks, therefore, about how empires are lost by unfair treatment of subjects are certainly meant to contain a lesson for his contemporaries in Rome.

In his lifetime, much of his native Sicily was plundered by venial Roman governors and fought over by its warring generals, and Agyrium suffered in particular. While accepting the fact of Roman rule, and even (necessarily) making the unification of the Mediterranean world under Rome a major theme of *The Library*, he avoids the customary effusive praise for Roman might and glory, and his history may well contain a tacit lesson for Rome: that empires fall as well as rise. Diodorus believed in some version of the theory of the succession of empires (see note 29), and may have believed that the Roman empire was not necessarily the last, the final end-point of history, as many of his contemporaries believed or professed to believe. In the first three books of *The Library*, Diodorus focused on the 'barbarian' nations that Rome had not conquered, and there were a lot of them, suggesting another limitation to Roman power.

He has high praise for certain Romans, especially Pompey the Great (38–39.9–10, 38–39.20) and Julius Caesar (especially 32.27.3), but criticizes others (e.g. 38–39.8.1–4; 40.4). There is a similar ambivalence as regards Rome's enemies, who are often portrayed as moral villains, as

---

[11] See also 37.29–30, 34–35.33.4–6.
[12] See also 34–35.25; 36.11.2 for criticism of Rome's imperial administration.

though it were the Romans' duty to subjugate them, but sometimes as men of honour (e.g. Arsaces and Viriathus in Book 33). But Diodorus seems to have thought little of the Romans collectively. He commends them only for their libraries, for their military prowess, and for having driven tyrants out of Sicily (1.4.2–3; 37.1; 19.1.5). Despite his long stay in Rome, he never acquired citizenship,[13] and does not seem to have gained a member of the Roman elite as a patron (otherwise, his name would have been Romanized, as a near contemporary, Diodorus of Lilybaeum in Sicily, became Quintus Lutatius Diodorus). There is no evidence that he belonged to one of the several literary circles that existed in Rome at the time, which was the usual route for a provincial intellectual to gain attention. Diodorus must have interacted with Romans—not least in order to gain access to private libraries—but he does not seem to have been taken up, as many other provincial artists and intellectuals were. He seems to have remained somewhat of an outsider in Rome.

But too much of Diodorus' narrative of Roman history is lost for us to be certain what his attitudes were towards the mistress of the Mediterranean. We can infer what he thought about certain aspects of Roman society at the time—that he approved of Julius Caesar's deification and thought that the Romans might benefit from a properly tempered monarchy—but these do not add up to a comprehensive stance on Rome as a whole. He certainly fell short of being a direct critic of Rome, just as he seems not to have used his writing as a platform for any other political stance, because we would know if he had gone that far. Even without the survival of any of his work, for instance, we know that Timagenes of Alexandria, a later contemporary of Diodorus, used his history-writing to criticize Rome and Augustus. It was expected that historians would use their work to comment on contemporary affairs, yet Diodorus seems largely to have avoided doing so. As far as our evidence goes, given the parlous state of the last twenty books of *The Library*, Diodorus comes across as a muted, apolitical historian. His Sicilian background shows in the proportion of *The Library* that he devotes to Sicilian affairs, but he is not otherwise a spokesman for Sicily, let alone Rome.

---

[13] He had a form of citizenship (Latin rights), along with all other Sicilians, originally awarded by Julius Caesar in 44 (see 16.70.6), but this was revoked by Octavian in 36.

The Library

The title of Diodorus' work is odd, and a novelty (later imitated by others), but he was trying to capture its most important feature—that he intended it to be in itself an entire library, a one-stop shop for information about the history of the known world.[14] As a library, it naturally incorporated the work of many writers. It was, in other words, a compendium of earlier historians' work.

This is important, because it means we should not expect more than Diodorus claims. He was not offering an original work of history, but a compilation. That was what all 'universal' historians offered; given the nature of their task, they had little choice. They selected from their predecessors and compressed the material. They could not carry out original research for the entirety of world history up to their time. In fact, compilation, or reliance on tradition, was the normal working method for all historians who dealt with the remote past, inaccessible to autopsy or interviews with eyewitnesses,[15] and so far from discrediting Diodorus we should commend him for the honesty implicit in his title.

The prefaces Diodorus composed for each book are probably original or largely so, along with other non-narrative material,[16] but a lot of the rest is paraphrase of others' work—shaped by Diodorus, to be sure, but essentially paraphrase. We rarely have extant the exact wording of the sources on which Diodorus drew, but when we do it is clear that he rephrases and abbreviates, rather than coming up with an original, new narrative; facts are taken over from his sources, and even opinions, if they fit in with Diodorus' own opinions.[17] At 31.10, for instance, he takes over more or less entirely from *Histories* 29.21

[14] The original title of the book was certainly *The Library*, but later writers often referred to it as *The Historical Library*, to make its nature clearer.

[15] See Meeus, 'Compilation or Tradition?'.

[16] Such as the few extended speeches, cross-references, citations of poetry (perhaps), further reflections on history-writing, criticisms of other historians, accounts of sights he has personally seen and interviews he has conducted, expressions of personal opinion (e.g. 18.10.4; 20.13.3), methodological asides (e.g. 20.1–2), and progress reports ('Now that I have covered X, I shall go on to Y'). Diodorus generally gives the impression of being an objective historian, but he covertly intrudes into the text in many ways.

[17] Compare e.g. Diodorus 25.2–5 with Polybius 1.65–88; Diodorus 31.15 with Polybius 30.18; Diodorus 31.35 with Polybius 32.15; Diodorus 32.26 with Polybius 38.1–4, 12–13; Diodorus 11.58.4–59 with Ephorus F 191. On the topic in general, see Hornblower, *Hieronymus of Cardia*, 22–32.

Polybius' reflections (by means of a quotation from Demetrius of Phalerum) on the passing of the kingdom of Macedon; Diodorus omits little more than Polybius' claim to autopsy, which of course he could not include. Diodorus was not a mere copyist, as we shall see, but at times he drew heavily on his sources.

The Library occupied forty books, but only fifteen have survived down to our day. The surviving books are 1–5 and 11–20; of the rest only tatters remain. The first six books covered prehistory (history prior to the Trojan War), and the geography and ethnography of the known world, Greek and non-Greek; these first books were organized by geography rather than chronology. The lost Books 7–10 would have whisked us from the Trojan War (the start of which was dated by Diodorus to 1183 BCE) to 481/0. Until the start of datable history with the first Olympiad (776–773), Diodorus structured his work by means of a web made up of generations, supposed synchronicities between events in one part of the world and another, and thalassocracies,[18] but also local counting systems, such as the lists of Spartan, Macedonian, Persian, and Argive kings, and Athenian Archon lists.

Book 11 opens with the year 480/79, by which date Diodorus was employing his familiar combination of three counting systems (Olympiads, Athenian Archons, and Roman consuls), and we then have continuous narrative—the only continuous history in Greek of such a long stretch of time—year by year up until 302, the end of Book 20. Like Books 6–10, Books 21–40 exist only in pitiful fragments, paraphrases, and excerpts, but, even so, what remains of *The Library* constitutes the largest surviving body of work from any ancient Greek historian.[19]

The task Diodorus set himself—an 'immense task' (1.3.6)[20] —was to compile a universal history, a history of the entirety of the known

[18] The Greeks believed that thalassocracy—control of the sea—passed periodically from one power to the other, much as land-based empires did.

[19] Diodorus himself saw his work as falling into three parts (1.4.6): the first six books contained 'the events and myths of the time before the Trojan War'; Books 7–17 constituted 'a general history of events from the Trojan War to the death of Alexander'; and then Books 18–40 contained 'all the remaining events down to the start of the Romans' war against the Gauls'.

[20] At 1.2.4 he compares the task to Heracles' famous labours (as other universal historians did too), and at 1.1.2 he compares himself to Odysseus, the other troubled hero of mythological times.

world from Creation down to his own day—which turned out to be 59 BCE, the year of Julius Caesar's first consulship and the start of his Gallic campaign. As far as we can tell from the remains of Book 40, the final book, he did indeed end at the year 60/59. The waters are muddied, however, since he says three times that he will cover Caesar's Gallic campaigns, and especially his conquest of the British Isles (3.38.2; 5.21.2; 5.22.1),[21] which took place after 59, and he also says at 1.5.1 that his work will end 730 years after the first Olympiad, which should be 46 BCE.

Probably, especially seeing that all these passages occur in early books, his original intention was to take his history down to 46,[22] thus including the Gallic campaigns, but at some point he changed his mind and effectively eliminated Caesar from his work (but did not get around to deleting from the text the statements promising a later stopping point). He may have thought that Caesar, who is mentioned a number of times in glowing terms, as we have seen, deserved a history of his own. In these turbulent times, he may have considered it dangerous (especially for a wealthy provincial) to write about contemporary events; in the surviving books, he mentions Octavian, the future emperor Augustus, who was at the heart of the violent politics of Rome in the 30s, only once, and that is a negative reference (16.7.1). His intention to end at 46 may have been derailed by Caesar's assassination in 44, which made the world peace of 46 seem less of an ending than it had seemed before. For whatever reasons, faced with the choice of either extending or shortening his work, to find a more suitable end-point, he chose to shorten it to 60/59, which, with the dominance of the First Triumvirate, was effectively the last year of the Republic.[23]

[21] He was attracted in particular to Caesar's campaigns in Britain, because they enhanced the universality of his work; it is only in his own lifetime, he says (3.38.2–3), that it has become possible to include Britain in a history.

[22] And probably in forty-two books. See C. Rubincam, 'How Many Books did Diodorus Siculus Originally Intend to Write?', *Classical Quarterly* 48 (1998), 229–33. If Rubincam is right that Diodorus saw *The Library* as being made up of sets of six books (with each set perhaps being publishable separately), then he spoiled this arrangement by deciding to eliminate the last two books. He must have had a good reason for doing so, and this makes the idea that he was too afraid to write about contemporary events a distinct possibility.

[23] Hence the year 60 was chosen as the start of his history of the downfall of the Republic by a somewhat later Augustan writer, Gaius Asinius Pollio.

Diodorus wanted his work to be useful, as we shall see. But useful to whom? To Everyman—because everyone can be influenced to be a better person (1.1.5) and many people enjoy reading history (1.3.6)[24]—but primarily to future leaders, who were the ones whose actions were writ large on the pages of history for all to see (and therefore imitate or avoid), and who were the ones who, if improved by the reading of history, would themselves become paradigms for yet further generations. Given current geopolitics, however, future leaders were bound to be Roman; most members of the Roman elite were able to read Greek, and since Diodorus quite often uses Roman history as a point of reference or comparison, he was certainly assuming a Roman readership.[25] His very choice of Roman consuls as one of his year-counting systems points in the same direction. On the other hand, since at 34–35.33 he explains what it takes for a Roman general to be acclaimed *imperator*, something which elite Romans already knew, and since he wrote in Greek, he was also assuming a Greek-reading audience. Diodorus was hoping to attract a very wide readership for *The Library*.

A Universal History

Diodorus' intention was not just to write a universal history, one that covered all the deeds of Greeks and non-Greeks alike from the beginning of time, but to improve on his predecessors' attempts to do so. At 1.3.2–3, he says that, of those who had undertaken to write universal histories, some had failed from a geographical perspective and others from a chronological perspective. That is, some had failed to incorporate the deeds of easterners (he was perhaps thinking of Polybius, among others), others—such as Ephorus (4.1.2–3)—had failed to incorporate the earliest myths and legends, and yet others had started later or stopped earlier than they might or should have. And it is true that universal historians earlier than Diodorus had tended to start their histories where some predecessor had finished (as Posidonius of Apamea carried on where Polybius left off), without bothering to start all over again at the beginning, and, for obvious

---

[24] Diodorus' statement is borne out by the contemporary assertion by Cicero that even 'members of the lower classes' enjoyed reading history (*On Moral Ends* 5.52).

[25] In our books: at 16.7.1 he gratuitously mentions the Roman colonization of Tauromenium; and at 19.35.5 he identifies Pyrrhus of Epirus by calling him 'the man who later fought the Romans'.

reasons, had avoided the mythological period. None of them, therefore, was a universal historian, strictly speaking.[26]

Moreover, in addition to improving on his predecessors' scope, Diodorus planned to bring the whole work to completion in forty books (papyrus rolls, much shorter than a 'book' in our terms). Diodorus knew he would have to compress events and miss out a lot, but he thought that the usefulness of his work would be enhanced by brevity. Since universal histories are the most useful kind, and since even those who professed to have written universal histories failed to do so, Diodorus claimed to have written the only truly useful history book. A competitive spirit, the desire to improve on one's peers and to be known for doing so, always prevailed among writers in all genres of Greek literature.

To be fair to his predecessors, we should note that Diodorus was in part the right person in the right place at the right time. Many of his predecessors lived before the campaigns of Alexander had opened up the non-Greek world and made a global perspective and the history of non-Greek peoples more feasible; long contact with the Persians in earlier centuries had gone some way towards informing the Greeks of eastern peoples and places, but Alexander's conquest vastly accelerated the process.

Then again, the unification of Mediterranean history under the Roman empire also made it easier for Diodorus to attempt a universal history. He was contemporary with Pompey the Great's conquest of Spain, pacification of Asia Minor, and incorporation of much of the former Seleucid empire under Rome in the 70s and 60s, and it may well have been Pompey's (and then Caesar's) campaigns that inspired him to write a universal history; at 40.4 he preserves a boastful inscription of Pompey's, listing the astonishing geographical extent of his victories. It could only have been such campaigns that allowed him to write (1.4.3) that Rome's power extended to the limits of the known world.

In short, the concept of universal history dovetailed perfectly with Roman aspirations at the time. There was even a coin, issued in the mid-70s, with the Roman people personified on the obverse, and on the reverse a globe flanked by a sceptre and a rudder, signifying Roman dominion of the world. Only a few decades later than Diodorus, the historians Pompeius Trogus and Nicolaus of Damascus composed

---

[26] Compare Polybius' sneering criticism of earlier attempts at universal history, at *Histories* 5.33.

universal histories, and Strabo tried to cover the whole world in his *Geography*.[27] Roman imperialism was arguably a catalyst of global histories and encyclopedic literature.

This innovative idea of Diodorus', to attempt a truly comprehensive world history, including the age of myth, and the relative brevity and accessibility of his work, guaranteed it a long after-life. Not only was it immediately popular (otherwise it would not have been pirated), but it was read and referred to by many later writers, and at some point, as we can tell from a Byzantine summary, someone even chose to extend it and take it down to the death of the emperor Augustus.[28]

Inevitably, it became more popular as the decades rolled by and the works on which Diodorus had based his history became harder to find, or even lost. In fact, the popularity of *The Library* in Byzantine times probably contributed to the process of the extinction of the earlier historians. Diodorus' single compendium was preferred to the many originals, and as a result there was no demand for scribes to reproduce the work of the latter. Then Christian writers came to dominate the West, and they liked Diodorus' moral streak, as well as his linear chronology, which they could adapt for their own purposes. Eusebius, for instance, the bishop of Caesarea in the early fourth century, whose lost *Chronicle* was intended to show that the march of historical events revealed God's plan for the salvation of the world, had nothing but the highest praise for Diodorus, despite the fact that he was a pagan, calling him 'a most distinguished man'.[29]

However, it has to be said that we are not given the universal history we were promised (at e.g. 1.3; 19.1.10). As the books translated in this volume attest (and despite Diodorus' choice to make Roman consuls one of his three chronographic indicators), Roman history was often relegated to a hasty paragraph or two at the end of a year, containing little or nothing more than the kind of sketchy information Diodorus

[27] Trogus' original is lost, but at least we have the epitome put together by Justin in the second or third century CE. Nicolaus' work occupied an incredible 144 books, Strabo's 47, and Trogus' 44. Trogus was the only one of these historians to write in Latin rather than Greek.

[28] Photius, *Library*, codex 244.

[29] *Preparation for the Gospel* 1.6.9. Christian writers were influenced by the theory of the four monarchies, as found in the Old Testament Book of Daniel. The idea was that there would be a succession of kingdoms on earth, followed by the kingdom of heaven. Daniel spoke of four kingdoms—Babylonia, Media, Persia, and Alexander and his Successors—but later writers such as Pompeius Trogus and Dionysius of Halicarnassus naturally added a fifth. For them, a typical sequence of empires went: Assyria, Media, Persia, Macedon, Rome.

found in an annalistic source; and there is no Roman history at all in Books 17 and 18. He could have done better, since a basic annalistic framework of the history of the Early Republic had been laid down by Quintus Fabius Pictor, a Roman historian writing in Greek, towards the end of the third century, and Diodorus was aware of his work (7.5.4). His treatment of Rome became more thorough in later books, as it had to, since Rome came to dominate the Mediterranean, but otherwise it is inadequate. The difficulty of researching even more far-flung places such as the kingdoms of Bosporus or Bithynia may excuse the paucity of information we receive about them. *The Library* ends up more a history of the Greeks than a thoroughly universal history, but, even so, there are more than a few years when we are given no history of the Greek mainland.

The basic problem—apart from the fundamental impossibility of 'giving a full account of all the events which have been handed down to memory and occurred in the known regions of the inhabited world' (1.9.1)—seems to be that Diodorus found it easy to get distracted. Book 17, for instance, is a good account of the career of Alexander the Great (though with more thorough coverage of the earlier stages than the later), but Diodorus has allowed his focus on Alexander to push out events in the central Mediterranean altogether, and much Greek history as well, unless it was relevant to Alexander. Book 17 is a more unified product than any of the other books—it forms a kind of chronologically organized monograph about Alexander's reign—and it is therefore easier to read, but it is not universal history. The same notion of Diodorus' distractibility can also account for a certain patchiness of presentation: whereas Books 18 and 19 are a good blend of material from East and West, by Book 20 the affairs of the western Greeks in Diodorus' native Sicily have squeezed out quite a bit of material about the doings of the Successors in the eastern Mediterranean. Diodorus was forced to select his material and omit a great deal, but that in itself undermines his grandiose claim to geographical as well as temporal universality.

The Character of The Library

Above all, Diodorus wanted his work to be useful. This was a standard claim of Greek historians, dating back as far as Thucydides.[30]

---

[30] *History* 1.22.4, 2.48.3. But for Diodorus (not for Thucydides) the usefulness of history was its ability to teach moral lessons.

Historiography was always a form of teaching. Diodorus felt that, if he could encompass all world history within a reasonable number of books, and if he could write it all down simply and clearly, he would have written a useful book, because readers would not have to go to multiple sources, each no more than a monograph, and because he would provide a clear, connected, sequential narrative (1.3.6–8; 16.1.1–2). This clarity and ease of reference would enable readers to profit from the work more easily than they would by reading other historians. One can even say that Diodorus' desire to be clear dictated the form of the work, because he felt that clarity would be enhanced by a year-by-year account (1.3.2, 1.3.8), with events expounded 'topically' (17.1.2)—that is, with the account of events in one part of the world completed before moving on to the next part of the world. He slightly qualifies this at 20.43.7, pointing out that a year-by-year account breaks up what would otherwise be a sequential narrative of, say, a single war into as many segments as there were years of warfare; but he still clearly prefers his system as the one that is most likely to be helpful to readers. Indeed, it is hard to think of an organizational system which would more readily have allowed Diodorus to display so much disparate information in an accessible fashion.

The reason history is a brilliant teacher, to Diodorus' mind, is that one can read about the successes and failures of others, and learn from them, without having to suffer oneself (1.1.1–2; 1.1.4–5).[31] The characters who appear on the historical stage are actors within their particular dramas, but they are also moral examples for future generations to emulate or avoid:

I shall mention certain men as exemplars, both because they deserve my praise and for the good it does society, so that bad men may be deterred from wicked impulses by the denunciations of history, and good men may be inspired by the praise conferred by history's everlasting glory to aspire to high standards of conduct. (37.4; see also 15.1.1)

The mere recording by a historian of good and bad deeds deters people from wickedness (1.1.5). It follows (1.3) that the more complete a history is—that is, the more examples it offers of success and failure and of good and bad deeds—the more its educational value is enhanced, because among so many examples there will be those that

---

[31] Polybius makes the same point at *Histories* 1.35.

are useful for every situation in which an individual might find himself. Hence Diodorus' desire to be complete.

The particular usefulness imparted by a knowledge of history, and delivered by those who write history, is moral guidance (1.1.5; 1.2.1–3).[32] For Diodorus, as for many of his peers, moralizing was one of the central roles of history-writing. Perhaps it was even the central role. He nowhere says that the purpose of history-writing is to preserve knowledge of past events for their own sake; the point is to guide future generations into the paths of righteousness and to alleviate distress. As he says at 18.59.6: 'In a world of inconstancy and change history has the power to remedy both the arrogance of the fortunate and the misery of the unfortunate.' At 1.2.2 we are told that history is the 'prophetess of truth' and 'the matrix of education', with the power 'to endow men's characters with noble integrity'.[33] These are hifalutin assertions, but they are almost conventional clichés in the context of contemporary historiography. They tell us little about Diodorus himself, because all of his peers felt the same.

History has these powers by itself, but sometimes the historian has to bring out the moral lesson; that is, even if sometimes the moral lesson is merely embedded within the narrative, at other times the historian pauses for explicit comment in a digression or aside. Like his predecessors, Diodorus was therefore inclined to select the episodes he recounted, and to spin his account of them, to bring out the lessons. He gives his readers the facts as he has been able to uncover them, but he tends to linger over those which contained useful moral lessons. In our books, for instance, more space is allotted to the exploits of Thibron than one might have expected (18.19–21) because of the great reversal of fortune he encountered, and the same goes for the adventures of the imprisoned generals (19.16).

A good example of the embedding of morally evaluative terminology within the text is 19.11.4–7, where we are left in no doubt how we are supposed to think of Olympias and Eurydice; at other times, Diodorus

[32] This was a commonplace and an integral element of Greek historiography, especially in the Hellenistic period, but stretching right back to Herodotus in the fifth century. One may of course doubt that reading a work of history could substantially alter one's behaviour, but that is what all the Greek historians believed, or pretended to believe. The idea recurs so often in the extant portions of *The Library* that it is safe to say that it was the chief thematic glue of the work.

[33] It is typical of the Greek historians to exaggerate the importance of what they were doing, because it made them seem more important.

might simply show that good men prosper (e.g. Philip II at 16.1.4 and 16.64.3; Ptolemy at 18.28.4–6), while bad men suffer (e.g. Tennes at 16.45.4). But explicit guidance by the historian is not uncommon. At 11.3.1, for instance, Diodorus chooses to name the Greeks who fought on the side of the Persians in 480, 'in the hope that the shame here visited upon them may, by the sheer force of its obloquy, deter any future traitors to the cause of common freedom' (trans. Green). An example from Books 16–20 occurs at 17.38.4–6, where Diodorus tells us in moral terms how to assess one of Alexander's acts. These are only a few examples, but any reader of *The Library* will be struck by how often Diodorus leaves her in no doubt about how he expects her to judge historical events and people.

Diodorus was a traditional moralist. The virtues he valued were courage, piety, justice, lawfulness, kindness, clemency, moderation, and humility in the face of success (this last virtue is particularly stressed). He subscribed to the belief that the gods would punish wrongdoing and reward good people. Again, it was up to the historian to bring this out where appropriate. The most sustained case is his account of the fate of the Phocians who had committed sacrilege by stealing the sacred treasures of Delphi (16.61–4). At 11.46.4, the arrogant behaviour of the Spartan regent Pausanias after the end of the Persian Wars was responsible, according to Diodorus, not only for Pausanias' own downfall, but for damaging Sparta as a whole, just as at 13.103.1–2 a miscarriage of justice in Athens is said to be responsible for their later falling under a savage oligarchy. Divine punishment often fits the crime perfectly, by mirroring it, and there are good examples of this in our books: 16.64.2–3; 19.103.4–5; 20.65.2; 20.70; 20.101.2–3. Examples from *The Library* could easily be multiplied, but the point is clear: thanks to the gods, individuals get what they deserve.

However, a slight tension arises in this theoretical framework because of Diodorus' frequent reference to the power Fortune has over human lives, and her fickleness. Demonstration of the power of Fortune was certainly one of the principles according to which Diodorus selected or spun his material, and as a result the gods become somewhat downplayed as agents capable of affecting human lives.

How could anyone with a sense of the inconstancy of human life fail to be astounded by the way luck ebbs and flows one way and then the other? Or how could he put such trust in the power he wields at a time of good fortune that he would give himself airs as though he were not subject to human frailty? Every person's life seems to be controlled by some divine helms-man, who makes it subject to cycles of alternating good and evil for ever. What is strange, then, is not that unexpected things happen, but that not everything that happens is unexpected. (18.59.5–6)

At 20.30.1, in one of his generalized statements about Fortune, Diodorus says: 'It would not be out of place to note here the incon-stancy of Fortune and the peculiar way in which men's achievements turn out contrary to expectations.' Logically, this means not just that bad men will be brought low, but even that good men could be brought low, or that (as happened to the king of Tyre at 17.47) a man might be raised up, or dashed down, without having done much to deserve such a fate in moral terms. Fortune is radically fickle; even 'hopeless cases' (20.70.2) can change under her influence. If so, then, presum-ably, bad men might prosper. But, if Fortune is so powerful, what happens to divine justice, which is supposed to ensure that bad men do not prosper?

It seems to me that Diodorus' thinking on this is not perfectly con-sistent. When he attributes something to Fortune, it is often no more than a way to say that a person met with bad or good luck—with fac-tors beyond his or her control. Where Fortune is more thoroughly anthropomorphized, so that she can be proactive, she rarely subverts the justice of the divine order, and in fact 'Fortune' is often little more than a way to say 'the divine' or 'the gods'. At 19.11.6–7, for instance, it is Fortune who sees that Olympias is punished as she deserved. But there are occasional cases where Fortune seems to act against divine justice. At 17.101.2 she lays low a good man who was not deserving of such treatment. At 17.35.7 she is responsible for the rape of innocent women. At 17.46.2 it is suggested that Fortune might be envious of a man's success and therefore see to his downfall—perhaps as she did Memnon at 17.29.4. So Diodorus has not fully made up his mind whether Fortune is a colleague of the gods or such an independent agent that she can even go against their wishes.

Apart from utility, a second and secondary intention of Diodorus was to entertain his readers. This is a subsidiary purpose because it is only meant to make the narrative more palatable and therefore more easy to understand and profit from. Entertainment comes in many forms in the pages of The Library—though there are many who might say that he should have embellished his plain narrative even more. Typical forms of entertainment are ethnographic asides, curiosities, and portents (e.g. 16.26; 17.7.5–7; 17.41.7; 17.105.1–5; 17.107; 17.116; 19.33.2–4; 19.98–9; 20.14.6; 20.58.2–5); the description of awesome structures (17.115; 18.26–7; 20.91.2–8); and the vivid and even sensational presentation of scenes (e.g. 17.13; 17.35.5–7; 17.58.5; 17.69.2–9; 17.92; 18.31.2–5; 20.51.3–4; 20.72.2–5), for which he sometimes even underlines the vividness by saying 'the scene before a spectator's eyes would have been . . .' (17.25.4; 17.34.1; 19.7.2–4). Invariably, in these cases, the reader's responses are guided by Diodorus, when, for instance, he allows the pathos of a scene to deliver the moral message. He relishes surprises, reversals, and unusual events in themselves, but also because they show the fickleness of Fortune and therefore suggest the need to be humble in the face of success (e.g. 17.5.6; 17.28; 17.46.6–47; 17.86.3–6; 17.100–1; 17.103.7–8; 20.13.3–4; 20.25.4).[34]

Many of these passages are examples of good writing. Analysis of the text has shown that the style in which it is written is pretty uniform throughout, and that it is the late Greek one would expect, rather than the earlier Greek used by his sources.[35] He was clearly rewriting as he paraphrased, and this means that we can attribute the good and bad points of style in the text to Diodorus himself. As one reads him, one gets the impression that he was not a confident writer, but he is always clear enough, and frequently very readable. The ninth-century Ecumenical Patriarch of Constantinople, Photius, summed up his style well: 'His style is clear, unadorned, and particularly suitable for history. He overuses neither Atticisms nor archaisms, but neither does he descend to the level of everyday language; he finds a happy medium between the two.'[36]

It is easy to detect his faults as a writer—a flatness of tone, repeated formulaic phrases, the relentless emphasis on warfare—but he is not uniformly dull or even plain. He knows, for instance, how to use short bursts of direct speech for dramatic effect (16.43.4; 16.87.2; 17.54.4–5; 17.66.5; 18.60.6; 19.97.3–5), although he largely eschewed the extended speeches beloved by most other historians (20.1–2.2). He throws in

---

[34] There are noticeably more of all these flourishes in Book 17 than in the other books, where presumably Diodorus' sources were less inclined to stress drama.

[35] J. Palm, *Über Sprache und Stil des Diodors von Sizilien* (Lund: Gleerup, 1955). For instance, where Ephorus uses *symprattein* for military cooperation (*FGrH* 70, F 186), Diodorus has the later *koinopragein*.

[36] Photius, *Library*, codex 70.

the occasional rhetorical question (e.g. 16.9.2; 18.59.5). His battle scenes—and battles loom large in *The Library*—are often thrilling, if somewhat formulaic: battles are invariably 'tough' or 'hard-fought' or 'fierce'; the outcome often hangs in the balance for a while, before Fortune, often using a single individual as her instrument, decides the issue. He was very aware that a work of literature should have what he calls 'proportion', by which he seems to mean that the length of a piece of narrative should reflect the importance of the events being narrated, and that a writer should not indulge in long set pieces (in our books, see the preface to Book 20, but then e.g. 1.9.4, 1.29.6, 1.41.10, 4.5.2, and 4.5.4). He likes neat, moralizing conclusions, such as 'Persepolis had exceeded all other cities in prosperity, and now to the same degree it exceeded them all in misery' (17.70.6), or 'Iniquitous behaviour may profit rulers because they can get away with it, but for ordinary people, their subjects, it generally leads to disaster' (19.48.4), or 'For the common people never like it when things stay the same, and every group that is not dominant finds change attractive' (19.81.3). *The Library* is not a difficult read, and its plainness is arguably not a fault in a historian.

Diodorus and His Sources[37]

It used to be the fashion to say that for long stretches of his work, even whole books, Diodorus followed only a single source and used him rather uncritically (so that much of Books 11–15, for instance, might be considered a lengthy 'fragment' of Ephorus of Cyme). This rather uncharitable view has given way in recent decades to the idea that, for any stretch of his work, Diodorus relied on a variety of sources (though often one main source) and created a patchwork narrative out of them, exercising a degree of originality and creativity in deciding what to include or exclude, in shaping the material, and in imposing his moral concerns on it. The early books are better examples of this than those translated in this volume, because in the early books Diodorus was faced with a vast mass of unorganized material from a great many sources, and had to work harder to impose order on it.

---

[37] For Diodorus' probable and possible sources for Books 16–20 in particular, see Appendix 1, pp. 537–42.

Diodorus' words at 3.11.2 are very telling: he distinguishes Agatharchides of Cnidus, Artemidorus of Ephesus, and other unnamed writers as more accurate than others who, he says, relied on false reports or even made things up themselves. This shows not only that he could approach his sources critically, but also that he relied on more than one source—here Agatharchides, Artemidorus, and the unnamed others. At 1.56.6 he says that he will record the different views of historians 'so that readers may judge the truth with an open mind'. At 20.79.5 and 20.89.5, it is clear that he has consulted Timaeus of Tauromenium along with several other sources for Sicilian history.[38] At 2.32 he goes so far as to give us two different accounts of an episode, each from a different historian he had consulted. He often refers to what 'some [unnamed] historians say' (e.g. 16.56.7; 17.23.1; 17.65.5; 17.73.4; 17.75.3; 17.117.5; 20.13.1), and it would be sheer lack of charity to think that he took even such phrases over unthinkingly from his sources.

Sometimes the joins between different sources are visible, thanks to near contradictions. There are plenty of examples of this in the books translated in this volume. The portrait of Philip II in Book 16 is invariably highly positive, for instance, but once in a while, when he is following another source (perhaps Theopompus of Chios), a different picture emerges (e.g. 16.87.1). The most telling case is at 16.54.4, where we are lucky enough to have the alternate source on which Diodorus was drawing—a famous speech by Demosthenes—and we can see how Diodorus has been influenced by Demosthenes to give a less than positive account of Philip, as a corrupter of men's morals, whereas otherwise one of the threads of the book is how Philip was rewarded by the gods for his piety. Similarly, in Book 17, Diodorus' invariable praise of Alexander yields once in a while (e.g. 17.79–80; 17.84) to a less flattering portrait. Again, we see indications that Diodorus did not thoroughly revise the work, otherwise he would presumably have ironed out such contradictions.

At 16.14.3 and 16.30.1, Philomelus is said to have plundered the sanctuary at Delphi, which is denied at 16.28.2 and 16.56.5. At 18.33.1, Diodorus says that news of Eumenes' successes in Asia Minor reached Perdiccas in Egypt, but at 18.37.1 he (correctly) says that the news did not arrive in time. These are examples of Diodoran carelessness

[38] See also e.g. 13.54.5; 13.60.5; 13.80.5; 13.109.2; 14.54.5–6.

(on which more below), but they also show that he was not merely copying from a single source. In Book 18, praise of Ptolemy occasionally (18.14.1; 18.28.5–6; 18.33.3; 18.34.2–4) intrudes into a narrative that otherwise avoids such effusion. At 18.59.3 the commanders of the Silver Shields display considerable loyalty to Eumenes, but at 18.60–1 Eumenes is doubtful of their loyalty.[39] In Book 19 we are given two rather different portraits of Seleucus, one in which he stands in Antigonus' shadow (19.12–48) and one in which his leadership is emphasized (19.49–92). Since Hieronymus of Cardia, Diodorus' primary source for Successor history in Book 19, wrote in the Antigonid court, the anti-Antigonid material of the second half of the book must come from elsewhere, perhaps Duris of Samos. At 19.9.6 Diodorus fails to reconcile the two different portraits of Agathocles that he received from his sources—the bloodthirsty tyrant or the benevolent king.

It is clear that Diodorus was not merely copying from a single source. He was more eclectic and better read than some scholars still allow him to be; he made use of multiple sources, or perhaps on occasion one main source garnished by pickings from others. He also approached them critically; let one more example stand for many. At 17.113.2, Alexander the Great has returned to Babylon and embassies from all over the known world come to honour him. We know that Cleitarchus, Diodorus' presumed chief source for Book 17, included a Roman embassy (*FGrH* 137, F 31), but Diodorus sensibly omits it. He does not argue against it, as Arrian does (*The Expedition of Alexander* 7.15.5–6), because as a universal historian he cannot allow himself the space to do that; so he just tacitly omits it.

Everyone agrees that Diodorus omitted a great deal of the material that he found in his sources; he had to, in order to fit everything that he wanted to cover into forty books. But any writer, when he omits something, takes care to paper over the cracks as much as possible. Omitting a certain event means that all traces of that event in future years must be omitted as well, along with any run-up to it in earlier years, and that its connections with the events immediately surrounding it have to be disguised. *The Library* usually reads coherently, and that is a sure sign that Diodorus put in considerable work to shape his

---

[39] This near contradiction is probably due to Diodorus' desire to stress the role of Fortune in Eumenes' career.

material. A good example of this is that in his battle scenes he often brings out the suffering of the civilians involved, the horrors of war, and the bravery of the underdogs, in order to tinge the accounts with a moral flavour. He does this so consistently, whatever sources he is drawing on, that it is safe to conclude that much of it is his own work.[40]

At least some of Diodorus' moralizing was given to him by his sources; the moralizing tendency is very pronounced in Greek historiography in general. The uniformity of the morality throughout *The Library* shows, however, that, even where Diodorus took over the moral to a story from one of his sources, he did so only when it was compatible with his own beliefs. He stamped the material he inherited with his own concerns. Here are a couple of slight but telling examples. First, as far as we can tell, Ephorus described the fifth-century Athenian empire as, among other things, 'very upright' (*FGrH* 70, F 191); Diodorus took over the other adjectives from Ephorus, but changed 'upright' to 'clement' or 'equitable', which is one of his preferred terms of commendation. Similarly, comparison with Plutarch, *Nicias* 28.2 suggests that Diodorus changed the original (Timaeus was the source common to Plutarch and Diodorus) from 'a noble use of victory' to 'a merciful use of victory'—mercy, like clemency, being a virtue Diodorus rated highly in leaders.

These are rare cases, however, where we have a means of checking the actual wording of one of Diodorus' sources, and therefore of assessing the extent of Diodorus' copying or creativity. Usually, all we have to go on is the fact, already mentioned, that stylistic analysis of the work reveals a uniformity that can only be explained by the hypothesis that Diodorus made all the material he inherited his own and wrote it up in his own way. Of course, some words, phrases, and even sentiments have been taken over from his sources, but it is clear that Diodorus was no mere scissors-and-paste writer, otherwise there would be more variety to his work; he has imposed his own style on it.[41]

Above all, the work has an overall intellectual unity, as we might call it; the consistency of the views expressed throughout *The Library* show that Diodorus introduced his own concerns, rather than slavishly taking

---

[40] See the chapter by N. Williams in Hau, Meeus, and Sheridan, *Diodoros of Sicily*.

[41] The 'scissors-and-paste' approach to Diodorus was dealt a severe blow by the demonstration that he did not slavishly take over cross-references from his sources: C. Rubincam, 'Did Diodorus Siculus Take Over Cross-references from His Sources?' *American Journal of Philology* 119 (1998), 67–87.

over every detail or opinion from his sources. Diodorus' views on the utility of history, on the role of Fortune in getting men to avoid arrogance at times of success and to take heart at the times of trouble, and on how power and empire are perpetuated by fair and moderate treatment of subordinates and lost by the opposite, are all independent of his sources.[42] These were his overriding concerns, and they form the threads that tie *The Library* together.

Diodorus as a Historian

Diodorus, then, paraphrased material from his sources, but was no mere copyist, because he imposed his own language and views on the material. That is about as creative as any compiler can be, and there is little reason to criticize him for not having done more. He certainly thought like a historian. He was aware of the importance of autopsy (3.11.3), and presumably therefore regretted that this was out of the question for him where most of his material was concerned. The number of times he summarizes or quotes inscriptions (over forty in the surviving books and fragments) shows that he was aware of their importance for the historian. Despite his emphasis on proportion (above, p. xxviii), he allowed himself to give detailed accounts where he felt that the material was interesting and informative, 'in order', as he said at 4.46.5, 'that nothing which is relevant to this history of mine may remain unknown'. He was aware of the importance of giving context to make his account more comprehensible (e.g. 18.5.1) and worried that his annalistic system might jeopardize that clarity (20.43.7). His cross-references are on the whole useful and accurate. He carried out his enormous task with diligence and organized the material well. He was well read in the earlier historians and read them critically. He is not to be criticized for including tall tales and myths in the early books; he was aware of their unreliable nature (1.5.1; 4.1.1–3, 4.8.1–3), but chose to include them for the sake of completeness. The border between myth and history was not as rigid in ancient times as in ours.

Nevertheless, it remains true that Diodorus' practice too often fails to live up to his or any other historiographical ideals. People are the focus of his history, and events are invariably due to their personal

---

[42] Sacks, *Diodorus Siculus*, 23–54.

qualities, rather than to more objective causes—but then almost all
the Greek historians wrote this kind of 'Great Man' history, and in
any case, in our books, great men such as Philip, Alexander, and the
Successors *were* largely responsible for events. There is too little politics in his work; we are given largely military narrative, but little
of the political background or aftermath to the wars and battles.
At 16.38.1, for instance, we read: 'Once he had completed the
reorganization of Thessaly, he advanced to Thermopylae to fight the
Phocians.' The military information is beyond price—but we would
also dearly like to know how Philip reorganized Thessaly. Diodorus
apologizes for his digressions—they 'demand to be told' (e.g. 17.27.7)—
but we wish there were more.

Apart from these general criticisms, there are many minor defi-
ciencies in *The Library*, which cumulatively do considerable damage to the value of Diodorus' work. Above all, there are frequent
problems with his chronology. We need to remember that he was
trying to do something very difficult. He was not only trying to
coordinate the various accounts he found in his sources, but he was
also trying to structure his work by means of three different dating
systems—Olympiads, Athenian Archon years, and Roman consul
years.[43] The reason this was likely to cause problems is that while
Athenian Archon years and Olympiads began fairly close to each
other after the midsummer of a year, Roman consuls took power on
1 March (in our terms), that is, at the beginning of a campaigning
season.[44]

This linking of two incompatible systems not infrequently tempted
Diodorus to write as if the consuls took office at the same time as the
Athenian Archon, and therefore to assign all the events of a campaigning season, from spring to winter, to a single Archon year, when
an Archon year began in July, not in the spring. Although in theory
he could have bundled the events of a consular year with either the
preceding or the succeeding Archon year, he tended to do the latter.

[43] At least one earlier chronicle (*FGrH* 255) combined Olympiads (with named win-
ners of the stade race) and Athenian Archons. Others added king lists to this combination.
The addition of the Roman consuls seems to be a Diodoran innovation, in which he was
followed by his later contemporary Dionysius of Halicarnassus (and later by others, such
as Phlegon of Tralles).

[44] From 153 the consuls took office on 1 January, but such is the state of the later books
of Diodorus that we have no way of knowing what difference, if any, that made to the
accuracy of his work.

This is his single most common fault. Here are a couple of examples from our books. We know from elsewhere that it was in the spring of 302 that Lysimachus crossed from Thrace to Asia Minor for the campaign that would culminate in the battle of Ipsus in 301. At 20.107.2, however, Diodorus places the crossing in the year 302/1—a clear case of a spring event being bundled together with the following Archon year. We know that the debate over the succession after Alexander the Great's death took place in June 323, before the beginning of the next Archon year, but in 18.2 Diodorus includes the debate among the events of 323/2.[45]

The difficulties were exacerbated by the different chronographic indicators that Diodorus found in his sources. Some histories were structured by the astronomical phenomena that determined the seasons—the rising or setting of a star, for instance. Or his sources might use a framework based on the campaigning season of each year, in which armies took to the field in spring and broke up for winter quarters late in the year, effectively structuring their histories by solar years. Plainly, any historian employing such a structure would have no need to interrupt his narrative in order to indicate the change-over of Athenian Archons, so Diodorus could only guess at which point in the narrative that happened. All this made it more difficult for him to assign events correctly to each year. In Book 17, the slippage becomes so great that events are misdated by as much as three years. I suspect that Diodorus was aware of the problems, and that is one reason why he makes very frequent use of lamentably vague phrases indicating intervals of time—phrases such as 'meanwhile', 'next', or 'some time later'.

Some events are summarized from start to finish under the heading of a single year, when they plainly lasted longer than a year. An innocent example of this is when he announces that a ruler came to power and then says, 'and he ruled for *n* years'. It is more misleading, however, when complex events are summarized in this way, making it impossible for us to place them accurately within the *n* years that are being summarized. In Book 16, for instance, the account of the Third Sacred War, begun in 355/4 and assiduously detailed under the headings of subsequent years, breaks off after 352/1 and resumes in 347/6,

[45] Further cases could be cited from Books 18–20: see L. Smith, 'The Chronology of Books XVIII–XX of Diodorus Siculus', *American Journal of Philology* 82 (1961), 283–90.

with the action of the intervening years summarized prospectively under 352/1 and retrospectively under 347/6 (and inadequately in both cases). Or again (a notorious case), the entirety of the exile of the famous Athenian statesman Themistocles is covered within a single year (11.54–8, in the year 471/0), despite the fact that it went on for several years. Examples could be multiplied.

It is right to criticize Diodorus for being sloppy with dates: chronology is, after all, one of the fundamentals of history. There is of course a lot more to history than dates, but alongside errors of chronology, the pages are also littered with errors of fact. In Book 20, for instance, he is undecided whether Agathocles' son is called Archagathus or Agatharchus; at 20.73.1 he writes 'Phoenix' instead of 'Philip' as the name of one of Antigonus' sons, and at 16.32.1 he wrote 'Eudemus' instead of 'Thoudemus'; at 16.53.2 he seems to think that the Chalcidice peninsula is near the Hellespont; at 16.93.9 Attalus is said to be the nephew rather than the uncle of Cleopatra; at 16.72.1 the Illyrian king is said to have died, when in fact he was deposed, but remained alive; in Book 17, a man whose name we know from elsewhere to be Abisares is called variously Embisarus (17.87.2) and Sasibisares (17.90.4). And so on: these and other mistakes (e.g. with his arithmetic) are pointed out in the Explanatory Notes. No doubt some of them are due to his sources rather than to Diodorus himself—but that only shifts the blame from carelessness to a lack of thorough research. We should also be aware of the way Diodorus probably wrote *The Library*; it would have been perfectly normal for him to have dictated the work to an educated slave, and some of the mistakes might be due to the slave's carelessness, not Diodorus', even though he still clearly failed adequately to revise the work. Perhaps he was slipshod, but I prefer to think that he was overtaken by death or incapacity.

There are also surprising omissions: the signing of the Peace of Philocrates between Philip II and the Athenians; Alexander III's birth; the formation of the League of Corinth; Alexander IV's birth; the Roman defeat at the battle of the Caudine Forks in 321—to name just a few. Any writer who has set his hand to a general history knows the painful decisions of omission and abbreviation that he has to make, but, even so, some of Diodorus' omissions seem ill chosen. Another form of omission consists of anacoloutha and non sequiturs—places where the information Diodorus gives us is isolated, with either no lead-in or no follow-up. 18.14.4 is a good example of the latter. We are told that Lysimachus and Seuthes were preparing for a final, decisive battle, but we never get to hear about it. At 16.25.1 the Boeotians send troops into the field to combat the Phocians, but we subsequently hear nothing more about them. At 17.71.7 we are told that a mountain was 'four plethra away', but we are not told what it is four plethra away from. At 18.23.4 Diodorus talks of 'the Athenian ships' as if we knew what ships they were, when they have not been mentioned earlier. At 18.38.1, the same happens with an agreement between Perdiccas and the Aetolians. There are occasional unfulfilled cross-references.

There are quite a few doublets in the text, where an event is covered more than once, with the inherent danger of confusing readers about which year it belongs to. Most of these are relatively innocuous, in that he merely mentions an event in a summary fashion at one point and then gives an account of it later; 18.73.3–4, for instance, is a summary of the action of 19.12–13. Doublets which actually repeat narrative are fortunately more rare—as at 16.24 and 16.28, or 16.25.1 and 16.30.1. The doublet of the siege of Methone in 16.31 (under 353/2) and then, in more detail, in 16.32 (under 352/1) is telling. Presumably, the siege ran over the year-break, so Diodorus found a mention of it in his sources under both years. But his common practice was to bring a simple event to a close at its first mention, and that is what he did in 16.31; his only mistake was to do it again in 16.32. For all we know, some of these doublets may be due to his sources—Ephorus certainly had the habit of repeating information—but, even so, Diodorus could have made things easier for his readers.

Leaving these faults aside, Diodorus has often been accused of more serious lapses, of a kind that would suggest great carelessness. The books translated in this volume have been held to contain such serious lapses, and a short discussion of two notorious cases will not be out of place.

First, the 'misplaced winter' of Book 19. At 19.68.5 and 19.69.2, under 314/13, we read of two armies going into winter quarters. This must be the winter of 314/13, then. Then at 19.77.7, under 312/11, we read about an army (the one of 19.69, as it happens) going into winter quarters, and we naturally take this to be the winter of 312/11. However, at 19.89.2, still under 312/11, we hear about another army being split up for winter quarters. Since no winter has been mentioned for 313/12, scholars have tended to think that Diodorus made a mistake, and that the middle winter, the one of 19.77.7, must be the unmentioned winter of 313/12. This, of course, had major consequences for the dating of events. But there is really no reason to think that Diodorus has made a mistake. The army that goes into winter quarters at 19.77 is that of Antigonus, and the one that goes into winter quarters at 19.89 is that of Cassander. It is more charitable to assume that they both refer to the winter of 312/11 and that Diodorus has been narrating two parallel campaigns that took place in that year.[46] It is not a problem that he has not mentioned the winter of 313/12, because he very often does not mention winters; they are just one tool in his chronographic box.

Second, the 'missing Archon years' of Book 18. At 18.26, we get Diodorus' usual chronographic indicators—the Athenian Archon and the Roman consuls—for the year 322/1. The next such indicators occur at 18.44, for the year 319/18. Two years have been omitted, or at least the chronographic indicators for these years have been omitted. Again, it has been usual to accuse Diodorus of a terrible lapse of concentration. But it is far more likely[47] that some original material has dropped out of our manuscripts. At 19.3.3 and 19.10.3, Diodorus says that he included in Book 18 an account of Sicilian history. There is no Sicilian history in Book 18, and it will by now surprise no reader to learn that Diodorus has been accused of carelessness. Surely, it is a more economical thesis, given the missing Archon years as well, to think that there is a lacuna—that our manuscripts have accidentally omitted a chunk of material, as they do also between 17.83 and 84 (see pp. 148–9). Diodorus is very careful to include the Archon names, since this was his fundamental indicator, so their omission through carelessness would be surprising. Book 18 is also noticeably shorter than other books, again pointing to a considerable lacuna. We can only guess what other material it might have contained.

So we can rehabilitate Diodorus to a certain extent, but he does make mistakes, and these faults are disturbing chiefly because he is often our only source for events. We can check in some cases—but what about all those many events and episodes where we have no

---

[46] See Meeus, 'Diodorus and the Chronology of the Third Diadoch War'.

[47] See Sheridan in Hauben and Meeus, *The Age of the Successors*.

external means of checking? We have to trust Diodorus, but he does not inspire complete confidence.[48] But many of these faults are correctable, and in any case they affect only a small proportion of *The Library*; on the whole he can be confidently used as a basis on which to reconstruct the histories of the peoples and states he covers.

[48] Some of the mistakes, however, are so egregious that it is better to explain them away. At 12.1.5, he dates three generations of philosophers—Socrates, Plato, and Aristotle—to the fifty years preceding the start of the Peloponnesian War in 431. But Diodorus certainly knew that Plato and Aristotle belonged to the fourth century (see 15.7.1 and 15.76.4), and is unlikely to have made such a gross error. The sentence is probably an interpolation into the text by some well-meaning but ignorant scribe.

SELECT BIBLIOGRAPHY

I have restricted this bibliography to the most useful and accessible works written in the English language. Some supplementary reading is included in the footnotes of the Introduction and in the Explanatory Notes.

Diodorus

Every relevant book covering the history of the period includes a paragraph or two in which the author expresses his or her opinion about Diodorus' value as a historian, but the following books and articles are dedicated to Diodoran studies, and especially to Books 16–20.

Atkinson, J., 'Originality and Its Limits in the Alexander Sources of the Early Empire', in A. B. Bosworth and E. Baynham (eds), *Alexander the Great in Fact and Fiction* (Oxford: Oxford University Press, 2000), 307–25.

Bigwood, J., 'Diodorus and Ctesias', *Phoenix* 34 (1980), 195–207.

Crawford, M., 'Greek Intellectuals and the Roman Aristocracy in the First Century BC', in P. Garnsey and C. Whittaker (eds), *Imperialism in the Ancient World* (Cambridge: Cambridge University Press, 1978), 193–207.

Drews, R., 'Diodorus and His Sources', *American Journal of Philology* 83 (1962), 383–92.

Green, P., *Diodorus Siculus, Books 11–12.37.1. Greek History, 480–431 BC: The Alternative Version* (Austin: University of Texas Press, 2006).

Green, P., 'Diodorus Siculus on the Third Sacred War', in J. Marincola (ed.), *A Companion to Greek and Roman Historiography* (Chichester: Wiley-Blackwell, 2007), 363–70.

Hadley, R., 'Diodorus 18.60.1–3: A Case of Remodelled Source Materials', *Ancient History Bulletin* 10 (1996), 131–47.

Hammond, N., 'Diodorus' Narrative of the Sacred War and the Chronological Problems of 357–352 BC', *Journal of Hellenic Studies* 57 (1937), 44–78.

Hammond, N., 'The Sources of Diodorus Siculus XVI: The Macedonian, Greek, and Persian Narrative', *Classical Quarterly* 31 (1937), 79–91.

Hammond, N., 'The Sources of Diodorus Siculus XVI: The Sicilian Narrative', *Classical Quarterly* 32 (1938), 137–51.

Hammond, N., *Three Historians of Alexander the Great* (Cambridge: Cambridge University Press, 1983).

Hau, L., 'The Burden of Good Fortune in Diodorus of Sicily: A Case for Originality?', *Historia* 58 (2009), 171–97.

Hau, L., Meeus, A., and Sheridan, B. (eds), *Diodoros of Sicily: Historiographical Theory and Practice in the* Bibliotheke (Leuven: Peeters, 2018).

Hornblower, J., *Hieronymus of Cardia* (Oxford: Oxford University Press, 1981).

McQueen, E., *Diodorus Siculus: The Reign of Philip II. The Greek and Macedonian Narrative from Book XVI* (London: Bristol Classical Press, 1995).

Markle, M., 'Diodorus' Sources for the Sacred War in Book 16', in I. Worthington (ed.), *Ventures into Greek History* (Oxford: Oxford University Press, 1994), 43–69.

Meeus, A., 'Diodorus and the Chronology of the Third Diadoch War', *Phoenix* 66 (2012), 74–96.

Muntz, C., 'Diodorus Siculus and Megasthenes: A Reappraisal', *Classical Philology* 107 (2012), 21–37.

Muntz, C., *Diodorus Siculus and the World of the Late Roman Republic* (Oxford: Oxford University Press, 2017).

Rubincam, C., 'The Organization and Composition of Diodorus' *Bibliotheke*', *Echos du Monde Classique* 31 (1987), 313–28.

Rubincam, C., 'Cross-references in the *Bibliotheke Historike* of Diodorus', *Phoenix* 42 (1989), 39–61.

Sacks, K., *Diodorus Siculus and the First Century* (Princeton: Princeton University Press, 1990).

Sacks, K., 'Diodorus and His Sources: Conformity and Creativity', in S. Hornblower (ed.), *Greek Historiography* (Oxford: Oxford University Press, 1994), 213–32.

Sacks, K., 'Dating Diodorus' *Bibliotheke*', *Mediterraneo Antico* 1 (1998), 437–42.

Sheridan, B., 'The Strange Case of the Missing Archons: Two Lost Years in Diodorus' History of the Successors', in H. Hauben and A. Meeus (eds), *The Age of the Successors and the Creation of the Hellenistic Kingdoms (323–276 BC)* (Leuven: Peeters, 2014), 115–33.

Sinclair, R., 'Diodorus Siculus and the Writing of History', *Proceedings of the African Classical Association* 6 (1963), 36–45.

Stronk, J., *Semiramis' Legacy: The History of Persia according to Diodorus of Sicily* (Edinburgh: Edinburgh University Press, 2017).

Stylianou, P., *A Historical Commentary on Diodorus Siculus Book 15* (Oxford: Oxford University Press, 1998).

Sulimani, I., *Diodorus' Mythistory and the Pagan Mission: Historiography and Culture Heroes in the First Pentad of the* Bibliotheke (Leiden: Brill, 2011).

Walsh, J., 'Historical Method and a Chronological Problem in Diodorus, Book 18', in P. Wheatley and R. Hannah (eds), *Alexander and His*

Successors: Essays from the Antipodes (Claremont, CA: Regina, 2009), 72–87.

Historiography

This section lists a few recent relevant works on Greek historiography, and focuses in particular on the kind of universal history that Diodorus was writing.

Alonso-Núñez, J., *The Idea of Universal History in Greece from Herodotus to the Age of Augustus* (Amsterdam: Gieben, 2002).

Bosworth, A. B., 'Plus ça change . . . Ancient Historians and Their Sources', *Classical Antiquity* 22 (2003), 167–97.

Clarke, K., 'Universal Perspectives in Historiography', in C. Kraus (ed.), *The Limits of Historiography: Genre and Narrative in Ancient Historical Texts* (Leiden: Brill, 1999), 249–79.

Clarke, K., *Making Time for the Past: Local History and the Polis* (Oxford: Oxford University Press, 2008).

Hau, L., *Moral History from Herodotus to Diodorus* (Edinburgh: Edinburgh University Press, 2016).

Liddel, P., and Fear, A. (eds), *Historiae Mundi: Studies in Universal Historiography* (London: Duckworth, 2010).

Marincola, J., *Authority and Tradition in Ancient Historiography* (Cambridge: Cambridge University Press, 1997).

Marincola, J., *Greek Historians* (Oxford: Oxford University Press, 2006).

Marincola, J., 'Universal History from Ephorus to Diodorus', in id. (ed.), *A Companion to Greek and Roman Historiography* (Chichester: Wiley-Blackwell, 2011), 171–9.

Marincola, J. (ed.), *A Companion to Greek and Roman Historiography* (Chichester: Wiley-Blackwell, 2011).

Meeus, A., 'Compilation or Tradition? Some Thoughts on the Methods of Historians and Other Scholars in Antiquity', *Sacris Erudiri* 56 (2017), 395–414.

Yarrow, L., *Historiography at the End of the Republic: Provincial Perspectives on Roman Rule* (Oxford: Oxford University Press, 2006).

History

I have made this section quite extensive, so that any reader can supplement Diodorus' account with what we know or think we know from other sources.

Anson, E., *Alexander the Great: Themes and Issues* (London: Bloomsbury, 2013).

Anson, E., *Alexander's Heirs: The Age of the Successors* (Chichester: Wiley-Blackwell, 2014).

Anson, E., *Eumenes of Cardia: A Greek among Macedonians* (2nd edn, Leiden: Brill, 2015).

Bayliss, A., *After Demosthenes: The Politics of Early Hellenistic Athens* (London: Continuum, 2011).

Berger, S., *Revolution and Society in Greek Sicily and Southern Italy* (Stuttgart: Steiner, 1992).

Billows, R., *Antigonos the One-Eyed and the Creation of the Hellenistic State* (Berkeley: University of California Press, 1990).

Boehm, R., *City and Empire in the Age of the Successors: Urbanization and Social Response in the Making of the Hellenistic Kingdoms* (Berkeley: University of California Press, 2018).

Bosworth, A. B., *Conquest and Empire: The Reign of Alexander the Great* (Cambridge: Cambridge University Press, 1988).

Bosworth, A. B., *The Legacy of Alexander: Politics, Warfare, and Propaganda under the Successors* (Oxford: Oxford University Press, 2002).

Briant, P., *From Cyrus to Alexander: A History of the Persian Empire* (University Park, PA: Eisenbrauns, 2002).

Buckler, J., *Philip II and the Sacred War* (Leiden: Brill, 1989).

Buckler, J., *Aegean Greece in the Fourth Century BC* (Leiden: Brill, 2003).

Buckler, J., and Beck, H., *Central Greece and the Politics of Power in the Fourth Century BC* (Cambridge: Cambridge University Press, 2008).

Campbell, D., 'Ancient Catapults: Some Hypotheses Reexamined', *Hesperia* 80 (2011), 677–700.

Carney, E., *Women and Monarchy in Macedonia* (Norman: University of Oklahoma Press, 2000).

Carney, E., *Olympias, Mother of Alexander the Great* (London: Routledge, 2006).

Cartledge, P., and Spawforth, A., *Hellenistic and Roman Sparta: A Tale of Two Cities* (London: Routledge, 1989).

Cornell, T., *The Beginnings of Rome: Italy and Rome from the Bronze Age to the Punic Wars* (London: Routledge, 1995).

Ellis, J., *Philip II and Macedonian Imperialism* (London: Thames and Hudson, 1976).

Engels, D., *Alexander the Great and the Logistics of the Macedonian Army* (Berkeley: University of California Press, 1978).

Evans, R., *Syracuse in Antiquity: History and Topography* (Pretoria: UNISA Press, 2009).

Finley, M., *Ancient Sicily* (London: Chatto & Windus, 1968).

Fraser, P., *Cities of Alexander the Great* (Oxford: Oxford University Press, 1996).

Habicht, C., *Athens from Alexander to Antony*, trans. by D. Schneider (Cambridge, MA: Harvard University Press, 1997).

Hammond, N., *Alexander the Great: King, Commander and Statesman* (2nd edn, Bristol: Bristol Classical Press, 1989).

Hauben, H., and Meeus, A. (eds), *The Age of the Successors and the Creation of the Hellenistic Kingdoms (323–276 BC)* (Leuven: Peeters, 2014).

Heckel, W., *Who's Who in the Age of Alexander the Great* (Oxford: Blackwell, 2006).

Heckel, W., and Tritle, L. (eds), *Alexander the Great: A New History* (Chichester: Wiley-Blackwell, 2009).

Hoyos, D., *The Carthaginians* (London: Routledge, 2010).

King, C., *Ancient Macedonia* (London: Routledge, 2018).

Lomas, K., *The Rise of Rome: From the Iron Age to the Punic Wars* (Cambridge, MA: Harvard University Press, 2018).

Markoe, G., *The Phoenicians* (London: British Museum Press, 2000).

Marsden, E., *Greek and Roman Artillery: Historical Development* (London: Oxford University Press, 1969).

Martin, T., 'Diodorus on Philip II and Thessaly in the 350s BC', *Classical Philology* 76 (1981), 188–201.

Meeus, A., 'The Power Struggle of the Diadochoi in Babylonia, 323 BC', *Ancient Society* 38 (2008), 39–82.

Murray, W., *The Age of Titans: The Rise and Fall of the Great Hellenistic Navies* (Oxford: Oxford University Press, 2012).

O'Sullivan, L., *The Regime of Demetrius of Phalerum in Athens, 317–307 BCE: A Philosopher in Politics* (Leiden: Brill, 2009).

Papazoglu, F., *The Central Balkan Tribes in Pre-Roman Times: Triballi, Autariatae, Dardanians, Scordisci and Moesians*, trans. by M. Stansfield-Popović (Amsterdam: Hakkert, 1978).

Roisman, J., *Alexander's Veterans and the Early Wars of the Successors* (Austin: University of Texas Press, 2012).

Roisman, J., and Worthington, I. (eds), *A Companion to Ancient Macedonia* (Chichester: Wiley-Blackwell, 2010).

Ruzicka, S., *Politics of a Persian Dynasty: The Hecatomnids in the Fourth Century BC* (Norman: University of Oklahoma Press, 1992).

Salmon, E., *Samnium and the Samnites* (Cambridge: Cambridge University Press, 1967).

Sanders, L., *The Legend of Dion* (Ontario: Edgar Kent, 2008).

van der Spek, R., 'Seleukos, Self-appointed General (*Strategos*) of Asia (311–305 BC), and the Satrapy of Babylonia', in H. Hauben and A. Meeus (eds), *The Age of the Successors and the Creation of the Hellenistic Kingdoms (323–276 BC)* (Leuven: Peeters, 2014), 323–42.

Talbert, R., *Timoleon and the Revival of Greek Sicily, 344–317 BC* (Cambridge: Cambridge University Press, 1974).

Vădan, P., 'The Inception of the Seleukid Empire', *Journal of Ancient History* 5 (2017), 2–25.

Waterfield, R., *Dividing the Spoils: The War for Alexander the Great's Empire* (Oxford: Oxford University Press, 2011).

Waterfield, R., *Creators, Conquerors, and Citizens: A History of Ancient Greece* (Oxford: Oxford University Press, 2018).

Worthington, I., *Philip II of Macedonia* (New Haven: Yale University Press, 2008).

Worthington, I., *Demosthenes of Athens and the Fall of Classical Athens* (Oxford: Oxford University Press, 2013).

Worthington, I., *Ptolemy I, King and Pharaoh of Egypt* (Oxford: Oxford University Press, 2016).

Worthington, I. (ed.), *Alexander the Great: A Reader* (2nd edn, London: Routledge, 2012).

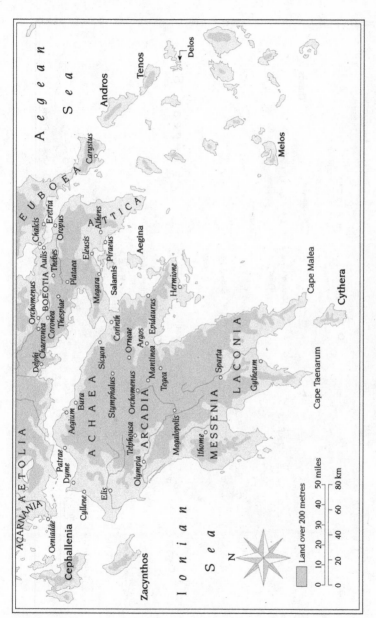

MAP A The Peloponnese and Central Greece

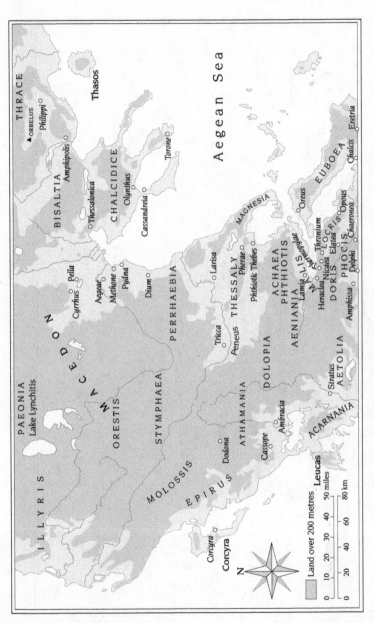

MAP B Northern Greece, Macedon, and Thrace

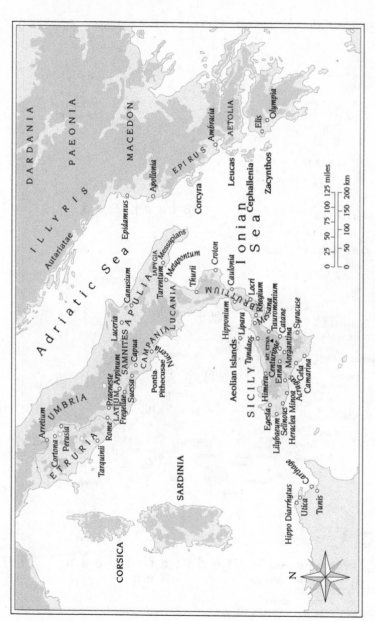

MAP C The Central Mediterranean

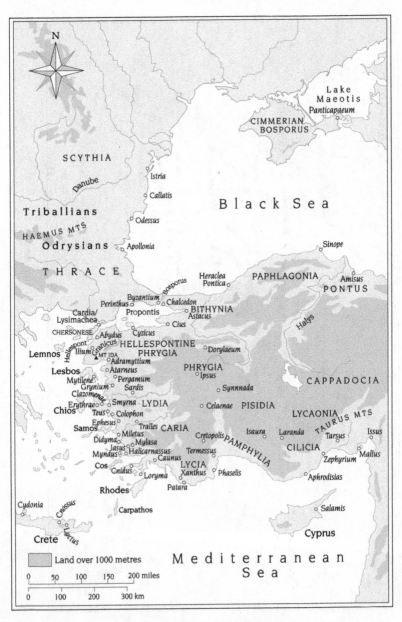

MAP D Asia Minor and the Black Sea

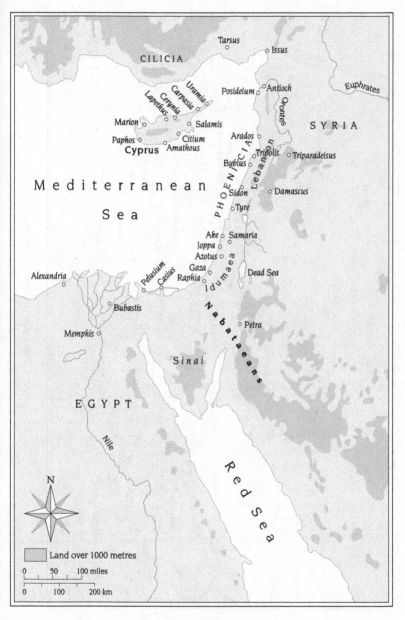

MAP E Syria and Egypt

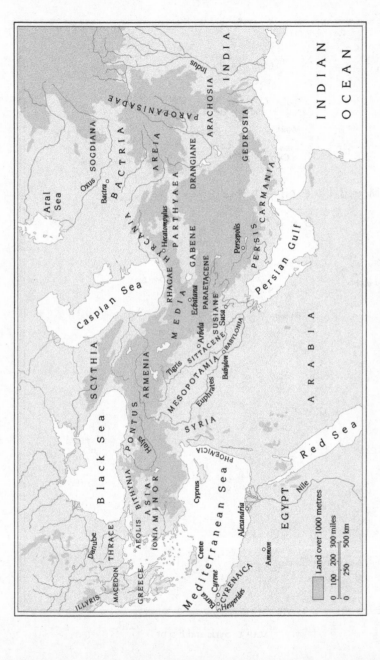

MAP F Alexander the Great's Empire

SYNOPSIS OF BOOKS 16–20

Given Diodorus' annalistic system, the narrative of every extended sequence of events is bound to be broken up into as many parts as there were years in which the events took place. Diodorus himself points out this weakness in the system, at 20.43.7. What follows is a synopsis of the books translated in this volume, to help the reader navigate around the text and follow particular threads. The Index will also help in this regard.

BOOK 19

In Book 16, approximately 69.5 chapters cover **Greece and Macedon**, approximately 25.5 chapters cover **Sicily**, and the rest receive no more than brief notices. The entirety of Book 17 is given over to the affairs of **Greece and Macedon** and **Asia**: that is, Alexander's eastern expedition, incorporating Egyptian and Persian affairs. Book 18 too contains nothing but material relating to **Greece and Macedon** and **Asia** (but see p. xxxvii: there is probably a lacuna in the text that would have contained material on **Sicily**). Book 19 consists of approximately 85.5 chapters on **Greece and Macedon**, 19.5 chapters on Sicily, and 4 chapters on **Rome**. Book 20 consists of 52 chapters on **Greece and Macedon**, the same number of chapters on **Sicily**, and 7 chapters on **Rome**.

THE LIBRARY

BOOK 16

1. The principle that a historian should have his books cover the affairs of states or of kings in their entirety, from beginning to end, applies to every work of history. There is no better way, in my opinion, to make one's account memorable and comprehensible to one's readers. [2] After all, when events are half finished, with beginning and end cut off from each other, the reader's desire to learn is frustrated, but when events are expounded in an unbroken account from beginning to end, the account is a rounded whole. And whenever events in themselves make the historian's task easier, then one must cleave without fail to this principle.*

[3] So, now that it is time for me to write about the affairs of Philip, the son of Amyntas, I intend to cover the affairs of this one king in just this one book,* since he ruled Macedon for twenty-four years. In the course of his reign, starting with the most meagre resources, he made his kingdom the greatest power in Europe; the Macedon he inherited was enslaved by the Illyrians, but he made it the master of many great peoples and cities. [4] His abilities were such that he gained the hegemony of all Greece, with the cities willingly submitting to him,* and because he protected the oracle and defeated those who had plundered the sanctuary at Delphi, he was given a seat on the Amphictyonic Council, and in recognition of his piety was awarded the votes of the defeated Phocians.

[5] Not content with subduing the Illyrians, Paeonians, Thracians, Scythians,* and all their neighbours, he planned to overthrow the Persian kingdom. He sent a force across to Asia and set about freeing the Greek cities, and, although Fate cut him short, he left an army of such competence and calibre that his son, Alexander, completed the overthrow of the Persian empire without needing further reinforcements.* [6] And it was not Fortune, but his own abilities that enabled him to achieve all this.* For Philip was a brilliant strategist and outstandingly brave,* and he had exceptional nobility of spirit. But I do not want to anticipate his achievements in the preface, so I shall proceed with my sequential account of events, after a brief summary of the background.

360/59*

2. *In the year of the Archonship of Callimedes in Athens, the 105th Olympic festival was celebrated, with Porus of Cyrene the victor in the stade race,* and the Romans appointed as their consuls Gnaeus Genucius and Lucius Aemilius.* In this year:*

Philip, the son of Amyntas, and the father of Alexander, the conqueror of the Persians, inherited the Macedonian throne. This is how it came about. [2] After Amyntas had been defeated by the Illyrians, he was compelled to pay tribute to them, as his conquerors, and the Illyrians received his youngest son, Philip, as a hostage and committed him to the care of the Thebans. The Thebans entrusted the young man to the father of Epaminondas, with instructions to take good care of his charge and see to his upbringing and education. [3] Since Epaminondas' tutor was a Pythagorean philosopher and Philip was being raised as Epaminondas' foster-brother,* he was exposed to a great deal of Pythagoreanism. Both of them were naturally talented and assiduous students, and each of them proved to be men of uncommon ability. Through the great battles and conflicts he endured, Epaminondas almost miraculously conferred the hegemony of Greece on his native city, while the fame that Philip won, with the same resources to draw on, was no less than that of Epaminondas.*

[4] This is what happened. After Amyntas' death, his eldest son, Alexander, succeeded to the throne, but was assassinated by Ptolemy of Alorus, who took over the kingdom. Perdiccas then did away with Ptolemy in the same fashion and made himself king, but when Perdiccas was defeated by the Illyrians in a major battle and lost his life in the course of the action, his brother, Philip, escaped from detention and took over the kingdom.*

Macedon was in a bad way. [5] More than four thousand Macedonians had been killed in the battle, and everyone else was in a state of shock, terrified of the Illyrian forces and with no stomach for continuing the war. [6] At much the same time their Paeonian neighbours were plundering the land, expecting no trouble from the Macedonians; the Illyrians were mobilizing in large numbers in preparation for a campaign against Macedon;* and a man called Pausanias, a member of the royal household, was planning to return and take the Macedonian throne with the help of the Thracian king. The Athenians, who were on bad terms with Philip, were up to something similar as well, since they were supporting Argaeus' claim to the throne, and had dispatched their general, Mantias, with three thousand hoplites and a substantial naval force, to see to his restoration.*

3. The catastrophic defeat and the magnitude of the dangers threatening them had reduced the Macedonians to a state of utter helplessness. The threats and hazards looming over them were indeed large, and terrible danger awaited them, but Philip did not lose heart. He convened a series of assemblies at which he addressed the Macedonians with such skill that he aroused their courage and raised their morale. Once he had improved discipline within the ranks, he equipped his men with suitable weaponry and had them constantly out on manoeuvres and training under battlefield conditions. [2] Moreover, reflecting on the close shield formation adopted by the heroes at Troy,* he came up with the idea of packing the phalanx closely and devised its structure; the Macedonian phalanx was his creation.*

[3] He was a good diplomat, and he set about not only using gifts and promises to induce the general populace of Macedon to feel unswerving loyalty towards him, but also devising clever ways to counter all the many looming dangers. When he realized that the sole object of all the Athenians' efforts was the recovery of Amphipolis* and that this was why they were trying to place Argaeus on the throne, he withdrew from the city of his own accord and left it independent. [4] Then he opened up negotiations with the Paeonians and, after winning them over with a combination of bribery and generous promises, he got them to agree to remain at peace for the time being. Likewise, he put an end to Pausanias' bid for the throne by bribing the Thracian king who was intending to see to his restoration.*

[5] Mantias, the Athenian general, sailed into Methone and stayed there while sending Argaeus on to Aegae with the mercenaries.* Argaeus approached the city and called on the inhabitants to recognize his return and become the instigators of his kingship. [6] His words fell on deaf ears, however, so he turned back towards Methone—and Philip appeared with his troops and attacked. He killed many of the mercenaries, but the remainder, who found refuge on a hill, he let go with a guarantee of safe passage, once they had surrendered the exiles to him.* This was Philip's first battle and he won it. Thanks to him, the Macedonians faced their next encounters with greater confidence.

[7] Meanwhile the Thasians founded a settlement at the place known as Crenides,* which the king subsequently named Philippi after himself and repopulated. [8] Among the historians, Theopompus of Chios made this year the start of his *History of Philip*, which consisted of fifty-eight books, of which five are lost.*

4. *In the year of the Archonship of Eucharistus in Athens, the Romans appointed as their consuls Quintus Servilius and Quintus Genucius. In this year:*

Philip sent ambassadors to Athens and persuaded the Athenians to enter into a peace treaty with him, since he was no longer claiming Amphipolis for himself.* [2] When the news arrived that Agis, the Paeonian king, had died, the fact that he was not encumbered by the war with Athens gave Philip what he regarded as an opportunity to go on the offensive against the Paeonians. He invaded Paeonia, defeated the barbarians in battle, and made them subjects of Macedon.*

[3] The Illyrians remained as enemies, however, and Philip was anxious to subdue them too. He convened an assembly at which he delivered a speech that effectively aroused his men's enthusiasm for the coming war, and then he immediately invaded Illyris with an army of at least ten thousand foot and six hundred horse. [4] When Bardylis, the Illyrian king, heard of their arrival, his first reaction was to send ambassadors to negotiate an end to hostilities, with both sides retaining the towns currently in their possession. Philip, however, replied that although he desired peace, he would never agree to it unless the Illyrians withdrew from all the Macedonian towns they occupied. The Illyrian ambassadors returned empty-handed, and Bardylis, made confident by his earlier victories and his men's valour, came out to meet Philip with an army of ten thousand foot, all picked men, and about five hundred horse.

[5] So the two armies drew near each other and their cries filled the air as they clashed. Philip, who was in command of the best of the Macedonian troops, who made up the right wing, ordered his cavalry to outflank the barbarians and attack them from the side, while he himself launched a frontal assault. A hard-fought battle ensued. [6] The Illyrians formed a square and put up a strong defence, and the

battle became evenly balanced for a long while because of the extraordinary valour displayed by both sides. Many died and even more were
injured as the battle inclined one way and then the other, swaying
constantly back and forth thanks to the bravery of the contestants.
But then, with the Macedonian cavalry exerting pressure on their
flank and rear, and with Philip fighting heroically alongside his elite
troops, the Illyrian army was forced to turn to flight. [7] The
Macedonians pursued the enemy for a considerable distance, and
many Illyrians lost their lives as they fled, but then Philip had the
trumpet recall his men. He erected a trophy and buried his dead,*
while the Illyrians asked for terms and obtained peace, once they had
withdrawn their troops from all the Macedonian towns. More than
seven thousand Illyrians lost their lives in this battle.*

5. Now that I have covered the conflict between Macedon and
Illyris, I shall turn to events elsewhere. In Sicily, Dionysius the
Younger, the Syracusan tyrant, who had succeeded to the throne some
years earlier, was an indolent man, far inferior to his father,* with
a tendency to use his indolence as a reason for claiming to be a man of
peace, non-aggressive by nature. [2] So he brought the war he had
inherited against the Carthaginians to an end with a peace treaty* and,
since the most recent battles in the war against the Lucanians (which
he had been pursuing just as sluggishly for some years) had delivered
him the advantage, he happily brought this war to an end as well. [3] In
an attempt to make the Ionian straits safe for shipping, he founded two
towns in Apulia, because the barbarian inhabitants of the coastline
were in the habit of putting to sea in their many pirate galleys and
making the entire Adriatic inaccessible to traders. [4] Then he gave
himself over to a life of peace. He released his troops from their military training, and although the empire he had inherited was the greatest
power in Europe and, in his father's words, was secured by adamantine
bonds,* he was such a weakling that, impossible though it may seem,
he lost it all. I shall do my best to record the reasons for the overthrow
of his empire and the particular events that led to it.

6. *In the year of the Archonship of Cephisodotus in Athens, the Romans
appointed as their consuls Gaius Licinius and Gaius Sulpicius. In this year:*

Dion, the son of Hipparinus and the most distinguished man in Syracuse, fled from Sicily* and, as a man of noble principles, liberated the Syracusans and the other Siceliots. This is how it happened. [2] Dionysius the Elder had children by two wives. From the first, who was a Locrian by birth, he had Dionysius, who succeeded to the tyranny, and from the second, whose father was Hipparinus (a very highly respected Syracusan), he had two sons, Hipparinus and Nysaeus. [3] Dion was the brother of this second wife.* He was an advanced philosopher,* and stood head and shoulders above his contemporaries in Syracuse for his courage and leadership. [4] But his high birth and the nobility of his spirit made him suspect to the tyrant, who believed him capable of overthrowing the tyranny. Out of fear, then, the tyrant decided to see to Dion's removal by having him charged with a crime that carried the death penalty.

The plan came to Dion's notice, however. At first, he hid in the homes of some of his friends, but then he fled from Sicily and went to the Peloponnese, along with his brother Megacles and Heracleides, whom the tyrant had put in charge of his army. [5] Dion sailed into Corinth* and asked the Corinthians to help him set about the freeing of the Syracusans, while he himself began to hire mercenaries and stockpile suits of armour. Many responded to his appeal, and before long he had plenty of suits of armour and mercenaries. He hired two transport ships, put the armour and the mercenaries on board, and then sailed to Sicily from Zacynthos (which is near Cephallenia), leaving Heracleides to come to Syracuse later with three triremes and further transport ships.

7. Meanwhile Andromachus of Tauromenium, a man of outstanding wealth and nobility of spirit (and the father of the historian Timaeus),* gathered together the survivors of the destruction of Naxos by Dionysius and settled them on a hill above Naxos called Taurus. After he had stayed there for quite a while, he named it Tauromenium after his 'stay on Taurus'.* Tauromenium's development was rapid, the inhabitants became very prosperous, and the city gained high status. But eventually, after Caesar* had expelled the people of Tauromenium from their homeland, it was made the site of a Roman colony. This happened in my own lifetime.

[2] Meanwhile the inhabitants of Euboea fell to fighting one another, and when one side called in the Boeotians and the other the Athenians war broke out all over the island. Several engagements

took place, and some skirmishing, in which honours were divided between the Boeotians and the Athenians. No major pitched battle was fought, but the island was devastated by civil war, and many lives were lost on both sides before the Euboeans, chastised by their misfortunes, belatedly settled their differences and made peace with one another.

On their return home, the Boeotians lived at peace, [3] but the Athenians became involved in what is known as the Social War, when the Chians, Rhodians, Coans, and Byzantines seceded from their alliance.* The war lasted for three years. The Athenians sent out Chares and Chabrias, their designated generals, with an army. Their objective was Chios, but when they arrived there they found that the Chians had been reinforced by troops supplied by Byzantium, Rhodes, and Cos, and by Mausolus as well, the dynast of Caria. The Athenian generals deployed their forces and put the city under siege by land and sea. Chares, who was in command of the infantry, approached the walls by land and became embroiled in a struggle with the enemy troops who poured out of the city to attack him. Chabrias, meanwhile, sailed up to the harbour. In the fierce fighting that ensued, his ship was shattered by rams and he found himself in bad trouble. [4] The crews of the other ships bowed to circumstances and were saved, but Chabrias preferred death with glory to defeat and fought on in defence of his ship, until dying of his wounds.

8. In the same year, Philip, the king of Macedon, returned home after defeating the Illyrians in a major battle* and turning the inhabitants of all the territory up to Lake Lychnitis into his subjects.* He had concluded an honourable peace with the Illyrians and was acclaimed by the Macedonians for his successes and the courage that won them. [2] Next,* since the people of Amphipolis were hostile to him and were giving him many reasons to go to war, he marched against them in considerable force.* He brought siege engines up to the city walls and succeeded in bringing down a section of wall with his rams after continuous, determined assaults. He entered the city through the breach, killed many of those who offered resistance, and made the city his. He banished his enemies,* but treated the rest mercifully.

[3] Given the favourable situation of this city in relation to Thrace and Thrace's neighbours, it made a major contribution towards the growth of Philip's power. In fact, he immediately took Pydna, and then

entered into an alliance with the Olynthians, one of the conditions of which was that he would give them Potidaea, a city which the Olynthians particularly wanted for their own.* [4] Since Olynthus was an important city, with a large enough population for it to tip the scales in warfare, it was always fought over by men who sought to increase their power. That is why the Athenians and Philip were in competition for alliance with the Olynthians. [5] Despite this rivalry, however, after Philip had assaulted and taken Potidaea, he allowed the Athenian garrison to leave the city unharmed, and sent them back to Athens. He always treated the Athenian people with great respect because of their city's importance and standing.* Once he had sold the inhabitants of Potidaea into slavery, he turned the city over to the Olynthians, granting them at the same time all the city's rural dependencies as well.

[6] He went next to the town of Crenides.* He enlarged it with many more settlers and renamed it Philippi after himself.* The gold mines attached to the city were wholly undeveloped and insignificant, but he built them up and increased their output until they were capable of providing him with an annual income of more than a thousand talents. [7] With the help of these mines he soon accumulated a lot of capital, and the ample supply of money enabled him to make the kingdom of Macedon ever more dominant. For with the gold coins he struck (which were named for him and known as 'Philips'),* he not only mustered a large force of mercenaries, but also bribed many Greeks to betray their homelands. All this will become clearer when we come to the particular events, but I shall now resume my sequential account of events.

357/6

9. *In the year of the Archonship of Agathocles in Athens, the Romans appointed as their consuls Marcus Fabius and Gaius Publius. In this year:*

Dion, the son of Hipparinus, returned to Sicily to overthrow Dionysius' tyranny, and to everyone's surprise, given that no one had ever had more meagre resources, he succeeded in overthrowing the greatest power in Europe. [2] Who could have believed it? He landed with only two transport ships, and overcame a tyrant who had four hundred warships and an army of about a hundred thousand foot and ten thousand horse, and who had stockpiled all the weaponry, grain,* and money that he was likely to need in order to supply these forces handsomely—a tyrant, moreover, who ruled the greatest of the Greek cities, who controlled harbours, dockyards, and unassailable citadels,* and who had a great many powerful allies. [3] The factors contributing to Dion's success were above all his noble spirit, his courage, and the support of his fellow freedom-fighters, but more important than all of these were the cowardice of the tyrant and the loathing his subjects felt for him. It was the conjunction of all these factors at a single critical moment that made it possible for Dion to succeed, contrary to expectations, where success had been considered impossible.

[4] But I must leave these reflections aside and turn to an account of the particular events.* Dion set sail with two transport ships from Zacynthos, which lies off Cephallenia, and put in at a place called Minoa, in the territory of Acragas. Minoa was founded in ancient times by Minos, the king of Crete, when, in the course of his hunt for Daedalus, he was made welcome by Cocalus, the king of the Sicanians.* At the time in question, it was subject to the Carthaginians, and its governor, a man called Paralus, was a friend of Dion, and readily let him in. [5] Dion brought five thousand suits of armour from the transport ships, gave them to Paralus, and asked him to convey them on carts to Syracuse, while he took the mercenaries, who numbered a thousand, and advanced on the city.

En route he persuaded the people of Acragas, Gela, some of the Sicanians and Sicels from the interior,* and also the people of Camarina to join his bid to free the Syracusans, and then he set out to overthrow the tyrant. [6] So many armed men poured into his camp from all quarters that soon an army had assembled of more than twenty thousand soldiers. Nevertheless, the Italian Greeks and the Messanians were sent for as well, in large numbers, and their commitment to his cause was such that they lost no time in joining him.

10. When Dion reached the borders of Syracuse, he was met by a great many unarmed people from both the countryside and the city—unarmed because Dionysius was suspicious of the Syracusans and had largely disarmed the population. [2] At this moment in time, the tyrant was on the Adriatic coast, along with a sizeable force, staying in the towns there that he had recently founded.* The officers he had left behind in Syracuse to guard the city first tried to get the Syracusans to call off their rebellion, but then they gave up† in the

face of the uncontainable determination of the citizens. Instead, they mustered their mercenaries and the tyrant's sympathizers, and, once they were at full strength, decided to attack the rebels.

[3] Dion distributed the five thousand suits of armour to the unarmed Syracusans and equipped the rest as well as he could with whatever weaponry was available. Then he convened a general assembly of all his troops, at which he informed them that he had come to liberate the Greeks of Sicily and called on them to choose as their Generals men who were capable of seeing to the utter overthrow of the tyranny and the restoration of independence. And, as if from a single throat, the crowd roared out that they chose Dion and his brother Megacles as Generals Plenipotentiary.

[4] Immediately after the assembly, then, Dion drew up his forces and set out towards the city. He met no resistance in the countryside, and he passed unmolested within the city walls and made his way, still without meeting any opposition, through Achradina* to the agora, where he halted. [5] The soldiers under his command numbered at least fifty thousand and all of them, with garlands on their heads, marched down from Achradina into the city, following the lead of Dion, Megacles, and thirty Syracusans, who were the only ones, of all those† who had been banished to the Peloponnese,* who were willing to risk joining the venture.

11. Now that the whole city had exchanged the rags of slavery for the robes of freedom, and Fortune was replacing the frown of tyranny with holiday smiles, every house was filled with sacrificing and rejoicing, as people burnt incense on their domestic altars, thanked the gods for their present blessings, and prayed for their favour in the future. A great cry arose from the women too for their unexpected good fortune, and everywhere in the city they gathered in bevies. [2] Every free man, every slave, every resident foreigner rushed to set eyes on Dion, and all were inclined to regard the man's abilities as more than human. Nor is it surprising that they should have felt like this, given the magnitude and unexpectedness of the change. After experiencing fifty years of slavery—after so much time had passed that they had forgotten that freedom existed—they had been released from their misery by the prowess of just one man.

[3] Dionysius, who at this time was at Caulonia in Italy,* summoned his general, Philistus,* from the Adriatic with his fleet and ordered him to Syracuse. Both men were racing to the same place, but

Dionysius reached Syracuse seven days later than Dion.* [4] As soon as he arrived, in an attempt to dupe the Syracusans he opened negotiations about an end to hostilities and dropped a number of hints to the effect that he would surrender his tyranny to the people and, in return for significant honours, would restore democracy. He also asked them to send him envoys, with whom he could meet and negotiate an end to the fighting. [5] The Syracusans, buoyed up by their hopes, sent as their representatives the most important men among them, but Dionysius placed them under guard and shelved the meeting. Then, noticing that their hopes for peace had made the Syracusans slipshod in their posting of pickets and unprepared for battle, he suddenly opened the gates of the Island acropolis, and he and his troops streamed out in battle order.

12. There was a defensive wall, built by the Syracusans across the peninsula from sea to sea, and Dionysius' mercenaries hurled themselves at it with loud and terrifying cries. They killed many of the guards and then, once they were inside the wall, they took on the reinforcements who were emerging from the city to join the fight. [2] The violation of the truce had taken Dion by surprise, but now he went to meet the enemy with his best men at his side, and in the engagement that ensued many died at their hands. Since the battle was taking place in a space no larger than a stadium, with men crammed together in a confined area, [3] it was the best fighters on both sides who chose to become involved in the mêlée. Incredible determination was displayed by both sides—Dionysius' mercenaries because of the great rewards they had been promised, and the Syracusans because of their hopes of freedom. For a while, the battle was finely balanced, since there was nothing to tell between the valour of either side, and of the many men who died or were wounded, there was not one who was not struck on the front of his body. For the front ranks fearlessly allowed themselves to be killed in defence of the others, while the rear ranks, using their shields to protect their falling comrades and standing fast against the danger, risked their lives to win victory.

[4] Then Dion, who wanted to put on a display of prowess and was determined to be personally responsible for victory, forced his way into the midst of the enemy. Many fell before his heroic onslaught, but by the time he had hacked his way right through the mercenary lines, he found himself cut off and surrounded by a large number of

enemies. Missiles rained down on him, striking his shield and helmet, and his well-made armour protected him from them, but then he was wounded in the right arm, and the force of the blow was such that he fell to the ground and only just avoided falling into enemy hands. [5] The Syracusans, fearing for their General's safety, packed closely together and slammed into the mercenaries, and they not only rescued Dion from his desperate plight, but the pressure they exerted on the enemy troops also forced them to turn and flee. Since the Syracusans also had the upper hand at the other stretch of the wall, the tyrant's mercenaries were all driven back inside the gates of the Island acropolis. This was a brilliant victory for the Syracusans, allowing them to recover and secure their freedom, and they erected a trophy to mark their defeat of the tyrant.

13. Dionysius had come to grief and was starting to think his tyranny a lost cause. Leaving substantial garrisons in the citadels,* he next arranged for the collection of his dead, who were eight hundred in number, and gave them a spectacular funeral. They were crowned with gold crowns and dressed in beautiful purple-dyed robes, because the tyrant hoped that the trouble he took over them would encourage the rest to be willing to risk their lives in defence of his tyranny. Likewise, those of the survivors who had fought with distinction received generous rewards.

He also sent men to the Syracusans with a view to negotiating an end to hostilities. [2] But Dion kept coming up with plausible excuses for postponing the meeting with the envoys, while in the meantime he quietly completed the building of the remainder of the wall—and only then asked for a meeting with Dionysius' envoys, once he had used his enemy's hopes of peace to outmanoeuvre him. When the envoys raised the matter of the terms of the settlement, Dion replied that there was only one condition, that Dionysius should resign his tyranny and be content with certain ordinary honours and offices.

Faced with such a presumptuous response, however, Dionysius convened his officers to consider how best to resist the Syracusans. [3] Since he was well supplied with everything except grain, and since he was dominant at sea, he set about raiding farmland and, given the difficulty of supplying himself with food by means of these foraging raids, he also sent out freighters and money to purchase grain. But, although the Syracusans had few warships,† they kept appearing at the critical locations and making off with a good proportion of what

Dionysius' merchants had purchased. That was how things stood in Syracuse.

14. In Greece, Alexander, the tyrant of Pherae, had been assassinated by his wife Thebe and her brothers Lycophron and Tisiphonus. At first, these three met with a high degree of popularity as tyrant-slayers, but later they changed, and their bribing of the mercenaries* showed them to be tyrants themselves. They killed many of their opponents, built up a noteworthy army, and held on to power by force. [2] Resistance to the tyrants came from the Aleuadae, as this Thessalian family is called, who were well known and highly regarded for their noble lineage.* But since on their own they did not stand a chance against the tyrants, they entered into an alliance with King Philip of Macedon. Philip returned† to Thessaly, subdued the tyrants, and demonstrated the depth of the goodwill he felt for the Thessalians by giving the cities back their freedom. That is why, in the years that followed, not only Philip, but also, later, his son Alexander, always had the support of the Thessalians.

[3] Among the historians,* Demophilus, the son of the historian Ephorus, wrote an account of the war—the Sacred War, as it is called—that his father had failed to cover.* Demophilus' account started with the capture of the sanctuary at Delphi and the despoiling of the oracular shrine by Philomelus of Phocis, which initiated eleven years of warfare* until those who had taken the sacred property for their own purposes were eliminated. [4] Callisthenes' history of Greece in ten books* ended with the capture of the sanctuary and Philomelus of Phocis' crime, [5] while Diyllus of Athens* began his history with the plundering of the sanctuary and wrote twenty-six books, covering everything that happened in this period in both Greece and Sicily.

15. *In the year of the Archonship of Elpines in Athens, the Romans appointed as their consuls Marcus Publius Laenates and Gnaeus Maemilius Imperiosus, and the 106th Olympic festival was celebrated, with Porus of Malis* the victor in the stade race. In this year:*

In Italy, masses of people came together in Lucania from all over the place—people of all sorts, but mostly runaway slaves. For a while, they took up a life of brigandage, but as they became trained and accustomed to warfare by the experience of living in the wild as marauders, they began to win their battles with the local inhabitants and their situation materially improved. [2] The first town they took was Terina, which they looted, but subsequently they took over Hipponium, Thurii, and a number of other towns, and formed a federation. They were called 'Bruttii' because the majority of them were slaves and in the local dialect 'Bruttii' was the word for runaway slaves.* That is how the Bruttian hordes became a distinct political entity in Italy.

16. As for Sicilian affairs, Philistus, Dionysius' general, sailed into Rhegium and brought a detachment of more than five hundred cavalry to Syracuse. Once he had added more than the same number again, and two thousand foot soldiers, he marched against Leontini, which had revolted from Dionysius. Under cover of darkness, he slipped inside the city and occupied a part of it, and a savage battle ensued. But when a relieving force arrived from Syracuse, Philistus was defeated and driven out of the city.

[2] Heracleides, the admiral of Dion's war fleet, who had been left by Dion in the Peloponnese, was delayed by storms and arrived (with twenty warships and 1,500 foot soldiers) too late for Dion's return and the liberation of Syracuse. Since he was a man of great distinction and acknowledged competence, the Syracusans made him their admiral, and it was as joint leader with Dion that he fought in the war against Dionysius.

[3] Next, Philistus, Dionysius' commander-in-chief, led sixty refitted triremes into battle with the Syracusans, who had more or less the same number of ships. A hard-fought battle ensued, and although at first Philistus' valour gave him the upper hand, his ship was later cut off and surrounded by the enemy. The Syracusans were anxious to take him alive, but Philistus killed himself to avoid being captured and tortured. After all, he had not only very often rendered the greatest of services to the tyrants, but he had also been their most reliable friend. [4] After this victory, the Syracusans dismembered Philistus' corpse, dragged it through the streets of the city, and threw it out unburied. Dionysius, who had lost the most effective of his friends and had no other general of sufficient calibre, found himself hard pressed in the war and sent emissaries to Dion. In the early stages of the negotiations, he offered to share power, but later he was prepared to relinquish it altogether.

17. Dion's position was that Dionysius should surrender the acropolis to the Syracusan people and receive certain specially selected valuables and honours in return, and when Dionysius proved willing to do that if he could take his mercenaries and money and move to Italy, Dion advised the Syracusans to accept this offer. However, the assembly speakers made a nuisance of themselves, and under their influence the Syracusan people turned down Dionysius' offer, in the belief that they could take the tyrant in his citadel by storm. [2] Dionysius therefore left the best of his mercenaries to guard the acropolis, while he loaded his property and all his regal paraphernalia on a ship, discreetly set sail, and came to land in Italy.

[3] There were two factions among the Syracusans. Some wanted to entrust the Generalship to Heracleides and make him the highest authority in the state, because it was thought that he would never try to make himself tyrant, while others insisted that Dion should have supreme power. Another issue was that the Peloponnesian mercenaries who had liberated Syracuse had not been paid their wages and had banded together. They were owed a lot of money, but the city was strapped for cash. There were more than three thousand of these mercenaries, they had all been chosen for their prowess, and they were all battle-hardened veterans, so they far outclassed the Syracusans.

[4] When the mercenaries suggested to Dion that he join their insurrection and repay the Syracusans, their common enemy, for the wrong they had done him, at first Dion refused, but later circumstances left him no choice* and he accepted the command of the mercenaries, joined them, and decamped for Leontini. [5] The Syracusans set out en masse after the mercenaries and engaged them while they were still on the way to Leontini, but withdrew after sustaining serious losses. Dion's victory was so spectacular that he could afford to be generous towards the Syracusans. In fact, when they sent a herald to him to arrange for the collection of their dead, he not only gave them permission to do so, but also freed the prisoners he had taken without ransom. And there were a lot of these prisoners, because, threatened with imminent death during the rout, many Syracusans had declared themselves to be sympathetic to Dion's cause, and all those who had done so had escaped death.

18. Dionysius next sent his general Nypsius of Naples to Syracuse, a man of exceptional courage and an excellent strategist, and along with him freighters filled with grain and other supplies. So Nypsius set sail from Locri* and was on his way to Syracuse. [2] Meanwhile, on the acropolis the tyrant's mercenaries, who had run out of grain and were suffering badly from the shortage of provisions, endured the ordeal bravely for a while, but eventually their plight became more than human nature could bear. No longer capable of seeing how they could otherwise survive, they convened an assembly by night and voted to surrender the acropolis and themselves to the Syracusans at daybreak. [3] Night was drawing to a close when the mercenaries sent heralds to the Syracusans to bring hostilities to an end, but as the sun rose Nypsius sailed in with his flotilla and anchored close to the Arethusa spring.* All at once, shortage of provisions was replaced by plenty. Nypsius, therefore, as commanding officer, convened a general assembly, including his troops once he had disembarked them, and, by pitching his words perfectly for the situation, he stiffened their resolve to face the coming dangers.

Thus the acropolis was unexpectedly saved, just as it was about to be surrendered to the Syracusans. [4] But the Syracusans manned all their triremes and sailed into the attack while the enemy were still busy unloading supplies from the ships. The suddenness of the attack, and the disorganized way in which the mercenaries from the acropolis lined up against the enemy triremes, gave victory in this sea-battle to the Syracusans, who sank some of the enemy ships, captured others, and harried the rest on to land. [5] Elated by their success, they performed magnificent sacrifices to the gods in thanks for the victory and gave themselves over to feasting and drinking—and, expecting no trouble from those they had defeated, they were slipshod in their posting of sentries.

19. But Nypsius, the commander of Dionysius' mercenaries, wanted to renew the battle and redeem the defeat, and that night he drew up his forces and led them in a surprise assault on the newly built wall. Finding that the guards had fallen asleep—they were expecting no trouble and had been drinking—he brought up the ladders that had been made for this purpose, [2] and with their help the pick of the mercenaries scaled the wall, killed the guards, and opened the gates. The soldiers poured into the city. The Syracusan generals, sobering up, tried to resist, but their efforts were hampered by the wine they had drunk, and their men either fled or were killed. Once almost all the soldiers from the acropolis were inside the wall and the city was in their hands, and seeing that the Syracusans were stunned by the

unexpectedness of the assault and in disarray, a great slaughter took place. [3] The tyrant's troops numbered more than ten thousand and they were drawn up in such good order that it was impossible for anyone to stand his ground against the pressure they exerted, especially since those who were on the receiving end were also hampered by the noise and confusion, and by their lack of good leaders.

[4] As soon as the agora had been taken by the enemy, the victors turned their attention to the residential houses. A lot of valuable property was carried off, and many women, children, and slaves were taken to be sold. The streets and alleys where the Syracusans offered resistance were scenes of relentless fighting, and many men were killed or injured. And so they spent the night killing one another blindly in the darkness, and there were corpses everywhere.

20. At daybreak, the extent of the catastrophe became visible. The only way the Syracusans could survive was if Dion came to their relief, so they sent riders to Leontini to ask him not to allow the city of his birth to fall, to forgive their mistakes, to take pity on their present misfortunes, and to remedy the terrible situation in which his native city found itself. [2] Now, Dion had a noble spirit, and his education in philosophy had given his mind a humane cast, so he bore no grudge against his fellow citizens. He won over his mercenaries and immediately set out for Syracuse, covering the ground to the city in very good time. When he reached the Hexapylon,* [3] he drew up his men in battle order and approached the city itself at a smart pace. He was met by an exodus of women, children, and elders, more than ten thousand of them—all of whom came up to him with tears in their eyes and begged him to avenge their suffering.

The mercenaries from the acropolis had by now attained their objective. After ransacking the houses around the agora they had set them on fire, and then they had turned to the remaining houses and were currently busy robbing them. [4] That was when Dion entered the city, at several points at once. He fell on the enemy as they were engaged in plundering the houses, and killed all the looters he met, who were carrying off various artefacts on their shoulders. The unexpectedness of his arrival, and the disorder and disorientation of the looters, made it easy for him to overpower them. Eventually, after more than four thousand had been killed, some in the houses and some in the streets, the rest saved their lives by fleeing en masse back to the acropolis and closing the gates.

[5] This was Dion's finest hour. He saved the burning houses by extinguishing the flames and had the defensive wall thoroughly repaired, which simultaneously strengthened the city and walled off the enemy, making it impossible for them to gain the mainland. After clearing the city of corpses and erecting a trophy, he sacrificed to the gods in gratitude for his preservation. [6] An assembly was convened, at which the grateful Syracusans elected Dion their General Plenipotentiary and instituted his worship as a hero.* In keeping with his past behaviour, Dion mercifully released all his political enemies from the charges outstanding against them, calmed the masses, and ushered in a period of general concord. And the Syracusans honoured their benefactor with unanimous accolades and ovations, as the only saviour of their homeland. That was how things stood in Sicily.

21. In Greece, the Chians, Rhodians, Coans, and Byzantines were fighting the Social War against the Athenians, and both sides were making large-scale preparations for what they wanted to be the decisive sea-battle of the war. Earlier, the Athenians had sent Chares on ahead with sixty ships,* and at the time in question they manned another sixty and placed them under the command of the most eminent men in Athens, Iphicrates and Timotheus. Then they dispatched this fleet as well, to join Chares and prosecute the war against their rebel allies.

[2] The Chians, Rhodians, Byzantines, and their allies ravaged the Athenian islands Imbros and Lemnos with their fleet of a hundred ships, and then they sent a strong force against Samos, where they plundered the farmland and put the city under siege by land and sea. They also raised money for the war by raiding a number of other islands that were subject to Athens. [3] Once all the Athenian generals had joined forces, they decided to prioritize the siege of Byzantium. Later, however, the Chians and their allies abandoned the siege of Samos and came to the aid of Byzantium—and that meant that all the fleets were together in the Hellespontine region. But a strong wind arose just as the battle was about to take place and frustrated their designs. [4] Chares wanted to fight even though the elements were against him, and when Iphicrates and Timotheus argued that the swell was too great for them to proceed, Chares called on the soldiers to act as witnesses and accused his colleagues before them† of treachery. Then he wrote a dispatch about them to the Athenian people, accusing them of having deliberately abstained from battle. The

Athenians were furious. They prosecuted Iphicrates and Timotheus, fined them an enormous sum of money,* and relieved them of their commands.

22. So Chares inherited the command of the entire fleet, and in his desire to spare the Athenians the costs, he embarked on a risky endeavour. Artabazus, who was in rebellion against the Persian king, was about to challenge the seventy thousand men under the command of the satraps with only a small force. So what Chares did was add his entire force to Artabazus', and once they had defeated the king's army, Artabazus expressed his gratitude for Chares' help by giving him a large amount of money, enough for him to maintain his entire army.* [2] At first, the Athenians thought Chares had done well, but they changed their minds later, after the Persian king had sent emissaries and denounced Chares, because it became widely known that the king had promised the Athenians' enemies three hundred warships to help them secure victory. The Athenians therefore chose caution and decided to bring the war against their rebel allies to an end. It turned out that the rebels wanted peace too, so a settlement was easily reached. So that was how the Social War, as it is known, came to an end, after a duration of four years.

[3] As for Macedonian affairs, three rulers joined forces against Philip—the Thracian king, the Paeonian king, and the Illyrian king.* They all shared borders with Macedon and therefore looked with suspicion on Philip's increasing power. Individually, they were no match for him and had been defeated by him before, but they thought it would be easy to get the better of him if they fought together. So Philip confronted them while they were still mustering their troops, before they had linked up, and they were terrified into alliance with the Macedonians.

355/4

23. *In the year of the Archonship of Callistratus in Athens, the Romans appointed as their consuls Marcus Fabius and Gaius Plautius. In this year:*
The so-called Sacred War broke out; it was to last nine years.* The war was ignited by Philomelus of Phocis, a particularly bold and lawless individual, when he seized the sanctuary of Delphi. This is how it happened.*

[2] After the Lacedaemonians had lost the Leuctran War against the Boeotians,* the Thebans brought a major suit against them in the Amphictyonic Council for having occupied the Cadmea* and succeeded in getting them condemned to pay a hefty fine. [3] The Phocians were also tried before the Council, for having cultivated a large tract of the so-called Cirrhaean sacred land,* and were also fined a very large sum of money. When the Phocians failed to pay what they owed,* the delegates* brought charges against them and demanded that, unless they paid the money to the god, the Council should declare their land sacred, on the grounds that they were stealing from the god.* At the same time, they said that any other state that had been condemned to pay a fine—and that included Sparta—should also discharge its debt, and that any state that disobeyed should be censured by all the Greeks in common as a malefactor.

[4] The Greeks* ratified these decrees of the Amphictyonic Council, and the Phocians' land was about to be consecrated when Philomelus, the most eminent man in Phocis, addressed the federal assembly. He explained that the fine was too much for them to pay, and that to allow their land to be consecrated would not only be cowardly, but also life-threatening, in the sense that they would lose the means of living that they all currently enjoyed. [5] He also argued, as persuasively as he could, that the verdicts handed down by the Amphictyonic Council were unfair, because a very large fine had been imposed for the cultivation of a very small amount of land. On these grounds, he advised them to regard the fine as invalid, and said that, in his view, the Phocians had strong reasons for defying the Council, because in ancient times it was the Phocians who had controlled and protected the oracle. And he said that this was proved by Homer, the most ancient and the greatest of the poets, in the lines that read:*

> Now the Phocians, to whom Cyparissus belonged
> And rocky Pytho,* were led by Schedius and Epistrophus.

[6] He argued, therefore, that they should lay claim to the right to protect the oracle, on the grounds that it was theirs by tradition. And he promised that, if they elected him General Plenipotentiary and made him responsible for the whole enterprise, he would see it through to a successful conclusion.

24. So the Phocians, alarmed by the size of the fine that had been imposed on them, elected Philomelus their General Plenipotentiary,*

and he energetically set about doing what he had promised to do. He went first to Sparta, where he held private talks with Archidamus, the Lacedaemonian king.* Philomelus argued that his attempt to annul the verdicts handed down by the Amphictyonic Council concerned Archidamus as much as anyone, because the Lacedaemonians too had had severe and unfair judgements passed down against them by the Council. So he let Archidamus know that he planned to seize Delphi, and told him that if he gained the right to protect the shrine, he would annul the Council's decrees.

[2] Archidamus liked what Philomelus was saying, and replied that, although he would not openly help for the time being, Philomelus would have his full cooperation in secret, and that he would provide him with both money and mercenaries. Philomelus was given fifteen talents by Archidamus, added the same or more himself, and used the money to hire mercenaries and create an elite force of a thousand Phocians, whom he called peltasts. [3] And once he had gathered a sizeable army, he seized the oracular shrine. Opposition was spear-headed by the Thracidae, as this Delphian family is known, so he killed them and confiscated their property. This made all the other Delphians fearful, but Philomelus assured them, when he heard about it, that they had nothing to worry about.

[4] As soon as news of the seizure of the sanctuary had got around, the neighbouring Locrians marched against Philomelus, and a battle was fought at Delphi, in which the Locrians sustained heavy losses. Defeated, they fled back home, while Philomelus, filled with pride at his victory, chiselled the Amphictyonic decrees out of the stones on which they had been engraved, and obliterated the letters* that recorded the fines. [5] He let it be known that he had no intention of plundering the oracle or of committing any other crime, and he said that, in claiming the Phocians' ancient right of protection of the shrine and wanting to annul the unfair decisions taken by the Amphictyonic Council, all he was doing was resurrecting the Phocians' ancestral customs.

25. The Boeotians voted in assembly to defend the oracular shrine, and before very long they sent troops into the field.* Meanwhile, Philomelus surrounded the sanctuary with a defensive wall and began to collect a large force of mercenaries by raising their pay to one and a half times the usual rate.* He also enlisted a picked force of the best Phocians, and before long he had a substantial army of more than five

thousand men. With this force defending Delphi, Philomelus was already a formidable opponent for anyone who wanted to make war on him.

[2] Next, he invaded Locris. After ravaging much of the enemy's farmland, he halted near a river that flowed past a strong hill-fort. He repeatedly assaulted this place, but found it impossible to take and abandoned the attempt. He had lost twenty men fighting the Locrians, but the bodies were out of his reach, so he sent a herald for permission to collect them.* But the Locrians refused him permission, and replied that it was a universal Greek custom that the bodies of temple-robbers should be cast out and left unburied. [3] The refusal irritated Philomelus and he joined battle with the Locrians. Fighting with the utmost determination, he killed some of the enemy soldiers and took possession of their bodies, thus forcing the Locrians to make an exchange of corpses. He was master of the countryside, and since his men had ravaged much of Locris, they returned to Delphi laden with booty. Then, because he wanted to hear what the oracle had to say about the war, he forced the Pythia to mount her tripod and go about her oracular business.

26. Since I have mentioned the tripod, it would not be inappropriate, I think, for me to retell the old, traditional story in which it features. In ancient times, the story goes, goats discovered the oracular shrine—and this is why, even now, the Delphians chiefly use goats for consultations of the oracle.* The discovery happened, we are told, as follows. [2] There was a fissure in the rock, at the place where nowadays there is the area of the temple which is called 'inaccessible',* and that was where the goats had been grazing, since Delphi was not yet inhabited. Any goat that went near the fissure and looked into it started to gambol about in a striking fashion and make a sound that was quite different from its usual bleating. [3] The man responsible for the goats was astonished by this weird behaviour and approached the fissure himself—and when he looked down into it, he had the same experience as the goats: they were acting as though they were possessed, and he began to foretell the future.

After this, when word got around among the locals about what happened when one approached the fissure, more and more people began to visit the place. The weirdness of the experience meant that everyone put it to the test, and indeed whenever anyone approached the place he did become possessed. That is how the oracular shrine became recognized as a place of wonder, and it was believed that it was the site of the oracle of the Earth.

[4] For a while, anyone who had a question about the future approached the fissure and people prophesied to one another. Later, however, after a number of people had leapt into the fissure in their frenzy, never to reappear, the local inhabitants decided, as a way of preventing further deaths, to station a woman there as a prophetess—just one prophetess for all comers—and to have her give voice to the oracles. And they constructed a device for her to mount, where she could safely become possessed and prophesy to those who sought answers.* [5] This device had three legs, and so it was called a 'tripod', and all† the bronze tripods that are made even to this day are, presumably, imitations of this original.

I think I have said enough about the discovery of the oracle and the making of the tripod. [6] In the old days, apparently, it was unmarried women who were the soothsayers, because of their physical purity and their similarity to Artemis,* and because such women were held to be able to keep the secrets of the prophecies. Some time between then and now, however, Echecrates of Thessaly visited the sanctuary. They say that when he set eyes on the maiden who was speaking the oracles, her beauty made him lust after her, and he abducted her and raped her. Because of this, the Delphians made a rule that, from then on, it should not be an unmarried woman who did the prophesying, but a woman aged over fifty, whom they dress up as though she were unmarried, to commemorate the prophetesses of old.

So much for the legend of the discovery of the oracle. Now I shall resume my account of Philomelus' exploits. 27. With the oracle in Philomelus' hands, he instructed the Pythia to continue prophesying from the tripod in the traditional way. When she refused,† he threatened her and compelled her to mount the tripod. To this display of excessive force, she responded by declaring that he could do whatever he wanted—and he was pleased by this and declared that he had the oracle that suited him.* He immediately had the oracle inscribed and set up for all to see, in order to make it clear that he had the god's permission to do whatever he wanted, [2] and he convened an assembly at which he boosted morale in the ranks by telling them about the prophecy. Then he turned his attention to the war.

He received another omen in the sanctuary of Apollo, when an eagle which was flying over the temple swooped down to the ground in pursuit of the doves which were kept in the sanctuary, and snatched some of them from the altars. According to the professional interpreters, the omen meant that Philomelus and the Phocians would control Delphi and its business.

[3] With his confidence riding high as a result of these portents, he appointed as ambassadors those of his friends who were best qualified, and sent them to Athens, Sparta, and Thebes,* as well as to the most eminent cities elsewhere in the Greek world. They were to explain that, so far from seizing Delphi because he had designs on the consecrated treasures, he had done so because he was laying claim to the right to protect the sanctuary, which had long ago been declared to belong to the Phocians. [4] As for the treasures, he promised to give an accounting of them to all the Greeks, and he said that, if anyone wanted to inspect the weight and the number of the dedications, he would gladly let him do so. He also asked them to join forces with him, or at least to remain neutral, if anyone, out of hatred or envy, made war on the Phocians. [5] After the ambassadors had carried out their missions, some states, including Athens and Sparta, entered into an alliance with him and promised their support; but the Boeotians, Locrians, and others voted to do the opposite, and went to war against the Phocians in defence of the god.

These were the events that took place in this year.

354/3

28. *In the year of the Archonship of Diotimus in Athens, the Romans appointed as their consuls Gaius Marcius and Gnaeus Manlius. In this year:*

Philomelus could tell that this was going to be a major war, so he started to hire mercenaries in large numbers and to enlist all Phocians who were fit for military service. [2] Although he still needed money for the war, he kept his hands off the sacred dedications, but he levied a large sum of money from the wealthiest and most prosperous Delphians, which was enough to cover the mercenaries' wages. Once he had built up a respectable army, he advanced into the countryside and made it clear that he was ready to take on any or all of the Phocians' enemies.

[3] The Locrians marched against him, and a battle was fought near the cliffs called the Phaedriades,* which Philomelus won after inflicting heavy casualties on the enemy and taking many prisoners,

some of whom he forced off the edge of the cliffs. After this battle, the Phocians were filled with pride at their success, but the humiliated Locrians sent emissaries to Thebes to request aid from the Boeotians for both themselves and the god. [4] Acting out of piety—but also because it was in their interests for the decrees of the Amphictyonic Council to remain in force—the Boeotians sent envoys to the Thessalians and the other members of the Amphictyonic Council, asking them to join forces and make war on the Phocians. And the Amphictyonic Council did vote for war against the Phocians, but this caused a great deal of confusion and dissension throughout Greece, as some decided to take the god's part and to try to punish the Phocians as temple-robbers, while others were inclining towards supporting the Phocians.

29. So the confederacies and cities* were split into two camps. The Boeotians, Locrians, Thessalians, and Perrhaebians decided to defend the sanctuary, and they were joined by the Dorians and Dolopians, and also by the Athamanians, Phthiotic Achaeans, Magnesians, Aenianes, and a few others. But the Athenians, Lacedaemonians, and some other Peloponnesian states joined the Phocians.* [2] The most determined support came from the Lacedaemonians, because, after defeating them in the Leuctran War,* the Thebans had brought a suit against the Spartiates in the Amphictyonic Council, on the charge that one of their number, Phoebidas, had occupied the Cadmea, and had got the Council to assess the crime at five hundred talents. They were duly sentenced to pay this fine, but when they failed to do so within the legally stipulated time, the Thebans brought another suit, for double damages. [3] With the fine imposed by the Amphictyonic Council standing at a thousand talents, the immensity of the debt was inducing the Lacedaemonians to echo the Phocians in protesting that the verdict handed down by the Amphictyonic Council was unfair. [4] Seeing that they and the Phocians had the same interest in the matter—and given that they were reluctant to initiate war themselves over the fine—they decided to use the Phocians as front men, judging that a more dignified way to get the Amphictyonic decrees annulled. So that is why the Lacedaemonians were so strongly motivated to support the Phocians in the war and to help them secure the right to protect the sanctuary.

30. When it became clear that the Boeotians were going to attack the Phocians in force, Philomelus decided to hire a large number of mercenaries. In need of further funds for the war, he had no choice but to lay his hands on the sacred dedications and to steal from the oracular shrine.* Given that he had set their pay at one and a half times the usual rate, it did not take him long to gather plenty of mercenaries, since many men responded to the call-up because of the high wages.* [2] But religious sensibility prevented any man of decent character from enlisting for the campaign, and only the worst kind, in whom greed had ousted reverence for the gods, rushed eagerly to join Philomelus, so that before long there existed a strong force of men whose object was to despoil the shrine.

[3] As soon as Philomelus had raised a substantial army with the help of his extensive resources, he invaded Locris with more than ten thousand men under his command, including both infantry and cavalry. When the Locrians, with Boeotian support, confronted him, a cavalry engagement took place which the Phocians won. [4] Next, the Thessalians and their allies from neighbouring states gathered an army of some six thousand men and advanced into Locris, but they were defeated by the Phocians in a battle at a hill called Argolas. Then the Boeotians appeared with thirteen thousand soldiers, and the Achaeans from the Peloponnese came with fifteen hundred to support the Phocians, and the armies encamped opposite each other, in close proximity.

31. The next thing to happen was that Boeotians captured quite a few of the mercenaries as they were out foraging, led them in front of the town,* and had their herald announce that, by order of the Amphictyonic Council, the men were to be executed for having fought alongside temple-robbers. Action followed immediately on words, and they were all massacred. [2] This made the mercenaries on the Phocian side furious, and they demanded that Philomelus should treat the enemy soldiers to the same punishment. With vengeful determination, they captured a good number of those who were serving with the enemy as they roamed around the countryside and brought them back—and Philomelus duly massacred them all. This act of revenge put an end to their adversaries' insolent and terrible reprisals.

[3] After this, the two armies went elsewhere, and as they were marching through rough and wooded countryside the vanguards suddenly encountered each other. This initial clash was followed by a tough battle, but with their considerable numerical superiority the Boeotians defeated the Phocians, [4] and many of the Phocians and

their mercenaries were cut down as they beat a hasty retreat through the precipitous and trackless countryside. Philomelus, who had fought with spirit and had been wounded a number of times, found himself trapped among crags and cliffs. There was no escape and, not wanting to face torture after he was taken prisoner, he hurled himself down from the rocks, punished by the gods with this terrible end to his life. [5] His command was inherited by his fellow general, Onomarchus, who retreated along with the survivors and then set about recovering his men as they returned from flight.

[6] Meanwhile, Philip, the Macedonian king, first besieged Methone into submission, ransacked it, and left it in ruins, and then took Pagae* and forced it to recognize his authority. On the Black Sea, Leucon, the king of Bosporus, died after a reign of forty years, and was succeeded by his son Spartacus,* who ruled for five years. [7] The Romans fought a war against the Falisci,* with no significant or memorable outcome, but Faliscan farmland was raided and plundered. In Sicily, Dion, the Syracusan General, was murdered by some mercenaries from Zacynthos, and Callippus,* who had arranged the assassination, took over and ruled for thirteen months.

32. *In the year of the Archonship of Eudemus* in Athens, the Romans appointed as their consuls Marcus Publius and Marcus Fabius. In this year:*

Since the Boeotians had defeated the Phocians, and since they believed that Philomelus, the man chiefly responsible for despoiling the temple, had been punished by gods and men so severely that others would be deterred from similar iniquity, they decamped and returned home.* [2] The Phocians too returned to Delphi, given the current lull in the fighting, and they convened a general assembly, including their allies, at which they discussed what to do about the war. The moderates among them were inclining towards peace, but the opposite policy was favoured by the predatory hotheads who cared nothing for the gods, and they were looking around for someone to argue for their lawless position.

[3] Onomarchus then swayed the masses towards war with a carefully worded speech in favour of keeping to their original plan, but he did

so not really because he had any concern for the common good, but because he was putting his own interests first. After all, he had been repeatedly and severely condemned by the Amphictyonic Council, just as they all had been, and had not discharged his debt. So, since in his view a state of war was better for him than peace, he used his eloquence to get the Phocians and their allies to keep to Philomelus' plan. [4] Once he had been elected General Plenipotentiary, he began to hire large numbers of mercenaries. He filled the gaps in the ranks left by the dead, enlarged his army by recruiting a great many mercenaries, and equipped himself on a massive scale with allies and everything that he might need for war.

33. Onomarchus was encouraged in this undertaking by a dream, which seemed to hint at great growth and glory.* In his sleep he saw himself remaking the colossal bronze statue which the Amphictyonic Council had erected in the sanctuary of Apollo, and making it much taller and larger. He thought that this was a sign from the gods that his Generalship would cause Phocian glory to grow, but that was not so, and in fact it indicated the opposite: because the Amphictyonic Council had used money raised by fining the Phocians to erect† the statue—the reason for the fine was that the Phocians had desecrated the shrine—what the dream was indicating was that the Phocian fine would increase thanks to Onomarchus' work. And so it proved.

[2] Once Onomarchus had been elected General Plenipotentiary, with the bronze and iron dedications he made a great store of weapons, and with the silver and gold he minted coins, which he distributed to the allied cities and which he used, above all, to bribe the leading men. He even bribed a number of his enemies, and either persuaded them to support his war effort or required them to remain neutral, [3] and human greed made it easy for him to get his way in everything. In fact, he even bribed the Thessalians to remain neutral,* and they enjoyed the highest status among the allies. As for his opponents among the Phocians, he had them arrested and put to death, and confiscated their property. Then he invaded Locris, where he took Thronium,* sold the population into slavery, and frightened the people of Amphissa into recognizing his authority. [4] In Doris he sacked the cities and laid waste their farmland, and then he invaded Boeotia, where he took Orchomenus and tried to put Chaeronea under siege, but returned home after losing a battle to the Boeotians.

34. Meanwhile, Artabazus,* who was in rebellion against the Persian king, was fighting the satraps who had been sent by the king to prosecute the war. For a while he had the support of Chares, the Athenian general, and he resisted the satraps energetically, but after Chares had left* and he was reduced to his own resources, he persuaded the Thebans to send him auxiliaries. The Thebans gave Pammenes the command and five thousand soldiers and sent him off to Asia. [2] Pammenes' support for Artabazus, and his defeat of the satraps in two major battles, made himself and the Boeotians celebrities. It seemed amazing that the Boeotians, who had been abandoned by the Thessalians and were facing great danger in the Phocian War, should be sending forces overseas and prevailing, for the most part, in their battles.

[3] Meanwhile, war broke out between the Argives and the Lacedaemonians. A battle was fought near the town of Orneae, which the Lacedaemonians won, and once they had assaulted and taken Orneae, they returned to Sparta.* Chares, the Athenian general, sailed to the Hellespont, where he took Sestus, massacred the adult males, and sold the rest of the population into slavery.* [4] Cersobleptes, the son of Cotys, who was an enemy of Philip and on good terms with the Athenians, entrusted the cities of the Chersonese, with the exception of Cardia,* to the protection of the Athenians, and the Athenians sent cleruchs* out to the cities.*

When it came to Philip's attention that the people of Methone were allowing their city to be used as a base for his enemies, he put the place under siege.* [5] For a while, the Methoneans held out, but Philip was too strong for them, and eventually they were compelled to surrender the city to him, on the condition that citizens of Methone should leave with just a single item of clothing each.* Then he razed the city to the ground and distributed the farmland to Macedonians. During this siege Philip lost the sight of one of his eyes, which was struck by an arrow.

35. Next, Philip led his forces to Thessaly in response to a request from aid from the Thessalians. At first, his help consisted in fighting Lycophron, the tyrant of Pherae,* but then Lycophron called for support from the Phocians and they sent Phayllus, Onomarchus' brother, with six thousand men. Philip defeated the Phocians and drove them out of Thessaly, [2] but before long Onomarchus came to Lycophron's assistance, bringing every available man with him, in the belief that he would gain control of all Thessaly. Philip and the Thessalians gave battle to the Phocians, but Onomarchus outnumbered them and defeated them twice,* with considerable loss of life on the Macedonian side. Philip's situation could not have been more hazardous, and his troops' morale was so low that there were desertions. But he finally managed to instil fresh hope in the majority of them and to make them obedient to his orders.

[3] Philip then withdrew back to Macedon, and Onomarchus invaded Boeotia, overcame the Boeotians in battle, and took the city of Coronea. In Thessaly, however, Philip had just returned from Macedon with his forces, and he marched against Lycophron, the tyrant of Pherae. [4] Since he stood no chance against Philip, Lycophron requested aid from the Phocians, and promised to help them establish their regime in Thessaly. Onomarchus therefore lost no time† in coming to his support with an army of twenty thousand foot and five hundred horse. Philip, however, who had persuaded the Thessalians to support his war effort, raised an army totalling more than twenty thousand foot and three thousand horse. [5] A fierce battle took place, which Philip won thanks to the numbers and exceptional skill of the Thessalian cavalry.*

Onomarchus fled to the coast, and Phocians were slaughtered there in droves. What happened was that Chares of Athens happened to be sailing by* with a fleet of triremes, and those who were trying to escape—Onomarchus was one of them—shed their armour and tried to swim over to the triremes. [6] In the end, more than six thousand Phocians and their mercenaries lost their lives, one of whom was the General himself, and at least three thousand were taken prisoner. Philip crucified Onomarchus' body and drowned the rest of the prisoners as temple-robbers.*

36. After Onomarchus' death, his brother Phayllus took over as leader of the Phocians. Wanting to remedy the disaster, he raised a large force of mercenaries, at double the usual rate of pay,* and summoned help from his allies. He also had a great many weapons made and minted both gold and silver coinage. [2] At much the same time, Mausolus, the dynast of Caria, died after a reign of twenty-four years, and was succeeded by Artemisia, his sister and wife,* who reigned for two years. [3] Clearchus, the tyrant of Heraclea, was killed as he was on his way to the theatre for the festival of Dionysus, after a reign of twelve years, and his rule passed to his son Timotheus, who

reigned for fifteen years.* [4] The Etruscans continued their war against the Romans; they despoiled a lot of farmland and marauded right up to the river Tiber,* before returning home. [5] In Syracuse, factional fighting broke out, with Dion's friends against Callippus, and Dion's friends came off worst and fled to Leontini. A short while later, however, Hipparinus, the son of Dionysius, sailed into Syracuse* with an army. Callippus was defeated and expelled from the city,* and Hipparinus recovered his father's throne and reigned for two years.

37. *In the year of the Archonship of Aristodemus in Athens, the Romans appointed as their consuls Gaius Sulpicius and Marcus Valerius, and the 107th Olympic festival was celebrated, with Micrinas of Tarentum the victor in the stade race. In this year:*

Phayllus, the Phocian General, built Phocis back up again after the death and defeat of his brother; its affairs were in a sorry state because of the defeat and the loss of so many soldiers. [2] With inexhaustible funds, he hired a large number of mercenaries and persuaded not a few of his allies to help him wage war. In fact, his unrestrained use of such an enormous amount of money not only won him the active support of many individuals, but also attracted the cooperation of the greatest states in Greece. [3] The Lacedaemonians, for instance, sent him a thousand soldiers, the Achaeans two thousand, and the Athenians five thousand foot and four hundred horse, commanded by Nausicles.*

The death of Onomarchus left Lycophron and Peitholaus, the tyrants of Pherae, without allies. They therefore surrendered Pherae to Philip, but they were allowed under a truce to collect their remaining mercenaries, two thousand in number. With these men, they found refuge with Phayllus and fought alongside the Phocians. [4] Quite a lot of the smaller towns also supported the Phocians, because of the amount of money that was being distributed. Under the influence of gold, that arouser of men's rapacity, they deserted to where they could advance their interests with financial gain.

[5] Phayllus led his forces into Boeotia, but he was beaten in a battle near the city of Orchomenus, with considerable loss of life. Then another battle took place by the Cephisus river, and the Boeotians

won again. They killed more than five hundred of the enemy and took at least four hundred prisoners. [6] And a few days later, the Boeotians won another victory near Coronea; they killed fifty of the Phocians, and took 130 prisoners. Now that I have covered the Boeotians and Phocians, I shall return to Philip.

38. After his glorious defeat of Onomarchus, Philip dissolved the tyranny in Pherae and gave the city back its freedom. Once he had completed the reorganization of Thessaly,* he advanced to Thermopylae to fight the Phocians— [2] but the Athenians blocked his way through the pass,* and Philip returned to Macedon.* A combination of military success and reverence for the gods had enabled him to increase the extent of his kingdom.

[3] Phayllus invaded Locris—Epicnemidian Locris, as it is called*—and captured all the cities except one, Naryx. It was betrayed to him one night by treachery, but he was driven out again with the loss of at least two hundred lives. [4] Next, while he was encamped near a place called Abae,* the Boeotians attacked under cover of darkness and killed quite a few of his men. Elated by their success, they crossed the border into Phocis, plundered a considerable portion of their farmland, and collected a great quantity of booty. [5] On their way back, they were trying to relieve the city of Naryx, which was under siege, when Phayllus appeared and put them to flight. Then he took the city by storm, ransacked it, and left it in ruins.

[6] However, Phayllus succumbed to a wasting disease* and died after an illness that was as long and painful as his sacrilege deserved. He bequeathed the Phocian Generalship to Phalaecus, the son of Onomarchus, the man who had ignited the Sacred War.* Phalaecus was only a teenager, so Phayllus assigned him one of his friends, Mnaseas, as both his guardian and commander-in-chief. [7] But next the Boeotians launched a night attack on the Phocians and killed both Mnaseas and about two hundred others. A short while later, a cavalry battle took place near Chaeronea in which Phalaecus was beaten and lost quite a few men.

39. Meanwhile, the Peloponnese was racked by disturbances and upheavals.* These began when the Lacedaemonians, who were enemies of the Megalopolitans, overran their farmland with an army under the command of King Archidamus.* The Megalopolitans urgently wanted to respond, but on their own they stood no chance against the Lacedaemonians, so they requested help from their allies.* [2] The Argives, Sicyonians, and Messenians quickly sent help in the form of their full

levies, and the Thebans sent four thousand foot and five hundred horse, under the command of Cephison. [3] So the Megalopolitans took to the field with their allies and encamped near the springs that are the sources of the Alpheius river.*

The Lacedaemonians were reinforced by three thousand foot from the Phocians and 150 horse from Lycophron and Peitholaus, the exiled tyrants of Pherae. Since the army they had assembled was combat-ready, they first threatened Mantinea, [4] but then descended on the city of Orneae in Argive territory, which was allied to Megalopolis, and quickly besieged it into submission before a relieving force could arrive. When the Argives took to the field against them, the Lacedaemonians defeated them in battle, killing more than two hundred men. [5] Then the Thebans arrived, who outnumbered the Lacedaemonians by a factor of two, but had poor discipline, and a closely fought engagement ensued. Once it was clear that there was going to be no outright winner, the Argives and their allies returned to their various cities, and the Lacedaemonians invaded Arcadia, took and plundered the town of Helissus,* and then returned to Sparta.

[6] Some time later,* the Thebans and their allies won a battle at Telphousa,* in which they inflicted serious casualties on the Lacedaemonians, and took more than sixty prisoners, including the commanding officer, Anaxander. Not long afterwards, they came off best in two further battles and slew quite a lot of their opponents. [7] But eventually the Lacedaemonians won a significant victory, and the forces of both sides returned to their various cities. Then, once the Lacedaemonians had made a truce with the Megalopolitans, the Thebans returned to Boeotia.

[8] Phalaecus was still in Boeotia, however. Chaeronea fell to him, but he was driven out when the Thebans came to the relief of the city. Then the Boeotians invaded Phocis in great strength, ravaged most of it, and ransacked farms. After taking some of the smaller towns as well, they returned to Boeotia, laden with booty.

40. In the year of the Archonship of Thessalus* in Athens, the Romans appointed as their consuls Marcus Fabius and Titus Quinctius. In this year:

The Thebans were overtaxed by the war against the Phocians and were running out of funds, so they sent an embassy to the Persian king, asking him to supply the city with a generous sum of money. [2] Artaxerxes was happy to comply and gave them three hundred talents of silver. The Boeotians and Phocians skirmished and raided each other's land, but did nothing memorable in the course of this year.

[3] In Asia, the Persian king, who had often campaigned against Egypt earlier without success, fought the Egyptians again in the current year, and this time his determination brought important results: he regained Egypt, Phoenicia, and Cyprus.* [4] But to ensure that my account of these events is comprehensible, I shall briefly return to the relevant period and explain the causes of the war.

The Egyptians were in revolt from the Persians, and earlier Artaxerxes, surnamed Ochus, had done nothing himself, not being a man of war. He repeatedly dispatched armies and generals, but he failed because of the cowardice and incompetence of his officers. [5] Hence, despite incurring the contempt of the Egyptians, his lethargic and unwarlike temperament left him no choice but to put up with the situation. In the current year, however, the Phoenicians and the Cypriot kings were induced by their contempt for him to follow the Egyptian example and set out on the path of rebellion, and in response Artaxerxes decided to make war on the insurgents. [6] He chose to fight for his empire in person, rather than send out generals, and accordingly, once he had equipped himself with great quantities of weaponry, artillery, grain, and men, he mustered an army of three hundred thousand foot, thirty thousand horse, three hundred triremes, and five hundred cargo and other ships to transport supplies.*

41. The war with the Phoenicians began as follows. In Phoenicia, there is an important city called Tripolis. Its name suits its nature, because it consists of three communities, those of the Aradians, Sidonians, and Tyrians,* at a distance of a stade from one another. It is the most important of the Phoenician cities, and it is the place where the Phoenician council used to meet to discuss issues of major concern.* [2] The Persian satraps and governors lived in the Sidonian quarter and behaved, in their management of affairs, in an overbearing and arrogant manner towards the Sidonians. This abuse was resented by its victims and they decided to revolt from the Persians. [3] They persuaded the rest of the Phoenicians to make a bid for independence

as well, and they sent a delegation to the Egyptian king Nectanebo, an enemy of the Persians, and got him to accept them as allies. Then they set about preparing for war.*

[4] Sidon was an especially prosperous city, and trade had made its citizens extremely wealthy, so before long a good number of triremes had been built and a large mercenary force had been hired, and in addition they had rapidly equipped themselves with weaponry, artillery, grain, and all other military necessaries. [5] Hostilities began when they destroyed the royal park, where the Persian kings used to come for rest and recreation, by cutting down the trees. Then they burnt the fodder that had been collected by the satraps to feed their horses in wartime, and finally they seized the Persians who had perpetrated the abuses and punished them. [6] That was how the war against the Phoenicians began. When Artaxerxes learnt of what the insurgents had dared to do, he warned all the Phoenicians, but especially the Sidonians, of the consequences of their actions.

42. As soon as he had mustered his infantry and cavalry in Babylon, he set out with them against the Phoenicians. While he was still on his way, Belesys and Mazaeus, the satraps respectively of Syria and Cilicia, joined forces and opened the Phoenician War. [2] But Tennes, the king of Sidon, had received from the Egyptians four thousand Greek mercenaries under the command of Mentor of Rhodes, and with them and his citizen soldiers he defeated these two satraps in battle and drove them out of Phoenicia.

[3] Meanwhile, war broke out on Cyprus, the course of which was intertwined with the war in Phoenicia. [4] The island contained nine important cities,* under which were ranged smaller communities that were their dependencies. Each of the nine had a king, who ruled his city, but was answerable to the Persian king. [5] All nine of these kings collaborated and, following the lead of the Phoenicians, rose up in rebellion, made their preparations for war, and declared their kingdoms self-governing. [6] In response, Artaxerxes wrote to Idrieus, the dynast of Caria, ordering him to collect a land army and a fleet with which to make war on the Cypriot kings. Idrieus, who had just recently acceded to the position,* was a friend and ally of the Persians, as his family had been for generations, [7] and he quickly got ready forty triremes and a force of eight thousand mercenaries, and sent them off to Cyprus under the command of Phocion of Athens* and Evagoras, who had formerly been one of the kings of the island.

[8] As soon as these two reached Cyprus, they led their forces against Salamis, the largest of the cities. They built a camp and fortified it, and then set about besieging Salamis by land and sea at once. Since the whole island had enjoyed peace for a long while and the farmland was flourishing, control of the countryside enabled the mercenaries to collect plenty of booty. [9] But when news of their enrichment got around, a lot of mercenaries from the coastlines of Syria and Cilicia which faced the island began to pour over of their own accord in the hope of gain, until the army of Evagoras and Phocion had doubled in size, to the alarm and terror of the Cypriot kings. That was how things stood in Cyprus.

43. Next, the Persian king decamped from Babylon and advanced on Phoenicia. When Tennes, the dynast of Sidon, learnt how large the army was that the king had brought with him, it seemed to him that the rebels did not stand a chance, and he decided to secure his own safety. [2] So, without the knowledge of the Sidonians, he sent the most trustworthy of his servants, a man called Thessalion,* to Artaxerxes, promising to betray Sidon to him. He also assured Artaxerxes of his support for the campaign against Egypt, and of his great usefulness, because he was acquainted with Egypt and had precise knowledge of where the landing places were along the Nile.

[3] When the king heard the details of Thessalion's message, he was overjoyed; he declared Tennes free of the charges arising from the rebellion, and promised that he would be richly rewarded if he did what he had undertaken to do. But when Thessalion mentioned that Tennes had also asked for a hand-token,* the king, angered by the suggestion that he was untrustworthy, handed Thessalion over to his minions and told them to remove his head. [4] But as Thessalion was being taken away to be punished, he said merely: 'You will do what you want, your majesty, but because you are refusing him a pledge Tennes will do nothing of what he has promised, even though he is capable of keeping his word in every particular.' This changed the king's mind back again. He recalled his subordinates, told them to release Thessalion, and gave him the hand-token, which is the most binding form of pledge for Persians. Thessalion then returned to Sidon and reported back to Tennes, without the Sidonians getting wind of it.

44. Because of his earlier defeat, the conquest of Egypt was a high priority for the Persian king, and he sent ambassadors to the most

important cities in Greece, asking for their support in his war against Egypt. The Athenians and Lacedaemonians replied that, without wishing to jeopardize their friendship with the Persians, they were opposed to sending him auxiliaries. [2] But the Thebans sent a thousand hoplites under the command of their designated general, Lacrates, and the Argives sent three thousand men. The Argives had left their men without a commanding officer, but when the king asked specifically for Nicostratus, they complied. [3] Nicostratus was effective both in battle and in the council chamber, but he combined good sense with eccentricity: he was exceptionally strong, and he used to imitate Heracles when he was out on campaign by wearing a lionskin and carrying a club during battles. [4] The Greeks who inhabited the coastline of Asia also sent six thousand soldiers, bringing the total number of Greek auxiliaries up to ten thousand.

Before these troops joined him, the king advanced into Phoenicia via Syria, and halted not far from Sidon. [5] While he had been slowly on his way, the Sidonians had painstakingly made themselves ready as regards grain, weaponry, and artillery, and they had also surrounded the city with three deep trenches and had increased the height of the walls. [6] They had an adequate force of citizen soldiers, who had worked hard at their exercises and drills, and were especially fit and strong. In terms of wealth and other resources, Sidon was far superior to the other Phoenician cities, and, most importantly, it had a fleet of more than a hundred triremes and quinqueremes.

45. Tennes shared his plan to betray the city with Mentor, the commander of the mercenaries from Egypt, and left him to watch over part of the city and to cooperate with the men to whom he was entrusting the betrayal, while he left the city with five hundred soldiers, making out that he was going to attend a general assembly of the Phoenicians. He took with him as advisers the hundred most eminent citizens of Sidon, [2] and when they were near Artaxerxes' camp, he seized these men and handed them over to him. The king welcomed Tennes as a friend, and had the hundred Sidonians executed as the instigators of the rebellion.

When five hundred of the foremost Sidonians came to meet him, carrying olive-branches as suppliants, he called Tennes back into his presence and asked if he was in a position to betray the city to him. The king was particularly anxious not to gain Sidon by making any kind of deal. He wanted the Sidonians to suffer cruelly at his hands;

he wanted their punishment to terrify the other cities. [3] When Tennes assured him that he would deliver up the city, the king, whose anger was no less implacable than before, had all the five hundred executed, with the suppliant branches still in their hands. And then Tennes approached the mercenaries from Egypt and prevailed upon them to open the city to him and the king.* [4] So Sidon fell into Persian hands by this act of treachery, but the king felt that he had no further use for Tennes and put him to death.

The Sidonians, however, had burnt all their ships before the king reached them,* to stop anyone in the city securing his own personal safety by sailing away, and when they saw that the city and the walls had been occupied and surrounded by tens of thousands of soldiers, they locked themselves and their families inside their houses and burnt them to the ground. [5] The tally, we hear, of those who died in the flames on that day exceeded forty thousand, including slaves. After this disaster struck the Sidonians and the entire city* was obliterated by fire, along with its residents, the king sold the funeral pyre for a very large sum of money—[6] and the prosperity of the inhabitants was such that a great deal of silver and gold was discovered, melted by the fire. That was the last act of the Sidonian tragedy; the other cities were terrified into surrendering to the Persians.

[7] Shortly before this, Artemisia, the ruler of Caria, died after a reign of two years, and was succeeded by her brother Idrieus, who reigned for seven years. [8] In Italy, the Romans made a truce with the people of Praeneste* and entered into a treaty with the Samnites;* they also carried out the public execution in the Forum of 260 men from Tarquinii.* [9] In Sicily, Leptines and Callippus, the Syracusan power-possessors,* took Rhegium,† threw out the garrison that had been installed by the tyrant Dionysius the Younger, and gave the people of Rhegium back their independence.

46. *In the year of the Archonship of Apollodorus in Athens, the Romans appointed as their consuls Marcus Valerius and Gaius Sulpicius. In this year:*

In Cyprus, Salamis was being invested by Evagoras and Phocion; all the other cities submitted to the Persians, and the only man to hold out against being besieged was Protagoras,* the king of Salamis. [2] Evagoras wanted to recover his father's rulership of Salamis and was trying to get himself restored to his kingdom with the help of the Persian king. But later, when calumnies about Evagoras reached Artaxerxes' ears, the king lent his support to Protagoras and Evagoras' hopes of restoration vanished. However, once he had defended himself against the calumnies, he was granted another charge, a more important one, in Asia.* [3] But his management of affairs in his domain was so bad that he fled once again to Cyprus, where he was arrested and punished as it was felt he deserved.* From then on, Protagoras, who had voluntarily submitted to the Persians, ruled undisturbed over Salamis.

[4] After the capture of Sidon, the Persian king mustered his entire army—including the auxiliaries from Argos, Thebes, and the Asiatic Greek cities, once they had arrived—and advanced against Egypt. [5] When he came to the great marshes where the so-called Pits are, his ignorance of the place caused him to lose some of his men. Since I have already described what the marsh is like and its strange properties in my first book,* I shall not repeat myself now.

[6] The king and his army marched past the Pits and came to the city of Pelusium, which lies on the first of the mouths of the Nile, where the river issues into the sea. While the Persians made camp about forty stades from Pelusium, the Greeks halted right by the city. [7] The Persians had left the Egyptians plenty of time to prepare, so they had all the mouths of Nile well fortified, but especially the one by Pelusium, because it was the first and therefore critical. [8] There was a garrison of five thousand soldiers in the city, under the command of a Spartiate† called Philophron.

The Thebans, wanting to be recognized as the best of the Greek auxiliaries, initiated the action when, with no support, they boldly risked crossing a deep and narrow canal. [9] Once they had made it across and were assailing the walls, the soldiers from the Pelusian garrison poured out of the city and battle was joined. The determination of both sides was such that a ferocious struggle ensued, which continued for the rest of the day, and the combatants were separated only by nightfall.

47. The next day the king divided his Greek forces into three. Each division had a Greek general, with a Persian as his co-commander, a man specially selected for his abilities and loyalty. [2] The forward

position was held by the Boeotians, with Lacrates of Thebes as general and Rhosaces as the Persian officer. Rhosaces was descended from one of the seven who had overthrown the Magi;* he was the satrap of Ionia and Lydia, and had brought with him a large cavalry contingent and a respectable force of native infantry. [3] The second division consisted of the Argives, with Nicostratus as general and Aristazanes as his Persian colleague. Aristazanes, the king's Grand Chamberlain and the most trusted of his Friends after Bagoas, had been assigned five thousand elite soldiers and eighty triremes. [4] The third division had as its general Mentor, the man who had betrayed Sidon, with the same mercenaries under his command as before, and his colleague was Bagoas, an exceptionally bold and lawless individual, who was closer than anyone else to the king. Bagoas had as his command the Greek mercenaries attached to the king, an adequate force of native troops, and a fair number of ships. [5] The king himself stayed on the sidelines of the whole affair, with the rest of the army under his command as reserves. These were the divisions of the Persian forces.

Nectanebo, despite being greatly outnumbered, was dismayed neither by the numbers of the enemy nor by their overall disposition, [6] because he had twenty thousand Greek mercenaries, about the same number of Libyan troops, and sixty thousand of the Warriors, as these Egyptians are called there.* He also had an incredible number of river boats, suitable for battles and engagements on the Nile, [7] and he had fortified the densely settled eastern bank of the river and entirely cut it off from the rest of the country with ramparts and trenches. The preparations he had made for the war in other respects as well were equally thorough, but, thanks to his poor judgement, he soon met with complete disaster.

48. He owed his defeat mainly to his inexperience as a general and to his triumph over the Persians in the previous campaign, [2] when his generals had been Diophantus of Athens and Lamius the Spartiate, both first-rate men, exceptionally brave, and brilliant strategists. His earlier success had been entirely due to them, but he imagined himself to be a competent general, and so at the time in question he shared the command with no one and his inexperience rendered him totally ineffective in military terms. [3] The towns he had under close guard by the large garrisons that he had installed in them, and the forces under his direct command—thirty thousand Egyptians, five thousand Greeks, and half the Libyans—he kept in reserve at the most critical of the mouths of the Nile.

That was the disposition of the troops on either side. Nicostratus, the Argive general, guided by Egyptians whose children and wives were hostages in the Persian camp, sailed along the coast with his fleet and found passage through a certain canal into a secluded part of the country, where he disembarked his troops, built a strong encampment, and bivouacked his men. [4] As soon as the mercenaries on the Egyptian side who were responsible for protecting the district realized that the enemy had arrived, they sallied forth, numbering at least seven thousand, [5] and Cleinius of Cos, their commanding officer, drew them up for battle. Once the disembarked troops had deployed opposite them, a fierce battle ensued in which the Greeks on the Persian side put on a dazzling display of martial prowess, killing the general Cleinius and cutting down more than five thousand of his men. [6] Nectanebo, the Egyptian king, was terrified when he heard of the annihilation of his men, because he thought the rest of the Persian forces would find it easy to cross the river as well. [7] He did not doubt that the enemy would reach the very gates of Memphis* and he decided to make its protection his priority. He therefore returned to Memphis with his troops and began to prepare for a siege.

49. Meanwhile, Lacrates of Thebes, the commander of the first division of the Persian army, embarked on the siege of Pelusium. He diverted the water of the canal to other parts, and when the bed was dry he filled it with earth and brought siege engines up to the city. A long section of wall came down, but the soldiers of the Pelusian garrison speedily erected further fortifications against the breach, and tall towers made of wood. [2] For some days a relentless battle was fought for the walls. At first, the Greeks in Pelusium defended themselves stoutly against the besiegers, but when they heard that the king had retreated to Memphis they lost heart and opened negotiations to end hostilities. [3] Lacrates assured them on oath that if they surrendered Pelusium they would all be shipped back to Greece with whatever they could carry out of the city, and on these terms they capitulated.

[4] The next thing Artaxerxes did, however, was send Bagoas* with some native troops to occupy Pelusium, and these soldiers, whose arrival at the place coincided with the departure of the Greeks, began to confiscate a lot of the items that the Greeks were carrying out of

the city. [5] The injustice of this made the Greeks angry and they cried out loud to the gods, as guardians of oaths. Lacrates was furious and he came to the defence of the victims of the truce-violation by scattering the native troops, some of whom died during the rout. [6] Bagoas fled to the king and denounced Lacrates, but Artaxerxes judged that Bagoas and his men had got their just deserts, and he put to death the Persians who were guilty of the thefts. So that is how Pelusium was surrendered to the Persians.

[7] Mentor, the commander of the third division of the Persian army, used a single stratagem to capture Bubastis and a lot of other cities, and make them subject to the Persian king. Since all the cities were garrisoned by two peoples, Greeks and Egyptians, Mentor spread the word among them that King Artaxerxes had decided to be lenient towards those who voluntarily surrendered their cities, but those who had to be subdued by force would receive the same punishment as had been meted out to the Sidonians; and he urged the men guarding the gates of the cities to allow anyone who wanted to desert from their side to do so. [8] Since Egyptian prisoners of war were being released from the Persian camp, Mentor's message was carried rapidly to all the cities in Egypt, and before very long the mercenaries and the native troops fell out with one another, and there was conflict between them throughout Egypt, as each group was striving to be the one to surrender its post and was hoping to benefit in exchange for rendering this service.

The first city to fall in this way was Bubastis. 50. Without telling the Greeks, the Egyptians in the city sent one of their number to Bagoas, since his and Mentor's camp was near by, promising to betray the city if they had a guarantee of safety from the Persians. [2] When the Greeks found out what was going on, they set out after the messenger and threatened him until he told them the truth. Enraged by the Egyptians' scheming, the Greeks attacked them. Some of the Egyptians were killed and some were wounded, and the rest were trapped in one of the quarters of the city.

[3] The victims of the assault let Bagoas know what had happened, and asked him to come quickly and take possession of the city from them. But what the Egyptians did not know is that the Greeks had been negotiating with Mentor, and Mentor had secretly encouraged them to attack the Persians when Bagoas entered the city. [4] Consequently, when Bagoas and the Persians began to enter the city without the

Greeks' approval, the Greeks waited until a number of soldiers were inside, and then suddenly shut the gates and attacked them. They killed all of those who were within the walls, except for Bagoas, who was taken alive. [5] Seeing that his hopes of safety lay with Mentor, Bagoas pleaded for his life and promised that in the future he would do nothing without consulting him, [6] and Mentor persuaded the Greeks to release Bagoas. He also persuaded them to entrust the negotiations for the betrayal of the city to him, so that he got all the credit for this coup.

As the man who had saved Bagoas' life, he imposed upon him a formal pact of cooperation, confirmed by an exchange of oaths. Mentor stuck by the agreement until the end of his life, [7] and the upshot was that, thanks to the concord between them in Artaxerxes' presence, these two later turned out to be the most influential of the Friends and Kinsmen at court. Mentor was chosen by Artaxerxes to govern the coastal regions of Asia, and in that capacity he performed very valuable services for the king by collecting mercenaries from Greece and sending them to him, and in general by the fearless and loyal way in which he handled all his tasks. [8] And Bagoas managed all the king's affairs in the upper satrapies and rose to such a position of power as a result of his partnership with Mentor that he became master of the kingdom* and Artaxerxes did nothing without consulting him. But where these matters are concerned, I shall cover the details in the appropriate years.*

51. In the current year, however, the surrender of Bubastis was followed by the surrender of the remaining cities, all of which were cowed into coming to terms with the Persians. The Egyptian king, Nectanebo, remained in Memphis, and even though he could see that the cities were heading towards capitulation, he considered it too risky to fight to preserve his kingship. He therefore abdicated and fled to Ethiopia with most of his fortune.

[2] Now that he had taken over all Egypt,* Artaxerxes demolished the walls of the most important cities, and collected plenty of gold and silver by plundering the temples. He also stole the archives from the ancient temples—the archives which Bagoas later returned to the Egyptian priests in exchange for a great deal of redemption money. [3] After generously rewarding the Greek auxiliaries, giving each man what he thought he deserved, Artaxerxes dismissed them to return to their homes. He installed Pherendates as satrap of Egypt* and

returned to Babylon with his army, laden with treasure and spoils, and with his reputation greatly enhanced by his successes.

349/8

52. *In the year of the Archonship of Callimachus in Athens, the Romans appointed as their consuls Marcus Gaius and Publius Valerius. In this year:*

In view of the great services that his general Mentor had rendered him during the Egyptian war, Artaxerxes promoted him more than any of his other Friends. [2] Reckoning that the man deserved the prize for valour,* he gave him a hundred talents of silver and the pick of the valuable artefacts;* he appointed him satrap of the coastal regions of Asia; and he entrusted him with the war against the rebels, giving him supreme command. [3] Moreover, since Mentor was related to Artabazus and Memnon,* both of whom had earlier fought against the Persians, but by then were staying with Philip as fugitives from Asia, he begged the king to release them from the charges against them, and the king granted his request. Mentor immediately asked the two of them to come to him, and to bring their entire families with them—[4] for Artabazus and the sister of Mentor and Memnon had eleven sons and ten daughters. Charmed by the number of Artabazus' children,* Mentor promoted his sons, giving them positions of the greatest distinction within the armed forces.

[5] Mentor's first campaign this year* was against Hermias, the tyrant of Atarneus, who was in rebellion against the Persian king and had many strongholds and towns under his sway. [6] He got him to come to a meeting by promising that he would persuade the king to drop the charges against him—but it was a lie, and he had him arrested.* This meant that Hermias' seal-ring fell into his hands. Mentor then wrote a letter to the towns, to the effect that with Mentor's help peace had been made with the king, sealed the missives with Hermias' ring, and sent them off along with the men to whom these places were to be surrendered. [7] Seeing no reason to doubt the letters, and pleased that peace had been made, the inhabitants duly surrendered all the garrison-posts and towns. Mentor had found a rapid and risk-free way of recovering the rebel towns, and he stood high in the king's favour, since he was clearly a competent and effective

commander; [8] and before long, either by force or deception, he had also subdued all the other leading men who were defying the Persians.*

So much for events in Asia. [9] In Europe, Philip, the Macedonian king, campaigned against the cities of Chalcidice. He besieged the fortress at Zereia*† into submission and razed the place to the ground, and several other towns submitted to him out of fear; then he went to Pherae in Thessaly and expelled Peitholaus, the dynast of the city.* [10] Meanwhile, on the Black Sea, Spartacus, the king of Pontus,* died after a reign of five years, and his brother Parysades succeeded to the kingdom and ruled for thirty-eight years.

348/7

53. *At the beginning of the following year, Theophilus became Archon in Athens, and Gaius Sulpicius and Gaius Quinctius were elected consuls in Rome, and the 108th Olympic festival was celebrated, with Polycles of Cyrene the victor in the stade race. In this year:*

[2] Philip, in pursuit of his ultimate goal of gaining the Hellespontine cities, took Mecyberna and Torone—the towns were betrayed to him, at no risk to himself—and then marched in force against the greatest of the cities in that part of the world,* Olynthus. In the early stages of the campaign, he defeated the Olynthians twice and pinned them inside the city under a siege. But the continuous assaults he was making on the walls cost him a lot of men, and in the end he bribed the leading men of Olynthus, Euthycrates and Lasthenes, and it was their treachery that enabled him to take the city.* [3] He then proceeded to sell as booty the spoils he plundered from the city and the enslaved inhabitants, which brought him plenty of money for the war and helped him to cow the other cities into submission. He rewarded those of his men who had fought valiantly in the battle as they deserved, and he freely distributed money to the men of power in the cities, thereby gaining the services of those—and there were plenty of them—who were prepared to betray their native cities. Philip himself used to say that the expansion of his kingdom owed far more to money than to arms.

54. The Athenians looked askance at Philip's rising power, and whenever he was at war they supported his opponents. They sent emissaries to the cities, calling on them to preserve their independence and to punish with death the potential traitors among them, and they promised all of them military support. By openly declaring their hostility towards Philip, they committed themselves to all-out war against him. [2] No one did more than the orator Demosthenes, the most persuasive speaker of his day in Greece, to get the Athenians to take the lead in defending the Greeks. Nevertheless, there was such a crop of traitors, so to speak,* at that time in Greece that it was impossible for Athens to check the impulse of members of the Greek cities towards treachery. [3] There is a story that once, when Philip wanted to take a particularly well fortified city and one of the locals claimed that the place was impregnable, he responded by asking whether the walls were unscalable by cash. [4] Experience had taught him that anything that could not be subdued by force of arms could be overcome by gold. So, by using bribery to make sure that he had traitors inside the cities, and by calling those who took his money his guest-friends and familiars,* he corrupted men's morals with this pernicious form of diplomacy.*

55. After the capture of Olynthus, he celebrated the Olympia,* at which he performed magnificent sacrifices to thank the gods for his victory. This was a major festival that he organized, with spectacular contests, and he invited many of the foreigners who were visiting Macedon to the banquet. [2] He was particularly courteous to his guests during the symposium:* he presented many of them with the cups that he raised to their health, bestowed gifts on quite a few of them, and gave the company at large a lengthy account of his activities, agreeably told. The upshot was that he made many of them desire his friendship.

[3] At one point in the course of the symposium, he noticed a frown on the face of the actor Satyrus* and asked why he was the only one who chose not to benefit from his generosity. When Satyrus replied that in fact there was a gift he would like from him, but he was afraid of being refused if he revealed what his chosen request was, Philip was overjoyed and assured him that, whatever it was, his request would be granted. So Satyrus said that among the captives were two daughters of a close friend of his, who were of an age to be married, and that it was these girls he wanted to be given, not so that he could profit from the gift, but so that he could endow them both and find husbands for them, and not leave them in a condition that was inappropriate for their age. [4] Philip welcomed this request from Satyrus and immediately

gave him the girls. But the return he got from the numerous and various favours and gifts that he spread around was worth many times more than his outlay, because a contest arose, with many participants tempted by the prospect of his generosity, to see who could be the first to attach themselves to him and to subject the cities of their birth to him.

56. *In the year of the Archonship of Themistocles in Athens, in Rome Gaius Cornelius and Marcus Popilius were the next to be appointed to the consulate. In this year:*

The Boeotians plundered a lot of the farmland near a Phocian city called Hya* and won a battle in which they killed about seventy of the enemy. [2] They clashed with the Phocians again at Coronea, but this time they lost and took heavy casualties. Then, when the Phocians occupied several important towns in Boeotia,* the Boeotians marched out and destroyed the grain in the enemy's fields, but they were badly mauled on their way back home.*

[3] Meanwhile, Phalaecus, the Phocian General, was accused of the wholesale theft of the consecrated treasures and was relieved of his post.* He was replaced by three generals,* Deinocrates, Callias, and Sophanes. An inquiry was instituted into the theft of the consecrated treasures and the Phocians asked those who had been responsible for them for an accounting. [4] Philon was the man chiefly responsible, and since he was unable to produce proper accounts he was found guilty. The generals had him tortured on the rack until he revealed the names of his accomplices in the theft, and then he was subjected to the most excruciating torments, so that he died the death that his sacrilege deserved. [5] The other thieves returned what remained intact of the treasures they had taken, and were then put to death as temple-robbers.

Of the earlier Generals, the first to hold the post, Philomelus, kept his hands off the dedications, but the second, whose name was Onomarchus, the brother of Philomelus,* helped himself freely to the god's treasures, and during his term of office the third, Phayllus, the brother of Onomarchus, turned a lot of the dedications into coin to pay his mercenaries. [6] The gold ingots dedicated by Croesus, the king of Lydia, of which there were 120, each weighing two talents, were turned into coin, and so were 360 golden goblets, each weighing two mnas, and golden statues of a lion and a woman,* together weighing thirty talents.* It follows that the amount of gold that was turned into coin, expressed as its equivalent in silver,* amounted to four thousand talents. As for the silver artefacts, whether dedicated by Croesus or anyone else, we hear† that what all the Generals together got through weighed more than six thousand talents, so that, including the golden dedications, they spent more than ten thousand talents. [7] Some historians say that the amount they stole was no less than the amount acquired by Alexander from the Persian treasuries.*

Phalaecus' captains even tried to dig up the temple. Someone told them there was a vault which held a great deal of silver and gold, and they determinedly set about digging up the ground around the hearth and the tripod. The man who gave them this information said that it was confirmed by Homer, the most distinguished and ancient of the poets, in the lines which read:*

> Not even all the wealth contained within the stone floor
> Of the archer god Phoebus Apollo, in rocky Pytho.

[8] But as the soldiers set about digging near the tripod, severe tremors shook the earth and terrified the Phocians, since it was clear that the gods were warning them that temple-robbers would be punished, and they stopped what they were doing. But it was not long before the man who instigated this crime, the aforementioned Philon, paid the appropriate penalty to the god.

57. The destruction of the sacred treasures was attributed entirely to the Phocians, but the Athenians and Lacedaemonians were partly responsible for the Phocians' decision, because they fought alongside the Phocians and were paid disproportionately well for the number of soldiers they supplied. [2] In fact, this was not the only occasion in these years when the Athenians were tempted to commit sacrilege. Not long before the Delphian affair, when Iphicrates was stationed at Corcyra with a fleet, Dionysius, the ruler of Syracuse, sent chryselephantine statues to Olympia and Delphi, which fell into Iphicrates' hands when he chanced upon the ships that were carrying them. He wrote to the Athenian people asking for instructions, and the Athenians ordered him not to concern himself with the gods' business, but to ensure that his men were well fed. [3] These were his official instructions,

and Iphicrates therefore obediently sold treasures that belonged to the gods as though they were war booty.

Incensed at the Athenians, the tyrant wrote them a letter, as follows:

Dionysius to the Athenian Council and Assembly. It would not be appropriate for me to wish you well,* since on land and sea you are stealing from the gods. You have seized and melted down for coin the statues sent by me for dedication to the gods, and you have committed sacrilege against the greatest of the gods, Apollo of Delphi and Zeus of Olympia.

[4] So much for the Athenian sacrilege, committed even though they claim Apollo as their ancestral deity and their forebear.* As for the Lacedaemonians, although it was through consulting the Delphic oracle that they gained their universally admired constitution,* and although even today they look to the god for answers to their most important questions, they still presumed to be partners in the lawless behaviour of those who violated the temple.

58. In Boeotia, the Phocians held three strongly fortified cities —Orchomenus, Coronea, and Corsiae—which they used as bases for their campaigns against the Boeotians. They were well supplied with mercenaries, so they freely plundered the farmland, and they came off best whenever they and the Boeotians clashed and fought. [2] The Boeotians therefore sent ambassadors to Philip to appeal for help; they were hard pressed by the war, they had lost thousands of men, and they were short of money. [3] The king, however, viewed their reduction with pleasure and, wanting to curb their post-Leuctra pride,* he sent a few soldiers, just enough to ensure that he was not taken to be indifferent to the violation of the oracular shrine. [4] The Phocians were building a hill-fort at Abae, where there is a sanctuary of Apollo, when the Boeotians marched out against them. Some of the Phocians immediately scattered and beat a hasty retreat to the nearest towns, while others, numbering about five hundred, sought refuge inside the temple of Apollo and died.

[5] There were a number of other occasions too in this period when the gods expressed their will concerning the Phocians, but the one I am about to relate was one of the most significant. The men who sought refuge in the temple imagined that they would be kept safe with the help of the gods, but exactly the opposite happened: the gods made sure that they met with the punishment appropriate for temple-robbers. [6] There was a lot of straw in the vicinity of the

temple, and when the men fled they left a fire burning in their camp. The straw caught fire, and such an inferno suddenly blazed up that the temple was devoured and the Phocians who had taken refuge inside it were burnt to death. The gods, then, were held to have refused the temple-robbers the protection conventionally accorded to suppliants.

346/5

59. *In the year of the Archonship of Archias in Athens, the Romans appointed as their consuls Marcus Aemilius and Titus Quinctius. In this year:*

The Phocian War, which had gone on for ten years, came to an end. This is how it happened. The length of the war had left the Boeotians and Phocians prostrate, and the Phocians sent envoys to Sparta to ask for help. The Spartiates sent a thousand hoplites and gave King Archidamus the command.* [2] By the same token, the Boeotians sent envoys to Philip to negotiate an alliance, and Philip arrived in Locris in force, having enlisted the Thessalians on his way. He caught up with Phalaecus (who had been reinstated to the Generalship), who had a respectable† force of mercenaries, and got ready to decide the war with a pitched battle.

But Phalaecus, who was stationed in Nicaea, could see that he was outclassed, so he opened negotiations with Philip about bringing the war to an end. [3] An agreement was reached whereby Phalaecus and his troops could leave and go wherever they wanted, and Phalaecus withdrew under a guarantee of safe passage to the Peloponnese along with his mercenaries, who were eight thousand in number. The Phocians' last hopes vanished and they surrendered to Philip. [4] Having unexpectedly brought the Sacred War to an end without having to fight, Philip held a meeting with the Boeotians and Thessalians, as a result of which he decided to convene the Amphictyonic Council and leave it to the councillors to make the final decisions about everything.

60. What the councillors decided to do, then, was allow Philip (and then his descendants) to join the council, and they gave him the two votes that had formerly belonged to the Phocians, before their defeat. They also decided to demolish the walls of the twenty-three† towns of Phocis; to ban the Phocians from the sanctuary and the Amphictyonic Council; to make it illegal for them to own horses or weaponry until they had repaid the money that had been stolen; to lay a curse on those of the Phocians who had fled and on anyone else who was implicated in the violation of the temple, and declare them liable to summary arrest; [2] and to destroy all the Phocian towns and to relocate the people in villages, each of which was limited to fifty households at the most and was to stand at least a stade distant from its neighbours. The Phocians were to farm their land and pay each year to the god a tribute of sixty talents, until they had repaid the full value of the treasures as recorded in the archives at the time of the robbery;* Philip was to manage the Pythian games,* and to do so along with the Boeotians and Thessalians, since the Corinthians were implicated in the Phocians' religious crimes;* [3] and the councillors and Philip were to break the arms and armour of the Phocians and their mercenaries against rocks, burn whatever remained after this, and sell their horses.* And, in keeping with these decisions, the Amphictyonic Council made arrangements for the care of the shrine and did everything else they could do to foster piety, universal peace, and concord among the Greeks.

[4] Then, once Philip had helped the Amphictyonic Council execute these decrees, dealing courteously with everyone throughout, he returned to Macedon. He had not only earned a reputation for piety and strategic skills, but he had also gone a long way towards laying the groundwork for the growth of his power in the future. [5] What he wanted was to be appointed General Plenipotentiary of Greece and as such to make war on the Persians. And that is exactly what happened. But where these matters are concerned, I shall cover the details in the appropriate years, and now I shall turn to sequential narrative.

61. I think it appropriate, however, first to record how the gods punished those who had sinned against the oracular shrine. In short, not only the actual perpetrators of the violation, but also all those who had the slightest connection with the crime, were visited with implacable punishment by the gods. [2] Philomelus, the instigator of the seizure of the sanctuary, hurled himself from a cliff at a critical point in the war; his brother Onomarchus, who took over the leadership of his now desperate people, was cut down in Thessaly, along with the Phocians and mercenaries who had fought alongside him, and crucified. [3] The third of them, Phayllus, who melted down a great many of the

dedications to coin money, suffered from a lingering illness and found no quick release from his punishment.

And finally Phalaecus, who appropriated what remained to be stolen from the temple, spent a fair amount of time living as a vagabond, frequently afraid and frequently in danger. So far from making him luckier than his fellow desecrators, this ensured that his torment went on for longer than theirs, and that, once his misfortune had become widely known, his suffering would become a famous object lesson. [4] For a while, after he had come to terms with Philip† and fled with his mercenaries, he lived in the Peloponnese, supporting his men with the remainder of the loot from the sanctuary. Later, however, he hired some large transport ships in Corinth and got ready to sail to Italy and Sicily with them and four *hēmioliae*.* His thinking was that in that part of the world he would either seize some city or other, or would obtain service as a mercenary, since the Lucanians and Tarentines were at war, but he told his companions that he was making the voyage because people in Italy and Sicily had asked for their help.

62. After they had left harbour and were on the high sea, some of the soldiers who were being transported on the largest of the ships, which had Phalaecus on board as well, spoke to one another of their suspicion that no one had asked for their help, based on the fact that there were obviously no officers on board from the states which were supposed to have summoned them. They were also concerned that this was no short voyage they were on, but that a long and difficult journey lay ahead of them. [2] So, because they both mistrusted what they were being told and did not relish the prospect of an overseas campaign, they banded together, with the captains of the mercenaries as the ringleaders, and eventually they threatened Phalaecus and the helmsman with drawn swords, and forced them to turn around. Once their friends on the other ships had done the same, they returned to the Peloponnese.

[3] They gathered at Cape Malea in Laconia, and found there some envoys from Cnossus who had sailed in from Crete precisely in order to assemble a force of mercenaries. The Cretans held talks with Phalaecus and his officers and offered them a decent rate of pay, so then they all put to sea together. No sooner had they landed in Crete, at Cnossus, than they captured a city called Lyctus with their first assault.* [4] But the Lyctians, thrown out of their homeland, soon

received help from an unexpected source. The Tarentines and the Lucanians were at war at this time, and the Tarentines sent envoys to the Lacedaemonians, from whom they were descended,* to appeal for help. Because of their kinship, the Spartans were keen to help, and they swiftly raised an infantry force and a fleet, and gave King Archidamus the command. Just as they were about to sail for Italy, the Lyctians arrived and asked them to prioritize their case.* The Lacedaemonians agreed, sailed for Crete, defeated the mercenaries, and restored the Lyctians to their homeland.

63. Then Archidamus sailed for Italy. He joined forces with the Tarentines, but lost his life in a battle, after putting on a dazzling display of martial prowess. People found nothing to criticize in his wartime leadership and his life in general, and he was censured only for the alliance with the Phocians, because this meant that a great deal of the responsibility for the seizure of Delphi was his. [2] Archidamus had been king of Sparta for twenty-three years, and he was succeeded by his son Agis, who reigned for fifteen years.* After Archidamus' death, his mercenaries, who had taken part in the plundering of the shrine, were massacred by the Lucanians.

Phalaecus, meanwhile, who had been expelled from Lyctus, had Cydonia under siege. [3] He built siege towers and was in the process of bringing them up to the city when they were struck by thunderbolts. Not only were the devices consumed by this fire from heaven, but a lot of the mercenaries who came to try to save them were burnt to death—including their commanding officer, Phalaecus. [4] There is an alternative version, however, according to which he was killed by one of his mercenaries, whom he had insulted.

The surviving mercenaries were recruited by Elean exiles* and were shipped to the Peloponnese, where they set about fighting the Eleans alongside the exiles. [5] But then the Arcadians came in on the side of the Eleans, and a battle was fought in which many of the mercenaries died, and the survivors of the defeat, some four thousand in number, were taken alive. The Arcadians and Eleans divided up the prisoners between them, and the Arcadians sold as booty all those who had been assigned to them, but the Eleans killed their prisoners to avenge the violation of the shrine.

64. Thus those who had been involved in the plundering of the sanctuary were punished as they deserved by the gods. And, for having played a part in the atrocity, the most renowned cities in Greece were

subsequently subdued by Antipater, and at a stroke lost both their influence in the Greek world and their freedom.* [2] The wives of the Phocian leaders, who had worn golden necklaces taken from Delphi, also met with the punishment their irreverence deserved. One of them, who had worn the necklace that had belonged to Helen, sank into a shameful life of prostitution and cast her beauty before any man who was disposed to degrade her. Another, who had put on Eriphyle's necklace, was burnt to death in her house when her eldest son set fire to it in a fit of madness.*

So those who were reckless enough to treat the divine with disrespect were punished as they deserved by the gods. [3] Philip, however, had come to the aid of the oracle, and from this time onward he went from strength to strength until eventually, thanks to his reverence for the gods, he was appointed to the leadership of all Greece and made his kingdom the greatest in Europe. But now that I have sufficiently covered the Sacred War, I shall resume my account of events elsewhere.

65. In Sicily, there was civil unrest in Syracuse and the people were constantly being forced to submit to various tyrannies,* so they sent envoys to Corinth,* asking the Corinthians to send them a general who would take charge of the city and put an end to the insatiable rapaciousness of those who aspired to tyranny. [2] The Corinthians thought it only right that they should help their descendants and by official decree the job was given to Timoleon, the son of Timaenetus,* who was unrivalled in Corinth for his bravery and generalship, and had been blessed with every virtue.

There had been an extraordinary event in Timoleon's life, which contributed towards his being chosen for this command. [3] His brother Timophanes was one of the wealthiest and most enterprising men in Corinth, and it had been clear for a long time that he wanted to be tyrant. In fact, at the time in question he was recruiting members of the lower classes, having suits of armour made for them, and going about in the agora accompanied by men of the worst sort; in short, he was acting like a tyrant* while maintaining the pretence that he was not one. [4] Now, there was nothing more repugnant to Timoleon than one-man rule, and at first he tried to persuade his brother to desist. So far from taking his advice, however, Timophanes every day became more and more committed to his brazen ways. And finding it impossible to reform his brother by argument, Timoleon murdered him as he was walking in the agora.

[5] There was uproar, and when the citizens ran up, drawn by the extraordinary and terrible nature of the incident, they fell to quarrelling. Some said that, as a murderer of his own kin, Timoleon should be punished as stipulated by law, but others, on the contrary, declared their intention† of officially commending the man as a tyrant-slayer.*
[6] The Council of Elders met in their chambers and the dispute about how to respond to what Timoleon had done was referred to them. Timoleon's enemies on the council denounced him, while men of the better sort spoke on his behalf and argued against killing him.

[7] A verdict had not yet been reached* when the envoys arrived from Syracuse, explained their mission to the Council of Elders, and asked them to send the military commander they required at the earliest possible opportunity. [8] So the council voted to send Timoleon, and in order to ensure his success they offered him a curious and unusual choice. They assured him that, if he proved to be a good ruler of Syracuse, he would be adjudged a tyrannicide—but a fratricide if he proved too rapacious. [9] And Timoleon did manage Sicilian affairs well and in the island's best interests, not because he felt pressured by the council's threat, but just because he was a good man. He defeated the Carthaginians, restored the Greek cities that had been destroyed by the barbarians to their original condition, and liberated all Sicily. In a word, he found Syracuse and the other Greek cities of the island empty, and left them brimming with people. But where these matters are concerned, I shall shortly be covering the details in the appropriate years, and I shall now resume my sequential account of events.

345/4

66. *In the year of the Archonship of Eubulus in Athens, the Romans appointed as their consuls Marcus Fabius and Servius Sulpicius.* In this year:*

Timoleon of Corinth, who had been chosen by his fellow citizens to take up the Generalship of Syracuse, got ready for his voyage to Sicily. [2] He hired seven hundred mercenaries, filled four triremes and three light galleys with soldiers, and set sail from Corinth. In the course of the voyage, he picked up three more ships from Leucas and Corcyra, and so it was with ten ships that he crossed the Ionian Sea.

[3] Timoleon had a curious and extraordinary experience during the voyage, when the gods lent their support to his enterprise and

gave advance notice of the fame that would accrue to him and the splendour of his achievements. For throughout the night a blazing torch in the sky showed the fleet the way forward, all the way to Italy.* [4] In fact, while in Corinth Timoleon had been told by the priestesses of Demeter and Korē that the goddesses had appeared to them in a dream and announced that they would accompany him on his voyage to their sacred island.* [5] So Timoleon and his companions were overjoyed to see that they had the goddesses' support, and he dedicated his best ship to them, giving it the name *Demeter and Korē*.

Just after the fleet arrived in Metapontum in Italy, after a trouble-free voyage, a Carthaginian trireme also put in there, with Carthaginian emissaries on board. [6] They held a meeting with Timoleon, at which they pleaded with him not to start a war or set foot on Sicilian soil. But the people of Rhegium were calling for Timoleon and promising an alliance, so he left Metapontum straight away, hoping to arrive before anyone knew of his coming, [7] since he was worried that the Carthaginians, with their dominance at sea, might stop him sailing over to Sicily.

So Timoleon was racing over the sea to Rhegium. **67.** Now, a little earlier, when the Carthaginians had realized how great a conflict they were facing, they initiated a programme of generous treatment of the Sicilian cities that were allied to them, and brought their quarrels with the tyrants of the island to an end with treaties of friendship. The most significant of these tyrants, given his formidable strength, was Hicetas, the ruler of Syracuse.* [2] They now got ready a large fleet and a land army, gave the command to Hanno, and sailed over to Sicily. Their fleet consisted of 150 warships, and their army of fifty thousand foot, two thousand horse,† three hundred war chariots, and over two thousand pairs of horses for the chariots.* And this is not to mention all the varied weaponry, artillery pieces of every description, countless siege devices, and an incredible quantity of grain and other necessaries.

[3] The first place they went to was Entella, where they ravaged the farmland and pinned the local residents inside the city with a siege. The Campanian inhabitants of the city were terrified by the size of the enemy army and sent messengers to the other cities which were hostile to the Carthaginians to ask for help. In the event, none of them responded except for Galeria, which sent a thousand men armed as hoplites. But the Carthaginians intercepted this force, overwhelmed it with their superior numbers, and wiped it out. [4] The Campanians

of Etna had started to muster auxiliaries to send to the people of Entella, on the basis of their kinship,* but then, when they heard what had happened to the Galerians, they judged it best to do nothing.

68. Dionysius was master of Syracuse* when Hicetas marched on the city at the head of a large army. As soon as he had built a camp at the Olympieium,* he took the fight to the tyrant, who held the city. [2] But the siege went on for so long that he ran out of supplies, so he decamped for Leontini, the city he had made his base. Dionysius went after him, caught up with the rearguard, and joined battle—[3] but Hicetas wheeled around to confront Dionysius, engaged him in battle, killed more than three thousand of his mercenaries, and routed the rest. He set out hot on the heels of the fugitives, burst into Syracuse along with them, and gained control of the entire city except the Island.

That was how things stood with Hicetas and Dionysius. [4] It was only three days after the capture of Syracuse by Hicetas that Timoleon sailed into Rhegium and anchored not far from the city. [5] The Carthaginians arrived as well, with twenty triremes*—but Timoleon was helped by the people of Rhegium. They convened a general assembly in the city to discuss the possibility of ending hostilities between the two sides, and since the Carthaginians felt certain that Timoleon would be prevailed upon to return to Corinth, they were careless in their posting of lookouts. Timoleon gave no indication of his intention to flee, and stayed close to the speaker's platform—but he secretly gave orders for all but one of his ten ships to leave as quickly as possible. [6] Then, while the Carthaginians' attention was occupied by the Rhegian speakers, who slyly prolonged their speeches, Timoleon stole off to the remaining ship and sailed rapidly away. The outmanoeuvred Carthaginians set out in pursuit, [7] but Timoleon had a good head start and the protection of darkness, and he reached Tauromenium before the Carthaginians could catch up with him. [8] The leading man of Tauromenium, Andromachus, had always favoured the Syracusans, so he let the escapees in and was largely responsible for their safety.

[9] Hicetas next put together a force consisting of his best five thousand men and marched against Adranum,* which was hostile towards him, and made camp near the city. Timoleon, however, reinforced by soldiers loaned by his hosts, set out from Tauromenium with a force numbering somewhat less than a thousand. [10] He left at nightfall, reached Adranum on the second day, and launched a surprise

attack on Hicetas' troops as they were busy with their evening meal. Once he had broken through the enemy's defences, he killed more than three hundred men, took about six hundred prisoners, and captured the camp. [11] Following this forced march with another, he immediately set out against Syracuse, and he covered the ground so quickly that his attack was completely unexpected by the Syracusans, since he had outstripped the fugitives from the rout at Adranum.

These were the events that took place in this year.

69. *In the year of the Archonship of Lyciscus in Athens, the Romans appointed as their consuls Marcus Valerius and Marcus Popilius, and the 109th Olympic festival was celebrated, with Aristolochus of Athens the victor in the stade race. In this year:*

The Romans and the Carthaginians for the first time entered into a treaty of friendship.* [2] In Caria, Idrieus, the ruler of the Carians, died after a reign of seven years; he was succeeded by his sister–wife Ada,* who ruled for four years.

[3] In Sicily, Timoleon gained the peoples of Adranum and Tyndaris as allies and received a fair number of soldiers from them. Syracuse was in utter chaos, with Dionysius holding the Island, Hicetas Achradina and New Town, and Timoleon the rest of the city, while the Carthaginians had sailed into the Great Harbour with 150 triremes and had fifty thousand men encamped on the shore.* The numbers of his enemies seemed overwhelming to Timoleon—but then the situation changed, against all odds and expectations. [4] First, Marcus,* the tyrant of Catane, came in on Timoleon's side with a decent-sized army; then quite a few of the garrisoned towns, which were bidding for independence, showed an inclination to join him; and, finally, the Corinthians manned ten ships, supplied them with money, and dispatched them to Syracuse.* [5] All this gave Timoleon fresh hope, but the Carthaginians panicked, abandoned the harbour for no good reason,* and sailed away, back to their part of the island. [6] Hicetas was left isolated, and Timoleon overcame him and gained control of the entire city. He also immediately regained Messana, which had gone over to the Carthaginians. That was how things stood in Sicily.

[7] In Macedon, Philip, who had inherited hostility towards the Illyrians from his father and had done nothing to reduce its bitterness, invaded Illyris in force.* He ravaged the farmland, captured a number of towns, and returned to Macedon laden with booty. [8] Then he went to Thessaly, where he expelled the tyrants from their cities,* thereby earning the Thessalians' gratitude and loyalty.* His hope was that, with the Thessalians as his allies, winning the goodwill of the Greeks as well would be a straightforward matter. And so it proved, because the Greeks who were neighbours of the Thessalians concurred with the Thessalians' decision, and before long became Philip's enthusiastic allies.

343/2

70. *In the year of the Archonship of Pythodotus in Athens, the Romans appointed as their consuls Gaius Plautius and Titus Manlius. In this year:*

The tyrant Dionysius became so alarmed by Timoleon's strength that he surrendered the acropolis to him, abdicated, and retired to the Peloponnese with a guarantee of safe passage, taking his property with him. [2] So, because of his weakness and ignoble spirit, Dionysius lost the far-famed tyranny that was secured, it was said, by adamantine bonds.* He spent the rest of his days in reduced circumstances in Corinth,* with his life and his changed situation serving as a warning to anyone who was foolishly inclined to congratulate himself on his good fortune. [3] After all, a man who a short while earlier had possessed four hundred triremes sailed into Corinth in a little tub, drawing attention to the dramatic change in his fortunes.

[4] Once Timoleon had taken over the Island and received the surrender of the outlying garrisons that had formerly been loyal to Dionysius, he destroyed the fortifications and the tyrant's mansion on the Island, and gave the garrisoned towns their independence. [5] He also immediately began to develop a new constitution for Syracuse, with democratic laws,* and he gave precise instructions about how the regulations governing private contracts and everything else should read, with his overriding objective being equality.

[6] One of the annual offices he created was the one that bears the most prestige in Syracuse, which they call the priesthood of Olympian Zeus. The first person to hold this post was Callimenes, the son of

Alcidas, and from then on the Syracusans have always designated years by the names of these office-holders. In fact, at the time of my writing this history, they still do, even though the political system has changed. For when the Romans granted citizenship to the Siceliots,* the priesthood lost its importance, but it still exists, after more than three hundred years. That was how things stood in Sicily.

71. In Macedon, Philip launched an offensive against Thrace, hoping to earn the goodwill of the Greek cities there. Cersobleptes, the Thracian king, was persistently trying to gain control of the Hellespontine cities whose territories lay on his borders, [2] and Philip's intention was to stop the barbarians in their tracks. He marched there at the head of a large army. After success in several battles against the Thracians, he ordered the defeated barbarians to pay a tenth of their revenues as tribute to Macedon, and by founding major cities at critical locations he curbed their aggressiveness.* The Greek cities now had nothing to fear, and they enthusiastically joined Philip's alliance.

[3] Among the historians, Theopompus of Chios devoted three books of his *History of Philip* to Sicilian affairs. He started with the tyranny of Dionysius the Elder, wrote up the next fifty years, and ended with the expulsion of Dionysius the Younger.* These three books are numbers 41 to 43.

342/1

72. *In the year of the Archonship of Sosigenes in Athens, the Romans appointed as their consuls Marcus Valerius and Gnaeus Publius. In this year:*

Arymbas, the king of the Molossians, died after a reign of ten years.* He left a son called Aeacides, the father of Pyrrhus, but it was Olympias' brother Alexander who succeeded to the kingdom, with the support of Philip of Macedon.

[2] In Sicily, Timoleon marched against Leontini, since that was where Hicetas was holed up with a large number of men. At first, he targeted the suburb known as New Town, but later he broke off the siege, since he was making no progress; there were a great many soldiers trapped inside and it was easy for them to put up a defence from the walls. [3] He moved instead against the town of Engyum, which was ruled by the tyrant Leptines. With the objective of expelling Leptines and restoring freedom to the city, Timoleon launched

a rapid series of assaults. [4] While Timoleon was preoccupied there, however, Hicetas marched out of Leontini at full strength and put Syracuse under siege, but his casualties were so heavy that he soon returned to Leontini. [5] Timoleon terrified Leptines into submission and shipped him off to the Peloponnese under a guarantee of safe conduct, so that the Greeks would know that the defeat of a tyrant would be followed only by his banishment. The town of Apollonia was also part of Leptines' dominion, and once it fell into his hands Timoleon restored its independence, just as he had with Engyum.*

73. Timoleon was short of money with which to pay his mercenaries, so he sent a thousand men under the command of his most senior officers to the territories that were under Carthaginian control. They gathered plenty of booty from all the farmland they plundered and turned it over to Timoleon. He raised a great deal of money by selling it, which he used to pay his mercenaries for an extended period of service. [2] He also took Entella,* where he put to death the fifteen men who had been the ringleaders of the Carthaginian faction and gave the rest of the citizens back their freedom. As Timoleon's power and reputation as a general grew, all the Greek cities of Sicily willingly submitted to him, because he never failed to restore their freedom. Moreover, many of the cities of the Sicels, Sicanians, and others who had been subjects of the Carthaginians opened negotiations with him, wanting to be accepted as his allies.

[3] Seeing that their generals in Sicily were making a pitiful job of the war, the Carthaginians decided to send replacements at the head of formidable armies. They set about it straight away. They recruited their best soldiers from the citizen body for the campaign, and drafted the most competent Libyans as well, and in addition, once they had set aside a large amount of money, they recruited Iberian, Celtic, and Ligurian mercenaries.* They also built warships, gathered a fleet of transport vessels, and made all the rest of their preparations on a vast scale.

341/0

74. *In the year of the Archonship of Nicomachus in Athens, the Romans appointed as their consuls Gaius Marcius and Titus Manlius Torquatus. In this year:*

Phocion of Athens defeated Cleitarchus, the tyrant of Eretria, who had been put in place by Philip.* [2] In Caria, Ada was thrown off her throne by Pixodarus, her younger brother, who then ruled for five years, until the arrival of Alexander in Asia.

Philip, who was going from strength to strength, marched against Perinthus, which was hostile to him and favoured the Athenians.* He instigated a siege and every day siege engines were brought up to the city in relays. [3] He built towers eighty cubits high, far taller than the Perinthian fortifications, and this advantage was enabling him to wear down the resistance of the defenders. At the same time, the walls were being weakened by his rams and sabotaged by his mines, and eventually a long stretch collapsed. But the Perinthians determinedly fought off the attackers and quickly built a counter-wall—and then the fighting and the onslaughts on the wall became unbelievably intense.

[4] Both sides displayed great determination. With his many bolt-shooting devices of various kinds, the king rained destruction down on his opponents on the battlements, but, although the Perinthians were losing many men every day, they received additional troops, missiles, and ordnance from the Byzantines. [5] Now that they were once again a match for the enemy, their spirits rose and they bravely endured all the dangers the defence of their homeland entailed. But the king's determination never slackened. He divided his forces into several parts and had his men assault the walls unrelentingly, in relays, by day and night. Faced with thirty thousand soldiers, a huge amount of artillery and siege engines, and an incredible quantity of other devices, the defenders' resistance was gradually crumbling.

75. As the siege dragged on, the numbers of dead and injured in the city mounted. When provisions began to run out as well, the fall of the city was expected imminently. But Fortune was not indifferent to the safety of the beleaguered Perinthians and saw to it that help arrived from an unexpected quarter. The growth of Philip's power had been widely reported in Asia and the Persian king was concerned enough to write to the satraps of the coastal provinces, telling them to spare no effort in helping the Perinthians. [2] So the satraps, working together, sent a large force of mercenaries to Perinthus, along with plenty of money, a good quantity of grain, artillery pieces, and all other military necessaries. And the Byzantines too sent the pick of their officers and men.

With the two sides matched, the intensity of the fighting revived and the siege was once again fought with incredible determination. [3] The constant battering of the walls by Philip's rams was starting to bring sections down, and since his artillery was also driving the defenders off the battlements, he had his men simultaneously force their way into the city in close formation through the breaches and bring their scaling ladders up to the cleared stretches of wall. In the hand-to-hand fighting that ensued, many died or fell with multiple wounds. The rewards of victory brought out the best in the fighters, [4] since the Macedonians, who were expecting to plunder a prosperous city and to be rewarded by Philip, were induced by their hope of gain to face danger without flinching, and the Perinthians, who could clearly imagine the horrors that would follow the fall of the city, stood undaunted in battle in the hope of securing their survival.

76. The defenders' ability to maintain their struggle for survival was helped a great deal by the physical nature of the city. Perinthus is a coastal town, situated on a lofty peninsula† with a neck only a stade wide, and its houses are closely packed together and particularly tall. [2] As they climb the hill, these houses are always built to overtop one another, and so they give the city as a whole the appearance of a theatre.* This explains why the Perinthians were not being beaten even though stretches of wall were constantly collapsing. What they did was barricade the streets and then whichever houses happened to be lowest at the time acted as a good, strong wall. [3] This meant that, even after Philip had expended a great deal of effort and taken huge risks to gain control of the outside wall, he was faced with an even tougher proposition in the form of the ready-made wall formed by the houses. Moreover, since all the Perinthians' military needs were being readily supplied by the Byzantines, Philip divided his forces into two.* One division he left at the siege under the command of his best officers, while he took the other and launched a surprise attack on Byzantium. He put the city under a close siege—[4] and the Byzantines found themselves in great difficulties, since everything that they might need, including soldiers and ordnance, was at Perinthus.

That was how things stood at Perinthus and Byzantium. [5] Among the historians, Ephorus of Cyme ended his work at this year with the siege of Perinthus. He covered almost 750 years of both Greek and non-Greek history, beginning with the return of the Heraclidae,* in thirty books, each of which began with a preface. [6] Diyllus of

Athens started the second part of his history where Ephorus left off, and gave a sequential account of both Greek and non-Greek history from then up until the death of Philip.

340/39

77. *In the year of the Archonship of Theophrastus in Athens, the Romans appointed as their consuls Marcus Valerius and Aulus Cornelius, and the 110th Olympic festival was celebrated, with Anticles of Athens the victor in the stade race. In this year:*

[2] Since Philip had Byzantium under siege, the Athenians judged him to be in breach of the peace that they had concluded with him,* and before long they dispatched a substantial fleet to relieve the Byzantines. Reinforcements were also sent there from Chios, Cos, Rhodes, and some other Greek states. [3] Alarmed by the convergence of so many Greeks, Philip broke off both sieges and made peace with the Athenians and the other Greeks.*

[4] As for Sicilian affairs, the Carthaginians completed their extensive preparations for the war and conveyed their forces across to the island. Including the forces already there, they had more than seventy thousand foot soldiers, and at least ten thousand cavalry, chariots, and pairs of horses for the chariots; they also had two hundred warships, and more than a thousand transport ships for the horses, artillery, grain, and so on. [5] Timoleon was not dismayed, however, when he was informed of the enemy's numbers, even though his own army had been reduced to just a few men.* He brought the ongoing war with Hicetas to an end, added Hicetas' men to his own,* and immeasurably increased the number of men under his command.

78. He decided to fight the Carthaginians in their own territory, the idea being to prevent any harm being done to his allies' farmland and to destroy only land that belonged to the barbarians. [2] He therefore immediately mustered his entire army—mercenaries, Syracusans, and all the auxiliaries—and convened a general assembly at which he delivered a speech that effectively aroused his men's ardour for the decisive battle. His words met with unanimous approval, with every man there calling on him to lead them straight against the barbarians, and he took to the field at the head of an army of close to twelve thousand men in all.

[3] Unexpectedly, however, by the time he reached Acragas, the troops were restive and mutinous. One of the mercenaries was behind it, a particularly brutal hothead called Thrasius.* He was one of those who had plundered the Delphic sanctuary along with the Phocians, and the way he behaved now was perfectly in keeping with all the outrages he had committed earlier. [4] Even though everyone else, I dare say, who had been involved in the violation of the sanctuary had met with the appropriate punishment from heaven, as I described a short while earlier,* he alone escaped the gods' notice, and now he set about encouraging the mercenaries to desert. [5] He said that Timoleon had lost his mind and was leading his troops to certain destruction. The Carthaginians had six times the number of men, he pointed out, and all their equipment was vastly superior, and yet Timoleon was promising victory, gambling with the lives of the mercenaries whose wages he had been too short of money to pay for a long time. [6] His advice was that they should return to Syracuse and demand their pay, and not accompany Timoleon any further on a doomed campaign.

79. The mercenaries agreed with Thrasius and committed themselves to mutiny, but by repeated appeals and promises of rewards Timoleon quelled their restiveness. A thousand men deserted with Thrasius, however. Timoleon deferred their punishment for a later occasion, and sent instructions to his friends in Syracuse that they were to treat the deserters well and pay them what they were due. This brought the last of the unrest to an end, although Timoleon stipulated that the mutineers were to have none of the credit for the victory. [2] Once his generous treatment had rekindled the rest of the men's loyalty, he advanced on the enemy, whose camp was not far distant. He assembled his troops† and stiffened their resolve with a speech in which he described how cowardly the Carthaginians were and reminded them of Gelon's victory.*

[3] As if from a single throat, the men were all calling on him to attack the barbarians and begin the battle, when it so happened that the supply train arrived with celery for their mattresses, and Timoleon said that they should see this as an omen of victory, because the crown of victory at the Isthmian games was made of celery. [4] At Timoleon's urging, the men wove the celery into crowns* and joyfully advanced into battle with their heads wreathed, confident that the gods were predicting their victory. And so it proved, [5] since against the odds

they got the better of the enemy, thanks to a combination of their own calibre and divine assistance.

Once Timoleon had drawn up his men for battle, he advanced down the slope of a line of hills towards the river,* which ten thousand of the enemy had already crossed, and immediately attacked these men, with himself positioned right in the centre of the phalanx. [6] A hard-fought battle ensued, but the Greeks' martial spirit and battle-field skills were superior, and the barbarians sustained terrible losses. The enemy soldiers who had crossed the river turned to flight, but then the entire Carthaginian army crossed the river and remedied the situation.

80. The battle was on again. With their superior numbers the Carthaginians were beginning to overwhelm the Greeks, when suddenly the heavens opened in a violent cloudburst, large hailstones pelted down, and thunder and lightning, accompanied by powerful gusts of wind, crashed all around them. The freak storm struck the Greeks from behind, but it drove right in the faces of the barbarians, so that, while it was easily endurable by Timoleon's men, it was all too much for the Carthaginians, and when the Greeks attacked they turned to flight.

[2] With the entire Carthaginian army wheeling and facing the river—horsemen and foot soldiers jumbled up together, and chariots adding to the chaos—they stood no chance at all. Some were trampled by their own side or were spitted by the swords and spears of their comrades, while others were driven like sheep into the river by the enemy cavalry and were struck down from behind. [3] The wounds that felled many of them were not even delivered by the enemy: what kept the bodies piling up were fear, congestion, and the hazards of the stream-bed. The worst thing was that the ferocity of the storm caused the river to bear down on them more violently than before, and many men were drowned as they tried to swim across in their armour.

[4] The upshot was that the soldiers of the Sacred Battalion—2,500 men, the foremost in Carthage for their calibre, prestige, and wealth—were annihilated, after putting on a dazzling display of martial prowess, [5] while from the other contingents of the army more than ten thousand were killed and at least fifteen thousand were taken prisoner. Most of the chariots were broken in the mêlée, and two hundred were captured. The pack animals, the draught animals, and the majority of

the carts with their supplies fell into Greek hands. [6] The arms and armour were mostly ruined by the river, but a thousand breastplates and more than ten thousand shields were delivered to Timoleon's tent. Some of these were subsequently dedicated in Syracusan temples, while others were distributed to the allies, and Timoleon sent some to Corinth, to be dedicated in the temple of Poseidon. 81. A great deal of valuable property was also captured, particularly because the Carthaginians had owned a great many silver and gold goblets, and all of this, along with the rest of the treasure (of which there was an excessive quantity because the Carthaginians were so rich), Timoleon allowed the soldiers to keep to reward their valour.

[2] The Carthaginians who escaped from the battlefield struggled through to safety at Lilybaeum, but they were so bewildered and frightened that they did not dare to board their ships and sail away to Libya; the hostility of the gods towards them seemed so great that they thought they would be swallowed up by the Libyan Sea. [3] When news of the scale of the disaster reached Carthage, their spirits were crushed and they anticipated the imminent arrival of Timoleon and his army. The first thing they did was recall Gisco, the son of Hanno, from exile and give him the command of the armed forces; he was widely believed to be an exceptionally bold and talented general. [4] They also decided that in the future they would not risk the lives of Carthaginian citizens in war, but would hire foreign mercenaries, especially Greeks, who, they were sure, would respond in large numbers to the call-up because of the high rate of pay and the wealth of Carthage. Finally, they sent competent ambassadors to Sicily, with the job of obtaining peace on whatever terms they could get.

339/8

82. *At the beginning of the following year, Lysimachides became Archon in Athens, and in Rome Quintus Servilius and Marcus Rutilius were elected consuls. In this year:*

After returning to Syracuse, the first thing Timoleon did was banish as traitors the mercenaries who had deserted with Thrasius. [2] They sailed over to Italy, and in Bruttium they occupied and pillaged a village on the coast. In response, the Bruttii immediately marched against them in strength, stormed into the village, and massacred them—and so the mercenaries who had abandoned Timoleon came to a wretched end and were repaid for their wrongdoing.

[3] Timoleon next arrested and put to death Postumius of Etruria, who had been preying on shipping with a fleet of twelve corsairs and had put in at Syracuse in the belief that it was a friendly city. He also received the settlers sent out from Corinth, who were five thousand in number. Then, when the Carthaginians opened negotiations and fervently begged for peace, he granted it to them, with the terms being that the Greek cities should all be free; that the Lycus river* should be the border between their two realms; and that the Carthaginians should give no assistance to the tyrants who were at war with the Syracusans.

[4] After this, he defeated Hicetas and put him to death, and then took the town of Etna and wiped out the Campanian inhabitants. He browbeat Nicodemus, the tyrant of Centuripae, into leaving the city, put an end to the tyranny of Apolloniades, the ruler of Agyrium, and gave Syracusan citizenship to all those he had liberated. In a word, he uprooted all the Sicilian tyrants, freed the cities, and accepted them into his alliance. [5] He had heralds proclaim in Greece that the Syracusans were offering land and houses to anyone who wanted Syracusan citizenship, and many Greeks moved there to take possession of a farm. Eventually, forty thousand new settlers were allotted unassigned land in Syracuse, and Agyrian farmland was so extensive and fertile that another ten thousand were settled there.

[6] He also prioritized the making of certain improvements to the existing Syracusan law code, as drawn up by Diocles.* He left the laws on private contracts and inheritance unchanged, but he revised all the legislation that covered public business in accordance with his conception of the city's best interests. [7] The person he made responsible for the revision of the laws was Cephalus of Corinth, who was well known as a man of culture and intelligence. And, once Timoleon had finished with that, he transferred the population of Leontini to Syracuse, and enlarged Camarina with a new batch of settlers.

83. In short, the peaceful conditions he established throughout Sicily made rapid economic progress possible for the cities. For a long time they had been drained of their inhabitants by civil strife and civil wars, and by the constant series of tyrants. Moreover, because their farmland had been left unworked it was running wild and was no

longer producing domesticated crops. But now, thanks to the large number of new settlers all over the place, and to the longevity of the peace that was instigated by Timoleon, the fields were reclaimed by tillage and produced a wide variety of crops in large quantities. And by selling these crops to traders at profitable rates, the Siceliots rapidly recovered their prosperity.

[2] Hence, with the money that was raised in this way, a great many monumental edifices were built around this time. In Syracuse, for instance, there was built on the Island the hall known as 'the Hall of Sixty Couches'.* Built by the dynast Agathocles, this was the largest and most magnificently appointed structure in Sicily, and was so imposing in its construction that it surpassed the gods' temples—and therefore received a sign of divine displeasure when it was damaged by a thunderbolt. Then there were the towers fringing the Small Harbour, with inscriptions, made out of different kinds of stones,* proclaiming the name of the man who had built them: Agathocles. Likewise, there were the structures built a little later by King Hieronymus, the Olympieium in the agora and the altar by the theatre, which is a stade in length and proportionately tall and wide.

[3] Among the lesser cities, a category that includes Agyrium,* the town was able, thanks to its involvement in the assignment of farmland to new settlers (which was due to the productivity of its fields), to build a theatre which is the second most beautiful in Sicily after the one in Syracuse, temples, a council chamber, and an agora, not to mention other significant work, such as towers, and many large and beautifully wrought pyramidal grave-markers.

338/7

84. *In the year of the Archonship of Chaerondas† in Athens, Lucius Aemilius and Gaius Plautius were the next to be appointed to the consulate. In this year:*

King Philip, who had by now gained the friendship of most of the Greeks, was determined to put his leadership of Greece beyond dispute by cowing the Athenians into submission. [2] He therefore unexpectedly seized the city of Elatea, assembled his forces there, and committed himself to war with Athens.* Given that the Athenians were unprepared—there was, after all, a peace treaty in place between them and Philip*—he was expecting an easy victory, and that is exactly what transpired.

Some men arrived one night in Athens with news of Philip's occupation of Elatea and of his imminent arrival in Attica with his forces. [3] The Athenian generals had not been expecting anything like this, and, in a state of shock, they summoned the trumpeters and told them to keep sounding the alarm all night long. By the time word had spread to every household, the city was alert with fear, and first thing in the morning the entire population converged on the theatre* without waiting for the customary proclamation by the Archons.* [4] When the generals arrived, they introduced one of the men who had brought the information, and after he had said his piece, a fearful silence gripped the theatre. None of the men who usually addressed the assembly dared to offer any advice, and although the herald called repeatedly for people to recommend courses of action that might save them all, not a single speaker came forward.*

[5] In a state of great uncertainty and fear, the people kept looking towards Demosthenes.* When he mounted the speaker's platform, he argued that it was not all doom and gloom, and recommended that they should immediately send ambassadors to Thebes and call on the Thebans to join them in the struggle for freedom.* There was no time to get in touch with their other allies to request help, he said, because Philip was expected to reach Attica in two days' time;* and given that his route would pass through Boeotia, the only course open to them was an alliance with the Boeotians, since Philip had a treaty of friendship and alliance with the Boeotians and therefore, as he passed through their territory, he was bound to try to enlist their help for the war against Athens.

85. The Athenians approved his proposal, and the decree authorizing the embassy was drafted by Demosthenes. Then the Athenians began to ask themselves who was best able to speak on their behalf—and Demosthenes voluntarily stepped up in their hour of need. To cut a long story short, he carried out his mission as ambassador promptly and returned to Athens with the allegiance of the Thebans.* The addition of the Thebans, doubling the size of their army, restored the Athenians' confidence, [2] and before long they sent a full levy of their soldiers under arms to Boeotia, with Chares and Lysicles as their commanding officers. Since all the men of military age were firmly committed to the struggle, they wasted no time on the road and soon

reached Chaeronea in Boeotia.* The Boeotians were impressed by the speed with which the Athenians had appeared and were equally prompt to arm themselves and join up with their allies. They set up camp together and awaited the approach of the enemy.

[3] Philip's first move was to send ambassadors to the Boeotian federal council. The most senior of these ambassadors was Python, who was famous for his eloquence, and in the course of the alliance debate before the Boeotians it became clear that although he was superior to every other speaker, he came off worst when compared with Demosthenes. [4] And Demosthenes himself, in his published works, boasts of the speech he delivered in response to Python, counting it one of his major achievements, when he says: 'On that occasion, with his confidence high Python bore down on you with a flood of words, but I stood firm.'*

[5] Despite having failed to win the alliance of the Boeotians, Philip was still committed to war, even against both the Athenians and Boeotians at once, so he waited for some of his allies to catch him up, and then marched to Boeotia with an army of more than thirty thousand foot and at least two thousand horse. [6] Both sides were ready for battle, resolute and determined, and both sides were evenly matched in valour, but Philip had superior numbers and was the better general; [7] he had fought many battles, under all sorts of conditions, and had usually been victorious, so that he had extensive experience of warfare. The finest Athenian generals—Iphicrates, Chabrias, and Timotheus—were already dead. The best of those who remained was Chares, but in terms of the forcefulness and planning required of a general, he was no better than the next man.

86. At daybreak the armies were drawn up for battle. Philip posted his son Alexander on one of the wings—he was only a teen-ager, but was already well known for his martial spirit and forceful energy—and gave him his most senior officers in support, while he took command of the other wing at the head of the crack troops and deployed all the other individual units as the situation demanded. [2] The Athenians, for their part, divided their forces by nationality, entrusting one wing to the Boeotians and taking command of the other themselves.*

A fierce and prolonged engagement ensued. So many men fell on both sides that for a while the battle allowed them both equally to anticipate victory. [3] But Alexander was anxious to put on a display

of valour for his father, and he was in any case excessively ambitious—and, besides, there were many good men fighting alongside
him in support—so it was he who was the first to create a breach in
the enemy lines.* He slew so many of those who were ranged opposite
him that the line was wearing thin, [4] and since his companions were
being just as effective, the enemy formation as a whole was constantly
in danger of being breached. The bodies were lying in heaps by the
time Alexander was first able to force the troops facing him to turn
and flee. Next it was Philip's turn to bear the brunt of the fighting.
Refusing to yield the credit for victory even to Alexander,* he first
drove the enemy back by main force, and then compelled them to
turn and flee. Victory was his.

[5] Athenian losses in the battle came to more than a thousand, and
at least two thousand were captured alive. [6] The Boeotians too lost
many men, and considerable numbers were taken prisoner. After the
battle, Philip erected a trophy, gave permission for the enemy dead to
be buried, sacrificed to the gods in thanks for the victory, and rewarded
as they deserved those of his men who had distinguished themselves
in the battle.

87. Some writers claim that, while celebrating, Philip imbibed a great
deal of unmixed wine* and led his friends in a victory revel through the
midst of the prisoners, sneering as he went at the misfortunes of these
miserable men. It so happened, however, that the orator Demades was
one of the prisoners, and he spoke his mind in terms that were able to
check the king's offensive behaviour. [2] Apparently, what he said was:
'My lord, when Fortune has cast you in the role of Agamemnon, doesn't
it embarrass you to act like Thersites?'* Philip was shaken by the accuracy
of the rebuke, they say, and so completely changed his attitude that he
tore off his garlands and repudiated the tokens of arrogance that are part
and parcel of a revel.* He was impressed by the freedom with which
Demades had spoken his mind, and he released him from captivity and
admitted him to an honoured position by his side. [3] The upshot was
that, charmed by the Attic grace of Demades' speech, he freed all the
prisoners unransomed, renounced all traces of post-victory arrogance,
sent emissaries to the Athenian people, and entered into a treaty of
friendship and alliance with them. He made peace with the Thebans too,
but he installed a garrison in the city.

88. Following their defeat, the Athenians condemned the general Lysicles to death, with the orator Lycurgus prosecuting.

Lycurgus was the leading politician in Athens at the time. He had done admirable service for twelve years as manager of the exchequer* and as one who had lived a famously virtuous life he was a particularly harsh prosecutor. [2] One can gain an impression of his abilities as an orator, and of his sternness, from the passage in *Against Lysicles* where he says:

You were general, Lysicles. A thousand of your fellow citizens died and two thousand were taken prisoner. A trophy commemorates our defeat and all Greece has been enslaved. All of these things happened under your command, when you were general—and yet you have the effrontery to live and see the light of day, and even to thrust yourself into the agora, a constant reminder of our country's shame and disgrace.

[3] A singular event took place in this year: at exactly the same hour of exactly the same day as the battle of Chaeronea, a battle was fought in Italy between the Tarentines, who had Archidamus, the Spartan king, on their side, and the Lucanians. Archidamus lost his life in the battle.* [4] He had been the king of Sparta for twenty-three years, and he was succeeded by his son Agis, who ruled for nine years. [5] Meanwhile, Timotheus, the tyrant of Heraclea Pontica, died after a reign of fifteen years and his brother Dionysius succeeded to the tyranny and ruled for thirty-two years.

89. *In the year of the Archonship of Phrynichus in Athens, the Romans appointed as their consuls Titus Manlius Torquatus and Publius Decius. In this year:*

King Philip was proud of his success at Chaeronea, and the fact that he had overpowered the most notable Greek cities* fuelled his desire to become the leader of Greece in its entirety. [2] He let it be widely known that he wanted to take on for the Greeks the job of waging war with the Persians and making them pay for their crimes against Greek sanctuaries.* This got him on the right side of the Greeks, and he continued to treat everyone with kindness both in private and in public. Then he told the cities that he wanted to hold talks with them on matters of mutual interest. [3] So a general congress was convened in Corinth, at which Philip addressed the issue of war against the

Persians, and inspired them with such hopes that he won their commitment to war. The upshot was that the Greeks elected him General Plenipotentiary of Greece,* and he set about making extensive preparations for the Persian campaign. He stipulated the quota of auxiliaries that every city should supply, and then returned to Macedon. That was how things stood with Philip.

90. In Sicily, Timoleon of Corinth, the man who had changed everything in Syracuse and Greek Sicily for the better, died after eight years as General. The Syracusans, who had the highest regard for him—for his abilities, and for all the great good he had done—gave him a magnificent funeral. A crowd gathered as his body was being taken to the place of burial and the following decree was read out by the herald, Demetrius, who had the most powerful voice of any herald at the time:

It has been decreed by the people of Syracuse that Timoleon the son of Timaenetus is to be buried at a cost of two hundred mnas and is to be honoured in perpetuity with musical, equestrian, and athletic contests, because he defeated the barbarians† and repopulated the greatest of the Greek cities, and thereby made himself the architect of freedom for the Siceliots.

[2] In this year also Ariobarzanes died after a reign of twenty-six years, and was succeeded by Mithridates,* who ruled for thirty-five years. The Romans fought and won a battle against the Latins and Campanians near the city of Suessa, and confiscated a portion of the enemy's land.* The consul Manlius, who was responsible for the victory, celebrated a triumph.

336/5

91. *In the year of the Archonship of Pythodorus* in Athens, the Romans appointed as their consuls Quintus Publius and Tiberius Aemilius Mamercus, and the 111th Olympic festival was celebrated, with Cleomantis of Cleitor the victor in the stade race. In this year:*

[2] King Philip, whom the Greeks had appointed their leader, opened the war against the Persians by sending Attalus and Parmenion ahead to Asia with some of his armed forces and instructions to free the Greek cities.* Philip himself, meanwhile, consulted the Pythia, since he wanted to embark on the war with the gods' blessing, and asked

whether he would defeat the Persian king. The response he received from her was: 'The bull is wreathed. Its end is nigh. The sacrificer is at hand.'

[3] Despite the enigmatic nature of this response, Philip was inclined to accept it as favourable to himself, as though the oracle were prophesying that the Persian king would be sacrificed like a ritual victim. In fact, however, that was not the case: the oracle's meaning, on the contrary, was that Philip would be slaughtered in the course of a festival involving sacrifices to the gods, when he would be wreathed like the bull. [4] Still, he thought that the gods were on his side, and he was delighted at the prospect of Asia becoming the spear-won possession of Macedon.

He therefore lost no time in performing magnificent sacrifices to the gods and celebrating the marriage of Cleopatra, his daughter by Olympias, to Alexander, the king of Epirus and Olympias' full brother.* [5] As well as honouring the gods, he wanted as many Greeks as possible to enjoy the festivities, so he laid on splendid musical contests and spectacular banquets for his friends and intimates. [6] From all over Greece he invited those who were closest to him, and he told his Friends to ask as many as possible of their acquaintances from abroad to come. For he particularly wanted to show favour to the Greeks, and to repay the honour they had granted him of supreme command with the appropriate courtesies.

92. The upshot was that large numbers of people poured in from every quarter to the festival—the contests and the marriage took place in Aegeae in Macedon—and Philip was awarded golden crowns* not just by distinguished individuals, but also by the majority of the important cities. Athens was one of them, [2] and when the herald proclaimed this crown, the last thing he said was that anyone who plotted against King Philip and sought refuge in Athens would be extradited to him. By means of this spontaneously prophetic utterance, the gods were clearly indicating, as though by divine foresight, that a plot was imminently to be launched against Philip's life. [3] Likewise, some other things that were said also seem to have been divinely inspired forecasts of the king's death.

During the royal symposium, for instance, Philip called on the tragic actor Neoptolemus, who had an unrivalled ability to project his voice and was the most popular actor of the day, to declaim some well-crafted verses, and especially any that related to the Persian

expedition. The artist picked a passage that he felt could be interpreted as relevant to Philip's invasion, intending it to reprove the
Persian king for his prosperity and to suggest that, for all its far-
famed magnitude, it could be overturned by Fortune. He began with
the following lines:*

> In your pride, now soaring higher than the sky,
> You think of estates more extensive than great plains,
> You think of palaces surpassing the dwellings of the gods,†
> Foolishly predisposing your life from afar.
> But the swift-footed one has you in his embrace,
> Hades, source of much grief.* He walks a path
> Shrouded in darkness, and of a sudden approaches
> Unseen to rob mortals of their best hopes.

And he continued with the rest of the passage, all of which was in the
same vein. [4] Philip enjoyed the recitation, and was completely and
utterly carried away with thoughts of overthrowing the Persian king,
especially since he was also taking into account the oracle he had
received at Delphi,* which had much the same import as what the
actor was saying.

[5] The symposium finally came to an end. Since the contests were
scheduled for the next day, the general populace flocked to the theatre
while it was still dark, and at daybreak the procession began. Along with
all the other magnificent artefacts, Philip paraded images of the twelve
gods,* exceptionally finely wrought pieces of work, marvellously
enhanced by the sheen of precious metals, and he accompanied these
with a thirteenth image, worthy of a god but of Philip himself, so that
the king was representing himself as enthroned among the twelve gods.

93. The theatre had filled up by the time Philip himself entered,
wearing a white *himation*.* He had ordered the bodyguards in his
train to keep their distance from him, since he wanted to show everyone that he had no need of their protection when he was shielded by
the goodwill of all the Greeks. [2] So high and mighty had he become,
and so universal were the praises and plaudits he was receiving, that
the plot against him, and his death, came as bolts out of the blue. [3]
But in order to ensure that my account of this incident is comprehensible, I shall first explain the reasons for the plot.

Pausanias, a Macedonian from Orestis, was one of the king's bodyguards and his good looks had attracted Philip's friendship. [4] When

he saw that another man, also called Pausanias, had become the object of the king's affection, he lambasted this second Pausanias, calling him an effeminate slut who was ready to accept the sexual advances of all and sundry. [5] This insult was too much for Pausanias to endure, and although at the time he kept his mouth shut, he told Attalus, who was a friend of his, what he intended to do, and then he deliberately let himself be killed. It was a remarkable event. [6] What happened was that, a few days later, a battle was being fought between Philip and the Illyrians, under their king, Pleurias, and Pausanias, who was positioned in front of Philip, took on himself all the blows that were meant for the king and died from his wounds.

[7] Pausanias' deed was widely praised, and Attalus, who was a courtier and highly influential with the king, invited the other Pausanias to dinner. After getting him drunk on a lot of unmixed wine, he handed his body over to his mule-drivers to be sodomized and abused as though he were a prostitute. [8] Pausanias was mortified by the rape and when he sobered up he denounced Attalus to the king.* Philip was outraged by the lawlessness of the act, but he was reluctant to condemn Attalus for it, because of their kinship and because Attalus was very important to him at the time. [9] It was not just that he was the nephew* of Cleopatra, Philip's most recent bride, but he had also been chosen to command the forces that had been sent ahead to Asia and was formidable on the battlefield. So, while recognizing that Pausanias' anger at what had happened was justified, the king tried to soothe him by giving him valuable gifts and promoting him to a higher rank in the corps of bodyguards.

94. Pausanias preserved his anger intact, however, and looked forward to punishing them both—the man who had wronged him and the man who was refusing to avenge him. The most important backing for the project came from the professor, Hermocrates. Pausanias was a student of his, and at one point during his studies he asked what was the best way of becoming truly famous. Hermocrates replied, 'By killing the man with the most significant achievements to his name, because then, whenever anyone mentions him, his killer will also be mentioned.'* [2] In his current angry state, Pausanias took this notion to heart, and since he was too worked up to tolerate any delay to the execution of his plan, he put it into effect during the aforementioned festival.

This is what happened. [3] Pausanias left horses at the city gates and made his way to the entrance of the theatre with a Celtic dagger concealed about his person. When, on Philip's orders, those of his Friends who were accompanying him preceded him into the theatre and at the same time the guards were some distance away, Pausanias saw that the king had been left alone, and he ran up and stabbed him through the ribs. The king fell lifeless to the ground, while Pausanias set out at a run for the gates and the horses he had prepared for his flight. [4] But, while some of the royal bodyguards immediately dashed over to the king, others, including Leonnatus, Perdiccas, and Attalus,* raced out of the theatre in pursuit of the assassin. Pausanias had a good start and would have reached his horse ahead of them and leapt on its back, had he not caught his foot in a vine and stumbled. This allowed Perdiccas and the others to catch up with him as he was getting to his feet, and together they stabbed him to death.*

95. So Philip met his end. In a reign of twenty-four years he had made himself greater than any other contemporary king, with an empire of such a size that he counted himself worthy to be enthroned among the twelve gods. [2] He is famous for having made himself king despite having started with the most meagre resources for such an enterprise; for having made his kingdom the greatest in the Greek world; and for having increased his empire more through his skill as a diplomat and his geniality than through his military valour. [3] Philip himself is said to have been prouder of his skills as a strategist and his diplomatic successes than of his abilities on the battlefield, [4] on the ground that while the army as a whole was partly responsible for his successes in battle, the credit for those which were the result of diplomacy was his alone.

[5] Now that I have reached the death of Philip, I shall end this book here, in accordance with my original plan. I shall start the next one with the accession of Alexander to the throne and try to cover all his exploits in a single book.*

BOOK 17

1. The previous book, the sixteenth of my history as a whole, began with the accession to the throne of Philip, the son of Amyntas; it covered both Philip's career in its entirety down to his death, and the history of other kings, peoples, and cities during the twenty-four years of Philip's reign. [2] In this book I shall begin the sequential narrative of events with the accession of Alexander, and cover his career down to his death, as well as contemporary events elsewhere in the known parts of the world.* It seems to me that this is the best way to make events memorable, when they are presented topically and with their ends joined to their beginnings.*

[3] In just a few years, Alexander achieved great things. In fact, thanks to his intelligence and courage, there is no other king, of all those whose memory has been preserved from ancient times, whose accomplishments come close to those of Alexander. [4] In just twelve years, he conquered much of Europe* and almost all of Asia, so it is not surprising that the glory that accrued to him equalled that of the heroes and demigods of old. But there is no need for me to anticipate in this preface any of Alexander's accomplishments, because the particular events themselves will sufficiently reveal the grandeur of his glory. [5] Being descended on his father's side from Heracles and on his mother's from the Aeacidae,* he innately possessed the qualities and abilities that were the foundation of his ancestors' fame. I shall now turn to the events of the period in question, presenting one by one the years that belong in the book.*

335/4

2. *In the year of the Archonship of Euaenetus in Athens, the Romans appointed as their consuls Lucius Furius and Gaius Manius.* In this year:*

Having inherited the Macedonian throne, the first thing Alexander did was punish his father's murderers as they deserved,* and then he devoted himself to seeing to his father's funeral. He proved to be a far better ruler than anyone had expected, [2] seeing that he was still very young. In fact, since his age was leading some people to think slightingly of him, he first won the Macedonians' loyalty with the appropriate promises—saying, that is, that only the name of the king had changed, and that everything would be managed just as it had been during his father's time—and then, by treating their embassies courteously, he encouraged the Greeks to preserve his father's legacy to him of their goodwill. [3] As for the troops, he accustomed them to respond readily to his commands by conducting frequent manoeuvres and tactical training exercises.

Attalus, however, was waiting in the wings to seize the throne, and Alexander decided to do away with him. Attalus was the brother of Philip's last wife Cleopatra,* and in fact Cleopatra had produced a child* for Philip just a few days before the king's death. [4] Attalus had been sent on ahead to Asia as joint commander with Parmenion of the expeditionary force; he had won the affection of the soldiers with his generosity and cordiality, and had become very popular in the army. Alexander had good reasons, then, to be concerned about the possibility that Attalus might link up with his opponents among the Greeks and claim the throne. [5] So he chose one of his friends, a man called Hecataeus, and sent him to Asia with sufficient soldiers and instructions to bring Attalus back alive, preferably, but if this was impossible, to murder him at the earliest opportunity. [6] So Hecataeus sailed over to Asia, joined Parmenion and Attalus, and waited for a chance to carry out his mission.

3. The realization that many of the Greeks were restive and heading towards rebellion caused Alexander a great deal of anxiety. [2] In Athens, Demosthenes was maintaining his anti-Macedonian stance and the news of Philip's death had been greeted with joy. The Athenians were not prepared to yield the leadership of Greece to the Macedonians. They entered into secret negotiations with Attalus and agreed to work with him, and they encouraged many of the Greek cities to espouse the cause of freedom. [3] Then the Aetolians voted to restore those of the Acarnanians who had known exile thanks to Philip. The Ambraciots, led by Aristarchus, threw out the garrison that had been installed by Philip, and changed their constitution to a democracy. [4] Likewise, the Thebans voted to expel the garrison on the Cadmea* from the city and not to recognize Alexander's leadership of Greece. The Arcadians were the only ones in Greece who had never acknowledged Philip's leadership* and now they were refusing to submit to Alexander as well. [5] Elsewhere in the Peloponnese, the

Argives, Eleans, Lacedaemonians, and a few others had set their sights on independence.* And several of the tribes who lived north of Macedon were resolved to rebel, so that unrest was widespread among the barbarians there. [6] Nevertheless, despite all the problems and threats that beset the kingdom, Alexander, though barely an adult,* unexpectedly and rapidly resolved all the difficulties. Some he won over by persuasive diplomacy, others were brought to heel by fear, and a few were forcibly subdued and compelled to recognize his authority.

4. He dealt first with the Thessalians.* He reminded them of their ancient kinship, based on their common descent from Heracles, and he stirred their hopes partly by speaking courteously to them, but mainly by making them great promises, and thereby got them to acknowledge, with an official vote of the Thessalian Confederacy, the leadership that he had inherited from his father.* [2] Next, he won a similar degree of loyalty from the tribes on his borders, and then he went to Thermopylae, convened a meeting of the Amphictyonic Council, and persuaded them to pass an official decree appointing him Leader of the Greeks. [3] He treated the Ambraciot ambassadors who came to him courteously and convinced them that their bid for independence had been only a few days premature, since he had been going to give them it of his own accord.

[4] In order to intimidate those who remained restive, he took to the field at the head of the Macedonian army in formidable battle array. A series of forced marches brought him to Boeotia, and he made camp not far from the Cadmea, much to the terror of the Thebans in the city. [5] When the Athenians heard of the king's march to Boeotia, they started to take him seriously for the first time, and indeed the young man's energy and his forcefulness in action tended to overawe all his enemies. [6] So the Athenians voted to fetch their property into the city from the countryside and to give their best attention to the state of the city walls, but they also sent ambassadors to Alexander, asking him to pardon their tardiness in acknowledging his leadership.

[7] Demosthenes was attached to this embassy, but he did not attend the meeting with Alexander. He went as far as Cithaeron,* but then turned back to Athens, perhaps out of fear, given his anti-Macedonian stance, or perhaps because he wanted to retain the good opinion of the Persian king. [8] After all, we are told that he received

a great deal of money from the Persians, to support his anti-Macedonian measures. This, apparently, is what Aeschines was referring to when he taunted Demosthenes in one of his speeches with venality, and said: 'It's true that at the moment his debts have been drowned by Persian gold, but even that will not be enough, because no amount of money has ever satisfied a crook.'* [9] Anyway, Alexander responded graciously to the ambassadors and relieved the Athenians' fears.

He next summoned the Greek ambassadors and delegates to a meeting in Corinth. Once the delegates were in session in the customary fashion,† he gave a speech and his arguments were so reasonable that he persuaded the Greeks to vote him General Plenipotentiary of Greece and to support his expedition to punish the Persians for their crimes against the Greeks.* Once he had gained this appointment, he returned with his troops to Macedon.

5. Now that I have covered Greece, I shall move on to what was happening in Asia. Immediately after Philip's death, Attalus embarked on a course of revolution and agreed to cooperate with the Athenians against Alexander, but later he changed his mind. He had in his keeping the letter he had received from Demosthenes* and he sent it off to Alexander along with expressions of goodwill, in an attempt to have the charges against him dropped. [2] But Hecataeus murdered Attalus, as ordered by the king,* and then the restiveness and rebelliousness of the Macedonian expeditionary force in Asia came to an end, though this was not just because of Attalus' murder, but also because Parmenion was squarely Alexander's man.

[3] Since I am about to write about the Persian kingdom, I must backtrack a few years and take up the narrative at an earlier point. During Philip's reign in Macedon, the Persian king was Ochus, who was a brutal and harsh ruler to his subjects. His cruel nature made him an object of loathing, and the chiliarch, Bagoas (physically a eunuch, and temperamentally corrupt and belligerent), had a doctor poison Ochus, and he placed on the throne the youngest of Ochus' sons, Arses.* [4] He also killed the brothers of the new king, who were still very young, the idea being that the young man would be more open to Bagoas' guidance if there was no one else to advise him. But when young Arses showed that he was appalled by these atrocities and was clearly intending to punish the criminal responsible for them, Bagoas struck before he could put his plans into action, and killed Arses and his children, in the third year of his reign.*

[5] Since the royal house was now extinct, there being no one of royal blood to succeed to the throne, Bagoas selected one of his friends, Darius by name, and helped him gain the kingdom.* Darius was the son of Arsanes and the grandson of Ostanes, who was the brother of Artaxerxes, a former Persian king.* [6] Bagoas came to an unusual end, one that is worth recording. Behaving with his usual savagery, he planned to poison Darius, but the king got wind of the plot; he invited Bagoas to join him, as if this were no more than a friendly gesture, and offered him the cup, leaving him no choice but to drink the poison.

6. If Darius was thought to be qualified for the kingship, this was because he was known to be by far the bravest man in Persis. Once, during Artaxerxes' reign, when the king was at war with the Cadusians,* one of the Cadusians, renowned as a spirited and fearless warrior, issued a general challenge to anyone in the Persian army who was prepared to fight him in single combat, and no one was brave enough to respond except Darius, who stepped up and slew the man who had issued the challenge. As a result, he was handsomely rewarded by the king and was hailed by the Persians as the first among them for courage. [2] It was because of this display of valour that he was considered to be qualified for kingship, and he took power at about the same time that Alexander succeeded to the throne on the death of Philip. [3] This was the man delivered up by Fortune to be Alexander's opposite number and to defy his prowess, and in fact it took many major battles to decide which of them was the best. But all this will become clear when we come to the particular events, and I shall now turn to sequential narrative.

7. Philip was still alive when Darius came to the throne, and Darius' desire at the time was to divert the coming war back to Macedon, but when Philip died he stopped worrying, because he thought that Alexander was too young to cause him any trouble. [2] But when, as a result of his forcefulness and energy, Alexander gained the supreme leadership of the Greeks and the young king's calibre became known far and wide, Darius had to face reality, and he began to give serious attention to his armed forces. He built a great many triremes, mustered significant numbers of troops, and appointed outstanding men as his officers. One of these was Memnon of Rhodes, a man of particular courage and an exceptional strategist. [3] The king gave Memnon five thousand mercenaries and ordered him to go to the city of Cyzicus and try to take it. So Memnon proceeded with these forces across Mount Ida.

[4] According to some of the mythologers, this mountain was named after Ida, the daughter of Melisseus.* It is the tallest mountain in the Hellespontine region, and in the middle of the range there is a wonderful cave, in which the goddesses are supposed to have been judged by Alexander.* [5] The Idaean Dactyls* are also said to have lived on this mountain, who were the first to work iron, once they had been taught how to do so by the Mother of the Gods. There is a singular and strange phenomenon associated with this mountain: [6] at the time of the rising of the Dog Star,* the surrounding air is so still on the highest peak of the mountain that the swirling of the winds is left far below, and the sun can be seen rising while it is still night, with its rays not concentrated† into a circular shape, but with its fire scattered here and there, so that it looks as though the horizon is lined with many bonfires. [7] Then, a short while later, these fires draw together and form a single mass with a diameter of three plethra. And finally, once day has dawned, the sun regains its usual size and the day continues as normal.

[8] Anyway, after crossing the mountain, Memnon launched a surprise attack on Cyzicus and very nearly took it.* After his failure, he plundered Cyzicene farmland and seized a lot of booty. [9] Meanwhile, Parmenion took the city of Grynium by main force and sold the inhabitants into slavery. He then put Pitane under siege,* but Memnon appeared and the Macedonians broke off the siege, seeing that they were no match for him. [10] Some time later, a force of Macedonians and mercenaries under the command of Callas fought a battle against the Persians in the Troad;* they lost the battle—they were greatly outnumbered—and retreated to Rhoeteum. That was how things stood in Asia.

8. Having quelled unrest in Greece, Alexander marched against Thrace, where the tribes were restive, and many of them submitted to him in fear. Then he attacked Paeonia, Illyris, and the neighbouring regions,* where a number of the barbarian tribes had rebelled, but he overcame them and in fact made all the barbarians in the region his subjects. [2] He was still occupied with this task when messengers arrived with news that rebelliousness was widespread in Greece, and that many of the Greek cities—Thebes above all—had already embarked on a course of insurrection. The news prompted him to

prioritize putting an end to the unrest in Greece and he returned to Macedon.

[3] In an attempt to force the garrison on the Cadmea out of the city, the Thebans had the acropolis under siege—but Alexander suddenly appeared* at the head of his full levy and encamped near the city. [4] Before his arrival, in addition to surrounding the Cadmea with deep trenches and solid palisades, so that neither help nor supplies could reach the garrison, [5] the Thebans had also sent for help from the Arcadians, Argives, and Eleans. They sent emissaries to Athens as well, to ask for an alliance, and when Demosthenes gave them a whole lot of weaponry, paid for out of his own pocket,* they were able to equip those of their men who were unarmed.

[6] As for the states the Thebans had asked for help: the Peloponnesians sent soldiers to the isthmus, but they then waited there to see what would happen, because Alexander was expected to arrive any day, and although the Athenians, on Demosthenes' proposal, voted to send help to Thebes, they did not actually dispatch the men, preferring to wait and see how the scales of the war fell. [7] Seeing all the ways in which the Thebans were getting ready for the siege, the commander of the Cadmea garrison, Philotas, strengthened his fortifications and made sure that he was well supplied with ordnance.

9. Alexander's unexpected arrival from Thrace with his full levy meant that the Thebans' allies had only a half-hearted presence, and the enemy forces were left with an obvious and undeniable superiority. Nevertheless, when the leading men of Boeotia met in council and debated the war, the unanimous opinion was that they should fight for their independence. The decree was passed by the assembly, and everyone was firmly committed and ready to risk conflict. [2] For a while, though, Alexander did nothing; he was giving the Thebans time to reflect and change their minds, and he could not believe that a single city would dare to fight such a large army.

[3] On this occasion, Alexander had more than thirty thousand foot and at least three thousand horse, and all of them were battle-hardened veterans of Philip's campaigns who had scarcely suffered a single reverse. These were men whose abilities and determination were such that Alexander was planning to overthrow the Persian empire with them. [4] If the Thebans had bowed to circumstances and entered into negotiations with the Macedonians with a view to reaching an

agreement and ending hostilities, Alexander would have welcomed
their petition and would have agreed to everything he was asked,
because he wanted to be rid of the troubles in Greece so that his hands
would be free for the war against the Persians. But, as things were, it
seemed to him that the Thebans were treating him with contempt,
and so he decided to destroy the city utterly and to use this act of
terror as a way of checking the momentum of those who were feeling
bold enough to rebel.

[5] Once he had got his army ready for the battle, he had a herald
proclaim that he would welcome any of the Thebans who wanted to
come over to his side and benefit from the peace that the Greeks were
enjoying in common. But the Thebans, giving as good as they got,
posted their herald on a high tower and had him proclaim in turn that
they would welcome anyone who wanted to join the Great King* and
themselves in the work of freeing the Greeks and ending the tyrannical
regime in Greece. [6] This cut Alexander to the quick. He flew into
a towering rage and decided to see that the Thebans were punished
with ultimate force. In a fury he saw to the construction of siege
engines and did everything else that was necessary to prepare for the
coming battle.

10. When the Greeks learnt how much danger the Thebans were
in, although they were appalled by the fact that the city was threatened with imminent disaster, they held back from sending help
because of the feeling that it was the Thebans' own precipitate and
ill-advised stance that had condemned them to certain destruction.
[2] As for the Thebans, it was not the danger that concerned
them—they had the courage to accept that willingly—but they were
disturbed by certain oracles and portents they had received from the
gods.

In the first place, a fine spider's web appeared in the sanctuary of
Demeter, which was not just as big as a *himation*,* but also was surrounded by an iridescent sheen like a rainbow in the sky. [3] When
they consulted the Delphic oracle about it, they received the following reply:

> This sign is intended by the gods for all men,
> But especially for the Boeotians and their neighbours.

And the national oracle of Thebes* gave them this reply:

> The woven web is bad for one but good for another.

[4] This sign appeared about three months before Alexander came to Thebes, and then, at the time of his arrival, the statues in the agora visibly dripped sweat and were covered with great gouts of it. And that was not all. The officers of the confederacy received reports from a number of people that a sound very like a bellow was coming from the marsh at Onchestus,* and that at Dirce a blood-coloured ripple was running over the surface of the water. [5] And others arrived from Delphi and reported that there was blood on the roof of the temple which the Thebans had built with Phocian spoils.*

The professional interpreters of signs said that the meaning of the web was that the gods were departing from the city,* while its many hues meant that there would be a storm of various troubles; that the sweating statues meant overwhelming disaster, and that the appearance of blood in several places meant that a great slaughter would take place in the city. [6] Since the gods were clearly predicting catastrophe for the city, the advice of the experts was that the Thebans should not commit themselves to deciding the war on the battlefield, but should rely on negotiation, as an alternative, safer way to settle matters.

Despite all this, the Thebans' resolve remained solid. In fact, so far from despairing, their determination led them to remind one another of their success at Leuctra and in other battles where, to everyone's surprise, they had gained victory against the odds by their valour.* So the Thebans hurtled, with a confidence that was brave rather than sensible, towards the total destruction of their city.

11. Meanwhile, Alexander took only three days to get everything ready for the assault on the city. He divided his forces into three. The first division was to assault the palisades which had been built in front of the city, the second was to confront the Thebans, and the third was to stay in reserve and in readiness to take over the fighting from any section of the army that was hard pressed. [2] The Thebans posted their cavalry behind the palisade, and deployed their freed slaves, resident exiles, and resident foreigners against those who were assaulting the wall, while they themselves made ready to engage Alexander and his Macedonians, who greatly outnumbered them, in front of the city. [3] The women and children crowded into the sanctuaries and besought the gods to save the city at this hour of peril.

When the Macedonians approached and each division of the army encountered its opposite number, the trumpets sounded the signal for engagement, and both sides together screamed out their battle-cries and hurled their javelins at the enemy. [4] Soon all the javelins were spent, and then everyone fell to fighting with swords and a brutal struggle took place. Because of their numbers and the weight of their phalanx, the Macedonians were exerting a virtually irresistible force, but the Thebans had the advantage in terms of physical fitness, especially because of their constant training in the gymnasia. Their self-confidence gave them an edge as well, and they stood their ground.

[5] On both sides, consequently, many men were wounded and many died from the frontal wounds they received. As the soldiers clashed and fought, the mingled sounds arose of groans and shouts and cries of encouragement, with the Macedonians urging their comrades to live up to the valour they had displayed in the past, and the Thebans exhorting one another to free their women, children, and parents from the threat of enslavement, to prevent their country and all their homes falling to Macedonian aggression, and to remember the battles of Leuctra and Mantinea,* and the valour they had displayed on those occasions to universal acclaim. For a long time, then, the courage displayed by both sides was so extraordinary that the battle hung in the balance.

12. After a while, however, seeing that the Macedonians were flagging in the battle, while the Thebans were still fighting keenly for their freedom, Alexander ordered the reserves to take over. Falling suddenly on the weary Thebans, the Macedonians pressed them hard and took many lives. [2] But the Thebans refused to give up; on the contrary, their desire to win led them to scorn every danger. Their valour induced them even to cry out to the Macedonians 'See! You're admitting your inferiority to us!', and although the invariable reaction when enemy reserves join the fray is to fear them for their freshness, on this occasion the Thebans proved to be the exception: when Alexander had those of his men who were falling back from exhaustion replaced, the danger roused the Thebans to an even greater degree of fortitude. [3] Their will to win was undaunted.

It came to Alexander's attention, however, that one of the postern gates had been left unguarded, and he sent Perdiccas with sufficient manpower to seize it and break into the city. [4] Perdiccas promptly carried out his orders, and the Macedonians slipped into the city through the gateway. The Thebans, meanwhile, had beaten back the first Macedonian phalanx, and were lined up steadfastly against the

second, with good hopes of victory. When they found out that a part
of the city was in enemy hands, however, they immediately withdrew
inside the walls. [5] But just as the infantry were racing inside the city,
the cavalry were doing the same, and they trampled and killed a lot of
their own men. Moreover, they rode into the city in such disarray that
some of them fell foul of their own weapons in the streets and trenches
and died like that. And then the soldiers of the garrison on the
Cadmea poured down from the acropolis and engaged the Thebans,
who in their disorganized state were slaughtered in droves.

13. Given the circumstances of the city's fall, many dramas of all
kinds were enacted within the walls. Because of the arrogance of the
proclamation by the herald, the Macedonians treated the Thebans
more harshly than is customary in war; howling out curses, they flung
themselves on the hapless creatures and killed everyone they came
across without mercy. [2] But the Thebans' desire to gain their freedom never wavered. So far from trying to save their lives, whenever
any of them encountered one of the enemy he engaged him, inviting
him to strike. As the city fell, no Theban was seen begging the
Macedonians to spare his life, and no Theban debased himself by
falling and grasping the knees of the victors.* [3] But no instance of
courage elicited mercy from the enemy, and there were not enough
hours of daylight for them to slake the savagery of their vengeance.
The entire city was sacked; children of both sexes were hauled away,
pitifully calling out to their mothers by name; in short, since every
member of every household was taken along with the property, the
enslavement of the city was total.

[4] Some Thebans were still alive. Fainting from their wounds,
they engaged the enemy, taking some of them with them as they died,
or, supporting themselves on the stumps of their spears, they sought
out their attackers and fought to the death with no thought of personal safety, but only of winning freedom. [5] A great slaughter took
place and corpses were piled everywhere in the city; it would have
been impossible for anyone not to have been moved by the sight to
pity the misfortunes of these miserable men. For there were even
Greeks in Alexander's army—Thespiaeans, Plataeans, Orchomenians,
and others who were enemies of the Thebans*—and they entered the
city along with him and demonstrated their hatred by the suffering
they caused the wretched Thebans. [6] The city therefore witnessed
terrible scenes: Greeks were being slaughtered without mercy by

fellow Greeks, men murdered by their close kin, and no hand was stayed by hearing the same language spoken.* By the time night fell, the houses had been plundered, and those who had taken refuge in the sanctuaries—the children, the womenfolk, and the elderly—were being hauled away and brutalized.

14. More than six thousand Thebans lost their lives, more than thirty thousand were taken prisoner, and an unbelievable amount of property was carried off. After burying the Macedonian dead, of whom there were more than five hundred, Alexander convened the Greek delegates and left it up to the common council of the Greeks* to decide how Thebes should be treated. [2] Once the council was in session, some of those who were hostile towards the Thebans proceeded to recommend that they should be punished severely because they had taken the side of the barbarians against the Greeks. They pointed out that, at the time of Xerxes' invasion,* the Thebans had actually joined the Persian army and fought against Greece, and that they were the only Greeks to be honoured as benefactors by Persian kings and whose ambassadors were allowed to be seated in the royal presence. [3] By listing a number of other similar examples, they aroused the feelings of the delegates against the Thebans so successfully that in the end they voted to destroy the city, to sell the prisoners, to declare any and all Theban exiles liable to summary arrest throughout Greece, and to make it illegal for any Greek to shelter a Theban. [4] So, in accordance with the will of the council,* Alexander razed the city to the ground, much to the terror of the other Greek rebels; and he also collected 440 talents of silver by selling the captives.

15. He next sent representatives to Athens to demand the extradition of the ten politicians who had been his main opponents—the most eminent being Demosthenes and Lycurgus. The Assembly met and Alexander's envoys were introduced. When the Athenian people heard what the envoys had to say, they were thrown into an agony of indecision. They wanted to preserve the city's reputation, but at the same time the destruction of Thebes had frightened them and, with the misfortunes of their neighbours before them as an object lesson, they were terrified of the awful consequences of refusal.

[2] After a number of speakers had addressed the Assembly, Phocion the Good, a political opponent of Demosthenes, said that the men whose extradition was being demanded should imitate the

daughters of Leos and Hyacinthus and go to their deaths willingly,* in order to keep irremediable disaster from the city of their birth, and he called men who refused to die for the good of the city weaklings and cowards. But the Athenians were disgusted by what he was saying and booed him off the speaker's platform. [3] Then a carefully worded speech by Demosthenes aroused sympathy in them for their politicians, and they made it clear that they wanted to keep them alive.

In the end, Demades—who, it is said, was given five talents of silver by Demosthenes to help him make up his mind*—advised the people to save the threatened men, and read out an artfully devised decree, which included a plea for the men's lives and a promise that they would be punished in accordance with the law, if they were found to deserve it. [4] The Athenians approved Demades' proposal. They ratified the decree and made him one of the members of an embassy they sent to Alexander, with instructions also to raise the issue of the Theban refugees and ask the king for permission to take them in. [5] And on this embassy Demades achieved everything he set out to do, thanks to his eloquence: he persuaded Alexander to release the men from the charges against them and to grant the Athenians all their other requests.

16. Alexander then returned with his troops to Macedon. He set up a meeting with the army officers and his most senior Friends, with the agenda being the invasion of Asia: when should the campaign be undertaken and how should the war be managed? [2] Antipater and Parmenion together recommended that, before setting his hand to such major exploits, he should first father an heir, but Alexander was an impatient man who could brook no delay under any circumstances, and he argued against them.* He said that it would be a disgrace if the man who had been chosen by the Greeks to take command of the war and had inherited his father's invincible army should sit at home celebrating marriages and waiting for children to be born. [3] He showed them where their true interests lay and spoke so well that he got them to look forward to the struggles ahead.

Then he performed magnificent sacrifices to the gods at Dium in Macedon, and held the theatrical contests in honour of Zeus and the Muses that his predecessor, Archelaus,* had instituted. [4] It was a nine-day festival, with each day named after one of the Muses. He had a pavilion made, large enough to hold a hundred couches, and he invited to the banquet his Friends and officers, and also the representatives of the Greek cities. All the arrangements were magnificent, a great many people enjoyed the fare and the entertainments, and he distributed to the entire army the sacrificial animals and everything else they might need to enjoy the celebrations. It was a time of rest and recreation for his troops.

334/3

17. *In the year of the Archonship of Ctesicles in Athens, the Romans appointed as their consuls Gaius Sulpicius and Lucius Papirius.*

Alexander led his army to the Hellespont and transported it over from Europe to Asia. [2] He sailed himself with sixty warships to the Troad,* and when he touched land he hurled his spear from his ship and it stuck in the earth. Then he leapt ashore, the first of the Macedonians to do so, and declared that he accepted Asia as a spear-won gift from the gods. [3] After honouring the tombs of the heroes, especially Achilles and Ajax, with offerings and other appropriate marks of respect, he carried out a precise count of the army that had accompanied him.*

The numbers came out as follows. The infantry consisted of 12,000 Macedonians, 7,000 auxiliaries, and 5,000 mercenaries, all under the command of Parmenion. [4] Then there were 7,000 Odrysians, Triballians, and Illyrians, and 1,000 archers and Agrianes,* so that the infantry totalled 32,000. The cavalry consisted of 1,800 Macedonians under the command of Philotas, the son of Parmenion, 1,800 Thessalians under the command of Callas, the son of Harpalus, and 600 men from elsewhere in Greece, under the command of Erigyius.* Then there were nine hundred Thracians,† scouts, and Paeonians, under the command of Cassander,* so that the cavalry totalled 4,500.* This was the strength of the army that crossed with Alexander from Europe to Asia. [5] And 12,000 foot and 1,500 horse were left behind in Macedon under Antipater's command.

[6] Before leaving the Troad, Alexander paid a visit to the sanctuary of Athena.* Now, the sacrificer, Aristander,† had noticed a statue of Ariobarzanes, the former satrap of Phrygia, lying on the ground in front of the temple,* and this was just one of a number of favourable omens that occurred. So he asked to see the king and assured him of victory in a cavalry battle, especially if it happened to take place in

Phrygia. [7] And he added that, in the course of a battle, Alexander would kill an eminent Persian governor with his own hands. These were the predictions vouchsafed to him by the gods, he said, and especially by Athena, who would help Alexander achieve success.

18. Alexander thanked the soothsayer for his predictions and performed a magnificent sacrifice to Athena. He dedicated his own shield to the goddess and replaced it with the best of the shields that had been presented to the temple, and it was with this shield that he fought his first battle, which was decided by his valour, and gained a famous victory. But this happened a few days later.

[2] The Persian satraps and generals had been too slow off the mark to impede the Macedonians' passage from Europe, but they met and discussed how to conduct the war against Alexander. Memnon of Rhodes, famous for his strategic brilliance, argued that they should not fight him directly, but should destroy the farmland so that shortage of provisions would prevent the Macedonians from advancing further; and he also argued that they should send both land and naval forces to Macedon, and make Europe rather than Asia the theatre of war. [3] Memnon's was the best advice, as subsequent events made clear, but he failed to win over the rest of the Persian high command, who thought the course of action he was recommending was beneath Persian dignity. [4] So, given that the prevailing view was that they should fight, the Persians mustered their forces from every quarter, until they greatly outnumbered the Macedonians,* and then they advanced to Hellespontine Phrygia. They made camp by the Granicus river, with the bed of the river as their forward defence.

19. When Alexander found out that the Persian forces had mustered, he advanced rapidly and halted within sight of the enemy, with the Granicus between the two camps. [2] This elicited no response from the barbarians, who had occupied the high ground; their plan was to fall on the enemy as they were crossing the river, when they thought it would be easy to gain the upper hand, since the Macedonian phalanx would be out of formation. [3] But Alexander boldly led his men at daybreak across the river, and before the enemy could react he had drawn up his forces in good order, ready for battle.*

The Persians posted their numerous cavalry, which they had decided was to bear the brunt of the fighting, all along the Macedonian front. [4] Memnon of Rhodes and the satrap Arsamenes, each with their own cavalry units, were in command of the left wing. Arsites and the Paphlagonian cavalry were deployed next to them, and then Spithrobates, the satrap of Ionia, with the Hyrcanian cavalry.* The right wing consisted of a thousand Medes, two thousand horsemen commanded by Rheomithres, and another two thousand Bactrians. Cavalry units from elsewhere, consisting of large numbers of men picked for their skill, occupied the centre. In all, the Persians had more than ten thousand cavalry. [5] Their infantry numbered at least a hundred thousand, but they were posted in the rear and did nothing, since the plan was that the cavalry would crush the Macedonians on their own.

[6] The cavalry of both sides set to with a will and battle was joined. On the Macedonian left, the Thessalians, under the command of Parmenion, stoutly withstood the assault of the units posted opposite them. On the right wing, Alexander had the elite cavalry under his command, and he was the first to mount a charge against the Persians. Once he was among them, he began to wreak havoc.

20. But the Persians were no mean fighters. For this contest of barbarian fervour against Macedonian calibre, Fortune had gathered together in one place the bravest men to decide the battle. [2] There was Spithrobates, for example, a man of exceptional courage, the satrap of Ionia, a Persian by birth and the son-in-law of King Darius. At the head of a large force of cavalry, and with forty Kinsmen* by his side, all men of outstanding ability, he attacked the Macedonians and began to press hard on his adversaries. Men were falling dead or wounded before his forceful onslaught, [3] and since the Macedonians were finding it hard to stand up to the pressure, Alexander turned his horse towards the Persian satrap and rode at him.

The Persian regarded this opportunity for single combat as a gift from the gods. There was a chance that, through his valour, Asia would be freed from the terrible fears that beset it, and it might be his own hands that would bring Alexander's bold enterprise to an end and redeem the glory of the Persians from shame. Before Alexander could do anything, Spithrobates hurled his javelin at him, and then fell on him with such vehemence and thrust his spear with such force that he drove it through Alexander's shield and the right shoulder strap, and pierced his breastplate.* [4] The weapon was impeding his arm, so Alexander shook it off, spurred his horse, and with the help of the force of his forward motion he drove his lance into the middle of the satrap's chest.

[5] Seeing the extraordinary bravery that this feat had entailed, the nearby ranks on both sides cried out in admiration, but in fact the tip of the lance broke off on the satrap's breastplate and the broken end of the shaft ricocheted off. The Persian then drew his sword and attacked Alexander, but the king took a firm grip on his sword† and quickly thrust at Spithrobates' face. He drove the blow home and the Persian fell, [6] but just then Rhosaces, his brother, rode up and slashed his sword down on to Alexander's head. The blow came very close to taking Alexander's life: it split open his helmet and lightly grazed his skin. [7] Rhosaces aimed another blow at the same gash—but Cleitus 'the Black' rode up and sliced off the Persian's arm.

21. The Kinsmen crowded around the two fallen men, and at first tried to pick off Alexander with their javelins, but then they closed in and risked being killed in their efforts to kill him. [2] Despite the difficulty and terrible danger of his situation, Alexander refused to succumb to the enemy, for all their numbers. He was struck twice on his breastplate, once on his helmet, and three times on the shield that he had found hanging in the temple of Athena, but still he did not give in; energized by his self-confidence, he rose to every challenge. [3] And then several more of the senior Persian officers also fell around him—the most distinguished of them being Atizyes, Pharnaces, who was Darius' brother-in-law, and Mithrobouzanes, the commander of the Cappadocian contingent.

[4] With a number of officers dead and every division of the Persian army proving inferior to the Macedonians, the first to be forced to retreat were those facing Alexander, and then all the others did the same. By common consent, the prize for valour was awarded to Alexander and responsibility for the victory was largely attributed to him. But in second place came the Thessalian cavalry, who gained a great reputation for martial prowess, thanks to the brilliant use to which they had put their squadrons and the exceptional valour with which they had fought.

[5] Once the Persian cavalry had fled the field, the infantry divisions engaged one another. The fighting was soon over, however. The barbarians had been demoralized and disheartened by the rout of their cavalry, and they quickly turned to flight. [6] In all, the Persians lost more than ten thousand foot and at least two thousand horse, and more than twenty thousand men were taken prisoner. After the battle, Alexander gave his dead a magnificent funeral, hoping that this

honour would increase the eagerness of his men to face the dangers of battle. [7] Then he took his army and marched through Lydia, where he gained the city of Sardis, along with its citadels and treasuries, when the satrap, Mithrines, surrendered it to him of his own accord.

22. Since the Persians who survived the battle—the general, Memnon, was one of them—took refuge in Miletus, Alexander made camp close to the city and every day launched continuous assaults on the walls in relays. [2] At first, the defenders found it easy to repulse the attacks from the walls, because a great many men had congregated inside the city, and they had plenty of artillery pieces and everything else they might need for a siege. [3] But when Alexander began to make a more determined use of his siege engines to breach the walls and increased the intensity of his assaults by land and sea at once, and the Macedonians began to force their way into the city through stretches of collapsed wall, then the defenders were overpowered and turned to flight.

[4] The Milesians hastened to abase themselves before Alexander, carrying olive-branches as suppliants, and they surrendered themselves and their city to him. As for the Persians, some were killed by the Macedonians, and some escaped from the city, but all the rest were captured. [5] Alexander treated the Milesians generously,* but the others were all sold into slavery. Since the fleet was now redundant and was hugely expensive, he disbanded it,* apart from a few ships (including a contingent of twenty from his Athenian allies), which were used to transport siege devices.

23. Some historians claim that the disbanding of the fleet was sound strategical thinking on Alexander's part, since he was expecting Darius' imminent arrival and the major land battle that would ensue, and also because he thought that the Macedonians would fight with more fervour if he deprived them of all hope of escape. [2] He employed the same tactic, they say, at the battle of the Granicus river, when he placed his army with the river at its rear, so that any thoughts of flight would be brought up short by the certainty that they would be killed in the river bed by their pursuers. And they point out that some years later Agathocles, the king of Syracuse, copied this tactic of Alexander's and thereby won a major battle that he had not been expected to win. [3] He took only a small force with him over to Libya, and what he did was burn the ships, which deprived his men of all hope of escape and compelled them to fight valiantly, with the result

that, when it came to battle with the Carthaginians, he defeated an army of theirs that numbered many tens of thousands.*

[4] After the fall of Miletus, most of the Persians and their mercenaries, and the most effective of the leading men, gathered in Halicarnassus. This city, where the residence of the Carian rulers is to be found, and well-appointed citadels, was the largest in Caria. [5] At this juncture, Memnon sent his wife* and children to Darius. His thinking was, first, that entrusting them to Darius was an excellent way of providing for their safety, and, second, that since the king now had good hostages, he would be more inclined to confer the supreme command on him. And this proved to be true, [6] because before very long Darius wrote to the coastal cities, telling them all to take their orders from Memnon. So, now that he had the supreme command, it was Memnon who was getting everything ready in Halicarnassus that he would need to withstand a siege.

24. King Alexander had the siege engines and grain taken to Halicarnassus by sea, while he marched with his whole army towards Caria, winning the cities on his route over to his side by treating them well. He was particularly generous to the Greek cities, which were given their independence and made exempt from paying tribute: after all, as Alexander remarked at the time, the freedom of the Greeks was the reason he had embarked on the war against the Persians in the first place.

[2] While he was en route, an elderly woman called Ada came to meet him, a member of the ruling family of Caria. She presented her petition, on her right to her family's traditional rulership of Caria, and asked for his help.* He decreed that she was to be entrusted with the rulership of Caria,* and his help for her also gained him the loyal support of the Carians. [3] All the cities immediately sent emissaries, honoured Alexander with golden crowns, and guaranteed to cooperate with him in everything.

Alexander made camp not far from Halicarnassus and set about the siege with a will, attempting to cow the defenders into submission. [4] At first, he launched continuous assaults on the walls in relays and the fighting went on day after day. Later, he brought up a variety of siege engines, and once his men, with the help of protective sheds, had filled in the trenches that lay in front of the city, he set about employing battering rams to try to demolish the towers and the curtain walls between the towers. And then, once he had brought down a stretch of wall, his subsequent efforts were focused on getting his men to break into the city over the rubble with hand-to-hand fighting.

[5] At first, Memnon found it easy to repel the Macedonians' assaults on the walls, since there were plenty of soldiers in the city. As for the siege engines, one night he slipped out of the city with a large body of men and tried to set fire to the contraptions. [6] Fierce fighting broke out in front of the city, in which the Macedonians had the superior abilities, but the Persians had the advantage of numbers and their situation was better, in the sense that they were helped by their comrades on the walls, who used their bolt-shooting catapults to kill and wound the Macedonians.

25. The air rang with the noise of the trumpets on both sides blaring out the signal for engagement, and the simultaneous cries of the soldiers applauding the feats of valour displayed by either side. [2] Some were trying to put out the flames that were rising into the sky among the siege engines; some were fighting the enemy hand to hand, and there were many casualties; some were building counter-walls behind those which were collapsing, far more sturdy constructions than the originals. [3] Memnon's officers formed a first line of defence and offered great rewards to any of their men who fought valiantly, so that on both sides the determination to win was formidable. [4] The scene before a spectator's eyes would therefore have been one of men falling with frontal wounds and being carried unconscious from the field, while others stood over their fallen comrades and fought fiercely to secure their safety; and of yet others who were on the point of giving up in the face of the overwhelming danger, but gained fresh heart and renewed confidence when urged on by their officers. [5] In the end, some of the Macedonians who fell died right by the city gates, among them an officer, a man of noble rank called Neoptolemus.*

Next, after two towers had totally collapsed and two curtain walls had been brought down, some of the men in Perdiccas' command, who were drunk, recklessly attacked the walls of the acropolis even though it was night-time. But when Memnon noticed the attackers' ineptitude, he sallied forth and, thanks to his far superior numbers, repulsed them and killed a good number of them. [6] Once they realized what had happened, the Macedonians emerged in force from their camp. The fighting grew intense and when Alexander arrived, the Persians were overcome and driven back inside the city. Alexander had his herald request a truce to recover the bodies of those of his men who had fallen in front of the wall, and Ephialtes and Thrasybulus, the Athenians who were fighting on the Persian side, advised Memnon not to give up the bodies for burial, but Memnon allowed the truce.

26. Next, at a meeting of the leading men, Ephialtes argued that there was no point in waiting for the city to fall and for them to be made prisoners, and proposed that the officers in command of the mercenaries should bear the brunt of the fighting and attack the enemy. [2] Memnon recognized Ephialtes' impulse towards valour, and since he placed great confidence in him because of his martial spirit and physical strength, he gave him permission to do as he wanted. [3] Ephialtes therefore put together a force of two thousand picked men, half of whom were given lighted torches, while the rest were to engage the enemy, and suddenly opened all the city gates. It was daybreak and, emerging from the city with his men, he had some of them set fire to the siege engines—the flames leapt up straight away—[4] while he led the rest, who were formed into a deep and closely packed phalanx, in an attack on the Macedonians who were coming to try to save the contraptions.

When Alexander realized what was happening, he posted the foremost fighters among his Macedonian troops in front, with a body of picked men to relieve them, and then behind these he posted a third division, all men of exceptional valour. Then he led this unit into battle, with himself at their head, and the enemy, who had thought that their numbers would deter opposition, found themselves having to fight. Alexander also dispatched men to put out the fires and save the siege engines.

[5] A great shout arose from both sides at once and the trumpets sounded the signal for battle. The soldiers fought with such skill and extraordinary determination that a ferocious struggle ensued. The Macedonians managed to stop the fire from spreading, [6] but Ephialtes and his men were winning the fight. He was by far the strongest man on the field and everyone who came up against him lost his life. The Macedonians were also losing many men to the relentless volleys of missiles fired from the top of the recently built counter-wall, where the defenders had built a wooden tower a hundred cubits high and filled it with bolt-shooting catapults. [7] Many Macedonians died and the rest were beginning to fall back under the onslaught of the countless missiles that were raining down on them, and when Memnon brought his reinforcements into play in large numbers, even Alexander had no real response.

27. At this point, just as the men from the city were gaining the upper hand, the scales of battle unexpectedly tipped† the other way. What happened was that the oldest of the Macedonians—men who had marched with Philip and had won many battles—had been excused from the battle because of their age, [2] but now felt impelled by the critical situation to help. They had far more pride and experience of warfare than their younger comrades, and they sharply rebuked them for their cowardly failure to stand firm in battle. They adopted a close formation with their shields overlapping and checked the enemy, who were already anticipating victory. [3] And in the end they killed Ephialtes and a lot of his men, and forced the rest to retreat into the city for safety.

[4] The Macedonians burst into the city along with the men they were pursuing, but night had fallen, so Alexander ordered the trumpeter to sound the recall and they returned to camp. [5] The governors and satraps on Memnon's side met and decided to abandon Halicarnassus. They garrisoned the acropolis with their best men and an adequate supply of provisions, and sailed with all the rest of the men and the matériel to Cos. [6] At daybreak, when Alexander learnt what had happened, he razed the city to the ground and surrounded the acropolis with a wall and a trench, both of a considerable size.* Then he dispatched a division of the army to the interior, with senior officers in command, who were tasked with subduing the neighbouring peoples. And in a vigorous campaign, they reduced the entire region up to Greater Phrygia while maintaining their men from the enemy's farmland.

[7] Meanwhile, Alexander subdued the entire coastline up to Cilicia.* In the course of this campaign, he added substantially to the number of towns under his sway. He also took a number of strongly defended hill-forts by force, following determined assaults, and the way one of these places fell to him was unusual. The adventure was so remarkable, in fact, that its story demands to be told. **28.** In the borderlands of Lycia there was a great rock fortress of exceptional strength, inhabited by people called the Marmares,* and, as Alexander marched past this place, the Marmares attacked the Macedonians who were bringing up the rear. They inflicted serious casualties and stole many of the captives and the draught animals, [2] and in response, Alexander put the place under siege. He focused all his efforts on taking it, but the Marmares were an exceptionally courageous people

and they bravely endured the siege, trusting in the natural impregnability of their fortress.

After two days of continuous assaults, however, it became clear that Alexander was not going to give up until the fortress had fallen to him. [3] At first, the elders of the Marmares advised the younger men to lay down their arms and make peace with the king on whatever terms they could obtain. The younger men, however, would not hear of it; none of them had the slightest desire to outlive his country's freedom. As a next alternative, then, the elders recommended that the young men should kill the children, the womenfolk, and the elderly, and then, since they had the strength to save themselves, break out at night through the enemy lines and find refuge in the nearby hill country.

[4] The young men agreed and told everyone to go home and spend time with their families, eating their greatest delicacies and drinking their finest wines, while waiting for the terrible event. But then the young men—there were about six hundred of them—changed their minds and decided that, rather than killing their families with their own hands, they would set fire to the houses, and then leave the city and retreat into the hills. [5] This was the plan they put into effect, and each of them turned their homes into their family's tombs, while they themselves slipped through the lines of the enemy encampment under cover of darkness and escaped into the nearby hill country.

These were the events that took place in this year.

333/2

29. *In the year of the Archonship of Nicostratus in Athens, in Rome Caeso Valerius and Lucius Papirius were the next to be appointed to the consulate. In this year:*

Darius sent a large amount of money to Memnon and appointed him commander-in-chief for the war. [2] Memnon raised a large force of mercenaries, manned three hundred ships, and fought a dynamic campaign. He won Chios over to his side and then sailed to Lesbos, where Antissa, Methymna, Pyrrha, and Eresus fell to him without any difficulty. The siege of Mytilene, however, which was a sizeable town with plentiful resources and defenders, took many days and cost him many men, but it did at last fall to him. [3] And once news of

Memnon's blitzkrieg got around, most of the Cycladic islands rushed to send embassies to him.

When word reached Greece that Memnon was intending to sail to Euboea with his fleet, the reaction in the Euboean cities was terror, but those Greeks who had sided with the Persians, such as the Spartiates, were excited by the prospect of political change. [4] With the help of bribes, Memnon got many of the Greeks to make common cause with the Persians. Nevertheless, Fortune put an end to his glorious progress: he caught a fatal disease and died, and his death also spelled the end of Darius' empire, 30. Because the king had been expecting Memnon to make Europe rather than Asia the sole theatre of war.

When Darius heard of Memnon's death,* he summoned his Friends for a meeting, with the agenda being to decide between two alternatives: should they fight the Macedonians by sending an army under the command of generals to the coast, or should the king go there with his entire levy? [2] Some of the Friends argued that the king should be present in person on the battlefield, because then the mass of Persians would fight with greater resolution, but Charidemus of Athens disagreed. This was a man who was widely admired for his martial spirit and strategic brilliance, and who had fought alongside King Philip and been the prime mover of all his victories and his chief counsellor,* and he warned Darius against staking his throne on a risky gamble; instead, he said, Darius should focus on stopping the great bulk of Asia that constituted his empire from falling apart, and should send against the enemy a general of proven ability. [3] In his view, a force of a hundred thousand would be enough, as long as a third of them were Greek mercenaries, and he gave the impression that he was guaranteeing personally to bring the enterprise to a successful conclusion.

[4] At first, the king agreed with Charidemus' plan, but some of his Friends vigorously opposed it, and thanks to them the king came to suspect Charidemus of aspiring to command just so that he could betray the Persian empire to the Macedonians. This made Charidemus furious, and he lashed out at the Persians, rebuking them as little better than women. But Darius found this even more offensive and, blinded by his anger to any sense of where his best interests lay, he seized Charidemus by the belt (which is the Persian method of arrest)* and turned him over to his attendants for execution. [5] But as he was being taken away to his death, Charidemus called out that

before long the king would regret what he was doing—that he would be paid back for punishing him in this unjust manner and would see the downfall of his kingdom.

So Charidemus died and his great prospects for the future came to nothing thanks to his inopportune frankness. [6] As for the king, as soon as he had calmed down again, he regretted his action and came to think that he had made a very serious mistake. But, of course, it was impossible for him, even with the Persian king's power, to undo what he had done. [7] Henceforth, in his dreams he was obsessed by the calibre of the Macedonians and, haunted by visions of Alexander's forcefulness, he set about finding a general who deserved to inherit Memnon's command. But there was no such person, and he had no choice but to march west himself to fight for his kingdom.

31. He immediately set about summoning his forces from all quarters*—they were ordered to meet him in Babylon—and selecting the most competent of his Friends and Kinsmen, who were either assigned commands suited to their talents or ordered to fight by his side. [2] So the day arrived for the army to set out. All the troops were there in Babylon—more than forty thousand foot and at least ten thousand horse. This was the size of the army with which Darius left Babylon and advanced into Cilicia. He also had with him his wife and children*—a son and two daughters—and his mother.

[3] Going back to before Memnon's death: the news of the submission of Chios and the cities of Lesbos, and the fall of Mytilene, on top of the information that Memnon was planning to take three hundred triremes and his infantry forces to campaign in Macedon and that most of the Greeks were poised to rebel, had put Alexander under a great deal of stress. [4] When news arrived of Memnon's death, therefore, he was hugely relieved. A few days later, however, he fell quite seriously ill and was in a lot of pain. He called for his doctors, [5] but they were all reluctant to recommend treatment, except for Philip of Acarnania, who promised that a course of risky but quick-acting medicines would make him better. [6] Philip's suggestion was very welcome to the king, because he had heard that Darius and his troops had set out from Babylon. So the doctor treated him with his potion and, aided by Alexander's robust constitution and Fortune, he very quickly cured the king of his illness. Alexander rewarded Philip magnificently for having so rapidly cured him of a dangerous illness, and counted him from then on as one of his most trusted friends.*

32. Alexander's mother wrote him a letter containing plenty of useful advice, including the recommendation that he should be on his guard against Alexander the Lyncestian, a man of exceptional bravery and high ambition, who accompanied the king and enjoyed his confidence as one of his Friends. [2] Since there were many other plausible pieces of evidence that combined to support the charge, Alexander was arrested and awaited his trial in prison.*

When Alexander found out that Darius was only a few days' march away, he sent Parmenion with his forces to seize the pass, the so-called Gates,† and when Parmenion reached the place, he drove off the Persians who were occupying the pass and secured it for himself. [3] Darius wanted to make his army more mobile, so he left the supply train and the non-combatants in Damascus in Syria, and when he heard that Alexander had already occupied the hills, he advanced rapidly towards him, feeling sure that he would not dare to fight on level ground. [4] The natives of the region scorned the small size of Alexander's force and were overawed by the huge size of the Persian army, so they had nothing to do with Alexander and supported Darius. They set about zealously supplying the Persians with provisions and other resources, and saw this decision of theirs as a way of predicting victory for the barbarians. Meanwhile, Alexander cowed the inhabitants of the city of Issus into submission and took it.

33. When the scouts told him that Darius was thirty stades away and was approaching in terrifying force with his troops drawn up for battle, Alexander regarded it as a gift from heaven that he had an opportunity to bring the Persian empire to an end by winning just a single battle.* He delivered a speech that effectively aroused his men's ardour for the decisive battle, and then deployed his regiments of foot and squadrons of horse in formations that suited the terrain with which he was faced; the cavalry he placed in front of the entire army, with the phalanx of foot soldiers behind, to act as reserves. [2] He himself faced the enemy at the head of the right wing, with the best of the cavalry under his command, while the Thessalian cavalry, by far the most valiant and experienced unit in the army, occupied the left wing.

[3] When the two armies were within missile range, the Persians let fly at Alexander with such a quantity of missiles that they collided with one another—such was the density of the objects flying through the air—and their deadliness was impaired. [4] On both sides, the

trumpets sounded the signal for engagement, and the Macedonians were the first to give throat to their fearful battle-cry, but then the Persians responded in kind and all the surrounding hills rang with the sound; the noise was so great that it swamped the shout that had gone before, since fifty thousand men were crying out with one voice.

[5] Alexander looked everywhere for Darius, and as soon as he spotted him he led the horsemen in his command in a charge straight at him, since he wanted not just to defeat the Persians, but also to make sure that it was he who was responsible for victory. [6] All the other cavalry units also engaged one another at the same time, and the loss of life was terrible, but the prowess of the fighters was such that the battle remained indecisive, with the balance shifting back and forth, now favouring one side and now the other. [7] Every javelin thrown or sword thrust found its mark, since the numbers of men involved made them easy targets. Many men therefore fell with frontal wounds, fighting desperately until their last breaths, preferring death to dishonour.

34. The officers in command of each unit led from the front and by their example stiffened the resolve of their men. The scene before a spectator's eyes would therefore have been one of men wounding and being wounded in countless different ways, and struggles of every imaginable kind erupting on the field in the pursuit of victory. [2] When the Persian Oxathres, a brother of Darius who was renowned for his courage, saw that Alexander was making for Darius in a seemingly unstoppable charge, he resolved to share his brother's fate. [3] He collected the best of the horsemen in his command and with them at his side he swooped down on Alexander. Certain that this demonstration of brotherly love would bring him great fame among the Persians, he fought in front of Darius' chariot, engaging the enemy fearlessly, and such was his skill that many fell dead before him. [4] But Alexander had the advantage in terms of valour, and soon a great pile of corpses was heaped up around Darius' chariot. For in his longing to break through to the Persian king every Macedonian contended passionately with his comrades and gave no thought to personal safety.

[5] Many eminent and high-ranking Persians fell in this battle, including Atizyes,* Rheomithres, and Tasiaces,* the satrap of Egypt. There were many casualties on the Macedonian side too, and Alexander himself was wounded in the thigh as the enemy crowded

around him. [6] The horses yoked to Darius' chariot received multiple wounds, and they were so startled by the number of corpses piling up around them that they attempted to shake off their bits,* and almost bore Darius off into the midst of the enemy. In the utmost peril, Darius grabbed hold of the reins himself; he was compelled to forgo the dignity that came with his pre-eminence and to contravene the custom that had long been established for Persian kings. [7] Another chariot was brought up for him by his minions, and in the confusion caused by his changing over from one to the other, even while he was being assaulted by the enemy, Darius became gripped by panic fear, and the Persians, seeing that their king was unnerved, turned to flight. And before long the rout became general, as every successive unit of cavalry did the same.

[8] The terrain over which they fled consisted of narrow defiles and rough ground, with the result that they impeded and trampled one another, and many men died without having been injured by the enemy. They became packed together, some unarmed and some still with their arms and armour, so that men were dying impaled on the swords of those who had them drawn. Most of them, however, escaped on to level ground, where they rode at a furious pace for towns that were friendly to them, where they found refuge. [9] The Macedonian phalanx and the Persian infantry were only briefly involved in the fighting, in the sense that the defeat of the cavalry became a harbinger, so to speak, of total victory, and soon all the barbarians were in flight. With so many thousands of men fleeing through narrow defiles, it did not take long for the whole region to be littered with corpses.

35. After dark it was easy for the Persians to scatter here and there, and the Macedonians called off their pursuit and turned to plundering. They focused especially on the king's pavilions because of the vast wealth they contained, [2] and the upshot was that a great deal of silver, not a little gold, and a huge quantity of valuable fabrics were carried off from the king's hoard. Much treasure was also seized from high-ranking Persians, especially from the king's Friends and Kinsmen, [3] since, in the traditional Persian fashion, the wives of the Kinsmen and Friends, as well as those of the royal household, had accompanied the army,* riding on gilded chariots, [4] and each of these women was so excessively rich and pampered that they never went anywhere without jewellery and other valuables galore.

The women who were taken prisoner suffered terribly. [5] Previously, given their pampered way of life, they had scarcely been able to bring themselves to travel on richly appointed wagons and never exposed any part of their bodies, but now they were evicted from their tents clad only in their undergarments. Bewailing their lot and tearing at their clothes,* they appealed to the gods and fell at the knees of the victors. [6] Ripping off the jewellery they were wearing with trembling hands, they fled with loosened hair over stony ground and huddled together, calling for help from those who were already in need of help themselves. [7] Some of their captors dragged the wretched women away by the hair, while others tore off their clothes and pawed at their naked bodies; they struck the women with the butts of their spears and acted as though Fortune had granted them the right to abuse the most precious and renowned of the barbarians' possessions.

36. The more decent Macedonians looked on this reversal of fortune with compassion and took pity on the hapless women for their suffering. Everything† that made them respectable and grand† had been taken far from them, while all that was alien and hostile was near at hand, and they were being forced† into a wretched and humiliating captivity. [2] It was above all Darius' family—his mother, wife, two nubile daughters, and a son who was still a child—who moved those present to tears and compassion; [3] in their case it was perfectly natural for those witnessing the reversal of their fortune and the magnitude of the disaster they were suddenly facing to sympathize with them for the calamity that had befallen them. [4] For they had no idea whether Darius was alive among the survivors or had died in the general destruction, and they could see armed men from the enemy camp plundering their pavilion, who did not know who their prisoners were and frequently behaved inappropriately because of their ignorance. The women had come to the realization that the whole of Asia had been captured along with them, and when they met the wives of the satraps and were appealed to for help, so far from having the power to assist any of them, they themselves fell to imploring the others to help them cope with their own misfortunes.

[5] The Royal Pages* took over Darius' pavilion and prepared the king's bath and evening meal. They lit a great blaze of torches and waited for Alexander, wanting him to find, on his return from the pursuit, all Darius' possessions laid out ready for him, as a portent of

his gaining control of all Asia. [6] More than a hundred thousand Persian infantry lost their lives in this battle, along with at least ten thousand cavalry, while on the Macedonian side about three hundred infantry died and about 150 cavalry. So that was the outcome of the battle at Issus in Cilicia.

37. As for the two kings, Darius turned to flight after his disastrous defeat and galloped away at a furious pace on one after another of his swiftest horses in relay, [2] while Alexander set out in pursuit with his best horsemen, including the Companion Cavalry. Darius' aim was to escape from Alexander's clutches and gain the upper satrapies, while Alexander's was to make Darius his prisoner. But after carrying on the pursuit for two hundred stades, Alexander turned back. He reached his camp in the middle of the night, and once he had bathed and recovered from the weariness all the stress had induced, he turned to relaxation and food.

[3] Someone came to Darius' wife and mother with the news that Alexander had returned from the pursuit, and told them that he had stripped Darius' corpse of his arms and armour. At this, a great cry of anguish burst from the women, and the rest of the prisoners, who were similarly affected by the news, also began howling out their grief. When Alexander heard how the women were suffering, he sent Leonnatus, one of his Friends, to quieten and calm Sisyngambris and her entourage—to assure them that Darius was still alive and that Alexander would treat them with all due respect. The king wanted to speak to them the following morning, Leonnatus said, and he added that his behaviour towards them would leave them in no doubt of his kindness. [4] And at this abrupt and altogether unexpected piece of good fortune, the captive women acclaimed Alexander as a god, and stopped their weeping and wailing.

[5] Early the next day, Alexander took one of his Friends, Hephaestion—there was no friend he valued more, in fact—and went to pay the women a visit. He and Hephaestion were both wearing similar clothes, but Hephaestion was taller and better-looking than Alexander, so Sisyngambris took him to be the king and did obeisance to him. The others who were there gestured to her, indicating with their hands which one was Alexander, and Sisyngambris, embarrassed by her mistake, made a fresh start and began to do obeisance to Alexander. [6] He interrupted her, however, and said: 'Don't worry, mother. He is Alexander too.'* In addressing the elderly

woman as 'mother', he was using this affectionate term to indicate
that a time of misfortune had given way to a time of kindliness. And
no sooner had he assured Sisyngambris that she would be his second
mother* than he put this verbal promise into practice.

38. What he did was furnish her with the trappings of royalty and
restore her former dignity with the appropriate honours. He not only
granted her the full complement of staff that had been given her by
Darius, but assigned her additional attendants as well from his own
staff, at least as many again as she already had. He also promised to
see to the marriages of her daughters, making a better selection of
husbands than Darius had, and to bring up her son as his own and
show him royal honour.* [2] He called the boy over and kissed him,
and seeing that the boy showed no fear and was basically perfectly
calm, he remarked to Hephaestion that, at the age of six, the boy was
displaying courage beyond his years and was far braver than his father.
As for Darius' wife and her dignity, he promised to make sure that she
would never have to submit to anything that would compromise her
former happy state.*

[3] This was far from all he said, and the compassion and kindness
of his words reduced the women to unquenchable tears, such was the
jolt of joy they felt on hearing him. He gave them his right hand to
guarantee his promises, and earned not only the thanks of those who
benefited from his kindness, but also the praise of his companions in
arms for his extraordinary clemency. [4] It is my opinion, in short,
that of all Alexander's many fine deeds, none was greater than this,
and none is more deserving of preservation in the historical record.
[5] Sieges, battles, and military successes in general are more commonly due to Fortune than ability, but when a man who has been
raised to power shows pity to those he has defeated, this is due entirely
to the cast of his mind. [6] I mean, most men are made proud by their
successes, which are due to luck, and at the time of their success are
too proud to remember that weakness is the collective lot of human-
kind. That is why a great many men are clearly incapable of enduring
success, as though it were too heavy a burden. [7] So, although
Alexander lived many generations before our time, his noble qualities
mean that he should meet from future generations too the praise that
is his due.

39. Meanwhile, Darius reached Babylon and collected the survivors
of the battle of Issus. Despite the terrible defeat he had suffered, he

was not downcast, and in fact in a letter to Alexander he advised him to remember, at this time of success, that he was only human, and offered him a large amount of money in exchange for the prisoners. He also said that he would cede all of Asia west of the Halys river to Alexander if he were prepared to enter into a treaty of friendship. [2] At the meeting of his Friends that Alexander convened, he concealed the genuine letter and presented to the council another one, written by himself, the tone of which suited him better,* and sent Darius' envoys away empty-handed.

[3] Darius therefore gave up trying to come to terms with Alexander by letter and set about preparing thoroughly for war. He re-equipped those who had lost their arms and armour in the course of the rout, recruited further troops and assigned them to regiments, and sent for the armies of the upper satrapies, which had remained unused earlier because of the speed of the previous campaign.* [4] In fact, thanks to the determined way he went about getting his army ready for war, he ended up with double the number of the troops that had taken to the field at Issus. He gathered a force of eight hundred thousand foot and two hundred thousand horse, and had a great many scythe-bearing chariots as well.

These were the events that took place in this year.

40. *In the year of the Archonship of Niceratus in Athens, the Romans appointed as their consuls Marcus Atilius and Marcus Valerius, and the 112th Olympic festival was celebrated, with Grylus of Chalcis the victor.* In this year:*

Following his victory at Issus, Alexander buried the dead, including those Persians who had displayed impressive valour. Then he carried out magnificent sacrifices to the gods and rewarded those of his men who had fought with distinction during the battle, giving each man what he deserved. [2] Then, after his troops had rested for several days, he advanced towards Egypt.*

In Phoenicia, he accepted the submission of all the other cities, whose inhabitants readily gave him a favourable reception, except for Tyre. When Alexander asked to sacrifice to Tyrian Heracles, the Tyrians rather foolishly prevented him from entering the city.* [3] This made Alexander angry and he threatened them with war, but the

Tyrians were undismayed by the prospect of a siege. In the first place, they wanted to please Darius and show him how unwavering their loyalty to him was, and they anticipated being rewarded magnificently for the good they were doing him—namely, drawing Alexander into a long and hazardous siege and buying Darius time to get ready. In the second place, they felt they could rely on the natural defences of their island and the armament they had there, and on the Carthaginians, who were originally their colonists.

[4] Alexander could see that the city could hardly be besieged by sea because of the artillery mounted on the walls and the existence of the Tyrian fleet, and also that it was virtually unassailable by land because it lay four stades off the mainland. Nevertheless, he decided to risk all and to do all in his power to ensure that the Macedonian army was not treated with contempt by a single, unexceptional city.* [5] He therefore immediately set about demolishing Old Tyre,* as it was called, and he had men in their tens of thousands carry stones with which to build a causeway, two plethra wide. He dragooned the entire populations of the neighbouring cities and the project made rapid progress because of the size of his workforce.

41. At first, the Tyrians sailed up to the causeway and mocked the king for thinking that he could get the better of Poseidon,* but later, as the causeway advanced with surprising rapidity, they voted to transfer their children, womenfolk, and elderly to Carthage,* assigned those who were young and fit to the defence of the walls, and got ready to fight at sea with their eighty triremes. [2] In the end, however, although they did manage to get a few women and children out of the city to safety in Carthage, they were overtaken by the speed at which Alexander's large workforce was able to progress, and since they were no match for him at sea, they were compelled to endure the siege with the entire population still inside the city.

[3] The Tyrians were extremely well supplied with catapults and other anti-siege devices, and there were engineers and all other kinds of craftsmen in the city, so that they easily made a great many more. [4] With the help of these craftsmen, all kinds of appliances were made, some of which were new inventions, and the entire circuit wall of the city bristled with artillery, but especially the stretch of wall which the causeway was approaching.

[5] The danger increased as the causeway began to come within missile range, and the gods sent the combatants certain omens. For

instance, the waves brought an incredibly large sea-creature* right up to the construction zone, and although it did no damage to the causeway by bumping into it, it stayed there for quite a while with part of its body pressed up against it before swimming off into the sea, and all who saw the marvel were filled with awe. [6] The portent brought out the superstitious sides of both the Macedonians and the Tyrians, and under the influence of wishful thinking both sides interpreted it as indicating that Poseidon would come to their aid.

[7] There were other strange and significant events too, designed to dismay and terrify the masses. Once, at mealtime in the Macedonian camp, the loaves of bread had a bloody appearance when broken open. Then a Tyrian reported that he had seen Apollo in a dream and that the god had told him he was going to leave the city. [8] It was widely believed that the man had made the story up in order to curry favour with Alexander, and on this assumption the younger Tyrians set out to stone him to death. He was spirited away by the authorities, however, and avoided their vengeance by seeking refuge in the temple of Heracles as a suppliant. Still, in their superstitious awe, the Tyrians tied the cult statue of Apollo to its pedestal with golden chains, supposing that this was the way to prevent the departure of the god from the city.

42. Alarmed by the advance of the causeway, the Tyrians next filled many of their smaller boats with bolt-shooters, catapults, archers, and slingers. They sailed up to the men who were working on the causeway, and succeeded in injuring a good number of them and killing quite a few as well, [2] since missiles of all kinds were flying repeatedly at men who were unarmed and in close proximity to one another. The workers made easy targets, then, and, since they had no protection, every single missile was effective. In fact, it was not only the men's fronts that were struck by missiles, but, since they were working face to face on the narrow causeway, their backs were vulnerable too. They were caught in a crossfire, with no way to protect themselves.*

[3] Alexander had not been expecting this and he urgently needed to redress the situation. He manned all his ships, took command of them himself, and sailed at speed for the Tyrian harbour, to cut off the Phoenician ships and prevent their return. [4] The possibility that he might gain control of their harbours* and seize the city while it was empty of soldiers worried the barbarians, and they set out at full speed back to Tyre. Both sides displayed an astonishing degree of

determination and rowed furiously, but the Macedonians were already close to the harbours and the Phoenicians almost lost all their men. But they forced their way in and saved the city, though they lost the ships that were bringing up the rear.

[5] Having failed at this critical venture, Alexander renewed his efforts over the causeway and used a large number of ships as a screen to make it safe for the labourers to go about their work. But just as the construction zone was drawing close to the city and its fall seemed inevitable, a fierce north-westerly arose and did a great deal of damage to the causeway. [6] The unlucky destruction of his construction frustrated Alexander and he almost regretted that he had undertaken the siege, but he was still powerfully motivated to succeed. So he cut down huge trees in the mountains and had them brought down, and by pouring rubble on to them, branches and all, he created a barrier against the force of the waves. [7] Before long he had repaired the damaged parts of the causeway and it had been brought by his workforce to within missile range. He then stationed his siege towers at the end of the causeway and began to try to bring the walls down with his stone-throwers, while using his bolt-shooters to inhibit defence from the battlements. The archers and slingers played their part in this too, and shot down many of those in the city who came to its defence.

43. The Tyrians, however, had metal-workers and engineers, and they constructed ingenious counter-measures. To defend against the bolts fired by catapults, they made multi-spoked wheels which, once they were set spinning by a certain contraption, broke or deflected some of the missiles and reduced the impact of all of them. And by getting the boulders hurled by the stone-throwers to land on soft and yielding materials, they lessened the force imparted by the power of the apparatus.

[2] While this assault was going on from the causeway, Alexander took his entire fleet and sailed around the city to inspect the walls, making it clear that he was going to besiege the city by land and sea at once. [3] The Tyrians now judged it too risky to come out against him with their fleet, and they had three ships anchored at the mouth of the harbour—but before returning to his camp Alexander sailed up and sank all three of them.

Wanting to make themselves doubly secure behind their walls, the Tyrians set about building a second wall inside the outer one at a distance of five cubits; this second wall was ten cubits thick and the space between the two walls was filled with rubble and earth. [4] But Alexander yoked his triremes together, mounted all kinds of siege engines on them, and brought down a plethron-long stretch of wall. The Macedonians poured through this breach into the city, [5] but the Tyrians fired volley after volley of missiles and gradually forced them back. And then, that night, the Tyrians rebuilt the collapsed part of the wall.

Now that the causeway had reached the wall and the city had become a peninsula, the fighting at the wall became frequent and intense. [6] With the threat right before their eyes, and imagining how disastrous it would be if the city fell, the Tyrians faced danger without caring about their personal safety. [7] As a matter of fact, when the Macedonians began to bring up towers as high as the walls which made it possible for them to lay down gangplanks, with which they boldly pressed their attack on the battlements, the Tyrians, relying on their engineers' inventiveness, developed a number of devices to counter the assaults on the walls. [8] For instance, they made long barbed tridents out of metal, and used them at close range against the men who were standing on the towers. The tridents, which had ropes attached, would get stuck in the attackers' shields and the defenders would take hold of the ropes and pull. [9] This left the attackers the choice either of letting go of their shields and exposing themselves to being shot down by the many missiles that were being fired at them, or of holding on to their shields out of shame and falling to their deaths from the lofty towers. [10] Others cast fishing nets over the Macedonians who were fighting their way along the gangplanks, pinioning their arms, and then, with a downward tug, bundled them off the planks and down to the ground.

44. Another ingenious device the Tyrians invented to counteract Macedonian daring enabled them to inflict terrible torments on the best of the enemy fighters, in such a way that they could do nothing to alleviate them. What they did was make shields out of bronze and iron, fill them with sand, light a strong fire under them, and heat them continuously until the sand was red-hot. [2] Then, with the help of a certain contraption, they tossed the heated sand on to the boldest of the enemy fighters. This was agony for those on whom the sand fell, because the sand trickled down inside their breastplates and undergarments, searing their flesh with its great heat, and there was no relief from the awful thing that was happening to them. [3]

Sounding just like men on the rack, they screamed out their entreaties, but no one could help them, and before dying they were driven mad by the terrible pain, because there was no escape from their appalling suffering.

[4] At the same time, the Phoenicians were also hurling fire on to the attackers, firing javelins at them, throwing stones, and overwhelming the valour of their opponents with a hail of missiles. Not only were they cutting the cords of the rams with scythe-bearing poles, which made the devices powerless and ineffective, but they were also using fire-throwing machines to hurl great red-hot lumps of iron into the mass of the enemy, where the men were so tightly packed together that they could not fail to hit a target, and with crows* and iron grapples they were snatching from their perches those who were standing at the breast walls of the towers. [5] They had so many men available that they were able to put all their apparatuses to work, and they inflicted heavy casualties on their assailants.

45. The situation was absolutely terrifying and the fighting unbearably horrific, but still the Macedonians refused to give up. Whenever men fell, others stepped over their bodies without being deterred by what was happening to their comrades. [2] Alexander had the stone-throwers set up in appropriate places and he began to batter the walls with the great boulders that they hurled, while with the bolt-shooters on the wooden towers he was firing missiles of all different kinds at the defenders, wreaking havoc among those who were standing on the walls. [3] The Tyrians responded with devices of their own. In front of the walls they set up wheels of marble and when they set these spinning by means of certain mechanisms they broke or deflected the catapult projectiles that were being fired at them and made them ineffective when they struck.* [4] Moreover, they sewed up skins and hides, folded double and stuffed with seaweed, for the missiles from the stone-throwers to land on, and the soft and yielding material reduced the impact of the boulders.

[5] In short, the Tyrians did all they could to mount a strong defence and, since they were well supplied with instruments of defence, they met the enemy with confidence; in fact, they even left the wall and their posts inside the towers and pressed forward on to the very gangplanks, matching their skills against the valour of the enemy. [6] As a result of their grappling with the enemy and engaging them at close quarters, the defence of the city became a ferocious

struggle. Some of the Tyrians were even using axes to hack off any part of an opponent's body that presented itself, and this was the point at which one of the leading Macedonians, Admetus by name, a man of exceptional courage and great bodily strength, who had been bravely resisting the Tyrians, was killed instantly, dying a hero's death, when he was struck square in the head by an axe.

[7] Seeing that the Macedonians were coming off worst in the battle, Alexander had the trumpet recall his troops. In any case, night had fallen. At first, he thought it better to call off the siege and march on towards Egypt, but then the idea of yielding all the glory of the siege to the Tyrians made him change his mind back again, and even though he secured the agreement of only one of his Friends, Amyntas the son of Andromenes, he committed himself again to the siege.*

46. In a speech to the Macedonians Alexander challenged them to match his own courage, and then, once he had got all his ships ready for battle, he launched a determined assault on the walls by land and sea at once. He had noticed that the wall in the location of the Tyrian harbour facilities was relatively weak, so this was the stretch against which he sent his triremes, yoked together and carrying the most formidable of his siege engines. [2] At this juncture, he did something that required such daring that even those who saw it could scarcely believe their eyes. He dropped a gangplank from the wooden tower on to the city walls and crossed over to the wall by himself, unconcerned about the envy of Fortune and uncowed by the fearsome Tyrians. With his fearlessness on display before the army that had defeated the Persians, he ordered the Macedonians to follow his lead. Any of the enemy who came within his reach he either killed with his spear or sword, or he knocked them over with the rim of his shield, and the high confidence that had been sustaining the enemy drained away.

[3] Meanwhile, a long stretch of wall in another part of the city had been battered down, and the city's fall was secured as the Macedonians poured in through this breach and as Alexander and his men gained the wall by crossing over the gangplank. Nevertheless, the Tyrians fought a defensive battle, and with cries of encouragement to one another they barricaded the streets, but only a few of them survived the fighting, and more than seven thousand were cut down. [4] Alexander sold the children and women into slavery and crucified all the men of military age, who numbered at least two thousand. There was such a vast crowd of prisoners that, even though a great many

people had been taken to Carthage,* there were still more than thirteen thousand left.

[5] This is a measure of the catastrophe that befell the Tyrians as a result of the siege, which lasted seven months and which they resisted with more courage than wisdom. [6] After having the golden chains and fetters removed from the statue of Apollo, the king said that the god should be called 'the Apollo of Alexander'. He also performed magnificent sacrifices to Heracles, rewarded those who had fought with distinction, and buried his dead with splendid ceremonies. He installed as the king of Tyre a man called Ballonymus, and some of his particulars demand to be recorded, because of the extraordinary reversal of fortune that was involved.

47. Once the former king, Straton,* had been deposed (he had been on good terms with Darius), Alexander gave Hephaestion permission to place on the throne of Tyre whichever of his friends he chose to nominate. [2] At first, Hephaestion favoured the man in whose house he was staying, where he had enjoyed pleasant lodging, and proposed that he should be put in charge of the city. There was no one in Tyre who was richer or more admired, but the man refused the offer because he had no family connection to the former kings. [3] Hephaestion left it up to him to nominate one of the king's relatives, and his host said that there was someone of royal descent who was basically a sound man and a good one, but he was extremely poor.

[4] Hephaestion agreed that the throne should be given to this man, and his host, the man to whom the decision had been entrusted, went off to find his nominee, taking the royal apparel with him. He found him watering a garden as a hired labourer, dressed in plain work clothes, [5] and told him about his change of station. Then he dressed him in all the appropriate finery, including the royal robes, conducted him to the agora, and proclaimed him king of Tyre. [6] The general populace was happy to have him as king and marvelled at the vicissitudes of fortune. And so, by becoming one of Alexander's friends and gaining the kingship of Tyre, he serves as a case study for people who are unaware of the sudden changes that Fortune can bring about.

Now that I have covered Alexander's deeds, it is time to move elsewhere. 48. In Europe, Agis, the king of the Lacedaemonians, hired the eight thousand mercenaries who had survived the battle of Issus and, as a favour to Darius, committed himself to rebellion. [2] Once he had received from Darius both ships and a large sum of money, he sailed to Crete, where he subdued most of the cities and forced them to join the Persian side.

Amyntas, who had been banished from Macedon and had made his way up country to Darius, fought for the Persians in Cilicia,* and after surviving the battle of Issus he went to Tripolis in Phoenicia with four thousand mercenaries. This was before Alexander arrived in Phoenicia. The entire Persian fleet was there, and Amyntas commandeered enough ships for his own troops and burnt the rest. [3] He sailed over to Cyprus, where he gained more men and ships, and then sailed over to Pelusium. Once he had made himself master of the city, he announced that he had been sent by King Darius to take command in Egypt because the satrap who had been responsible for the country had died fighting in Cilicia, at Issus. [4] He sailed up river to Memphis and at first things went well: he defeated the local forces in a battle in front of the city. But then, after his men had turned to looting, the Egyptians emerged from the city and attacked Amyntas' troops while they were out of formation, plundering farms in the countryside, and they killed not only Amyntas, but every single one of his men as well. [5] So Amyntas met his end in the midst of the great enterprise he had undertaken, a failure when he had had every expectation of success.

Some of the other leading men and generals who escaped from the battle of Issus with their men, and continued to pin their hopes on the Persians, did much the same as Amyntas. [6] That is, some of them too seized critical cities and held them for Darius, while others won over tribes and, once they had equipped themselves with troops, provided whatever services were appropriate for the situation.*

The delegates of the Greek states* voted to send an embassy of fifteen men to take a golden crown to Alexander, as a prize for valour awarded by the Greeks to express their shared joy at his victory in Cilicia. [7] Meanwhile, Alexander marched to Gaza, which had a Persian garrison, and took the city by storm after a siege of two months.

331/0

49. *In the year of the Archonship of Aristophanes in Athens, Spurius Postumius and Titus Veturius were elected consuls in Rome. In this year:*

Once King Alexander had ordered affairs in Gaza, he sent Amyntas with ten ships to Macedon to recruit men of military age who were fit for service,* while he made his way to Egypt with his entire army. All the cities there capitulated without a fight; [2] the harshness of Persian rule, and the disrespect with which they had treated temples, made the Macedonians welcome to the Egyptians. After settling matters in Egypt, Alexander paid a visit to the temple of Ammon,* because he had a question for the god. When he was about halfway there, he was met by emissaries from Cyrene, bringing him a crown and magnificent gifts, which included three hundred warhorses and five superb four-horse chariots. [3] He made the envoys welcome and concluded a treaty of alliance and friendship with them, before carrying on to the temple with his travelling companions.

When he reached the part of the country that was uninhabited and waterless, he loaded up with water and set out to cross it. It was an endless expanse of sand, and within four days all their water had been used up and they began to suffer terribly from thirst. [4] Everyone was getting desperate—but suddenly the heavens opened and a heavy downpour began, bringing their shortage of water to an unexpected end. In fact, because they had been rescued when they had given up hope, they decided that what had happened was due to divine providence. [5] After taking on water from a hollow in the ground, they once more had enough to see them through four days, and that is how long it took them to complete their crossing of the desert.† At one point, there was so much sand that they were uncertain of their route, but the guides told Alexander about some crows that were cawing to their right, as a way of showing where the road was that led to the temple. [6] Alexander took this as an omen and pressed on urgently, believing that the god was indicating his pleasure at his visit. First he came to the Bitter Lake, and then after another hundred stades he passed the Communities of Ammon, and from there it took him only one more day of travel to reach the sanctuary.

50. The place where this sanctuary is located is surrounded by sandy, waterless desert—a completely hostile environment for humans. But the place itself, which forms a square with sides of about fifty stades, is drenched with the water of numerous fine springs, and there are abundant trees there of all kinds, especially fruit-bearing species. The ambient temperature of the air is spring-like, and since the oasis is surrounded by torrid regions, it is the only place where the

inhabitants can get relief and find a moderate climate. [2] It is said that the sanctuary was founded by Danaus of Egypt.* The land, which is consecrated to the god,* is inhabited to the south and west by Ethiopians, to the north by a tribe of Libyan nomads, and in the direction of the interior by a tribe called the Nasamonians.

[3] The people of Ammon live in villages, and in the middle of their land there is a fortress, surrounded by three defensive walls. The innermost circuit of the fortress contains the royal court buildings of the ancient rulers of the land; the next contains the women's quarters, the residences of the children, womenfolk, and relatives of the rulers, the soldiers' guardrooms,† the god's precinct, and the sacred spring which is used to purify offerings to the god; and the outermost circuit contains the barracks of the king's bodyguard and their guardrooms. [4] At no great distance from the fortress there is a second temple of Ammon, in the shade of many tall trees. Near this temple there is a spring which is called the Spring of the Sun because of its behaviour: its water changes temperature according to the time of day, in a paradoxical fashion.* [5] At daybreak, the water that comes up is warm, but as the day advances it cools down in proportion to the passing of the hours, until its coldness peaks in the heat of midday. Then, and once more in proportion with the passing of time, the coldness wanes towards evening, and after nightfall the water continues to warm up again until midnight, after which the heat again wanes, until at dawn the water has regained its original state.

[6] The cult statue of Ammon is encrusted with emeralds and other jewels and it responds in a most peculiar fashion to questions that are put to it. It is carried around on a golden boat by eighty priests who walk, with the god on their shoulders, not in accordance with their own volition, but in whichever direction is indicated by an inclination of the god's head.* [7] Throughout this process, the priests are followed by a train of girls and women, singing paeans and a traditional hymn of praise of the god.

51. Once Alexander had been led inside the temple by the priests and had contemplated the god, the elderly man who spoke for the god approached and said: 'Greetings, my son! And you may take it that this greeting comes from the god too.' [2] In response, Alexander said: 'I thank you, father, and from now on I shall be called your son.* But tell me if you will grant me dominion over the whole world.' The priest approached the precinct, and when the men lifted the god on to

their shoulders and moved around according to certain traditional cues,† he declared to Alexander that the god was certainly granting his request. And then Alexander said: 'I have one final question for you, lord Ammon. Have I caught all my father's murderers, or have some escaped?' [3] But the prophet cried out in a loud voice: 'Sacrilege! The one who begot him* is invulnerable to human schemes, but all the murderers of Philip have been punished. The greatness of the deeds that he accomplishes will serve as proof of his divine parentage. For up until now he has never known defeat, and from now on he shall be invincible for ever!' [4] Alexander was delighted with these responses, and he honoured the god with magnificent dedications in the temple before returning to Egypt.

52. Having decided to found a great city in Egypt,* he told the men to whom he entrusted responsibility for the task to build it between the lake and the sea. [2] He skilfully established the dimensions of the site and designed the layout of the streets,* and gave orders that the city was to be called Alexandria after him.* The city was in an excellent location near the harbour of Pharos, and he laid out the streets so cleverly that the city breathed with the etesian winds.* Since these winds blow over a very large expanse of open sea and cool the air in the city, he was making sure that the inhabitants had a tempered climate and good health. [3] He also designed the outer wall of the city, which was exceptionally tall and incredibly secure, because, lying as the city does between a great lake and the sea, there are only two ways to approach it from a landward direction, and both of them are narrow and easily guarded. In outline, the city resembles a military cloak,* and it has a central street of unbelievable size and beauty which more or less divides the city in two. This main street, forty stades long and a plethron wide, runs from gate to gate, and has been embellished all along its length by sumptuous edifices, both private houses and temples.

[4] Alexander also ordered the construction of a palace, the size and grandeur of which are astounding. But the palace is not only Alexander's work, because almost all the later rulers of Egypt, right up until the present day, have spent large amounts of money on extensions. [5] In fact, the city as a whole has made such progress in recent years that many people reckon it to be the greatest in the world,* and it is true that it leaves the rest a long way behind in terms of its beauty, size, financial liquidity, and everything that contributes to graceful

living. [6] It has a larger population than any other city, and I know this because when I visited Egypt the men who kept the census returns of the inhabitants told me that, not counting slaves, there were three hundred thousand people living there, and I was also told that the king's annual revenues from Egypt amounted to more than six thousand talents. [7] Be that as it may, Alexander made some of his Friends responsible for the building of Alexandria, and once he had seen to the reorganization of Egypt* he returned with his army to Syria.

53. By the time he heard of Alexander's arrival, Darius had already mustered his forces from all over the empire and equipped himself with everything he would need for battle. The swords and spears that he made, for instance, were much longer than the kinds he had used before, because it was widely held that the extra length of his weaponry had given Alexander a clear advantage in Cilicia. Darius also built two hundred scythe-bearing chariots, which were designed to overawe and terrify the enemy. [2] On each of them long scythes (three spans long,* in fact), which were attached to the yoke, projected beyond the two trace horses and had their curved edges turned towards the front, and moreover there were another two blades attached to the linchpins of the axles, in line with each other, which were like the others in having their cutting edges turned towards the front, but were longer and broader.†

[3] After equipping all his troops with first-rate weaponry and appointing talented officers, Darius left Babylon with an army of more than eight hundred thousand foot and at least two hundred thousand horse. He travelled with the Tigris on his right and the Euphrates on his left, through land which was fertile enough to provide the animals with plenty of fodder and even such a large force of soldiers with sufficient food. [4] His intention was to fight near Nineveh,* since the plains there were perfect for a pitched battle: there was plenty of open ground for an army of the size he had collected. After making camp near a village called Arbela,* he drilled his troops every day. He had them continually out on manoeuvres and exercises, so that they would learn to obey orders, because his chief concern was to see that no confusion arose during the battle, given that he had gathered together a large number of peoples, who spoke different languages.

54. Now, Darius had earlier sent emissaries to Alexander to discuss bringing hostilities to an end, on the basis of his offering to cede to Alexander the land west of the Halys river and promising twenty

thousand talents of silver as well.* [2] Alexander had refused, how-ever, and so now Darius sent further ambassadors. He thanked Alexander for his good treatment of his mother and the other cap-tives, and invited him to become one of his Friends and to take all the land west of the Euphrates for himself, along with thirty thousand talents of silver and one of his two daughters for a wife. In short, he was suggesting that, by marrying his daughter, Alexander should become a full partner in his kingdom, with the rank of one of his sons.

[3] Alexander called all his Friends to a meeting. He explained the available alternatives and asked each of them to speak his mind freely. [4] The issue was so important, however, that no one else dared to offer any advice, and Parmenion was the first to speak. 'If I were Alexander,' he said, 'I would accept the offer and make peace.' [5] And in response Alexander said: 'Yes, I too would accept the offer, if I were Parmenion!'*

To cut a long story short, Alexander continued in the same proud vein and rejected the arguments that the Persians were advancing. Preferring glory to the gifts that were being offered him, he replied to the ambassadors that, just as the universe could not maintain its orderly arrangement if there were two suns, so the earth could not remain free of unrest and strife if two kings were in power. [6] So he told them to offer Darius a choice: if he desired supremacy, he would have to fight Alexander for it, to decide who would be the sole ruler of the empire, but if he cared nothing for glory and preferred a life of wealth and indolent luxury, all he had to do was leave supreme com-mand to Alexander, while Darius would rule over other kings, once Alexander in his goodness had ceded him the power to do so.* [7] Alexander then brought the meeting to an end and advanced with his troops towards the enemy encampment. Meanwhile, however, Darius' wife died* and Alexander buried her with full honour.

55. When Darius heard Alexander's response, he realized that there was no chance of a diplomatic settlement, and he continued to drill his forces every day and train them in battlefield obedience. He dispatched one of his Friends, Mazaeus, with a body of crack troops to seize the ford and guard the river crossing, and he sent others to scorch with fire the farmland on the route the enemy was bound to take. His original plan was to use the bed of the river as a first line of defence against the approach of the Macedonians, [2] but when Mazaeus saw that the river was too deep to cross and had too strong

a current, he did not bother to guard it,* but joined those who were burning the farmland. He laid waste to a great deal of land, until he judged that shortage of food would make it impossible for the enemy to pass that way.

[3] When Alexander reached the Tigris crossing and was told about the ford by some of the local inhabitants, he had his troops cross over, which proved to be not merely difficult, but extremely dangerous. [4] The water came up over the men's chests, and many of them, as they attempted the crossing, found that the strength of the current was threatening to sweep them away and make them lose their footing. The buffeting of the water on their shields carried a lot of men off and put their lives in the greatest danger. [5] But Alexander devised a measure to counteract the force of the current. He got his men to link arms and to press close to their neighbours so that, all together, they formed a kind of barrage. [6] Since the crossing had been hazardous and the Macedonians had barely come out of it alive, Alexander let his men take their ease for the rest of the day, and then the next day he drew them up in formation, advanced towards the enemy, and made camp close to the Persian position.

56. With his mind dwelling on the size of the Persian army and the momentous nature of the coming battle, and because he was aware that the fateful moment was at hand, Alexander spent a sleepless night, worrying over what lay ahead. He finally fell asleep around the time of the morning watch, and slept so soundly that the next day he could not be woken up. [2] At first his Friends were pleased about this, thinking that, being well rested, the king would have more energy for the coming battle. But as time passed and sleep still continued to claim him, Parmenion, who was the most senior of his Friends, took it upon himself to give the order for the troops to prepare for battle.

[3] When he still did not wake up, his Friends came and finally managed to rouse him. They all expressed astonishment at how soundly he had slept and asked the reason for it, and Alexander said that Darius had relieved all his stress by assembling his forces in one place, [4] because this meant that everything would be decided in a single day, and there would be an end to their troubles and the dangers they had faced for so long. And so, once he had effectively encouraged his marshals and inspired them with confidence for the coming battle, he led his army in formation towards the barbarians, with the cavalry units ahead of the infantry.

57. On the right wing, Alexander stationed the Royal Squadron, under the command of Cleitus 'the Black'.* Next came the rest of his Friends,* under the command of Philotas, the son of Parmenion, and then the other seven cavalry units,* also commanded by Philotas. [2] Behind them was stationed the infantry battalion called the Silver Shields,* distinguished by their gleaming shields and their calibre; Nicanor, the son of Parmenion, was their commanding officer. Next came the Elimiote Battalion, as it is called,* under the command of Coenus, and then the units from Orestis and Lyncestis, under the command of Perdiccas. The next battalion was led by Meleager, and the one after that by Polyperchon, who had the Stymphaeans under him. [3] Philip, the son of Balacrus, held the command of the next unit, and the one after that was led by Craterus. The position next to the cavalry units that I have already mentioned was filled by a brigade made up of cavalry from Achaea and elsewhere in the Peloponnese, who formed a single contingent, along with men from Phthiotis and Malis, and from Locris and Phocis, with Erigyius of Mytilene in command. [4] Then came the Thessalians, whose courage and horsemanship were by far the best in the army, under the command of Philip. Next to them were stationed the Cretan archers and the Achaean mercenaries.*

[5] On both wings, Alexander had the units form up slantwise,* so that the enemy would not be able to use their superior numbers to outflank the relatively few Macedonians. [6] He came up with a plan to counter the threat of the scythed chariots, and gave orders that, as the chariots approached, the infantrymen who made up the phalanx were to take up a tight formation with overlapping shields and beat their shields with their pikes. The idea was that the noise would frighten the horses and make them turn tail, and if any of the chariots did manage to get through, his men were to open up gaps in the line, through which the chariots might pass without endangering the Macedonians.* Alexander took personal command of the right wing, which on his orders took up an oblique formation, and his intention was that it would be he who was responsible for the decisive victory.*

58. Darius deployed his troops according to the region from which the tribes and peoples came and posted himself opposite Alexander. Then he gave the order to advance. When the two armies were close to each other, the trumpeters on both sides gave the signal for battle, and the men charged at one another with shrill cries. [2] At first, the scythed chariots, bearing down at a furious pace, sowed fear and panic in the Macedonian lines—and Mazaeus, the cavalry commander, made the chariot charge even more fearsome by having squadrons of horse in close formation ride along with the chariots. [3] But when all the phalangites overlapped their shields and began to beat on them with their pikes, as Alexander had ordered, the huge racket they created frightened the horses [4] and most of the chariots turned around and bore hard with irresistible force against their own lines.

Some of the chariots did get through to the phalanx, however, and the Macedonians opened up sizeable gaps through which the chariots sped. Some of these were stopped by a hail of javelins, while others rode through and escaped, but some were moving so fast and using the blades of their scythes so effectively that death in many different forms ensued. [5] Such were the sharpness and the destructive force of the tempered blades that many men had their arms sliced off, shields and all. Quite a few others were decapitated, and their heads fell to the ground with eyes still open and facial expressions unchanged, and in some cases the blades lethally tore open men's sides and brought a swift death.

59. When the armies were close to each other, the airborne missiles began to be used up as the bows, slings, and javelins went about their business, and then it came to close combat. [2] The cavalry were the first to engage, and specifically the Macedonians who were fighting on the right wing, but Darius, who was in command of his left wing, had the Kinsmen Cavalry by his side, a single regiment of a thousand chosen for their prowess and loyalty. [3] With the king as a witness of their valour, they willingly braved the missiles that were raining down on them in large numbers. They were supported by the Apple-bearers,* a large regiment made up of men of exceptional valour; by the Mardians and Cossaeans,* distinguished for their exceptional physical strength and their nobility of spirit; [4] and also by the Palace Guard and the best fighters among the Indians. With a loud cry, these men hurled themselves against the Macedonians, and there were so many of them, and they fought so ferociously, that they started to gain the upper hand.

[5] On the right wing, Mazaeus, who had the pick of the cavalry under him, killed many of his opponents straight away, in the first charge. Then he sent a picked force of two thousand Cadusian and a thousand Scythian horsemen to ride around the enemy's wing to

their camp and take the baggage.* [6] They rapidly carried out their orders, and when they burst into the Macedonian camp, some of the prisoners snatched up weapons and helped them plunder the baggage. The entire camp resounded with shouts and was plunged into confusion by the unexpectedness of the attack.

[7] All the rest of the female prisoners flew from their quarters to the barbarians, but not Darius' mother, Sisyngambris. She paid no attention when the others called out to her, but kept quiet and stayed composedly where she was, since she did not trust accidents of Fortune, and also because she felt grateful to Alexander and did not want to sully that sense of gratitude. [8] Eventually, after taking a great deal of the baggage, the Scythians rode back to Mazaeus and told him of their success. Meanwhile, some of the cavalry deployed in Darius' part of the field had got the better of the Macedonians ranged opposite them, whom they outnumbered, and had forced them to flee.

60. This defeat was a second success for the Persians, and Alexander decided that it was up to him to remedy the situation, so he took the best of his cavalry, including the Royal Squadron, and rode straight for Darius. [2] The Persian king stood his ground and fired javelins at his attackers from his chariot, and alongside him there were many others fighting too. The kings were focused only on each other, however, and Alexander aimed his javelin at Darius, but missed him and hit the driver standing next to him instead, who toppled off the chariot and on to the ground. [3] A loud cry arose from the vicinity of Darius, and men who were some way off, thinking that it was the king himself who had fallen, turned to flight. Their neighbours then followed their lead, and, ever so gradually,† Darius' wing began to crumble. When his other side was exposed too, as men fell away, Darius became alarmed and turned to flight.* [4] So the Persian left wing was in flight, with the dust from the cavalry rising high into the air and Alexander's men in close pursuit—but there was so much dust and it was so thick that it was impossible to see which way Darius had gone, and only the groans of the wounded could be heard, and the thudding of horses' hoofs, and the continuous cracking of whips.*

[5] Meanwhile, Mazaeus, the commander of the right wing, who had a large force of first-rate cavalry under him, was pressing hard on the Macedonian left, but Parmenion, with the Thessalian cavalry and the rest of his troops, managed to stand his ground. [6] At first, in fact, in a dazzling display of martial prowess, he gained the upper

hand, thanks to the skill of the Thessalians, but then Mazaeus bore down on him, making good use of the large numbers of men at his disposal and the weight of his formation, and began to get the better of the enemy cavalry. [7] Many lives were lost on the Macedonian side and it was becoming hard for them to resist the pressure exerted by the barbarians, so Parmenion sent some of his horsemen to Alexander, asking him to respond rapidly with help. These men lost no time in carrying out their orders, but they found that Alexander had been drawn far from the field in his pursuit of the enemy.* They returned empty-handed, then, [8] but Parmenion brought all his experience to bear in deploying the Thessalian squadrons, and after he had inflicted many casualties on the barbarians, whose morale had plummeted, especially with the flight of Darius, he finally managed to turn them.

61. Mazaeus† was no slouch in military matters and he made good use of the great quantity of dust. He did not retreat along with the rest of the barbarians, but set out in the opposite direction and, with his route concealed by the thickness of the dust cloud, he not only escaped without trouble himself, but he also brought all of those who were with him to safety in the villages to the rear of the Macedonian position. [2] But in the end, with the entire Persian army in flight and the Macedonians mopping up any stragglers they came across, the whole region around the plain was covered with corpses. [3] So in this battle, counting cavalry and infantry together, the Persians lost more than ninety thousand men,* while the Macedonian dead numbered only about five hundred, although a great many men were injured. The wounded included one of the most distinguished of Alexander's marshals, Hephaestion, the commander of the bodyguards,* who had been wounded by a spear thrust in the arm, and several governors and senior officers, including Perdiccas, Coenus, and Menidas. So that was the outcome of the battle of Arbela.

62. *In the year of the Archonship of Aristophon in Athens, in Rome Gaius Domitius and Aulus Cornelius were the next to be appointed to the consulate. In this year:*

When news of the battle of Arbela reached Greece many of the cities, disturbed by the growth of Macedonian power, decided to make a bid

for freedom while the Persian empire still remained.* [2] Their thinking was that Darius would help them by providing them with ample
money for a large force of mercenaries, and that Alexander would be
unable to divide his forces—[3] and that if they just stood by and
watched as the Persians were defeated, they would be isolated and
freedom would no longer be a viable issue.

[4] The Greeks were also encouraged to rebel by the concurrent
outbreak of unrest in Thrace, [5] when Memnon, the military commander of the region, who had an army at his disposal and no
shortage of ambition, persuaded the Thracians to rise up against
Alexander.* Soon he had the command of a great many men, and
since he made no secret of his warlike intentions, [6] Antipater raised
his full levy, marched through Macedon to Thrace, and set about
fighting him.

Antipater's preoccupation with this business seemed to the Lacedaemonians to be an opportunity to prepare for war, and they called on
the Greeks to join them in a bid for freedom. [7] The Athenians did
nothing, because they had been especially favoured by Alexander, more
than any other Greek state,* but most of the Peloponnesians and some
others joined together and signed up for war. They recruited the best
men of fighting age, according to the capacity of the cities, and raised
an army of at least twenty thousand infantry and about two thousand
cavalry. [8] The Lacedaemonians had overall command, and they set
out at full strength for the decisive battle, with their king, Agis, as the
commander-in-chief.

63. When Antipater found out that the Greeks had banded
together, he brought the Thracian war to an end on the best terms he
could arrange and marched into the Peloponnese with his entire
army. He acquired further troops from his Greek allies* and ended
up with a force of at least forty thousand. [2] A great battle took place,
and Agis died on the field, but the Lacedaemonians resolutely fought
on and held out for a long time. When their allies were overcome,
however, the Lacedaemonians too retreated back to Sparta. [3] They
and their allies lost more than 5,300 men in the battle, while Antipater's
losses came to 3,500.

[4] Agis' death came about under unusual circumstances. After
putting on a dazzling display of martial prowess, in the course of
which he received many frontal wounds, he was being carried back to
Sparta by his men when he was overtaken by the enemy. He gave up

hope of saving himself, but he ordered the rest of his troops to race away—to stay alive for the good of their city. Then he armed himself, raised himself on to one knee, and defended himself against the enemy. He even managed to kill a few of them, but he died in a hail of javelins. He had been king for nine years.

[5] Having covered events in Europe, I shall turn next to Asia. 64. Following his defeat in the battle of Arbela, Darius fled to the upper satrapies, the idea being that these regions were far enough away for him to gain a breathing space and sufficient time to raise another army. At first, he went to Ecbatana in Media and stayed there, making it the collection point for the survivors of the battle and arming those who had lost their weapons. [2] He also requisitioned troops from the nearby tribes, and wrote to the satraps and governors in Bactria and the upper satrapies, asking them to remain loyal to him.

[3] Once Alexander had buried his dead, he followed up his victory with an offensive against Arbela, where he found abundant stores of food, plenty of valuables and precious objects of eastern workmanship, and three thousand talents of silver. Realizing that the air thereabouts would be befouled by the thousands of corpses, he quickly broke camp and made his way with his entire army to Babylon. [4] The Babylonians welcomed him enthusiastically and provided the Macedonians in their billets with sumptuous fare, and Alexander let his men rest and recover from the ordeals they had been through. Given the vast quantity of provisions there and the hospitality of the local people, he stayed in the city for more than thirty days.*

[5] Next, he entrusted the security of the Babylonian acropolis* to Agathon of Pydna and formed a unit of seven hundred Macedonian soldiers to support him. Apollodorus of Amphipolis and Menes of Pella were his choices as the military governors of, respectively, Babylonia and the other satrapies up to Cilicia, and he gave them a thousand talents of silver with which to recruit as many mercenaries as possible. [6] To Mithrines, who had betrayed the acropolis of Sardis to him, he gave Armenia, and with the money he had captured he made a present of six mnas to every Macedonian cavalryman, five to every allied cavalryman, and two to every phalangite; and he paid all the mercenaries two months' wages.

65. After Alexander had left Babylon, he was met en route by fresh troops from Antipater: 500 Macedonian horse and 6,000 foot; 600 horse from Thrace; 3,500 Trallians;* 4,000 foot and almost 1,000

horse from the Peloponnese; and from Macedon fifty sons of the king's Friends, who had been sent out by their fathers to serve as the king's bodyguards.* [2] Once these men had been added to the army, Alexander carried on and five days later he reached the district of Sittacene. Since the land there was blessed with everything he might need in ample quantities, he stayed there for quite a few days, not just because he wanted to rest his men, who needed a break from marching, but also because he intended to give some thought to the organization of his army. He wanted to promote some officers, so that the army would be strengthened by having plenty of talented men in senior positions. [3] By carrying out these plans—that is, by giving a great deal of thought to deciding who were the best men for the job,† and by promoting many junior† officers to positions of great responsibility—he moved all his officers up the ranks and bound them to him with strong ties of affection.* [4] He also rethought the normal deployment of the troops and came up with a number of improvements to increase their effectiveness.* Having raised to exceptional levels the loyalty of his men towards their leader and their obedience to his commands, and aroused their fighting spirit to an extraordinary degree, he felt ready for the battles that remained.

[5] He met no resistance on his journey to Susiane. The satrap, Abouleutes, surrendered the city to him and Alexander took over the famous royal palace of Susa. Some historians claim that Abouleutes was obeying orders issued by Darius to his most trusted subordinates, and they say that the Persian king did this so that Alexander would be preoccupied by all these major distractions and by his acquisition of world-famous cities and rich treasuries, while Darius bought time by his flight to prepare for war.

66. Once he had control of the city, Alexander found in the royal treasuries more than forty thousand talents of uncoined gold and silver. [2] For many years, the Persian kings had kept this money safe without touching it, leaving it as a last resort against the vicissitudes of Fortune. As well as this bullion, there were nine thousand talents of minted gold in the form of darics.*

[3] A curious thing happened while Alexander was taking possession of this money. He was seated on the royal throne, which happened to be disproportionately large for his body, and when one of his slaves saw that his feet were a long way off the footstool that went with the throne, he picked up the table that Darius had used and placed it

under Alexander's dangling feet. [4] Now that he was comfortable, Alexander thanked the slave for his thoughtfulness—but among the people standing near the throne was a certain eunuch, who was so affected by the way everything had changed that tears came to his eyes. [5] When Alexander noticed this, he asked him: 'Why are you crying? Did you see something that troubled you?' And the eunuch replied: 'I am your slave now, but previously I belonged to Darius, and since I am by nature devoted to my masters, it upset me to see the item of furniture that was most precious to him being treated as something of no worth.'

[6] This reply gave Alexander a sense of the completeness of the change that had come over the Persian empire, and it occurred to him that he had acted arrogantly, and in a way that was totally at odds with his moderate treatment of the captive women. [7] He called over the slave who had placed the table under his feet and told him to take it away again. At this, Philotas, who was standing near by, said: 'But this was not arrogance, because the order was not given by you. This was the outcome of the foresight and wishes of some benign deity.' And Alexander, taking what Philotas had said as an omen, ordered the slave to leave the table standing at the foot of the throne.

67. Alexander arranged for Darius' mother, daughters, and son to have tutors in the Greek language, and left them in Susa when he set out with his troops. Three days later he reached the Tigris river.* [2] This river, which rises in the mountains inhabited by the Uxians,* passes for the first thousand stades of its course through regions which are rugged and fractured by deep ravines, but then it flows through level terrain, with its current gradually decreasing in strength, and after another six hundred stades, by which time it is in Persis, it issues into the sea. [3] Alexander crossed the river and marched into Uxiana. The farmland there is extremely fertile and well watered, and produces a wide variety of crops in abundance, and so, at the time when the ripe fruits are being dried, the traders who ply the waters of the Tigris* bring down to Babylonia all kinds of enjoyable sweets.

[4] Alexander found that the pass was guarded by Madetes, a Kinsman of Darius,* with a large number of men, and, on inspection, he could see how difficult it would be to seize it. The cliffs were unscalable, but a native of the region, an Uxian, who knew these parts, assured Alexander that he would guide his men along a narrow

and dangerous path to a position above the enemy. [5] Alexander trusted him and dispatched him along with an adequate number of men, while he himself first cleared as much of a pathway as he could and then sent wave after wave of troops to attack the men stationed at the pass. The fighting was intense and the barbarians who were defending the pass were distracted by it, so that the appearance of the troops Alexander had dispatched took them by surprise. In terror, the Persians turned to flight, and Alexander gained control not only of the pass, but before long of all the Uxian towns as well.

68. His destination on leaving Uxiana was Persis,* and four days later he arrived at the so-called Susian Rocks, which had already been occupied by Ariobarzanes with twenty-five thousand foot and three hundred horse. [2] Alexander thought it would be possible for him to force his way through, and he advanced, making his way through narrow defiles and over broken ground. He met no trouble at first, but the Persians were allowing the Macedonians to get a certain distance into the pass, and when they were right in the middle of the badlands, they launched a surprise assault. They rolled many boulders down, as big as wagons, and since the Macedonians were bunched together, a lot of them lost their lives when the boulders suddenly struck. Meanwhile, a good number of the Persians were hurling their javelins down from the cliffs, and with the Macedonians packed closely together they could not fail to make a hit. Still others threw stones from close at hand at those Macedonians who continued to push forward. The broken terrain gave the barbarians a considerable advantage, and the numbers of dead and wounded were mounting.

[3] Alexander could do nothing to alleviate the dreadful situation and, seeing that his own losses were considerable, while not one of the enemy was dead or even injured, he had the trumpet recall his men from the fray. [4] He pulled back three hundred stades* from the pass and made camp. When he asked the local inhabitants whether there was some other way through, they all claimed that there was no other direct route, but only a circuitous route of several days. But Alexander could not stand the shame of leaving his dead unburied, and at the same time he could not countenance the idea of asking for permission to recover them, since that entailed an admission of defeat.* He therefore ordered all the prisoners to be brought up for questioning.

[5] Among the prisoners who appeared before him was a man who was bilingual in Greek and Persian. He said that he was a Lycian by

birth, that he had been captured in war, and that for quite a few years he had been a shepherd in these mountains. He knew the land well, he said, and could guide the army through thickly wooded parts to a position behind those who were guarding the pass. [6] The king promised the man a fortune, and with him as guide he did manage to cross the mountain under cover of darkness. The going was very difficult: they had to tramp through thick snow and find a way through terrain that was nothing but cliffs and was fractured by deep ravines and numerous chasms. [7] But when they came within sight of the enemy's pickets, they cut down those who had been assigned the forward position, made prisoners of the men in the second line of defence, and forced the third to turn and flee. Alexander then gained control of the pass, and killed most of Ariobarzanes' men.

69. Alexander next set out for Persepolis. While he was en route a letter came from Tiridates, who was responsible for the city.* In the letter Tiridates wrote that if Alexander could get there ahead of those who were coming to defend Persepolis for Darius, the city would be his because Tiridates would surrender it to him. [2] Alexander therefore led his men on at a fast pace, bridged the Araxes river, and brought his men over to the other side.

As he marched onward, he encountered the kind of weird and terrible sight that is guaranteed to arouse condemnation of the men who carry out such crimes, and pity and compassion for the victims of wrongdoing for which there is no remedy. [3] What happened was that he came across a band of men bearing suppliant branches, and they were Greeks, the descendants of Greeks whom earlier Persian kings had evicted from their homes and resettled.* There were about eight hundred of them, most of them elderly, and all of them had been mutilated, with either their hands or their feet or their ears and noses cut off. [4] They were professionals and craftsmen, experts in their fields, and all their extremities had been cut off except those they needed for their work. The sight of the dignified bearing of these elderly men, and the ways in which their bodies had been abused, aroused pity in everyone, but especially in Alexander, who felt such compassion for the wretches that he was unable to hold back his tears.

[5] The pitiful men all cried out at once, asking Alexander to relieve their suffering, and the king called their leaders forward. Treating them with the respect that one would expect from a man with his nobility of spirit, he promised to do his best to see them restored to

their homes. [6] But they met and talked things over, and decided that it would be better for them to stay where they were rather than return to Greece. Their thinking was that, if they were restored to Greece, they would become separated into small groups, and, as they went around in public in the cities, they would come to feel that the atrocious way they had been treated by Fortune was something of which they should be ashamed. If they continued to live together, however, as companions in misfortune, each of them would find that their shared experience of misery would alleviate his own misery. [7] So they arranged another meeting with Alexander, at which they explained their preference and asked him to give them the kind of assistance that would enable them to put this plan into effect.

[8] Alexander agreed that they had made the right decision, and gave each man three thousand drachmas, five sets of male apparel and five of female apparel, two teams of oxen, fifty sheep, and fifty *medimnoi* of wheat.* He also made them exempt from paying any of the royal taxes, and told his governors to see that they suffered no wrong from anyone. [9] With these benefactions, then, which were typical of his sense of justice, he alleviated the suffering of these wretched men.

70.   Arguing that there was no city in Asia that was more inimical to the Macedonians than Persepolis, the capital of the Persian empire,* Alexander gave his men permission to plunder it all except for the palace. [2] There was no wealthier city on earth, and over the course of many years the private houses had been filled with every token of prosperity, so the Macedonians went at it with a will. They killed all the men and plundered the houses; many of the houses belonged to ordinary people, but they were crammed with all kinds of furniture and finery. [3] Much silver was therefore carried off from them, and quite a lot of gold was stolen too, and the rewards of victory also included a great deal of valuable clothing, some dyed with sea purple,* some with gold embroidery. But the great palace, famed throughout the world, was slated for violation and utter destruction.

[4] After a full day of looting the Macedonians still could not satisfy their rapacity. [5] In fact, during this orgy of plundering, their greed exceeded all bounds, so that they even fought with one another, and many of those who had taken most of the booty for themselves were killed. Some men cut the most valuable of the finds in two with their swords and carried off their own portions; others, driven mad by their lust, cut off the hands of those who were trying to make off with

disputed property. [6] The women they manhandled and hauled away, finery and all, treating the prisoners of war as slaves. Persepolis had exceeded all other cities in prosperity, and now to the same degree it exceeded them all in misery.

71. Alexander made his way to the citadel and helped himself to the treasure that had been deposited there. The citadel was stuffed with silver and gold, because the treasure had been added to continuously from the time of Cyrus, the first Persian king, up until the time of Alexander's arrival. In fact, it was found to contain the equivalent of 120,000 silver talents, once the gold-to-silver ratio* was taken into account. [2] Alexander wanted to take some of the money with him to meet the costs of the war, and to deposit the rest in Susa and keep it under guard there, so he requisitioned a large number of mules from Babylon, Mesopotamia, and Susa, some to work as pack animals and some to draw carts in teams, and three thousand pack camels as well, and used them to convey all the treasure to the places he had selected. He sent for animals from so far away [3] because, given the bitter state of enmity between him and the local inhabitants, he did not trust them. Their hostility was also why he was planning to destroy Persepolis utterly.*

The Persepolis palace was such a superb piece of work that I think a brief description of it would not be out of place. [4] Three circuit walls* enclose the remarkable citadel. The first, which was built on a foundation on which no expense was spared, had a height of sixteen cubits and was enhanced by battlements. [5] The second is structurally the same as the first, except that it is twice as tall. The third circuit wall is oblong in shape, has a height of sixty cubits, and is made out of a hard stone which can never be worn down. [6] Each of its sides has a gateway with bronze gates, flanked by bronze poles twenty cubits high. The poles were designed to be impressive, but the gates were made for security.

[7] Four plethra away,* in the eastern part of the citadel, there is the mountain called the Mountain of the Kings, where the kings' graves are to be found. The rock has been hollowed out until it is honeycombed with chambers, in which the dead kings are laid to rest. No pathway has been cut up to these chambers: the corpses are hoisted up by machines and the sarcophagi inserted into them. [8] It was in this citadel that the several richly appointed residences of the kings and generals were to be found, and treasuries for keeping the royal hoard safe.

72. Alexander held a triumphal festival to celebrate his victories, at which he performed magnificent sacrifices to the gods and feasted his friends sumptuously. They were enjoying themselves in a companionable atmosphere, but at a certain point, when the celebrations were quite advanced and they were getting more and more drunk, a fit of madness gained thorough possession of their addled minds. [2] It was brought on when one of the women present—Thais, an Athenian by birth*—suggested to Alexander that it would crown all his fine achievements in Asia if he were to join them in a revel* and set fire to the palace, with the hands of women seeing to the swift extinction of this source of Persian glory.

[3] Now, the audience for this suggestion by Thais consisted of young men whose minds had been inflamed and robbed of reason by drink, and so, as was only to be expected, someone called on them to form a procession and light torches, and urged them to pay the Persians back for their crimes against Greek temples.* [4] Others chimed in with their approval and said that, if there was one person on earth who should properly carry out such a deed, it was Alexander. Once the king had been stirred into action by their words, they all leapt to their feet, abandoning the celebrations and calling on one another to honour Dionysus with a triumphal revel.

[5] Soon a large number of brands had been gathered, and since female musicians had been invited to the party, the sound of singing and of reed and wind pipes accompanied the king as he led them out for the revel, with Thais the courtesan taking command of the operation. [6] She was the first, after the king, to hurl her blazing brand into the palace. Before long, everyone else had done likewise, and so great was the conflagration that not just the palace, but the whole area around it caught fire. It was truly astonishing that it took just one woman, a fellow citizen of those whom Xerxes had wronged, to repay the Persian king in kind, so many years later, for his impious treatment of the Athenian acropolis, and that she should have done so for fun.*

73. After this, Alexander made the rounds of the cities of Persis, subduing some by force and winning others over by his clemency. Then he set out against Darius. [2] The Persian king's intention had been to gather the armies of Bactria and the upper satrapies, but he had run out of time and was fleeing to Bactra* with a force of thirty thousand Persians and Greek mercenaries. But in the course of his

retreat he was seized and murdered by Bessus, the satrap of Bactria. [3] Alexander was in hot pursuit with his cavalry, and Darius was not long dead when Alexander came upon his corpse and granted him a kingly funeral. [4] Some historians, however, say that Darius was still breathing when Alexander found him. According to this version, Alexander commiserated with him for his downfall, and when Darius implored him to avenge his death, Alexander agreed and set out after Bessus. The satrap was a long way ahead, however, and found refuge in Bactria, so Alexander gave up his pursuit and turned back.

That was how things stood in Asia. [5] In Europe, the calamitous defeat of the Lacedaemonians in a major battle* forced them to approach Antipater for terms. He passed the right of deciding their fate on to the common council of the Greeks,* and after the Greek delegates had convened in Corinth and had heard speech after speech for this position or that, they decided to refer the matter to Alexander for him to resolve.* [6] Antipater took the fifty most eminent Spartiates as hostages, and the Lacedaemonians sent envoys to Asia to beg Alexander to forgive their mistakes.

329/8

74. *At the beginning of the following year, Cephisophon became Archon in Athens, and Gaius Valerius and Marcus Claudius were elected consuls in Rome. In this year:*

In his flight from Alexander, trying to avoid falling into his hands, Bessus and his many companions (who included Nabarzanes and Barxaes)* reached Bactria. Bessus had been the satrap of Bactria under Darius, a position that had made him a familiar figure to the Bactrians, and he now called upon them to make a bid for freedom. [2] The land would give them valuable help, he argued, since it was not an easy place to invade, and it supported a large enough population for them to secure their independence. He announced that he would take command of the war and designated himself king,* with the approval of the general populace. Then he set about enlisting troops, having arms and armour made in quantity, and assiduously making sure that he had everything else that he would need to face the impending crisis.

[3] Alexander could see that the Macedonians were counting Darius' death as the end of the expedition and were impatient to go

back home, so he convened an army assembly,* at which he delivered a speech that effectively raised their morale and made them willing to continue with what remained of the campaign. He also convened the contingents supplied by the Greek cities, thanked them for all they had done and released them from service. He gave every cavalryman a talent, and every infantryman ten mnas, in addition to paying them their outstanding wages and giving them enough extra to see them through their return journey until they reached their homes. [4] But he gave three talents to any of them who chose to stay in the army under his command. He rewarded the soldiers so generously not just because it was his nature to be magnanimous, but also because he had gained a great deal of money in the course of his pursuit of Darius. [5] Eight thousand talents had been handed over to him by Darius' treasurers, but that was not all, because his disbursements to his troops, including jewellery and goblets, amounted to thirteen thousand talents, and it was suspected that more was stolen and embezzled.

75. Alexander set out for Hyrcania, and on the third day he made camp near a city called Hecatontapylus.* This is a prosperous city, where everything that makes life pleasant is to be found in great abundance, so he rested his troops there for a while. [2] Then, 150 stades further on, he encamped near a huge rock, which had a wonderful cave at its base, out of which flowed a great river called the Stiboetes. The current of this river is very rapid and turbulent for three stades, and then it divides into two around a rock shaped like a woman's breast, at the base of which there is a vast chasm in the ground. The river falls down into this chasm with a great roar, foaming from being dashed against the rock, and then flows underground for three hundred stades before issuing once more into the open air.*

[3] Alexander entered Hyrcania with his army and subdued all the cities there up to the Caspian Sea, which some call the Hyrcanian Sea. It is said that in this sea there are spawned large numbers of great snakes, and all kinds of fish as well, which are quite different in appearance from those found in our part of the world. [4] He crossed Hyrcania and came to the Prosperous Villages, as they are called—deservedly so, because their farmland is far more productive than anywhere else.* [5] Each vine, for instance, is said to produce a *metrētēs* of wine, and some fig trees to produce ten *medimnoi* of dried figs. The grain that is left over at harvest time and falls to the ground is said to

sprout without having to be sown and to bring a bounteous crop to maturity.

[6] There is also a tree in this region, the leaves of which drip honey; it resembles an oak in appearance, and the honey, which people collect, is extremely pleasant.* [7] There is also a winged creature there, called an *anthrēdōn*, which is smaller than a bee, but otherwise extremely similar,† since it roams the mountains, gathering pollen from all kinds of flowers, and then it constructs combs of wax in the hollow rocks and lightning-blasted trees where it lives, and makes a liquid of exceptional sweetness, which is almost as good as the honey found in our part of the world.*

76. While Alexander was in the process of adding the Hyrcanians and their neighbours to his dominion, he also received the surrender of many of the senior Persians who had fled with Darius. He treated them decently and acquired such a reputation for clemency [2] that the Greek mercenaries who had served with Darius, who numbered about 1,500 and were exceptional soldiers, immediately surrendered. They obtained his pardon and were enrolled in the army at the same rate of pay as the rest of the mercenaries.

[3] Alexander marched along the coastline of Hyrcania and entered the territory of the Mardians.* They were men of spirit, and they scorned the growing power of the king. So far from granting him a meeting or any token of respect, [4] eight thousand of them occupied the passes and confidently awaited the approach of the Macedonians. Alexander attacked, and in the battle that ensued he killed most of them and chased the rest into the hill country. [5] He then proceeded to put their farmland to the torch.

Seeing that the slaves who were driving the royal horses were some distance away from the king, some of the barbarians attacked them and made off with Bucephalas, the best of Alexander's horses. [6] It had been a gift from Demaratus of Corinth,* and it had been with the king in every battle he had fought in Asia. While it was still unharnessed, it would allow itself to be mounted only by its groom, but once it had on the royal livery, it no longer accepted even the groom, and submitted only to Alexander, and only for him would it lower its body to facilitate mounting.

[7] Furious at the loss of such an excellent creature, Alexander ordered his men to begin clearing the land of trees, and he had people who spoke the local language tell the Mardians that if they did not

return the horse, they would see their land utterly devastated and the inhabitants slaughtered to a man. [8] He immediately set about carrying out these threats, and the terrified barbarians returned the horse. They sent along with it gifts of the greatest value, and also fifty men to beg forgiveness. The most important of these men Alexander took as hostages.

77. On his return to Hyrcania, the queen of the Amazons paid him a visit.* Her name was Thallestris, and the land between the Phasis river and the Thermodon was her domain.* She was a woman of exceptional beauty and physical strength, and her martial prowess had won the admiration of her compatriots. She left most of her army on the border with Hyrcania and came to Alexander with three hundred Amazons in full armour. [2] The king expressed surprise both at their unexpected visit and at the impressive bearing of the women, and when he asked Thallestris why she had come, she said that she wanted to conceive his child. [3] She explained that his achievements proved that there was no man on earth to compare with him, and that since her strength and courage made her superior to other women, it was likely that any child with two such outstanding parents would surpass all others in valour. The king was charmed, and in the end he granted her request. They spent thirteen days together, and then he honoured her with valuable gifts and sent her back home.

[4] After the conquest of Hyrcania, it seemed to Alexander that by now he had done what he set out to do and that his hold on his kingdom was incontestable. He began, then, to imitate the luxurious Persian lifestyle and the extravagance of eastern kings. The first thing he did was introduce into his court ushers of eastern origin,* and then he formed a bodyguard for himself consisting of the most eminent easterners, including Darius' brother, Oxathres. [5] He also took to wearing the Persian diadem,* and dressed in white clothes with no coloured border, a Persian sash, and everything else except trousers and *kandys*.* He had his companions wear purple-bordered robes, and he equipped the horses with Persian tack. [6] As if that were not enough, he also installed concubines in his retinue, just as Darius had; there were as many of them as the days of the year, and they were outstandingly beautiful, as might be expected given that they had been selected from all the women of Asia. [7] Every evening, these women paraded around the king's bed, for him to choose the one who would spend the night with him. But in fact Alexander made little use

of such practices, and largely stuck to his former habits, since he had
no desire to offend Macedonian sensibilities. 78. His behaviour still
found many critics, but he bribed them into acquiescence.

When Alexander found out that Satibarzanes, the satrap of Areia,
had killed the soldiers he had left with him and was cooperating with
Bessus—and had, in fact, decided to join Bessus in resisting the
Macedonians—he marched against him.* Satibarzanes mustered his
forces in Chortacana,* which was the most notable city in those parts
and was endowed with exceptional natural strength, [2] but at the
approach of the king the size of his army and the reputation of the
Macedonians as fighters filled him with consternation. He therefore
took two thousand men and rode off to Bessus, to ask him to send help
as soon as possible, and he told the rest of his men to take refuge in
a mountain range called [...],† the broken terrain of which offered
plenty of places where men who lacked the courage to face their
enemies in battle could find refuge.

[3] They did as he had told them and took refuge on a certain rock,
tall and easily defensible, but the king, with his usual determination,
put them under a close siege and forced them to surrender. [4] He
followed this success by gaining the submission of all the cities in the
satrapy. This took him no more than thirty days, and then he left
Areia† and went to the main city of Drangiane, where he halted and
rested his men.

79. It was around this time that Alexander found himself compelled to commit a despicable act, one that was alien to his fundamental goodness. What happened was that one of his Friends, a man
called Dimnus, who disapproved of some of what the king was doing,*
became angry enough to form a conspiracy against him. [2] He
persuaded Nicomachus, his boyfriend, to join the conspiracy, but
Nicomachus, who was very young,* told his brother Cebalinus about
it, and Cebalinus, terrified that one of the conspirators might warn
the king before he did, decided to turn informer himself.

[3] He went to the court, fell in with Philotas, and told him about
the plot. He asked him to inform the king without delay, but Philotas,
who may have been in on the plot, or may just have been careless,
failed to do anything about the information he had received. Although
he saw Alexander and took part in a long and wide-ranging conversation, he made no mention at all of what Cebalinus had told him. [4]
After leaving Alexander, he told Cebalinus that he had not found

a suitable opportunity to divulge the plot to the king, but he assured him that he would be meeting with the king alone the next day, and would tell him everything. But Philotas did the same thing the next day as well, so Cebalinus, who was worried about the danger he would find himself in if the king got the news from someone else, went behind Philotas' back and approached one of the Royal Pages. He gave him a detailed account of all that had happened and asked him to tell the king as soon as possible.

[5] The page took Cebalinus into the armoury and hid him there, and then went in to see the king, whom he found bathing. He passed on the information Cebalinus had given him, and said that he had Cebalinus hidden and in his care. The king was astounded. He immediately had Dimnus arrested, and once he was in possession of all the facts, he sent for Cebalinus and Philotas. [6] While everyone was being interrogated and the investigation was still ongoing, Dimnus committed suicide. As for Philotas, although he admitted that he had been careless, he denied any involvement in the conspiracy, and the king left the decision in his case up to the Macedonians.

80. After a great deal of discussion, the Macedonians condemned Philotas to death. The others who were accused along with him were also condemned, and they included Parmenion, who was regarded as the foremost of Alexander's Friends.* He was not there, but it was believed that he was actually the prime mover of the conspiracy, and that his son Philotas had been acting as his agent. [2] Philotas was tortured, and then, once he had confessed to the plot, he was put to death in the Macedonian manner,* as were the others who had been condemned along with him. Another similar case was that of Alexander the Lyncestian. Accused of plotting against the king, he had been held in prison for three years,* with the decision in his case delayed because of his kinship to Antigonus.* But now he was brought to trial before the Macedonians, and when he failed to find anything to say in his defence, he was put to death.

[3] Alexander saw to the assassination of Parmenion, Philotas' father, by sending men out on dromedaries,* so that they would get to him before the news of Philotas' death. Parmenion had been the governor of Media, and had been entrusted with the royal treasuries in Ecbatana, which held 180,000 talents. [4] Alexander also withdrew from their units any Macedonians who had ever criticized him, and those who were angry at Parmenion's death, and anyone who had ever

written anything detrimental to his interests in their letters to relatives back in Macedon, and formed them into a single regiment called
the Refractory Regiment, so that the rest of the Macedonians would
not be corrupted by their inappropriate talk and the bluntness with
which they spoke.*

81. Once all this was behind him and he had made his arrangements for Drangiane, Alexander set out with his troops to launch an
offensive against the people who were formerly known as the
Ariaspians,† but were now called the Benefactors. The change of
name came about as follows. Cyrus, the man who engineered the
Persian takeover of the Median empire, once became trapped in the
course of a campaign in an uninhabited region and found himself in
extreme danger because of lack of provisions. In fact, for want of
anything else to eat, his men were compelled to resort to cannibal-
ism. But he was saved in the nick of time when the Arimaspians
brought thirty thousand carts laden with food. Exemption from
taxes was just one of the ways he rewarded them, and he revoked the
name by which they had formerly been known and called them the
Benefactors instead. [2] So now, when Alexander marched into their
territory, they made him welcome, and he honoured them with
appropriate gifts.*

Their neighbours, the Gedrosians, did the same and they too
received suitable tokens of Alexander's favour in return. He made
Tiridates the governor of these two peoples. [3] While he was busy
with these arrangements, messengers arrived with the news that
Satibarzanes had returned to Areia from Bactria with a large force of
cavalry, and had stirred the local people into rebellion.* Alexander's
response to the news was to send a division of his army under the
command of Erigyius and Stasanor to deal with Satibarzanes,
while he conquered Arachosia, the subjection of which took only
a few days.*

328/7

82. *At the beginning of the following year, Euthycritus became Archon in
Athens, in Rome Lucius Platius and Lucius Papirius were the next to be
appointed to the consulate, and the 113th Olympic festival was celebrated.† In this year:*

Alexander marched against the Paropanisadae, as they are called. [2] Their country lies right under the Greater and Lesser Bear constellations;* it is entirely blanketed with snow, and the extreme cold makes it a hostile environment for other peoples. Most of the country consists of a treeless plain, which is divided among a large number of villages. [3] The houses in these villages have vaulted brick roofs contracted to a peak.† In the middle of the roof there is an aperture through which smoke escapes, and since the building is closed on all sides,* the inhabitants are very well protected. [4] Because of the amount of snow, the natives spend most of the year inside their homes, with their food ready at hand. They bank up earth around their vines and fruit trees, leave them like that for the duration of winter, and then remove the earth at the time of new growth. [5] Nowhere is there anything green or cultivated to be seen; being gripped by snow and ice, the land is all white and sparkling. This means that no birds settle there, nor is it trodden by any wild animals; every part of the country is inhospitable and inaccessible.*

[6] Even though the army had all these difficulties to contend with, Alexander overcame the obstacles put in his way by the country with typically Macedonian boldness and grit. [7] One result of this was that many soldiers and non-combatants from the baggage train could not keep up and were abandoned, and others were blinded by the glare of the snow and the harshness of the reflected light.* [8] It was impossible to see anything clearly in the distance; it was only when smoke revealed the presence of villages that the Macedonians found that they were close to where some natives lived. That was how they managed to capture the villages. The amount of booty they took recompensed the soldiers for the ordeals they had been through, and before long the king had subdued the entire native population.

83. Next, Alexander drew near Mount Caucasus (or Mount Paropanisus, as it is also known) and made camp.* It took him sixteen days to cross this mountain range from one side to the other, and in the pass which leads to India he founded a city called Alexandria.* Deep in the Caucasus there is a rock with a perimeter of ten stades and a height of four stades, with a cave in it which the local inhabitants identify as the cave of Prometheus, and they also point out where the eagle that features in the story had its nest, and the marks of the chains.* [2] Alexander founded other towns as well,* a day's march away from Alexandria,† and populated them with seven thousand barbarians, three thousand of his camp followers, and volunteers

from the mercenary contingents. [3] Then he led his army into Bactria, because he had learnt that Bessus had assumed the diadem and was gathering his forces.

That was how things stood with Alexander. [4] The generals who had been sent to Areia found that the rebels had gathered a substantial army, and had as their general Satibarzanes, who was a skilled strategist and a man of exceptional courage. They made camp near the enemy. There was a lot of skirmishing, and for a while there were only limited engagements, [5] but then they fought a pitched battle. The barbarians were holding their own, but then the rebel commander, Satibarzanes, pulled the helmet from his head so that everyone could see who he was, and offered to fight any of the senior officers among the Macedonians in single combat. [6] Erigyius accepted the challenge and a titanic clash took place, which Erigyius won. At the death of their general the barbarians lost heart, and once they had received a guarantee of safety they surrendered to the king.

[7] After proclaiming himself king, Bessus sacrificed to the gods and invited his Friends to the celebratory banquet. In the course of the celebrations, Bessus and one of his companions, a man called Bagodaras, got into an argument.* The quarrel heated up until Bessus lost his temper and made it plain that he wanted to kill Bagodaras, but his Friends persuaded him to think better of it. [8] Although he was out of immediate danger, Bagodaras still fled that night to Alexander, and the fact that Alexander made him safe and promised to reward him for his defection tempted the most senior of Bessus' generals. They formed a conspiracy, seized Bessus, and brought him to Alexander. [9] The king rewarded them generously and handed Bessus over to the brother and the other kinsmen of Darius for punishment.* After subjecting him to every imaginable kind of abuse and torture, they chopped him up into little pieces and disposed of the remnants here and there.

A major gap occurs in all the manuscripts at this point, covering the end of the year 328/7 and the beginning of 327/6 (the Archonship of Hegemon in Athens). We know from the Table of Contents that was at some point drawn up for each of Diodorus' books that fifteen full chapters are missing. We have lost his account of the difficult conquest of Bactria and Sogdiana, Alexander's increasing orientalization and its unpopularity (and probably his deification), and the early phases of Alexander's Indian campaign. Some famous incidents took place during these months: Alexander's marriage to Sogdianian Rhoxane; the drunken killing of Cleitus the Black; the Pages' Conspiracy and the arrest of Callisthenes.

84. ...Once a truce had been arranged on these terms, the queen,* who was astounded at Alexander's generosity, sent him fabulous gifts and promised to be his loyal subject. In accordance with the terms of the truce, the mercenaries immediately left the city* and made camp about eighty stades away. They met with no interference and had no idea what was going to happen. [2] But Alexander was unyielding in his hostility towards them. He had kept his army in a state of readiness, and now he followed the barbarians and launched a surprise attack, intending to slaughter them.* The mercenaries' immediate response was to shout out that fighting them contravened the truce oaths, and they invoked the gods who were being wronged by Alexander's sacrilege; but Alexander shouted back at the top of his voice that he may have allowed them to leave the city, but that did not mean that the Macedonians would treat them as friends for ever.

[3] Undismayed by the severity of the danger, the mercenaries closed ranks and had the entire company adopt a circular formation (with the children and women corralled in the centre), so that they could securely defend against their attackers in every direction. The courage and calibre of these men, who fought with desperate fury, made the fighting so fierce that, in combination with the Macedonians' determination to match and surpass barbarian valour, the battle became a scene of horror. [4] With the fighters engaging one another at close quarters, there were all kinds of ways for men to be killed or wounded. The Macedonians tore through the barbarians' shields with their pikes and drove the iron heads into their lungs, while the mercenaries hurled their lances into the close-packed ranks of the enemy, who were so close that they could not miss.

[5] The number of mercenaries who were being wounded or killed was mounting—and the women began to take up the weapons of those who had fallen and fight alongside the men. The severity of the danger and the ferocity of the action forced them to find resources of courage untypical of their kind. Some of them even wore armour and stood in line next to their husbands, while others, lacking arms or armour, dashed forward, grabbed hold of their opponents' shields, and impeded them very effectively. [6] In the end, overwhelmed by

the superior numbers of the Macedonians, all the mercenaries and the women fighters were cut down, preferring death and glory to a cowardly clinging to life. Alexander separated out all those who had no military function and were unarmed, and the surviving women too, and gave them into the care of the cavalry.

85. After the successful assault of a number of other cities, and the killing of those who offered resistance, he came to the rock called Aornus, where the surviving natives had fled for refuge, trusting in its incredible strength. [2] It is said that, long ago, Heracles* planned to put the rock under siege, but refrained after receiving warning signs from the gods, including several severe earthquakes. But the effect of this story on Alexander was just to make him even more determined to besiege the stronghold and to pit his reputation against that of the god.

[3] The rock had a circumference of a hundred stades and a height of sixteen, and its surface was all smooth and rounded. Its southern flank was washed by the Indus, the greatest river in India, and its other flanks were protected by deep ravines with sheer sides. [4] After inspecting the place and seeing how rugged it was, Alexander despaired of taking it by force, but then an old man came to him, accompanied by his two sons. [5] The old man was extremely poor and had lived thereabouts for a long time—his home being a cave with three crude beds cut into the rock, where he spent the nights with his sons—so that he had come to know the area very well. He approached Alexander, explained his situation, and offered to guide the king through the rough hills and to a favourable point in relation to the position of the barbarians who had occupied the rock.

[6] Alexander promised to reward him generously, and after the old man had taken him there, the first thing he did was occupy the defile that led to the rock, thereby trapping the barbarians and denying them any hope of relief, since there was no other way out. Then, taking advantage of the great workforce at his disposal, he filled in the ravine at the base of the rock, which allowed him to draw near it and put it under a close siege. He assaulted it continuously for seven days and seven nights, with his men working in relays. [7] At first, the barbarians had the upper hand, because they held the higher ground, and many of Alexander's men lost their lives as they pushed their way recklessly forward. But once the ravine had been filled in and the bolt-shooting catapults and other siege devices were in place—and once it had also become clear that the king was not going to give

up—the Indians became terrified. Alexander cleverly foresaw what would happen, and he withdrew† the men who had been guarding the defile, so as to allow anyone who wanted to leave the rock to do so. And indeed the barbarians did abandon the rock by night, out of fear of Macedonian martial skill and the king's determination.

86. So Alexander overcame the Indians by employing the ruse of inciting needless alarm, and took the rock without further loss of life. He gave the guide his promised reward, and then broke camp and led his troops away. [2] Coincidentally, an Indian called Aphrices was close by with an army of twenty thousand men and fifteen elephants,* but some of his men killed him and brought his head to Alexander, doing him a good turn in return for their lives. [3] The king took these men into his service, and rounded up the elephants, which were roaming free in the countryside.

Alexander next reached the Indus river, where he found that his thirty-oared ships were ready and that the river had been bridged. He rested his men for thirty days and then, after performing magnificent sacrifices to the gods, he led them across the river—and into an unusual adventure. [4] The king, Taxiles, had died. He had been succeeded by his son, Mophis, who had already made contact with Alexander while he was in Sogdiana, and had promised his support if Alexander would help him against his Indian enemies. And Mophis followed this up now by sending emissaries to Alexander and offering to surrender his kingdom to him.

[5] However, when Alexander was forty stades away, Mophis drew up his troops, seemingly for battle, deployed his elephants, and marched forward to meet him, with his Friends by his side. At the approach of this sizeable army in battle array, Alexander assumed that the Indian's promises had been a deception, so that he would find the Macedonians unprepared when he launched his attack, and he ordered his trumpeters to give the signal for battle, formed up his men, and advanced to confront the Indians. [6] But when Mophis saw all the tumult in the Macedonian camp, he guessed what had happened. He left his army and rode forward with just a few men, and once he had corrected the Macedonians' misapprehension, he surrendered himself and his troops to the king. [7] Alexander was very relieved, and returned his kingdom to him; he changed his name to Taxiles,* and from then on treated him as a friend and ally.

These were the events that took place in this year.

326/5

87. *In the year of the Archonship of Chremes in Athens, the Romans appointed as their consuls Publius Cornelius and Aulus Postumius. In this year:*

While he was in Taxiles' realm, Alexander brought his army back up to strength and then marched against Porus, whose kingdom bordered that of Taxiles. [2] Porus had an army of more than fifty thousand foot, about three thousand horse, more than a thousand chariots, and 130 elephants, and he also had the support of another of the neighbouring kings, who was called Embisarus and who had almost as large an army as Porus. [3] When Alexander heard that Embisarus was four hundred stades away, he decided to attack Porus before his ally showed up, and he halted close to the Indians.*

[4] As soon as Porus found out that the enemy was near by, he drew up his men for battle. He divided the cavalry between the two wings, and posted the elephants in a terrifying array at regular intervals along the front. In the gaps between the elephants, he posted the remainder of his men, the heavy infantry, whose job it was to support the creatures and to make sure that they could not be attacked from the sides by the enemy's javelins. [5] The overall effect of the arrangement was to make his army look like a city, with the elephants in the position of towers and the soldiers between them resembling the curtain walls. Alexander took good note of the enemy's arrangements and disposed his men accordingly, in response to the formation he was facing.

88. In the first phase of the battle, almost all the Indians' chariots were destroyed by Alexander's cavalry. But then the elephants began to make good use of their great height and massive strength. Some of Alexander's men were trampled in the dirt, armour and all, and died with their bones crushed; others were grasped by the elephants' trunks and died a terrible death when they were raised up high and dashed back down to the ground. Many were transfixed by the elephants' tusks and lost their lives in an instant, with their bodies run clean through.

[2] But the Macedonians firmly stood their ground against the horrific danger, and the battle became evenly balanced as their pikes thinned the ranks of those who were posted between the elephants. [3] After that, the elephants began to be struck by javelins—and they

were wounded so often, and were in such agony as a result, that the Indians mounted on them lost control of the creatures' movements, and they changed direction and charged uncontrollably into their own ranks, trampling their friends. [4] There was considerable confusion, but Porus could see what was happening. He had taken the most powerful of the elephants for himself, and he gathered about him forty others which had not yet been driven wild and launched an attack. They slammed into the enemy and took many lives, not least because Porus himself was by far the strongest man in his army. He was five cubits tall, and his chest was twice as broad as that of the most muscle-bound of his soldiers. [5] He was so strong that javelins thrown by him packed almost as great a punch as missiles fired by catapults.

The Macedonians facing Porus had found his courage too much for them, but Alexander called up his archers and light infantry and told them all to make Porus their target. [6] The men did as they had been told and soon many missiles were hurtling towards the Indian, who was so big that they could not miss. Porus fought on heroically, until the amount of blood he had lost from his many wounds made him faint, and he slumped down on the elephant and fell to the ground. [7] The rumour spread that the king was dead, and the rest of the Indians turned to flight.

89. Many Indians lost their lives in the course of their flight, but then Alexander, who had won a notable victory, had the trumpets recall his men. More than twelve thousand Indians died in the battle, and the casualties included two of Porus' sons, his generals, and the most eminent of the leading men of his kingdom. [2] More than nine thousand men were taken prisoner as well, along with eighty elephants. Porus himself, who was still alive, was handed over to the Indians for treatment. [3] On the Macedonian side, 280 cavalry died and more than seven hundred infantry. Alexander buried his dead, rewarded those of his men who had fought with valour as they deserved, and sacrificed to Helios, the Sun, on the grounds that it was he who had made his conquest of the East possible.

[4] The hill country near by had plenty of good fir trees, along with quite a bit of cedar and pine, and a more than ample supply of other materials needed for ship-building, so Alexander built a good number of ships. [5] His plan was to get to the end of India, subduing all the inhabitants of the country on the way, and then to sail down to the

Ocean.* [6] He founded two cities, one on the far side of the river at the point where he had crossed, and the other at the spot where he had defeated Porus. He had such a large workforce at his disposal that the work was soon completed. Once Porus had recovered, Alexander acknowledged his merits by restoring him to the kingship of the country he had formerly ruled. Then he let his men rest for thirty days, since there was no shortage of provisions where they were.

90. The nearby hill country was not without interest. In addition to ship-quality timber, there were also a great many snakes there, and at sixteen cubits they were exceptionally long.* There were many different species of monkey as well, of various sizes, and they themselves show the way in which they can be caught. Force is not a good way to capture them, because they are strong creatures, and canny as well, [2] but they imitate everything, so this is what the hunters do.* Some of them smear their eyes with honey, while others—this is while the animals are watching—tie on sandals or hang mirrors around their necks. Then they leave, but first they join the sandals together with straps, put out gum instead of honey, and attach nooses to the mirrors. [3] So when the animals try to do what they saw the hunters doing, they become helpless, with their eyelids stuck together, their feet bound, and their bodies immobilized. Then they become easy prey for the hunters.

[4] Alexander next cowed Sasibisares* into submission—he was the king who had failed to arrive in time to help Porus in battle—and forced him to become his vassal. Then he crossed the river with his army and marched on, through land of exceptional fertility. [5] Various kinds of tree grew there, which attained a height of seventy cubits and a girth that could hardly be encompassed by four men, and overshadowed three plethra of ground.* This land too was infested by snakes, which were small in size and variously patterned. [6] Some of them looked like sticks made of bronze, while others had thick, hairy crests. Death followed quickly from their bites, and their victims were seized by terrible pain and burst out in a bloody sweat. [7] The Macedonians, who fared badly from the bites, therefore hung hammocks in the trees to sleep in and passed restless nights. Subsequently, however, the natives told them of a root that acted as an antidote,* and they got over their fear.

91. As Alexander and his men continued on their way, he received word that King Porus, a cousin of the Porus who had been defeated,

had left his kingdom and fled to the Gandaridae.* [2] Alexander responded by sending a force under Hephaestion to Porus' kingdom, to see to its takeover by the friendly Porus. Meanwhile, he campaigned against the Adrestae, as they are called. Some of their cities fell to him by main force and some he won over by diplomacy, and then he came to the land of the Cathaeans.* [3] It was the custom among these people for wives to be cremated along with their husbands—a regulation that came into force thanks to one woman in particular, who poisoned her husband.* [4] Anyway, after a great deal of fighting, Alexander succeeded in taking their largest and strongest city, which he put to the torch. He had another of their important cities under siege when the Indians came to him as suppliants and begged him for mercy, and he brought the hostilities to an end.

The targets of his next campaign were the cities that fell within Sopeithes' domain. These cities have an exceptionally fine legal system, because in all their measures they focus on what others will think of them. [5] One consequence of this is that, at infancy, children there are separated into categories. Those who are physically sound and have the potential to grow into fair and fit adults are brought up, while those who are physically defective are judged not to be worth rearing and are killed. [6] In keeping with this, when it comes to arranging marriages there, people are not bothered about dowries or profit in any form, but think only of beauty and physical excellence. [7] As a result, very many of the inhabitants of these cities have particularly dignified bearings. With a height of over four cubits, the beauty and stature of their king, Sopeithes, was unrivalled among his subjects. He emerged from his capital city, and surrendered himself and his kingdom to Alexander, but such was the conqueror's sense of justice that he received it back again.* [8] And Sopeithes devoted himself to arranging for the entire army to be treated for several days to lavish banquets.

92. Alexander was given many valuable gifts by Sopeithes, including 150 impressively large and strong dogs, which were said to have some tiger in them. [2] Sopeithes wanted Alexander to recognize the quality of the dogs by seeing them in action, so he had a mature lion let into an enclosure and he set on it two of the poorest of the dogs he had given Alexander. The lion started to overpower these two, however, so he released two more, [3] and then the four dogs began to get the better of the lion. At this point, Sopeithes had a man enter the

enclosure with a knife and make as if to cut off the right leg of one of the dogs. Alexander cried out, and his bodyguards dashed up and stayed the hand of the Indian, but Sopeithes promised to give him three dogs to compensate for this one, and then the handler took hold of the dog's leg and slowly but surely cut through it. No yelp or whimper was heard from the dog, and it stayed with its jaws clamped shut in the lion's flesh until it bled to death, still attached to the beast.

93. Meanwhile, Hephaestion arrived with the army that had accompanied him on his mission. He had successfully conquered a large chunk of India, and Alexander commended him for his valour and then entered the land ruled by Phegeus. The local inhabitants welcomed the Macedonians, and Phegeus brought Alexander a great many gifts. Alexander allowed him to retain his kingdom, and Phegeus provided very generously for the army for two days. Then Alexander marched on to the Hyphasis river,* which was seven stades wide and six fathoms deep, and had a powerful current that made it hard to cross.

[2] Phegeus told him that on the far side of the river there was a desert* that would take twelve days to cross, and that then he would come to a river called the Ganges, which was thirty-two stades wide and the deepest river in India. Beyond the Ganges, Phegeus went on, lived the Tabraesi and the Gandaridae.* The king of the Gandaridae was called Xandrames, and he had an army of twenty thousand horse, two hundred thousand foot, two thousand chariots, and four thousand elephants equipped for war. Alexander found this unbelievable, and he sent for Porus and asked him whether or not the information he was receiving was accurate. [3] Porus confirmed that it was, but added that the king of the Gandaridae was an utterly ordinary and undistinguished individual, rumoured to be the son of a barber. His father had been an attractive man and a great favourite of the queen, and when the king was murdered by his wife, the kingdom had fallen to him. [4] Although Alexander could see that it would be difficult to wage a successful campaign against the Gandaridae, he was still determined to try. His faith in the calibre of his Macedonian troops and in the oracles he had received made him confident that he would defeat the barbarians. After all, the Pythia had called him invincible, and Ammon had granted him dominion over the whole world.*

94. Alexander could see, however, that the continuous campaigning had exhausted his men. For almost eight years they had been beaten down by hard work and danger, and he was sure that he would

have to find good arguments to persuade them to undertake a campaign against the Gandaridae, [2] since there had already been considerable loss of life and there was no prospect of an end to the fighting. The horses' hoofs had been worn thin by non-stop travel,* most of the men's weaponry had become blunt, their Greek clothing was long gone, and they were forced to make use of foreign fabrics and re-tailor Indian garments. [3] And, as luck would have it, there had been ferocious storms for seventy days,* with continuous thunder, and thunderbolts constantly crashing around them.

All this was clearly going to make it difficult for him, and he realized that the only way he was going to attain his goal was if he could improve his men's lives to such an extent that they were won over and gave him their absolute loyalty. [4] He therefore let them plunder the farmland beside the river,† where there was plenty of booty for the taking, and while the men were busy foraging, he gathered together their wives and the children who had been born to them. He promised the women a monthly allowance of grain, and awarded the children military stipends that depended on their fathers' ranks. [5] Then, when the soldiers came back laden with all the good things they had found in the course of their foraging, he convened a general assembly. He delivered a carefully worded speech about the expedition against the Gandaridae, but he completely failed to win the Macedonians over, and he abandoned the plan.*

95. Having decided that this spot constituted the furthest limit of the expedition, he first raised altars to the twelve gods,* each fifty cubits high, and then he marked out the circuit of a camp that was three times as large as the existing one, dug a ditch around it with a width of fifty feet and a depth of forty feet, and constructed a formidable rampart out of the earth that was excavated from the trench and heaped up on the side nearest the camp. [2] Then he ordered every infantryman to build a two-bed hut, with each bed five cubits long, and every cavalryman to build not just a hut, but also two mangers, each double the usual size; and similarly outsized versions were made of everything else that was to be left behind. His intention in doing this was not just to construct a camp fit for heroes, but to leave the natives with evidence that great men had been there, men of superhuman strength.

[3] Once he had finished with this, Alexander and his entire army retraced their route back to the Acesines river. He found some completed

hulls there, and he fitted out these boats and ordered more to be made. [4] At this juncture, a number of auxiliaries and mercenaries arrived from Greece, who had been led there by their commanding officers. There were thirty thousand foot and almost six thousand horse, and they also brought with them twenty-five thousand superb suits of infantry armour and a hundred talents of medicinal herbs. All of these supplies were distributed among the men. [5] When the fleet was ready—it consisted of two hundred undecked galleys and eight hundred transports—his final act was to name the two cities that had been founded on the river: he called one Nicaea in commemoration of his victory, and the other Bucephala after the horse of his that had died in the battle with Porus.*

96. So Alexander embarked with his Friends and sailed down the river towards the southern Ocean,* while the bulk of his army marched alongside the river, led by Craterus and Hephaestion.* When they reached the junction of the Acesines and the Hydaspes, he disembarked his men and led them against the Sibi, as they are known, [2] who are said to be descended from the men who served with Heracles in the campaign against the Rock of Aornus, and to have been settled in this region by Heracles after they had failed to capture the rock.* Alexander made camp close to a splendid city, and the most eminent of the citizens came out to meet him. In their meeting with the king, in addition to giving him the magnificent gifts they had brought, they reminded him of their kinship and said that, as kin,* they would willingly support his every enterprise. [3] Alexander thanked them for their loyalty, declared their cities free, and then marched against their neighbours.

Finding that the Agalasseis had raised an army of forty thousand foot and three thousand horse, he brought them to battle and inflicted very heavy casualties on them in the course of defeating them. The survivors were sold into slavery, once Alexander had taken the nearby towns where they had fled for safety. [4] The other local peoples had also massed together, and he stormed into a great city where twenty thousand of them had sought refuge, but the Indians barricaded the streets and fought so valiantly from the houses that Alexander had a hard time of it, and quite a few Macedonian lives were lost. [5] This made the king angry, and he put the city to the torch and burnt a great many of the inhabitants to death. About three thousand survivors withdrew to the acropolis for safety, and when they came to him as suppliants to beg for mercy, he let them go free.

97. Alexander embarked once more with his Friends and sailed downstream until he came to the confluence of the rivers I have already mentioned with the Indus.* The collision of three great rivers at this one point created many fearsome eddies, which spun the boats around and threatened to destroy them. The current was so fierce and strong that the helmsmen were unable to cope, for all their skill, and two of the long ships were sunk, while many vessels ran aground. [2] The command ship became trapped in a long stretch of rapids, and the king found himself in extreme danger. With death staring him in the face, Alexander shed his clothes and, naked, clung on to anything that seemed to offer the prospect of safety. His Friends swam alongside the boat in order to catch him, since the ship was in danger of capsizing.* [3] On board the ship, there was utter chaos as the crew struggled to master the violent current, but there was nothing that human skill or strength could do against the power of the water, and Alexander made it ashore with the help of the swimmers.† It was a close-run thing, but he had beaten the odds and survived, and he sacrificed to the gods in thanks for having escaped death, and in celebration of the fact that he had fought a battle with a river, just as Achilles had.*

98. Next, he campaigned against two populous and warlike peoples, the Sydracae and the Malli, who, he found, had collected an army of more than eighty thousand foot, ten thousand horse, and seven hundred chariots. Before Alexander's arrival, these two peoples had been enemies, but on his approach they had banded together; each gave the other ten thousand unmarried girls, and their reconciliation was confirmed by granting each other in this way the right of intermarriage. [2] Nevertheless, they failed to put a joint force in the field for a battle, because they fell out once more, this time over which of them should have overall command and withdrew into the nearby towns.

Alexander drew near the first of these towns. His intention was to take it by storm, [3] but just then one of the army diviners, a man called Demophon, approached him and said that it had been revealed to him by certain omens that the king would find himself in mortal danger from a wound received in the course of the assault. He asked Alexander, therefore, to leave this town alone for the time being and to turn his attention elsewhere. [4] Alexander told the man off for sapping the army's morale, deployed his troops for the assault, and took the lead himself as they advanced on the town, which he was determined to capture by main force. It was taking time for the siege engines to be moved up into place, but Alexander took the lead, broke down a postern gate, and burst into the town. He cut down many of the enemy, forced the rest to retreat, and pursued them to the acropolis.

[5] The Macedonians were still busy trying to secure the outer wall, so Alexander grabbed a ladder, leant it up against the wall of the citadel, and climbed up, holding his shield over his head. He was so quick to act that he reached the top of the wall before the foremost barbarian soldiers could intercept him. [6] The Indians did not dare to come to close quarters, but fired javelins and arrows at him from a distance—such a hail of missiles that the king found himself in trouble. Some Macedonians brought up a couple of ladders and tried to climb up to the top of the wall, but the ladders broke, because they were all on them at once, and the men fell to the ground.

99. Finding himself isolated and with no hope of support, Alexander did something that was unexpected in its boldness, and well worth recording. He felt it would betray the success of his expedition if he were to retreat from the wall and back to his men without having achieved anything, so he leapt down into the citadel, fully armed but all alone. [2] The Indians ran up to attack him, but he defended himself valiantly against their onslaught. His right side was protected by a tree that had sunk its roots right by the wall, the wall itself stopped the Indians attacking him from the left, and he displayed the kind of courage that one would have expected from a king whose valour had already accomplished so much, and who was determined to end his life in a blaze of glory.

[3] His helmet and shield were struck time and again, but eventually an arrow hit him below the breast and he fell to one knee, reeling from the wound. The Indian who had shot him ran straight up, not expecting any trouble, and aimed a blow at him, but Alexander thrust his sword up and into the man's side. The wound was fatal and the barbarian fell to the ground, but the king grabbed hold of a nearby branch, pulled himself to his feet, and challenged the Indians to fight. [4] Just then, Peucestas, one of the king's foot guards, who had climbed up on another ladder, reached the king—he was the first to do so—and covered him with his shield. Then several others arrived, the barbarians lost heart, and Alexander was saved.* But the wounding of their king made the Macedonians furious, and once the town

had fallen to them they killed everyone they came across and filled the town with corpses.

[5] Alexander was laid up for many days while he underwent treatment. For a long time resentment had been building up among the Greeks who had been settled in Bactria and Sogdiana because they had been made to live among barbarians, and now, when the rumour reached them that the king had died from his wounds, they defected from Macedon. [6] They banded together—there were about three thousand of them—and suffered terribly in the course of their journey home; later they were slaughtered by the Macedonians after Alexander's death.*

100. When Alexander had recovered from his wound, he sacrificed to the gods to thank them for saving his life and arranged great banquets for his friends. In the course of the celebrations, an unusual incident occurred which should not go unrecorded. [2] Among the invited guests was a Macedonian called Coragus, an exceptionally strong man who had often distinguished himself in battle, and, under the influence of alcohol, he challenged Dioxippus to single combat—Dioxippus being an Athenian athlete who had won crowns in the most notable games.* [3] Naturally, the guests at the symposium stoked their rivalry, and Dioxippus accepted the challenge. Alexander named a day for the contest, and when the time came for the duel to take place, tens of thousands of men gathered to watch it. [4] The Macedonians and Alexander backed Coragus because he was one of them, while the Greeks were on Dioxippus' side.*

The Macedonian stepped up for the competition fully armed and arrayed in expensive armour, but the Athenian was naked, with an oiled body, and carried only a moderately sized club. [5] Both men were remarkably well-built and exceptionally strong, so what was about to take place was expected to be little short of a battle between gods. Since the Macedonian's physique and gleaming armour inspired terror, he was taken to be the image of Ares, while Dioxippus, with his exceptional strength, his athletic training, and his choice of a club as his weapon, resembled Heracles.

[6] As they closed in on each other, the Macedonian hurled his javelin, but there was still quite a gap between them, and the Greek merely leant aside a little to let it fly harmlessly past. Then the Macedonian couched his pike and advanced, but as soon as he was close the Greek struck the pike with his club and broke it. [7] After

these two failures, the Macedonian resorted to his sword, and he was just drawing it when the Greek pounced. With his left hand he seized the Macedonian's right hand, which was drawing the sword, and at the same time he used his other hand to force his opponent off balance and knock him off his feet. [8] Once he was down on the ground, the Greek stood over him, with his foot on his neck, raised his club, and looked expectantly at the spectators.

101. The crowd erupted, partly because this was not the result they had expected, and partly in appreciation of the extraordinary courage the Greek had displayed, and the king ordered him to let the Macedonian live. He then brought the performance to an end and left, fuming at the Macedonian's defeat. [2] Dioxippus released his fallen opponent. He had won a famous victory, and he left the arena bedecked with wreaths by his fellow Greeks, who felt that he had earned glory not just for himself but for all Greeks. But Fortune did not allow the man much time to enjoy his victory.

[3] Alexander's ill will towards Dioxippus only increased as the days went by, and eventually his Friends and all the Macedonians in his court, who resented the Greek's success, persuaded his chamberlain to slip a golden goblet under his pillow. Then, at the next symposium, they accused him of theft and pretended to discover the goblet, thus stigmatizing him as a thief and ruining his reputation. [4] It was clear to Dioxippus that the Macedonians were ganging up against him. He left the symposium at this point, and a short while later, back in his quarters, he wrote a letter to Alexander explaining the foul trick that had been played on him and gave it to his servants to deliver. Then he committed suicide. It was rash of him to have accepted the challenge to the duel, but it was far more stupid of him to have taken his own life. [5] His folly came in for a lot of criticism from his detractors, with people saying that it was hard to have a super-strong body, but a weak mind.

[6] Alexander read the letter and was upset that the man had died. There were many occasions when he missed him for his merits—which is to say that, after neglecting the man while he was there, he missed him when he was gone. The iniquity of Dioxippus' detractors eventually taught him to recognize the man's true goodness, but by then it was too late.

102. Alexander ordered the army to continue its march alongside the river, shadowing the fleet, while he sailed downstream towards the

Ocean. He came to land in the country of the Sambastae, as they are known, [2] who were at least as populous as any other Indian people, and just as skilled at warfare. They lived in cities which were run as democracies,* and when they heard about the approach of the Macedonians they mustered an army of sixty thousand foot, six thousand horse, and five hundred chariots. [3] But the arrival of the fleet frightened them—it was an unfamiliar and unexpected sight—and, besides, they were aware of the reputation of the Macedonians and it terrified them. So, seeing that their elders also advised them not to fight, they sent a delegation of fifty of their most distinguished men to ask Alexander to treat them mercifully. [4] The king complimented the men and agreed to a peace treaty, and the Indians showered him with valuable gifts and instituted his worship as a hero.*

The next peoples to submit to him were the Sodrae* and Massani, who lived on opposite banks of the river. He founded a riverside city here called Alexandria, and picked the ten thousand settlers who were to inhabit it.* [5] Then he came to the country of King Musicanus, where he got the king into his power, killed him, and made the people his subjects. After that, he invaded the country where Porticanus was king. He assaulted and took two towns, which he put to the torch after allowing his soldiers to plunder them. Porticanus himself escaped to the safety of a stronghold, but Alexander captured it and killed the king, who refused to surrender. He then proceeded to capture every single one of the cities which had been in Porticanus' realm, and he left them all in ruins, in order to strike terror into Porticanus' neighbours.

[6] Next, in the realm of King Sambus, he destroyed farmland and left a great many towns in ruins; the inhabitants were sold into slavery, but over eighty thousand of the barbarians were slaughtered as well. [7] He visited a similar catastrophe on the people known as Brahmans,* but when the survivors came to him as suppliants and begged for mercy, he granted clemency to everyone except the ringleaders, who were punished. King Sambus saved his life by fleeing with thirty elephants into the country on the other side of the Indus.

103. The last of the Brahman towns, called Harmatelia,* was confident that the courage of its citizens and the ruggedness of its location would keep it safe. Alexander sent a small force of light-armed troops there, with orders to engage the enemy and withdraw if they came out against them. [2] There were only about five hundred of them, and the inhabitants of Harmatelia scoffed at their attack on the

walls. Three thousand soldiers sallied out of the town, and Alexander's
men ran away, pretending to do so out of fear. The barbarians set out
in pursuit, [3] but they had not gone far when Alexander checked
them and initiated a hard-fought battle in which the barbarians lost
many men, killed or captured.

Quite a few of Alexander's soldiers were also wounded, however,
and found themselves in mortal danger. [4] The barbarians had
smeared their weapons with a deadly poison—in fact, it was this that
gave them the confidence to risk a battle. The way they made the poison was by catching and killing certain snakes, and leaving their bodies
out in the sun. [5] As the heat of the sun dissolved the flesh, drops of
sweat appeared on the surface, and the poison was drawn out of the
flesh along with the moisture. As soon as a man was wounded, his body
went numb, but this was quickly followed by severe pain, and by con-
vulsions and juddering which racked the whole body. The skin became
cold and livid, and vomiting occurred as a means of expelling black
bile, while a dark foam bubbled up from the wound and gangrene set
in. The gangrene spread rapidly, overran the vital parts of the body,
and a terrible death followed. [6] It made no difference whether a man
was wounded badly, or received only a flesh wound or a scratch.

An appalling death, then, awaited anyone who was wounded, and
although Alexander found every case distressing, he was particularly
upset by Ptolemy. This was the Ptolemy who later became a king, and
who at that time was a great favourite of Alexander's.* [7] Something
curious and unusual occurred in Ptolemy's case, and there were those
who were inclined to attribute it to divine providence, in the sense
that his abilities and his extraordinary generosity towards others had
endeared him to everyone, and the help he received was no more than
his decency deserved. What happened was that Alexander had a dream
in which he saw a snake holding a plant in its mouth, and in the dream
the snake showed him what the plant looked like, explained its virtue,
and pointed out where it grew. [8] When he woke up, therefore, he
tracked the plant down and ground it up.* He not only rubbed it on
Ptolemy's body, but also gave him an infusion to drink, and he did
indeed cure his friend. Now that the plant's efficacy had been recognized, everyone else received the same treatment and recovered. As
for the city of Harmatelia, Alexander planned to assault it, despite its
strength and size, but then the inhabitants came to him as suppliants
and capitulated, and he spared them any punishment.

104. So he and his Friends reached the Ocean. He performed magnificent sacrifices to the gods on two islands that he found there,* and while pouring libations he also let a large number of golden goblets fall into the sea and sink. Finally, he built altars to Tethys and to Ocean,* and then it seemed to him that the campaign he had undertaken was at an end.

After leaving these islands, he sailed back up the Indus to a notable city called Patala.* [2] Its constitution was very similar to that of Sparta, in the sense that it had two kings from two royal houses who gained their thrones by inheritance. At times of war, the kings were in charge, but overall responsibility for the state was in the hands of the Board of Elders. [3] At Patala, Alexander burnt those of his ships that were in poor condition, and entrusted the rest of the fleet to Nearchus and some of his other Friends; their orders were to sail along the Ocean, hugging the coastline all the way, to take note of everything they saw,* and then to meet him at the mouth of the Euphrates.

[4] He himself took the army. Over the course of the next lengthy phase of the march, he used force to overcome any opposition he met, but was generous in his treatment of those who submitted to him. The Abritae,* for instance, and the inhabitants of Gedrosia he won over peacefully. [5] But after Patala, he crossed a long stretch of waterless land, much of which was also uninhabited, and then he came to the borders of Oreitis. Here he divided the army into three, with Ptolemy and Leonnatus in charge of the other two divisions. [6] Ptolemy's job was to plunder the coastal regions, while Leonnatus did the same inland and Alexander ravaged the uplands and the hill country. The simultaneous devastation of so much land meant that there was no part of the country that was not ablaze, with its goods being plundered and its inhabitants slaughtered. [7] It did not take the soldiers long, then, to acquire a great deal of booty, nor did it take long for the number of dead to reach countless thousands. But the destruction of these peoples frightened all their neighbours into submission. [8] Alexander wanted to found a city by the sea, and finding a sheltered harbour which was close to a spot that was suitable for a new settlement, he founded a city there called Alexandria.*

105. He next entered the country of the Oreitae through the mountain passes, and before long he had made the entire population subject to him. The Oreitan way of life is fundamentally the same as the Indian; there is only one practice that is significantly different,

but it is quite a strange one. [2] When someone dies there, his body is carried off for burial by his relatives, who are naked and carry spears. They place the body in some undergrowth in the countryside, and then strip it of its clothing and finery, and leave the corpse to be eaten by wild animals. They divide the dead man's clothes among themselves, sacrifice to the chthonian heroes, and feast all the members of the dead man's household.

[3] On his way towards Gedrosia, marching along the coast, Alexander next encountered a people who were wary of strangers and lived utterly brutish lives. [4] The inhabitants of this part of the world never cut their nails from birth to death, nor comb their hair, their skin has been burnt by the sun, and they dress in animal skins. [5] Their food is the flesh of monstrous sea-creatures that are cast up on the shore, and the houses they build have walls made of seashells and roofs made of the ribs of these creatures, which they used as beams, eighteen cubits long. And instead of tiles, they covered their roofs with the creatures' scales.*

[6] Shortage of provisions made this stage of Alexander's journey arduous, and then the next region he came to was completely uninhabited and lacking in everything that sustains life. As the number of men dying of hunger grew, the Macedonians lost heart and Alexander became extremely upset and concerned. The idea that men whose prowess had enabled them to conquer the world should die ingloriously in a desert, starved of all resources, appalled him. [7] He therefore dispatched lightly clad messengers to Parthyaea, Drangiane, Areia, and the other provinces that bordered the desert, who were instructed to see that dromedaries and other species† which were regularly used as pack animals arrived as soon as possible at the border with Carmania, laden with food and other supplies.* [8] These messengers raced off to the satraps of these provinces and arranged for large quantities of provisions to be transported to the appointed place. Alexander still lost a lot of men, however, first because of the desperate shortage of food, and then because during the march some of the Oreitae attacked Leonnatus' division and inflicted heavy casualties before withdrawing safely back into their own territory.

106. Eventually, however, Alexander made it across the desert and came to a land that was inhabited and well supplied with everything he might need. Once his men had recovered, he marched on for seven days with the army adorned as though for a festival, and he turned the

whole journey into a Dionysian revel, with feasting and drinking and celebrations.* [2] This revel was just over when he heard that many of his satraps and governors had been doing wrong, abusing their powers and treating their subjects with high-handed abusiveness, and he punished them as they deserved. As word spread of Alexander's intolerance of wrongdoing among his officials, many of his governors became frightened, because they knew they had been acting in an arrogant and lawless manner. Some of them, who had mercenary forces under their command, rebelled, while others packed up their valuables and fled. [3] When Alexander found out about this, he wrote to all the generals and satraps in Asia, ordering them to disband their mercenary forces as soon as they had read the letter.

[4] Just then, while the king was staying in a coastal town called Salmous* and was in the middle of holding a dramatic contest in the theatre, there arrived in the harbour the fleet that had been given the mission of sailing along the coastline of the Ocean. The officers came straight to the theatre, hailed Alexander, and gave him an account of their adventures. [5] The Macedonians, delighted that they had arrived safely, marked the occasion with loud applause, and the whole theatre was filled with unrestrained celebration.

[6] In their report, the returning sailors said that the Ocean had astonishing tides. When it was on the ebb, a large number of sizeable islands* became visible just offshore, but when it was in flood all these islands were inundated by the substantial body of water that sped towards land, and there was enough foam to turn the surface of the water white. But the strangest adventure of all, they said, was when they encountered a large number of unbelievably enormous sea-creatures.* [7] They were terrified at first and gave up any hope of survival, since they were sure that the ships were going to be destroyed in the next instant and that they would die along with them. But when they all yelled at once and made a terrific noise by beating on their shields, and when the trumpets joined in as well, the unexpected noise frightened the monsters, and they disappeared into the depths of the sea.

107. After hearing their report, Alexander told the officers in command of the fleet to sail on to the Euphrates, while he took the army all the way up to the borders of Susiane. This was when Caranus,* an advanced Indian philosopher who stood high in Alexander's estimation, brought his life to an end. The circumstances were unusual. [2]

He had lived for seventy-three years without having experienced a day of illness, and so he decided that, since both Nature and Fortune had given him unalloyed happiness, it was time to end his life. [3] He had fallen ill and was getting worse day by day, so he asked the king to build him a great pyre. He would climb to the top of this, he said, and then Alexander should get his servants to set fire to it.

[4] At first, Alexander tried to dissuade him, but his words fell on deaf ears, so he said that he would do as Caranus asked. Word got around about what was going to happen, and when the pyre had been built, a large crowd came to witness the unusual spectacle. [5] True to his beliefs, Caranus cheerfully climbed up to the top of the pyre and was burnt to death along with it. Some of those present judged him insane, while others thought he was making a conceited display of fortitude, but there were also those who were impressed by his courage and his contempt for death. [6] Alexander gave Caranus a lavish funeral, and then went on to Susa. While he was there, he married Stateira, the eldest daughter of Darius, and gave the other daughter, Drypetis, to be Hephaestion's wife.* He also persuaded the most illustrious of his Friends to marry, and he gave them as their wives young Persian women from the most noble families.*

108. At this juncture, thirty thousand Persians arrived in Susa. They were very young, but they had been selected for their good looks and strength. [2] They had been formed into a unit on Alexander's orders, and for quite a long time they had been under supervisors and instructors, training them in the arts of war. All of them were decked out in costly Macedonian-style suits of armour. They made camp in front of the city and put on a demonstration for the king of their discipline and proficiency with weapons, and won high praise from him. [3] It was not just that the Macedonians had refused an order to cross the Ganges river;* they were also given to heckling him in assemblies and they thought the idea that Alexander's father was the god Ammon was absurd. The reason, then, that Alexander had formed this unit from Persians (all drawn from one and the same age-group) was to have it act as a counterweight to the Macedonian phalanx.*

That was how things stood with Alexander. [4] Harpalus had been entrusted with the treasury in Babylon and the public revenues, but no sooner had Alexander marched into India than he turned to a life of debauchery, since he did not expect Alexander to return. Harpalus had been put in charge of a large satrapy, but what he prioritized and devoted himself to was the violation of women and illicit sex with natives. He spent a lot of the treasure on the most intemperate pleasures imaginable, and earned himself a bad name by having fish brought in large quantities all the way from the Red Sea* and instituting similarly extravagant practices. [5] Then he had the most famous courtesan in the world, a woman called Pythonice, brought to him from Athens. He honoured this woman with gifts fit for a queen while she was alive, and when she died he gave her a lavish funeral and built a costly tomb for her in Attica.* [6] Next he sent for another Athenian courtesan, called Glycera, and with her he lived a life of extraordinary luxury and extravagance. But, knowing the vicissitudes of Fortune, he made sure that his generosity towards the Athenian democracy secured him a bolt-hole there.*

On his return from India, Alexander accused a lot of the satraps of crimes and put them to death, and Harpalus was afraid of being punished. He packed up five thousand talents of silver, gathered an army of six thousand mercenaries, and left Asia.* He sailed to Attica, [7] but his plea for refuge fell on deaf ears in Athens, so he left his mercenaries at Cape Taenarum in Laconia,* returned to Athens with a portion of his money, and appealed to the people as a suppliant. Antipater and Olympias demanded his extradition,* and although Harpalus distributed a great deal of money to politicians so that they would support his appeal, he slipped away by boat and joined his mercenaries at Taenarum. [8] From there, he sailed to Crete, where he was murdered by a friend of his called Thibron. The Athenians carried out an investigation into Harpalus' finances, and Demosthenes and some other politicians were found guilty of accepting money from him.

109. When the Olympic festival was held,* Alexander had a herald in Olympia proclaim that everyone who had been sent into exile from his homeland was to be taken back, unless they were temple-robbers or murderers. He himself selected the oldest of the Macedonians and released them from service. There were about ten thousand of them. [2] When he found out that many of them were heavily in debt, he paid off what they owed in a single day, which cost him just short of ten thousand talents.

The remaining Macedonians, however, were tending towards mutiny and, when he convened an assembly, they tried to shout him down. With no thought of the danger, Alexander's response was to condemn their behaviour. This cowed the majority, and then he boldly leapt down from the speaker's platform, seized the ringleaders of the disturbance with his own hands, and turned them over to his attendants for punishment. [3] The disaffection became far worse, however, and the king gave positions in the army to some of the Persians he had singled out, and began to promote them to the highest command. Then the Macedonians had a change of heart, and they repeatedly begged Alexander, with tears in their eyes, to forgive them, and eventually he was won over and made his peace with them.

325/4

110. *In the Archonship of Anticles in Athens, the Romans appointed as their consuls Lucius Cornelius and Quintus Popillius. In this year:*

Alexander made up the number of those he had released from service by recruiting Persians, a thousand of whom were assigned to the Household Guard, and on the whole he placed no less trust in these Persians than he did in his Macedonians. [2] Peucestas arrived around this time as well, bringing twenty thousand Persian archers and slingers,* whom Alexander added to already existing units of the army—a revolutionary innovation that enabled him to create the kind of integrated army that he aimed to have.* [3] Some of the Macedonians had sons whose mothers were female prisoners, and Alexander did an accurate count of them. There were not far short of ten thousand of them, and he set aside enough money for all of them to receive a liberal education and appointed men to teach them the appropriate subjects.

Then he gathered his troops and left Susa.* After crossing the Tigris, he halted at the Carian Villages,* as they are called, [4] and then he marched through Sittacene, which took him four days, and arrived at a place called Sambana. He stayed there for seven days, resting his men, and then three days later he reached the land occupied by the Celones. There were Boeotians living there, as they still do today, who had been uprooted during Xerxes' expedition to Greece,* but still remembered their ancestral customs. [5] They were bilingual, for instance—scarcely distinguishable from the natives when they spoke one language, but with very many Greek words and idioms preserved in the other.

Finally, after waiting there for several days, he broke camp, but made a detour from his itinerary and went to Bagistana* to see the sights. This is a truly wonderful country, filled with fruit trees and everything else that makes life good. [6] Next he came to land that was capable of supporting vast herds of horses. It was said that in the old days there were 160,000 horses at pasture there, but when Alexander was there the number was found to be sixty thousand.* He stayed there for thirty days, and then on the seventh day after leaving he arrived at Ecbatana in Media. [7] This is a city the circuit of which is said to be two hundred and fifty stades; the royal court buildings are there, which constitute the centre of all Media, and very well-stocked treasuries as well.

He let the army rest in Ecbatana for quite a long time. While he was there, he put on a festival with theatrical competitions and held continuous symposia for his Friends. [8] Hephaestion drank to excess during these symposia—so much so that he fell ill and died. The grieving king gave Perdiccas the job of conveying the dead man's body to Babylon, where he intended to give him a spectacular funeral.

111. Meanwhile, in Greece unrest and revolution were widespread, and turned out to be the first rumbles of the so-called Lamian War.* The cause of the war was as follows. Alexander had ordered all the satraps to discharge their mercenaries, and so they did, but that meant that the whole of Asia was overrun by all those former professional soldiers, now drifters who got their food by foraging. Subsequently, they sailed over to Cape Taenarum in Laconia,* [2] and then the last of the Persian satraps and other leading men sailed over to Taenarum as well, taking with them the money and troops they had collected, and joined forces with those who were already there.

[3] Ultimately, they chose as their supreme commander Leosthenes, a man endowed with exceptional nobility of spirit and a bitter opponent of Alexander. After secret consultations with the Athenian Council, he was given fifty talents with which to pay his troops, and enough weapons for his immediate needs. He contacted the Aetolians to see about an alliance, since they were no friends of Alexander,* and made thorough preparations for war.

[4] While Leosthenes was occupied with getting ready for what he could see was going to be a critical war, Alexander marched with his light-armed troops against the Cossaeans, who were refusing to submit to him. The Cossaeans were an exceptionally spirited people, living in

the mountains of Media.* They had always relied on the ruggedness of their homeland and their courage to keep them out of the control of foreign masters. They had remained free even in the days of the Persian empire, and at the time in question Macedonian prowess caused them no alarm or loss of confidence. [5] But Alexander occupied the passes and ravaged most of the country, and came off best every time they met in battle. Many of the barbarians lost their lives, and a great many more were taken prisoner.

The Cossaeans had been utter failures on the battlefield and were finding it hard to endure the loss of all their men who had been captured. Under the circumstances, they had no choice but to accept subjugation as the price of the recovery of the prisoners. [6] So they surrendered to Alexander and gained peace on the condition that they would be his obedient subjects. It had taken Alexander a total of forty days to defeat the Cossaeans. He founded noteworthy towns in the hills, and then let his men rest.

112. After his defeat of the Cossaeans, Alexander decamped and marched on towards Babylon at a leisurely pace, halting constantly and resting his men. [2] When he was about three hundred stades from the city, the Chaldaeans (as these priests are called) sent to him a delegation of their oldest and most experienced men. These Chaldaeans are particularly famous as astrologers, and their practice is to predict the future on the basis of perpetual observation of the stars.* They had learnt through their astral divination that death awaited the king in Babylon, so they instructed their delegates to warn him of the danger and to recommend that he avoid entering the city altogether. [3] They said that he could escape the danger if he rebuilt the temple of Bel,* which had been destroyed by the Persians, but that he must desist from his intended route and bypass the city.

The leader of the Chaldaean delegation, whose name was Belephantes,* was too afraid to talk directly to the king, but he obtained a private meeting with Nearchus, one of Alexander's Friends, at which he briefed him thoroughly and asked him to explain matters to the king. [4] Nearchus' report of the Chaldaeans' prophecy frightened Alexander, and he only became more troubled as he recalled their reputation for wisdom. In the end, he sent most of his Friends into the city, while taking another road himself. He avoided Babylon, made camp two hundred stades away, and stayed quietly there.

No one knew what to make of this, and many Greeks came to visit him. One of their number was the philosopher Anaxarchus, [5] and when he found out the reason for Alexander's behaviour he forcefully advanced arguments drawn from philosophical texts,* and worked such a change in the king that he came to despise all forms of divination, and especially the kind preferred by the Chaldaeans. It was as though Alexander had been wounded in the mind and then healed by the words of the philosophers.* And so he entered Babylon with his troops. [6] As they had on his previous visit, the Babylonians made his men welcome, and the whole army gave itself over to relaxation and easy living, since everything that they might want had been made ready for them in abundance.

These were the events that took place in this year.

324/3

113. *In the year of the Archonship of Agesias* in Athens, the Romans appointed as their consuls Gaius Publius and Papirius, and the 114th Olympic festival was celebrated, with Micinas of Rhodes the victor in the stade race. In the course of this year:*

Envoys arrived in Babylon from almost every part of the known world. Some came to congratulate Alexander on his conquests, some to honour him with crowns, and others to conclude treaties of friendship and alliance. Many of them brought him magnificent gifts, and a few came to defend themselves against charges that had been brought against them. [2] Nor was it only the peoples and cities of Asia who were represented: many dynasts also came from Europe and Libya. From Libya came the Carthaginians, the Libyphoenicians,* and all the peoples who inhabit the coast up to the Pillars of Heracles.* From Europe came representatives of the Greek cities, the Macedonians, the Illyrians, most of the peoples who live on the Adriatic coastline, the Thracian tribes, and the Celts who were neighbours of the Thracians. This was the first time that Greeks had ever come across Celts.*

[3] When the register of the envoys was submitted to Alexander, he ordered the names according to which of them he would respond to first, which second, and so on for all of them. He met first with those whose business concerned sanctuaries, second with those who had

brought gifts, third with those who were in dispute with their neighbours, fourth with those who had come on personal business, and fifth
with those who were protesting the return of the exiles.* [4] The
first to be granted an audience were the Eleans, and then there followed
the Ammonians, the Delphians, the Corinthians, the Epidaurians,
and so on, with the meetings ordered according to the importance of
the sanctuary.* He did his best to give favourable replies to all the
embassies and to send them away as satisfied as they might be.

114. Once he had dismissed the embassies, the king occupied himself with Hephaestion's funeral. He was so obsessed with the arrangements that it not only eclipsed every funeral ceremony there had ever
been on earth, but will never be surpassed in the future either. For he
had loved Hephaestion more than† any of his other Friends, however
fond he seemed to be of them, and no one could have done more to
honour a man after his death than Alexander did for Hephaestion.
While he was alive, he had preferred him to all his other Friends,*
even though Craterus was a rival for his affection. [2] In fact, when
one of the king's companions said that Craterus and Hephaestion were
equal in the king's affection, Alexander agreed, adding that Craterus
loved him as a king, but Hephaestion loved him as Alexander. And
when Darius' mother, on her first meeting with Alexander, mistakenly
started to do obeisance before Hephaestion, taking him to be the king,
and became flustered when she learnt of her mistake, Alexander said:
'Don't worry, mother. He is Alexander too.'*

[3] As Alexander's friend, Hephaestion generally enjoyed so many
privileges and was allowed so much freedom of speech that Olympias
became jealous. She turned hostile towards him, and wrote him
letters in which she rebuked him harshly and threatened him. To
these he responded with a letter written in a reproachful tone and
concluding: 'Do, please, stop thinking badly of us, and do put an end
to your anger and threats. If you don't stop, though, it won't particularly bother us. For you know that there is no one greater than
Alexander.'*

[4] Be that as it may, as part of his preparations for the funeral
ceremony, the king ordered the nearby cities to do what they could,
depending on their means, to see that it was a splendid affair. He also
ordered all the inhabitants of Asia to be sure to extinguish their
fires—fire is sacred to the Persians—and not to re-light them until
the ceremony was over. But this was the Persian custom at the death

of a king, [5] and most people took the order to be a bad omen and thought that it was the gods' way of foretelling the king's death. There were other unusual signs as well that foreshadowed Alexander's death, which I shall come to shortly, after my account of the funeral.

115. With the intention of ingratiating themselves to the king, every one of his officers and friends had likenesses of Hephaestion made out of all the materials that men find precious, such as ivory and gold. Meanwhile, Alexander gathered his master builders and a large number of craftsmen. He tore down a ten-stade stretch of the city wall,* and once he had collected all the baked brick and had levelled the ground where the pyre was going to stand, he built a four-sided pyre, with each side a stade in length. [2] He divided the space into thirty courses, laid out the roofs of each course with palm-tree trunks, and squared off the whole structure.

The next job was to attach the ornamentation to the facade, all the way round the outside wall. Two hundred and forty golden quinquereme prows occupied the bottom level, with two archers, four cubits in height, each kneeling on one knee on the outriggers, and five-cubit-high statues of armed marines, while the interstices were filled with stylized palm-trees made of felt. [3] The next level up, the second, consisted of carved torches, each fifteen cubits long and with a golden wreath on its handle; above the flaming ends of the torches were eagles with their wings spread and heads bowed, looking down, and at their bases were serpents looking up at the eagles. On the third level was depicted a hunting scene, involving a great many wild animals. [4] Then the fourth level consisted of a centauromachy rendered in gold,* while the fifth was made up of alternating lions and bulls, all in gold. The next part was occupied by Macedonian and barbarian arms and armour, arranged so as to signify the martial prowess of the former and the military failures of the latter. Finally, on top of these six levels stood Sirens, which had been hollowed out so that they could conceal people within them who would sing a funeral lament for the deceased. [5] The total height of the structure was more than 130 cubits.

In short, with everyone eager to contribute to the splendour of the funeral ceremony—not just officers, but also ordinary soldiers, the envoys from other states, and native Babylonians—the money spent on it is said to have amounted to more than twelve thousand talents. [6] In keeping with this grandeur, the last of the honours that

Alexander ordained in the context of the funeral ceremony was that everyone was to sacrifice to Hephaestion as an adjunct deity.* And, by a happy coincidence, one of Alexander's Friends, Philip, arrived in Babylon just then, bringing back from Ammon the god's permission for Hephaestion to receive sacrifices as a god.* Alexander was delighted that Ammon had confirmed his opinion, and he was the first to perform the sacrifice. Since it consisted of ten thousand victims of all kinds, the accompanying feast for the army was a sumptuous affair.

116. After the funeral ceremony, the king gave himself over to diversions and filled his days with feasting. But just when his power and prosperity seemed to have peaked, Fate curtailed the span of life that had been granted him by Nature. Immediately after the funeral, even the gods began to signal his impending death, and many strange omens and signs occurred. [2] Once, for instance, when the king was being rubbed with oil and the royal robes and diadem had been laid on a chair, a Babylonian prisoner, whose fetters had come loose all by themselves, passed through the entrance of the court without the guards noticing and without anyone impeding his progress. [3] He came up to the chair, and once he had dressed himself in the royal robes and tied the diadem on his head, he sat down and remained quiet.

When the king was told what was going on, it struck him as weird and disquieting, but he approached the chair, and without giving any indication of his fear he calmly asked the man who he was and why he had acted in this way. [4] The man said not a word in reply, however, and Alexander referred the interpretation of the portent to his diviners. Their opinion was that the man should be killed, so that whatever the trouble was that was being portended would descend on his head, not Alexander's, and that is what Alexander did.* He then recovered his clothes and sacrificed in thanks to the gods who protect men from evil, but he remained anxious. He recalled the Chaldaeans' prediction, found fault with the philosophers who had persuaded him to enter Babylon, expressed his admiration of Chaldaean skill and acumen, and in general maligned those who used sophistical ingenuity to deny the power of Fate.

[5] A short while later, the gods sent him another omen that related to his kingship. Alexander wanted to visit the Babylonian marshes, and he and his Friends were being rowed in some skiffs when Alexander's boat became separated from the rest. He was lost for several days, and even came to doubt that he would survive. [6] As he was

passing through a narrow channel which was choked with trees, his diadem was whisked off his head by overhanging branches and then fell into the water. One of the oarsmen swam over to it and put it on his head, because he wanted to keep it safe, before swimming back to the boat. [7] Alexander was lost for three days and three nights before being rescued, and, since he was once again wearing his diadem when it might have been lost, he consulted his diviners about what it was that was being foretold.

117. The diviners told Alexander that he should perform lavish sacrifices to the gods, but then he was invited to a heavy drinking session hosted by one of his Friends, a Thessalian called Medius, who was very insistent. While he was there, he drank a great deal of undiluted wine, and ended up by filling and draining the great 'Cup of Heracles'. [2] Suddenly, he cried out in pain, as though he had been struck a violent blow, and he was supported out of the party by his Friends. As soon as he was in the hands of his attendants, they put him to bed and kept a careful eye on him, [3] but the pain got worse. Doctors were summoned, but none of them was able to help, and Alexander continued to be racked by frequent and agonizing pains.

Eventually, Alexander realized that he was dying, and he took off his seal ring and gave it to Perdiccas. [4] When one of his Friends asked him to whom he was leaving the kingdom, he said: 'To the strongest!' And he added—the last words he ever spoke—that his funeral games would take the form of a great contest among all his foremost Friends.* [5] So that is how Alexander died. He had reigned for twelve years and seven months, and no king before him, nor any of those who came after him, right down to the present day, has achievements to his name that come close to Alexander's in scale.

Some historians, however, have a different account of Alexander's death, claiming that he was killed by a deadly poison, and I feel bound to include this version of events as well. 118. It goes like this. Antipater, who had been left behind by Alexander as his General in Europe, had fallen out with Olympias,* the king's mother. At first, he expected no trouble from her because Alexander was paying no attention to the complaints she was making about him, but later, with the enmity between them going from bad to worse, the king, as a man who was obedient to the gods' commandments,* seemed inclined to indulge his mother in everything, and at that point Antipater began to give many indications of his hostility towards Alexander. The final straw was the killing of Parmenion and Philotas, which induced terror in all Alexander's friends, and Antipater then administered a deadly poison to the king through the agency of his son, who served as the king's cup-bearer.* [2] Following Alexander's death, Antipater was the most powerful man in Europe, and then his son Cassander succeeded to the throne, so that it would have taken real courage to mention the poison, and few historians dared to do so. Cassander's extreme hostility towards Alexander was revealed, however, by his actions: he murdered Olympias and threw her body out unburied, and determinedly refounded Thebes,* which had been razed by Alexander.

[3] The king's death left Sisyngambris, the mother of Darius, prostrate with grief for his death and her bereavement, and since she was approaching the end of her life anyway, she refused to take food and died four days later. [4] As for me, now that I have reached Alexander's death, I shall next—in conformity with the programme that I announced at the beginning of the book—use the books that follow to cover, as best I can, the history of the Successors.

BOOK 18

1. It was the opinion of several of the ancient natural scientists, not least Pythagoras of Samos, that men's souls are immortal, and in keeping with this view they said that at the moment of death, when the soul is separating from the body, it can foresee the future. [2] The poet Homer seems to have agreed with them, because he has Hector, at the moment of his death, telling Achilles about his impending death.* [3] There have been many recorded instances of the same phenomenon in more recent times as well, when men were on the verge of death, and a signal case in point is the death of Alexander the Great. [4] As he lay dying in Babylon, he was asked by his Friends to whom he was leaving the kingdom, and with his last breath he said: 'To the best. For I foresee that my funeral games will take the form of a memorable contest among my Friends.'* [5] And that is what actually happened: his foremost Friends fell out over the issue of supremacy and fought a large number of major battles after his death.

This book, which contains an account of their deeds, will shed light on this saying of Alexander's for the interested reader. [6] The previous book covered all of Alexander's achievements and ended with his death; this one contains the history of the Successors to his kingdom and covers seven years, ending with the year before the accession of the tyrant Agathocles.

2. *In the year of the Archonship of Cephisodorus in Athens, the Romans appointed as their consuls Lucius Frurius and Decius Junius.* In this year:*
Since the king, Alexander, died childless, the throne was left vacant and supremacy became a major bone of contention.* [2] The infantry phalanx was pushing for Arrhidaeus—who was the son of Philip, but was afflicted with incurable mental problems—to become king.* But the most important of Alexander's Friends and Bodyguards* talked things over among themselves and, since they had the support of the cavalry unit known as the Companion Cavalry, they decided at first to contest the issue with the phalanx, and they sent a delegation of

high-ranking men—the most distinguished of them being Meleager—
as emissaries to the infantry to demand their obedience.

[3] When Meleager reached the phalangites, however, he made no
mention of the mission with which he had been entrusted; on the
contrary, he congratulated them on the decision they had taken and
stirred them up against their adversaries. The Macedonians therefore
made Meleager their leader and advanced under arms against their
opponents. [4] The Bodyguards retreated out of Babylon and got
ready to fight, but there were men of noble principles present,* and
they persuaded the two sides to make peace. Arrhidaeus, the son of
Philip, was immediately raised to the kingship, under the name of
Philip;* Perdiccas, the man to whom the dying king had given his seal
ring,* was made custodian of the kingdom;* and the most important
of Alexander's Friends received satrapies as subordinates of the king
and Perdiccas.

3. So Perdiccas assumed supreme command. After conferring with
his officers, he gave Egypt to Ptolemy, the son of Lagus, Syria to
Laomedon of Mytilene, Cilicia to Philotas, and Media to Pithon.
Eumenes received Paphlagonia, Cappadocia, and all the neighbouring territories, which had been bypassed by Alexander because at the
time the war with Darius had allowed him no opportunity to invade
them.* Antigonus was given Pamphylia, Lycia, and Greater Phrygia;
Asander* got Caria, Menander* Lydia, and Leonnatus Hellespontine
Phrygia. That is how these satrapies were distributed.

[2] In Europe, Lysimachus received Thrace and the nearby peoples
of the Black Sea coast,* while Macedon and its neighbours were
assigned to Antipater. As for the remaining Asian satrapies, Perdiccas
decided to make no changes and to leave them under the governors
they already had. He likewise left Taxiles and Porus as masters of
their kingdoms, keeping to the arrangements put in place by Alexander
himself. [3] The satrapy next to Taxiles' kingdom Perdiccas granted
to Pithon,*† and the satrapy that lies at the foot of the Caucasus,*
which is called Paropanisadae, he assigned to Oxyartes of Bactria,
whose daughter Rhoxane had been Alexander's wife. He gave Arachosia
and Gedrosia to Sibyrtius, Areia and Drangiane to Stasanor of
Soli, Bactria and Sogdiana to Philip, Parthyaea and Hyrcania to
Phratapheres, Persis to Peucestas, Carmania to Tlepolemus, Media
to Atropates,* Babylonia to Archon, and Mesopotamia to Arcesilaus.
He gave Seleucus the enormously prestigious command of the

Companion Cavalry; Hephaestion had been the original commander, and he was followed by Perdiccas, and now Seleucus. And he† gave Arrhidaeus* the job of transporting the corpse and building the carriage that would convey the body of the dead king to Ammon.

4. Now, it so happened that Craterus, one of the leading men, had been sent ahead to Cilicia by Alexander with the ten thousand discharged soldiers.* At the same time, Alexander gave him written instructions to carry out, but after his death the Successors decided not to implement these plans. [2] Perdiccas found in the king's notebooks plans not only for the completion of Hephaestion's funeral monument, which required a great deal of money, but for a number of other major projects involving enormous expenditure. It was Perdiccas' opinion that the best course was for him to cancel these plans, [3] but he did not want to appear to have diminished Alexander's glory on his own authority, so he referred the decision on these matters to the general assembly of the Macedonians.

[4] The greatest and most remarkable of the plans in the notebooks were as follows.* A thousand warships larger than triremes were to be built in Phoenicia, Syria, Cilicia, and Cyprus for an expedition against the Carthaginians and the other inhabitants of the coastlines of Libya, Iberia, and so on up to Sicily; a road was to be laid along the coast of Libya all the way to the Pillars of Heracles,* with harbours and dockyards constructed at suitable points because of the great size of the fleet; six very lavish temples were to be built, each costing 1,500 talents; and in addition there were cities to be founded and populations to be transferred from Asia to Europe, and also the other way around, from Europe to Asia, the intention being to use intermarriage and the creation of family ties to bring the two largest continents into concord and the kind of solidarity that is only found among relatives.

[5] The temples I have mentioned were to be built at Delos, Delphi, and Dodona,* and the other three in Macedon: a temple of Zeus at Dium, a temple of Artemis Tauropolus at Amphipolis, and a temple of Athena at Cyrrhus.† There was also another temple of Athena to be built at Ilium, designed to match any temple in the world for grandeur. And a tomb was to be built for his father, Philip, to rival the single greatest pyramid in Egypt, which some people count as one of the Seven Wonders of the World.* [6] The Macedonians had no quarrel with Alexander, but once the notebooks had been read out, they

appreciated how grandiose and impractical the projects were, and they decided not to put any of them into effect.

[7] The first thing Perdiccas did was put to death the thirty men in the army who were chiefly responsible for the turmoil and were particularly hostile towards him. Next, it was the turn of Meleager, who had acted treacherously during the crisis and on his mission to the infantry; seizing on aspersions† and denunciations of a personal nature, he punished Meleager on the charge of having plotted against him.* [8] Next, since the Greeks who had been settled in the upper satrapies had revolted and raised a substantial army, he sent one of the leading men, Pithon, to put them down by force.*

5. Given the events I am about to describe, I feel that I should first clarify not just the causes of the revolt, but also the overall disposition of Asia and the sizes and characteristics of the satrapies. I want my account to be easy for readers to follow, and nothing will help more towards that goal than if I give them some idea of the overall topography and the distances involved.

[2] From the Taurus in Cilicia, through the entirety of Asia to the Caucasus and the eastern Ocean is one continuous range of mountains.* Each stretch of this mountain range has its own name, because it is divided into distinct sections by various prominences. [3] Thanks to this continuous mountain range, Asia is divided into two parts, one facing north and one facing south. Because of these two different orientations, the rivers flow in opposite directions: those to the north debouch into the Caspian Sea or the Black Sea or the northern Ocean, while their opposite numbers issue either into the Ocean off India or the Ocean that hugs the Indian coastline, or are carried down to the so-called Red Sea.*

[4] The satrapies are similarly divided into those that face north and those that face south.* The easternmost of those that face north, Sogdiana–Bactria, lies on the Tanais river,* and then the next ones to the west are Areia, Parthyaea, and Hyrcania. This last satrapy envelops the Hyrcanian Sea, which is a distinct body of water.* Next comes Media, which includes many regions with their own individual names and is the largest of all the satrapies. Then there are Armenia, Lycaonia, and Cappadocia, all of which have cold climates. Carrying on due west, their neighbours are Greater Phrygia and Hellespontine Phrygia, which have Lydia and Caria off their southern flanks, while Pisidia occupies the high ground beside southern Phrygia, and has

Lycia as its neighbour. [5] The coastlines of these last satrapies are
where the Greek cities are to be found, but for present purposes there
is no need for me to record their names. So much for the positions of
the north-facing satrapies.

6. The first of the south-facing satrapies, next to the Caucasus, is
India, a large and populous country, ruled by kings and inhabited by
many Indian peoples. The greatest of these are the Gandaridae, who
avoided being attacked by Alexander because of the great many war
elephants they had.* [2] The border between the Gandaridae and the
next part of India is formed by a river called the Ganges, which is the
greatest river in India and has a width of thirty stades. Then comes
the rest of India, the part that Alexander conquered, which is irrigated by the waters of five rivers*† and is famous for its prosperity.
This region was where the realms of Porus and Taxiles were, along
with many other kingdoms, and through it flows the Indus river, after
which the whole country is named.

[3] The next satrapy across the border from India is Arachosia,
which is followed by Gedrosia and then Carmania. Next comes Persis,
which includes Susiane and Sittacene. Persis is followed by Babylonia,
which goes up to the Arabian desert. On the other side of Babylonia,
in the opposite direction from that which we take when we journey
inland, is Mesopotamia, which is encompassed by two rivers, the
Euphrates and the Tigris, which have given the satrapy its name.*
The next satrapy to Babylonia is Upper Syria, which is bordered by
the coastal satrapies of Cilicia and Pamphylia, and by Coele Syria,
which includes Phoenicia.* Beyond the border of Coele Syria and its
adjacent desert (the desert through which the Nile flows, forming the
border between Syria and Egypt) lies Egypt, which is traditionally
regarded as the best of all the satrapies for the amount of wealth it
generates. [4] All these satrapies are hot, since the southern climate is
the opposite of that which prevails in the north. So much for the
locations of the satrapies conquered by Alexander. These were the
satrapies that were distributed among the most important of his
Friends.

7. The Greeks who had been settled by Alexander in the upper
satrapies missed Greek customs and the Greek way of life, cast away
as they were in the remotest regions of the empire. While the king was
alive they put up with their situation out of fear, but they rose up in
rebellion after his death. [2] They collaborated, chose as their general

Philon the Aenianian, and raised a large army of more than twenty thousand foot and three thousand horse. All the men were hardened veterans of war, noted for their valour.

[3] When Perdiccas heard of the Greek rebellion, he put together a force of three thousand foot and eight hundred horse, drawn by lot from among his Macedonians. He chose as their commander Pithon— a former Bodyguard of Alexander's, a proud man and a competent general—and passed the soldiers he had selected by lot on to him. He gave him letters for the satraps, in which he ordered them to supply Pithon with troops, specifically with ten thousand foot and eight thousand horse, and sent him off to deal with the rebels. [4] Now, Pithon was a highly ambitious man, and he was delighted to accept command of the expedition because he intended to attach the Greeks to himself by treating them well. Then, once he had enlarged his army by taking them on as auxiliaries, he planned to go independent and rule over the upper satrapies. [5] But Perdiccas suspected that this was what Pithon was planning, and he gave him express orders to kill all the rebels, once he had defeated them, and to share the spoils among his men.*

Pithon set off with the soldiers he had been given, and once he had added the troops supplied by the satraps, he marched to confront the rebels at full strength. Through the agency of a man from Aenis, he bribed Lipodorus,† whom the rebels had put in charge of a contingent of three thousand of their soldiers, and won a decisive victory. [6] Battle had been joined and the outcome was hanging in the balance when, with no warning, the traitor deserted his allies and took himself and three thousand men off to a hill. Discipline broke down in the rest of the army, because they believed that these men had been routed, and they turned and fled.

[7] After his victory, Pithon sent a herald to the defeated rebels, ordering them to lay down their arms and promising that they could return to their homes with their safety guaranteed. [8] Oaths were exchanged to this effect, and the Greeks fraternized with the Macedonians. Pithon was delighted, because things were developing according to his plan, but the Macedonians remembered Perdiccas' orders and, ignoring their sworn oaths, they violated their agreement with the Greeks. [9] They launched a surprise attack on them, caught them off guard, massacred them to a man, and took their property for themselves. With his hopes dashed, Pithon returned to Perdiccas with the Macedonians. That was how things stood in Asia.

8. In Europe, the Rhodians* threw out their Macedonian garrison and gave their city back its liberty, while the Athenians embarked on the Lamian War against Antipater. It will help to make the course of the war more comprehensible if I preface my account of it with an explanation of its causes. [2] Not long before his death, Alexander decided that all the exiles from the various Greek cities were to be restored to their homelands.* He did this not just to enhance his glory, but also because he wanted every city to contain a good number of individuals who were loyal to him, in order to counteract the revolutionary and rebellious tendencies of the Greeks. [3] So, since the Olympic festival was in the offing, he sent Nicanor of Stagira to Greece with a dispatch on the matter of the restoration of the exiles, and told him to have it read out by the victorious herald* to the mass of people who had come for the festival. [4] Nicanor carried out his orders, and the dispatch that he gave the herald to read out was as follows:

King Alexander to the exiles from the Greek cities: Although we were not and are not responsible for your banishment, we will be responsible for restoring you to your homelands. Only those of you who are under a curse are excluded. We have written to Antipater about this, instructing him to use force in the case of cities that refuse to comply.

[5] This announcement was loudly acclaimed by the crowd. The people attending the festival showed their appreciation of the king's gift and expressed their happiness by responding to his benefaction with shouts of gratitude. [6] All the exiles had assembled for the festival, and there were more than twenty thousand of them.

On the whole, people thought the restoration of the exiles was a good thing and they welcomed it, but it angered and worried the Aetolians and Athenians. The Aetolians had expelled the people of Oeniadae from their homeland, and now began to expect that they would be punished for their wrongdoing—and in fact the king had already threatened them by saying that it would not be the sons of the people of Oeniadae who would make them pay, but that he himself would see to it. [7] And the Athenians had established a cleruchy* on Samos and were flatly refusing to give up the island. But since they were no match for Alexander's forces, they kept quiet for the time being. They were waiting for a favourable opportunity, and Fortune soon supplied them with one.

9. When Alexander died shortly afterwards, leaving no sons to succeed to the kingdom, the Athenians made a bold bid for freedom and for the general leadership of the Greeks. As resources for the war, they had not only the great quantity of money abandoned by Harpalus (I gave a detailed account of the affair in the previous book),* but also the eight thousand mercenaries who had been dismissed from service in Asia by the satraps and who were biding their time at Cape Taenarum in the Peloponnese.* [2] So they issued secret orders to Leosthenes of Athens about the mercenaries, stressing that he was to recruit them as though he were acting in his own interests, not on behalf of the Athenian people. Antipater would then hardly trouble himself with making any preparations, since Leosthenes would not appear to him to constitute any kind of threat,* and it would buy time for the Athenians to get ahead in their preparations for war. [3] Proceeding with great discretion, then, Leosthenes hired these mercenaries, and before anyone was aware of it he had a substantial force under his command. They were ready for action as well, because they had served for a long while in Asia, where they had taken part in a large number of major battles and had become trained experts in war.

[4] All this was going on before the news of Alexander's death had been confirmed, but then some people arrived from Babylon who had personally witnessed the king's death, and at that point the Athenian people stopped disguising their warlike intentions. They sent Leosthenes some of Harpalus' money and many suits of armour, and told him that the time for secrecy had passed and he could now openly act in their interests. [5] Once he had paid the mercenaries and equipped those who lacked armour, he went to Aetolia to conclude an agreement about joint action. The Aetolians were happy to comply and they gave him seven thousand soldiers. Leosthenes next wrote to the Locrians and Phocians and their neighbours, urging them to espouse the cause of independence and free Greece from Macedonian domination.

10. The Athenian people <met to decide what to do. In the course of the debate,>† the men of property advised them not to break the peace, while the demagogues tried to stir them up and stiffen their resolve for war, but those who were in favour of war were in the great majority. They were men who customarily made their living as mercenaries—men of whom Philip once remarked that, for them, war

was peace and peace war. [2] The politicians accordingly gave shape to the popular impulse by formulating a decree to the effect that the Athenian people should make the freedom of the Greeks their business. They were to liberate any cities that had been garrisoned and make seaworthy forty quadriremes and two hundred triremes, all Athenians under the age of forty were to be called up, and seven tribes were to be ready to serve abroad, leaving the protection of Attica to the other three tribes.* [3] Moreover, envoys were to be sent around the Greek cities with the job of explaining that, just as, in the past, it was because the Athenian people judged Greece to be the common homeland of the Greeks* that they had used their navy to repel the barbarians* who had invaded Greece in order to enslave its inhabitants, so now they were of the opinion that the survival of the Greeks required them to put their lives, wealth, and ships at the service of defending them.

[4] So this decree was ratified, with more haste than prudence. The more intelligent Greeks thought that, if their aim was glory, the Athenian people had made the right decision, but that they had mistaken where their own best interests lay. For they had revolted prematurely and were intending to go to war when there was no urgent necessity for them to do so, against armies made up of a great many men who had never known defeat. Moreover, although the Athenians were reputed to be especially clever, they had failed to learn the lesson of the renowned Theban catastrophe.* [5] Nevertheless, as their ambassadors toured the cities, and tried with typically Athenian eloquence to motivate them for war, most cities did join the alliance, whether they did so as members of a confederacy or as individual city-states.*

11. As for the Greeks who remained outside the alliance, some sided with the Macedonians, while others chose neutrality. The Aetolians, as I have already said, were the first to join the alliance, and they did so unanimously. They were followed by all the Thessalians (except the people of Pelinna), the Oetaeans (except the people of Heraclea), the Phthiotic Achaeans (except for the Thebans), and the Malians (except for the Lamians). Then all the Dorians signed up, and the Locrians, the Phocians, the Aenianians, the Alyzaeans, the Dolopians, the Athamanians, the Leucadians, and the Molossians who were ruled by Arhyptaeus.* But Arhyptaeus' commitment to the alliance was false, and later he treacherously cooperated with the

Macedonians. As for the Illyrians and Thracians, a few joined the alliance out of hatred of Macedon. [2] Then the people of Carystus in Euboea also contributed to the allied war effort, as (to complete the list) did a number of Peloponnesian peoples: the Argives, Sicyonians, Eleans, Messenians, and the inhabitants of the Headland.* These were the Greeks who joined the alliance.

[3] The Athenian people strengthened Leosthenes' position by sending some of their citizen soldiers to him—five thousand foot and five hundred horse—and two thousand mercenaries. These men had to pass through Boeotia,* but it so happened that the Boeotians were at odds with the Athenians. The reason for their hostility was as follows. When Alexander razed Thebes, he gave its land to the Boeotians who lived near by, [4] and these Boeotians divided the farms of the hapless Thebans among themselves. The land they gained was very profitable for them, and so, since they knew that Athenian victory in the war would be followed by the restoration to the Thebans of their land as well as their city, they had sided with the Macedonians. [5] The Boeotians were encamped near Plataea when Leosthenes arrived in Boeotia with part of his army. Battle was joined and, with the help of the Athenian contingents, Leosthenes defeated the Boeotians. After his victory—and after erecting a trophy—he quickly returned to Thermopylae, where he had been based for a while. The passes were already in his hands, and now he waited for the Macedonian army.

12. The news of Alexander's death in Babylon and the distribution of the satrapies prompted Antipater—the man who had been left behind by Alexander as his General in Europe—to write to Craterus in Cilicia, asking him to come with reinforcements as quickly as possible. Craterus had been sent ahead to Cilicia and was due to repatriate the Macedonian troops who had been discharged from service, who numbered over ten thousand. Antipater also wrote to Philotas,* who had received the satrapy of Hellespontine Phrygia, asking him too for help, and offering him one of his daughters in marriage.* [2] Then, when he found out that the Greeks had united against him, he left Sippas in charge of Macedon, with an adequate number of soldiers and orders to recruit as many more as he could, while he took thirteen thousand Macedonian infantry† and six hundred cavalry (no more than that, because Macedon was short of citizen soldiers, since so many of them had been sent to Asia as replacements for the army) and left Macedon for Thessaly, with his

entire fleet shadowing the army along the coast. This was the fleet of 110 ships which Alexander had sent to convoy a large amount of money from the imperial treasuries to Macedon.

[3] At first, the Thessalians fought for Antipater and supplied him with many fine horsemen, but later they were persuaded by the Athenians to change sides. They rode off to Leosthenes, who posted them alongside the Athenians, and fought for Greek freedom. [4] This substantial addition to the Athenian contingent gave the Greeks considerable numerical superiority and they began to gain the upper hand. After he had been worsted in battle, Antipater had no desire to fight again. At the same time, however, he could not return safely to Macedon, so he fled for safety to the town of Lamia.* He kept his army confined there, improved the city walls, furnished himself with weaponry, catapults, and grain, and waited for his allies from Asia.

13. So Leosthenes and his army halted near Lamia. He fortified his camp with a deep trench and a palisade, and his opening gambit was to approach the town with his men in battle array and challenge the Macedonians to battle. When they proved to have no stomach for a fight, he began to assault the wall day in and day out, with his men working in relays. [2] The Macedonians fought back well, however, and many Greek lives were lost as they pushed forward recklessly. It was not difficult for the defenders to have the advantage: there were a great many soldiers in the town, they were well stocked with all kinds of artillery, and the defensive wall was superb. At this point, the Aetolians asked Leosthenes for permission to return home for a while, to take care of some internal business,* and the entire contingent returned to Aetolia.†

[3] Leosthenes abandoned the idea of taking the place by storm. Instead, he made it impossible for supplies to continue to enter the town, thinking that shortage of food would soon force those who were trapped inside to submit, and he built a rampart and dug a huge, deep trench, so that there was no way for any of the besieged to get out. [4] But just when Antipater had been worn down by this tactic, and imminent famine had brought the city close to surrender, Fortune granted the Macedonians an unexpected piece of good luck.

[5] What happened was that Leosthenes went to the assistance of some of his men—they had been working on the trench, and had become involved in a fight when Antipater had attacked them—and he was struck on the head by a stone. He fell straight to the ground

and was carried unconscious back to his camp, but two days later he died. His conduct of the war had brought him great fame, and he was awarded a hero's funeral. The Athenian people gave Hypereides, the foremost politician in Athens for his eloquence and hostility towards Macedon, the job of delivering the funeral eulogy.* [6] They gave it to Hypereides because the most important Athenian politician, Demosthenes, had been found guilty of accepting a bribe from Harpalus and was in exile at the time.* Leosthenes' replacement as general was Antiphilus, a brilliant strategist and an outstandingly brave man. That was how things stood in Europe.

14. In Asia, of those who had been assigned satrapies, Ptolemy took over Egypt* without any trouble. The native Egyptians he treated well, and with the chest of eight thousand talents that he inherited* he began to hire mercenaries and build up his forces. A number of his Friends were also attracted to Egypt by his moral integrity. [2] He approached Antipater with a view to entering into a treaty of cooperation, which was duly concluded, because there was no doubt in his mind that Perdiccas intended to try to take the satrapy of Egypt away from him.

Lysimachus launched an offensive in the Thracian countryside and found King Seuthes encamped with twenty thousand foot and eight thousand horse, but he was not fazed by the size of the enemy army. He brought the barbarians to battle, with an army consisting of no more than four thousand foot and two thousand horse, [3] and although he was numerically inferior, his men's martial skills were superior, and a hard-fought battle took place in which his losses were great, but nowhere near as great as those of the enemy. In the end, he returned to camp the victor of an inconclusive battle. [4] For the time being, then, both sides withdrew from the countryside and occupied themselves with larger-scale preparations for the final struggle.*

As for Leonnatus, when Hecataeus* came to him as Antipater's ambassador and said that his help was urgently needed by Antipater and the Macedonians, he promised his support. [5] He crossed over to Europe and marched to Macedon, where he enlisted Macedonians in large numbers for his army.* He ended up with a total of more than twenty thousand foot and 1,500 horse, and then he marched through Thessaly to confront the enemy.

15. The Greeks abandoned the siege. They burnt their camp and sent the baggage and the camp followers, who would be useless in a fight, to Meliteia,* while the soldiers, now lightened and ready for

battle, advanced to meet Leonnatus before he could link up with Antipater and unite the two armies. [2] The Greeks had an infantry force of only twenty-two thousand in all, because all the Aetolians had already left and returned home, and quite a few of the other Greeks had by then scattered to their various homes. But they had a cavalry force of more than 3,500, two thousand of whom were exceptionally skilled Thessalians, and it was they, above all, on whom the Greeks were depending for victory. [3] And indeed, when a fierce and protracted cavalry engagement took place, the Thessalians' skill gave them the upper hand. After putting on a dazzling display of martial prowess, Leonnatus found himself trapped in a marsh, with no chance of getting out alive. He died of his many wounds, and his men took up his corpse and carried it back to the baggage train.*

[4] This battle, with Menon of Thessaly in command, was a resounding victory for the Greeks, and the Macedonian infantry, fearful of the Greek cavalry, rapidly retreated from the plain to the nearby hills, where the strength of their position kept them safe. The Thessalian cavalry rode up, but the fractured terrain meant that there was nothing they could do. The Greeks therefore erected a trophy, collected their dead, and left the field of battle.

[5] The next day, however, Antipater and his men arrived and linked up with their defeated comrades. All the Macedonians now formed a single camp, and Antipater took overall command. [6] Under the circumstances, he decided not to continue fighting, and since the enemy had cavalry superiority, he chose not to retreat across level terrain, but instead made good his withdrawal by leading his men over broken ground and by speedily occupying the high points. [7] Antiphilus, the commander of the Greeks, had won a brilliant victory against the Macedonians, and he remained on guard in Thessaly, waiting for the enemy to make a move.

So the Greeks were enjoying a high degree of success. [8] But at sea the Macedonians were supreme, and so the Athenians fitted out extra ships to supplement those at their disposal, until they had 170 in all. The Macedonian fleet, however, consisted of 240 ships, under the command of Cleitus, [9] and when Cleitus engaged his Athenian counterpart, Euetion, in battle, he beat him twice and destroyed many enemy ships off the islands called the Echinades.*

16. Meanwhile, Perdiccas, with King Philip and the Royal Army, marched against Ariarathes, the dynast of Cappadocia. Ariarathes

had refused to submit to Macedon, and Alexander had been too distracted by his conflict with Darius to deal with him, so he had enjoyed an extended respite as master of Cappadocia. [2] This had enabled him to put aside a large amount of money from his revenues, and he had gathered a large force of Cappadocians and mercenaries. Styling himself king of Cappadocia, he was ready to fight Perdiccas with an army of thirty thousand foot and 10,500 horse. But when they met in battle,* Perdiccas won, and in doing so killed about four thousand of his men and took more than five thousand prisoners, one of whom was Ariarathes. [3] After torturing him and all his relatives, Perdiccas had them impaled,* but he pardoned the defeated Cappadocians, and once he had settled their affairs, he gave the satrapy to Eumenes of Cardia, to whom it had originally been assigned.*

[4] It was also about now that Craterus left Cilicia and arrived in Macedon, to reinforce Antipater and to redress the balance after the defeats the Macedonians had suffered. He brought with him six thousand foot soldiers who had been with Alexander from the moment he crossed from Europe into Asia,* four thousand who had been added in the course of the march, a thousand Persian archers and slingers, and 1,500 cavalry. [5] Once he arrived in Thessaly, he willingly yielded supreme command of the army to Antipater and they encamped together by the river Peneus.* Their forces in total, including those who had come with Leonnatus, amounted to more than forty thousand heavy infantry, three thousand archers and slingers, and five thousand cavalry.

17. The Greeks now made camp not far from the Macedonians, but with considerably depleted numbers, because a lot of men had returned home to take care of domestic business, since their earlier successes had led them to belittle the enemy's abilities. [2] With many† soldiers neglecting their duty in this way, there remained in camp only twenty-five thousand foot and 3,500 horse. They were pinning their hopes of victory on the cavalry, because of their calibre and because the terrain where they were was level. [3] After a while, Antipater began to lead his forces up to the Greek camp every day and challenge them to battle. At first, the Greeks waited for their missing men to come back from their towns and cities, but eventually circumstances compelled them to commit themselves to the decisive battle.

They drew up their forces with the cavalry posted in front of the infantry phalanx, since it was the cavalry that they were hoping would win the battle for them. [4] And indeed, when battle was joined, the skill of the Thessalian cavalry gave them the advantage over the enemy cavalry—but Antipater called up his infantry, who smashed into the enemy phalanx and inflicted heavy casualties. The Greek infantry were unable to withstand the pressure exerted by so many men and retreated straight away to the hills. They took care to remain in formation, and so, once they had seized the high ground, the superiority of their position made it easy for them to keep the Macedonians at bay. [5] The Greek cavalry were getting the better of their opposite numbers, but as soon as they realized that the infantry had retreated, they rode off to join them. At that point, with the battle having gone as I have described, the two sides separated, with the scales of victory favouring the Macedonians. More than five hundred Greeks lost their lives in the fighting, but only 130 Macedonians.

[6] The next day, the two senior Greek officers, Menon and Antiphilus, met to determine whether they should wait for their allies to reappear from their homelands, and then fight the decisive battle once they were in a position to meet the enemy on equal terms, or whether they should bow to circumstances and send a delegation to negotiate terms. They decided to send heralds to arrange an end to hostilities, [7] but in response, once the heralds had carried out their mission, Antipater flatly refused to consider a collective settlement and insisted that each city should negotiate separately. But city-by-city solutions were unacceptable to the Greeks, so Antipater and Craterus set about laying siege to the Thessalian cities and taking them by main force, since the Greeks were in no position to send help. The terrified towns therefore began unilaterally to send envoys to discuss terms, and because Antipater treated them decently and never failed to grant peace, [8] the desire to secure safety for themselves swept through the rest of the Greeks, and before long they all obtained peace—except those whose hostility towards Macedon was most bitter, the Aetolians and Athenians. Now abandoned by their allies, they waited for the return of their troops† and then met to try to decide what to do about the war.

18. Having successfully dismantled Greek unity by this manoeuvre, Antipater led his entire army against Athens.* With no help forthcoming from their allies, the Athenian people had no idea what to do. Everyone in the Assembly looked to Demades and called out that he should be sent as an ambassador to Antipater to sue for peace,* but

although he was asked to recommend a course of action, he refused to do so. [2] He had been found guilty three times of illegal procedures, and had therefore lost his citizenship privileges and was legally debarred from offering advice. But as soon as the people had given him back his citizenship, he was sent off as a member of an embassy that included Phocion and several others.

[3] After listening to their speeches, Antipater replied that the only way he would end the war with Athens was if they left their fate entirely up to him—the point being that this was the reply the Athenians had given Antipater's envoys when they had him trapped inside Lamia and he had sued for peace. Since the Athenians were no match for him in military terms, they had no choice but to surrender unconditionally and allow Antipater complete authority over the city. [4] He was lenient in his treatment of them, in the sense that he let them keep their city, their farms, and everything else, but he changed the constitution from democracy* and ordered that citizenship and the ability to play a political role in the city were to depend on a means test—that is, that only those with property worth more than two thousand drachmas should play a role in the administration and be allowed to vote, while all those whose property fell below this level were excluded from political life, on the grounds that their politics was disruptive and hawkish.* However, he offered land in Thrace to anyone who wanted to settle there, [5] and more than twenty-two thousand*† moved there from Athens.

So those with the stipulated level of property, who numbered about nine thousand, were made responsible for the city and its land, and proceeded to govern in accordance with the laws of Solon.* They were all allowed to keep their property in its entirety, but they had to accept a garrison (commanded by Menyllus), whose job was to prevent any sedition.* [6] The decision regarding Samos was referred to the kings.* So the Athenians obtained peace. They had been better treated than they had expected, and from then on their political life proceeded smoothly; they could profit from their land without fear of attack, and it was not long before they had recovered their prosperity.

[7] On his return to Macedon, Antipater enhanced Craterus' prestige with appropriate honours and gifts, gave him one of his daughters—the eldest, Phila—to be his wife, and helped him get ready to return to Asia.* [8] He treated the rest of the Greek cities just as equitably as he had treated Athens—reducing their citizenship

rolls and putting good constitutions in place*—and for this he was formally thanked and awarded crowns.* [9] Perdiccas gave the Samians back both their city and their farmland and restored them to their homeland after an exile of forty-three years.

19. Now that I have covered the course of the Lamian War, I shall move on to the war that took place in Cyrene, so as to keep events in their proper sequential order as much as possible.* But I must first briefly summarize the background, to make my account of particular events more comprehensible. [2] After Harpalus had fled from Asia and landed on Crete with his mercenaries, as I explained in the previous book,* Thibron, who was supposed to be a friend of his, murdered him and took possession of both his money and his seven thousand soldiers. [3] Once he gained his ships as well, he embarked his men and sailed over to Cyrene. He had brought with him a number of exiles from Cyrene, who knew the terrain and were acting as his guides for this venture.*

The Cyreneans confronted him and a battle took place which Thibron won, taking a lot of lives in the process and plenty of prisoners. [4] Once he had gained control of the port,* he put the city under siege and forced the terrified Cyreneans to make a pact with him whereby they were to give him five hundred talents of silver and contribute half of the chariots for the campaigns he planned. [5] He also sent envoys around the other cities of Cyrenaica, asking for treaties of alliance, seeing that he was going to conquer the part of Libya that lay across their borders; and he stole the merchandise that he found in the port from the traders and gave it to his soldiers as plunder, to arouse their enthusiasm for the war.

20. So things were going well for Thibron, but Fortune soon altered course and brought him low. This is what happened. One of his officers, a Cretan called Mnasicles, a man with plenty of experience and knowledge of warfare, held a grudge against him over what he claimed was the unfair division of the spoils, and, hot-headed trouble-maker that he was, he deserted and went over to the Cyreneans. [2] He went on and on to them about Thibron's cruelty and dishonesty, until he persuaded the Cyreneans to break their agreement and make a bid for freedom. Only sixty talents had been paid up to that point, and when the rest of the money was not forthcoming, Thibron denounced the rebels and arrested the eighty or so Cyreneans he found in the port. Then he immediately led his men against the

city and assaulted it, but that got him nowhere and he returned to the port.

[3] Since the people of Barca and Hesperides were on Thibron's side, the Cyreneans took to the field with half of their army, leaving the other half in the city, and ravaged their neighbours' farmland. [4] The victims of this expedition appealed for help from Thibron and he set out at full strength to fight alongside his allies. At this juncture, the Cretan, realizing that the port was undefended, persuaded those who remained in Cyrene to attack it. [5] As soon as he had won their agreement, he assaulted the port, with himself leading the operation, and because of Thibron's absence he easily gained control of it. He gave the traders back what remained of their cargoes and put the port under close guard.

[6] At first, Thibron was despondent, because he had lost a favourable position and his men's baggage, but later his morale improved, and after taking the town called Taucheira, he fully recovered his confidence. As luck would have it, however, a short while later he met with further serious setbacks. [7] Since they had no access to the port and were short of food, the crews of his ships were in the habit of going out every day into the countryside and foraging for their food. But the Libyans ambushed them as they were roaming around the countryside, and killed or captured a lot of men. The survivors of the affair fled for safety to their ships and set sail for the cities that were allied to them, but a violent wind arose and most of the ships were swallowed up by the sea. Of the few survivors, some were driven ashore on Cyprus and others in Egypt.

21. Despite the magnitude of this catastrophe, Thibron did not give up the fight. He selected those of his friends who were qualified for the job and sent them to the Peloponnese to recruit the mercenaries who were encamped at Cape Taenarum,* where many discharged mercenaries were still on the loose and on the lookout for paymasters. In fact, at that time there were more than 2,500 mercenaries at Taenarum, [2] and Thibron's agents set about recruiting them, and then set sail for Cyrene. But before the mercenaries arrived,† the Cyreneans, encouraged by the successes they had enjoyed, fought a battle with Thibron, in which they took a lot of lives and came off victorious.

[3] By now these setbacks had made Thibron ready to abandon his attempt on Cyrene, but his spirits abruptly rose again when the

soldiers from Taenarum arrived. The addition of this large force to his army gave him renewed confidence. [4] Seeing that the war was intensifying once more, the Cyreneans asked their Libyan neighbours and the Carthaginians for help, and when they had gathered an army of thirty thousand, including their own citizen soldiers, they prepared to settle things once and for all.

A major battle took place, in which Thibron was victorious and killed many of the enemy. He was delighted, believing that the nearby cities would fall to him in short order, [5] but the Cyreneans, all of whose generals had been killed in the battle, elected a new board of generals, which included the Cretan, Mnasicles. With his confidence high as a result of his victory, Thibron put the Cyreneans' port under siege and launched daily assaults on Cyrene itself. [6] As the fighting dragged on and the Cyreneans became short of food, political strife broke out among them. The democrats came out on top and threw the men of property out of the city, and these outcasts fled either to Thibron or to Egypt. [7] The ones who went to Egypt persuaded Ptolemy to restore them to their homeland, and came back with a large land army and fleet, under the command of Ophellas. When the exiles who had gone to Thibron heard of the arrival of this army, they tried surreptitiously to leave under cover of darkness and join them, but they were spotted and cut down to a man.

[8] The return of the exiles frightened the democratic generals in Cyrene, and they came to terms with Thibron and the former enemies got ready to fight Ophellas together. [9] But Ophellas defeated Thibron and took him prisoner, and then, once the cities had fallen to him, he turned both them and their land over to King Ptolemy.* So Cyrene and its neighbours lost their freedom and became dependencies of the Ptolemaic kingdom.*

22. After Perdiccas and King Philip had defeated Ariarathes and turned the satrapy over to Eumenes, they left Cappadocia and went to Pisidia, where they had decided utterly to destroy two towns, Laranda and Isaura. While Alexander was still alive, the people of these towns had killed Balacrus, the son of Nicanor, who was simultaneously satrap and military governor.* [2] Laranda fell to Perdiccas straight away, and after massacring the men of military age and selling the rest of the population into slavery, he razed the town to the ground. Isaura, however, was large and strong, and brimming with brave defenders. The Macedonians assaulted it vigorously for two days, but

then pulled back after sustaining heavy losses. [3] For the Isaurians not only had a good supply of artillery and everything that was required to counter a siege, but they had also steeled themselves mentally to endure the ordeal with desperate courage, and were giving their lives willingly in defence of their freedom.

[4] On the third day, after many men had lost their lives and so few remained that the walls were only thinly defended, the Isaurians did something so heroic that it demands to be recorded. They could see that there was no way to avoid the punishment that awaited them, and that they lacked the strength to make defence a viable option. But they decided not to surrender the town and entrust their fate to the enemy, since there was no doubt not only that they would be punished, but also that it would be a degrading form of punishment. So one night all of them, to a man, resolved to die with dignity. They shut their children, womenfolk, and parents inside their houses and set fire to them, making fire the instrument of their communal death and burial.

[5] As the flames rose into the air, the Isaurians threw their possessions into the fire along with everything that could enrich the victors, while Perdiccas, who could scarcely believe his eyes, stationed his men around the town. Wherever there was a possibility of forcing their way inside, they made the attempt, [6] but the Isaurians fought back from the walls and slew many of the Macedonians, until Perdiccas, now thoroughly perplexed, was left wondering why men who had consigned their houses and everything else to the flames were still determinedly defending the walls. [7] Eventually, Perdiccas and the Macedonians pulled back from the town, and then the Isaurians threw themselves into the fire and were buried along with their families in their homes. [8] The next morning, Perdiccas gave his troops permission to plunder the town, and once they had extinguished the flames they found a great deal of silver and gold, since the town had enjoyed many years of prosperity.

23. The next thing that happened after the destruction of these towns was that two women arrived, both of them aiming to marry Perdiccas. They were Nicaea, the daughter of Antipater, whose hand Perdiccas had actively sought, and Cleopatra, the full sister of Alexander and daughter of Philip, the son of Amyntas. [2] Originally, Perdiccas had decided to work with Antipater, and that was why he had courted Nicaea. That, however, had been before he had consolidated and

secured his position, and once he had taken over the king's forces and the protection of the kings, he changed his mind. [3] He was now aiming for the kingship, and that made marriage to Cleopatra attractive, because her influence, he thought, would help him to persuade the Macedonians to confer supreme power on him. However, since he was not yet ready to reveal his true intentions, he married Nicaea as a temporary measure, so that his plans would not be impeded by Antipater's hostility.*

Next, however, Antigonus got wind of what Perdiccas was up to,* and Perdiccas decided to get rid of him.* It was not just that Antigonus was on good terms with Antipater, but also that he was the most effective of the leading men. [4] Perdiccas launched a smear campaign against Antigonus, denouncing him for things he had never done, and made no secret of the fact that he wanted to see him dead. But Antigonus was an exceptionally clever and resourceful man, and although in public he let it be known that he wanted the opportunity to defend himself against the charges, he surreptitiously got ready everything he would need for flight, without Perdiccas getting wind of it, and one night he boarded the Athenian ships* with his friends and his son Demetrius.* Once he had reached Europe in this way, he set out to find Antipater.

24. At this time, Antipater and Craterus were engaged on a campaign against the Aetolians, with an army of thirty thousand foot and 2,500 horse. The Aetolians were the only ones of those who had fought in the Lamian War who had never submitted. [2] So far from being alarmed by the size of the army that was sent against them, they raised a force of ten thousand men, every one of them in his prime, and took to the rugged hill country, where they secreted their children and womenfolk, the elderly, and the bulk of their valuables. Towns that were unfortified were abandoned, while those with particularly strong defences they secured by installing strong garrisons in them, and then they fearlessly awaited the enemy.

25. When Antipater and Craterus invaded Aetolia and found that any cities which would have been easy to take had been abandoned, they marched against the Aetolians who had fallen back on the hills. At first, the Macedonian troops suffered considerable losses, as they were attacking places that were easily defended and situated in broken ground. The natural defensibility of the Aetolians' positions, in combination with their bravery, made it easy for them to ward off men

who recklessly rushed forward into desperate danger. Later, however, Craterus had his men build shelters, and he blockaded the Aetolians where they were for the winter, forcing them to endeavour to survive in places that were blanketed in snow and short of food.

The Aetolians found themselves in the gravest danger. [2] They had to either come down from the mountains and fight an army which outnumbered them by far and was commanded by notable generals, or stay where they were and die of hunger and cold. But just when they thought there was no chance of survival, their troubles were resolved without their having to do anything, as though one of the gods had taken pity on them for their courage. [3] What happened was that Antigonus, who had fled from Asia, met up with Antipater, revealed all the details of Perdiccas' designs, and explained that as soon as Perdiccas had married Cleopatra* he would come to Macedon with his army as king and depose Antipater.

[4] Craterus and Antipater were astonished at the news; they had not been expecting anything like this. They consulted their officers, and the outcome of their deliberations was that they unanimously decided to make peace with the Aetolians on the best terms they could arrange, and then take their forces across to Asia as soon as possible. They planned to make Asia Craterus' domain and Europe Antipater's. They also decided to get in touch with Ptolemy with a view to gaining his cooperation. After all, he was on the worst possible terms with Perdiccas, but on good terms with them,* and Perdiccas was scheming against him no less than them. [5] They lost no time in making a truce with the Aetolians, though they were determined to subdue them later, and to move them all, with their households, to the remotest part of Asia where no people lived. And then, once they had drafted a decree to that effect, they busied themselves with preparing for the expedition.

[6] Perdiccas convened a meeting of his Friends and officers, with the agenda of deciding whether they should march against Macedon or make Ptolemy their first target. They all thought that it would be best to defeat Ptolemy first, to forestall the possibility of any interference from him when they went on the offensive against Macedon, so Perdiccas gave Eumenes a substantial army and sent him to watch over the Hellespontine region and stop Craterus and Antipater from reaching Asia. Meanwhile, he left Pisidia and marched on Egypt with his army.

These were the events that took place in this year.

26. *In the year of the Archonship of Philocles in Athens, Gaius Sulpicius and Gaius Aelius were elected consuls in Rome. In this year:**

Arrhidaeus, the man who had been given the job of transporting Alexander's body, completed the carriage on which the king's corpse was due to be conveyed, and then turned to preparations for the journey. [2] The carriage was built to reflect Alexander's glory, and since it was the most expensive such vehicle that has ever been made, costing many talents to build, and was famous also for the exceptional artistry that went into it, I think it only right that I should give a description of it.

[3] They started by making a casket of hammered gold, the right size to accommodate the body,† and they filled the inside of it with aromatics which had the property of both imparting a sweet smell to the corpse and preserving it.* [4] On top of the casket was laid a lid of gold, which was a perfect fit and covered the upper rim of the chest. Over the casket was draped a magnificent piece of purple cloth, embroidered with gold, beside which they placed the dead man's weapons. Their intention was that the overall appearance should reflect what he had accomplished in his lifetime.

[5] Next, they brought up the carriage that was to transport this casket. It was topped by a golden vault, the surface of which was studded with precious stones, and which was eight cubits wide and twelve cubits long. Under the roof, running along the whole length of each side, was a rectangular golden beam,† on which were carved the heads of goat-stags. From the beams hung golden rings, with diameters of two palms, and through them was threaded a brightly and variously coloured festoon, of the kind that might be used in a parade, that hung down from the rings. [6] On the ends of the beams were network fringes furnished with bells that were large enough to ensure that the sound would be heard from a long way off as the carriage approached. On each corner of the roof, where the sides met, there was a golden Victory bearing a trophy. The colonnade on which the vault rested was of gold, with Ionic capitals.* Set back from the colonnade was a golden net, made of strands twined as thick as a finger, on which were fixed four painted panels at the same height as one another, with each panel occupying an entire side.

27. The first of the panels had a chariot in relief, in which Alexander was sitting, holding a magnificent sceptre in his hands and escorted by two units of the Household Guard, one consisting of Macedonians and the other of Persian Apple-bearers,* with their shield-bearers in front of them. The second panel showed the elephants that used to follow the Household Guard, accoutred for war and with mahouts mounted in front and Macedonians, armed in their usual fashion, behind. The third had cavalry squadrons made to look as though they were engaging in combat, and the fourth had ships in battle formation. Golden lions flanked the entrance to the vault, with their gaze turned towards people as they entered. [2] Climbing its way gradually up the centre of each column all the way to the capital was a golden acanthus. On top of the vault, in the middle of the roof, exposed to the open air, there was a stylized palm tree, bearing a large golden olive wreath, which shone with a bright and scintillating light when struck by the sun's rays, so that from a long way off it looked like a flash of lightning.

[3] The bed of the chariot, under the vault, was fitted with two axles on which four Persian-style wheels revolved;* the felloes and the spokes of the wheels were gilded, while the part that made contact with the ground was made of iron. The projecting parts of the axles were golden and had the foreparts of lions on them, each gripping a spear in its teeth. [4] Halfway along each axle was a rod which was ingeniously inserted inside the vault so as to allow it to remain stable even when shaken or passing over uneven ground.* [5] The carriage had four shafts, and each shaft had four rows of yokes, with four mules harnessed to each yoke, making a total of sixty-four mules, every one selected for its strength and height. Each mule wore a golden crown, golden bells hung down either cheek, and around their necks were collars studded with precious stones.

28. The design of the carriage, and the fact that no description of its splendour did justice to its appearance, made it so famous that it drew large crowds of spectators. In fact, whenever it came to a town, the entire population came out to meet it and then escorted it on its way out again, since they had not exhausted the pleasure of seeing it. [2] And it was in keeping with its magnificence that it was accompanied not just by an armed escort, but also by gangs of road-menders and engineers.

Arrhidaeus spent almost two years on its construction and then conveyed the king's body from Babylon to Egypt. [3] As a way of honouring Alexander, Ptolemy went all the way to Syria with an army to meet the catafalque,* and after he had received the body, he lavished care on it. He decided not to take it to Ammon for the time being, but to lay it to rest in the city founded by Alexander,* which was close to being the most famous city in the world. [4] So he built a precinct, the size and design of which were worthy of Alexander's glory, and there he buried him. He instituted sacrifices to honour him as a hero and a magnificent athletic festival.

Ptolemy was well repaid for all this, however, by both men and gods. [5] Men began to flock to Alexandria from everywhere, drawn by his benevolence and generosity, and they did not hesitate to make themselves available for the coming campaign, even though it was the Royal Army that was getting ready to make war on Ptolemy. Despite the obvious risks and the great danger they would face, they were all prepared to risk their own lives in Ptolemy's defence. [6] And the gods, because of his goodness and the equitable way in which he treated all his friends, saved him unexpectedly from almost certain disaster.

29. Perdiccas was mistrustful of the growth of Ptolemy's power and decided to march on Egypt with the kings and the bulk of his army, while sending Eumenes to the Hellespont with enough men to prevent an invasion of Asia by Antipater and Craterus. [2] He also attached to Eumenes a number of high-ranking officers, of whom the most senior were his brother Alcetas and Neoptolemus, and ordered them to obey Eumenes in everything, because of his skill as a strategist* and his steadfast loyalty. [3] So Eumenes went to the Hellespont. The army he had been given was deficient in horse, but he had already raised a large cavalry force from his own satrapy, and he made good the deficiency.

[4] When Craterus and Antipater brought their forces over from Europe,* Neoptolemus, who was jealous of Eumenes and had a substantial number of Macedonian troops under his command, secretly got in touch with Antipater.* They came to an agreement and the idea was for Neoptolemus to find a way to kill Eumenes. His treachery was discovered, however, and he was forced to fight. In the battle he came close to losing his life and he did lose almost all his men, not just because a lot of them were killed during the battle, [5] but also because, after his victory, Eumenes won the rest of them over to his side,* so that his strength grew just as much from the addition of a good number of Macedonian soldiers as it did from the victory itself.

[6] Neoptolemus rode off to Antipater with the three hundred cavalrymen who had survived the battle along with him, [7] and Antipater called a meeting of his advisers to discuss how to go about the war. They decided to divide the army into two, with Antipater taking one half and setting out for Cilicia to fight Perdiccas, while Craterus attacked Eumenes with the other half, and then joined Antipater after defeating Eumenes. That way, they thought, once they had reunited the army, and once Ptolemy had been added to the alliance, they would be able to get the better of the Royal Army.

30. When Eumenes found out that the enemy was advancing against him, he gathered his troops together from all quarters, and especially the cavalry. Since his infantry was no match for the Macedonian phalanx, he had been putting together a good-sized cavalry corps, and it was they who, he hoped, would bring him victory. [2] When the two armies were close to each other, Craterus convened an army assembly and delivered a speech that effectively aroused his men's ardour for the battle, by promising that, in the event of victory, he would allow them the whole of the enemy's baggage train to plunder.* [3] Once they were fired up, he deployed his forces for battle, taking command of the right wing himself and giving the left to Neoptolemus. [4] He had in all twenty thousand foot, most of whom were Macedonians, famed for their prowess, on whom he was chiefly relying for victory, and he also had two thousand horse under his command. [5] Eumenes had an ethnically diverse infantry division of twenty thousand, and five thousand horse, who he expected to win the battle for him.

Once the two generals had divided their cavalry contingents up between the wings and had led them a long way forward from the infantry, Craterus started the action by leading the best of his men in a ferocious charge against the enemy. He fought superbly, but then his horse stumbled and he fell to the ground. In the swirling, dense mass of horsemen, he went unrecognized; he was trampled and died an inglorious death. [6] His fall boosted the morale of Eumenes' men, and they swarmed around the enemy and took many lives. The pressure they exerted was too much for Craterus' right wing and, overwhelmed by the enemy, they were forced to retreat for safety to the infantry phalanx.

31. On Craterus' left, where Neoptolemus was facing Eumenes himself, the charge of these two generals at each other showed clearly

what men can do when driven by love of glory. [2] Once they had recognized each other by their horses and other distinguishing marks, they engaged, and made victory in the battle depend on the outcome of the single combat between them. At first, they went at each other with their swords, but then the duel became unusual, and in fact quite extraordinary, because they were so carried away by their passion and their loathing of each other that they let the reins drop from their left hands and grabbed hold of each other. As they grappled, their horses ran out from under them, carried forward by their impetus, and the two men fell to the ground.

[3] The abruptness and violence of the fall meant that both of them struggled to stand, especially since they were impeded by their armour, but it was Eumenes who found his feet first and got in the first blow, when he struck Neoptolemus behind the knee. [4] It was a bad wound, and Neoptolemus collapsed. He lay disabled on the ground, with the wound making it impossible for him to get to his feet. Yet his mental courage was stronger than his physical impairment, and he raised himself on to his knees and wounded his adversary three times, in the arm and thighs. [5] None of the blows was fatal, however, and with his wounds still fresh Eumenes struck Neoptolemus a second time, in the neck, and killed him.

32. Meanwhile, the rest of the cavalry had also joined battle and a great slaughter was taking place. With so many men falling dead or wounded, for a while there was nothing to tell between the two sides, but then, once it became known that Neoptolemus had died and that the other wing was in flight, his men all turned tail and fled for safety to the infantry phalanx, as though it were a strong rampart. [2] Eumenes was gratified by his success, and once he had taken possession of the bodies of the two enemy generals,* he had the trumpeter recall his men. After erecting a trophy and burying his dead, he sent envoys to the defeated infantry, encouraging them to enlist under him, but also giving any of them who wanted to leave permission to go wherever he wanted.

[3] Once the Macedonians had agreed to end hostilities on these terms, which they guaranteed under oath to honour, they were given leave to replenish their supplies in certain nearby villages—and they played Eumenes false. As soon as they were rested and had stocked up on provisions, they left one night and surreptitiously made their way to Antipater. [4] Eumenes wanted to punish the oath-breakers for

their faithlessness, and he set out after the infantry, hot on their heels, but they fought a superb rearguard action, and this, on top of the handicap of his wounds, forced him to abandon the pursuit. But he had won a notable victory and killed two important generals, and this earned him great glory.

33. Antipater took in the survivors of the rout and incorporated them into his forces, and then marched towards Cilicia in support of Ptolemy. At the news of Eumenes' victory, Perdiccas went about the Egyptian campaign with far more daring,* and he reached the Nile and made camp close to the city of Pelusium. [2] But during an attempt to dredge an old canal the river violently burst its banks and ruined the siegeworks, and at that point many of his friends abandoned him and went over to Ptolemy. [3] For Perdiccas was a man of blood, who tended to restrict the extent to which his officers could act on their own authority, and in general used force to get everyone to obey him, whereas Ptolemy, by contrast, was generous and equitable, and allowed all his officers to speak their minds. Besides, Ptolemy had secured all the most important places in Egypt with strong garrisons, and supplied them with all the equipment they might need, including all kinds of artillery pieces. [4] The reason, then, why his ventures were generally successful was that many men gave him their loyalty and were prepared to fight for him.

[5] Nevertheless, when Perdiccas convened his officers in an attempt to repair the damage, he won their loyalty—gifts or extravagant promises were needed in some cases, but generally it was his courteous and tactful behaviour that did the trick—and motivated them to face the coming dangers. After ordering them to get ready to break camp, he set out with the army in the evening, without telling anyone where he was taking them. [6] All through the night they marched at a fast pace, and then he had them halt by the Nile, not far from a fortress called Camel Fort. At daybreak, he got his men to begin crossing the river, with the elephants going first, then the Hypaspists,* who were carrying scaling ladders, and everyone else he was going to use to assault the fortress. The rear was made up of his best cavalry, whom he was planning to send against Ptolemy, if he happened to appear.

34. His men were only halfway across when Ptolemy and his men did in fact appear, racing up to relieve the fortress. They reached the place before Perdiccas, threw themselves inside, and signalled their

presence by sounding their trumpets and shouting, but, nothing daunted, Perdiccas' men boldly approached the fortifications. [2] The Hypaspists lost no time in bringing up the ladders and starting to ascend, while the riders mounted on the elephants tried to breach the palisade and tear down the parapet. But Ptolemy, who had his best men by his side and wanted to encourage his officers and Friends not to shrink from danger, stood, pike in hand, on top of the bulwarks. First, with the help of his superior position, he put out the eyes of the leading elephant and wounded the mahout mounted on it, and then he turned to those who were climbing up the ladders. Disdainfully he struck at them and sent them tumbling down into the river in their armour, sorely wounded. [3] Following his example, Ptolemy's Friends also took up the fight, and they neutralized the next elephant by shooting down its mahout controller.

[4] The battle for the wall went on for a long while, with Perdiccas sending in his troops in relays and doing his utmost to take the place by storm, and Ptolemy proving himself the most valiant of his men, encouraging his Friends to show him just how loyal and brave they were, and fighting like a hero. Thanks to the incredible determination of these two generals, [5] there was severe loss of life on both sides, because Ptolemy's men had the advantage of height, while Perdiccas had superior numbers. Finally, after the fighting had gone on all day, Perdiccas gave up the assault and returned to camp.

[6] That night, he secretly broke camp and set out on the march. His destination was the river bank opposite Memphis, where the Nile divides and creates an island capable of accommodating and offering security to a very large army and its camp. [7] He had his men cross over to this island, but the depth of the river made the going very difficult for them. The water came up to their chins, and its buffeting of their bodies as they crossed threatened to knock them off their feet, especially since they were hampered by their arms and armour.

35. When Perdiccas noticed the problems the current was causing, he placed the elephants to the left of the ford† to break the force of the water and lessen the strength of the current,† and he posted the cavalry to the right, their job being to catch any men who were swept away by the river and to see them safely across to the other side. [2] There was a curious and unusual aspect to this crossing of the river by the army. Although the first to cross did so safely, those who followed them found it extremely dangerous. For no apparent reason, the river

had become far deeper and, with their bodies completely submerged, the men were little short of helpless.

[3] When they asked themselves what was causing the water level to rise, they could not figure it out at all. Some said that somewhere upstream a silted-up canal had been cleared, and that the ford had got deeper when the canal water had joined the river; others thought that rainfall upstream had increased the volume of water in the Nile. [4] Neither of these ideas was right, however. The first crossing of the ford had been safer because the sand that formed the bed of the ford was undisturbed, but during subsequent crossings the sand had been trampled and set in motion by the horses and elephants, who had crossed early, and then by the feet of the infantry; the disturbed sand had been carried downstream, leaving the ford hollowed out, and that was why the crossing had become deeper mid-river.

[5] The fact that the rest of the army was prevented in this way from crossing the river left Perdiccas in a considerable quandary. Since not enough of his men had reached the other side to stand up to the enemy, and those who remained on the near side were unable to go to their support, he ordered them all to retrace their steps back again. [6] But this meant that they would have to get across the stream. Some of them—those who were good swimmers and in excellent physical shape—did manage to cross the Nile, although it was a horrific ordeal and they lost much of their weaponry and armour, but the rest, who were not so good at swimming, were less fortunate. Some were swallowed up by the river, some were cast ashore on the bank occupied by the enemy, but most of them were carried a long way downstream and were eaten by river-dwelling creatures.*

36. More than two thousand men lost their lives, including some high-ranking officers, and the army turned against Perdiccas. Ptolemy, however, cremated the corpses of those who had been cast ashore on his side of the river, gave them a proper funeral, and then sent the bones of the dead men back to their relatives and friends. [2] The upshot was that the more the Macedonians on Perdiccas' side became disaffected with him, the more they were inclined to give their allegiance to Ptolemy. [3] That night, the camp was filled with lamentation, as they mourned the loss of so many men—men who had died for no good reason, not as a result of enemy action, and of whom at least a thousand had been eaten by animals.

[4] So a large number of Perdiccas' officers met and denounced him, and the threatening shouts coming from the infantry, who had all turned against him, left no one in any doubt of their hostility. [5] It was the officers, then, who were the first to mutiny. There were about a hundred of them, with the most senior being Pithon, the man who had suppressed the Greek rebellion,* and was as valiant and illustrious as any of Alexander's Friends. Then some of the cavalry joined the conspiracy as well, and they went to Perdiccas' tent, fell on him all at once, and murdered him.

[6] The next day an assembly was convened, and Ptolemy came to address it. He paid his respects to the Macedonians and defended his actions, and then, seeing that provisions were low, he supplied the army with a lavish amount of grain and made sure that the camp was replete with provisions. This went down very well, and he could have used the favour of the army to assume the custodianship of the kings, but this was not a position he wanted, and as a way of thanking Pithon and Arrhidaeus he arranged for them to share the supreme command. [7] That is, when the Macedonians met to decide what to do about the leadership, Ptolemy made his recommendation, and they all enthusiastically chose Pithon and Arrhidaeus (the man who had been responsible for the king's cortège) as plenipotentiary custodians of the kings. So Perdiccas lost both his leadership and his life, after having been at the helm for three years.

37. Very soon after his death, messengers arrived with news of Eumenes' victory in Cappadocia, and of the deaths of Craterus and Neoptolemus in the course of their defeat. If the news had arrived two days before Perdiccas' death, his great good fortune would have deterred anyone from laying hands on him. [2] But now, when the Macedonians heard how things stood with Eumenes, they condemned him to death, along with fifty of his senior associates, including Alcetas, the brother of Perdiccas. They also killed Perdiccas' closest friends and his sister Atalante, who was the wife of Attalus, the man who had been given command of the fleet.

[3] At the time of Perdiccas' murder, Attalus, as Admiral of the Fleet, was based at Pelusium, but on hearing of the deaths of his wife and Perdiccas he sailed off with the fleet and put in at Tyre. [4] A Macedonian, Archelaus, was in command of the garrison at Tyre, and he made Attalus welcome, and surrendered to him not just the city, but also the money—eight hundred talents—which had been

given him by Perdiccas, and which he now dutifully returned. Attalus was joined in Tyre by those of Perdiccas' friends who managed to escape from the camp at Memphis.*

38. After Antipater took his forces to Asia, the Aetolians invaded Thessaly. This was an attempt to distract his attention, which they were obliged to do by their agreement with Perdiccas.* On their way to Thessaly, the Aetolian army of twelve thousand foot and four hundred horse, under the command of Alexander the Aetolian, [2] assaulted the Locrian city of Amphissa,* overran their farmland, and captured some of the nearby towns. They met and defeated Antipater's general Polycles in a battle in which they killed him and many of his men as well. The captives were either sold or ransomed.

[3] Then the Aetolians invaded Thessaly. They persuaded most of the Thessalians to make common cause with them against Antipater, and before long they had an army totalling twenty-five thousand foot and 1,500 horse. [4] However, while they were winning the cities over to their cause, the Acarnanians, who were their enemies, invaded Aetolia and set about ravaging farmland and assaulting towns. [5] When the Aetolians heard of the threat to their country, they left the non-citizen soldiers in Thessaly under the command of Menon of Pharsalus, while the citizen contingent returned rapidly to Aetolia, cowed the Acarnanians into submission, and freed their country from danger. [6] While they were occupied with this, however, Polyperchon, whom Antipater had left as the governor of Macedon, marched into Thessaly with a large army. A pitched battle was fought, which Polyperchon won.* The Thessalians lost most of their men, including Menon, and Polyperchon recovered Thessaly.

39. In Asia, Arrhidaeus and Pithon, the custodians of the kings, left the Nile and took the kings and the army to Triparadeisus in inland Syria.* [2] But while they were there, Queen Eurydice* began to make a thorough nuisance of herself and to obstruct their projects. This annoyed Pithon and his colleague and, since it was clear that the Macedonians were increasingly taking their orders from her, they convened an assembly at which they renounced their custodianship, [3] and the Macedonians chose Antipater to replace them, with plenipotentiary power. When Antipater arrived in Triparadeisus a few days later, he found Eurydice stirring up trouble and turning the Macedonians against him. [4] There was virtual anarchy in the camp, but Antipater addressed the troops at a general

assembly and calmed things down. He also frightened Eurydice into quiescence.*

[5] He then went on to make a new division of the satrapies. He re-assigned to Ptolemy the satrapy he already had: his possession of Egypt was widely regarded as being due to his personal courage, as though it were spear-won land, and so it was impossible to remove him anyway.* [6] He gave Syria to Laomedon of Mytilene, and Cilicia to Philoxenus.* Of the upper satrapies, he gave Mesopotamia and Arbelitis* to Amphimachus, Babylonia to Seleucus,* Susiane to Antigenes (a reward for his having been the first to attack Perdiccas), Persis to Peucestas, Carmania to Tlepolemus, Media to Pithon, Parthyaea to Philip,* Areia and Drangiane to Stasander of Cyprus, and Bactria and Sogdiana to another Cypriot, Stasanor of Soli.* He re-assigned Paropanisadae to Oxyartes, the father of Alexander's wife Rhoxane, and the parts of India bordering Paropanisadae to Pithon, the son of Agenor. As for the adjacent kingdoms, the one on the Indus he left in Porus' hands, and the one on the Hydaspes in Taxiles' hands, since it would take the Royal Army and a senior general to remove these kings. As for the north-facing satrapies,* he gave Cappadocia to Nicanor; Greater Phrygia and Lycia to Antigonus, as before; Caria to Asander;* Lydia to Cleitus; and Hellespontine Phrygia to Arrhidaeus. [7] He appointed Antigonus General of the Royal Army and tasked him with the defeat of Eumenes and Alcetas. And he attached his son Cassander to Antigonus as his chiliarch, so that Antigonus would not be able to pursue his own interests without Antipater hearing about it.* Then he set off for Macedon with the kings and his army, to restore the kings to their homeland.

40. Antigonus, appointed General in Asia for the war against Eumenes, collected his forces from their winter quarters, and once he felt ready for battle, he set out against Eumenes, who was in Cappadocia. [2] One of Eumenes' senior officers, a man called Perdiccas, had broken with him and was encamped at a distance of three days' march with the troops who had joined his mutiny, three thousand foot and five hundred horse. Eumenes sent Phoenix of Tenedos to deal with them, with four thousand foot—all picked men—and a thousand horse. [3] Phoenix made a forced march by night and fell on the rebels unexpectedly at about the second watch, while they were asleep. He captured Perdiccas and contained the rebel forces. [4] Eumenes put the ringleaders of the mutiny to death,

but he incorporated the rank-and-file soldiers back into his army, and this merciful treatment won him their loyalty.

[5] Next, however, Antigonus got in touch with a man called Apollonides, the commander of Eumenes' cavalry, and secretly bribed him, with promises of generous rewards, to turn traitor and desert during the battle. [6] Eumenes was encamped on a plain in Cappadocia* that was suitable for cavalry action when Antigonus brought up his entire army and occupied the high ground overlooking the plain. [7] At this time Antigonus had more than ten thousand foot (of whom half were Macedonians, widely admired for their valour), two thousand horse, and thirty elephants,* while Eumenes had at least twenty thousand foot and five thousand horse. [8] A ferocious battle took place, but when Apollonides and the cavalry under his command abruptly abandoned their comrades, victory fell to Antigonus and about eight thousand of Eumenes' men died. Antigonus also gained possession of all Eumenes' baggage, and the combination of the defeat and the loss of the baggage caused morale to plummet in Eumenes' camp.*

41. Eumenes' next plan was to escape to Armenia and replenish his army from among the inhabitants there, but Antigonus was coming up behind him, and when it became clear that his men were starting to desert to the enemy, Eumenes seized a stronghold called Nora instead.* [2] This was a very small fortress, with a circuit of no more than two stades, but it was astonishingly strong. The place had been built on a lofty crag, and the combination of natural defences and the work of men's hands afforded it a remarkable degree of security. [3] It was also well enough stocked with grain, wood, and salt to supply all the needs of the fugitives for many years. Eumenes was accompanied by those of his friends who were so exceptionally loyal that they had decided to continue the fight to the bitter end and die along with him. All told, counting both cavalry and infantry, there were about six hundred men.

[4] The incorporation of Eumenes' forces into his army, his takeover of Eumenes' satrapies and their revenues, and the large amount of money that he gained prompted Antigonus to aspire to greater things, seeing that none of the leading men in Asia any longer had an army that was capable of deciding the issue of supremacy with him by battle. [5] One result of this was that, although for the time being he kept up a pretence of being well disposed towards Antipater, he had decided

that, once he had consolidated his position, he would stop taking orders from either the kings or Antipater.

[6] At first, Antigonus surrounded the fortress and the fugitives with two sets of ramparts, ditches, and remarkably strong palisades, but subsequently* he arranged a meeting, at which he renewed their former friendship and persuaded Eumenes to come in with him. Knowing full well how rapidly luck can change, Eumenes pushed harder for concessions than might have been expected from someone in his position, [7] and insisted on being granted the satrapies he had originally been given and a full pardon in respect of the charges that were outstanding against him. Antigonus referred Eumenes' demands to Antipater and, leaving an adequate guard, he set out to tackle the surviving† enemy generals who had armies at their disposal, namely Perdiccas' brother Alcetas and Attalus, who had the entire fleet at his disposal.

42. Eumenes next sent envoys to Antipater to negotiate the terms of the agreement. The delegation was led by Hieronymus, the author of the *History of the Successors.** Eumenes had experienced a number of changes of various kinds in his lifetime, and so he remained sanguine, because he was well aware of Fortune's habit of rapidly changing, for better or for worse. [2] He could see that the current kings of Macedon had no more than the empty trappings of royalty, and that many highly ambitious men were in the process of trying to succeed to the rulership of the empire, each of them interested only in working for his own ends. Eumenes was hoping, then, that there would be plenty of demand for his services, because of his practical intelligence, his military expertise, and his absolutely steadfast loyalty.* And this turned out to be true.

[3] Since the fortress offered only cramped conditions and uneven surfaces, Eumenes could see that it was impossible to exercise the horses and that they would become useless for employment in battle conditions, and so he devised a strange and novel form of exercise for them. [4] He tied their heads with ropes to beams or projecting pegs and then raised them by four or six palms. This forced them to put their weight on their hind legs, with their forefeet just failing to graze the ground. The immediate reaction of the horse, as it strove to take its weight on its forelegs, was to work its whole torso and its legs, with every part of its body being equally affected. This activity caused sweat to pour off its body, and the incredible effort the creatures had to put in made this a perfect form of exercise for them.

[5] All his men received the same rations, and Eumenes joined
them himself in their spare diet. The fact that he treated himself no
differently from everyone else won him the firm loyalty of his men,
and allowed him to ensure that concord reigned in this community of
fugitives. That was how things stood with Eumenes and those who
had joined him in his rock-bound fastness.

43. In Egypt, after his surprising success in eliminating the threat
of Perdiccas and the Royal Army, Ptolemy held the country as though
it were spear-won land.† However, since he could see that Phoenicia
and Coele Syria, as it is called, would be perfect launching points for
an attack on Egypt, he was very keen to annex these territories. [2] He
therefore dispatched an adequate army and appointed one of his
Friends, Nicanor, as its general. Nicanor marched into Syria, made
the satrap Laomedon his prisoner, and gained the submission of the
entire province. He also secured the allegiance of the Phoenician cities, and once he had installed garrisons in them, he returned to Egypt,
after a brief and effective campaign.*

319/18

44. *In the Archonship of Apollodorus in Athens, the Romans appointed
as their consuls Quintus Popillius and Quintus Publius. In this year:*

Having defeated Eumenes, Antigonus decided to campaign against
Alcetas and Attalus. They were the last of Perdiccas' Friends and
relatives, and they were notable generals with enough troops to make
a bid for power. He therefore left Cappadocia and advanced on Pisidia,
where Alcetas was based. [2] By making forced marches that tested
the limits of his men's endurance, he covered 2,500 stades in seven
days* and arrived at the city called Cretopolis. The speed of his march
meant that he took the enemy by surprise. They still did not know
about his arrival even when he was near by, and he quickly seized and
occupied some rugged hills.

[3] As soon as Alcetas was aware of the enemy's presence, he drew
up his infantry for battle, and had his cavalry assault the hills, since he
was determined to take them by storm and dislodge Antigonus' men
from the high ground they had occupied. [4] A fierce battle ensued,
with both sides taking heavy losses, but then Antigonus led six thousand horsemen in a furious charge against the enemy phalanx, with

the intention of making it impossible for Alcetas to use it as a point of refuge on which to fall back. [5] He succeeded in this, and then the troops of his who were occupying the high ground, who greatly outnumbered their opponents and had the advantage of superior height, routed their assailants. With his line of retreat to the infantry phalanx cut off and the enemy army between him and safety, Alcetas was facing certain death. The situation was desperate, but, though it cost the lives of many of his men, he just managed to break through to the infantry phalanx.

45. Antigonus led his entire army, elephants and all, down from the heights and his greatly superior numbers struck terror into the enemy. Alcetas had in all sixteen thousand foot and nine hundred horse, while, leaving aside the elephants, Antigonus had more than forty thousand foot and over seven thousand horse. [2] With the elephants coming at them from the front, with thousands of horsemen harassing them on all sides, and with the infantry, who vastly outnumbered them and also outclassed them as fighters, holding the superior position, Alcetas' men were gripped by confusion and fear. The speed and intensity of the attack were such that Alcetas was unable even to deploy his phalanx effectively. [3] The rout was complete, and the prisoners included Attalus, Docimus, Polemon, and many high-ranking officers, but Alcetas, along with his bodyguards and pages, escaped with his Pisidian allies to a city in Pisidia called Termessus.

[4] After receiving the surrender of the officers on terms, Antigonus enrolled the rest of Alcetas' men in his own ranks—which is to say that, by treating them kindly, he enormously increased his strength. [5] But the Pisidians, six thousand men of exceptional courage, told Alcetas not to worry and guaranteed to stick with him through thick and thin. The reason for their extraordinary devotion was as follows.

46. After Perdiccas' death, Alcetas found himself short of allies in Asia and he began to think it advisable for him to favour the Pisidians, the idea being that he would gain as allies men who were skilled at war, and who inhabited a country which was rugged enough to discourage invasion and had plenty of strong fortresses. [2] In the course of his campaigns, therefore, he rewarded them disproportionately, compared to his other allies, by sharing the profits of war with them and giving them half of the booty. Moreover, he never spoke harshly to them when they met, every day he invited the most important of them in turns to join him at his table for a banquet, and he honoured

many of them with valuable gifts. That is how he gained their devotion. [3] At the time in question, then, Alcetas was resting his hopes on the Pisidians, and he was not disappointed. In fact, when Antigonus and his entire army made camp near Termessus and demanded Alcetas' surrender, and the elders of the community wanted him to be handed over, the younger ones united against their fathers, set up on their own, and undertook to keep him safe at all costs.

[4] The elders at first argued that their sons should not let the land of their birth fall to a conqueror for the sake of a Macedonian, but when they realized that they were talking to people whose will was unshakeable, they met together in secret and, one night, they sent representatives to Antigonus, promising to hand Alcetas over to him, alive or dead. [5] They asked him to attack the city in a few days' time† and to have his light-armed skirmishers draw the defenders out from behind the wall by pulling back as though they were in flight. When this happened, they said, and the young men were busy fighting away from the city, they would be presented with a perfect opportunity for executing their plan. [6] Antigonus approved of their scheme. He moved his camp a long way off and used his skirmishers to lure the young men into fighting away from the city. [7] When the elders saw that Alcetas had been left alone, they selected their most trustworthy slaves and those of their citizens who were of military age, but had not sided with Alcetas, and took advantage of the absence of the young men to launch an attack on him. They were unable to take him alive, because he quickly killed himself in order to avoid falling into hostile hands, but they put his body on a bier, draped a plain cloak over it, bore it out of the city gates, and handed it over to Antigonus without attracting the attention of the skirmishers.

47. This contrivance of theirs enabled them to free their city from danger and avert war, but they were unable to avoid the hostility of the young men. When they returned from the battle and heard what had happened, the extraordinary degree of loyalty they felt for Alcetas made them furious with their fellow citizens. [2] They took over part of the city, and at first they voted to burn down the houses and then rush out of the burning city with their weapons and take to the hills. From there, they intended to raid the farmland that was subject to Antigonus. Later, however, they changed their minds and refrained from setting fire to the city, but they still turned to brigandage, and in the course of their raids they destroyed a lot of enemy farmland.

[3] After being given Alcetas' corpse, Antigonus mutilated it, and then three days later, when it began to rot, he left it unburied* and set out to leave Pisidia. But the mutilated wretch retained the devotion of the young men of the city, and they recovered the body and buried it with full honour.* This is the nature of doing good to others: it has the peculiar property of casting a spell, so to speak, which works in the favour of benefactors by guaranteeing the unswerving devotion of those who are in their debt. [4] Anyway, having decided to leave Pisidia, Antigonus and his entire army set out for Phrygia. When he was at Cretopolis, Aristodemus of Miletus met him with the news that Antipater had died, and that rulership of Macedon and the custody of the kings had been inherited by Polyperchon of Macedon. [5] The news gave Antigonus great pleasure. He was excited by his prospects, and his intention was to retain Asia—to keep supremacy there for himself and no one else. That was how things stood with Antigonus.

48. In Macedon, Antipater fell ill with a rather serious illness, which, with old age a factor as well,* was likely to be terminal. The Athenians sent Demades as an envoy to him—choosing Demades because he was known as an advocate of the Macedonian cause—to ask him to honour his long-standing promise to remove the garrison from Munychia.* [2] Antipater had originally been well disposed towards Demades, but after Perdiccas' death some letters were discovered in the royal archives in which Demades urged Perdiccas to cross from Asia to Europe at the earliest possible opportunity and attack Antipater.* Without revealing that he now regarded Demades as an enemy, Antipater had therefore withdrawn his favour. [3] So when Demades, following the instructions he had been given by the Athenian people, began to ask Antipater to keep his promise and, speaking rather too directly, made threats about what would happen to the garrison, Antipater said not a word in reply, but merely handed Demades over to the executioners along with his son Demeas, who had accompanied his father on this mission. [4] They were taken away to a shack and put to death, for the reasons I have given.

On his death bed Antipater appointed Polyperchon* the custodian of the kings and General Plenipotentiary—Polyperchon was almost the oldest of those who had campaigned with Alexander, and was held in great respect in Macedon—and he made his son Cassander Polyperchon's chiliarch and second-in-command. [5] The chiliarchy was first developed as a position of prestige and glory by the Persian kings, and then later, under Alexander, when he started to emulate Persian customs, it became a very powerful and highly regarded post.* So Antipater was following this tradition when he appointed his son Cassander, who was still young, to the chiliarchy.

49. Cassander, however, was dissatisfied with the arrangement. He regarded it as outrageous that his father's command should be inherited by a man who had no connection with the family, especially given that Antipater had a son who was capable of command and had already given sufficient proof of his abilities and courage. [2] At first, then, he took trips with his friends into the countryside, where he had the opportunity and the time to raise the question of supremacy with them. He took them aside one by one, entreated them to help him seize power, and by promising them substantial rewards he won their willing support. [3] He also secretly sent emissaries to Ptolemy, to renew their friendship, to ask for an alliance, and to request that a fleet be dispatched at the earliest possible opportunity from Phoenicia to the Hellespont. He sent envoys to ask the other leading men and cit-ies for alliances as well, and he arranged a long hunting trip for him-self, in an attempt to dispel any suspicion that he was about to revolt.

[4] After Polyperchon had assumed the custodianship of the kings, he consulted with his Friends and gained their approval for his notion of sending for Olympias. He asked her to take on the custodianship of Alexander's son,* who was just a child, and to stay in Macedon, where she would have royal rank. For Olympias had fallen out with Antipater a few years earlier and fled to Epirus. That was how things stood in Macedon.

50. In Asia, the dissemination of the news of Antipater's death triggered unrest and the first stirrings of political change, as the power-possessors set about working for their own ends. Antigonus took the lead in this. He had already vanquished Eumenes in Cappadocia and taken over his army; he had defeated Alcetas and Attalus in Pisidia and taken over their armies; and he had also been made General Plenipotentiary of Asia by Antipater, which brought with it the com-mand of a large army.* All this had filled him with arrogance and self-importance, [2] and since his goal was rulership of the entire empire, he decided to take orders from neither the kings nor their custodians, since it seemed certain to him that, with the most power-ful army in Asia, he would gain control of the treasuries.* There was no one who was capable of standing up to him. [3] At that time, he had

sixty thousand foot, ten thousand horse, and thirty elephants, and he expected to be able to raise more, should he need them, because Asia had the resources to pay for the recruitment of mercenaries for ever.

[4] Bearing all this in mind, Antigonus sent for Hieronymus, the historian, who was a friend and fellow citizen of Eumenes of Cardia, with whom he had taken refuge in the stronghold called Nora.* After giving him valuable gifts as a way of persuading him to act as his agent, he sent him to Eumenes. His job was to ask Eumenes to forget the battle they had fought in Cappadocia, to accept a treaty of friendship and alliance, gifts that would make him far wealthier than he had been before, and a larger satrapy, and in general to be the foremost of Antigonus' Friends and his partner in the whole enterprise. [5] At the earliest opportunity, Antigonus also convened a council of his Friends at which he informed them of his intention to gain supreme power and distributed satrapies or military commands to the most senior of them. But he held out great prospects for all of them, and made them full of zeal for his endeavours. For his intention was to overrun Asia, deposing the current satraps and re-assigning positions of command in his friends' favour.

51. While Antigonus was occupied with all this, Arrhidaeus, the satrap of Hellespontine Phrygia, who realized what Antigonus was up to, decided not just to protect his own satrapy, but also to install garrisons in the most important cities.* The largest of the cities, and the one that was strategically the most important, was Cyzicus, so Arrhidaeus set out to attack it with a force made up of more than ten thousand mercenary infantrymen, a thousand Macedonians, five hundred Persian archers and slingers, eight hundred cavalry, all kinds of artillery pieces, both bolt-shooting and stone-throwing catapults, and every other variety of siege equipment.* [2] His attack took the city by surprise and he trapped the majority of the population in the countryside. He then set about the siege, trying to intimidate the Cyzicenes into accepting a garrison.

Given the unexpectedness of the attack and the fact that most of their fellow citizens were stranded in the countryside, leaving few in the city, the Cyzicenes were utterly unprepared for the siege. [3] All the same, they decided to defend their freedom. Openly, they sent envoys to try to persuade Arrhidaeus to call off the siege, on the understanding that they would do anything he wanted, short of accepting a garrison; but, secretly, they set about raising a force large enough to line the city walls with defenders, consisting of young men of military age and selected slaves, who were chosen on the basis of their competence and supplied with arms. [4] When Arrhidaeus insisted on their accepting a garrison, the Cyzicene envoys said that they wanted to put the matter to the popular assembly. The satrap agreed, and the Cyzicenes were granted a truce—and they spent that day and the following night improving their ability to resist a siege.

[5] Arrhidaeus had been outmanoeuvred. His window of opportunity had closed and his hopes came to nothing, because it was not hard for the Cyzicenes to keep enemies at bay: the city, which was well fortified, was extremely easy to defend by land because it is on a peninsula, and they had control of the sea.* [6] They also sent for reinforcements from Byzantium, and ordnance, and everything else that might help them withstand a siege, and the promptness and willingness with which the Byzantines got everything to them boosted their morale, so that they found the courage to face whatever dangers were in store for them. [7] They also hastily launched some warships, which sailed along the coast, picking up people from the countryside, and brought them back to the city. Before long, they had plenty of soldiers and they killed enough of the besiegers to thwart the siege. Arrhidaeus returned to his satrapy, then, outmanoeuvred by the Cyzicenes and without having achieved anything.

52. Antigonus happened to be in Celaenae when he heard that Cyzicus was under siege. It seemed to him that it would help him attain his objectives if he made the endangered city his, so he put together a force of twenty thousand foot and three thousand horse, picking the best men from the entire army, [2] and hurried off with them to help the Cyzicenes. He arrived a little too late, but he made it clear that he favoured the city, even if he failed to achieve his entire objective.

[3] He sent envoys to Arrhidaeus, accusing him, first, of having presumed to put under siege a Greek city which was an ally and had done no wrong, and, second, of plainly contemplating rebellion and wanting to make his satrapy his personal domain. He ended by ordering him to quit his satrapy and to keep the peace, as a resident of just a single city, which would be assigned to him. [4] After listening to what the envoys had to say and reprimanding them for their highhanded words, Arrhidaeus refused to leave his satrapy, and said that what he was doing, in garrisoning the cities, was getting ready† for

war with Antigonus. In keeping with this response, once he had secured the cities, he dispatched one of his generals with a division of his army. His mission was to link up with Eumenes, raise the siege of Nora, and then, as his saviour, gain him as an ally.*

[5] Antigonus had no intention of letting Arrhidaeus get away with it, and he sent an army to deal with him, while he himself set out for Lydia with sufficient manpower to attain his objective, which was the expulsion of the satrap, Cleitus. [6] But Cleitus had guessed that Antigonus would attack him, and once he had secured the most important cities with garrisons, he sailed to Macedon to tell the kings and Polyperchon about Antigonus' presumptuous rebellion, and to ask for help. [7] Ephesus fell to Antigonus at his approach, because he had inside help, and then, when Aeschylus of Rhodes sailed into the harbour with four ships with which he was bringing from Cilicia six hundred talents of silver that was on its way to Macedon for the kings, Antigonus seized the money, saying that he needed it to pay his mercenaries.* [8] This action of his proved that he was focusing only on his own interests and was an enemy of the kings. Then, once he had Cyme under siege,† he proceeded against the rest of the cities, one by one, and either subdued them by force or won them over by diplomacy.

53. I shall move on now from a narrative centred on Antigonus to an account of what happened to Eumenes, who was experiencing great and unexpected shifts of fortune, constantly encountering both good and bad when he least expected them. [2] Earlier, as an ally of Perdiccas and the kings, he had been awarded the satrapy of Cappadocia and its neighbouring territories, where, with large armies and plenty of money at his disposal, he became famous for his good fortune, [3] since he defeated Craterus and Neoptolemus in a set battle, and they were renowned generals with Macedonian troops under their command who had never previously been beaten. [4] But just when he had acquired a reputation for invincibility, he experienced a change of fortune, losing a major battle to Antigonus and being forced to retreat to a tiny stronghold. Shut up inside this place and surrounded by two sets of walls built by his enemies, there was no one to whom he could turn to help him recover from this disaster.

[5] After the siege had gone on for a year, however, and he was beginning to give up any hope of being rescued, an end to his misery suddenly appeared out of the blue. Antigonus, who was the one who had him under siege and wanted to see him dead, changed his mind

and invited him to work with him. And as soon as he had received pledges in the form of oaths, he brought the siege to an end. [6] So Eumenes was unexpectedly saved after a period of misfortune. He stayed for the time being in Cappadocia, recruiting his former friends and those of his former soldiers who were at large in the countryside. Thanks to his extraordinary popularity, he had soon gained a large number of men who shared his hopes for the future and accepted his invitation to serve under him. [7] He ended up, after only a few days, with more than two thousand soldiers who had voluntarily joined him, and that is not counting the five hundred friends who had been besieged with him in the fortress.* Then, with Fortune's help, he became so powerful that he was assigned the Royal Army and became the protector of the kings against those who presumed to bring their rule to an end. But I shall cover this in more detail a little later, at the appropriate points of the narrative.*

54. It is time now to leave Asian affairs and move on to events in Europe. Cassander, undaunted by his failure to be appointed to the command in Macedon, decided to make a bid for it anyway, because he thought it disgraceful for his father's office to be administered by anyone else. [2] The Macedonians, he could see, were inclining towards Polyperchon, so he talked in private with his trusted friends and sent them as his agents to the Hellespont, as a way of avoiding suspicion, while he took a break of some days' duration in the countryside, organizing hunting expeditions,* and succeeded in creating the impression that he had no interest in trying to gain his father's position.

[3] When everything was ready for his departure, he surreptitiously left Macedon and reached the Hellespont via the Chersonese. He sailed across to Antigonus in Asia, to ask for his help, and told him that Ptolemy had promised an alliance as well. Antigonus made him very welcome, guaranteed his full and unstinting support, and told Cassander that he had an infantry force and a fleet available for him straight away.* [4] In doing so, although he pretended that his help was due to the fact that Antipater had been his friend, in fact he wanted Polyperchon to be so thoroughly preoccupied by major troubles that he, Antigonus, could get away with overrunning Asia and securing supreme power there for himself.

55. Meanwhile in Macedon, Cassander's departure made it clear to Polyperchon, the custodian of the kings, that a major war was

brewing, and since he had decided to do nothing without the approval of his Friends, he called a meeting of all his commanders and the most important of the Macedonians. [2] Now that the threat posed by Cassander had been given substance by Antigonus, there could be no doubt that Cassander would retain the Greek cities, some of which were guarded by garrisons imposed by his father, while others were governed by oligarchies which were controlled by Antipater's friends and by mercenaries. It was also clear that Cassander would gain the military support of both Ptolemy, the ruler of Egypt, and Antigonus, who was already in open rebellion against the kings, and these two had mighty armies at their disposal and plenty of money, and included many peoples and major towns among their subjects. Under these circumstances, the agenda before the meeting was how they should go about fighting these enemies. Many speeches were delivered, stating various views on how to conduct the war, and in the end they decided to free the cities of Greece and to put an end to the oligarchies established by Antipater, [3] on the grounds that this was the best way simultaneously to undermine Cassander's influence and win for themselves great glory and many important alliances.

[4] They immediately invited all the ambassadors who were there representing their cities to a meeting, at which they told them that they had good news and promised to re-establish democracies in the cities. Once an edict to this effect had been approved and written up, they gave copies to the ambassadors, and asked them to hasten back to their cities and countries, and proclaim to the people the goodwill of the kings and leaders of Macedon for the Greeks. The resolution was as follows:*

56. Since earlier occupants of our throne performed numerous services for the Greeks, we* wish to maintain this tradition and make clear to all the goodwill which we continue to have for the Greeks. [2] Earlier, when Alexander departed from this world and the throne devolved on to us, we thought it our duty to reinstate peace for all our subjects and the political systems which our father Philip had put in place, and we wrote to the cities along these lines. [3] But then some of the Greeks took advantage of our absence far abroad* and unwisely made war on Macedon and were defeated by our generals, and consequently life became difficult for the cities in many ways, but you should know that it was the generals* who were responsible for this, and that we, out of respect for the original policy, are reinstating peace, the political systems that were current in the time of Philip and

Alexander, and the right to act entirely in accordance with the resolutions issued in years past by them. [4] Moreover, those who, from the start of Alexander's Asian expedition onward, left their cities or were banished from them by our generals, we restore. And those who are restored by us are to have full possession of their property and play their parts in the public lives of their communities without being subject to politically inspired antagonism* and without having any of their past wrongs held against them; and if there are any decrees outstanding against them, they are to be made null and void, except in the case of those who were sent into exile after due process of law for murder or impiety. [5] Of the Megalopolitans, those who were sent into exile along with Polyaenetus for treason are not to be restored, nor are the exiles from Amphissa, Tricca, Pharcadon, and Heraclea,* but all the others are to be re-admitted before the thirtieth of Xanthicus.* [6] If Philip or Alexander proscribed any institution in any city as inimical to their interests, the cities concerned are to present their petitions to us, so that improvements can be made and in the future they will act in ways that benefit both us and their cities. The Athenians are to have everything they had in the time of Philip and Alexander, except that Oropus shall remain in the hands of the Oropians, as it is at present.* [7] Samos we give to the Athenians, just as our father Philip did.* All the Greeks are to pass a resolution to the effect that none of their citizens is to bear arms against us or act in any way that is inimical to our interests, and that if anyone does so he and his family are to be punished with exile and confiscation of property. We have instructed Polyperchon to see that these and future measures are carried out, [8] and we urge you, as we did in an earlier letter, to obey him. For we will not tolerate failure to carry out any of the measures included in this decree.

57. Once this resolution had been published and every city had received a copy, Polyperchon wrote to Argos and all the other cities, ordering them to send into exile the politicians who had been their leaders in Antipater's time—and even to condemn some of them to death—and to confiscate their property, so that they would be so utterly ruined that they would be of no help to Cassander. [2] He also wrote to Olympias, Alexander's mother, who was living in Epirus because of her hatred of Antipater, asking her to come as soon as she could to Macedon and take charge of Alexander's child as his custodian, until he came of age and inherited his father's kingdom.*

[3] Polyperchon also sent messengers to Eumenes with a letter written in the names of the kings, asking him not to bring his enmity with Antigonus to an end, but to take the kings' side instead. He

suggested that Eumenes could either come to Macedon, if that was what he wanted, and work with him as one of the custodians of the kings, or, if he preferred, stay in Asia, where he would be given an army and funds to fight Antigonus, who had already made it clear that he was in rebellion against the kings. The kings, he wrote, hereby restored to him both the satrapy which Antigonus had taken from him and all the prerogatives that he had enjoyed before in Asia. [4] To cut a long story short, he argued that consistency with the services Eumenes had earlier rendered the royal house made it more appropriate for him than for anyone else to care for and concern himself with its fate. And he said that if Eumenes needed more forces, he would come in person from Macedon with the kings and the entire Royal Army.

These were the events that took place in this year.

318/17

58. *In the year of the Archonship of Archippus in Athens, the Romans appointed as their consuls Quintus Aelius and Lucius Papirius. In this year:*

Eumenes, newly released from Nora, received Polyperchon's letter, in which, in addition to what I have already mentioned, it was written that the kings were giving him five hundred talents with which he was to redress the balance after the defeats he had suffered, and that they had written to the generals in Cilicia and the guardians of the treasury, instructing them to give Eumenes the five hundred talents and more, if he needed it for mercenary recruitment and other pressing needs. He also said that the kings were writing to the leaders of the Macedonian Silver Shields, three thousand strong, ordering them to put themselves at Eumenes' disposal and cooperate fully with him in everything, since he had been appointed the General Plenipotentiary of all Asia.

[2] Eumenes also received a letter from Olympias, in which she passionately pleaded with him to help the kings and herself; he was the only one left of her friends that she really trusted, she said, and he was in a position to remedy the royal house's lack of allies. [3] Olympias also asked him for advice: in his opinion, was it better for her to remain in Epirus—that is, for her to remain suspicious of

those who were at any given time supposed to be the custodians of the kings, but who in reality were trying to take over the kingdom themselves—or should she return to Macedon? [4] Eumenes wrote straight back to Olympias, advising her to stay in Epirus for the time being, until the outcome of the war was clear. As for himself, since he had always been consistently loyal to the kings, he decided not to take orders from Antigonus, who wanted to appropriate the kingship for himself. Since his help was needed by Alexander's son, a fatherless boy who was up against rapacious generals, it seemed to Eumenes that the right course for him was to lay his life on the line, if need be, to try to ensure the kings' safety.

59. He therefore immediately ordered his men to break camp, and he set out from Cappadocia with about five hundred horse and more than two thousand foot. There were others who had promised their support, but they had not yet arrived and Eumenes did not have the time to wait for them, because a large force was on its way, sent by Antigonus. Menander was in command, and his job was to make it impossible for Eumenes, now that he had become an enemy of Antigonus, to stay in Cappadocia. [2] But in fact, when Menander and his men arrived three days later, they found they had missed Eumenes. They set out after him and his column, but they could not catch him, and they returned to Cappadocia.

[3] By putting his men on forced marches, Eumenes made it through the Taurus mountains and into Cilicia in good time. Antigenes and Teutamus, the commanders of the Silver Shields, obedient to the orders they had received in the kings' letter, came from a considerable distance to meet Eumenes and his friends. They gave him a courteous reception, congratulated him on his unexpected delivery from deadly peril, and promised their full and unstinting support. The Macedonian Silver Shields, numbering about three thousand, also came to meet him, and declared their loyalty and commitment.* [4] Everyone expressed astonishment at the mutability and unpredictability of Fortune, seeing that just a short while earlier both the kings and the Macedonian troops had condemned Eumenes and his friends to death, but now they were ignoring their own ruling,* and had not only let him off his punishment, but had even trusted him with the command of the entire kingdom.

[5] It was hardly surprising that everyone who observed the fluctuations in Eumenes' fortunes at that time responded with astonishment.

For how could anyone with a sense of the inconstancy of human life fail to be astounded by the way luck ebbs and flows one way and then the other? Or how could he put such trust in the power he wields at a time of good fortune that he would give himself airs as though he were not subject to human frailty? [6] Every person's life seems to be controlled by some divine helmsman, who makes it subject to cycles of alternating good and evil for ever. What is strange, then, is not that unexpected things happen, but that not everything that happens is unexpected. This also gives one a good reason for valuing history, because in a world of inconstancy and change history has the power to remedy both the arrogance of the fortunate and the misery of the unfortunate.*

60. All this was going through Eumenes' mind as well at the time in question, and in anticipation of further changes at Fortune's hands, he sensibly secured his own position, since he was not a Macedonian and had no connection to the throne. Moreover, since he was aware that he had been condemned to death by the Macedonians who were now under his command, and that his senior officers were proud men with great ambitions, it seemed likely to him that before long he would come to be despised and envied, and that in the end his life would be in danger. After all, no one is happy to take orders from a man he regards as his inferior, and no one can tolerate having as his master a man who ought to be subject to others.

[2] As a result of turning all this over in his mind, when the five hundred talents for recruitment and construction was offered to him in accordance with the kings' letters, at first he refused it, saying that he had no need of such a large amount of money, since leadership was the last thing he wanted. [3] Even now, he said, it was not as if he had volunteered for the job; he had been coerced by the kings into undertaking this form of service. Apart from anything else, after so long constantly on campaign, he could no longer stand the hardship and the rootlessness, he said, especially when there was no prospect of high office for him, since he was not a Macedonian and was excluded from the prerogatives that were reserved for ethnic Macedonians.

[4] But he then went on to tell them about a dream he had had, saying that he felt obliged to divulge it, since he believed that it would make an important contribution towards concord and the common good. [5] In this dream, he said, he saw King Alexander alive and bedecked with his royal insignia; he was conducting business, giving

orders to his officers, and playing an active part in managing all aspects of his kingdom. [6] 'It seems to me, then,' Eumenes said, 'that we should draw on the royal treasure and build a golden throne, and on this throne we should place all his insignia, especially his diadem, sceptre, and crown. Every day, as the sun rises, all of us officers should make an offering to him, and then we should meet in council with the throne near by, and receive our orders in the name of the king, as though he were alive and at the head of his kingdom.'*

61. This proposal met with universal approval, and everything that was needed was soon made ready, since the royal treasury was not short of gold. A magnificent tent was made, the throne was set up, and the diadem, sceptre, and Alexander's usual panoply* were placed on it. Finally, a fire altar* was put in place, on which all the leading men would burn frankincense and other precious aromatics, drawn from a golden casket, and worship Alexander as a god. [2] The tent was likewise furnished with plenty of chairs, and it was on these that the commanders used to sit in council and discuss whatever business required their attention at any time.

Whenever they met on official business, Eumenes presented himself as the equal of the other officers. By treating them with the utmost courtesy, he won them all over and not only eradicated the envy they felt for him, but even won a high degree of loyalty from his officers. [3] At the same time, their growing reverence for Alexander filled them all with confidence for the future, as though the way forward were being shown to them by a god. Eumenes was equally diplomatic towards the Macedonian Silver Shields as well, and he became very popular with them, since they regarded him as worthy of the trust the kings placed in him.

[4] Eumenes selected the most suitable of his friends, gave them ample funds, and sent them off to recruit mercenaries, with the rate of pay set at an inflated level. Some of them set out straight away for Pisidia, Lycia, and the neighbouring provinces, where they diligently hired mercenaries, while others travelled through Cilicia, or Coele Syria and Phoenicia, or the cities of Cyprus. [5] Word got around that mercenaries were in demand and, with a generous rate of pay on offer, many came even from the cities of Greece to volunteer their services and were enrolled for the campaign. It was not long before a force had been raised of more than ten thousand foot and two thousand horse, not counting the Silver Shields and Eumenes' original companions.

62. The astonishingly rapid growth of Eumenes' power prompted Ptolemy to take a fleet to Zephyrium in Cilicia, from where he got a message to the commanders of the Silver Shields, urging them not to take orders from a man who had been unanimously condemned to death by the Macedonians.* [2] He also got in touch with the commanders of the garrisons at Cyinda,* adjuring them not to give any money to Eumenes and promising his protection. But no one paid any attention to him, because they had received orders in letters written by the kings, by Polyperchon, the custodian of the kings, and by Olympias, Alexander's mother, that they were to give Eumenes their full support, since he was the General Plenipotentiary of the kingdom.

[3] No one was more displeased at the time by Eumenes' prefer- ment and all the power that was accruing to him than Antigonus. He understood that, in Eumenes, Polyperchon was creating the strongest possible counterweight to himself, now that he was in rebellion against the monarchy. [4] He therefore decided to hatch a plot against Eumenes, and chose one of his Friends, Philotas, as his agent.* He gave Philotas a letter addressed to both the Silver Shields and the other Macedonian troops in Eumenes' army, and he sent along with him thirty other Macedonians as well, chosen for their enquiring minds and ready tongues. Their job was to meet in private with Antigenes and Teutamus, the commanders of the Silver Shields, and once they had gained their support by offering to enrich them and set them up in larger satrapies, they were to devise a plot against Eumenes with their help. If any of the Silver Shields were known to them or were fellow citizens, they were to meet with them as well, and bribe them to join the conspiracy against Eumenes' life.

[5] The only person they succeeded in winning over was Teutamus, the commander of the Silver Shields, who accepted the bribes that were offered him and undertook to try to recruit his fellow com- mander, Antigenes, for the conspiracy as well. [6] But Antigenes, a man of remarkable intelligence and unswerving loyalty, not only refused to be persuaded, but even got his colleague to change his mind, despite the fact that he had already accepted a bribe, by pointing out to him that he was better off with Eumenes alive than with Antigonus. [7] He argued that if Antigonus became more powerful, he would deprive them of their satrapies and install some of his friends instead, whereas Eumenes, as a non-Macedonian, would

never dare to work for his own ends; in his capacity as general, he would treat them as his friends, protect their satrapies for them as long as they cooperated with him, and possibly give them others as well. That, then, was how the plot against Eumenes' life failed.

63. However, once the commanders had taken delivery from Philotas of Antigonus' open letter, the Silver Shields and the other Macedonians held their own meeting, without Eumenes, and had the letter read out. [2] In it, Antigonus denounced Eumenes and invited the Macedonians to arrest him as a matter of urgency and put him to death. Otherwise, he said, he would come at full strength and make war on them, and anyone who failed to carry out his order would be appropriately punished. [3] After the letter had been read out, all the Macedonians, including the two commanders, found themselves on the horns of a vicious dilemma: they could either side with the kings and draw Antigonus' vengeful wrath, or obey Antigonus and be punished by Polyperchon and the kings.

[4] While the troops were in this state of uncertainty, Eumenes arrived. After reading the letter, he called on the Macedonians to comply with the kings' decrees and not to listen to a man who had chosen to rebel. [5] He brought up many arguments to support his case, and not only succeeded in averting the danger with which he was threatened, but also made the troops feel even more loyalty for him than before. [6] Once again, then, after finding himself unexpectedly in danger, Eumenes managed, against the odds, to strengthen his position. He told his men to get ready for departure and then set out for Phoenicia, since he planned to build up a substantial fleet by getting all the cities to send him ships.* The idea was that these additional ships from Phoenicia would give Polyperchon control of the sea, so that he would be able to take his Macedonians safely over to Asia to go on the offensive against Antigonus whenever he wanted.

So Eumenes was in Phoenicia improving his naval capacity. **64.** Meanwhile, when Nicanor, the captain of the Munychia garrison, heard that Cassander had left Macedon and gone to Antigonus, and that Polyperchon was expected to reach Attica before long with his forces, he asked the Athenians to stay loyal to Cassander.* [2] Not only did his request fall on deaf ears, however, but the Athenians were unanimous in holding that they should evict the garrison as soon as possible. So what Nicanor did was trick the Athenian people. First, by assuring them that he was going to act in their interests he persuaded them to wait a few days, and then he spent the few days of Athenian passivity sneaking troops into Munychia a few at a time under cover of darkness, until there was a large enough force there to maintain the guard and to resist any attempt to besiege the garrison.

[3] When the Athenians realized that Nicanor was up to no good, they sent an embassy to the kings and Polyperchon, asking them to send help, as they were obliged to by the terms of the resolution on Greek independence,* while they themselves held frequent meetings of the Assembly and debated how to handle the conflict with Nicanor. [4] Before the Athenians had reached a resolution, however, Nicanor, who had hired many mercenaries, surreptitiously led his men out of the fortress one night and seized the Piraeus walls and the harbour booms. Now, in addition to not recovering Munychia, the Athenians had lost Piraeus as well, and they were furious. [5] They formed a delegation of eminent men who were on good terms with Nicanor—Phocion, the son of Phocus, Conon, the son of Timotheus, and Clearchus, the son of Nausicles—and sent them off to him. They were to protest at what he had done and ask him to obey the edict and give them back their independence. [6] Nicanor, however, replied that they should take their petition to Cassander, because he owed his command of the garrison to Cassander and did not have the right to act independently.

65. Just then, however, a letter reached Nicanor from Olympias, in which she ordered him to return Munychia and Piraeus to the Athenians.* Now, Nicanor was hearing it said that the kings and Polyperchon were intending to bring Olympias back to Macedon,* give her the custody of the boy king, and restore the prestige and respect she had enjoyed while Alexander was alive, so out of fear he promised to go ahead with the restoration, but then he kept finding reasons for procrastination. [2] In the past, Olympias had been well liked in Athens, and now, thinking that the honours that had been decreed for her had worked to their advantage,† they relished the prospect of the trouble-free recovery of their independence with her help. [3] Nicanor's promises had still not come to anything, however, when Polyperchon's son Alexander arrived in Attica with an army. The Athenians supposed that he had come to return Munychia and Piraeus to them, but that was an illusion. His intention, on the contrary, was to take both for himself, since they would be valuable possessions in wartime.

[4] Some Athenians—they included Phocion—who had been on good terms with Antipater were worried that there might be legal grounds for punishing them, and they went to meet Alexander. They argued that it was in his best interests to seize the fortresses for himself, without turning them over to the Athenians, at least until Cassander had been defeated, and Alexander agreed. [5] He was encamped close to Piraeus, and he did not invite the Athenians to have a presence at his conferences with Nicanor, but met with him in private and negotiated with him in secret—which made it clear that he was not intending to deal fairly with the Athenians. [6] An Assembly was convened, at which the Athenian people deprived the incumbent officers of their posts and replaced them with boards made up of the most committed democrats. Those who had held office under the oligarchy were either condemned to death or punished with exile and the confiscation of their property. Among those condemned was Phocion, who, in Antipater's day, had been the most powerful man in Athens.

66. On being thrown out of the city, these men fled to Alexander, the son of Polyperchon, in the hope that, with his help, they would be able to secure safety for themselves. He made them welcome and gave them letters for his father, Polyperchon, to the effect that Phocion and his colleagues should be protected from harm, since they had looked after his interests and were still promising their full cooperation. [2] But the Athenian people also sent an embassy to Polyperchon, denouncing Phocion and the others, and demanding that he give them Munychia and along with it their independence. Polyperchon had been wanting to occupy Piraeus with a garrison, because the harbour could be very useful to him during the war. But he was embarrassed to go against what he had written in the resolution, and reckoned that the Greeks would judge him untrustworthy if he behaved unscrupulously towards the most distinguished of their cities, so he changed his mind. [3] After he had heard the embassies, he gave a favourable and sympathetic response to the representatives of the Athenian people, but he arrested Phocion and his colleagues and sent them to Athens in chains, leaving it up to the Athenian people to execute them or dismiss the charges against them, as they pleased.*

[4] An Assembly was held in Athens, with the trial of Phocion and the others on the agenda, and those who had been exiled during Antipater's regime and were the oligarchs' political opponents spoke

up in large numbers, accusing them of crimes that deserved the death penalty. [5] Their accusations rested entirely on the claim that after the Lamian War these men had been responsible for the enslavement of Athens, and for the dissolution of the democratic constitution and legal code. When the time came for the defendants to make their pleas and Phocion began to address his own case, the assembled people made enough noise with their heckling to derail the speech, which left the defendants with no recourse. [6] After the disturbance had died down, Phocion made another attempt to deliver his speech, but the crowd shouted him down and made it impossible for the accused man's voice to be heard. For there were a great many democrats who had been denied their rights as citizens and had now unexpectedly had those rights restored, and they were bitterly hostile towards those who had deprived Athens of its independence.

67. Phocion was overwhelmed; he was faced with a hopeless situation in which to fight for his life. Those who were near by could hear the justice of his case, but the noise generated by those who were disrupting the proceedings was so great that people who were further away could not hear a single word, and all they could do was see the gestures he was making—gestures that were becoming increasingly emphatic and wild because of the great danger he was in. [2] Eventually, seeing that there was no way to save himself, he called on the Athenians at the top of his voice to condemn him to death, but spare the others. But the mob's violent fury was implacable, and when some of Phocion's friends stepped up beside him to speak on his behalf, the people listened to their opening sentences, but it soon became clear that the speech they were trying to get through was a defence speech, and then they were driven off the podium by hostile jeers and howls. [3] In the end, the defendants were condemned unanimously by the people and were taken off to prison for execution.

They were accompanied on their way to prison by many men of the better sort, expressing grief and sorrow at their miserable fate. [4] A lot of people found it shocking that men whose standing in society and families were second to none, and who in their lifetimes had performed numerous services for the city, should be denied a hearing and a fair trial—and they were frightened too, by the insight that Fortune was fickle and that everyone was subject to her. [5] Many of the democrats, however, who were ferociously hostile to Phocion, were vicious in their denunciations and bitterly laid responsibility for

the city's misfortunes at his door. Although hatred is silent at times of
good fortune, it changes and erupts furiously instead at times of misfortune, and under the influence of rage it becomes truly savage. [6]
And when these men had brought their lives to an end with a draught
of hemlock, which was the traditional method of execution,* all of
their bodies were thrown out unburied beyond the borders of Attica.*
So perished Phocion and his colleagues, the victims of vilification.*

68. Cassander sailed into Piraeus with thirty-five warships and
four thousand men he had been given by Antigonus. The garrison
commander, Nicanor, let him in and transferred Piraeus and the
harbour booms over to him, while retaining the command of Munychia,
since he had enough of his own soldiers to guard the fortress. [2]
Polyperchon was in Phocis with the kings, but when he found out that
Cassander had arrived in Piraeus he marched into Attica and set up
camp near by. [3] He had twenty thousand Macedonian infantry
under his command, along with four thousand from his allies, and
then a thousand cavalry and sixty-five elephants. His plan was to subject Cassander to a siege, but he was short of food, and since the siege
was likely to be prolonged, he was forced to leave some of his army in
Attica under the command of his son Alexander—as much of it as
could be fed by the available supplies—while he took the larger
division into the Peloponnese. He wanted to coerce the Megalopolitans
into obedience to the kings, because they had sided with Cassander
and were governed by the oligarchy that had been established by
Antipater.

69. While Polyperchon was engaged with these operations,
Cassander sailed with his fleet over to Aegina, which submitted without resistance, and then to the island of Salamis, where the people had
come out against him. He pinned them inside the city and put them
under siege. Every day he assaulted the walls, and since he was short
of neither ordnance nor men, the Salaminians found themselves in
the direst of straits. [2] The city was extremely close to falling when
a large force of infantry and ships arrived from Polyperchon to attack
the besiegers. Cassander was frightened into breaking off the siege,
and he sailed back to Piraeus.*

[3] Polyperchon's intention was to settle Peloponnesian affairs to
his own advantage, and on his arrival he called on the cities to send
representatives for a meeting, at which he raised the question of their
entering into an alliance with him.* He also sent emissaries around

the cities, to convey his order that the political leaders who had been raised to power by Antipater during the time of oligarchy were to be put to death, and the right of self-government was to be returned to the people. [4] This order was widely obeyed, and massacres took place throughout the cities, although some men were sent into exile. It was the end of the road for Antipater's supporters, and the states, having recovered the democratic right of free speech, formed alliances with Polyperchon. The only city to remain attached to Cassander was Megalopolis, and Polyperchon decided to put it under siege.

70. When the Megalopolitans discovered what Polyperchon's intentions were, they voted to move their rural property into the city and, after counting up citizens, foreigners, and slaves, they found they had fifteen thousand men who were capable of military service. They lost no time in either enrolling these men in regiments, or assigning them to work crews, or having them tend to the city walls. [2] At any given moment, men were surrounding the city with a deep trench, fetching wood from the countryside with which to make a palisade, repairing damaged sections of wall, or occupied with the making of weapons and the construction of bolt-shooting catapults. Everyone was so determined, and the dangers they were facing were so great, that the entire city set to work. [3] For rumours were spreading about the size of the Royal Army and the number of elephants that were attached to it—elephants which were believed to possess such spirit and physical aggressiveness that they were unstoppable.

[4] It did not take long for them to be fully prepared. When Polyperchon arrived, at the head of his entire army, he halted near the city and made two camps, one for the Macedonians and one for the auxiliaries. He built wooden towers that would overtop the city walls and brought them up to the city at suitable points. He had placed all kinds of artillery pieces in them, as well as soldiers, and he set about clearing the battlements of the defenders who were stationed there. [5] Meanwhile, his sappers undermined the walls, and when they set fire to the support posts they brought down three of the largest towers and the same number of stretches of curtain wall.

Suddenly, there was a gaping breach in the wall, and the Macedonians shouted in triumph, while the Megalopolitans reacted with terror and dismay. [6] Then, as the Macedonians began to pour into the city through the breach, the Megalopolitans divided their forces, giving some of their men the job of resisting the enemy—and these men succeeded in putting up a strong fight, not least by taking advantage of the uneven surface of the breach—and setting the rest to block the inner part of the breach with a palisade and to work without a break, both day and night, at building another wall. [7] It did not take long for the work to be finished, not just because of the large workforce they had available, but also because they were well supplied with all the materials they needed, and so the Megalopolitans quickly redressed the setback they had suffered with the collapse of the wall. They were also making good use of their bolt-shooting catapults, as well as their slingers and archers, against the enemy soldiers on the wooden towers, many of whom were struck by missiles.

71. Many were falling dead or wounded on both sides, and as night closed in Polyperchon had the trumpets sound the recall and returned to camp. [2] The next day, he cleared the rubble from the area of the breach and made it passable for the elephants, whose great strength he proposed to use for the capture of the city. But the Megalopolitans gained a signal victory over Polyperchon, thanks to their commander, Damis. He had been in Asia with Alexander and knew what elephants were like and the uses to which they were put, [3] and by pitting his brain against the brawn of the animals, he neutralized their great strength. What he did was fix sharp spikes close together in a large number of sizeable boards, which were laid in shallow trenches with the points of the spikes concealed. He left a corridor into the city, formed of these devices, and he posted none of his troops in front of this corridor, but deployed a great many javelineers, archers, and catapults on either side of it.

[4] Polyperchon did† a thorough job of clearing the area where the walls had collapsed, but as he began to advance with his elephants in close formation through the breach, the outcome was far from what he had expected. Since there was no one straight ahead offering resistance to the elephants, the mahouts drove them on into the city, and the elephants charged forward and encountered the spike-studded boards. [5] With their feet wounded by the spikes—and their own weight drove the points deep—they were so impaired that they were unable to carry on and equally unable to turn back. At the same time, with missiles of all kinds coming at them from both sides, the mahouts were being killed, or at any rate were so weakened by their wounds that they were failing to fulfil their potential. [6] The creatures were in great pain as a result of the hail of missiles and the unfamiliar

wounds caused by the spikes, and they started to turn back into the ranks of their own friends, many of whom were trampled to death. In the end, the bravest and most formidable elephant fell, and the rest either had no effect at all or killed large numbers of men from their own side.

72. This success gave a great boost to the Megalopolitans' confidence, but Polyperchon regretted having undertaken the siege, and as he was unable to spend much time there, he left a division of his army to maintain the siege, while he turned his attention to more pressing matters.* [2] Cleitus, his admiral, he sent out at full strength to the Hellespont, where he was to patrol the region and make it impossible for the forces that were trying to cross from Asia to reach Europe. Cleitus was also to enlist the help of Arrhidaeus, who had taken refuge with his troops in Cius and was an enemy of Antigonus.*

[3] So Cleitus sailed to the Hellespont. He gained the allegiance of the cities on the Propontis and added Arrhidaeus' forces to his own, but then Nicanor arrived in the region, the commander of the Munychia garrison. He had been sent there by Cassander with the entire fleet, and he had also been given the use of Antigonus' ships, so that in all he had more than a hundred. [4] A battle was fought not far from Byzantium, and Cleitus won. He sank seventeen of the enemy ships and captured at least forty, along with their crews, while the rest fled for safety to the harbour of Chalcedon.

[5] After such a convincing victory, Cleitus imagined that the magnitude of the defeat would deter the enemy from fighting, but when Antigonus heard about the fleet's losses, to everyone's surprise he repaired the damage, by quick thinking and sound strategy. [6] What he did was arrange for the Byzantines to send him transport vessels under cover of darkness, which he used to ferry archers and slingers across to the other shore, along with an adequate number of other light-armed troops, and while it was still dark these men launched an attack on the enemy, who had disembarked from their ships and made camp on land. Cleitus' forces took fright, and before long the entire camp was a scene of panic and turmoil. They rushed for their ships, but that only created chaos because of the baggage and the large number of prisoners.

[7] Meanwhile, Antigonus had made ready his warships and put on board a large force of marines drawn from the bravest of his foot soldiers. He sent his fleet on its way, urging them to attack the enemy

with confidence, since victory was sure to be theirs. [8] Nicanor put to sea with these ships during the night, and at daybreak his men fell suddenly on the enemy, who were in utter disarray. They scattered them straight away, with their first attack. The enemy ships were either holed by Nicanor's rams, or had their oars broken, or were captured without a fight when they surrendered with their entire crews. In the end, Antigonus' men gained possession of every enemy ship, with the sole exception of the command ship. [9] Cleitus got ashore safely, abandoned his ship, and tried to make his way through to Macedon and safety, but he lost his life when he ran into some of Lysimachus' soldiers.*

73. The severity of the defeat Antigonus had inflicted on the enemy won him great glory, and he was widely recognized as a skilled and intelligent general. His aims now were to keep control of the sea and to place his supremacy in Asia beyond dispute. He therefore selected from the entire army twenty thousand light infantry and four thousand horse, and set out for Cilicia, with the intention of finishing off Eumenes before he could increase the size and strength of his forces.

[2] When Eumenes heard about Antigonus' move, he decided to try to regain Phoenicia for the kings, which had been illegally occupied by Ptolemy,* but he ran out of time, and he left Phoenicia with his army and marched through Coele Syria, with his plan now being to reach the so-called upper satrapies. [3] Near the Tigris river he was attacked one night by some of the natives and lost some men, and he was attacked again at the Euphrates river in Babylonia, by Seleucus.* A canal was breached and Eumenes came close to losing his entire army when his camp was totally inundated, but nevertheless, good general that he was, he managed to escape to a rise and saved himself and his men by returning the canal to its original course. [4] Following this narrow escape from Seleucus' clutches, Eumenes succeeded in reaching Persis with his army, which consisted of fifteen thousand foot and 3,300 horse. He let his men rest and recover from their efforts, and then he sent messengers to the satraps and governors of the upper satrapies, requesting men and money.

So much for the progress of events in Asia in this year. 74. In Europe, Polyperchon's failure at the siege of Megalopolis earned him a reputation for ineffectiveness, and most of the Greek cities forsook the kings and aligned themselves with Cassander. As for the Athenians, since the help of neither Polyperchon nor Olympias had enabled them to get rid of the garrison, one of their citizens, a highly regarded man, summoned up his courage and suggested that it might be a good idea to come to terms with Cassander. [2] This immediately provoked a stormy debate about the pros and cons of the proposal, but after they had carefully considered where their best interests lay, they unanimously decided to send an embassy to Cassander and to arrange the best settlement with him that they could.

[3] It took a number of meetings, but then a peace treaty was drawn up, according to which the Athenians would keep everything—their city, farmland, revenues, ships, and so on—as friends and allies of Cassander, but Munychia would remain for the time being in Cassander's control, until the war against the kings was over. Moreover, a regime was instituted based on a property qualification of at least ten mnas,* and the city was to be made the responsibility of a single individual, an Athenian citizen nominated by Cassander. The man Cassander chose was Demetrius of Phalerum, and under his regime political strife died down and his fellow citizens were treated well.

75. Some time later, Nicanor sailed into Piraeus with his fleet adorned with the enemy's stemposts, as trophies of victory. For a while, his success raised him high in Cassander's favour, but later, when Cassander saw how arrogant and presumptuous Nicanor had become—and when he realized that the Munychia garrison consisted of Nicanor's own men—he judged him an enemy and had him murdered. Cassander also campaigned in Macedon, where many of the inhabitants came over to his side. [2] Likewise, the general trend in the Greek cities was to ally themselves with Cassander.*† For Polyperchon was widely held to perform his duties as protector of the kingdom and his allies in an indolent and ill-considered manner, whereas Cassander treated everyone with clemency and went about everything he did energetically. As a result his rule was becoming increasingly popular.

[3] Since it was in the following year that Agathocles became the tyrant of Syracuse, I shall end the present book here, in accordance with my original intention.* I shall begin the next book with the tyranny of Agathocles and give an account of the events that merit inclusion in my work.

1. An old saying has come down to us to the effect that democracies are undone not by ordinary people, but by men who stand out for their exceptional qualities. This is why some cities mistrust the most powerful of their citizens and curtail their opportunities for distinction. [2] For men who hold power year after year, the enslavement of their country seems no more than a small step to take, and it is hard for them to abstain from autocracy when their eminence has led them to entertain hopes of rulership. [3] After all, it is perfectly natural for men with great ambitions and limitless desires to want more. It was for these reasons, therefore, that the Athenians sent the foremost of their citizens into exile, by including among their statutes the process called ostracism.* This was not intended to punish a man for past crimes; it was a way of denying men who had the power to disregard the laws the ability to wrong the city. [4] In fact, they used to treat as a kind of oracular utterance those verses of Solon's in which he predicted Peisistratus' tyranny and included the following couplet:*

> The city is being destroyed by great men, and the people,
> All unwitting, succumb to the slavery of tyranny.

[5] Nowhere was this impulse towards autocracy more prevalent than in Sicily before the Romans gained possession of the island.* The cities there, duped by demagoguery, even went so far as to raise the weak to positions of such power that they became the masters of those they had duped. [6] The clearest case of this was when Agathocles became tyrant of Syracuse. This is a man who started with very meagre resources, and yet became the agent of the direst misfortunes for not just Syracuse, but all Sicily and Libya as well. [7] As a poor man, and one of no standing in society, he worked as a potter,* but later he gained so much power, and became so dreadfully thirsty for blood, that he enslaved the largest and fairest island in the world,* possessed, albeit briefly, a large chunk of Libya* and parts of Italy, and filled the Sicilian cities with violence and slaughter. [8] None of his predecessors as tyrants did anything this terrible,* and none of them used to act with such cruelty towards their subjects either. For example, Agathocles used to punish private citizens by wiping out their entire

families, and his way of chastising cities was to slaughter every adult male. He would impose the punishment due to a few alleged wrong-doers on the general populace of a city, people who were entirely inno-cent; the entire populations of cities were condemned to death.

[9] But in fact Agathocles' tyranny is not the only subject of this book, and I shall therefore forgo preliminary remarks about it. Instead, I shall continue with my sequential account of events, sup-plying, as a preliminary, only some indication of the period of time that is appropriate for this book. [10] In the previous eighteen books, I have, to the best of my ability, written up the histories of the known parts of the world from the earliest times until the year before Agathocles became tyrant, which was the 866th after the fall of Troy.* In this book, I shall start with the start of his reign and end with the battle at the Himeras river between Agathocles and the Carthaginians, covering seven years.*

317/16

2. *In the year of the Archonship of Demogenes in Athens, the Romans appointed as their consuls Lucius Plautius and Manius Fulvius,* and Agathocles of Syracuse became tyrant of the city.*

It will help to make the particular events I shall be narrating more comprehensible if I first briefly recapitulate the career of this dynast. [2] After having been exiled from his native city, Carcinus of Rhegium settled in Therma in Sicily, a city which was subject to the Carthagin-ians. He took up with a native woman, but after she became pregnant he began to be troubled every night by bad dreams. [3] This made him worried about what kind of a child he had fathered, and he instructed some Carthaginians who were setting sail for Delphi as sacred ambassadors* to ask the god about the child that was expected. The Carthaginians diligently carried out their instructions, and the oracle replied that the child that was born would be the cause of catastrophe for the Carthaginians and all Sicily. [4] The information alarmed Carcinus, and he exposed the child in a public place and posted men to make sure it died.* But several days later the child was still alive, and the men who had been given the job of watching over it began to get careless. [5] That, then, was when the mother came at night and sneaked the baby away. She did not take him back to her own house, because she was afraid of her husband's reaction, but she left him with her brother, Heracleides, and named him Agathocles after her father.

[6] So the boy was brought up in Heracleides' house. He became far better looking and physically stronger than was normal for his age, and when he was seven years old,* Carcinus, who had been invited by Heracleides to join him for a sacrifice, saw Agathocles playing with some other children of his own age, and expressed astonishment at how handsome and strong he was. The mother remarked that the child who had been exposed would be the same age, if he had lived, and Carcinus told her that he regretted what he had done and the tears poured from his eyes. [7] At that point, realizing that her husband was disposed to accept and approve of what she had done, she told him the whole truth. He was delighted, and he took back his son, but out of fear of the Carthaginians he moved his household to Syracuse. Since he was not well off, he arranged for young Agathocles to learn pottery.

[8] At this juncture, Timoleon of Corinth, who had recently defeated the Carthaginians at the Crimisus river,* offered Syracusan citizenship to all and sundry, and Carcinus had his name entered on the citizenship rolls along with that of Agathocles. Carcinus lived only a short while longer before dying. [9] The mother erected a marble statue of her son in a temple precinct as a dedication,* and a swarm of bees settled on it and made a comb of wax on its haunches. The professional interpreters were consulted about this portent, and they unanimously declared that at the prime of his life he would become very eminent—as, of course, he did.

3. A man called Damas, who was accounted one of the notables of Syracuse, became Agathocles' lover, and in the early stages of their relationship it was thanks to him that Agathocles acquired a modest fortune, since he supplied all his needs with ample generosity. Then, some years later, Damas was appointed to the command of a war against Acragas, and when one of his chiliarchs died, he replaced him with Agathocles.* [2] Even before this campaign, Agathocles had been regarded with considerable awe because of the weight of his armour—he was accustomed to take part in military reviews wearing a suit of armour that was so heavy that everyone else found it too much of a burden—and after he had become chiliarch his fame increased by leaps and bounds, as someone who positively relished the dangers of battle and had a bold and fluent tongue when addressing

the troops. And when Damas fell ill and died, Agathocles married his wife, who had inherited Damas' entire estate, and so became accounted one of the wealthiest men in Syracuse.

[3] Some time later, the Bruttii had Croton under siege, and the Syracusans sent a strong force to help the Crotonians. One of the senior officers for this expedition was Antander, the brother of Agathocles, but the commanders-in-chief were Heracleides and Sosistratus*—scheming, murderous men, and perpetrators of horrors on a grand scale. I gave a thorough account of them in the previous book.* [4] Agathocles was serving as well, and since his calibre was recognized by the people, he had been given the rank of chiliarch. In the early stages of the campaign, he performed better than anyone else in fighting the barbarians, but even so he was denied the prize for valour by the envy of Sosistratus. [5] This hurt Agathocles badly, and in a speech to the popular assembly he accused Sosistratus of aspiring to tyranny. The Syracusans did not believe his allegations, but on his return from the Crotonian expedition Sosistratus and his friends did seize power in Syracuse.

4. Since Agathocles was not on good terms with Sosistratus, he and his supporters remained for a while in Italy. He tried to seize Croton, but was driven out of the city and escaped with a few friends to Tarentum. The Tarentines engaged him as a mercenary officer, but his involvement in a number of foolhardy enterprises led to his being suspected of plotting the overthrow of the government, [2] and he was discharged from their service as well. Next, he raised an army by collecting exiles from all over Italy, and went to help the people of Rhegium, who were under attack by Heracleides and Sosistratus. [3] Then, once the regime in Syracuse had been dissolved and Sosistratus and his friends were sent into exile,* Agathocles returned to the city.

Many eminent men were banished along with the leaders of the regime, on the grounds that they had been members of the oligarchy of the Six Hundred, which consisted of the foremost men in Syracuse, and war broke out between these exiles and the partisans of democracy. With the Carthaginians as allies of Sosistratus and the exiles, the fighting was relentless, and battle after battle took place between mighty armies. In the course of these battles Agathocles, whether or not he had been appointed to a command, gained a reputation as an effective and inventive tactician. Whatever the situation, he could always find some way of turning it to advantage.

One of these exploits of his is well worth recording. [4] It occurred at a time when the Syracusans were encamped near Gela. One night he slipped into the city with a thousand soldiers, but Sosistratus appeared with a large and disciplined force and forced them to flee, killing about three hundred in the process. [5] The remainder tried to escape, but found themselves in a confined space, where their annihilation seemed certain—but then, against the odds, Agathocles saved their lives. [6] No one had put up a more brilliant display of martial prowess than him; he had been wounded seven times and had lost so much blood that his strength was ebbing away. Nevertheless, with the enemy pressing hard, he ordered his trumpeters to go, some to the left and some to the right, and stand on the city walls and sound the signal for battle. [7] The order was promptly carried out, and because it was dark the Geloans who were attacking them were unable to see clearly and assumed that the rest of the Syracusan army had entered the city at these two points. They called off their pursuit, divided their forces in two, and raced off towards the sound of the trumpets to help defend their city. In the meantime, Agathocles and his men used the reprieve to return to their camp in complete safety. So that was how, on this occasion, Agathocles outwitted the enemy and, against the odds, saved the lives not only of his men, but of seven hundred auxiliaries as well.

5. Some time later,* when Acestoridas of Corinth had been elected General in Syracuse,* Agathocles was suspected of aspiring to tyranny, and he had to use his wits to escape with his life. Acestoridas was reluctant to do away with Agathocles openly, because he did not want to provoke civil unrest, so he ordered him to leave the city and sent men out at night to kill him on the road. [2] But Agathocles had guessed what Acestoridas was planning, and he selected from among his slaves the one who most closely resembled himself in height and general appearance. By giving this slave his own suit of armour, horse, and clothing, he tricked the men who had been sent to kill him. [3] As for himself, he dressed in rags and travelled across country. So the assassins, judging from the armour and other tokens that the slave was Agathocles, and prevented by the darkness from seeing clearly, did indeed commit murder—but they failed to carry out their mission.

[4] Next, the Syracusans took back the men who had been exiled along with Sosistratus and made peace with the Carthaginians. Agathocles, in exile, raised an army of his own in the interior. Once he

had made himself an object of fear not only to his fellow citizens, but to the Carthaginians as well,* he let himself be persuaded to return to Syracuse. He was taken to the sanctuary of Demeter by the Syracusans, where he swore that he would do nothing to harm the democracy. [5] By pretending to be a champion of democracy, and by practising various forms of demagoguery on the masses, he got himself elected General and guardian of the peace, until such time as there was genuine concord among the inhabitants of the city. [6] For the clubs formed by like-minded people were divided into many factions, and every one of them had major differences of opinion with the others. But the most serious opposition to Agathocles came from the Council of the Six Hundred (which had governed the city during the oligarchy), because its membership consisted of the most eminent and wealthy men in Syracuse.

6. Agathocles was hungry for power, and he was well equipped to achieve his aim. As General, he had command of the army, but in addition the news that some rebels were mustering at Erbita,* in the interior, made it possible for him to enlist soldiers of his own choosing without arousing suspicion. [2] So, on the pretext of a campaign against Erbita, he enrolled in the army, from Morgantina and other cities of the interior, men who had earlier served with him against the Carthaginians. [3] Every one of these men was utterly loyal to Agathocles, since, thanks to him, they had done very well for themselves in the course of their campaigns. Moreover, they had always been hostile to the Six Hundred, the former oligarchs,† and were fundamentally opposed to the democracy because they hated having to take orders from the Syracusan people. There were about three thousand of these men, and their principles and their politics made them perfect instruments for the dissolution of the democracy. Agathocles also added to their number by selecting from the citizen body men who were poor and envious enough to be opposed to the ascendancy of the men of means.

[4] When he had everything ready, he ordered his soldiers to assemble at daybreak at the Timoleontium,* while he invited Peisarchus and Diocles to a meeting. These two were regarded as the political leaders of the Six Hundred, and Agathocles pretended that he wanted to discuss with them some matters of common interest. As soon as they arrived, however, with about forty of their friends, Agathocles had them arrested, on the pretext that they were plotting his death.

He denounced them in an army assembly, claiming that the Six Hundred wanted to seize him because of his devotion to the common people, and deploring the way Fortune was treating him. [5] His men became incensed. They began to call on him to act immediately and summarily to punish those who had wronged him, and he ordered the trumpeters to sound the signal for battle. To his troops, his instructions were that they should kill the guilty and take for themselves the property of the Six Hundred and their sympathizers.

[6] So his men with one accord turned to plundering. The city descended into chaos and calamity stalked the streets, as members of the elite, unaware that they had been marked down for destruction, dashed out of their houses into the streets to find out what was causing the disturbance, and met death at the hands of Agathocles' men. These men had been whipped up into a frenzy by a combination of greed and anger, and they set about killing men who, in their ignorance, appeared before them wearing no protective armour.

7. One after another, the streets were closed off by soldiers, and the massacre began both out in the open and in the houses. Many were killed even though they were not among those who were accused of anything, but just because they asked the reason for the killing. An armed mob had been let loose, and they were not inclined to distinguish friend from foe—or, rather, they regarded as an enemy anyone who seemed likely to enrich them.

[2] Everywhere in the city, then, the scene before a spectator's eyes would have been one of violence, slaughter, and all kinds of criminal activity. There was no form of brutality that some of Agathocles' men, who had long-standing grievances, did not employ against their enemies, now that they had the power to arrange everything for the gratification of their anger. Others imagined that slaughtering the rich was the way to remedy their own poverty and went out of their way to kill them. [3] While some broke down the courtyard doors of houses* or used ladders to climb on to the roofs, others fought those who had taken to the rooftops to defend themselves. Even supplicating the gods afforded no protection to those who had taken refuge in the temple precincts;* reverence for gods was overruled by men. [4] At a time of peace and within the borders of their own country, Greeks dared to use violence on Greeks, kin on kin. Nothing made them hesitate—no natural feeling of kinship, no sworn truce, no fear of the gods. The atrocities they committed would have provoked pity for the

victims in anyone, even a confirmed enemy (assuming he was temperamentally not entirely given to excess), let alone a friend.

8. All the gates of the city were shut, and more than four thousand
people were slain in a single day, whose only crime was to have been
a cut above the others. Many turned to flight, but those who made for
the gates were seized. Some jumped down from the walls and escaped
to nearby cities, but others, too frightened to look before they leapt,
landed badly. [2] In all, more than six thousand people were driven
from the city. Most of them sought refuge in Acragas, where they
were cared for as they deserved. [3] Agathocles and his men spent the
day killing their fellow citizens, and so far from refraining from rap-
ing and violating women, they thought that defiling them in this way
would constitute a suitable punishment for those of their menfolk
who had escaped death. It was, after all, likely that the awareness that
their wives had been violated and their daughters dishonoured would
cause husbands and fathers more pain than death.

[4] I should keep my account free of the tragic effects that one commonly finds in the historians,* mainly out of respect for the victims,
but also because none of my readers needs to hear details he can easily
supply from his own understanding. [5] When men had no qualms, in
the hours of daylight, about slaughtering their innocent victims in the
streets and the agora, it hardly needs a writer to reveal what they got
up to at night when they were on their own inside houses, and how
they treated orphaned girls and women who had no one to help them
and had fallen under the absolute power of their bitterest enemies.*
[6] Two days later, then, by which time Agathocles was sated with
the blood of his fellow citizens, he assembled the prisoners. He let
Deinocrates live, in recognition of their former friendship, but the
others were either killed, if they were unremittingly hostile to him, or
sent into exile.

9. Next, he convened an assembly and gave a speech in which he
denounced the Six Hundred and the oligarchic regime that they had
earlier instituted. He claimed to have purged the city of men whose
intention was to rule and to have given the people back their freedom
in an untarnished form. Now that the struggle was over, he said, he
wanted to live as an ordinary citizen with the same status as everyone
else. [2] And with these words he tore off his military cloak, replaced
it with a civilian *himation*,* and made as though to leave, having
demonstrated that he was a man of the people. But in doing this he

was merely assuming a democratic mask. Besides, he was well aware that the majority of those attending the assembly were implicated in his crimes, and would therefore never willingly choose anyone else as General. [3] And indeed, the men who had looted the homes of their hapless victims began loudly to beg him not to abandon them, but to accept supreme command.

At first, Agathocles kept quiet, but when the crowd became more insistent he agreed to accept the Generalship, but only if he held the office alone, [4] because he refused to be held legally accountable, he said, as a member of a board, for the illegal actions of others. The mob had no objection to his becoming sole ruler, and he was elected General Plenipotentiary. From then on, there was no doubt that he was the ruler of the city and that its administration was in his hands. [5] As for those Syracusans who were untainted by his crimes, some were too frightened to do anything except put up with the situation, and others, finding their strength less than that of the mob, did not dare to show their hostility when it would do no good. Many of those who were poor and in debt, however, welcomed the change, because in the assembly Agathocles kept promising to abolish debts and give land to the poor.*

[6] Now that he had got what he wanted, Agathocles called a halt to the killings and the punishments, and became a completely different kind of person.* He treated the masses with courtesy and made himself highly popular by improving a lot of people's lives, by raising hopes of a better future in many others, and by never speaking harshly to everyone. [7] For all his great power, he did not behave like a typical tyrant: he did not adopt a diadem,* he did not surround himself with bodyguards, and he had no interest in making himself inaccessible. He managed the city's finances, supervised the preparation of weaponry and artillery, and increased the strength of his war fleet by having extra ships built. He also gained the submission of most of the villages and towns in the interior of the island. That was how things stood in Sicily.

10. In Italy, the Romans were at war with the Samnites, as they had been for eight years.* In previous years they had fielded substantial armies, but this year, although they invaded Samnite territory, they achieved nothing important or worth recording. Nevertheless, they carried on attacking strongholds and ravaging farmland. [2] They pillaged all of Daunia in Apulia as well, and gained the submission of

Canusium,* from where they took hostages. They also added two new tribes to the existing set, Falerna and Oufentina.*

[3] Meanwhile, the Crotonians made peace with the Bruttii, and elected two distinguished men, Paron and Menedemus, to take command of the war—now in its second year—against those of their citizens who had been exiled by the democracy because they had made common cause with Heracleides and Sosistratus. I gave the details in the previous book.* [4] The exiles recruited three hundred mercenaries, set out from Thurii, and tried to break into the city by night, but they were beaten back by the Crotonians and made camp on the borders between Croton and Bruttian territory. It was not long, however, before they were attacked by the Crotonian citizen militia, who greatly outnumbered them, and they were wiped out to a man in the battle.

Now that I have given an account of what was happening in Sicily and Italy, I shall move on to the rest of Europe. 11. In Macedon, Eurydice had become the effective head of state, and when she found out that Olympias was planning to return to Macedon,* she sent a courier to Cassander in the Peloponnese* with an urgent request for help, and set about making the most competent of the Macedonians personally loyal to herself by enticing them with gifts and promises of a brilliant future.

[2] Polyperchon, however, had the support of Aeacides of Epirus, and he raised an army and brought Olympias and Alexander's son back to Macedon. When he heard that Eurydice was in Evia (a Macedonian town)* with her army, he took to the field against her, intending to settle the business with a single battle. The two armies formed up opposite each other, but the Macedonians, respectful of Olympias' high rank and mindful of all the good Alexander had done them, deserted to Polyperchon's side. [3] King Philip was captured straight away along with his retinue, and Eurydice was arrested as she was making her way to Amphipolis with one of her advisers, a man called Polycles.

[4] So the king and queen fell into Olympias' hands and she gained the kingdom without a fight, but she made cruel use of her good fortune. The first thing she did was imprison both Eurydice and her husband Philip in particularly vile conditions: she walled them up in a tiny cell, leaving only a single narrow opening through which they were supplied with what they needed. [5] This abuse of the wretched prisoners went on for many days, but then the Macedonians began to

feel sorry for Olympias' victims and to think badly of her. She therefore arranged for Philip to be stabbed to death by some Thracians—he
had been king for six years and four months—but to her mind
Eurydice deserved a worse form of punishment, since she had been
making her views known and crying out that the kingdom belonged to
her rather than to Olympias. [6] She therefore sent her a sword,
a noose, and some hemlock, and told her to use one of them, whichever she wanted, to kill herself. The former rank of her victim gave
her not the slightest pause, nor was she moved to tears by the thought
that all human lives are subject to Fortune—[7] and that is why,
when it was her turn to fall, she died the kind of death that her savagery deserved. In fact, while the man who had brought the objects
was still there, Eurydice prayed that the same gifts might come
Olympias' way. She prepared her husband's body for burial, taking
care of the wounds as well as she could under the circumstances, and
then she hanged herself with her girdle. She shed no tears for her fate
as she brought her life to an end, nor was she crushed by the weight
of her misfortunes.*

[8] After killing Philip and Eurydice, Olympias did away with
Nicanor, the brother of Cassander, and destroyed the tomb of Iollas,
as a way, she said, of avenging Alexander's death.* From among
Cassander's friends, she selected a hundred Macedonians of great
distinction and slaughtered them all. [9] But glutting her anger with
atrocities such as these soon made the Macedonians hate her for her
savagery, and everyone remembered what Antipater had said. As
though he were foretelling the future at the point of death,* he had
warned them never to let a woman become the head of state. It was
clear, then, given the way in which Macedonian affairs had been handled, that change was due.

12. In Asia, Eumenes wintered in Babylonia, along with the
Macedonian Silver Shields and their commanding officer, Antigenes,
at the Carian Villages, as they are called. While he was there, he sent
embassies to Seleucus and Pithon, asking for their support in the
kings' cause—for them to join him in resisting Antigonus. [2] Pithon
had been given the satrapy of Media, and Seleucus Babylonia, at
the time of the second division of the satrapies at Triparadeisus.*
Seleucus, however, said that, although he was ready to serve the kings,
he would never agree to take orders from Eumenes, who had been
condemned to death by the Macedonians in assembly.* And having

formulated this policy, after thorough talks with his advisers, he sent an envoy off to Antigenes and the Silver Shields, calling on them to remove Eumenes from his command.

[3] The Macedonians ignored him, however, and after thanking them for their commitment to his cause, Eumenes marched off with his army and made camp by the Tigris river, three hundred stades from Babylon. His plan was to make his way to Susa, where he intended to send for the armies of the upper satrapies and draw on the royal treasury for his immediate expenses, [4] He had to cross over to the other side of the river, however, because the land to his rear had already been stripped by foraging, whereas the other side was untouched and had an ample supply of food for his men, [5] so he collected vessels from wherever he could find them. But then Seleucus and Pithon sailed down with two triremes and a large number of wherries,* the remainder of the boats that Alexander had built at Babylon.

13. After having come ashore at the landing, they renewed their attempt to persuade the Macedonians to remove Eumenes from his command, arguing that they should not prefer over themselves a man who was not a Macedonian and had indeed killed a great many Macedonians. [2] Antigenes was utterly unreceptive, however, and so Seleucus sailed off to an ancient canal, the opening of which had become blocked over the course of time, and breached it. The Macedonians' camp was surrounded by water, and since the whole area around them had become a lake, there was a good chance that the entire army might be wiped out by the flood.*

[3] They stayed where they were without doing anything for the rest of the day, since they had no idea what to do, but the next day they appropriated the wherries—there were about three hundred of them—and got most of the army across the river. No one tried to stop them at the landing, because Seleucus had no infantry, and his cavalry were well outnumbered by their opposite numbers. [4] Eumenes was worried about the baggage, however, and after dark he had the Macedonians cross back over the river. With one of the locals directing the operation, he set about clearing a tract through which it would be easy to divert the canal and thus drain the surrounding land. [5] When Seleucus realized what he was up to, he sent heralds to arrange a truce, since he could do nothing to prevent Eumenes crossing and wanted him out of his satrapy as soon as possible. But he also lost no

time in dispatching a courier to Antigonus in Mesopotamia, asking
him to bring his army as soon as he could, before the satraps arrived
with their armies.

[6] After crossing the Tigris and reaching Susiane, shortage of
provisions forced Eumenes to divide his army into three, and they
marched on in separate columns. There was no grain to be had at all,
but the land was rich in crops such as rice, sesame, and dates, and
Eumenes made sure that these were distributed to his men. [7] Even
earlier,* he had sent the leading men of the upper satrapies the kings'
letters, which directed them to obey him in everything, and now he
sent couriers, calling on them all to bring their armies and meet him
in Susiane. Coincidentally, however, they had already mustered and
united their forces for another purpose, which I must first explain.

14. Pithon had been made satrap of Media, but after he had become
General of the Upper Satrapies,* he killed Philotas, the incumbent
satrap of Parthyaea,* and replaced him with his own brother, Eudamus.
[2] At this, all the other satraps joined forces, since they were afraid of
the same kind of treatment, seeing that Pithon was restive and highly
ambitious. They defeated him in a battle, inflicting heavy casualties
on his men, and drove him out of Parthyaea. [3] At first, he withdrew to Media, but a short while later he went to Babylon, where he
asked for Seleucus' help and invited him to make common cause
with him. [4] That, then, was why the governors of the upper satrapies
had joined forces and Eumenes' couriers found their armies ready
and waiting.

The most distinguished of the leading men and the one who had
officially been chosen as commander-in-chief was Peucestas. He had
been one of Alexander's Bodyguards, a promotion awarded him by the
king for his courage.* [5] He had been satrap of Persis for a number
of years and was well liked by the natives. We are told, in fact, that this
is why he was the only Macedonian whom Alexander allowed to dress
in the Persian style—because Alexander wanted the Persians to be
content and thought he could use Peucestas to keep them utterly submissive. At the time in question, Peucestas had under his command
ten thousand Persian archers and slingers, three thousand men of
diverse origins armed in the Macedonian manner, six hundred Greek
and Thracian cavalry, and more than four hundred Persian cavalry.
[6] Polemon, the Macedonian who had been appointed the satrap of
Carmania,* had 1,500 foot and seven hundred horse. Sibyrtius, the

satrap of Arachosia, supplied a thousand foot and 610 horse, and
Androbazus had been sent from Paropanisadae, Oxyartes' satrapy,
with 1,200 foot and four hundred horse. [7] Stasander, the satrap of
Areia and Drangiane, had been joined by the Bactrian contingent and
had 1,500 foot and a thousand horse. [8] And Eudamus came from
India* with five hundred horse, three hundred foot, and 120 elephants.
He had gained these elephants after Alexander's death by assassinating
King Porus. In all, then, the forces mustered by the satraps consisted
of more than 18,700 foot and 4,600 horse.

15. When they reached Eumenes in Susiane, they convened a general assembly, in the course of which a fierce contest arose over who
should be commander-in-chief. [2] Peucestas thought that he should
have supreme command, not just because of the number of troops he
was supplying, but also because of his seniority under Alexander.
Antigenes, however, the general of the Macedonian Silver Shields,
argued that the right to choose the commander should be granted to
his Macedonians, since they had conquered Asia with Alexander and
their calibre was such that they had never been beaten.

[3] Eumenes was afraid that if the commanders fell out with one
another they would become easy prey for Antigonus, and his advice
was that they should not choose a single leader, but that all the satraps
and generals who had already been chosen by the army should meet
every day in the royal tent and arrive at policy decisions by consensus.
[4] His practice was to set up† a tent for the dead Alexander, with
a throne in it,* at which the generals were accustomed to sacrifice and
by which they met to discuss business that required their attention.
Everyone indicated his approval of the suggestion as being in their
best interests, and so every day Eumenes convened a council similar
to that of a democratic city.

[5] Susa was their next destination. In their letters, the kings had
made it clear that Eumenes was to be given as much money as he
wanted, and the guardians of the treasury released enough for him to
meet his commitments. He paid the Macedonians for six months and
gave Eudamus, the man who had brought the elephants from India,
two hundred talents. He claimed that the money was for the upkeep
of the animals, but in fact this gift was a way of currying favour with
the man, because, since it was the elephants' job to strike terror, if
Eudamus attached himself to one of the rival commanders, he would
tip the scales decisively in that man's favour. Each of the other satraps

was responsible for the maintenance of the men he had brought from
his country.

[6] So Eumenes was in Susiane, resting his troops. Antigonus,
meanwhile, had wintered in Mesopotamia, and his original plan was
to harry Eumenes before he became too strong. But when he heard
that the Macedonians had been joined by the satraps and their armies,
he checked his haste and let his men rest instead, while he recruited
additional soldiers. It was clear to him that a large army and an
unusual degree of forward planning were needed for this war.

16. Meanwhile, the generals who had been captured along with
Alcetas' army—Attalus, Polemon, Docimus, Antipater, and Philotas*—
were being held in an especially secure fortress. The news that Antigonus
was on his way to the upper satrapies, however, seemed to present them
with a favourable opportunity, and they persuaded some of their keep-
ers to release them. Then, in the middle of the night, they set upon
their guards. They were only eight and the guard consisted of four
hundred men, but campaigning with Alexander had honed their courage and skill. They seized Xenopeithes, the captain of the garrison,
and threw him from the wall where the cliff was six hundred feet high.
The rest they either killed or drove out of the fortress, and then they
set fire to the buildings. [2] They were joined by about fifty men, who
were waiting outside.

Since there was no shortage of grain and other supplies in the
fortress, they debated whether they should stay and take advantage of
the strength of the place while waiting for help to arrive from Eumenes,
or escape as soon as possible and range around the countryside until
the situation changed. [3] The discussion became quite heated, with
Docimus arguing for departure and Attalus claiming to be in such
poor health as a result of his time in prison that he would be unable to
endure any hardship. But before they had settled their differences,
soldiers from the nearby hill-forts formed themselves into a force of
more than five hundred infantry and four hundred cavalry, and they
were joined by some of the local inhabitants from various places, who
numbered more than three thousand. These men selected a general
from their own ranks and put the fortress under siege.

[4] Suddenly they were trapped inside again. Docimus, however,
noticed that one of the ways down from the fortress had been left
unguarded, and he sent a message to Stratonice, Antigonus' wife, who
was in the region. With her help, he and one other man escaped from

the fortress, but he was considered untrustworthy and was handed over to her bodyguard.* The man who escaped with him, meanwhile, acted as a guide for the enemy; he led a sizeable force up to the fortress, and they occupied the top of one of the cliffs. [5] However, even though Attalus and his men were easily outnumbered, their prowess enabled them to put up a stiff resistance and keep fighting day after day. In fact, it was only after they had been under siege for a year and four months that they were overwhelmed and captured.

17. *In the year of the Archonship of Democleides in Athens, the Romans appointed as their consuls Gaius Junius and Quintus Aemilius, and the 116th Olympic festival took place, with Deinomenes* of Laconia the victor in the stade race. In the course of this year:*

[2] Antigonus left Mesopotamia and went to Babylonia, where he came to an agreement with Seleucus and Pithon for common action. Once he had received extra troops from them, he built a pontoon bridge across the Tigris, crossed his forces over, and set out against the enemy.* [3] When Eumenes heard the news, he ordered Xenophilus, who was responsible for the security of the Susa acropolis,* not to give Antigonus any money and not to parley with him either, and then he and his men set out for the Tigris.* The point where the river flows out of the mountains (which are inhabited by the Uxians, an independent people) is a day's journey from Susa; the river is often three or even four stades wide, and in the middle of the stream its depth is about the height of an elephant. After the mountains, it flows for seven hundred stades and issues into the Red Sea;* there are plenty of saltwater fish in the river, and sea monsters as well, which are found especially at the time of the rising of the Dog Star.*

[4] With this river as his forward defence, Eumenes posted pickets all the way down the bank from its sources to the sea, and awaited the approach of the enemy. Guarding the river like this required a great many soldiers because of the distance involved, and so Eumenes and Antigenes asked Peucestas to send ten thousand bowmen from Persis. [5] At first, he failed to comply with their request, because he resented the fact that he had not obtained the supreme command, but later, after he had thought things through, he appreciated that the result,

for him, of a victory for Antigonus would be the loss of his satrapy and possibly his life. [6] Out of self-interested concern, then, and because he thought that he was more likely to gain the supreme command if he had as many soldiers as possible, he brought up ten thousand bowmen, as requested.

Some Persians lived thirty days' journey away, but even they received their orders on the very day they were sent out, because of their ingenious system of lookouts, which deserves a mention. [7] Persis is corrugated with many valleys, and there are a great many lofty observation points, one after another, on which the men with the loudest voices are posted. Since the places are separated by the distance a human voice can carry, those who received the order passed it on in the same way to others, who did the same again, until the message reached the limits of the satrapy.

18. While Eumenes and Peucestas were taking these measures, Antigonus continued to advance with his army and reached Susa, the royal capital. He appointed Seleucus satrap of the country, supplied him with troops, and ordered him to besiege the citadel, since Xenophilus, the treasurer, was refusing to obey his orders. Then he led his army off towards the enemy, along a road that was exposed to the blazing sun and was highly dangerous for foreign armies to take. Antigonus was forced to march by night and make camp by the river before sunrise. [2] Even so, he was unable to remain altogether unaffected by the hazards of the land, and despite his best efforts he lost many men to the extreme heat; it was, after all, the time of the rising of the Dog Star.

[3] When Antigonus reached the Coprates, he set about preparing to cross. The Coprates emerges from a mountainous region and joins the Pasitigris at a point which is eighty stades away from where Eumenes was encamped. The river is only about four plethra wide, but its current is swift, and boats or a bridge are needed to cross it. [4] Antigonus got hold of a few wherries and sent some of his men across in them, with the job of digging a trench and throwing up a palisade to accommodate the rest of the army.

However, when Eumenes heard from his scouts of Antigonus' intentions, he marched across the Tigris bridge with four thousand foot and 1,300 horse, and fell on those of Antigonus' men who had crossed the Coprates—more than three thousand foot and four hundred horse, and at least six thousand of the men who usually crossed in small groups to forage for food.* [5] Eumenes launched a surprise attack before they had a chance to form up, and most of them turned to flight straight away, but the Macedonians resisted, until Eumenes overwhelmed them with his superior power and numbers and forced them all to beat a hasty retreat to the river. [6] There was a general rush for the boats, but the number of men on board made them sink, while most of those who dared to try to swim across were carried away by the current and killed, although a few saved themselves in this way. [7] About four thousand non-swimmers chose captivity over drowning and were taken prisoner. Antigonus could see the scale of the losses he was incurring, but he lacked the boats to send help.

19. Since it seemed that there was no way he could get across the river, Antigonus left and made for the city of Badace, which lies on the river Eulaeus.* His route was open to the sun and the heat was so intense that losses were heavy and the army's morale plummeted. [2] Nevertheless, after staying in Badace for a few days and letting his men recover from the ordeal they had been through, he decided that his best bet was to go to Ecbatana in Media, and to use that as a base from which to gain control of the upper satrapies.

There were two ways into Media, neither of them altogether straightforward. The road to Calon† was good, and was part of the Royal Road system,* but it was blazingly hot, and it was also long, since it took up to forty days to complete the journey. The road that went via Cossaean territory, on the other hand, was rough, narrow, and precipitous, and it also involved travelling through hostile territory where little was to be found in the way of supplies, but it was short and cool. [3] It was not easy for an army to take this route without having gained the consent of the barbarians who inhabit the mountains. They have been independent since ancient times,* and they live in caves on a diet of acorns, mushrooms, and the smoked flesh of wild animals.

[4] Antigonus considered it weak to gain the Cossaeans' consent by diplomacy or bribery when he led such a strong army. He selected the best of the peltasts and divided them into two, with each division supported by archers, slingers, and other light infantry. He gave the command of one division to Nearchus, and ordered him to go on ahead and occupy the valleys and the hills, while he stationed the men of the other division all along the route. Then he advanced with the heavy infantry, and gave Pithon the command of the rear.

[5] The men who had been sent on ahead with Nearchus managed to seize a few peaks, but they found most of them, including the particularly important ones, already in enemy hands. They incurred heavy losses and barely made it through against the barbarians' assaults. [6] As for Antigonus and his men, whenever they came to rough terrain they found themselves in desperate danger. The natives, who were on familiar ground, occupied the heights and set about rolling huge boulders, one after another, down on to his column, and they were also pouring arrows into the ranks of men who were unable to defend themselves or get out of the way of the missiles because of the ruggedness of the terrain. [7] The road was so precipitous and difficult to negotiate that the elephants, the cavalry, and even the heavy infantry found themselves both at risk and suffering from the fact that there was nothing they could do to help themselves. [8] In these dire straits, Antigonus regretted that he had not listened to Pithon when he recommended purchasing the right of passage. Nevertheless, after losing a lot of men and facing the prospect of annihilation, he eventually made it through, eight days later, to the civilized part of Media.

20. But the constant adversity and the extraordinary degree to which they had suffered turned the army against Antigonus, and they held him responsible for the three great setbacks with which they had been afflicted within the space of forty days.

Nevertheless, by treating the soldiers tactfully and making sure they had plenty of everything they needed, Antigonus managed to raise their spirits. [2] He dispatched Pithon to travel throughout Media and collect as many horsemen and war-horses as he could, and also large numbers of draught animals. [3] There is never any shortage of four-footed creatures in Media, so it was not difficult for Pithon to fulfil his mission, and he arrived back with two thousand horsemen, more than a thousand horses with their tack, and enough draught animals to furnish the whole army. He also brought five hundred talents from the royal treasury. Antigonus assigned the horsemen to regiments, gave the horses to men who had lost theirs, and restored himself to the army's favour by distributing all the draught animals as gifts.

21. The news that the enemy was encamped in Media caused a dispute to arise among the satraps and generals in Eumenes' camp. Eumenes, Antigenes (the commander of the Silver Shields), and all

those who had come up from the coast held that they should go back there again, but those who had come down from the upper satrapies argued, out of concern for their territories, that they should stand by the inland provinces.* [2] The argument became increasingly heated, and since it was clear to Eumenes that, if the army split up, neither division would be able on its own to stand up to the enemy, he deferred to the wishes of the satraps who had come down from the upper satrapies. They therefore left the Pasitigris and went on to Persepolis, the royal capital of Persis, a journey of twenty-four days.

For the first stages of the journey, up to the so-called Ladder,* the road was sunken, it was stiflingly hot, and provisions were scarce, but the rest took place over high ground, with a wonderfully healthful atmosphere and plenty of fruits in season. [3] There were shady glens one after another, and parks with their varied stands, as well as naturally growing coppices of all kinds of trees, and streams of water, so that travellers thoroughly enjoyed the time they spent in places that were made to refresh them in the most delightful way. There was also a great deal of livestock of various kinds, and Peucestas arranged for the creatures to be delivered by the local inhabitants and distributed them in ample quantities to the troops, in order to win their allegiance. [4] The inhabitants of that land are the most warlike of the Persians, all of them being archers and slingers, and it is far more densely populated than the other satrapies.

22. When they reached Persepolis, the royal capital, Peucestas, the satrap of the province, performed a magnificent sacrifice to the gods, to Alexander, and to Philip. From almost the entirety of Persis he sent for sacrificial victims and ample quantities of everything else that was needed for festive merry-making, and he treated the army to a banquet. [2] He filled four concentric circles* with the couching† for the celebrants. The outer circle, with a circumference of ten stades, was occupied by the mercenaries and auxiliaries. The second circle, with a circumference of eight stades, contained the Macedonian Silver Shields and those members of the Companion Cavalry who had fought with Alexander. The circumference of the next circle was four stades, and the space was filled with reclining officers of the second rank, Friends, senior officers who had not been assigned posts, and the cavalry. The final circle had a circumference of two stades and the couches were occupied by the generals, the cavalry commanders, and the highest-ranking Persians. [3] In the middle of the circles were the

altars for the gods, Alexander, and Philip. The couches were made
from foliage and covered with tapestries and carpets of every description, since Persis has a bountiful supply of everything that contributes towards gracious and easy living. And the gaps between the
concentric circles were large enough to ensure that the banqueters
were not inconvenienced at all and that all the fare was ready to hand.

23. Everyone was being looked after to perfection and the assembled
crowd applauded Peucestas' zeal. It was clear that his popularity was
increasing by leaps and bounds. Eumenes could see this too, and in his
opinion it was because Peucestas wanted supreme command that he
was behaving in this public-spirited way towards the masses. So
Eumenes forged a letter, which he used not just to inspire his men with
confidence for the coming battle, but also to reduce Peucestas' authority and prestige by improving his own standing and making the rank-
and-file soldiers believe that he had great prospects. [2] The gist of the
letter was that Olympias had taken over responsibility for Alexander's
son; that Cassander had been killed and Olympias had also resumed
control of the kingdom of Macedon; and that Polyperchon had entered
Asia to deal with Antigonus, accompanied by the best regiments of
the Royal Army and the elephants, and was already drawing near
Cappadocia.* [3] The letter, written in Syrian,* allegedly came from
Orontes,* who was the satrap of Armenia and a friend of Peucestas. The
friendship between these two satraps afforded the letter credibility, and
Eumenes ordered it to be taken around and shown not just to the commanders, but also to the troops, most of whom got to see it.

The entire army had a change of heart, and everyone's thoughts
turned to Eumenes and his prospects, because they supposed that,
thanks to the support of the kings, he would also be able to advance
anyone he wanted and punish anyone who got on the wrong side of
him. [4] Wanting to intimidate those who were refusing to take orders
from him or had their sights set on the generalship, after the banquet
Eumenes brought charges against Sibyrtius, who was the satrap of
Arachosia and a close friend of Peucestas. Without Sibyrtius' knowledge, he sent some horsemen into Arachosia with orders to seize his
baggage, and made things so hazardous for him that, if he had not managed to slip away out of the camp, he would have been condemned to
death by the army assembly.*

24. Having cowed the others by this attack on Sibyrtius, and with
his authority and prestige greatly enhanced, Eumenes changed tack

and won Peucestas' loyalty and his commitment to fight for the kings by treating him tactfully and promising him a splendid future. [2] As a hedge against betrayal by the other satraps and generals, he decided to take hostages from them, so to speak: he made out that he was short of money and asked each of them to lend the kings as much as he could spare. [3] From the leading men for whom this tactic seemed to him to be useful he received four hundred talents, and so men whom he had previously suspected of plotting against him or of intending to desert him became the most trustworthy protectors of his person and resolute fighters for his cause.

[4] While Eumenes was securing his future by outwitting these men like this, messengers arrived from Media with the news that Antigonus had broken camp and was on his way to Persis with his army. In response, Eumenes broke camp as well, since he had decided to meet the enemy and risk a decisive battle. [5] On the second day of the journey, however, he sacrificed to the gods and treated his men to a sumptuous feast. This may have made him popular with the troops, but in the course of the symposium he let himself be prevailed upon by those of the guests who were determined drinkers, and he fell ill. The march was delayed for several days, therefore, while he was incapacitated by his sickness. Morale in the ranks fell, because the enemy was expected to make contact with them before long and the most competent of their generals was laid low by illness. [6] Nevertheless, once the critical phase of the illness was past and he had somewhat recovered, he had the army advance under the leadership of Peucestas and Antigenes, while he was carried in a litter behind the rearguard, so that he would not be troubled by the noise and the crush.

25. When the armies were a day's march away from each other, both sides sent out scouts, and once they had learnt the enemy's numbers and intentions, they got ready for battle—but then they stood down without a fight. [2] What happened was that both armies formed up with a river and a gully in front of them as their forward defence, and the awkwardness of the terrain made it impossible for them to join battle. For four days, the armies, which were encamped at a distance of three stades from each other, spent the time skirmishing and foraging for food in the countryside, since all their supplies were low, but on the fifth day Antigonus sent a delegation to the satraps and the Macedonians, asking them to repudiate Eumenes and give their loyalty to him instead. [3] He guaranteed that the satraps would be

allowed to keep their satrapies, and promised that everyone else would
either receive a substantial amount of land or be sent back home laden
with rewards and gifts, while those who chose to serve with him would
be assigned to the appropriate units of his army.

[4] Not only did the Macedonians refuse to comply with Antigonus'
request, however, but they even threatened the lives of his emissaries.
Eumenes came and thanked them, and told them a story—a traditional
tale passed down from ancient times, but not inappropriate for the
occasion. [5] In this fable a lion fell in love with a human girl and
spoke to her father about marriage. The father said that he would gladly
betroth his daughter to the lion, but that its claws and teeth had him
worried. Suppose that, after the marriage, he lost his temper for some
reason and treated his daughter with the ferocity of a wild beast. [6]
The lion pulled out its claws and teeth, and when the father saw that
it had lost everything that made it fearsome, he had no difficulty in
beating it to death with a club. Eumenes said that Antigonus was
doing much the same kind of thing—[7] that he would honour his
promises until he had made the army his, and at that point would
punish its leaders. The army was still applauding in agreement when
he dismissed the assembly.

26. That night, however, some men arrived, deserters from Antigonus' army, with the news that Antigonus had ordered his men to break
camp at the second watch. After thinking it over, Eumenes correctly
concluded that the enemy were going to withdraw to Gabene,* [2]
which was three days' march away, because its fields were unravaged
and had plenty of grain and fodder, and in general because it was
capable of supplying, more than adequately, the needs of large armies.
[3] Moreover, these advantages were enhanced by the very geography
of the place, with its rivers and steep-sided ravines.

Eumenes wanted to get there before the enemy, and he replicated
Antigonus' plan. He paid some of his mercenaries and sent them off
as though they were deserters, having instructed them to say that he
had decided to attack Antigonus' camp that night.* Meanwhile, he
sent the baggage on ahead and ordered his men to take as little time as
possible over their evening meal and then to break camp. [4] All his
orders were promptly carried out. When Antigonus heard from the
'deserters' that the enemy had decided to attack that night, he cancelled his departure and disposed his forces for the coming battle. [5]
What with the confusion entailed by this, and his worrying about the

future, he failed to notice that Eumenes had stolen a march on him and was making his way at speed towards Gabene.

Antigonus kept his men under arms for a while, until he found out from his scouts that the enemy had left and realized that he had been outmanoeuvred. He still kept to his original plan, however. [6] He ordered his troops to break camp and advanced at a rapid pace—almost as fast as a pursuit. But Eumenes had a start of two watches, and Antigonus knew that it would be hard for his whole army to catch up with a force that was so far ahead, and so he came up with the following plan. [7] He consigned the rest of the army to Pithon and ordered him to follow without undue haste, while he himself took the cavalry and rode hard after the enemy. By the time day was dawning, he had made contact with Eumenes' rearguard as they were on their way down a line of ridges, and he took up a position on the ridges, where he could be seen by the enemy. [8] Eumenes was quite a way distant, but he could see the enemy cavalry, and since he supposed that the whole army was not far behind, he halted his troops and deployed them for the battle that he imagined was imminent.

[9] So the generals of both armies outwitted each other in this way. It was as though they were engaged in a preliminary contest of intelligence and were making it clear that, if victory came their way, it would be entirely their doing. [10] Be that as it may, this ploy of Antigonus' enabled him to halt the enemy's progress and bought him time for the rest of his army to catch up. When they arrived, he drew the entire army up for battle and marched his formidable forces down against the enemy. 27. Including the additional troops supplied by Pithon and Seleucus, he had in all more than 28,000 foot, 8,500 horse, and sixty-five elephants.*

The two generals deployed their troops differently, competing with each other to see which of them was the best tactician as well. [2] On his left wing, in contact with the rising ground of the foothills, Eumenes posted Eudamus, the man who had brought the elephants from India, with his personal guard of 150 heavy cavalry. Eudamus' front was protected by two elite units of mounted lancers, each consisting of fifty men.† [3] Next, he posted the satrap Stasander, with 950 of his own cavalry, [4] and then Amphimachus, the satrap of Mesopotamia, who had six hundred cavalry under his command. Their neighbours were the six hundred horsemen from Arachosia who had formerly been led by Sibyrtius, but were now under the command of Cephalon, since Sibyrtius' flight. [5] Next came five hundred horse from Paropanisadae and the same number of Thracians drawn from the military settlements of the upper satrapies.* On the flank of the whole wing, he stationed forty-five elephants slantwise, with a good number of archers and slingers in the spaces between the elephants.

[6] Once he had made these dispositions for securing the left wing, he arrayed the heavy infantry alongside it. The far left of the infantry phalanx was occupied by the mercenaries, of whom there were more than six thousand, and next to them came about five thousand infantrymen armed in the Macedonian manner, though they were of different races. 28. Next came the Macedonian Silver Shields, who numbered more than three thousand; they had never been beaten, and their prowess struck terror into every enemy they faced. Finally, there were more than three thousand Hypaspists, who, along with the Silver Shields, were commanded by Antigenes and Teutamus. [2] In front of the entire phalanx, Eumenes posted forty elephants, and filled the gaps between them with light infantry units.

[3] Next, he arranged his cavalry on the right wing. Immediately next to the phalanx were the Carmanians, led by Tlepolemus, their satrap. Then came the regiment known as the Companion Cavalry, nine hundred strong, and then the personal guard of Peucestas and Antigenes, which consisted of three hundred heavy cavalry amalgamated into a single unit. The far right of the wing was occupied by Eumenes' personal guard, also three hundred in number, with his front protected by two squadrons of his Pages, each consisting of fifty horsemen; and beyond the wing, guarding its flank, were two hundred cavalry in a slanting formation, divided into four squadrons.* [4] In addition, he stationed three hundred horsemen, selected from all the cavalry regiments for their speed and strength, behind his personal guard. Along the front of the whole wing he posted forty elephants. In all, Eumenes' army consisted of 35,000 foot, 6,100 horse, and 114 elephants.*

29. Looking down from a high place, Antigonus could see the enemy formation, and he made his own dispositions accordingly. Seeing that the enemy's right wing had been strengthened by the elephants and the best of the cavalry, he stationed his lightest cavalry opposite them. They were to adopt an open order, avoid direct engagement, and wheel in and away from their opponents in order to

neutralize this division of the enemy army, which was the one on which Eumenes was chiefly relying. [2] On this wing,† therefore, Antigonus posted the thousand horse-archers and lancers from Media and Parthyaea, who were perfect for a contest involving such harrying. Next to them, he placed the 2,200 Tarentines who had come up with him from the coast; they had been selected for their skill at catching an enemy unawares, and were staunchly loyal to him.* Then there were a thousand cavalry from Phrygia and Lydia, 1,500 of Pithon's cavalry, the four hundred lancers under Lysanias, and finally the cavalry known as the 'two-horsers'* and eight hundred Thracians from the military colonies of the upper satrapies. [3] These were the horsemen that made up Antigonus' left wing, with Pithon in overall command.

As for the infantry, immediately next to the left wing were posted the mercenaries, of whom there were more than nine thousand, then three thousand Lycians and Pamphylians, then at least eight thousand men of different races armed in the Macedonian manner, and finally almost eight thousand Macedonians, who had been given to Antigonus by Antipater when he had been made custodian of the kingdom.*

[4] The first of the cavalry on the right wing, adjacent to the heavy infantry, were five hundred mercenaries of different races, then a thousand Thracians, five hundred auxiliaries, and next to them the thousand-strong regiment known as the Companion Cavalry. These men were under the command of Demetrius, the son of Antigonus, who was now about to fight alongside his father for the first time.* [5] At the outer end of the wing was the personal guard of three hundred cavalry, with whom Antigonus himself would fight. They were protected by three squadrons of Antigonus' Pages, again numbering three hundred, who were posted alongside them† and were reinforced by a hundred Tarentines. [6] Slantwise, covering† the whole wing, Antigonus posted his thirty best elephants, and he filled the gaps between the elephants with selected light-armed units. The other elephants were mostly stationed in front of the heavy infantry, but there were also a few with the cavalry on the left wing.

[7] When he had formed his troops up in this order, Antigonus marched down against the enemy. He adopted an oblique front, in the sense that he pushed forward the right wing, on which he was chiefly relying, and held back the other, since he had decided that the one

wing was to avoid battle while the other was to bear the brunt of the fighting.

30. When the armies were close to each other and the standard had been raised on both sides, the troops shouted out their battle-cries, first one side and then the other, several times each, and the trumpets sounded the signal for battle. Pithon's cavalry units initiated the action. They were in open formation and their front was more or less unprotected, but they outnumbered their opponents and were more mobile, and they tried to make use of these advantages. [2] They judged it too hazardous to make a frontal attack on the elephants, but by riding around the enemy wing and taking it in the flank they began to wound the creatures with dense volleys of javelins and arrows. Thanks to their mobility they remained completely unscathed, but they injured the elephants a great deal, which were too heavy to give chase and could not retreat either when the occasion demanded it. [3] Seeing that his right wing was finding it hard to cope with the large number of horse-archers, Eumenes called up his lightest cavalry from Eudamus on the left wing [4] and led the entire unit out in column. He fell on the enemy with his light infantry and his lightest cavalry, and with the elephants backing him up he easily routed Pithon's cavalry and pursued them as far as the foothills.

[5] Meanwhile, the infantry phalanxes had also been engaged for some time, but in the end, after heavy losses on both sides, Eumenes' men won. They owed their success to the valour of the Macedonian Silver Shields. [6] Even though they were quite elderly,* the number of battles they had fought had honed their courage and their skills to an exceptional degree, until their sheer power overwhelmed everyone who confronted them. Hence, although at the time there were only three thousand of them, they had become the spearhead, so to speak, of the whole army.

[7] Antigonus' left wing was in flight and his entire phalanx had been turned. He was aware of this, and he was being advised to pull back, while his division of the army was still intact, to the high ground where he could collect the survivors of the rout. He did not take this advice, however. Instead, by making clever use of the advantages afforded by the situation, he not only saved the lives of the fugitives, but also won the day. [8] What happened was that, as soon as Antigonus' infantry turned to flight, Eumenes' Silver Shields and the rest of his infantry forces set out in pursuit and followed them as far as the

closest† foothills. [9] This opened a gap in the enemy's formation, and Antigonus charged through it with some of his cavalry and attacked the flank of the troops stationed with Eudamus on the left wing. [10] Before long, because of the unexpectedness of the attack, he had put the enemy to flight and taken many lives. He then dispatched his lightest cavalry here and there, and used them to rally the fugitives and reorganize them in a line along the foothills. When Eumenes heard that his left wing had been turned, he had his trumpeters recall his men from the pursuit, because he needed to go and help Eudamus.

31. By then it was the time of night when lamps are lit, but even so, such was the determination to win that gripped not only the generals, but even the rank-and-file soldiers, that once they had rallied their fugitives, both sides set about marshalling their entire forces to renew the battle. [2] It was a clear night, with a full moon, and the armies were deploying with a distance of about four plethra between them, so the clattering of weapons and the whinnying of horses seemed to all the combatants to be very close by. But while they were still regrouping, at a point that was about thirty stades from the bodies of those who had fallen in the battle, the hour of midnight arrived, and both sides were so exhausted by their marching, their efforts on the battlefield, and lack of food, that they were forced to abandon the idea of renewing the battle and make camp instead.

[3] Eumenes wanted control of the collection of the dead, to put his victory beyond dispute,* so he endeavoured to go back to the battlefield, but when his men refused and loudly insisted on returning to their baggage, which was a good way off, he yielded to the majority. He had no choice in this, [4] because he was not in a position to censure the troops sharply when there were plenty of men who disputed his right to command, and this was obviously not the right time to punish disobedience in the ranks. Antigonus, however, was secure in his command and had no need to take account of the wishes of the majority, and he prevailed upon his men to make camp near the bodies. Since he had control of their burial, he declared himself the winner, on the ground that possession of the dead constituted victory in battle. [5] On Antigonus' side about 3,700 infantry lost their lives in the battle, and fifty-four horsemen, while more than four thousand were injured, and on Eumenes' side 540 infantry died—his cavalry was more or less unscathed, however—and more than nine hundred men were wounded.

32. After withdrawing from the battle, Antigonus could see that his men were disheartened and he decided, as a matter of urgency, to get as far away from the enemy as possible. Wanting the army to be unencumbered for the retreat, he sent the wounded men and the heaviest baggage on ahead to a nearby town, and as soon as it was light he buried his dead. He detained the herald who had come from the enemy camp to arrange for the collection of their dead,* and ordered his men to eat their main meal early. [2] In the evening, he sent Eumenes' herald back, having granted permission for the dead to be collected the next day. Then, just as the first watch was beginning, he marched off with his entire army. By forcing the pace he managed to put a considerable distance between himself and the enemy, and ended up in a part of the country that had not been plundered, where his men could rest and recover. In fact, he went as far as Gamarga, a place in Media (Pithon's satrapy), which was capable of supplying, more than adequately, everything a large army might need in the way of sustenance. [3] When Eumenes was informed by his scouts that Antigonus had left, he decided not to go after him, because his own men were also short of food and suffering greatly from battle fatigue, and instead he focused on disposing of the dead and made sure that they received a magnificent funeral.

A curious thing happened at this point, something that was quite different from the way things were done in Greece. **33.** Ceteus, the commander of the Indian troops, died in the battle after putting on a dazzling display of valour, and he left two wives, who were with him in the camp, one of whom he had recently married, while the other had been his wife for a few years. Both the women were very fond of him. [2] Now, it is a long-standing custom in India that husbands and wives do not get married as a result of a decision taken by their parents, but by mutual agreement. In the past, this courtship took place when the people involved were rather young, and they often found that they had made the wrong choice and came to regret what they had done. Many wives allowed themselves to be seduced and out of moral weakness gave their love to other men. But since they could not leave the husbands they had originally chosen without bringing shame on themselves, they used to kill their husbands with poison. The land, it has to be said, furnished them with plenty of means for doing so, since it produced a wide variety of poisons, some of which caused death simply by being spread on food or drinking-cups.

[3] Eventually, this form of wickedness became so widespread that many men were being killed in this way. The women who committed the murders were punished, but this failed to deter the rest from their criminal ways. So they passed a law to the effect that wives were to be cremated along with their husbands, unless they were pregnant or had children, and that anyone who refused to obey the regulation should not only remain unmarried, but should also be regarded as unclean and be banned for life from attending sacrifices and other rites. [4] Once this law was in force, it brought about a complete and utter change in the women's lawless behaviour. The dishonour they faced was so severe that they all preferred to endure death, and every wife therefore began not only to protect her husband, since his safety was hers too, but even to vie with the other wives as though she were competing for the greatest of honours.*

34. The occasion about which I am writing was a case in point. Although the law states that only one wife is cremated along with her husband, both of Ceteus' wives turned up for his funeral, vying as keenly with each other for the right to die with him as one would over an award for valour in battle. [2] The generals took on the job of arbitrating the dispute, and the younger woman claimed that her rival was pregnant and was therefore ruled out, but the older woman argued that, in all justice, the one with more years should have more honour too, seeing that in all other matters older people are regarded as deserving far more respect and honour than their juniors.

[3] Anyway, with the help of experts in midwifery the generals determined that the older woman was indeed pregnant, so they chose the younger. When this happened, the woman against whom the decision had gone left in a flood of tears, shredding the diadem she wore on her head and tearing at her hair, just as if she had received news of a terrible disaster. But the other woman, made jubilant by her victory, withdrew to the pyre. Her hair bound with fillets by her maidservants, and clothed in finery as though for a wedding, she was escorted by her relatives, who were celebrating in song the excellence of her character.

[4] When she came near the pyre, she began stripping off her jewellery and giving it to her family and friends, so as to leave those who loved her with a memorial, as one might call it. Her jewellery consisted of a number of rings for her hands, set with colourful precious stones; a headband with a large number of golden stars alternating with precious stones; and a number of necklaces for her throat, which

started small and became progressively larger row by row. [5] Finally, after embracing her family, she was helped on to the pyre by her brother and, with the crowd that had gathered for the spectacle looking on in admiration, she brought her life to an end with consummate bravery. [6] The entire army marched under arms three times around the pyre before it was lit, while she lay down next to her husband. As the flames rapidly spread, she let no cry of weakness escape her lips, and while some spectators were moved to pity, others found her deserving of the highest praise. Some of the Greeks, however, denounced the practice as cruel and inhuman.

[7] After he had seen to the burial of the dead, Eumenes left Paraetacene* and went to Gabene, which had not been plundered and was capable of supplying, more than adequately, everything an army might need. [8] Antigonus' camp was a journey of twenty-five days away from his, if one travelled through civilized parts, but nine days if one crossed the uninhabited and waterless desert.* So Eumenes and Antigonus were wintering this far apart from each other in the places I have mentioned, allowing their men time to recover.

35. In Europe, Cassander was in the Peloponnese, where he had Tegea under siege,* but when he heard that Olympias had returned to Macedon and that Eurydice and King Philip had been killed—and when he heard how the tomb of his brother Iollas had been treated*—he came to terms with the Tegeans and marched on Macedon with his army. This disturbed his allies a great deal, because Polyperchon's son Alexander was waiting with an army for an opportunity to attack the Peloponnesian cities.

[2] The Aetolians wanted to get on good terms with Olympias and Polyperchon,* so they occupied the narrows at Thermopylae and blocked Cassander's passage. He decided against forcing his way through, given the difficulty of the terrain, and arranged instead for boats and scows to come from Euboea and Locris, and transported his forces to Thessaly by sea. [3] When he was informed that Polyperchon and his army were protecting Perrhaebia, he left it up to his general Callas to deal with that division of the enemy, and sent him on his way with an army, while Deinias, who was to occupy the passes into Macedon, went to confront the troops who had been sent into the field by Olympias and succeeded in gaining control of the passes before they did.

[4] The news that Cassander was close to Macedon with a large army prompted Olympias to appoint Aristonous her general, and she

ordered him to deal with Cassander, [5] while she went to Pydna
with her companions: Alexander's son; the boy's mother, Rhoxane;
Thessalonice, the daughter of Philip, the son of Amyntas; Deidameia,
who was the daughter of King Aeacides of Epirus and the sister of
Pyrrhus, the man who later fought the Romans;* the daughters of
Attalus; and also the relatives of other eminent friends of hers. This
meant that although there were a great many people gathered around
her, most of them were of no use in military terms; and in fact there
was not enough food there for them either, if they were to face a protracted siege. [6] The risk she was running in all this was obvious, but
she still decided to stay in Pydna, since she hoped that plenty of
Greeks and Macedonians would come to her aid by sea. [7] She had
with her some of the Ambraciot cavalry, most of the troops who were
usually attached to the court, and also the remainder of Polyperchon's
elephants—the remainder, because the rest had been captured by
Cassander during his previous invasion of Macedon.*

36. This time, he marched through the narrows of Perrhaebia and
halted close to Pydna. He surrounded the city from sea to sea with a palisade, and from those who wanted to become his allies he requisitioned
ships, all kinds of artillery, and siege engines, because his intention
was to besiege Olympias by land and sea. [2] When he found out that
Aeacides, the king of Epirus, was planning to come in force to help
Olympias, he put Atarrhias in charge of an army and ordered him to
go and meet the Epirotes. [3] Atarrhias smartly carried out his orders:
he occupied the passes from Epirus and succeeded in neutralizing
Aeacides.* In fact, most of the Epirotes had been pressed against their
will into campaigning in Macedon and were making trouble in the
camp. Aeacides was desperate to help Olympias,* and he discharged
those who were disaffected and took with him only men who were
willing to fight alongside him. But although he remained determined
to fight, the number of men who stayed with him was too small and he
was no match for the enemy.

[4] The Epirotes who left the expedition and returned to their
country rebelled against the king in his absence; they officially
condemned him to exile and entered into an alliance with Cassander.
Nothing like this had ever happened before in Epirote history, ever
since the reign of Neoptolemus, the son of Achilles;* up until then,
sons had always succeeded to their fathers' rule and had died while
still occupying the throne. [5] Cassander accepted Epirus into his

alliance, and sent Lyciscus there as both civil and military governor.*
At this juncture, those Macedonians who had previously been undecided
about whom to side with saw that Olympias' position was hopeless
and joined Cassander. The only chance Olympias had of receiving
help lay with Polyperchon, but this hope too was unexpectedly extinguished. [6] When Callas, whom Cassander had dispatched with an
army, drew near Polyperchon's position in Perrhaebia, he made camp
and set about bribing most of Polyperchon's troops to defect, until
only his most loyal men remained, and there were not many of them.
So, in just a short time, Olympias' hopes were crushed.

37. In Asia, Antigonus was wintering in Media, in Gadamela.* It was
clear to him that he was outclassed by the enemy, so he wanted to take
them by surprise and outmanoeuvre them. Now, Eumenes' forces had
scattered for their winter quarters, so much so that some divisions were
six days' journey away from others. [2] Antigonus therefore decided
against taking the route that passed through civilized parts, because of
its length and because it was easily visible to the enemy, and opted for the
bold tactic of marching through the uninhabited and waterless desert.
This would certainly be arduous, but it would best serve the kind of
offensive he had in mind, not just because it would reduce the amount
of time spent on the march, but also because it would not be difficult for
him to remain unobserved by the enemy, and then he could take them by
surprise, seeing that they had been stupid enough to disperse among
separate villages and were taking few precautions.

[3] Once he had formulated this plan, he ordered his troops to be
ready to break camp and to prepare ten days' worth of food that would
not require cooking. Then, after disseminating the rumour that he
was about to set off for Armenia, he suddenly confounded everyone's
expectations by setting out through the desert, even though it was
about the time of the winter solstice. [4] His instructions to his men
as regards their encampments were that they could light cooking fires
in the daytime, but they had to extinguish them completely after
dark, so that people living in the hills could not spot them and inform
the enemy of what was happening. [5] The point being that, although
the desert was almost entirely level, it was surrounded by high hills
from which the gleam of campfires would be easily visible at a considerable distance.

However, after the army had been on the march for five days, under
very difficult conditions, the soldiers began to light fires in their

camps at night as well as in the daytime, because of the cold and other pressing needs, [6] and this was indeed noticed by some of the inhabitants of the margins of the desert. They sent messengers on dromedaries to Eumenes and Peucestas, because these creatures can keep going for almost 1,500 stades.

38. When Peucestas found out that the enemy encampment had been observed halfway across the desert, he decided to withdraw to the furthest limits of the territory in which they were wintering. He was afraid of being caught by the enemy before all the contingents of the army had reunited from their various quarters. [2] When Eumenes saw how discouraged Peucestas was, he told him that there was no need for it. He could safely stay on the margins of the desert, he said, because he had found a way to delay Antigonus' arrival for three or four days. If that happened, he pointed out, their own forces would be assembled with time to spare, and the enemy would be at their mercy, since they would be weary and their provisions would be utterly exhausted.

[3] Everyone expressed surprise at this unexpected promise. They asked what he was going to do to slow down the enemy's advance, and Eumenes told all the commanders to gather their men and come with him, bringing a great many pots filled with fire. He chose a spot in the hills which faced the desert and was easily visible from all directions, and marked out an area with a perimeter of about seventy stades. He divided this space up into sectors, one for each of the officers who had come with him, and ordered them to light fires at night, at a distance of about twenty cubits from one another. During the first watch, they were to have the fires blaze up, as though men were still awake, and were tending the fires and cooking their evening meal. In the second watch, they were to let the fires die down a bit, and then in the third watch they were to leave just a very few burning, so that anyone watching from a distance would gain the impression that this was a genuine encampment.

[4] The soldiers carried out his orders, and the fires were noticed by some shepherds on the facing hills who were on good terms with Pithon, the satrap of Media. Since they supposed that there really was a camp there, they hurried down to the plain and told Antigonus and Pithon, who were taken aback. [5] They had not been expecting anything like this, and they halted the march while they talked over how they should respond to the information, seeing that it would be

risky for men who were weary and utterly provisionless to join battle with an enemy who had already reunited his forces and had plenty of supplies. [6] The conclusion they came to was that someone had betrayed them—that the enemy had reassembled because they had been warned—and so they abandoned the idea of carrying on straight ahead. They turned right instead, and marched to unplundered† parts of the inhabited country, because their men needed to recover from their ordeal.

39. Having outwitted the enemy with this stratagem, Eumenes recalled from their various quarters the soldiers who were spending the winter dispersed among the villages. He erected a palisade and protected the encampment with a deep trench, and began to receive the allied troops as they turned up. He also stocked the camp with everything the army might need. [2] But after crossing the desert, Antigonus was told by the locals that, although all the rest of Eumenes' army had assembled, the elephants' departure from their winter quarters had been delayed—and they were not far from his position, all by themselves with no support.

Antigonus sent some of his cavalry against the elephants—two thousand Median lancers and two hundred Tarentines—and all his light infantry. [3] He was hoping that an attack on the creatures while they were isolated would make it easy for him to capture them and deprive the enemy of the strongest division of his army. But Eumenes guessed what was going to happen, and sent 1,500 of his best cavalry and three thousand light infantry to the aid of the elephants. [4] Antigonus' troops got there first, however, and the commanders of the elephants formed a square and carried on, with their baggage safe in the middle, and in the rear the cavalry unit of four hundred or so men which was attached to them. [5] Antigonus' men threw all their weight into their assault and attacked with extreme force. The cavalry was overwhelmed by their superior numbers, and turned to flight, but the men mounted on the elephants resisted and persevered for a while under a hail of fire from all directions, but were unable to inflict any harm on the enemy. [6] Just as they were beginning to give in, however, the troops sent by Eumenes appeared and snatched them from the jaws of danger.

A few days later, with the two armies encamped facing each other, forty stades apart, both sides drew up their forces for what they expected would be the decisive battle. 40. Antigonus distributed his

cavalry between the wings. The command of the left wing he gave to
Pithon and that of the right to his son Demetrius. As for himself, he
decided to fight alongside his son. He stationed the infantry in the
centre, deployed the elephants along the whole front, and filled the
gaps between them with light infantry units. In all, his army consisted of 22,000 foot,* nine thousand horse (this included the extra
troops raised in Media),* and sixty-five elephants.

[2] When Eumenes found out that Antigonus had positioned himself on the right wing with his best cavalry, he drew up his forces in
response, with his best men posted on the left wing. In fact, he posted
most of the satraps there, with their accompanying elite cavalry units,
and he himself intended to fight alongside them as well. On this wing
there was also Mithridates, the son of Ariobarzanes; a descendant of
one of the seven Persians who killed the Magus, Smerdis,* he had
been trained from childhood onwards as a soldier and was a man of
exceptional courage. [3] On the flank of the whole wing, he deployed
his sixty best elephants slantwise, with the gaps between them occupied by light infantry units.

Immediately next to the left wing he posted the Hypaspists, then
the Silver Shields, and finally the mercenaries and those of the
remaining contingents which were armed in the Macedonian manner.
In front of the infantry, he stationed elephants and an adequate force
of light infantry. [4] On the right wing, he posted the weakest of his
cavalry and elephants, with Philip in overall command. Philip's
orders were to avoid battle and to watch the other wing, to see how the
battle there turned out. In all Eumenes had under his command at the
time 36,700 foot, six thousand horse, and 114 elephants.

41. Shortly before the battle, Antigenes, the general of the Silver
Shields, sent a Macedonian cavalryman to the enemy phalanx, with
the job of delivering a shouted message when he was close enough.
He rode up all alone to a point where his voice would carry to
Antigonus' Macedonian heavy infantry and called out: 'You scum!
Are you really going to fight your fathers, who conquered the world
with Philip and Alexander? You will soon see that they are worthy of
the kings and of their past battles.' [2] The point was that, even
though at this time the youngest of the Silver Shields were about sixty
years old, and most of the rest were about seventy or, in a few cases,
even older, their experience and strength were such that they were
invincible. They had gained an extraordinary degree of skill and

daring as a result of the constant battles they had fought. [3] The effect on Antigonus' men of this declaration was to make them give voice to their disgust that they were being forced to fight men who were kin and their elders, while in Eumenes' ranks cheers could be heard, and they called on him to lead them straight against the enemy. When Eumenes saw how determined they were, he raised the standard, which was the cue† for the trumpeters to sound the signal for battle and for the whole army to raise the battle-cry.

42. The first to engage were the elephants, and then the majority of the cavalry.* Now, the plain was very extensive, and was completely uncultivated because of the amount of salt that permeated it, and as a result so much dust was raised by the cavalry that no one could make out what was happening just a short distance away. [2] When Antigonus noticed this, he sent the Median cavalry and a good number of the Tarentines against the enemy's baggage train, hoping—and he was not deceived—that the dust would keep them hidden and that the capture of the baggage would bring him an easy victory. [3] The detachment rode around the enemy wing and attacked the baggage train, which was about five stades away from the battlefield, without being noticed. They found it packed with non-combatants, but poorly defended, and it did not take them long to scatter those who offered resistance and capture all the rest.

[4] Meanwhile, Antigonus joined battle with his immediate opponents. His appearance at the head of a large body of horsemen panicked Peucestas, the satrap of Persis, and when he retreated out of the dust clouds with his cavalry he drew with him about 1,500 of the others as well. [5] Eumenes was left isolated at the outer end of the wing with only a few men, but he judged it disgraceful to yield to Fortune and flee. Preferring to die as a result of taking the noble decision to remain true to the trust placed in him by the kings, he made a push for Antigonus himself. [6] A hard-fought cavalry battle ensued, in which losses were heavy on both sides, because while Eumenes' men had the advantage in terms of determination, they were outnumbered by their opponents.

There was also a battle going on between the elephants, and just then Eumenes' premier elephant fell, after a fight with the strongest of Antigonus' creatures. [7] Eumenes could see that everywhere his men were getting the worse of it, so he extracted the remainder of the cavalry from the fighting and went to the other wing, where he assumed command of the troops he had assigned to Philip, whose job had been to avoid battle. That was the outcome of the cavalry engagement.

43. As for the infantry, the Silver Shields adopted a compact formation and overwhelmed their immediate opponents, who either died on the battlefield or were forced to flee. The Silver Shields were unstoppable, and when they turned to engage the enemy phalanx as a whole, they were so superior in terms of skill and strength that not a single one of them lost his life, while they killed over five thousand and routed all the rest of the enemy infantry, despite the fact that they were greatly outnumbered.*

[2] Eumenes was informed about the capture of the baggage, but he also found out that Peucestas and his cavalry were still close at hand, so he tried to rally all the cavalry and renew the fight against Antigonus, in the hope that victory would enable him not just to save his own baggage, but to gain the enemy's as well.* [3] But so far from obeying him, Peucestas retreated to an even more remote spot, and since at the same time it began to get dark, Eumenes had no choice but to bow to circumstances.

[4] Antigonus divided his cavalry into two. He took charge of one division and waited to respond to Eumenes' next move, while he put Pithon in charge of the rest of the cavalry and ordered him to attack the Silver Shields, now that they were isolated and there was no chance of their receiving cavalry support. [5] Pithon promptly carried out his orders, but the Macedonians formed a square and retreated safely to the river,* where they began to denounce Peucestas as the one who was to blame for the defeat of the cavalry.

When Eumenes joined them as well, at about the time that lamps are lit, they met and tried to decide what to do. [6] The satraps argued that they should beat a hasty retreat to the upper satrapies, but Eumenes said that they should stay and continue the fight, since the enemy phalanx had been shattered and the cavalry forces of both sides were equally matched. [7] The Macedonians, however, were unhappy with both suggestions because of the capture of their baggage, which left their children and womenfolk, and others they could not live without,* in enemy hands. [8] The meeting therefore broke up for the time being without their having come up with a plan that met with everyone's approval, and the Macedonians then entered into secret negotiations with Antigonus. They seized Eumenes and handed him over,* recovered their baggage, and, once they had received guarantees of safety, were enrolled in Antigonus' army.* [9] Likewise, the satraps and most of the other officers and ordinary soldiers abandoned their general and thought only of their own safety.

44. So Eumenes and the entire enemy army suddenly fell into Antigonus' hands. Antigenes, the commander of the Silver Shields, Antigonus arrested, placed in a pit, and burnt alive. Eudamus, who had brought the elephants from India, and Celbanus, and some others who had been unremittingly hostile to him, he executed. [2] Eumenes was put under guard while Antigonus tried to decide what to do with him. As a good general—and as one who would be in his debt—he wanted Eumenes on his side, but he had little faith in his promises because of his loyalty to Olympias and the kings. Earlier, in fact, even after he had spared his life at Nora in Phrygia,* Eumenes had still committed himself absolutely to fighting for the kings. Since Antigonus could also see that the Macedonians were not going to give up their desire to see Eumenes punished,* he put him to death. But because of their earlier friendship, after he had cremated the body he put the bones in a container and sent them to his family. [3] Among the wounded who were brought in as prisoners was the historian Hieronymus of Cardia, who in earlier years had always been held in high regard by Eumenes, and who after Eumenes' death was treated well by Antigonus and won his trust.

[4] Antigonus took his whole army into Media, where he spent the winter in a village near Ecbatana, the royal capital of Media, while accommodating his men here and there throughout the whole satrapy, and especially in the district called Rhagae, which was named after a disaster that happened there in the past.* [5] There was nowhere in that part of the world that had more or more prosperous cities, but it experienced earthquakes of such violence that both the cities and all their inhabitants were obliterated, and the countryside was completely transformed, with new rivers and lakes replacing those that had been there before.

45. In this year the third inundation of the city of Rhodes took place, in which many of the inhabitants lost their lives. The first inundation caused little disruption to people, since the city had only recently been founded* and therefore had plenty of open spaces. [2] The second was more serious and more people lost their lives. The last one occurred at the beginning of spring, when suddenly a storm broke out, with torrential rain and hailstones of an unbelievable size.

Some weighed as much as a mna or even more, and as a result many houses collapsed under their weight and quite a few people died. [3] The town was shaped like a theatre, which meant that most of the water that poured down the slopes ended up in the same place and the lowest-lying parts of the town immediately began to be flooded. The drains had been neglected, because the rainy season was supposed to be over, and the drainage slits in the walls had become blocked.

[4] The water rose at an alarming rate, and soon the whole area around the wholesale market and the temple of Dionysus was flooded. By the time the temple of Asclepius was threatened with inundation panic was rife and everyone began trying to find some way or another of saving their lives. [5] Some ran to the ships, others raced to the theatre, while a few, who had already been caught up in the disaster and had no other recourse, climbed up on to the tallest altars or statue bases. [6] The city was in danger of being wiped out along with its inhabitants, but then luck came to the rescue: a long stretch of the city wall collapsed, the accumulated water poured out through the breach into the sea, and life soon returned to normal for everyone. [7] It helped that the flood happened in daylight, because most of those who were threatened by it had time to escape from their homes to the higher parts of the city, and it also helped that the houses were made out of stone rather than brick, which meant that people who took refuge on rooftops remained safe and sound.* [8] All the same, it was a major disaster; more than five hundred people lost their lives, and many buildings either collapsed completely or were badly damaged. That was how close the city of Rhodes came to destruction.

46. When Antigonus, who was wintering in Media, heard that Pithon was winning over many of the soldiers in their winter quarters by making them promises and giving them gifts—in other words, that he was planning to rebel—he concealed his intentions and made out that he did not believe those who were bringing these charges against Pithon. He told them off in front of many witnesses for trying to break up their friendship, and had the rumour spread abroad that he was going to leave Pithon as General of the Upper Satrapies and give him an army that was large enough to protect them. [2] He even wrote to Pithon, asking him to come as soon as possible, so that they could meet face to face and make all the necessary arrangements, and then he could go down to the coast without further delay.

The point of this ploy was to keep Pithon from suspecting the truth, and to seduce him into his grasp by convincing him that he was going to be entrusted with the satrapies when Antigonus left. After all, it was hardly practicable to use force to arrest a man whose abilities had led to his advancement by Alexander, who was the current satrap of Media, and who had made himself popular with the whole army. [3] Pithon was spending the winter in the most remote part of Media, and he already had the assurances of a large number of men, whom he had bribed, that they would join his rebellion, but when his friends wrote to him about Antigonus' plans and hinted at his great prospects for the future, he was deceived by vain expectations and went to Antigonus, who promptly arrested him. [4] Antigonus formally accused him, easily won a conviction from the members of his council, and put him to death straight away.

[5] After he had reunited the army, he entrusted the satrapy of Media to Orontobates the Mede, and appointed Hippostratus the military governor,* with an infantry force of three thousand mercenaries and five hundred horse.† [6] He next took the army to Ecbatana, where he withdrew five thousand talents of uncoined silver, and then he advanced into Persis, reaching the royal capital, which is called Persepolis, after a journey of about twenty days.

47. While Antigonus was still en route, Pithon's friends and fellow conspirators, the most eminent of whom were Meleager and Menoetas, put together a force of about eight hundred cavalry from those of Eumenes' and Pithon's friends who were at large. [2] At first, they plundered the land of those Medes who had refused to join their rebellion, but then, when they found out that Hippostratus and Orontobates were in the habit of making a slipshod camp, they launched an attack on them one night. They came very close to making a success of the enterprise, but the enemy was too numerous for them and they withdrew again, after persuading some of the soldiers to join their rebellion. [3] Since the rebels were mobile and were all mounted, their raids were impossible to anticipate and caused turmoil throughout the countryside. Some time later, however, they were trapped in a gorge, and were either killed or captured. [4] A number of leading men lost their lives, refusing to surrender: Meleager, Ocranes the Mede, and several other notables. That was the outcome of the Median rebellion.

48. As soon as Antigonus reached Persis, he was acclaimed king by the Persians, as the acknowledged master of Asia, and he met with his

Friends in council to discuss what to do with the satrapies.* He allowed Tlepolemus to keep Carmania, and he also retained Stasanor in Bactria, since it would take more than a letter to oust them, when they were popular with the locals and had large armies at their disposal. [2] He sent Evitus to Areia,* and when he died a short while later, he replaced him with Evagoras, a man of remarkable courage and intelligence. He allowed Oxyartes, the father of Rhoxane, to keep the satrapy of Paropanisadae, which had been his before, since it would take a lot of time and a strong army to evict him.

[3] He summoned Sibyrtius, who was a friend, from Arachosia, and not only permitted him to keep the satrapy, but also put him in charge of the chief trouble-makers among the Silver Shields. In theory, these men were for Sibyrtius to use in war, but in fact Antigonus was arranging for them to die, because he told Sibyrtius in private to send them out a few at a time on the kinds of missions that would get them killed. [4] It so happened that the men assigned to Sibyrtius included those who had betrayed Eumenes, so that they did not long escape punishment for their faithless treatment of their general. Iniquitous behaviour may profit rulers because they can get away with it, but for ordinary people, their subjects, it generally leads to disaster.

[5] Anyway, seeing Peucestas' growing popularity among the Persians, Antigonus first removed him from office, and then, when Thespius, one of the most eminent men in Persis, bluntly declared that the Persians would tolerate no other leader, he killed Thespius and installed Asclepiodorus as satrap, with an adequate force of soldiers. He made empty promises to Peucestas and hinted that he might still have a glorious future, but when he left the country he took him with him.*

[6] While he was at the Pasitigris river, en route for Susa, he was met by Xenophilus, the man responsible for the Susa treasury, who had been ordered by Seleucus to place himself entirely at Antigonus' disposal.* Antigonus made him welcome and pretended to value him as much as any of his friends, because he did not want Xenophilus to change his mind and shut him out again. [7] And when the Susa acropolis was surrendered to him, he found there the golden, vine-entwined tree* and a large number of other works of art, the combined weight of which was fifteen thousand talents. [8] Other gifts that had been given to the Persian kings, such as golden crowns, and the spoils

of war together amounted to another large sum—five thousand talents, in fact—and, on top of these valuables in the Susa treasury, there was the same amount again in Media, which meant that, in all, he amassed twenty-five thousand talents. That was how things stood with Antigonus.

49. Now that I have covered events in Asia, I shall move on to Europe and continue my account from where I left off. Cassander had Olympias trapped in Macedon, in Pydna, and wintry weather was thwarting his assaults on the walls, but he had the city under siege. He threw up a palisade from sea to sea and blockaded the harbour, making it impossible for anyone who wanted to bring help to do so. [2] Before long, all supplies in the city had been exhausted, and then the besieged were reduced to such extreme hunger that they were completely undone. The situation became so grim that each soldier received as his rations for a month a mere five choenixes of grain,* they sawed wood to feed the elephants that were trapped inside the city,* and the draught animals and horses were slaughtered for food. [3] Over the course of the catastrophe that struck the city, while Olympias was still hoping to be rescued from outside, the elephants died of starvation, almost every horse-owner died who was not on active service and therefore was not receiving rations, and many ordinary soldiers met the same fate as well. [4] Some barbarians* found their natural needs too strong for their scruples; they began to collect the bodies of the dead and eat their flesh. The city was quickly becoming glutted with corpses, and although the commanders of the queen's guard saw to the burial of some of them, they threw a lot over the city wall. The sight of these corpses was ghastly and the foul smell was unbearable, not just to women of royal blood who were used to gracious living, but even to soldiers who were accustomed to hardship.

50. As winter turned to spring and the famine became ever more acute, a large body of soldiers came and implored Olympias to let them go because of the lack of supplies. Since she had no rations at all for them and could not make the siege go away, she gave them permission to leave. [2] Everyone who deserted was taken in by Cassander. He treated them well and sent them back to their cities, in the hope that, when the Macedonians heard from these men how precarious Olympias' position was, they would give up on her. [3] And his hunch about what would happen was right: those who had decided to try to relieve the town by military means changed their minds and went

over to Cassander, and the only men in Macedon who remained loyal were Aristonous in Amphipolis and Monimus in Pella.

[4] When Olympias saw that most of her sympathizers had gone over to Cassander, and that those who remained were too weak to help her, she tried to have a quinquereme launched, with which to secure her own safety and that of her friends. [5] But a deserter informed on her, and when Cassander sailed up and captured the ship, Olympias realized that her position was hopeless, and sent envoys to Cassander to sue for peace. Although Cassander insisted on an unconditional surrender, she managed eventually to persuade him to make an exception in her case alone and guarantee that she would be allowed to live.

[6] Once Pydna was in his hands, Cassander dispatched troops to take over Pella and Amphipolis. [7] The news of what had happened to Olympias prompted Monimus, who held Pella, to surrender the city, but Aristonous initially decided to resist, since he had a large force of soldiers and had recently won a battle. A few days earlier he had fought Cassander's general Cratevas; he had killed most of the enemy soldiers, and when Cratevas and two thousand others had taken refuge in Bedyndia in Bisaltia,* he had besieged the place and taken it, disarmed them, and let them go under a truce. [8] His military strength was not the only factor that made him confident: he was also unaware that Eumenes had died, and he was expecting Alexander and Polyperchon to come to his aid. And so he refused to surrender Amphipolis. But when Olympias wrote to him, asking him to trust her and ordering him to surrender, he could see that he had no choice but to obey; he handed over the city and received a guarantee that he would not be killed.

51. Cassander was aware of the respect that Aristonous enjoyed as a result of his advancement by Alexander,* and he felt he had to do away with anyone who was capable of leading a rebellion, so he used Cratevas' relatives to kill the man. He also got the relatives of the people who had been killed by Olympias to prosecute her* before a general assembly of the Macedonians. [2] They duly did so, and even though Olympias was not present and there was no one to speak in her defence, the Macedonians condemned her to death. But Cassander sent some of his friends to her with the suggestion that she should slip quietly away, and promised to provide her with a ship and see that she got to Athens. [3] He was not acting out of concern for her safety; he wanted her to condemn herself to exile, so that, when she

died during the voyage, this might seem to be a deserved punishment. He had to proceed carefully, not just because of her standing in Macedon, but also because of the fickleness of the Macedonians.

[4] Olympias refused to escape, however. In fact, she wanted a trial before the assembled Macedonians.* But Cassander was afraid that, if the Macedonians heard the queen's defence speech and were reminded of all the good Alexander and Philip had done the country as a whole, they would change their minds, and he therefore sent two hundred of his most competent men to her, with orders to do away with her immediately. [5] They broke into the queen's house, but when they confronted her, they were overawed by her high rank and they retraced their steps without having carried out their mission. But the relatives of the people she had killed, who wanted to curry favour with Cassander as well as avenge their dead, did murder the queen, and she died without uttering any weak or womanish plea. [6] So ended the life of Olympias, the most eminent woman of her time. She was the daughter of Neoptolemus, the King of Epirus; the sister of Alexander, who campaigned in Italy;* the wife of Philip, the most powerful ruler there had ever been in Europe; and the mother of Alexander, the scale and glory of whose achievements have never been rivalled.

52. Everything was going well for Cassander, and he began to entertain hopes of gaining the Macedonian throne. That was why he married Thessalonice, one of Philip's daughters* and Alexander's half-sister, because he wanted to present himself as a member of the royal family. [2] He also founded a city on Pallene, named Cassandreia after himself, by uniting as a single community all the towns of the peninsula, Potidaea, and a large number of nearby villages. There were quite a few surviving Olynthians, and he had them take up residence there as well.* [3] Since the borders of Cassandreia encompassed a large amount of good farmland, and since Cassander worked hard to see that the city flourished, it quickly made great progress and soon became the most important city in Macedon.

[4] Cassander had decided to kill Alexander's son and the child's mother, Rhoxane, to make sure that there was no natural successor to the throne,* but for the time being, since he wanted to see how people would react to the killing of Olympias, and also since he had no news of Antigonus, he moved Rhoxane and her son to the acropolis of Amphipolis, which he placed under the command of one of his most

trusted friends, Glaucias, and imprisoned them there. He also deprived the boy of the pages who were being brought up with him in the customary manner,* and gave orders that he was no longer to be treated as royalty, but was to receive the kind of upbringing that was suitable for an ordinary member of the public. [5] Next, since he was already behaving like a king in administering the realm, he followed the traditional practice of Macedonian kings and buried at Aegeae Queen Eurydice and King Philip, and also Cynna, whom Alcetas had killed.* After holding funeral games in honour of the dead, he put together a select force of Macedonians for a campaign he had decided to conduct in the Peloponnese.

[6] Meanwhile, Polyperchon was under siege in Azorius in Perrhaebia. The news of Olympias' death, however, made him give up on Macedon, and he made his way out of the city with a few companions and left Thessaly. He picked up Aeacides and his men as well and then withdrew to Aetolia. He was on good terms with the Aetolians,* and thought that this would be the safest place for him to wait for things to change.

53. Once Cassander had mustered a large enough force, he left Macedon with the intention of driving Alexander, Polyperchon's son, from the Peloponnese.* Alexander was the last of Cassander's opponents with an army, and he had occupied strategically located cities and strongpoints. Cassander marched through Thessaly safely, but he found the pass at Thermopylae guarded by Aetolians, and he struggled to force his way past them. [2] Once he was in Boeotia, he gathered the scattered Theban survivors and set about refounding Thebes.* He doubted he would ever have a better opportunity to re-establish a city of such renown, known not just for its achievements, but also because of all the legends in which it featured, and he expected this good deed of his to earn him undying glory.

[3] In fact, Thebes had experienced a great many major upheavals, since it had been depopulated a number of times, and a sketch of its history will not be out of place here. [4] Following the deluge that took place in the time of Deucalion, Cadmus founded a settlement on the Cadmea (named after him), and he was joined there by a people who are known either as the Sparti, because they had come together from various locations,* or as the Indigenous Thebans, because they had originally come from Thebes, but had been driven out and scattered by the deluge. [5] Anyway, these people, the inhabitants of Thebes at

that time, were later defeated by the Encheleans and driven out of the city,* and this was the occasion when Cadmus too was expelled from the city and went to Illyris.

Later, Amphion and Zethus gained control of the place, and they began to develop the lower town; in the words of the poet: 'They were the first to found the seven-gated city of Thebes.'* Then the inhabitants of Thebes were expelled for a second time when Polydorus, the son of Cadmus, returned, knowing that Amphion had been hurt too badly by what had happened to his children* to give him any trouble. [6] Then, when Polydorus' descendants were the rulers of Thebes* (by which time the whole district was known as Boeotia, after Boeotus, a former king of Thebes, the son of Melanippe and Poseidon), the Thebans were expelled for a third time when the Epigoni from Argos took the city by siege. [7] The survivors of the expulsion escaped to Alalcomenae and Mount Tilphosium,* and returned to the city once the Argives had withdrawn.

Next, when the Thebans had left the city and gone to Asia for the Trojan War, those who stayed behind were expelled by the Pelasgians, as were all the other Boeotians as well. [8] This was far from the end of the misfortunes they suffered in subsequent years, but eventually, four generations later, they returned to Boeotia and re-established Thebes, in accordance with the oracle of the crows.* After that, the city lasted for almost eight hundred years, and the Thebans, who at first were the leaders of just their own people, were later in contention for hegemony of the Greeks, but then Alexander, the son of Philip, took the city by storm and razed it to the ground.

54. Twenty years later, in a bid for glory, Cassander gained the agreement of the Boeotians and re-established the city for the Theban survivors. [2] Many Greek cities contributed to the refoundation, partly out of pity for the hapless Thebans and partly because of the city's fame. Most of the wall, for instance, was rebuilt by the Athenians, and other cities played a part as well—cities from Sicily and Italy, not just from Greece—either by contributing as best they could to the building, or by sending money for the work that needed doing.* [3] That is how the Thebans got their city back.

Cassander then set out for the Peloponnese with his army, but he found that Alexander, the son of Polyperchon, had secured the isthmus. So he went to Megara instead, where he built flatboats, which he used to transport the elephants over to Epidaurus, while the rest of his forces made the crossing on ships. When he reached Argos, he forced the city to secede from Alexander's alliance and side with him, [4] and then he won over all the towns of Messenia except for Ithome,* and entered into an agreement with the people of Hermione which gained him that city too. Alexander refused battle, however, so Cassander left two thousand men at the Gerania isthmus* under the command of Molyccus, and returned to Macedon.

315/14

55. *At the beginning of the following year, Praxibulus became Archon in Athens, and in Rome Nautius Spurius and Marcus Popillius were elected consuls. In this year:*

Antigonus decided to take all the money down to the coast personally, so he left a local man, Aspisas, as satrap of Susiane, while he equipped himself with carts and camels and set out with the army for Babylonia. [2] He reached Babylon twenty-two days later, and Seleucus, who was satrap there, honoured him with gifts fit for a king and feasted his entire army. [3] But when Antigonus demanded an accounting of his revenues, Seleucus refused, saying that he was not obliged to submit to an audit when the land concerned had been given to him by the Macedonians in recognition of the services he had undertaken during Alexander's lifetime.* [4] Day by day, the quarrel became more acerbic, and Seleucus, bearing in mind what had happened to Pithon,* was terrified that Antigonus would find some pretext for doing away with him, since it looked as though he wanted to get rid of every man of worth who had the potential to take power.* [5] To be on the safe side, then, he fled, accompanied by only fifty horsemen, with the intention of making his way to Ptolemy in Egypt, because word had spread of Ptolemy's goodness, and of the warm friendship he extended to all who turned to him for safety.

[6] Antigonus was delighted when he heard of Seleucus' flight. It was not just that it freed him from the necessity of laying hands on a man who was a friend and who had actively cooperated with him; he was also pleased because Seleucus' self-enforced exile delivered Babylonia to him without his having to fight or face danger for it. [7] But then the Chaldaeans paid him a visit and warned him of the consequences of letting Seleucus slip out of his grasp—that Seleucus

would become the master of all Asia, and that Antigonus himself
would lose his life in battle against him*—and Antigonus regretted
what he had done. He sent men after Seleucus and they followed him
for a while, but then came back empty-handed.

[8] Although Antigonus generally despised such prophetic warn-
ings, this one disturbed him a great deal. What troubled him was
the reputation the Chaldaeans had as men of real expertise whose
observation of the heavenly bodies was particularly accurate. The
Chaldaeans claim, in fact, to have been devoting themselves to these
matters for thousands upon thousands of years. They are also supposed to have warned Alexander that he would die if he entered
Babylon,* [9] and the outcome of the prophecy about Seleucus was
the same as the one about Alexander: in both cases, the Chaldaeans'
assertions turned out to be true. I shall go into more detail about this
when we come to the relevant period of time.*

56. Seleucus reached Egypt safely and met with nothing but kindness from Ptolemy. He bitterly denounced Antigonus, accusing him
of having decided to expel every man of worth from his satrapy and
of picking especially on those who had campaigned with Alexander.
He cited as examples the killing of Pithon, the removal of Peucestas
from Persis, and his own case. [2] None of these men had done any
wrong; in fact, while they had been on good terms with Antigonus
they had often served him well, and had been expecting their good
services to be rewarded. He described the size of Antigonus' army
and the extent of his wealth, and suggested that his recent good fortune had made him presumptuous and had led him to hope that the
entirety of the Macedonian empire might be his.

[3] These arguments convinced Ptolemy that he had better get
ready for war, and Seleucus also sent some of his friends to Europe, to
see if they could sway Cassander and Lysimachus with similar arguments to come out against Antigonus. [4] His emissaries swiftly
carried out their orders, sowing the seeds of conflict and major warfare. Antigonus, however, who had guessed what course of action
Seleucus was likely to take, sent envoys to Ptolemy, Lysimachus, and
Cassander, asking them not to jeopardize their good relations. And
once he had appointed Pithon satrap of Babylonia—the Pithon who
had come from India—he marched away from Babylon and made for
Cilicia. [5] By the time he reached Mallus, Orion had already set and
he divided his forces for the winter. He also took the money—ten

thousand talents—from the treasury at Cyinda. Even without this money, he had a regular annual income of eleven thousand talents. That is what made him so formidable: not just the size of his army, but his great wealth as well.

57. While Antigonus was advancing into Upper Syria, he was met by the envoys sent by Ptolemy, Lysimachus, and Cassander. Their demands, which they presented when they were brought before Antigonus' council, were that Cappadocia and Lycia should be given to Cassander, Hellespontine Phrygia to Lysimachus, all Syria to Ptolemy,* and Babylonia to Seleucus, and that Antigonus should share with them the money he had gained after the battle with Eumenes, seeing that they too had played their parts in the war. If he failed to meet their demands, they said that they would unite and make war on him. [2] But Antigonus gave them a very harsh response, telling them to make ready for war, which meant that the envoys returned with their mission unfulfilled.

Next, then, Ptolemy, Lysimachus, and Cassander entered into a formal alliance with one another, and set about mustering their forces and equipping themselves with armour, artillery, and everything else that they might need. [3] When Antigonus saw the strength of the coalition that had formed against him, and the stature of the men involved, he realized that the coming war would be a major one, and he began to invite peoples, cities, and dynasts to become his allies. [4] He sent Agesilaus to the Cypriot kings, Idomeneus and Moschion to Rhodes, and his nephew Ptolemaeus to Cappadocia with an army. He was to relieve Amisus, which was under siege, drive out all the troops who had been sent there by Cassander,* and finally go to the Hellespont and wait in case Cassander tried to sail over from Europe. [5] He sent Aristodemus of Miletus to the Peloponnese with a thousand talents and the job of entering into a treaty of friendship with Alexander and Polyperchon and raising a large enough force of mercenaries to make war on Cassander. And he established beacons and couriers throughout the length and breadth of as much of Asia as was his to command, which would enable the rapid execution of his orders.

58. Once Antigonus had attended to these matters, he set out for Phoenicia. He wanted to build a fleet, because at that time his enemies had large navies and control of the sea, while he had hardly any ships at all. In Phoenicia, he made camp at Tyre, and since he intended to

besiege the city he sent for the kings of the Phoenician cities and the governors of Syria. [2] He prevailed upon the kings to help him with the ship-building, since Ptolemy was keeping all the ships of Phoenicia, along with their crews, in Egypt; and he ordered the governors swiftly to prepare four and a half million *medimnoi* of wheat <and . . . *medimnoi* of barley>,*† which was the amount the army consumed in a year. He took personal charge of the task of gathering lumberjacks, carpenters, and shipwrights from wherever they could be found, and saw to the transportation of timber from Mount Lebanon to the coast. [3] This mountain range stretches from Tripolis to Sidon via Byblus, and is covered with wonderfully beautiful cedar and cypress trees, which grow there to an amazing height. Eight thousand men were employed as lumberjacks and sawyers, and a thousand teams of oxen were used to transport the timber from the mountain.† [4] He established three shipyards in Phoenicia—at Tripolis, Byblus, and Sidon—and a fourth in Cilicia, the timber for which was brought from the Taurus mountains. [5] There was another one in Rhodes, where the democracy had agreed to build ships out of imported wood.

Now, Antigonus had established his camp by the sea, and while he was busy with all these preparations, Seleucus came from Egypt with a hundred ships, good sailers which were decked out as a royal fleet. He sailed contemptuously past the camp, sending morale plummeting among the men from the allied cities and everyone who had taken Antigonus' side, [6] because there could be no doubt that, since the enemy controlled the sea, they would ravage the land of those who had been induced by their friendship with Antigonus to make common cause with their adversaries. But Antigonus told them not to worry, and assured them that he would take to the sea that very summer with five hundred ships.

59. At this juncture, Agesilaus, the man Antigonus had sent to Cyprus, arrived back with the news that Nicocreon and the most powerful of the other kings had made an alliance with Ptolemy,* but that the kings of Citium, Lapithus, Marion, and Cerynia had concluded a treaty of friendship with him. [2] Upon receipt of this news, Antigonus left three thousand soldiers under the command of Andronicus to press on with the siege of Tyre, while he marched off with the rest of the army and took Joppa and Gaza,* which had refused to submit to him. All the soldiers of Ptolemy's that he captured were incorporated into units of his own army, and he

installed garrisons in the cities to make sure that the inhabitants remained submissive. [3] Then he returned to the camp at Old Tyre* and continued his preparations for the siege.

This was also when Ariston, the man who had been entrusted by Eumenes with Craterus' remains, passed them on for burial to Phila, Craterus' former wife, who was now married to Demetrius, the son of Antigonus. [4] Phila seems to have been an exceptionally intelligent woman. If there was unrest in the army, for instance, she calmed the malcontents down by dealing judiciously with them on an individual basis; she used her own money to pay for the marriages of poor men's sisters and daughters; and she often came to the rescue of people who were being falsely accused of crimes. [5] We even hear that her father, Antipater, who is widely held to have been one of the most astute rulers of the time, used to ask for Phila's advice on critical matters while she was still a child. [6] But the woman's character will be revealed more precisely at a later stage of my narrative, especially as her situation changed in the final crisis of Demetrius' reign.* Anyway, that was how things stood with Antigonus and Phila, the wife of Demetrius.

60. Meanwhile, the generals Antigonus had sent out were carrying out their missions. Aristodemus sailed to Laconia, and once the Spartiates had given him leave to recruit soldiers, he raised a force of eight thousand men from the Peloponnese. He met with Alexander and Polyperchon, entered into a treaty of friendship with them in Antigonus' name, appointed Polyperchon General of the Peloponnese, and prevailed upon Alexander to go and join Antigonus in Asia.

[2] The other general, Ptolemaeus, proceeded with his army into Cappadocia, where Cassander's general, Asclepiodorus, had Amisus under siege. Ptolemaeus' arrival freed the city from danger; he let Asclepiodorus and his men leave under a truce and recovered the satrapy for Antigonus. [3] His route took him next across Bithynia, where he found that the Bithynian king, Zibytes, had both Astacus and Chalcedon under siege. He forced him to abandon both sieges, and once he had brought these cities and Zibytes into the Antigonid alliance, and had been given hostages, he set off towards Ionia and Lydia, because Antigonus had ordered him by letter to go straight to the coast, where his help was needed since Seleucus was about to arrive there with a fleet. [4] By the time Ptolemaeus reached the coast, Seleucus had Erythrae under siege, but when he found out that the

enemy army was in the vicinity, he sailed away without having achieved anything.

61. When Polyperchon's son Alexander reached Tyre, Antigonus formally confirmed their friendship. He then convened a general assembly, consisting of both soldiers and visitors,* and indicted Cassander for his killing of Olympias and his treatment of Rhoxane and the king. [2] He also accused him of having forced Thessalonice to marry him against her will, of openly trying to appropriate the kingdom of Macedon, of having resettled the Olynthians, who were deadly enemies of Macedon, in a city named after himself, and of having refounded Thebes, even though it had been destroyed by the Macedonians.*

[3] The assembled masses made it clear that they shared his anger, and Antigonus introduced a motion that Cassander was to be regarded as an enemy of Macedon unless he destroyed the two cities, released the king and his mother, Rhoxane, from prison and restored them to the Macedonians, and in general submitted to Antigonus as the officially appointed general and legitimate custodian of the kingdom.* The Greeks, moreover, were to be free, ungarrisoned, and self-governing. Once the troops had voted in favour of these stipulations, Antigonus had couriers disseminate the decree far and wide. [4] His thinking was that the prospect of freedom would gain him the Greeks' active support in the war, and also that if the generals and satraps of the upper satrapies, who suspected him of having decided to depose the kings who had succeeded Alexander, saw that he was going to war on their behalf, they would all have a change of heart and be prepared to take orders from him.

[5] Once he had finished with this, he gave Alexander five hundred talents and sent him back to the Peloponnese with great hopes for the future. Then he sent for the ships from Rhodes, fitted out the majority of the newly built ones as well, and had them sail for Tyre. As a result of his control of the sea, no food could be brought in to the city, and he maintained the siege for a year and three months. Eventually, the besieged were starved into submission. He allowed Ptolemy's soldiers to leave with their property, and after negotiating the terms of the city's surrender he installed a garrison to defend it.

62. Meanwhile, when Ptolemy heard about the decree that had been passed by Antigonus' Macedonians on the freedom of the Greeks,* he drew up a similar decree of his own, because he wanted the Greeks to

know that their independence was just as important to him as it was to Antigonus. [2] Both men could see that there was no little advantage in acquiring the goodwill of the Greeks, and they were competing with each other to see who could do them more good. Ptolemy also brought into his alliance Asander,* the satrap of Caria, who owed his strength to the number of cities in his domain.

[3] The Cypriot kings had already received three thousand soldiers from Ptolemy, and he now sent a formidable army, because he wanted to force the kings who were defying him to acknowledge his supremacy. [4] So he sent ten thousand soldiers under the command of Myrmidon of Athens and a hundred ships under Polycleitus, and gave overall command to his brother Menelaus. They sailed to Cyprus, where they found Seleucus with his fleet, and they met in council and considered what to do. [5] They decided that Polycleitus should sail to the Peloponnese with fifty ships and fight it out with Aristodemus, Alexander, and Polyperchon; that Myrmidon and the mercenaries were to go to Caria to help Asander,* who had been attacked by Antigonus' general Ptolemaeus; and that Seleucus and Menelaus should remain on Cyprus with King Nicocreon and the rest of their allies, and make war on their opponents there. [6] Once their forces had been divided up along these lines, Seleucus set to work. He took Cerynia and Lapithus, gained the support of Stasioecus, the king of Marion, and forced the ruler of Amathous to give hostages. At Citium, however, diplomacy failed, and he subjected it to continuous assaults with all the men he had available.

[7] At this juncture, forty ships reached Antigonus from the Hellespont under the command of Themison, and Dioscourides also brought eighty ships from the Hellespont and Rhodes. [8] The first to be completed of the Phoenician-built ships had already been fitted out and were available to him, and they and the ships that had been captured at Tyre made a combined total of 120, so that the total number of seaworthy warships he assembled was 240. Among these, there were ninety quadriremes, ten quinqueremes, three niners, ten deceremes, and thirty were undecked galleys.* [9] Antigonus sent fifty ships, one division of the fleet, to the Peloponnese, and he put his nephew, Dioscourides, in charge of the rest and ordered him to cruise around, keeping their allies safe and trying to win over those of the islands which had not yet joined the alliance. That was how things stood with Antigonus.

63. Now that I have covered the affairs of Asia in this year, I shall return next to Europe and give an account of events there. Apollonides, the man appointed by Cassander as military governor of Argos, marched out one night into Arcadia and captured the town of Stymphalus. [2] But while he was away, the Argive faction that was hostile to Cassander sent for Alexander, Polyperchon's son, and promised to surrender the city to him. Alexander was slow to respond, however, and Apollonides reached Argos before him. Finding about five hundred of his opponents in council in the town hall, he prevented them from leaving and burnt them alive. Most of the others he exiled, but a few were arrested and put to death.

[3] When Cassander learnt of Aristodemus' mission to the Peloponnese and the number of mercenaries he had collected, his first move was to try to persuade Polyperchon to abandon Antigonus. His words fell on deaf ears, however, so he raised an army and marched through Thessaly into Boeotia, [4] where he helped the Thebans with the building of their walls, before continuing on into the Peloponnese. After taking Cenchreae* and ravaging Corinthian farmland, he captured two hill-forts by sheer force, but he allowed the men who had been placed in them by Alexander on garrison duty to leave under a truce. [5] Next, he attacked Orchomenus, where he was let into the city by the faction that was hostile to Alexander. He installed a guard to protect the town, and when Alexander's friends took refuge in the sanctuary of Artemis, he gave their fellow citizens permission to do what they wanted with them. So the Orchomenians dragged the suppliants out of the sanctuary and killed them all, contrary to the common laws of the Greeks.

64. Cassander next went to Messenia, but finding the city* garrisoned by Polyperchon, he chose not to put it under siege for the time being and marched into Arcadia. Leaving Damis as governor of Megalopolis, he carried on into Argolis, where he celebrated the Nemean festival* and then returned to Macedon. [2] After he had left, Alexander and Aristodemus marched against the Peloponnesian cities in an attempt to expel the garrisons installed by Cassander and give the cities back their freedom. [3] When Cassander found out, he sent Prepelaus to Alexander, with the job of asking him to abandon Antigonus and make a formal alliance with Cassander instead. If Alexander complied, Cassander said that he would make him the military governor of the entire Peloponnese, with an army at his

disposal, and would honour him as he deserved. [4] Seeing that he was being offered exactly what had motivated him to go to war with Cassander in the first place, Alexander entered into an alliance with him and was made General of the Peloponnese.

Meanwhile, Polycleitus, who had been sent by Seleucus from Cyprus, sailed into Cenchreae, [5] where he learnt that Alexander had changed sides. Since there was obviously no enemy force to fight there, he set sail for Pamphylia. From there, he sailed along the coast to Aphrodisias in Cilicia, but then he received the news that Theodotus, Antigonus' admiral, was coming from Patara in Lycia with the Rhodian ships,* crewed by Carians, and that Perilaus was shadowing the fleet on land with his troops in order to keep it safe during the voyage. Polycleitus came up with a stratagem that was the undoing of both of these generals at once. [6] He disembarked his soldiers and concealed them in a suitable spot, one the enemy was bound to pass, while he put to sea with his entire fleet, hid behind a headland, and waited for the enemy to arrive.

The land army was the first to fall into the trap. Perilaus was taken prisoner, and the rest either died fighting or were captured. [7] Then, when the Rhodian ships came to help their comrades, Polycleitus suddenly sailed up with his fleet in battle order. He easily routed the enemy, who were thrown into confusion, and in the end he captured every single ship and a great many men too, including Theodotus himself, who was wounded and died a few days later. [8] After having achieved this great success at no risk to himself, Polycleitus sailed off to Cyprus and then Pelusium. Ptolemy commended him for his victory, showed by the size of his gifts how highly he thought of him, and gave him a more prominent position in court as the architect of a significant victory. When Antigonus sent envoys to treat for the prisoners, Ptolemy released Perilaus and a few others, and then he went to the town known as Ecregma* for a meeting with Antigonus. But Antigonus refused to agree to his demands, so he left again.

65. Now that I have covered the affairs of the European Greeks in Greece and Macedon, I shall next describe what was happening in the West. Agathocles, the ruler of Syracuse, had taken over a fortress belonging to the people of Messana, but he promised to surrender the position if they gave him thirty talents. [2] The Messanians duly gave him the money, but so far from keeping faith with those who had believed his promises, he even tried to take Messana itself. When he

was told that a section of the wall had collapsed, he dispatched his cavalry overland from Syracuse, while he sailed up close to the city under cover of darkness with a fleet of *hēmioliae*.* [3] The Messanians learnt in advance about the scheme, however, and the attack failed, but Agathocles sailed to Mylae where the fort capitulated after a siege.*

He then returned to Syracuse, but at harvest time he marched once more against Messana. [4] He made camp near the city and assaulted it unceasingly, but he was unable to injure the enemy to any significant extent because many of the exiles from Syracuse had gathered in the city, and they put up a spirited resistance, not just to keep themselves safe, but also because of their hatred of the tyrant. [5] At this juncture envoys arrived from Carthage, who rebuked Agathocles on the grounds that his actions contravened the terms of their treaty and arranged peace for the Messanians. Once they had also forced the tyrant to restore the fortress, they sailed back to Libya. [6] Agathocles went to Abacaenum,* a town that was in his alliance, where he put to death over forty men whom he believed to be his political enemies.

[7] Meanwhile, the Romans, who were at war with the Samnites, assaulted and took Ferente, a town in Apulia,* and the people of Nuceria Alfaterna were persuaded by some of their number to break off their friendship with Rome and enter into an alliance with the Samnites.*

314/13

66. *At the beginning of the following year, Nicodorus became Archon in Athens, and the consuls in Rome were Lucius Papirius, for the fourth time, and Quintus Publius, for the second time.* In this year:*

[2] When Aristodemus, Antigonus' general, found out about the defection of Alexander, the son of Polyperchon, he delivered a speech at the meeting of the Aetolian assembly,* in which he pleaded his case, and he obtained a majority vote in favour of siding with Antigonus. He then sailed across with his mercenaries from Aetolia to the Peloponnese, where he found Alexander and the Eleans besieging Cyllene.* His arrival was very opportune for the endangered Cyllenians, and he raised the siege. [3] He left men there to keep the stronghold safe and then marched into Achaea. He freed Patrae from

the garrison Cassander had installed and took Aegium. He forced the
garrison there to submit, and he wanted to give the Aegians back their
freedom, as promised in the decree,* but circumstances prevented
him from doing so, because his soldiers turned to looting, and many
Aegians were killed and very many buildings were damaged beyond
repair.

[4] Later, after Aristodemus had sailed across to Aetolia, the people
of Dyme, which was garrisoned by Cassander's men, built a wall
across the city, cutting the acropolis off and separating it from the
lower town. Calling on one another to espouse the cause of independence, they surrounded the acropolis and never slackened their assaults
on it. [5] When Alexander found out, he went there in force, broke
inside, and gained control of the city. He killed or imprisoned some
Dymaeans, and sent a great many into exile. [6] After Alexander had
left, the remaining Dymaeans did nothing for a while, not just because
they were crushed by the magnitude of the disaster, but also because
they had no allies. But after a while they asked Aristodemus' mercenaries
in Aegium for help, and attacked the garrison once again. The acropolis
fell to them and they freed the city. They killed most of the garrison,
and then they also put to death any of their fellow citizens who had
been supporters of Alexander.

67. Meanwhile, as Alexander, the son of Polyperchon, was setting
out with his army from Sicyon, he was killed by Alexion of Sicyon
and some others, who were pretending to be his friends.* But his wife,
Cratesipolis,* took over the reins of government, and she was able to
keep the army together because she was exceptionally popular with the
soldiers. This was due to her benefactions; she used to help men who
were down on their luck and she often supported those who were short
of money. [2] She also had a pragmatic intelligence and an unusual
degree of daring for a woman. After her husband's death, in fact, the
Sicyonians did not expect any trouble from her and they assembled
under arms in a bid for freedom, but she drew up her forces and
defeated them. Many of her opponents died in the battle, and she also
arrested and crucified about thirty others. Once she had a secure grip
on the city, she governed Sicyon as the sole ruler, since she had a large
force of soldiers who would brave any danger for her. That was how
things stood in the Peloponnese.

[3] Seeing that the Aetolians had sided with Antigonus and were
also engaged in a border war with the Acarnanians, Cassander decided

that it would be best for him to form an alliance with the Acarnanians and weaken the Aetolians. He therefore set out from Macedon at the head of a large army and halted in Aetolia at the Campylus river.* [4] He convened a general assembly of the Acarnanians, and after running through their long history of border wars, he advised them to move from their small, unfortified villages into a few cities, because living as they did in dispersed villages made it impossible for them to come to one another's help and made it difficult for them to mobilize when faced with an unexpected enemy attack. The Acarnanians thought he was right, and most of them started to live together in Stratus, which was their largest and most defensible town, but the Oeniadae and some others made Sauria their collective home, as the Derieis and others did Agrinium.* [5] Cassander left a fair-sized army in Acarnania under the command of Lyciscus, to reinforce the Acarnanians, while he went to Leucas and won the city over by diplomacy. [6] Then he went to the Adriatic coast, where Apollonia fell to him straight away. He advanced into Illyris, crossed the Hebrus river,* and fought a battle against the Illyrian king, Glaucias.* [7] Following his victory, he entered into a treaty with Glaucias, the terms of which forbade the Illyrian king from attacking any of Cassander's allies. Then he gained Epidamnus, and after garrisoning the city he returned to Macedon.*

68. After Cassander left Aetolia, about three thousand Aetolians formed a war party, surrounded Agrinium with a palisade, and put it under siege. The inhabitants negotiated a deal with the Aetolians, whereby, on surrendering the city, they could leave under a guarantee of safety, and they duly left, counting on the compact to keep them safe. But, in violation of the agreement, the Aetolians hunted them down—men who thought they had nothing to fear—and slaughtered all but a few of them.

[2] When Cassander reached Macedon and heard about the war that was being made on all the cities of Caria which were allies of Ptolemy and Seleucus, he sent an army there. It was not just that he wished to help his allies, but he also wanted to involve Antigonus in situations that would distract him and make him too busy to cross over to Europe. [3] He also wrote to Demetrius of Phalerum and to Dionysius, the commander of the Munychia garrison, telling them to send twenty ships to Lemnos, and they immediately dispatched the ships with Aristotle in command. Once he had arrived on Lemnos, he

asked Seleucus to bring a fleet, and set about persuading the Lemnians
to defect from Antigonus' alliance. When they refused, he ravaged
their farmland, surrounded the city with a palisade, and put it under
siege. [4] But later Seleucus sailed off to Cos, and when Dioscourides,
Antigonus' admiral, learnt of Seleucus' departure, he swooped down
on Lemnos, drove Aristotle off the island, and captured most of his
ships along with their crews.

[5] Asander* and Prepelaus were the commanders of the expeditionary force dispatched to Caria by Cassander, and when they found out
that Ptolemaeus, Antigonus' general, had split his army up for the winter and was preoccupied by his father's funeral,* they sent Eupolemus
to lie in wait for the enemy at Caprima, in Caria.* The force they sent
along with him consisted of eight thousand foot and two hundred
horse. [6] At the same time, however, Ptolemaeus, who had been
informed by some deserters of the enemy's plan, rounded up 8,300
foot and six hundred horse from the troops who were wintering in the
vicinity. [7] He fell on the enemy camp without warning at around
midnight and caught them off guard and asleep; Eupolemus was taken
prisoner and his men had no choice but to surrender. That was the
outcome of the Asian offensive of Cassander's generals.

69. It was clear that Cassander wanted Asia for himself, so Antigonus
divided his forces, leaving his son Demetrius in Syria with the job of
watching out for Ptolemy, whom Antigonus suspected of planning to
march on Syria from Egypt. He left Demetrius with an infantry force
consisting of ten thousand mercenaries, two thousand Macedonians,
five hundred Lycians and Pamphylians, four hundred Persian bowmen and slingers, a cavalry force of five hundred, and more than forty
elephants. He also assigned him four advisers to act as his right-hand
men: Nearchus of Crete, Pithon, the son of Agenor (who had just
arrived back from Babylon a few days earlier), Andronicus of Olynthus,
and Philip. These were all senior men who had served with Alexander
throughout his campaign—the point being that Demetrius was still
young, since he was only twenty-two years old.

[2] The other division of the army Antigonus took himself. At first,
however, he lost many men as he was trying to cross the Taurus, where
he found deep snow. He turned back to Cilicia, therefore, and waited
for another opportunity. He then crossed the Taurus mountains in relative safety, and when he reached Celaenae in Phrygia, he dismissed
the army to its separate winter quarters. [3] He then sent to Phoenicia

for his fleet, which was commanded by Medius. As Medius was on his way, he came across thirty-six ships from Pydna; he defeated them and captured the ships along with their crews.* That was how things stood in Greece and Asia.

70. In Sicily, the Syracusan exiles who were resident in Acragas urged the rulers of the city not to stand idly by while Agathocles seized control of the cities. It would be better, they argued, to go to war of their own free will before the tyrant got strong, rather than wait for his strength to increase and then be forced to fight against an enemy who outclassed them. [2] This seemed to be no more than the truth, and the Acragan assembly voted for war. They gained Gela and Messana as allies, and sent some of the exiles to Sparta, with the job of trying to find a general to bring back who was capable of taking charge of the war. [3] They did this because they suspected their own political leaders of inclining towards tyranny and thought (because they remembered the Generalship of Timoleon of Corinth) that a general from abroad would exercise supreme command without playing them false.

[4] When the envoys reached Laconia, they found that Acrotatus, the son of King Cleomenes, had provoked widespread resentment among the men of military age, and was therefore on the lookout for opportunities abroad. [5] What happened was that after the battle against Antipater* the Lacedaemonians had exempted the survivors of the defeat from dishonour, and Acrotatus alone had opposed the decree.* This of course irritated many of his fellow citizens, but especially those who were liable to the conventional penalty; a gang of them beat him up, and they were constantly trying to do him down. [6] He was wanting a foreign command, then, and was delighted at the proposal from Acragas.

He took his leave without the approval of the Ephors* and set sail with a few ships with the intention of making straight for Acragas, [7] but he was blown off course into the Adriatic and came to land within the territory of Apollonia. Finding the city under siege by Glaucias, the Illyrian king, he raised the siege by persuading the king to agree to a treaty with the Apollonians. [8] From there he sailed to Tarentum, where he called on the people to join him in liberating Syracuse and succeeded in getting them to vote to send help in the form of twenty ships. They were inclined to find his arguments plausible and compelling because of their kinship* and because of the prestige of his house.

71. Leaving the Tarentines busy with their preparations, Acrotatus sailed with his men to Acragas and assumed the office of General. At first, the common people were greatly encouraged and he led everyone to expect the imminent fall of the tyrant, [2] but as time went on he lost their favour; he achieved nothing worthy of either Sparta or his distinguished lineage, but on the contrary proved to be a man of blood and more savage than the tyrants. [3] Moreover, he abandoned the traditional lifestyle of his native city and indulged in pleasures with such lack of restraint that he seemed to be more Persian than Spartiate.

[4] After he had got through most of the city's revenues by profligacy† and embezzlement, the last straw was when he invited Sosistratus to dinner and murdered him. Sosistratus was the most eminent of the exiles, a man who had often commanded armies, and Acrotatus killed him not because he thought him guilty of any crime, but just because he wanted to get rid of an effective man who was in a position to wait for an opportunity to attack those who abused the leadership with which they had been entrusted. [5] As soon as what he had done became public knowledge, the exiles began to mobilize against him and everyone else fell out of sympathy with him. The first thing they did was take away his Generalship and a short while later they tried to stone him to death. Terrified by the general mood in the city, Acrotatus fled one night and sailed surreptitiously across to Laconia.

[6] Once he had gone, the Tarentines recalled the fleet they had sent to Sicily, and the Acragans, Geloans, and Messanians* brought their war against Agathocles to an end, with Hamilcar of Carthage acting as the mediator between the two parties to the agreement. [7] The most important aspect of the treaty was as follows: of the Sicilian Greek cities, Heraclea,* Selinous, and Himera were to be subject to the Carthaginians, as they had been before, but all the others were to be self-governing under the hegemony of Syracuse.

72. Seeing that there were no hostile armies remaining in Sicily, Agathocles set about bringing the cities and villages under his sway, with no one to stop him. Before long, he had gained control of many places and confirmed his position as sole ruler, in the sense that he had equipped himself with a large number of allies, ample revenues, and a substantial army. [2] Not counting his allies and the Syracusans who were enrolled in the army, he had an infantry force of ten thousand

picked mercenaries and 3,500 cavalry. He also stocked up on weapons and ordnance of all kinds, since it seemed certain that the Carthaginians would soon go to war against him; after all, they had censured Hamilcar over the treaty. That was the situation in Sicily at this time.

[3] In Italy, the Samnites were engaged in their long struggle with the Romans for supremacy. They took Plestice,* which had a Roman garrison, and persuaded the people of Sora to kill all the Romans in the town and enter into an alliance with themselves. [4] Next, while the Romans were besieging Saticula,* the Samnites suddenly appeared in force with the relief of the town as their objective. A fierce battle was fought in which many lives were lost on both sides, but eventually the Romans won. After the battle, they took the town and then marched unimpeded against the nearby towns and villages and set about gaining control of them.

[5] With the war now being fought in the vicinity of the Apulian towns,* the Samnites enrolled every man of military age and encamped near the enemy, hoping to fight the decisive battle. [6] When the Roman people were informed of this, their anxiety about the future was such that they sent a large army out into the field. Since in a crisis it was their custom to give one of their eminent citizens full powers to see to the war, they now appointed Quintus Fabius to this position and made Quintus Aulius his Master of Horse.* [7] Once these men had been given command of the armed forces, they fought a battle against the Samnites at a place called Laustolae,* in which they incurred severe losses. The entire Roman army turned to flight, and Aulius, overcome by shame at the rout, stood alone against the massed enemy—not that he expected to prevail, but he wanted to show that Rome was undefeated, at least in his person.

[8] By refusing to join his fellow citizens in their flight and disgrace, Aulius earned himself a glorious death, but the Romans, faced with the disheartening possibility that they might lose control of Apulia, sent a colony to Luceria, the chief city of the region. They used it as a base from which to wage war on the Samnites, and this turned out to have been an excellent provision as far as their survival was concerned, [9] because the city not only enabled the Romans to gain the upper hand in this particular war, but they have continued to use it as a base of operations against the nearby peoples for all the subsequent wars they have fought, right up until today.*

313/12

73. *At the beginning of the following year, Theophrastus became Archon in Athens, and Marcus Publius and Gaius Sulpicius were elected consuls in Rome. In this year:*

The people of Callatis, a town on the left coast of the Black Sea* which was garrisoned by Lysimachus, evicted the garrison and made a bid for independence. [2] They liberated Istria and the other nearby towns in the same way, and formed them into an alliance for the purpose of making war together against the dynast. They established friendly relations with their Thracian and Scythian neighbours, so that in the end they had a substantial coalition with the ability to stand up to powerful armies.

[3] When Lysimachus found out what they had done, he set out in force against the rebels. He marched through Thrace,* crossed the Haemus mountains, and halted near Odessus. He put the city under siege, and before long the terrified inhabitants surrendered the city to him on terms. [4] Once he had recovered Istria in much the same way, he marched against Callatis. But just then the Scythians and Thracians arrived with a sizeable army to help their allies, as they were obliged to by their agreement. [5] Lysimachus confronted them and engaged them straight away, which terrified the Thracians into changing sides, but he had to fight the Scythians. He won the battle, inflicting heavy casualties on the enemy, and harried the survivors out of the country. Then he surrounded Callatis and put the city under siege, since he was absolutely determined to punish them for having instigated the rebellion.

[6] While Lysimachus was occupied with this, some messengers arrived with the news that Antigonus had dispatched two forces to reinforce Callatis, one by land and one by sea. His general Lycon had brought a fleet into the Black Sea, and Pausanias, with a good number of men under his command, had encamped at the place called Hieron.* [7] The news thoroughly unsettled Lysimachus.* He left an adequate number of soldiers to continue the siege, but he hurried off with the strongest division of the army himself, with the intention of bringing the enemy to battle. [8] When he reached the pass through the Haemus mountains, however, he found that the Thracian king, Seuthes, who had sided with Antigonus, was guarding it with a large

number of soldiers. [9] He engaged Seuthes in a battle that went on for quite a long time, but in the end he overcame the barbarians. The battle cost him a lot of men, but the cost to the enemy was enormous. [10] He also went to meet Pausanias and, finding that he had taken refuge on a hill, he assaulted it, killed Pausanias, and either ransomed the survivors or incorporated them into his own army. That was how things stood with Lysimachus.

74. After this setback, Antigonus sent Telesphorus* to the Peloponnese. He gave him fifty ships and an adequate number of soldiers, and his orders were to free the cities. He hoped that by doing this he would convince the Greeks that he really did care about their freedom, and at the same time it would of course harm† Cassander. [2] As soon as Telesphorus reached the Peloponnese, he marched against the cities that had been garrisoned by Alexander and freed them all except Sicyon and Corinth. He failed with these two because they were serving as Polyperchon's headquarters,* and Polyperchon was keeping strong forces in them, since he had only these forces and the defensibility of the places to keep him safe.

[3] Meanwhile, no sooner had Philip arrived in Acarnania with his army—he had been sent by Cassander to take command of the war against the Aetolians*—than he immediately set out on a plundering raid in Aetolia, and then a little later, when he found out that Aeacides of Epirus had returned to his kingdom* and had raised a mighty army, he swiftly marched against him, because he wanted to fight him on his own, before he joined forces with the Aetolians. [4] He found the Epirotes ready for battle, and he engaged them straight away;* many lives were lost on the enemy side, and many prisoners were captured as well, among whom, as it happened, were about fifty of the men who had been responsible for the king's return. Philip bound these men in chains and sent them to Cassander. [5] But Aeacides and his men regrouped after their flight and linked up with the Aetolians, so Philip advanced once more. He defeated them in battle and took many lives, including that of Aeacides, the king. [6] It had taken him only a few days to win significant victories, and many of the Aetolians became so disheartened that they abandoned their unfortified towns and fled with their children and womenfolk to the most inaccessible mountains. That was how events in Greece turned out.

75. In Asia, Asander, the governor of Caria, was suffering badly in the war and made peace with Antigonus. He was required to hand all his

soldiers over to Antigonus and allow the Greek cities self-determination, but, as a close friend of Antigonus, he would retain his former satrapy as a gift. [2] As a hostage for his observance of these terms, Asander gave his brother Agathon—but then, a few days later, he felt that he had made a mistake in entering into this agreement. He stealthily removed his brother from custody, and he got in touch with Ptolemy and Seleucus, asking them to send help at the earliest possible opportunity.

[3] Antigonus was furious. He sent troops by both land and sea to free the cities, with Medius in command of the fleet and Docimus of the army. [4] When they reached Miletus, they called on the citizens to free themselves, and once they had besieged the garrison on the acropolis into submission, they gave the state back its freedom. [5] While they were going about this, Antigonus took Tralles and then moved on to Caunus. He summoned the fleet there to help him, and captured this city as well, except for the citadel. He put the citadel under siege and began to assault it continuously at the point where it could be approached and attacked. And Ptolemaeus, who had been sent against the town of Iasus with a good-sized army, compelled it to come over to Antigonus' side. [6] And so these Carian cities became subject to Antigonus.

A few days later, ambassadors arrived from the Aetolians and the Boeotians and he entered into an alliance with them;* but negotiations with Cassander about peace in the Hellespont came to nothing, because they could find no common ground at all.* Cassander therefore abandoned the idea of coming to terms with Antigonus and decided to renew his involvement in the affairs of Greece. [7] He sailed with a fleet of thirty ships to Oreus and put the city under siege. He assaulted the city fiercely, and in fact it was about to fall to him when help arrived for the people of Oreus—Telesphorus from the Peloponnese with twenty ships and a thousand soldiers, and Medius from Asia with a hundred ships. [8] They found Cassander's ships lying at anchor in the harbour and set fire to them. Four were destroyed, and they came close to destroying them all. Cassander's men were getting the worst of it, but reinforcements arrived from Athens, and then Cassander sailed into the attack, expecting to make short work of the enemy. He joined battle, sank one of the enemy ships, and captured three others with their crews. So much for the events of Greece and the Black Sea.

76. In Italy, the Samnites advanced in force, ransacking all the Italian cities which were supporting the enemy, but the Roman consuls appeared with an army and endeavoured to help their threatened allies. [2] They freed the town of Cinna* from the danger threatening it as soon as they encamped there close to the enemy, and then a few days later the two armies fought a pitched battle. It was a ferocious business and casualties were heavy on both sides, but in the end the Romans overpowered the Samnites and prevailed; in fact, they took more than ten thousand lives, since they carried on the pursuit for a long time.*

[3] Before they heard about this battle, the Campanians, expecting the Romans to be preoccupied, rose up in revolt, but the Roman people immediately sent an adequate force against them under the command of the dictator Gaius Manius, who was accompanied, in the traditional fashion, by Manius Fulvius as his Master of Horse.* [4] They halted near Capua and at first the Campanians resolved to fight, but once they heard about the defeat of the Samnites, they made peace with the Romans, since they thought that the full force of the Roman armies would now be directed against them. They surrendered those who had been responsible for the uprising, but the men committed suicide without waiting for the outcome of the trial that had been proposed for them. The Campanian cities, however, were pardoned and reincorporated into the Roman alliance, as before.

77. *At the beginning of the following year, Polemon became Archon in Athens, Lucius Papirius (for the fifth time) and Gaius Junius were the consuls in Rome, and in this year the 117th Olympic festival was celebrated, with Parmenion of Mytilene* the victor in the stade race. In this year:*

[2] Antigonus sent his general Ptolemaeus to Greece to free the Greeks,* and sent with him 150 warships under the command of Medius, and a land army of five thousand foot and five hundred horse. [3] He also entered into an alliance with the Rhodians and received from them ten ships that they had fitted out for the war, to support the enterprise of freeing the Greeks. [4] Ptolemaeus took the entire fleet to Boeotia, landing at the harbour known as Bathys, and

the Boeotian Confederacy gave him 2,200 foot and 1,300 horse. He also sent for the ships that were at Oreus, and once he had fortified Salganeus* he made it the collection point for the entire army. He was hoping to gain Chalcis, which was the only city on Euboea to have been garrisoned by the enemy, [5] but Cassander was so concerned about Chalcis that he abandoned the siege of Oreus, sailed to Chalcis, and concentrated his forces there.

When Antigonus heard that each of the land armies in Euboea was waiting for the other to make a move, he recalled Medius and the fleet to Asia, and immediately set out with his army for the Hellespont, forcing the pace of the march, as if he were planning to cross over and invade Macedon. Either Cassander could stay in Euboea, in which case Antigonus would find Macedon undefended, or he could defend his kingdom, in which case he would lose the Greek cities. [6] But Cassander realized what Antigonus was up to and, leaving Pleistarchus* in command of the Chalcis garrison, he marched off at full strength. He took Oropus and made an alliance with the Thebans, but then, after arranging a ceasefire with the other Boeotians and leaving Eupolemus in command of Greece, he returned to Macedon, with the possibility that the enemy might cross over into Europe weighing on his mind.

[7] When Antigonus reached the Propontis, he sent envoys to ask the people of Byzantium to join his alliance. But there were envoys there from Lysimachus as well, asking the Byzantines to do nothing to harm either his or Cassander's interests, and the Byzantines decided to remain neutral and to stay on peaceful and friendly terms with both sides. Foiled in this attempt, and also because winter was drawing in, Antigonus distributed his men among the cities for the winter.

78. Meanwhile, the Corcyraeans, who had gone to help the people of Apollonia and Epidamnus, let Cassander's soldiers leave under a truce. One of the two cities—Apollonia—they left free, but they turned Epidamnus over to Glaucias, the Illyrian king.

[2] Once Cassander had left for Macedon, Ptolemaeus, Antigonus' general, cowed the soldiers who were garrisoning Chalcis into submission and received the surrender of the city. He left Chalcis ungarrisoned as a way of making it clear that Antigonus really did intend to free the Greeks, given that the city was of critical importance for anyone who wanted a base from which to wage a war for supremacy in

Greece.* [3] Anyway, Ptolemaeus next took Oropus, which he turned over to the Boeotians, while making prisoners of Cassander's troops. Then, after gaining Eretria and Carystus as allies, he invaded Attica, where Demetrius of Phalerum was the governor of Athens. [4] The Athenians had for a while secretly been sending messages to Antigonus, asking him to free the city, but now, encouraged by the fact that Ptolemaeus was close by, they forced Demetrius to make a truce and send heralds to Antigonus with a view to making an alliance.*

[5] After Attica,* Ptolemaeus went to Boeotia. He captured the Cadmea, expelled the garrison from Thebes, and gave the city back its freedom. Then he marched into Phocis, where he won over most of the cities and evicted Cassander's garrisons wherever they were to be found. He also proceeded against Locris, and since the Opountians were on Cassander's side he put Opus under siege and subjected it to continuous assaults.*

79. In the summer of this year, the people of Cyrene rose up in rebellion against Ptolemy. They blockaded the acropolis of the city in order to make short work of expelling the garrison, and when envoys arrived from Alexandria and called on them to put an end to their presumptuousness, they killed them and put even more energy into their siege of the acropolis. [2] In response, Ptolemy sent his general Agis there with a land army, and he also sent out a fleet to play a support role in the war, with Epaenetus as its admiral. [3] Agis conducted a forceful campaign against the rebels and took the city by storm. He sent the ringleaders of the rebellion in chains to Alexandria, and disarmed the rest of the population. Then, once he had ordered the city's affairs as he thought best, he returned to Egypt.

[4] With Cyrene settled to his satisfaction, Ptolemy sailed over from Egypt to Cyprus to deal with the kings who had not yet submitted to him. He found that Pygmalion* was negotiating with Antigonus, so he had him killed; and he arrested Praxippus, the king of Lapithus, and <. . .>,† the ruler of Cerynia, whom he suspected of being hostile towards him. He also arrested Stasioecus, the ruler of Marion,*† and he demolished the town and moved the inhabitants to Paphos. [5] He had done what he came to do, and he appointed Nicocreon as the governor of Cyprus, giving him both the cities and the revenues of the kings who had been expelled.

[6] Ptolemy then sailed over with the army to Upper Syria, where he took and sacked Posideium and Potami Caron.* He sailed straight

on to Cilicia, where he took Mallus and sold the captives as booty. He also ravaged the nearby farmland, and once his men had their fill of plunder, he returned to Cyprus. [7] He was deliberately courting the favour of his troops in this way, as a way of making them eagerly anticipate the battles that were to come.

80. Antigonus' son, Demetrius, had remained all this time in Coele Syria, waiting to see if the Egyptian forces would come. But when he heard about the fall of the towns, he appointed Pithon to govern the region in his absence, giving him the elephants and the heavy units of the army, while he took the cavalry and the light units and advanced swiftly towards Cilicia in order to bring help to the embattled towns. [2] He arrived too late, however, and found that the enemy had already left, so he hurried back to his camp. He lost most of his horses in the course of the return journey, because in six days after leaving Mallus he covered twenty-four stages,* which was too punishing a pace for the camp-followers and horse-minders, not one of whom was able to keep up.

[3] Since the expedition had turned out satisfactorily for Ptolemy, he returned to Egypt, but a short while later, with Seleucus urging him on because of his loathing for Antigonus, he decided to attack Coele Syria and confront Demetrius. [4] He therefore rounded up his soldiers from wherever they were based and left Alexandria for Pelusium. His army consisted of eighteen thousand foot and four thousand horse. There were Macedonians and mercenaries in the army, but there were also a great many Egyptians, some of who were responsible for transporting the artillery and the rest of the equipment, while others were armed and equipped for battle. [5] After leaving Pelusium, he crossed the desert and camped near the enemy in Syria, at Old Gaza. Demetrius, who had also ordered his troops to leave their winter quarters and join him at Old Gaza, had been waiting for the enemy to approach.

81. Demetrius' Friends advised him not to fight a pitched battle against a general of such calibre and superior numbers, but Demetrius refused to listen and his confidence was high as he made his preparations, even though he was very young and was about to fight such an important battle without his father. [2] He convened an assembly of his men under arms and stood on a dais, anxious and flustered, but the crowd called on him with one voice not to worry, and before the herald had given the command to quieten the din they all fell silent.

[3] He had not long been in command, and so his conduct as a general and as a statesman had not yet attracted criticism of the sort that tends to be brought against men who have held command for a long time, when all the many reasons for dissatisfaction come together at a particular moment as a single grievance. For the common people never like it when things stay the same, and every group that is not dominant finds change attractive.

By now his father was elderly,* so along with the expectation that Demetrius would succeed to the kingdom came not only generalship, but also the goodwill of the masses. [4] Moreover, he was exceptionally handsome and tall,* and when dressed in royal armour he looked very distinguished and imposing, which led the masses to expect great things of him. And he was also blessed with a certain gentleness, suitable for a young king, which won him universal devotion. The upshot was that even the non-combatants flocked to hear him address the assembly, because they shared in the general anxiety about his youth and about the outcome of the impending battle. [5] After all, not only was he intending to fight against superior numbers, but it would have been hard to find generals greater than the two he was going up against, Ptolemy and Seleucus. They had fought alongside Alexander in all his wars, had often led armies on their own, and had so far never been defeated. [6] Anyway, Demetrius found the right words with which to address the assembled troops— that is, he promised that valour would be rewarded and said that he would leave all the spoils for them—and then he drew up his forces for battle.

82. On his left wing, where he himself was going to be stationed for the battle, he first placed the two hundred picked cavalrymen who formed his guard; they included all his Friends and especially Pithon, who had fought with Alexander, and whom Antigonus had made joint general with Demetrius and his colleague in supreme command. [2] He stationed three cavalry squadrons in front of this guard, and the same number on the flank, and he also placed three squadrons of Tarentines in a detached position beyond the wing. In other words, his person was protected by five hundred mounted lancers and a hundred Tarentines.* [3] The next position was taken by the Companion Cavalry, as they were called, of whom there were eight hundred, and then by at least 1,500 cavalrymen from various parts of the world. In front of the entire wing he posted thirty elephants and filled the gaps

between them with light infantry—a thousand javelineers and bow-men, and five hundred Persian slingers.

[4] That was the arrangement of the left wing, with which he was planning to decide the battle. Next to the left wing he placed the infantry phalanx, which consisted of eleven thousand men: two thousand Macedonians, a thousand Lycians and Pamphylians, and eight thousand mercenaries. On the right wing, he posted the remaining cavalry, numbering 1,500 and commanded by Andronicus. His orders to Andronicus were that he was to maintain an oblique line and avoid battle while waiting to see the outcome of the action initiated by himself. The remaining thirteen elephants he posted in front of the infantry phalanx, and they were joined by an adequate number of light troops in the gaps between them.

So that was how Demetrius disposed his forces. 83. Ptolemy's and Seleucus' original dispositions made their left wing strong, because they were unaware of Demetrius' tactics. But when they learnt the facts from their scouts, they quickly redeployed their forces so that the right wing was strong and included the best troops, who would confront Demetrius and his men on the left wing. On this wing, they stationed their three thousand best cavalry, and they had also decided to fight there themselves. [2] In front of this position they stationed men who carried a palisade clad in iron and bound with chains; this had been made to baffle the charge of the enemy elephants, because when it was stretched out it became easy to stop the creatures moving forward.* [3] In front of this wing, they too posted light infantry units, whose job was to ply the elephants and their riders with a relentless hail of javelins and arrows. Once they had made the right wing strong in this way, they skilfully deployed the rest of their forces and then advanced towards the enemy with a great cry.

Their opponents also advanced, and the first clash came between the cavalry squadrons which had been posted out in front at the outer ends of the wings. Demetrius had much the better of this engagement, [4] but a short while later Ptolemy and Seleucus outflanked Demetrius' wing and launched a more effective attack with their squadrons in column formation, and such was the determination of both sides that a fierce battle took place. [5] In the first charge, in fact, when the combatants were wielding spears, nearly all the spears were broken and many men were wounded. When they wheeled around for the second charge, they hastened to join battle with their swords, and many men died on both sides in the fighting. By risking their lives out in front of the entire formation, the generals themselves inspired the men under their command to face danger without flinching, and on both sides the horsemen, every one of whom had been selected for his skill, vied with one another, since the generals, fighting alongside them, were witnesses of their courage.

84. The cavalry were evenly matched and the engagement went on for a long time. Then the elephants, urged into combat by their mahouts, advanced in a terrifying array, expecting to sweep all before them. But after they had advanced a certain distance, they encountered the iron-clad palisade and a barrage of missiles from the massed javelineers and archers, who began to wound the elephants and their riders. [2] As the mahouts drove the creatures forward with their goads, some of them were impaled on the ingenious palisade and, driven mad by their wounds and the damaging hail of missiles, they began to cause chaos. [3] When these creatures advance over smooth, soft ground, their power overwhelms all opposition, but on uneven, rough terrain their strength is completely negated by the tenderness of their feet. [4] That is why on this occasion Ptolemy negated their strength by installing the palisade, the effects of which he had cleverly foreseen. In the end, after the majority of the mahouts had been shot down, all the elephants were captured. [5] When this happened, most of Demetrius' cavalry turned to terrified flight, leaving Demetrius with only a few men. Although he implored each of them to stand with him and not desert him, no one listened, and he had no choice but to retreat along with them.

[6] As far as Gaza, most of the cavalrymen who were with him maintained discipline and remained in formation, which deterred their pursuers, who were out of order, from attacking. The plain was broad and the terrain soft, which made it easier for those who wanted to retreat in good order to do so. [7] They were accompanied also by some of the infantry, who had chosen to desert and save themselves by travelling light, without their armour.* But as Demetrius was passing Gaza at sunset, some of his cavalry broke off and entered the city, because they wanted to fetch their baggage. [8] That meant that the gates were opened and a large number of draught animals were crowded together there, and since everyone was trying to be the first to lead his own animals out, the situation at the gates became so confused that when Ptolemy came up no one was able to close them

against him. The enemy got inside the defences, then, and the city fell
to Ptolemy.

85. That was the outcome of the battle. Demetrius reached Azotus
around the middle of the night, after a journey of 270 stades. From
there, he sent a herald to request permission to collect his dead, since
he was extremely anxious to honour the dead with proper funerals. [2]
Most of his Friends had fallen, of whom the most eminent were
Pithon, who shared the command on equal terms with Demetrius, and
Boeotus, who had lived for a long time with Demetrius' father Antigonus
and had been privy to all state secrets. [3] More than five hundred
men* fell in the course of the battle, most of whom were cavalrymen of
distinction, and more than eight thousand were captured.

Ptolemy and Seleucus granted permission for the dead to be collected, and sent back to Demetrius, without demanding ransom money,
the royal baggage they had captured and those of the prisoners who
were habitués of Antigonus' court, because, they said, they had nothing to do with the reasons why they were at odds with Antigonus.
Their grievances were that, even though he and they had fought
together, first against Perdiccas and later against Eumenes, he had not
given his friends their share of the spear-won land, and that, even
though there was a pact of friendship in existence between him and
Seleucus, he had still deprived Seleucus of his satrapy, Babylonia, without the slightest justification.

[4] Ptolemy sent the prisoners to Egypt, ordering them to be distributed among the nomes,* and gave all of his men who had died
in the battle a magnificent funeral. Then he advanced against the
Phoenician cities with his army, and either besieged them into submission or won them over by diplomacy. [5] Demetrius' army was
now below strength and he sent a courier to his father with an urgent
request for reinforcements. He made his way to Tripolis in Phoenicia,
and sent for the troops he had stationed in Cilicia and also all those
who were guarding either cities or hill-forts that were a long way from
the enemy.

86. In the course of taking control of the open countryside,
Ptolemy first gained Sidon and then encamped near Tyre. He called
on Andronicus, the garrison commander, to surrender the city, and
promised to reward him with both money and great prestige. [2]
Andronicus replied, however, that there was no way in which he would
betray the trust placed in him by Antigonus and Demetrius, and he

cast coarse insults at Ptolemy. Later, when his troops mutinied and he was expelled from Tyre, Andronicus fell into Ptolemy's hands and expected to be punished for the insults as well as for having refused to surrender Tyre, but Ptolemy bore him no grudge; on the contrary, he gave him gifts and kept him by his side, making him one of his Friends and raising him high in honour. [3] For Ptolemy was exceptionally fair and forgiving, and generous to a fault. In fact, this was a very important factor in the growth of his power, in that he made many men desire his friendship.* [4] Take Seleucus, for example: when he was thrown out of Babylonia, Ptolemy had no hesitation in taking him in, and shared his prosperity with him just as much as with his other friends. [5] And at the time in question as well, when Seleucus asked him for soldiers for an expedition to Babylon, he was happy to comply, and he also promised to do everything he could to help him until he regained his former satrapy. That was how things stood in Asia.

87. In Europe, Telesphorus, the commander of Antigonus' fleet, was based at Corinth. When he saw that Ptolemaeus was being preferred to him and was being entrusted with overall responsibility for Greece, it seemed to him that Antigonus was treating him unjustly. He sold all the ships he had, enlisted those of his soldiers who were willing to join his enterprise, and set about consolidating his position as an independent agent. Pretending that there was no change in his good relations with Antigonus, [2] he went to Elis, where he fortified the acropolis and reduced the population to slavery.* He also plundered the sanctuary at Olympia,* and when he had collected more than fifty talents of silver he began to hire mercenaries. [3] So, out of jealousy of Ptolemaeus' advancement, Telesphorus betrayed the friendship of Antigonus.

When Ptolemaeus, the general Antigonus had made responsible for Greece, heard that Telesphorus had defected and seized Elis—and also that he had helped himself to the sacrosanct valuables of Olympia—he marched to the Peloponnese at the head of an army. When he reached Elis, he demolished the new acropolis fortifications, gave the Eleans back their freedom, and returned the god's property.* Telesphorus had garrisoned Cyllene, but Ptolemaeus persuaded him to turn it over to him and gave it back to the Eleans.*

88. Meanwhile, on the death of their king, Aeacides,* the Epirotes gave the kingship to Alcetas, who had been banished from the kingdom by his father Arymbas.* Alcetas was hostile to Cassander, [2] and so

Lyciscus, Cassander's governor of Acarnania, took an army into Epirus, hoping that it would be easy for him to remove Alcetas from his throne while the kingdom was still in turmoil. [3] When he encamped near Cassope, Alcetas sent his sons Alexander and Teucer around the Epirote communities, ordering them to raise as many soldiers as possible, while he took to the field with all the men he had at his disposal. He drew close to the enemy and waited for his sons to arrive. [4] But when Lyciscus bore down on him with far superior numbers, the terrified Epirotes surrendered to the enemy, and Alcetas, abandoned by his troops, fled for safety to Eurymenae, a town in Epirus.*

[5] While he was under siege there, Alexander arrived with reinforcements for his father and a fierce battle took place, with heavy losses. A number of high-ranking men died, including the general, Micythus, and Lysander of Athens, Cassander's governor of Leucas. [6] But then Deinias arrived with reinforcements for the defeated army and a second battle was fought, which Alexander and Teucer lost. They fled with their father to a stronghold, while Lyciscus took Eurymenae, plundered it, and razed it to the ground.

89. Just then Cassander arrived. He had heard about the defeat his men had suffered, but he was unaware of the subsequent victory, and so he hurried into Epirus to aid Lyciscus. When he found that Lyciscus had won, he made peace with Alcetas and entered into a pact of friendship with him, and then he marched with a division of his army to the Adriatic coast in order to besiege Apollonia, which had thrown out his garrison and gone over to the Illyrians.* [2] The Apollonians were not intimidated, however; they called up reinforcements from their other allies and drew up their forces in front of the city walls. The ensuing battle was closely fought and went on for a long time, but in the end the Apollonians, who had superior numbers, turned their opponents. Cassander lost a lot of men. Since his army was below strength and seeing that winter was on its way, he returned to Macedon. [3] After he left, the Leucadians, with the help of the Corcyraeans, expelled Cassander's garrison. The Epirotes endured Alcetas' kingship for a while, but his treatment of the common people was excessively harsh, and in the end they murdered not just him, but two of his sons as well, Esioneus and Nisus, who were just children.

90. In Asia, after the defeat of Demetrius in Syria, at the battle of Gaza, Seleucus was given some men by Ptolemy—no more than

eight hundred infantrymen and about two hundred cavalrymen—and set out for Babylon. So positive were his expectations that, even if he had had no soldiers at all, he would have taken his friends and slaves and travelled up into the interior with them. He reckoned that the Babylonians would readily side with him because of the goodwill they already held for him, and that, by taking his forces far off, Antigonus had presented him with a perfect opportunity to accomplish his goal. [2] But although he himself was all eagerness, the friends who accompanied him felt extremely discouraged. They could see how few soldiers they were accompanied by and they knew that the adversaries against whom they were advancing had large armies at their ready disposal, abundant supplies, and a great many allies.

[3] When Seleucus saw how frightened they were, he encouraged them by explaining that, when faced with adversity, men who had campaigned with Alexander and had been promoted by him because of their abilities should not rely entirely on military power and financial resources to realize their ambitions, but on experience and intelligence, without which even Alexander would never have achieved his great and universally admired successes. He also argued that they should trust in the predictions of the gods, who had indicated that the outcome of the expedition would match his aspirations. [4] When he had consulted the oracle at Branchidae the god had addressed him as 'King Seleucus',* and Alexander had appeared to him in a dream and given him an unambiguous sign of the supremacy that lay in his future, which he was bound to gain in the fullness of time. [5] And he added that nothing fine or admirable is achieved in this life without toil and danger. But he also courted the favour of the soldiers who were with him: he treated them unfailingly as equals, and this earned him the respect of all his men and made them willing to endure the risks that would attend the bold venture.

91. On he marched, and when he reached Mesopotamia, a combination of persuasion and pressure enabled him to get the Macedonians who had been settled in Carrhae* to join his expedition. When he entered Babylonia, most of the inhabitants came to meet him, declared their loyalty, and promised to help him whatever he chose to do. [2] He had been the satrap of Babylonia for four years, and had always treated everyone well, so that he had gained the loyalty of the people and had ensured well in advance that there were men there who would support him if he was ever granted the opportunity to try to recover

his leadership. [3] He was joined also by Polyarchus, the superintendent of an administrative district of Babylonia, who brought more than a thousand soldiers with him.

When those who remained loyal to Antigonus realized that there was no way they could check the popular impulse, they retreated for safety to the acropolis, the garrison of which was commanded by Diphilus. [4] Seleucus besieged the citadel and, once he had taken it, released from captivity the friends and pages of his who had been in custody there; they had been imprisoned by Antigonus after Seleucus had left Babylon for Egypt. [5] When he had done this, he enlisted more troops and collected horses, which were given to those who were competent riders. By treating everyone well and raising their hopes, he kept those who joined him in this hazardous venture ready and willing to face any situation that might arise in the future. So Seleucus was in the process of recovering Babylonia by these means.*

92. When Nicanor, the governor of Media, raised an army of more than ten thousand foot and about seven thousand horse from Media, Persis, and the neighbouring territories, Seleucus lost no time in setting out to confront him. [2] He had in all somewhat over three thousand foot and four hundred horse. He crossed the Tigris, and when he was informed that it would take the enemy no more than a few days to get there, he concealed his men in the nearby marshes, intending to make a surprise attack. [3] When Nicanor reached the Tigris and found no trace of the enemy, he made camp by one of the staging posts on the Royal Road,* supposing that they had made themselves scarce. Nicanor's men were therefore careless and slipshod in their posting of pickets, and during the night Seleucus attacked. The unexpectedness of the attack sowed confusion and terror in Nicanor's camp, [4] not least because when the Persians became involved in the fighting, both their satrap, Evagrus,* and some of their senior officers were killed.

At this, most of the ordinary soldiers went over to Seleucus, not just because they were frightened and their lives were in danger, but also because they had been finding Antigonus' behaviour offensive. [5] Nicanor was left with only a few men, and since he thought there was a good possibility that he might be betrayed to the enemy, he fled with his friends through the desert. Seleucus now had a powerful army, and his generous treatment of everyone soon gained him Susiane, Media, and some of the neighbouring territories.* He wrote to Ptolemy and his other friends about the measures he had taken, since he now had the stature of a king and glory that was worthy of supreme power.

93. Meanwhile, Ptolemy had stayed in Coele Syria after his defeat of Demetrius, the son of Antigonus, in a major battle.* When he heard that Demetrius had returned from Cilicia and was encamped in Upper Syria, he chose one of his Friends, a Macedonian called Cilles, [2] gave him an adequate army, and ordered him either to chase Demetrius out of Syria altogether, or to confine him there and crush him. But while Cilles was still en route, Demetrius' spies told him that the camp he had established at Myous* was carelessly defended. Demetrius left his baggage train behind and took only mobile troops with him. He marched at speed through the night and fell on the enemy unexpectedly at around the dawn watch; the army surrendered without a fight and the general was taken alive.

Demetrius felt that a victory of this magnitude cancelled out his earlier defeat, [3] but all the same he was sure that Ptolemy would proceed against him at full strength, so when he made camp he used the marshes and swamps as his forward defences. He also wrote to his father about his victory, and asked him either to send him an army as soon as possible or to come to Syria himself. [4] Antigonus happened to be in Phrygia, at Celaenae, and when he received the letter he was extremely pleased because his son, despite his youth, seemed to have redressed the situation on his own and to have shown himself worthy of kingship. He set out with his army from Phrygia, and a few days after crossing the Taurus he joined Demetrius.

[5] When Ptolemy learnt of Antigonus' arrival, he convened a meeting of his officers and Friends, with the agenda of deciding whether it was better for him to stay where he was and fight the decisive battle in Syria, or return to Egypt and fight there, as earlier he had fought Perdiccas.* [6] The unanimous advice he received was that he should not take on an army that considerably outnumbered his and had a great many elephants, and that was led, besides, by a general who had never been beaten. It would be far easier to fight in Egypt, they said, where they had abundant supplies and could rely on the natural defences of the region.* [7] So Ptolemy decided to leave Syria. He destroyed the most important of the towns he had captured—Ake in Phoenician Syria, and Joppa, Samaria, and Gaza in Syria—and then he returned to Egypt with his army and all the valuables that could be driven or carried away.

94. Having recovered all Syria and Phoenicia without striking a blow, Antigonus' next project was a campaign against the land of the Arabs known as the Nabataeans,* who he had decided were hostile to his interests. He delegated the job to one of his Friends, Athenaeus, and gave him a force consisting of four thousand light infantry and six hundred cavalry who were capable of moving at speed. His orders to Athenaeus were that he was to attack the barbarians without warning and take their livestock for himself.

[2] It will be useful, for the sake of those of my readers who are unfamiliar with the Nabataeans, for me to give an account of the customs of this Arabian people—customs which are thought to enable them to preserve their freedom. They live in the open countryside, claiming as their homeland a wilderness that has no rivers or springs plentiful enough to provide an enemy army with water. [3] It is their way to sow no grain, cultivate no fruit- or crop-bearing plants, drink no wine, and build no houses. If anyone is found contravening these rules, the penalty is death. [4] These practices are based on the belief that people who possess such things are dependent on them, and that makes them vulnerable to being compelled by powerful men to do their bidding. They do raise camels and sheep, however, pasturing them in the desert. This is common practice among the Arabian peoples, but the Nabataeans are far wealthier than the rest, even though there are scarcely more than ten thousand of them. [5] The reason is that quite a few of them regularly bring down to the coast frankincense, myrrh, and other precious aromatics, which they procure from people who bring them from Arabia Felix, as it is called.*

[6] They are exceptionally attached to their freedom, and when an enemy approaches in strength, they retreat into the desert. The desert serves as their defences, because, being waterless, it is inaccessible to others, but the Nabataeans have built stucco-lined tanks underground, so that they are the only ones for whom the desert is safe. [7] The ground consists partly of clay† and partly of soft rock, so the holes they dig are large; they make the mouths of the holes very small indeed, but by constantly increasing the width as they dig deeper, they eventually end up with a space with sides a plethron in length. [8] After filling these tanks with rain water, they close the mouths and make them level with the rest of the terrain, leaving markers which are known to them but unrecognizable by others. [9] They also let

their sheep drink only once every three days, so that when they flee
into the desert the creatures will not require regular access to water.

Their diet consists of meat, milk, and edible wild plants; [10] pep-
per grows there, for instance, and the trees produce plenty of so-called
wild honey,* which they drink mixed with water. There are also other
Arabian peoples, some of whom even work the land; they live among
the tribute-paying peoples of the empire, and have the same customs
as the Syrians, except the custom of living in houses. 95. So much for
the practices of these Arabs.

When it is time for their general assembly (which is traditionally
attended by all the local inhabitants, some of whom come to sell
goods, others to buy what they need), before going there they leave
their property, along with the elderly, the children, and the womenfolk, at a certain rock.* [2] This place has superb natural strength,
despite being unwalled, and the nearest inhabited place is two days'
journey away. Athenaeus waited until it was time for the assembly and
then set out to attack the rock with his troops equipped for mobility.
It took him three days and three nights to complete the journey of
2,200 stades* from the province of Idumaea, and the Arabs had no
idea that he was coming. He seized the rock in the middle of the night
[3] and, wasting no time, killed or made prisoners of the people he
found there, leaving behind only a few wounded. He packed up most
of the frankincense and myrrh, and also about five hundred talents of
silver. He stayed there for no longer than one watch,† and then hurried back the way he had come, since he expected that the barbarians
would come after him. After marching for two hundred stades, he
and his men made camp; they were tired and they posted their pickets
in a slipshod manner, since they did not think that the enemy would
be able to set out for two or three days.

[4] But people who had seen the army brought news of it to the
Arabs, and they immediately regrouped, cancelled the assembly, and
marched to the rock. The wounded men there told them what had
happened, and they hurried after the Greeks. [5] In their camp,
Athenaeus and his men were not expecting any trouble, and while they
were deep in exhausted sleep some of the prisoners escaped and told
the Nabataeans about the situation in the enemy camp. The Nabataeans—
there were at least eight thousand of them—attacked at about the third
watch. They slaughtered most of the Greeks where they lay, still in
their beds, and those who woke up and ran for their weapons were

massacred. In the end, all the infantrymen were killed, but about fifty cavalrymen escaped, though most of them were wounded.

[6] So that is how, thanks to his own indiscretion, Athenaeus came to fail after initial success. In fact, success is invariably followed by carelessness and negligence, [7] and that is why some people rightly hold that it is easier to endure disaster wisely than it is to keep one's wits about one at a time of great success. Disaster leaves one no choice but to be cautious, out of fear of what might happen next, but success encourages men to be totally careless, because they have already met with good fortune.

96. After having manfully punished the enemy, the Nabataeans returned to the rock with the property they had recovered. They wrote to Antigonus—the letter was written in Syrian*—denouncing Athenaeus and justifying themselves. [2] When Antigonus wrote back to them, he endorsed their claim that they had been justified in defending themselves, and he placed the blame on Athenaeus, claiming that the attack on the Nabataeans went beyond the orders he had received. This was a way of disguising his intentions and duping the barbarians into relaxing their vigilance, so that they would not be expecting his attack when it came and he would make a success of the enterprise. After all, trickery was really the only feasible way to get the better of men who had adopted a nomadic way of life and had the desert as an inaccessible refuge.

[3] The Arabs were delighted at having apparently been released from great fear, but they did not altogether trust Antigonus' words, and, since they were uncertain what the future might hold, they posted lookouts on the hills, which afforded a fine, long-distance view of the passes into Arabia, and once they had got themselves properly organized they waited to see what would happen. [4] Antigonus treated the barbarians as friends for a while, until he thought he had them thoroughly fooled and was being presented with the opportunity to go against them. Then he selected from the entire army four thousand infantrymen, who were lightly armed and physically capable of speed, and more than four thousand horsemen, and ordered them to carry several days' worth of food that would not need cooking. He gave the command to his son, Demetrius, and sent him out at the first watch, to do his best to punish the Arabs.

Demetrius marched for three days without using roads to avoid being spotted by the barbarians, 97. but their lookouts saw that a hostile force had invaded and informed the Nabataeans by means of their system of beacons. Reckoning that it would not take long for the Greeks to get there, the barbarians stored their belongings in the rock and posted a guard of sufficient strength, given that there was only a single, man-made way up to it;* they also divided their flocks and drove them here and there into the desert. [2] When Demetrius reached the rock and found that the booty was missing, he made repeated assaults on the stronghold, but the men inside resisted well. In fact, the height of their position gave them a clear advantage, and on this first day Demetrius fought on until evening and then had the trumpeter recall his men.

[3] The next day, as he approached the rock, one of the barbarians called out to him. 'King Demetrius,' he said, 'why are you making war on us? What is it you want? What is driving you to this? We live in the desert, in a part of the world that has no water, grain, or wine—in other words, that has none of the things which, in your world, count as the necessities of life. [4] It is our unequivocal desire to avoid enslavement that has led us to take refuge in a land that lacks everything that is valued by others, and to choose to live just like wild beasts, remote from civilization, doing no harm at all to the rest of you. We ask you and your father, then, to cease your aggression against us. We ask you to accept gifts from us, withdraw your men, and henceforth regard the Nabataeans as friends. [5] However much you want to, you cannot stay here long, since you lack water and all other provisions, nor will the application of force make us change our way of life, though you might gain a few prisoners to turn into unhappy slaves suffering under an alien culture.'

[6] After listening to this appeal, Demetrius pulled his men back and told the Arabs to send him an embassy to negotiate terms. They sent their most senior men, who, making use of much the same line of argument, persuaded Demetrius to accept as gifts the most valuable things they had to give, and to make peace with them.

98. Once he had been given hostages and the promised gifts, Demetrius left the rock. After a march of three hundred stades, he halted close to the Asphalt Lake,* which I should describe before moving on. It lies in the middle of the satrapy of Idumaea,* and is approximately five hundred stades long and about sixty wide. Its water is very bitter and extremely foul-smelling, which means that it is unable to support fish or any other familiar kind of aquatic animal,

and although great rivers with exceptionally sweet waters flow into it, it overwhelms them with its foul smell. Every year, a mass of solid asphalt erupts up to the surface in the middle of the lake. It varies in length from more than three plethra down to a little less than one plethron, and the barbarians who live near by have special terms for it: they call the larger mass a 'bull' and the smaller one a 'calf'. Since the asphalt floats, that part of the lake looks from a distance like an island. There are signs twenty days before the event that an eruption is going to take place: the stench of asphalt spreads for many stades all around the lake, accompanied by a vile exhalation, and everything in the district that is made of silver, gold, or bronze loses its character- istic colouring,* though it comes back again once the eruption of the asphalt has completely finished. Since the whole region thereabouts is torrid and foul-smelling, the inhabitants are physically sickly and do not live for very long. But the land—or as much of it as is intersected by serviceable rivers or by springs with enough water for irrigation—is good for growing palm trees. And there is a valley in the district where the plant called balsam grows, which is a good source of income because this is the only place in the world where it grows and doctors find it extremely effective as a medicine.

99. Once the asphalt has erupted, the people who live on either shore of the lake treat it as plunder, because they are enemies of each other. They have a peculiar way of collecting it, without boats. What they do is make large bundles of reeds and throw them into the lake. Three men, but no more, sit on one of these bundles; two of them row, using blades that are attached to the bundles, and the third man carries a bow to ward off adversaries from the opposite shore or anyone who dares to offer violence. [2] When they are close to the asphalt, they jump on to it with axes, cut off chunks as if it were soft stone, load them on to the bundle of reeds, and then row back. If the bundle breaks apart and someone falls into the water who is unable to swim, he does not sink, as he would in other bodies of water, but stays afloat just as a swimmer would.* [3] For it is a characteristic of this liquid that it supports any heavy body that has the properties of growth and breathing. Only solid bodies sink, and I suppose this is because they are almost as dense as silver, gold, lead, and so on; but even these sink much more slowly than they do when they are cast into other bodies of water. The barbarians who make a living in this way take the asphalt to Egypt and sell it for the embalming of the

dead, because it is only if asphalt is blended with the other aromatics that the preservation of the corpse can be permanent.*

100. On Demetrius' return, he gave his father a detailed report about what he had done, and Antigonus told him off for coming to terms with the Nabataeans. He said that by leaving them unpunished Demetrius had made the barbarians far bolder; they would assume that they had been pardoned not because he had been moved by a sense of justice, but because he had been unable to defeat them. However, he commended Demetrius for his survey of the lake and for having apparently discovered a new source of income for the kingdom. He made the historian Hieronymus responsible for this; [2] he was to get some boats ready, collect all the asphalt, and take it to a certain place.

The outcome, however, was not at all what Antigonus had hoped. The Arabs formed a war party of about six thousand men, sailed on their bundled-reed rafts against the men in the boats, and shot down almost all of them. [3] After that, Antigonus gave up on this source of income, not just because of the setback he had suffered, but also because he had more important matters on his mind. A courier had recently arrived with a letter from Nicanor, the governor of Media and the upper satrapies, telling of Seleucus' journey back to Babylon and the defeats he had suffered at Seleucus' hands. [4] Worried about the upper satrapies, Antigonus dispatched his son, Demetrius, with an infantry force of five thousand Macedonians and ten thousand mercenaries, and four thousand horse. His orders were to march inland to Babylon, recover the satrapy, and return promptly to the coast.*

[5] Demetrius set out from Damascus in Syria and rapidly put his father's orders into effect. When Patrocles, Seleucus' military commander of Babylon, found out that Demetrius was in Mesopotamia, he did not dare to wait for his arrival, because he had only a few men. He ordered the civilian population to evacuate the city—some of them were to cross the Euphrates and take refuge in the desert, while others were to cross the Tigris into Susiane and make their way to Euteles on the Red Sea*— [6] while he and the few men he had, using river-beds and canals as cover, moved around the satrapy, keeping an eye on the enemy,* but also keeping Seleucus in Media up to date about what was happening and asking him to send reinforcements as soon as he could.

[7] When Demetrius reached Babylon and found the city abandoned, he set about assaulting the citadels. The first of them fell to
him and he gave his men permission to plunder it, but after besieging
the other one for a few days, by which time it was clear that it would
be a lengthy process, he left one of his Friends, Archelaus, to persevere with the siege with a force of five thousand foot and a thousand
horse, while he set out for the coast with the rest of the army because
he would soon be due back as ordered.*

101. Meanwhile, in Italy the war between the Romans and the
Samnites continued; farmland was raided, towns were assaulted,
armies were constantly out in the field. There was no let-up, and
fighting of every kind and description occurred as the two most
warlike peoples of Italy struggled for supremacy. [2] At one point,
the Roman consuls were encamped with a division of the army
within sight of the enemy camp, waiting for a suitable opportunity
for battle and protecting the allied towns. [3] The rest of the army
was with Quintus Fabius, who had been appointed dictator, and he
took Fregellae* and made prisoners of the foremost opponents of
Rome, who numbered more than two hundred. He marched them
off to Rome and took them into the Forum for public execution
in the traditional manner; they were flogged and then beheaded.
A short while later he invaded enemy territory and took Calatia and
the citadel of Nola.* He sold most of the spoils, and divided up the
farmland into allotments for his soldiers. Since matters were progressing satisfactorily, the Roman people sent a colony to the island
known as Pontia.*

102. In Sicily, Agathocles had reconciled his differences with the
Siceliots, apart from the Messanians, and the Syracusan exiles gathered in Messana, since this was the only city that remained hostile to
the dynast. [2] Agathocles wanted to break up this coalition and he sent
his general Pasiphilus to Messana at the head of an army, with instructions, privately delivered,* as to what he should do. [3] Pasiphilus'
arrival in Messanian territory came like a bolt out of the blue, and he
took a lot of prisoners and captured a great deal of booty. Then he asked
the Messanians to actively seek his friendship and not to be forced to
negotiate terms along with his bitterest enemies. [4] The prospect of
a bloodless resolution to the war inspired the Messanians to expel the
Syracusan exiles, and they welcomed Agathocles when he came with
an army.

[5] At first, Agathocles treated them well and persuaded them to take back the exiles he had with him in his camp, who had been officially banished from Messana. [6] Later, however, he rounded up from Tauromenium and Messana those who had formerly been opposed to his rule—about six hundred men in total—and slaughtered them all. [7] He was intending to go to war against the Carthaginians and he wanted to clear all opposition out of Sicily first. The Messanians had already driven out of the city the mercenaries who were most loyal to them and were capable of protecting them from the tyrant, and now those of their citizens who were hostile to Agathocles had been killed and they had been forced to take back men who had been officially convicted of criminal activity. When they saw how things stood, they regretted what they had done, but they had no choice but to put up with the situation, since the great power wielded by their masters cowed them into submission.

[8] Agathocles began by marching against Acragas, which he planned to annex, but when a Carthaginian fleet of sixty ships sailed in he abandoned the project. Instead, he invaded territory that was subject to the Carthaginians. He plundered the farmland, and the hill-forts either fell to his assault or came to terms with him.

103. Meanwhile, Deinocrates, the leader of the Syracusan exiles, got in touch with the Carthaginians and asked them to send help before Agathocles made himself master of all Sicily. [2] Having taken in the exiles who had been banished from Messana, Deinocrates had a strong army, and he now sent one of his associates, Nymphodorus, with a division of his forces to Centuripae. [3] The town had been garrisoned by Agathocles, but some of its citizens had promised to surrender it, provided the people were allowed political independence afterwards. So one night Nymphodorus broke into the town, but when the commanders of the garrison realized what was going on, they killed both Nymphodorus himself and his companions as they were forcing their way inside the walls.

[4] Agathocles availed himself of this opportunity. He brought charges against the people of Centuripae and put to death all the alleged ringleaders of the sedition. While the dynast was occupied with this, fifty Carthaginian ships sailed into the Great Harbour of Syracuse, but all they were able to do was sink two freighters from Athens that they found there† and cut off the hands of the crews.* [5] It was widely held that this was a savage way to have treated people

who had done them not the slightest harm, and it did not take long for the gods to indicate their displeasure: immediately on leaving Syracuse, some of the ships became separated from the rest of the Carthaginian fleet off Bruttium; they were captured by Agathocles' generals, and the Phoenicians* who were taken prisoner suffered the same fate that they had inflicted on their prisoners.

104. The exiles who were with Deinocrates had at their disposal more than three thousand infantry and at least two thousand horse, and they accepted an invitation from the citizens of Galeria to occupy the town. They drove out Agathocles' garrison, but remained outside the town themselves. [2] Agathocles swiftly sent Pasiphilus and Demophilus against them with five thousand soldiers, and they joined battle with the exiles, who were led by Deinocrates and Philonides, each in command of one of the wings. Both sides fought with such determination that the outcome hung in the balance for quite a while, but when Philonides fell, one of the two generals, and his division of the army turned to flight, Deinocrates too was forced to retreat. Pasiphilus inflicted heavy casualties on the enemy as they fled. With Galeria recovered, he killed those who were responsible for the uprising.

[3] When Agathocles found out that the Carthaginians had occupied the hill called Ecnomus in the territory of Gela, he decided to commit his entire army to do battle with them. He took to the field, and when he was near their position, flushed with his earlier victory he challenged them to battle. [4] The barbarians refused the challenge, and Agathocles took this to mean that the open countryside was now his, gained by default. He returned to Syracuse, where he embellished the most important of the temples with the spoils of war.

These were the events that took place in this year, as far as I have been able to discover.

105. *In the year of the Archonship of Simonides in Athens, the Romans appointed as their consuls Marcus Valerius and Publius Decius. In this year:*

Cassander, Ptolemy, and Lysimachus brought the war with Antigonus to an end and concluded a treaty with him.* The treaty specified that Cassander was to be the General of Europe until Alexander, Rhoxane's

328 THE LIBRARY BOOK 19 311/10

son, should come of age; that Lysimachus should be master of Thrace and Ptolemy of Egypt and the neighbouring cities in Libya and Arabia;* that Antigonus should have supremacy in all Asia; and that the Greeks should be autonomous.* But they failed to abide by this agreement; instead, each of them came up with plausible pretexts for trying to increase his own power.

[2] Cassander could see that Rhoxane's son, Alexander, was growing towards maturity, and he was aware that there were people in Macedon who were disseminating the idea that the boy should be released from custody and his father's kingdom should be turned over to him. Fearful for purely personal reasons, Cassander ordered Glaucias, who was responsible for the boy's custody, to murder Rhoxane and the king, hide their bodies, and to keep the matter completely secret.* [3] Glaucias carried out his orders—and Cassander, Lysimachus, Ptolemy, and Antigonus were freed from the threat they had been expecting the king to pose in the future. [4] Since there was no longer anyone to inherit the empire, from then on anyone who ruled peoples or cities could entertain hopes of kingship and the territory under his sway was in effect a kingdom, won by the spear.

That was how things stood in Asia, Europe, Greece, and Macedon.* [5] In Italy, the Romans marched against Pollitium, a town belonging to the Marrucini,* with a strong force of combined foot and horse. They also sent out some of their citizens as colonists to settle the place known as Interamna.*

106. In Sicily, Agathocles was growing in strength day by day and increasing the size of his forces. When the Carthaginians found out that the dynast was annexing the cities in the island and that his forces outnumbered theirs, they decided to put more effort into the war. [2] In a very short time, they had fitted out† 130 triremes, and as general they chose one of their most distinguished men, Hamilcar. They gave him an army consisting of two thousand citizen soldiers (among whom were many eminent men), ten thousand from Libya, a thousand mercenaries and two hundred chariot-riders* from Etruria, and a thousand Balearic slingers. They also gave him plenty of money and made sure that he had all that he might need in the way of ordnance, grain, and other military necessaries. [3] The whole fleet set sail from Carthage, but a storm suddenly struck when they were out at sea. Sixty triremes were sunk and two hundred grain-carriers destroyed. The rest of the fleet barely managed to make it safely to Sicily against the storms they encountered. [4] Many leading Carthaginians lost their lives, and the city instituted a period of public mourning for them; the walls were covered in black sackcloth, which is the Carthaginian custom when great misfortune strikes the city.

[5] Hamilcar, the general, reassembled the survivors of the storm, enrolled mercenaries, and recruited the pick of his Sicilian allies. He also took over command of the forces that were already on the island and, once he had taken care of everything that needed to be done for the war, he mustered his army in the open countryside. It consisted of about forty thousand infantry and not far short of five thousand cavalry. Since it had not taken him long to redress the disaster at sea, and since he was widely held to be a skilled general, he dispelled the gloom that had taken hold of his men's minds and gave his enemies plenty of cause for anxiety.

107. It was clear to Agathocles that the Carthaginian forces were superior to his, and he assumed that many of the fortresses would go over to the Phoenicians, along with all the towns and cities that bore him a grudge. [2] He was particularly uncertain about the Geloans when he found out that the entire enemy army was in their territory. His fleet also suffered a considerable setback at this time when twenty ships were captured at the strait* by the Carthaginians along with their crews. [3] Nevertheless, he decided to secure Gela with a garrison, but he did not dare to introduce a force openly, in case it gave the Geloans the excuse they had been looking for to thwart him, and he lost the city and the important resources it gave him. [4] He therefore sent his men off a few at a time, as if they had some business to attend to, until the citizens were far outnumbered by his soldiers.

When Agathocles himself arrived a short while later, he accused the Geloans of treachery and desertion, either because they really were planning some such move, or because he had believed the lies of the exiles, or perhaps because he wanted to enrich himself with their wealth. In any case, he had more than four thousand Geloans killed and confiscated their property. He also ordered all the remaining Geloans to bring out their coined money and their uncoined gold and silver bullion, and warned that disobedience would be punished. [5] Everyone rushed fearfully to carry out this order of his, and as a result he collected a very large sum of money and made all his subjects petrified of him. He was thought to have treated the Geloans with undue savagery, and after he had dumped the bodies of those he had killed in the trenches outside the city walls and had left an adequate garrison in the city, he marched off and halted within sight of the enemy.

108. The Carthaginians were occupying the hill Ecnomus, which is said to have been one of Phalaris' strongholds; in fact, it is said to have been where the tyrant had the infamous bronze bull made, a contraption which was an instrument of punishment by torture when a fire was lit underneath it. Hence the place was called Ecnomus because of his heinous treatment of his unfortunate victims.* [2] Opposite them, Agathocles had occupied another of Phalaris' strongholds, which was called Phalarium after him. A river ran between the two camps, and both sides had made it their forward defence against the enemy. There was an old rumour flying around to the effect that a large number of men were destined to die in battle in that spot, and since it was unclear to which of the two sides this disaster would occur, both camps were filled with superstitious dread and neither of them was looking forward to combat.

[3] For quite a while, then, neither army dared to cross the river in a massed formation, and it took an unusual event to bring about a full-scale battle. Libyan incursions into his territory provoked Agathocles to respond in kind, and on one occasion, when the Greeks were driving away some livestock and draught animals that they had stolen from the Carthaginians, troops issued from the Carthaginian camp and gave chase. [4] Agathocles guessed what was going to happen, and he placed a force of men, picked for their valour, in ambush beside the river. As the Carthaginians crossed the river in pursuit of the rustlers, these men suddenly sprang from concealment into the attack, and since the enemy were out of order they easily turned them.

[5] With the barbarians being cut down and running for their camp, Agathocles felt that this was an opportune moment for battle and he led his entire army against the enemy position. The attack took the Carthaginians by surprise and before long Agathocles had filled up a section of the trench, torn down the palisade, and forced his way into the camp. [6] The Carthaginians, who had been thrown into a panic by the unexpected attack and had no time to form up, confronted the enemy and fought just as they were. A ferocious battle took place between the two sides at the trench and soon the whole area was strewn with corpses, because on the one side Carthaginians of the highest rank* rushed up to help when they saw that the camp was

being taken, and on the other side Agathocles, encouraged by the advantage he had gained and thinking that he could conclude the entire war with a single battle, piled the pressure on the barbarians.

109. Seeing that his men were being overpowered and that more and more Greeks were pouring into the camp, Hamilcar brought up the slingers from the Balearic Islands. There were at least a thousand of them, [2] and they kept up such a relentless barrage of large stones that many of the attackers were injured or even killed, and very many of them had their protective armour shattered. These Balearic slingers normally employ stones a mna in weight, and they make a major contribution towards victory in battle, since in their part of the world they practise constantly with the sling from childhood onwards. [3] So the barbarians drove the Greeks from the camp and got the better of them.

But Agathocles returned to the attack at other points, and the camp was actually on the point of falling when ships arrived fortuitously from Libya, bringing reinforcements for the Carthaginians. [4] With fresh confidence, the men from the camp fought the Greeks from the front, while the newly arrived reinforcements covered all the other angles. These unexpected blows swiftly reversed the course of the battle, and the Greeks fled either to the Himeras river or back to their camp. The retreat went on for forty stades, and since almost all of this was level terrain the barbarian cavalry, five thousand strong, harried them all the way. The intervening space therefore became filled with corpses, and the river also played a major part in the destruction of the Greeks in the sense that, since it was the season of the Dog Star* and the pursuit was taking place in the middle of the day, many of the fugitives became parched by the heat and the effort of running and drank to excess, even though it was salt water.* As a result, as many men were found dead beside the river without a scratch on their bodies as were killed in the course of the pursuit. About five hundred of the barbarians lost their lives in this battle, and at least seven thousand Greeks.

110. It was a complete disaster for Agathocles. He rallied the survivors of the rout, burnt his camp, and retreated to Gela. He had spread the word around that he intended to leave before long for Syracuse, and when three hundred Libyan horsemen encountered some of his soldiers in the countryside, they were told that Agathocles had left for Syracuse. So the Libyans entered Gela as friends, but this turned out to be a false assumption and they were massacred.

[2] Agathocles shut himself up in Gela, not because he could not get through safely to Syracuse, but because he wanted to tempt the Carthaginians into besieging Gela, so that the Syracusans would be able to harvest their crops, as the season demanded, in complete safety. [3] Hamilcar did think at first about besieging Gela, but when he found out that there were troops in the city to defend it and that Agathocles was very well off for supplies, he gave up the idea. Instead, he did the rounds of the fortresses and towns, gaining their allegiance and treating everyone with kindness in an attempt to win the loyalty of the Siceliots. In fact, Camarina, Leontini, Catane, and Tauromenium sent embassies straight away and went over to the Carthaginians, [4] and a few days later Messana, Abacaenum, and many other towns raced one another to see who could be the first to transfer their allegiance to Hamilcar.* This shows how powerful the mood was, generated by their loathing for the tyrant, that swept over the common people after the defeat.

[5] Agathocles led the remnants of his army back to Syracuse, repaired the ruined stretches of the defensive wall, and brought the grain in from the fields. His plan was to leave a strong enough guard to protect the city, while he took the bulk of the army over to Libya and made the mainland the theatre of war instead of the island. But, in keeping with the plan announced at the beginning of this book, I shall make Agathocles' invasion of Libya the starting point for the next book.

1. Writers who insert lengthy speeches into their history or resort time and again to oratory* lay themselves open to criticism on two counts: they break up the sequence of the narrative with the disproportionateness of the speeches they introduce, and they frustrate the enthusiasm of readers who are keen to acquire a knowledge of history.* [2] Surely, if someone wants to display his rhetorical skill, there is nothing to stop him composing speeches for politicians and ambassadors as a distinct pursuit, and the same goes for all other kinds of speeches—those that praise or find fault with their subjects,* for instance. After all, if he acknowledges that they are different genres of writing and works at each of these two pursuits separately, he might well expect to become highly regarded in both fields. [3] At present, however, some writers—those who over-indulge in rhetorical speeches—make history-writing a mere adjunct to oratory.

It is not only bad writing that puts readers off; they also dislike it when a work that seems to be successful in other respects fails in respect of the structure and proportionality* that properly belong to its genre. [4] Faced with such a work, some readers skip the speeches, however well done they appear to be, while the disproportionate wordiness of the author makes others lose interest, and they give up reading the work altogether. And this is not an unreasonable thing for them to do, [5] because a work of history should properly be a simple and organic whole. In short, it resembles a living body in that, if it is not unified, it loses its ability to please the mind, while if it retains its essential unity, its proportionality preserves that ability, and its overall organic unity makes the work enjoyable to read and comprehensible.

2. All the same, I do not entirely disapprove of the use of rhetorical speeches in a work of history and think they have absolutely no place at all. History should be embellished by variety, and there are passages where it is necessary to enlist the aid even of rhetorical speeches—and I too would not want to deny myself the opportunity to do so—which means that when the situation calls for a speech by an ambassador or a politician, or whatever kind of speech it may be, a writer who failed boldly to enter the rhetorical fray would be the one to deserve criticism. [2] I mean, there are a good many obvious reasons for feeling

obliged to enlist the aid of rhetoric on a number of occasions. There have been many well-argued and elegant speeches, so one should not contemptuously omit those that deserve to be remembered and are valuable in a historical context, nor, when the subject is an important and glorious event, should one allow one's language manifestly to fall short of the deeds being described. From time to time, when something unexpected happens, I shall have no choice but to make use of speeches* that are suitable for the purpose of casting light on an otherwise inexplicable event.

[3] But I have said enough on this, and I should now turn to the events of the period before us. But first I shall explain which years belong to the present book. In the preceding books, I have covered both Greek and non-Greek history from the earliest times down to the year before Agathocles' expedition to Libya, which took place a total of 883 years after the sack of Troy.* In this book I shall add the history of the subsequent years; I shall cover nine years, starting with Agathocles' invasion of Libya and ending with the year in which the kings formed a coalition and went to war against Antigonus, the son of Philip.

310/9

3. *In the year of the Archonship of Hieromnemon in Athens, the Romans appointed as their consuls Gaius Julius and Quintus Aemilius.**

In Sicily, after his defeat by the Carthaginians at the Himeras river and the loss of the largest and best part of his army, Agathocles had taken refuge in Syracuse. [2] Under the circumstances—with all his allies having changed sides, and the barbarians in control of almost all Sicily except for Syracuse and outclassing him by far on land and at sea—he did something so utterly bold that no one could have foreseen it. [3] No one thought that he would even try to resist the Carthaginians, but he planned to leave an adequate guard for the city and to sail over to Libya with a select force of suitable soldiers.

In doing this, he had various hopes and expectations. He hoped to find the Carthaginians softened by long years of peace and, since they therefore had no experience of battles and fighting, he expected that they would easily be defeated by men who had been schooled by danger.* He hoped that the Libyan auxiliaries, who had long resented

Carthaginian dominion, would seize the opportunity to rebel. He hoped, above all, that his unexpected appearance would enable him to plunder a land which had remained unravaged and which, thanks to Carthaginian prosperity, was filled with all kinds of good things. And, in general, he hoped to distract the barbarians from Syracuse and from Sicily as a whole, and transfer the war entirely over to Libya—which is exactly what happened.

4. He told none of his friends about this plan. He made his brother Antander responsible for the city and gave him an adequate guard, while he selected and enrolled suitable soldiers for the expedition. His orders to the infantry were that they should be ready with their arms and armour, and he told the cavalry to bring not only their panoplies, but also saddlecloths and bridles, so that, once he had captured some horses, there would be men with the necessary equipment ready to mount them. [2] The point was that, in the course of his recent defeat, even though it was the majority of his infantrymen who had been killed, while almost all the cavalrymen had survived, he was unable to transport their horses over to Libya. [3] To make sure that the Syracusans did not rise up in rebellion in his absence, he broke families up, focusing especially on separating brothers from brothers and fathers from sons, leaving some in the city and taking others with him over to Libya. [4] Obviously, affection for their offspring would deter those who remained in Syracuse from doing the slightest harm to Agathocles' interests, even if they happened to be bitter enemies of the tyrant.

[5] To solve his money problems, he confiscated the estates of the city's orphans from their trustees, claiming that he would make a far better guardian of the property than them and could be more relied on to return it to the children when they came of age, and in addition he took out loans from traders, seized some of the dedications that had been given to the temples,* and stripped the women of their jewellery. [6] Then, since it was clear that the majority of the wealthiest Syracusans found what he was doing abhorrent and were bitterly opposed to him, he convened an assembly. At this assembly he played up both the earlier defeat and the dangerous future that awaited them, saying that while he would† have no difficulty in enduring the siege, because he was accustomed to all kinds of hardship, he pitied his fellow citizens if they were shut up and forced to endure one. [7] If there were any men who were unwilling to endure what Fortune

had in store for them, he said, they should save themselves and take their property with them. But once the wealthiest men, those who were particularly hostile to the dynast, had set out from the city, he sent some of his mercenaries after them, killed them, and took their property for himself. [8] At one fell swoop, he enriched himself and purged the city of his enemies, and then he gave all the slaves who were capable of military service their freedom.*

5. When everything was ready, Agathocles manned sixty ships and waited for a suitable opportunity to set sail. Since no one knew what his intentions were, people supposed either that he was planning to campaign in Italy or that he was going to lay waste to the Carthaginian-controlled part of Sicily. Everyone expected it to be a suicide mission and condemned the dynast for his lunacy. [2] But the enemy was blockading the harbour with a far larger number of ships than Agathocles had, so for a while he was forced to keep his soldiers on board, since he was unable to get out of the harbour. A few days later, however, some grain ships were running for the city and the Carthaginians set out with their entire fleet to attack them. Agathocles, who by then had begun to think that he would have to abandon the expedition, saw that the mouth of the harbour was clear of the blockading ships and rowed out at top speed.

[3] Next, when the Carthaginians, who were already closing in on the freighters, saw the enemy sailing in close formation, their initial assumption was that they were coming to the rescue of the grain ships, and they turned and made their fleet ready for battle. But when they saw Agathocles' ships sailing straight past and pulling away, they set out in pursuit. [4] With the two fleets contending against each other, however, the freighters were suddenly out of danger, and they brought their plentiful supplies into Syracuse, which was already short of grain. And then Agathocles, who was about to be overtaken by the Carthaginians, was unexpectedly saved by nightfall. [5] On the next day, there occurred such a total solar eclipse that it might as well have been night, with stars visible all over the heavens.* But this only made Agathocles even more worried about what might happen, because he took the portent to be a harbinger of evil for him.

6. After a voyage of six days and nights, at dawn the Carthaginian fleet was suddenly spotted near by. Forced by this into awareness of the urgency of the situation, the two sides vied to out-row each other. The Phoenicians were motivated by the belief that the capture of the

enemy ships would leave Syracuse at their mercy and at the same time free their country from extreme peril; the Greeks saw clearly the fate that awaited them if they did not make land before the Carthaginians reached them, and the horrors of slavery that awaited those who had been left behind at home. [2] When the Libyan coast came in sight, the crews of each fleet urged themselves on and redoubled their efforts. The barbarians' ships were faster, because their oarsmen had put a lot of time and effort into their training, but the Greeks had a sufficient lead. The remaining distance was very quickly covered, and when they were close to land, the Greek ships drove for the beach together, like men in a race. [3] In fact, the last of Agathocles' ships were within missile range, and the first of the Carthaginian ships were beginning to shoot at them. There was a brief engagement, involving bows and slings, and the barbarians joined battle with a few of the Greek ships, but with his superior numbers Agathocles had the best of it. At that point, the Carthaginians withdrew a short distance and lay at anchor outside of missile range, while Agathocles disembarked his forces (the place was called the Quarries), threw up a palisade from sea to sea, and beached his ships.

7. As if this venture had not been hazardous enough, Agathocles next set about another one, even more dangerous. He called for those of his senior officers who would do his bidding in this enterprise and with them by his side he sacrificed to Demeter and Korē* and then convened an assembly. [2] When the men had assembled, he stepped forward to speak, wearing a garland on his head and a magnificent *himation*.* After some preliminary remarks concerning the mission they had undertaken, he said that, while they were being pursued by the Carthaginians, he had made a vow to Demeter and Korē, the patron goddesses of Sicily, that he would make a burnt offering to them of the entire fleet.* [3] Now that they were safe, he said, it was right that he should fulfil his vow, and he said that these ships were nothing compared to the numbers he would replace them with if his men fought with determination. And in fact, he added, the goddesses had indicated by means of the sacrificial victims* that victory in the war as a whole would be his.

[4] While he was speaking, one of his attendants brought up a lighted brand. He took it in his hand and ordered brands to be distributed to all the captains of the ships, and then, calling on the goddesses as witnesses, he led the way by setting out for the command

ship. He stood by the stern* and ordered the others to do the same. Then all the captains tossed their brands into their ships, and before long flames had risen into the air. The trumpeters sounded the signal for battle, the soldiers followed this with their battle-cry, and everyone prayed that they might return home safely.

[5] Agathocles' main reason for doing this was to force his men to banish the idea of flight from their minds when they were in danger.* If there was no chance of their falling back on the ships, obviously their only hope of safety lay in victory. Besides, he did not have a large army, and plainly, if he had to protect the ships, he would have to divide his forces and that would make him no match for the enemy, whereas if he left them undefended he would be making a present of them to the Carthaginians.

8. Nevertheless, when all the ships were ablaze and the fire had taken extensive hold, fear gripped the Siceliots. Initially, they had been misled by Agathocles' sorcery* and, since the speed with which he executed his plans allowed them no time for reflection, they had all gone along with what was happening. But when they had time to think about it in detail, they were overtaken by regret, and the thought of the vastness of the sea that lay between them and home made them despair of survival.

[2] Wanting to raise his men's spirits, Agathocles led them against a Carthaginian town called Megalopolis. [3] The intervening countryside, through which they had to march, was divided into plots and fields growing every conceivable kind of plant, since the whole region was irrigated by water channelled through numerous sluices. Estate followed estate, with richly appointed, meticulously whitewashed houses which indicated the wealth of the owners. [4] The farm buildings were filled with things that were good to eat, since the locals had had many years of peace in which to lay in abundant stores of their products. The land was partly given over to vines and partly to a profusion of olives and other fruit-bearing trees. To left and right, herds of cattle and flocks of goats were being pastured on the plain, and the nearby fens teemed with horses out at grass. In short, the region was prosperous in every imaginable way, because the several owners of the estates were the most eminent Carthaginians and they had used their wealth to beautify them and make them pleasing.*

[5] The Siceliots were astounded by the beauty of the land and its prosperity, and they began to be more eager for the coming conflict

when they saw that the prizes that would readily fall to the victors were commensurate with the risks they were running. [6] As soon as Agathocles saw that his men's spirits were improving and that they were looking forward eagerly to battle, he launched an assault on the walls of Megalopolis. Partly because of the unexpectedness of the attack, and partly because of the inhabitants' ignorance and inexperience of warfare, resistance was brief and he overran the town. He gave his troops permission to plunder, and this had the effect of simultaneously filling the camp with booty and his men with confidence.

[7] Agathocles next set out immediately for White Tunis,* as it is called, which lies about two thousand stades from Carthage, and gained the town's submission. The soldiers were expecting to protect both the towns that had fallen to them, and they began depositing their booty in them, but Agathocles had further plans along the lines of what he had already done, and he explained to his men that it was in their interests to leave behind them no place of refuge until they had won a major battle. He therefore razed the towns to the ground and camped in the open countryside.

9. At first, the Carthaginians who were lying at anchor off the Siceliot beachhead were delighted when they saw the ships on fire, because they supposed that it was fear of them that had driven the Greeks to destroy their ships. But when they saw the enemy army advancing into the countryside, they thought over the consequences of the destruction of the ships and concluded that it was a disaster for them. They therefore draped hides over the prows of their ships, which is their invariable practice when something has happened that is held to be bad for the city of Carthage as a whole.* [2] They also took the bronze ram-sheaths of Agathocles' ships and stowed them in their own vessels,* and sent messengers to Carthage to deliver a precise report about what had happened. But before these messengers arrived to deliver the news, some country folk who had seen Agathocles' ships arrive rushed to Carthage with the information. [3] The Carthaginians had not been expecting anything like this, and in their fear they assumed that their own forces had been wiped out in Sicily—both the land army and the navy, they thought, because it seemed to them that Agathocles would never have dared to leave Syracuse undefended unless he had been victorious, and would never have ventured to transport his army across to Libya if the sea was still controlled by his enemies.

[4] Panic and confusion therefore gripped the city, the masses gathered in the agora, and the Council of Elders met to decide what to do. There was no armed force available with the ability to stand up to the enemy, the mass of citizens had no experience of war and were therefore already inclined to defeatism, and the enemy was expected outside the city walls. [5] Some of the Carthaginians were in favour of sending envoys to Agathocles to sue for peace—envoys who would double as spies to assess the enemy's situation—while others thought they should wait until they had found out exactly what had happened. While the city was in this state of chaos, however, the messengers who had been sent by their admiral sailed in and explained what had happened.

10. Everyone's confidence revived. The Council of Elders issued a collective reprimand to the officers of their navy for having let an enemy army land in Libya when they had control of the sea, and they gave the command of their forces to Hanno and Bomilcar. There was an ancestral feud between these two men, [2] and the Carthaginians thought that their mutual mistrust and enmity would secure the safety of the city as a whole,* but that was far from the truth. In fact, Bomilcar had for a long time aspired to tyranny, but he had not been strong enough and had never found the right moment for putting his plans into effect; but now, by being appointed general, it became significantly more feasible.

[3] The fundamental issue was the harshness of the Carthaginian system of punishment. At a time of war, they promote their leading men to commands, since they think it the duty of such men to be the first to brave danger for the state; but at a time of peace, out of envy they take these men to court on trumped-up charges and punish them. [4] Hence some of those who are given commands become rebels because they are afraid of being taken to court, while others attempt to set themselves up as tyrants. This is what one of the two generals, Bomilcar, did at the time in question, and I shall come back to him later.*

[5] Anyway, the Carthaginian generals could see that the situation did not favour the slightest delay, and without waiting for troops to arrive from the countryside and the allied cities,* they took the citizen militia out into the field. With this army of at least forty thousand foot, a thousand horse, and two thousand war chariots,* [6] they occupied a rise not far from the enemy and drew up their troops for

battle. Hanno had the command of the right wing, which included the men assigned to the Sacred Battalion.* Bomilcar, in command of the left wing, drew up his men in a deep phalanx, since the terrain was not conducive to an extended front. They stationed the cavalry and the chariots in front of the phalanx, because they had decided to attack first with these units and test the mettle of the Greeks.

11. After checking the formation adopted by the barbarians, Agathocles gave the right wing to his son, Archagathus,* with the 2,500 foot that he had assigned him. Next to the right wing he posted the 3,500 Syracusans, then three thousand Greek mercenaries, and finally three thousand Samnites, Etruscans, and Celts. He himself, along with his bodyguard, fought at the head of the left wing,† pitting a thousand hoplites against the Carthaginian Sacred Battalion, and he divided the archers and slingers between the two wings. [2] His troops barely had sufficient arms and armour and, seeing that the galley crews were unarmed, he had stretchers of sticks made for the shield covers,* so that they had the circular appearance of a shield, and he distributed these fake shields to the men; they were completely useless, but from a distance they were able to give an impression of armour to anyone who did not know better.

[3] It was clear, however, that his troops were terrified by the numbers of the enemy cavalry and infantry,† so Agathocles ordered owls to be released into the lines at various points. He had laid in these owls beforehand as a way of dealing with poor morale among the rank-and-file soldiers. [4] They flew among the infantry lines, settling on shields and helmets, and the soldiers' morale was boosted by what they all took as a portent, since the bird is supposed to be sacred to Athena.* [5] Some people might think the idea ridiculous, but this kind of thing† has often been responsible for significant victories.* And that is what happened on this occasion as well: their spirits rose, word was passed among the ranks that the goddess was unequivocally indicating that victory would be theirs, and they awaited the onset of battle with increased courage.

12. And so, when the battle opened with the chariots being sent against them, the Greeks shot some of them down and let others pass through their lines,* but they forced most of them to turn back towards their own infantry lines. [2] They withstood the cavalry charge too with equal success, shooting down enough of them to make the rest flee to the rear. But while they had been putting on a dazzling

display of martial prowess in these preliminary stages of the battle, the entire barbarian infantry had come to close quarters [3] and a monumental battle took place. Hanno, who had the elite Sacred Battalion under his command and wanted to be personally responsible for victory, pressed hard on the Greeks and took many lives. He did not yield even under the barrage of missiles he encountered, but pushed forward despite being wounded many times, until at last he was worn down and died.

[4] After his death, Carthaginian spirits in that part of the field sank, while Agathocles' men took heart and were greatly encouraged. [5] When messengers brought the news to Bomilcar, the other general, he thought that this was a gift from the gods and that the moment had come for him to seize the opportunity for his attempt on the tyranny. His reasoning was as follows: if Agathocles' army was destroyed, he would not be able to launch his attempt to seize power because his fellow citizens would be strong. However, if Agathocles won, that would crush the Carthaginians' spirits; the defeated people would readily submit to him and it would be easy for him to defeat Agathocles whenever he liked.

[6] Having come to this conclusion, he fell back, taking with him the soldiers of the front rank. To the enemy, this gift of a withdrawal was incomprehensible, but Bomilcar told his men about Hanno's death and ordered them to pull back in good order to the rise, claiming that this was in their best interests. [7] But under the enemy's assaults the whole retreat was beginning to resemble a rout, and the Libyans of the next ranks gained the impression that the first rank was being defeated by main force and turned to flight themselves. However, the officers who had taken charge of the Sacred Battalion since the death of Hanno, their general, put up a strong resistance for a while. Stepping over the bodies of those of their comrades who had fallen, they endured every hazard, but when they realized that the bulk of the army had turned to flight and that the enemy was starting to come at them from the rear, they had no choice but to fall back. [8] So, with the rout spreading throughout their army, the barbarians began fleeing in the direction of Carthage. Agathocles pursued them for a while, but then turned back and plundered their camp.

13. The Greeks lost about two hundred men in the battle, and the Carthaginians a thousand at the most, though some historians say they lost more than six thousand. Along with all the other booty, there was

found in the Carthaginian camp a large number of carts which were being used to transport more than twenty thousand pairs of handcuffs. [2] The barbarians had been expecting to get the better of the Greeks without any difficulty, and had urged one another to take as many prisoners as possible and to throw them, cuffed, into slave workhouses. [3] But the gods, I think, make sure that, when people have arrogant expectations, the outcome is the opposite of what they had hoped. At any rate, Agathocles, after his unexpected victory, had the Carthaginians trapped within their city walls. But Fortune had success and failure play their parts alternately and humbled the victors no less than the defeated. [4] For in Sicily the Carthaginians had Syracuse under siege after their great defeat of Agathocles, while in Libya Agathocles had the Carthaginians pinned inside their city and under siege after having won a major battle, and the most surprising thing of all was that on the island, where Agathocles had had fresh forces, he proved inferior to the barbarians, while on the mainland he got the better of his conquerors with only a fraction of the army that had earlier been defeated.

14. That is why the Carthaginians believed that the disaster had been visited upon them by the gods and devoted themselves to supplicating heaven in every way imaginable. They thought that it was above all Heracles, the god of their founders,* who was angry with them, and they sent a very large sum of money and many of their most valuable dedications to Tyre. [2] Carthage was originally a colony of Tyre and it had been their custom in times past to send a tenth of all their revenues to the god, but later, even though they became very wealthy and had more substantial revenues, they sent hardly anything and neglected the god. But now this misfortune made them regret their neglect and remember all the gods of Tyre. [3] They even sent the golden temples, simulacra and all,* that had been dedicated in their sanctuaries, thinking that they would be more likely to mitigate the god's wrath if his dedications were sent to appease him. [4] They thought that Cronus had turned against them as well,* because in times past they had sacrificed the best of their sons to this god, but later they started sending for sacrifice children they had secretly bought and brought up in their homes. An investigation took place, which revealed that a number of the children who had been destined for sacrifice were supposititious.

[5] Weighing these things in their minds, and seeing the enemy encamped right by the city walls, they were frightened that they had

offended the gods by having abandoned the traditional ways of honouring them and were eager to redress their error. So they selected
two hundred sons of the most distinguished families and sacrificed
them in public, and in addition at least three hundred of those who
were suspect volunteered to be sacrificed. [6] In Carthage, there was
a bronze statue of Cronus with his arms stretched out, palms up, and
inclining towards the ground, so that a child placed on the out-
stretched arms would roll off and fall into a fiery pit.* It seems likely
that this is where Euripides got the idea for what he says about the
legendary sacrifice in Tauris, in the lines where he has Orestes ask
Iphigeneia 'But what tomb will receive me when I die?', and she
replies: 'A great pit in the earth, with sacred fire within.'* [7] And the
traditional story the Greeks tell, based on ancient legend, that Cronus
did away with his children,* seems to have been perpetuated among
the Carthaginians by means of this custom.

15. Be that as it may, after this reversal in Libya, the Carthaginians
wrote to Hamilcar in Sicily, asking him to send reinforcements at the
earliest possible opportunity, and they sent him the bronze ram-
sheaths they had taken from Agathocles' ships. When the messengers
arrived, Hamilcar ordered them to keep quiet about the defeat they
had suffered, and instead to spread the word among the troops that
not just Agathocles' ships, but his entire army had been completely
wiped out.* [2] Then he sent some of these new arrivals from Carthage
into Syracuse as envoys to demand the surrender of the city on the
grounds that their army had been annihilated by the Carthaginians
and their fleet burnt. If anyone doubted the truth of this, he offered
proof in the form of his possession of the rams.

[3] When the inhabitants of the city were told about the alleged
disaster that Agathocles had suffered, the masses believed it to be
true, but the city officials were not entirely convinced. They made
sure that the city remained peaceful and they lost no time in sending
the envoys out of the city, but they also banished at least eight
thousand people, who were either the relatives and friends of men
they had exiled or others who were opposed to what they were doing.*
[4] With such a large number of people suddenly forced to leave their
homeland, the streets were filled with people running here and there,
and with confused noise and wailing women, because there was no
household that did not have its share of grief at this time. [5] Some of
Agathocles' sympathizers were lamenting the fate of the tyrant and

his children; some of the ordinary citizens were mourning those who (as they thought) had been lost in Libya, while others were weeping for the men who were being expelled from hearth and ancestral gods, who were not allowed to stay in the city, but could not go outside the walls either because of the ongoing siege by the barbarians, and who, on top of all this misery, great as it was, were also being forced to involve their infant children and wives as well, and drag them too into exile. [6] In fact, however, any exiles who turned to Hamilcar for safety were afforded his protection. He then got his army ready and led it against Syracuse. He expected the city to fall to him, not just because there was no one left to defend it, but also because those who remained in the city knew of the alleged disaster in Libya.

16. Hamilcar sent envoys to convey his offer of safety for Antander and his colleagues in return for their surrendering the city. The most senior of the city's leaders met in council, and after a lot of discussion Antander—who was a weak man,* with none of his brother's boldness and energy—concluded that it would be best if they surrendered the city. Erymnon of Aetolia,* however, who had been appointed by Agathocles to join his brother on the council, expressed the opposite opinion and persuaded the council to persevere until they had accurate information about what had happened. [2] When Hamilcar learnt of the council's decision, he set about constructing various siege engines, since he had decided to go on the offensive.

[3] But Agathocles had built two thirty-oared ships after the battle, and he sent one of them to Syracuse, rowed by his best oarsmen and commanded by Nearchus, a trusted friend, to bring news of his victory. [4] After an easy voyage they approached Syracuse during the night of the fifth day and at dawn they were about to sail into the harbour, garlanded and singing paeans as they went, [5] but the Carthaginians' picket ships saw them coming and hastened to intercept them. Since the ship they were pursuing had no great lead, it became a rowing race, and while they were vying with each other in this way, both the Syracusans and the besiegers, who had seen what was happening, ran to the harbour and each side began to shout encouragement to their men. [6] Soon the thirty-oared ship was on the point of being overtaken, and the barbarians cried out in triumph, while the Syracusans, unable to bring concrete help, prayed that the gods would save the lives of those who were trying to sail in. Now they were close to land and one of the Carthaginian ships was manoeuvring

to ram its quarry, but the Greeks thwarted their pursuers by coming within missile range, and now that the men from the city could help, the ship escaped danger.

[7] However, when Hamilcar saw that in their anxiety and in anticipation of some extraordinary news the Syracusans had flocked to the harbour, it occurred to him that a certain part of the wall might be unguarded and he sent his best men there with scaling ladders. Finding that the guards had indeed left their posts, they scaled the wall without interference and had almost completed their takeover of an entire stretch of curtain wall when a patrol, making its usual rounds, arrived and spotted them, [8] and battle was joined. The Syracusans ran up to help and, since they arrived before their opponents could reinforce the men who had scaled the wall, a massacre ensued, with some of the enemy being thrown from the battlements. [9] Hamilcar was deeply disappointed by this, and he withdrew his forces from the city and sent help to Carthage in the form of five thousand soldiers.

17. Meanwhile, Agathocles, who already had control of the countryside, was engaged in taking the strongholds near Carthage by storm, and he won the towns over to his side either by frightening them into submission or, in some cases, by exploiting their hatred of the Carthaginians. After building a fortified camp near Tunis and leaving a fair-sized guard for it, he set out against the cities on the coast. The first, Neapolis,* he took by storm, but he treated the inhabitants well once they had fallen into his hands. Then he marched against Hadrumetum,* which he put under siege, and he gained Aelymas, the king of the Libyans, as an ally.

[2] When the Carthaginians found out what was happening, they marched against Tunis at full strength. They captured Agathocles' camp, brought siege engines up to the city, and began to launch wave after wave of assaults. [3] When messengers brought news of the loss of his camp, Agathocles left the bulk of his forces to continue the siege, and with his bodyguard and a few other soldiers he stealthily made his way to a place in the mountains from where he could be seen by both the people of Hadrumetum and the Carthaginians who were besieging Tunis. [4] That night, he had his men light fires over a large area, which gave the Carthaginians the impression that he was bringing a substantial army against them, and made the people pinned inside Hadrumetum believe that another powerful army had arrived

to support their enemies. [5] Both the Carthaginians and the people of Hadrumetum were taken in by the stratagem* and suffered unexpected defeats as a result, with those who were besieging Tunis abandoning their engines and fleeing to Carthage, and the people of Hadrumetum surrendering their city out of fear. [6] After negotiating the terms of the surrender, Agathocles next took Thapsus by force, and the other towns in the region were either besieged into submission or negotiated their surrender. Once all the towns and cities had submitted to him—and there were more than two hundred of them—he planned to campaign next in inland Libya.

18. After Agathocles had set out and had been on the march for quite a few days, the Carthaginians took to the field with the army that had been brought over from Sicily and with the rest of their forces. They set about besieging Tunis for a second time and recaptured many of the strongholds that were in enemy hands. As soon as messengers arrived from Tunis and informed Agathocles about the Phoenician offensive, he turned back, [2] and when he was two hundred stades away from the enemy, he made camp and ordered his soldiers to light no fires. Then he marched through the night, and at dawn fell on those who were foraging in the countryside and others who were wandering around outside the camp and out of formation. He killed over two thousand of these men and took many prisoners. This gave his confidence a substantial boost for the future, [3] because the addition of the reinforcements from Sicily and the support of their Libyan allies had seemed to give the Carthaginians the advantage, but after this successful strike of his the barbarians' spirits were again crushed. In fact, Agathocles also defeated Aelymas, the Libyan king, who had deserted his cause, and in the battle many of the barbarians lost their lives, including the king. That was how things stood in Sicily and Libya.

19. As for Macedonian affairs, Cassander went to help Audoleon, the king of the Paeonians, in his war with the Autariatae.* He not only saved his life, but he also resettled about twenty thousand of the Autariatae, along with the children and womenfolk who went with them, at Mount Orbelus. [2] While he was engaged with this, Ptolemaeus, who was responsible for Antigonus' Peloponnesian army, feeling that the dynast had treated him badly and that he was not being treated with the respect he deserved, defected from Antigonus and entered into an alliance with Cassander. Moreover, he deputized Phoenix, one

of his closest friends who was the governor of the satrapy on the
Hellespont, sent him soldiers, and asked him to garrison the fortresses
and towns and to defy Antigonus.

[3] By the terms of the mutual agreement entered into by the
dynasts,* the Greek cities were to be left free, so Ptolemy, the ruler of
Egypt, accused Antigonus of garrisoning the cities* and prepared to
go to war. [4] He dispatched his army with Leonidas in command and
gained the submission of the cities in Rough Cilicia that were subject
to Antigonus. He also wrote to the cities that were subject to Cassander
and Lysimachus, asking them to help him put an end to the growth of
Antigonus' power.* [5] But Antigonus sent his youngest son Philip to
the Hellespont to tackle Phoenix and the rebels there, and he sent
Demetrius to Cilicia, where he conducted a vigorous campaign in
which he defeated Ptolemy's generals and recovered the cities.

20. Meanwhile, Polyperchon was in the Peloponnese, nursing his
grudge against Cassander.* He had for a long time aspired to supremacy in Macedon, and he now summoned Heracles, the son of Barsine,
from Pergamum.* Heracles, who was about seventeen years old, was
the son of Alexander the Great and was being brought up in Pergamum.
[2] Polyperchon wrote around to his personal friends and anyone
who was hostile towards Cassander, asking them to restore the young
man to his father's kingdom, [3] and he also wrote to the Aetolian
Confederacy, asking them to grant him safe passage through their
territory and to support his war effort, and promising to repay the
favour many times over if they helped restore the young man to his
father's kingdom. Everything went according to plan. The Aetolians
had no hesitation in complying with his wishes,* many others joined
forces for the purpose of restoring the king, and they ended up with
an army of more than twenty thousand foot and at least a thousand
horse. [4] In the course of preparing for war, Polyperchon also set
about collecting money and writing to solicit support from his friends
in Macedon.

21. When Ptolemy, who held sway over the cities of Cyprus, was
told by some informants that Nicocles, the king of Paphos,* had
secretly entered into a pact of friendship with Antigonus, he sent two
of his friends, Argaeus and Callicrates, to kill Nicocles. He was keen
to guard against the possibility that any of the other kings might be
moved to change sides by seeing that earlier rebels had got away with
it. So Argaeus and Callicrates sailed to the island, and once they had

been given soldiers by Menelaus, the governor, they surrounded Nicocles' house, informed him of the king's wishes, and ordered him to take his own life.

[2] At first, Nicocles tried to defend himself against the charges, but when his pleas fell on deaf ears he killed himself. When Axiothea, Nicocles' wife, heard of her husband's death, she killed her daughters, who were virgins, to make sure that no enemy possessed them, and urged the wives of Nicocles' brothers to join her in choosing death, although Ptolemy had not ordered the wives' deaths and had even agreed to leave them alive. [3] With the royal residence a bloodbath, overwhelmed by unforeseen calamity, Nicocles' brothers locked the doors, set fire to the house, and committed suicide. So the house of the kings of Paphos came to an end in this tragic fashion.* And now that I have given an account of what happened in Cyprus, I shall resume my sequential account of events.

22. In the Black Sea region, in the course of this year, following the death of Parysades, the king of the Cimmerian Bosporus,* his sons, Eumelus, Satyrus, and Prytanis, were fighting one another for supremacy. [2] The eldest son, Satyrus, had been bequeathed the throne by his father (who had reigned for thirty-eight years), but Eumelus had entered into a pact of friendship with some of the neighbouring barbarians and, once he had raised a formidable army, he began to challenge his brother's claim to the throne. [3] When Satyrus found out, he took to the field against Eumelus in strength. He crossed the river Thates,* halted close to the enemy position, and protected his camp by surrounding it with the very large number of wagons he had used to transport supplies. Then he drew up his men for battle, with himself in the centre, in command of the phalanx, as is the Scythian custom. [4] In his army there were close to two thousand Greek mercenaries and the same number of Thracians, and all the rest were his Scythian allies, numbering twenty thousand foot and at least ten thousand horse. But Eumelus had Aripharnes, the king of the Siraces, as an ally, who had twenty thousand horse and twenty-two thousand foot under his command.

[5] A fierce battle took place, and Satyrus, supported by his elite cavalry, joined battle with Aripharnes, who had stationed himself in the middle of the line. After heavy losses on both sides, Satyrus eventually overwhelmed and routed the barbarian king. [6] He harried the fugitives for a while, killing those he caught up with, but before long

it was brought to his attention that his brother Eumelus was winning on the right wing, where his mercenaries had been routed, so he gave up the pursuit and went to help his defeated men. And so for the second time he became responsible for victory; he forced the entire enemy army to turn and flee, making it clear to everyone that, in addition to being the eldest, he also had the prowess that made him the proper successor to his father's kingdom.

23. After their defeat in this battle, Aripharnes and Eumelus fled to Aripharnes' capital city, which was situated on the Thates river. Since the river flowed around the fortress city and was good and deep, access was difficult, and it was also surrounded by lofty crags and dense woods. In fact, there were no more than two means of entry, both man-made. One of them was in the royal castle itself and was protected by high towers and outworks, while the other approach, in marshy ground on the opposite side of the city, was protected by wooden barricades and supported at intervals by piles, and there were houses on it, raised above the water. Given how secure the place was, Satyrus at first ravaged the enemy's farmland and set fire to villages, where he obtained captives and a great deal of booty, [2] but then he turned to an attempt to force the approaches. On the side where there were the outworks and towers, he lost a lot of men and pulled back, but on the marshy side, he overran and captured the wooden barricades. [3] After tearing these down† and crossing the river, he began to cut down the trees in the woodland through which he had to pass in order to reach the royal castle.

While Satyrus' men were going about this with a will, King Aripharnes, worried that his citadel might end up being overrun, fought back with great boldness, since he knew that only victory would bring him safety. [4] He sent archers to positions on both sides of the approach, which made it easy for him to shoot down the men who were cutting down the trees, because they were prevented by the density of the woods from having advance warning of incoming arrows and from fighting back against those who were firing them. [5] For three days Satyrus' men cleared the woods and created a way through them, barely enduring the ordeal, and on the fourth day they drew near the city wall, but victory was denied them by the barrage of arrows and the cramped conditions, and they sustained great losses. [6] In fact, Meniscus, the commander of the mercenaries, a man of exceptional intelligence and daring, pushed on along the approach and reached the walls, but after a brilliant display of martial prowess he and his men were forced back when a far stronger force made a sortie against them.

[7] When Satyrus saw that Meniscus was in trouble, he came to help. He stood firm against the enemy charge, but was wounded in the arm by a spear. He returned to the encampment, but in the night he died, after a reign of only nine months following the death of his father, Parysades. [8] Meniscus, the commander of the mercenaries, abandoned the siege and led the army away to Gargaza, and from there he conveyed the king's body by way of the river to his brother Prytanis at Panticapaeum.

24. After giving his brother a magnificent funeral and laying his body to rest in the royal tombs, Prytanis went to Gargaza and took over both the army and the reins of power. Through envoys, Eumelus raised the possibility of dividing the kingdom between them, but Prytanis ignored him, and after leaving a garrison in Gargaza he returned to Panticapaeum in order to secure the kingdom for himself. But Eumelus used this time to seize Gargaza with the help of his barbarian allies, and also a number of other towns and strongholds. [2] When Prytanis marched against him, Eumelus defeated his brother in battle, trapped him on the isthmus near Lake Maeotis, and forced him to come to terms, according to which he was to hand over the army and cede the kingdom. But when Prytanis arrived in Panticapaeum, which had always been the royal seat of the rulers of Bosporus, he made another attempt to recover the kingdom; he lacked the strength to succeed, however, and he fled to the so-called Gardens, where he was killed. [3] After his brother's death, in order to secure his rule, Eumelus killed not just the friends of Satyrus and Prytanis, but also their wives and children. The only one to escape was Satyrus' son Parysades, who was very young; he fled on horseback out of the city and found refuge with Agarus, the king of the Scythians.*

[4] The murder of their friends and relatives angered the citizens of Panticapaeum, however, so Eumelus convened an assembly, at which he justified the killings and restored the ancestral political system.* In addition to granting them the exemption from taxes which the residents of Panticapaeum had enjoyed in the time of their forebears, he promised to impose no more wealth taxes at all* and raised the possibility of other measures in his desire to win the favour of the masses. [5] Soon the concord of earlier times was restored

throughout the city thanks to his benefactions, and from then on he ruled as Archon* over his subjects, abiding by the laws and winning an extraordinary degree of admiration for his goodness.

25. He was a constant benefactor of the Byzantines and the Sinopeans, for instance, as well as the other Greeks living on the Black Sea. When Lysimachus had Callatis under siege* and the inhabitants were suffering badly from lack of provisions, he took in a thousand men who had been driven out by starvation. Not only did he make them safe by granting them refuge, but he even gave them a place to live, and also divided up Psoa, as it is called, and its farmland into lots for them. [2] In order to protect shipping in the Black Sea, he waged war against the barbarians who practised piracy—the Heniochians, the Taurians, and the Achaeans*—and cleared the sea of pirates. The upshot was that he reaped the finest harvest from his good deeds—the harvest of acclaim—not only in his kingdom, but throughout almost all the world, as merchants spread the news of his magnanimity. [3] He also annexed much of the neighbouring barbarian land, thereby adding considerably to the lustre of his kingdom.

In a word, Eumelus made it his objective to subdue all the peoples who lived on the Black Sea, and he probably would have succeeded if his life had not been cut short. But in fact he died after a reign of five years and five months, as a result of an unusual accident. [4] He was returning home one day from Sindice,* hurrying to get back in time for a sacrifice, and was heading towards the royal residence on a wagon drawn by four horses—one of those wagons with four wheels and a canopy—when the horses took fright and bolted with him. The driver was unable to keep hold of the reins and Eumelus, afraid of being carried down a ravine, tried to jump out of the wagon. But his sword got caught in one of the wheels, and he was dragged along at high speed and died instantly.

26. There were oracles in existence about the deaths of the brothers, Eumelus and Satyrus—oracles that were rather inane, but were nevertheless believed by the people of Bosporus. They say that Satyrus had been warned by the god to beware lest a mouse caused his death. Because of this, first he allowed none of those in his service, slave or free, to have that name, and then he was afraid of mice, whether in the home or the fields, and was always ordering his slaves to kill them and block up their holes. But, although he did everything possible and employed every means he could think of to cheat his

THE LIBRARY BOOK 20

353

309/8

destiny, he died after being wounded in the arm—in the 'mouse'.* [2]
In Eumelus' case, the oracle warned him to beware of a moving house,
and so he, in his turn, was never comfortable entering a house unless
his slaves had first inspected the roof and the foundations. But when
he died, everyone considered the prophecy fulfilled because of the
canopy on his wagon.

Moving on from events in Bosporus, [3] in Italy the Roman consuls
invaded enemy territory† and defeated the Samnites at a place called
Talium. After the defeat, the Samnites occupied Sacred Hill, as it is
called, and since night had fallen the Romans pulled back to their
camp. On the next day, however, battle was joined once more. Many
of the Samnites were killed and more than 2,200 were taken prisoner.
[4] These victories were so decisive for the Romans that from then on
the consuls had secure control of the countryside and set about subduing rebel towns. They besieged Cataracta and Ceraunilia* into submission and installed garrisons in them, but they used diplomacy to
gain the submission of some of the other towns.

309/8

27. *In the year of the Archonship of Demetrius of Phalerum* in Athens,
in Rome Quintus Fabius (for the second time) and Gaius Marcius obtained
the consulate. In this year:*

King Ptolemy* of Egypt's response to the news that his generals had
lost the Cilician cities was to sail at strength to Phaselis. He besieged
the city into submission and then moved on to Lycia, where he
assaulted and took Xanthus, which had been garrisoned by Antigonus.
[2] Then he sailed on to Caunus, and once he had made the lower
town his, he turned his attention to the acropolises, which had
garrisons. He had to use force to take the Heracleum, but the Persicum
fell to him when the garrison surrendered. [3] After that,* he sailed to
Cos, where he sent for Ptolemaeus, who, despite being Antigonus'
nephew and despite having been entrusted with an army, had for-
saken his uncle* and was offering to cooperate with Ptolemy.* So
Ptolemaeus sailed from Chalcis and arrived in Cos. At first, Ptolemy
received him graciously, but then it came to his attention that
Ptolemaeus had started to act impudently and was using diplomacy
and gifts to try to gain the personal loyalty of Ptolemy's officers.

Afraid that Ptolemaeus might be hatching a plot against him, Ptolemy arrested him before he could act and compelled him to drink hemlock.* As for the soldiers who had come with Ptolemaeus, he won them over with promises and had them join his own army.

28. Meanwhile, Polyperchon, with the substantial army he had raised, brought Heracles, the son of Alexander and Barsine, back to his father's kingdom. He made camp in Stymphaea,* and while he was there Cassander arrived with an army. The two camps were quite close to each other, and since the Macedonians were not displeased at the return of the king, Cassander became afraid, given their habitual fickleness, that they might desert and go over to Heracles.* He therefore sent envoys to Polyperchon [2] and tried to get him to understand that, once restored, the king would be under the influence of others, not Polyperchon. However, he said, if Polyperchon joined forces with him and killed the young man, in the first place he would immediately receive the estates that had formerly been his in Macedon; secondly, he would be given an army and appointed General of the Peloponnese;* and thirdly, he would be an equal partner in everything in Cassander's realm and would occupy the highest rank.

Cassander eventually won Polyperchon over with his plentiful and bountiful promises; he entered into a secret agreement with him and persuaded him to assassinate the king. [3] Once Polyperchon had done away with the young man* and was openly working with Cassander, he recovered his estates in Macedon and, in accordance with his agreement with Cassander, was given four thousand Macedonian foot soldiers and five hundred Thessalian horsemen. [4] Once he had also gained the support of a number of other volunteers, he tried to lead his army through Boeotia to the Peloponnese, but he was prevented from doing so by the Boeotians and Peloponnesians,* so he turned back to Locris and passed the winter there.

29. Meanwhile, Lysimachus founded a city in the Chersonese which was called Lysimachea after himself, and Cleomenes, the king of the Lacedaemonians, died after a reign of sixty years and ten months.* He was succeeded by <Areus, the grandson of Cleomenes and son of Acrotatus,>† who reigned for forty-four years.

[2] In this year, the last of the outposts fell to Hamilcar, the commander of the Carthaginian forces in Sicily, and then he advanced with his army against Syracuse, intent on taking it by storm, just as he had the outposts. [3] His long-established control of the sea

enabled him to prevent any grain from getting into the city, and after destroying the crops that were growing on the farmland, he intended to take over the area around the Olympieium*—an area that lay close to the city walls. But no sooner had he got there than he decided to launch his assault on the city straight away, because his seer had assured him, after inspecting the sacrificial victims, that he would dine in Syracuse on the following day.

[4] When the Syracusans saw what the enemy were up to, they sent out under cover of darkness about three thousand foot and about four hundred horse to occupy Euryelus,* [5] and these men promptly carried out their mission. But the Carthaginians brought up their forces during the night, thinking that they would not be spotted by the enemy. Hamilcar was out in front with his usual bodyguard, and he was followed by Deinocrates, who had been put in charge of the cavalry. [6] Then came the infantry, which had been divided into two phalanxes, one made up of non-Greeks and the other of Greek auxiliaries. And the army was followed by a varied horde of non-combatants who were there to enrich themselves. So far from having any use at all in military terms, such people are the cause of confusion and mindless turmoil, factors which are often responsible for endangering an entire campaign. [7] On this occasion too, since the roads were narrow and rough, the men who were carrying equipment and some of the non-combatant camp-followers kept jostling one another as they competed for space on the road. With large numbers of people crowded together in a narrow space, inevitably brawls broke out here and there, and many men joined in on one side or the other to help their comrades. The upshot was that the army became predominantly a scene of shouting and considerable confusion.

[8] At this point, the Syracusans on Euryelus, who could see that their adversaries were approaching in disorder and who had the superior position, charged the Carthaginians. [9] Some stood on the heights and shot at the enemy as they approached; some seized favourable positions and made it impossible for the barbarians to proceed down the road; others forced fugitives to hurl themselves down from the crags. Because of the darkness, which prevented them from knowing the truth, the Carthaginians assumed that the Syracusans were attacking in force. [10] They were already at a disadvantage because of the confusion in their ranks, and the sudden appearance of the enemy was another factor, but the main determinants of their

discomfiture were their ignorance of the terrain and the lack of space. And so they turned and fled, but since the terrain offered no open escape route, some were trampled by their own horsemen, of whom there were many, while others mistook one another for enemies and fell to fighting, since the darkness prevented them from knowing the truth. [11] Hamilcar stood his ground bravely against the enemy for a while and expected his guard to face the danger along with him; but after a while, demoralized and frightened, they abandoned him. Left all alone, he was seized and carried off by the Syracusans.

30. It would not be out of place to note here the inconstancy of Fortune and the peculiar way in which men's achievements turn out contrary to expectations. After all, Agathocles, an exceptionally brave man who had a substantial army fighting with him at the Himeras river, was not only decisively defeated by the barbarians, but also lost the best and largest part of his army, whereas the men who had been left behind in Syracuse to defend the walls, who constituted only a fraction of the army that had already been beaten, not only defeated the barbarian besieging force, but also captured their general, Hamilcar, the most illustrious of the Carthaginians. And the most amazing thing of all was that 120,000 foot and five thousand horse were overwhelmingly defeated by the clever use, by only a small number of enemies, of deception and the terrain—thus proving the truth of the saying that there are many needless alarms in war.

[2] After the rout, the Carthaginians scattered here and there, and it was only with difficulty that they regrouped on the following day. Meanwhile, the Syracusans returned to the city laden with booty and handed Hamilcar over to those who wanted to punish him. People also recalled the pronouncement of the seer who had said that Hamilcar would dine the next day in Syracuse; the gods were telling the truth, but in a misleading manner. [3] The relatives of those who had died led Hamilcar in chains through the city, tortured him horribly, and then killed him in the most humiliating fashion imaginable. Then the rulers of the city cut off his head and sent it to Agathocles in Libya, along with news of their victory.

31. Understanding how they had come to be defeated, as the Carthaginian soldiers did after the defeat, hardly relieved them of their fears. Since there was no overall leadership, the barbarians and their Greek allies went separate ways: [2] the exiles and the other Greeks chose Deinocrates as their general, and the Carthaginians put

themselves in the hands of the officers who had been second in rank behind Hamilcar.

At this juncture, the Acragantines decided to make a bid for supremacy on Sicily; they could see that, given the situation there, they would never have a better opportunity. [3] Their thinking was that the Carthaginians would continue to resist Agathocles, even if with difficulty; that Deinocrates would be easy to defeat since he had only an army of exiles at his disposal; that the Syracusans were too reduced by starvation to attempt to make a bid for pre-eminence themselves; and, most importantly, that since the purpose of the campaign was the liberation of the Greek cities,* everyone would gladly follow their lead, partly out of hatred of the barbarians, and partly because of the desire for self-determination that is innate in all men.

[4] They therefore chose Xenodicus* as their general, gave him an appropriately large army, and sent him out to wage war. His first target was Gela. He was let in by personal friends of his under cover of darkness, and gained control of the city along with its powerful army and its wealth. [5] After their liberation, the Geloans committed their entire levy to the campaign and wholeheartedly set about freeing the cities. As word spread throughout the island about what the Acragantines were up to, the desire for freedom took hold in the cities. The people of Enna were first: they sent envoys and surrendered their city to the Acragantines, who freed the city and then went to Herbessus,* where the town was defended by a garrison. A fierce battle took place, in which the people of Herbessus supported the Acragantines, and in the end the garrison was captured; losses on the barbarian side were heavy, but about five hundred of them laid down their weapons and surrendered.

32. While the Acragantines were engaged in freeing these cities, some of the troops whom Agathocles had left in Syracuse seized Echetla* and plundered land belonging to Leontini and Camarina. [2] The ravaging of their farmland and the utter destruction of their crops left the cities in a bad way, so Xenodicus went there and not only made the people of Leontini and Camarina safe, but he also besieged the stronghold of Echetla into submission, gave the citizens back their former democratic constitution, and cowed the Syracusans into withdrawing. But, essentially, wherever he went he freed fortresses and towns from Carthaginian dominion.

[3] Meanwhile, the Syracusans, stricken by starvation, heard that grain ships were setting out for their city. They manned twenty triremes, waited until the barbarians who usually blockaded the harbour were off guard, and then slipped out of the harbour and sailed up the coast to Megara,* where they looked for the arrival of the traders. [4] But then the Carthaginians sent thirty ships against them. At first, the fighting took place at sea, as the Syracusans intended, but before long they had been driven ashore at a certain temple of Hera, where they leapt overboard. [5] Then a battle was fought for the ships. The Carthaginians attached grappling hooks and captured ten triremes by dragging them from the shore by sheer force, but the rest were saved when men came to help from Megara. That was how things stood in Sicily.

33. In Libya, when the Syracusans who were bringing Hamilcar's head arrived, Agathocles took it and rode past the enemy camp, close enough to be within hearing distance, showing it to the enemy and making it clear that their army had been defeated. [2] The Carthaginians were deeply distressed. Treating the king's death as catastrophic for themselves, they prostrated themselves on the ground, like the barbarians they were, and they were plunged into deep despair as regards the war as a whole. In Agathocles' case, however, since he was already elated by his victories in Libya, these further great successes served to make his hopes soar with the thought that he need be afraid no longer.

[3] Fortune, however, did not allow success to take up a permanent post, but arranged for Agathocles' own soldiers to be the cause of the greatest danger for him. What happened was that Agathocles invited one of his senior officers, Lysiscus, to dine with him, and in his cups Lysiscus insulted the dynast. [4] Agathocles, for his part, passed off his words as a jest, even though they had been spoken in bitter anger, because he valued the man for his usefulness in war. But his son Archagathus was furious, and he reprimanded Lysiscus and threatened him. [5] As they were returning to their quarters after the symposium was over, Lysiscus reviled Archagathus for his illicit affair with his stepmother—it was widely believed that he was having sex with Alcia (that was the woman's name) behind his father's back. [6] Goaded into an overpowering rage, Archagathus snatched a spear from one of the Household Guard and thrust it through Lysiscus' ribs.

Lysiscus died instantly and his body was carried back to his quarters by his attendants. In the morning the friends of the murdered man met. They were incensed about the murder, and once they had also been joined by many of the other soldiers, they threw the entire camp into disorder. [7] A number of the senior officers as well, who feared for their lives because the mob had its doubts about them, turned the situation to their advantage and fanned the flames of what became a prodigious mutiny. With the whole army condemning the murder, men set about donning their armour with the intention of punishing the killer. The upshot was that the mob decided that Archagathus should be put to death, and that if Agathocles failed to surrender his son to them, he should be punished in Archagathus' place; [8] and another of their demands was that they should be paid their overdue wages. They chose generals to take command of the army, and in the end some of them seized the walls of Tunis, so that, wherever they turned, the dynasts found themselves surrounded by armed guards.

34. When the Carthaginians learnt of the mutiny in the enemy camp, they sent agents to try to persuade Agathocles' men to change sides, by promising them a pay increase and substantial rewards, and not a few of Agathocles' officers did undertake to bring their forces over to them.* [2] Agathocles, however, who could see that his life was hanging in the balance and was afraid of being handed over to the enemy and dying a humiliating death, decided that it would be better, if he was bound to die anyway, for him to be killed by his own men. [3] So he exchanged his purple-dyed robes for humble, everyday apparel and stepped up to face the mob.

Silence fell at this unusual behaviour, and when a large crowd had gathered he addressed them in words that suited the seriousness of the situation. He reminded them of his earlier achievements and said that he was ready to die, if that was what his men decided was best for them, [4] because he had never been the kind of man who, under the influence of cowardice, allowed himself to be treated monstrously just in order to save his life. They themselves would witness the truth of this, he said as he drew his sword and made as if to kill himself. But just as he was about to strike, the army shouted out and stayed his hand, and from every side voices arose exonerating him from the charges. [5] The crowd urged him to take up his royal robes once more, so with tears in his eyes and expressions of gratitude to the people on his lips, he dressed himself as suited his station, as the crowd smoothed the way to his restoration with cheers and applause.

All this time the Carthaginians had been waiting, in the expectation that the Greeks would be defecting at any moment, but instead Agathocles seized the opportunity and led his forces against them. [6] The barbarians had no idea of what was really going on and thought that the enemy were coming over to their side. When Agathocles was quite close to the enemy position, he suddenly ordered the signal for battle to be sounded, launched into the attack, and set about slaughtering them. This misadventure was the last thing the Carthaginians had been expecting, and after taking heavy casualties they fled for safety to their camp. [7] So Agathocles, who had come close to losing his life thanks to his son, not only found a way out of his difficulties by drawing on his natural gifts, but defeated the enemy as well. But the ringleaders of the mutiny and others who were hostile towards Agathocles—more than two hundred men in all—did indeed go so far as to desert to the Carthaginians.

Having covered what was happening in Libya and Sicily, I shall now give an account of events in Italy. 35. When the Etruscans marched against Sutrium,* a Roman colony, the consuls took to the field at strength to relieve the town. They defeated the Etruscans in battle and drove them back to their camp, [2] but the Samnites used this time, while the Roman forces were far away, to raid the territory of the Iapygian communities which were loyal to Rome,* knowing that they would not meet any opposition. The consuls were therefore obliged to divide their forces, and while Fabius stayed in Etruria, Marcius set out against the Samnites. He assaulted and took the town of Allifae,* and brought relief to the cities allied to Rome which were being besieged by the Samnites.

[3] As Etruscan reinforcements arrived in large numbers to renew their attack on Sutrium, Fabius stealthily marched through the territory of their neighbours and invaded inland Etruria, which had remained unplundered for many years. [4] No one had been expecting this, and he laid waste a great deal of farmland. He defeated the local inhabitants whenever they came out against him and, although many were killed, he also took a good number alive as prisoners. Then he won a second battle at Perusia against the Etruscans, who suffered heavy casualties and became disheartened, because no Roman army had ever before been seen in those parts. [5] He arranged a truce with the peoples of Arretium, Cortona, and Perusia,* and his siege of Castola* forced the Etruscans to raise the siege of Sutrium.

36. In Rome in this year censors were elected,* and one of them, Appius Claudius (his colleague was Lucius Plautius),* made a number of changes to the ways in which things had traditionally been done, because his measures were designed to please the common people and he took no account of the Senate. In the first place, he built the so-called Appian Aqueduct to bring water to Rome from a distance of eighty stades* and spent a large amount of public money on its construction without obtaining a senatorial decree. [2] Then he paved most of the Appian Way (named after him) with solid blocks of stone—all the way from Rome to Capua, a distance of more than a thousand stades; since the work involved cutting through elevated ground and creating substantial embankments to raise gullies and hollows to ground level, he expended the entire revenue of the state,* but left an undying monument to himself, as one who worked tirelessly for the public good.

[3] He also diluted the purity of the Senate by enrolling not just well-born men of high rank, as was customary, but also many sons of freedmen as well—a measure which was deeply offensive to men who were proud of their noble birth. [4] He also gave citizens the right to be registered in whichever tribes they wanted and to be included in the census classes of their choice.* In short, seeing the great store of enmity that the most eminent men in Rome had amassed against him, he was careful not to give offence to the rest of the citizen body; in effect, he was making the goodwill of the masses a counterweight to the hostility the nobles felt for him. [5] When it came to assessing the Knights, he deprived none of them of his horse,* and when it came to drawing up the senatorial roll he expelled none of them as unworthy,* as censors customarily did.

But then the consuls,* who found his measures offensive and wanted to please the nobility, convoked the Senate not as reconstituted by him, but as constituted by the previous censors. [6] So, in order to thwart the nobles and provide support for Appius' programme, and also because they wanted to confirm the advancement of members of their own class, the people elected to the most prestigious of the aedileships* Gnaeus Flavius, the son of a freedman, who thereby became the first Roman to gain this office whose father had been a slave. After completing his term of office, as a precaution against the enmity of the Senate, Appius pretended to be blind and stayed at home.*

308/7

37. *In the year of the Archonship of Charinus in Athens, the Romans entrusted the consulship to Publius Decius and Quintus Fabius, and in Elis the 118th Olympic festival was celebrated, with Apollonides of Tegea* the victor in the stade race. In this year:*

Ptolemy put to sea from Myndus with a strong fleet. As he sailed through the Aegean islands, he liberated Andros and installed a garrison.* When he reached the isthmus, he was ceded Sicyon and Corinth by Cratesipolis. I have already explained in the previous book* how she came to possess such great cities, so I shall not repeat myself by covering the same ground again. [2] Ptolemy's plan was to liberate the rest of the Greek cities as well, the idea being that the goodwill of the Greeks would greatly increase his power.* But when the Peloponnesians, who had undertaken to supply him with grain and money, did nothing of the kind, the aggravated dynast made peace with Cassander, by the terms of which each of them would retain the cities he currently possessed. Then, after securing Sicyon and Corinth with garrisons, he sailed back to Egypt.*

[3] Meanwhile, Cleopatra fell out with Antigonus, and since she was inclining towards choosing Ptolemy as her husband, she set out from Sardis in order to make the voyage to Egypt. She was the sister of Alexander, the conqueror of the Persians, and daughter of Philip, the son of Amyntas, and she had been the wife of the Alexander who campaigned in Italy.* [4] Her lineage was so distinguished that Cassander, Lysimachus, Antigonus, Ptolemy, and in short all the most important leaders who emerged after the death of Alexander had sought her hand in marriage. Each of them hoped that a consequence of the marriage would be Macedonian loyalty, and so they wanted an alliance with the royal house as a stepping-stone to supreme power. [5] The governor of Sardis, however, who had been instructed by Antigonus to keep an eye on Cleopatra, prevented her from leaving, and then later, acting on orders from Antigonus, he had her murdered by some women. [6] In an attempt to divert blame for her death from himself, Antigonus punished some of the women for their murderous conspiracy against Cleopatra and made sure that she was buried in fine style, as befitted a member of the royal family. And so Cleopatra,

who had been fought over by the greatest men of power, died before the marriage with Ptolemy could go ahead.

[7] Now that I have covered Asia and Greece, I shall move on to other parts of the world. 38. In Libya, the Carthaginians sent out an army to win back the allegiance of the Numidians* who had seceded from their alliance, and Agathocles left his son Archagathus with a division of the army at Tunis, while he set out after the enemy at speed, taking with him the cream of the army, a force of eight thousand foot, eight hundred horse, and fifty Libyan war chariots. [2] When the Carthaginians came to the part of Numidia inhabited by a people called the Zouphones, they won many of the natives over to their side and brought some of the rebels back into alliance, as they had been before.

When they were informed that the enemy was approaching, they made camp on a hill which was surrounded by deep and virtually uncrossable branches of a river. [3] These streams were to act as their forward defences against surprise attacks by their adversaries, and they ordered the most competent of the Numidians to stick closely to the Greeks and to harry them until they halted their advance. The Numidians duly carried out their orders, but Agathocles sent his slingers and archers against them, while advancing against the enemy camp himself with the rest of his army. [4] As soon as they understood his design, the Carthaginians brought their forces out of the camp, formed them up in battle order, and got ready to fight.

When they saw that Agathocles was already starting to cross the river, they attacked in formation and took many enemy lives at the river bed, which was awkward to cross. [5] Agathocles pushed on, however, and while the Greeks were the better fighters, the barbarians had numerical superiority. After a long period of spirited fighting, the Numidians on both sides withdrew from the battle and waited to see what the outcome would be, since they had decided to plunder the baggage of whichever side was defeated. [6] But Agathocles still had his best soldiers, and before long he had forced his immediate opponents to turn, and their flight caused the rest of the barbarians to flee as well. Only the Carthaginians' Greek cavalry auxiliaries, who were commanded by Clinon, continued to resist the onset of Agathocles' heavy troops. They put on a brilliant display of martial prowess, but most of them were killed, fighting bravely, and the survivors were lucky to remain alive.

39. Agathocles did not bother to pursue these men and set out instead against the barbarians who had taken refuge in the camp, but he had to force his way over steep and difficult ground, and he found himself taking as many losses as he had earlier inflicted on the Carthaginians. So far from giving up, however, he pressed on; he had been successful up until then and he confidently expected to take the camp by main force. [2] Meanwhile, however, the Numidians had been awaiting the outcome of the battle. Since they could not get to the Carthaginians' baggage because the fighting between the two armies was taking place near the Carthaginian camp, they set out against the Greek camp, knowing that Agathocles had been drawn a long way off. Since the camp had no defenders who were capable of standing up to them, assaulting it presented no difficulties. They killed the few men who offered resistance and captured a great deal of booty, including a large number of prisoners.

[3] When Agathocles found out, he led his forces back at the double. He recovered some of the stolen property, but most of it remained in Numidian hands, and that night they moved a long way off. [4] After erecting a trophy, Agathocles distributed the spoils to his men, so that there would be no complaints about the lost baggage. As for the Greeks he had captured, who had been fighting for the Carthaginians, he shut them up in a fortress, [5] but they did not want to face whatever punishment the dynast had in store for them, and at night they attacked the garrison. Even though they came off worst in the fighting, they managed to occupy a strong position, and there were at least a thousand of them, of whom more than five hundred were Syracusans. [6] When Agathocles was informed about what had happened, he brought his forces up and induced the Greeks to leave their strongpoint under a truce—and then slaughtered all those who had been involved in the attack on the garrison.

40. After this battle, Agathocles put his mind to considering all kinds of ways in which he might get the better of the Carthaginians. The upshot was that he sent Orthon of Syracuse as an envoy to Ophellas in Cyrene.* Ophellas was one of Alexander's Friends and a veteran of the eastern expedition, but now he was master of the cities of Cyrenaica, with a powerful army at his disposal, and he saw himself increasing his dominion. [2] So he was already entertaining these kinds of hopes when Agathocles' envoy arrived and asked for his help in defeating the Carthaginians. In return for this service,

Orthon promised that Agathocles would allow Ophellas to be the master of Libya. [3] Sicily was enough for Agathocles, he said, as long as he could free himself from the threat posed by Carthage and rule the whole island without fear. If Agathocles decided to try to increase his sway, Italy was available near by and he could extend his rule there. [4] After all, Libya was separated from Sicily by a large and difficult stretch of sea, which made it very unsuitable for him; even now, he said, Agathocles had not gone there because of any aspirations he entertained, but because he had no choice.

[5] With this new hope added to his long-standing resolution, Ophellas had no hesitation about falling in with the plan, and he sent an envoy to arrange an alliance with the Athenians; his wife was Euthydice, the daughter of Miltiades, the namesake of the man who had commanded the victorious army at Marathon.* [6] Because of this marriage connection, and in general because of the partiality he had often displayed for the city, a good many Athenians committed themselves to joining the expedition.* Many other Greeks also wanted to take part in the enterprise, hoping to gain a share of the best land in Libya and to plunder the wealth of Carthage. [7] Conditions in Greece were poor and depressed, thanks to the relentless warfare and the rivalries of the dynasts, so men were hoping not just to do well for themselves, but also to leave their present troubles behind.

41. So, once Ophellas had completed his preparations for the expedition, which were on an impressive scale, he set out with his army. He had more than ten thousand foot, six hundred horse, a hundred war chariots, and more than three hundred charioteers and chariot-mounted fighters. The army was also accompanied by at least ten thousand non-combatants, as we call them, many of whom were bringing their families and other belongings, so that the army resembled nothing so much as a colonizing expedition. [2] After a march of eighteen days and three thousand stades, they made camp at Automalax.

On the next stage of their journey, there was a mountain which was sheer on both sides, but had a deep ravine running through it, from which a precipitous cliff rose straight up to a peak.* [3] At the foot of this cliff there was a large cave, with its entrance thickly covered by ivy and bindweed, and this is the cave in which, in myth, Queen Lamia is supposed to have been born. She was a woman of extraordinary beauty, but it is said that, because of her savage temperament, she subsequently came to look like a wild beast. What happened was that, after all the children born to her had died,* she became so depressed and so envious of other women's flourishing families that she gave orders that infants were to be snatched from their mother's arms and killed on the spot. [4] That is why even nowadays, in our own time, this woman's tale is still told to children and her name still terrifies them.* [5] When she was drunk, however, everyone could get away with doing what they wanted without being watched over by her, and since on these occasions she was not an intrusive presence in their lives, the people of the land assumed that she could not see them. And that explains why, in some versions of the myth, it is said that she threw her eyes into a basket, which is to transfer to this measure* the heedlessness brought on by drinking, since it was a measure of wine that had robbed her of her sight. [6] One could also adduce evidence from Euripides to prove that she was born in Libya, since he says:*

> Is there anyone on earth who does not know the name
> Of Libyan-born Lamia, a name to horrify mortal men?

42. Anyway, Ophellas was advancing with his army over terrain that was waterless and teeming with wild creatures. It was hard going, not only because of the shortage of water, but also because he had no more dry food left and was therefore in danger of losing the entire army. [2] Fanged creatures of all kinds make the desert near the Syrtis* their home, most of them with deadly bites, and Ophellas and his men found themselves in considerable difficulty, since no remedy doctors or friends might suggest was effective. Some of the snakes had skin that was similar in colour to the ground on which they lay,* so that they could not be seen for what they were. Many men therefore unwittingly trod on them and received bites that were fatal. Eventually, however, after over two months of misery on the road, Ophellas at last reached Agathocles and had his men make camp, with the two armies a short distance apart.

[3] When the Carthaginians learnt of Ophellas' arrival and saw how large an army he had brought against them, they were terrified. But Agathocles went to meet Ophellas, cordially supplied him with all his needs, and suggested that he let his men recover from their ordeal. In fact, he stayed for several days, observing all that went on in the camp of the new arrivals. Then, when most of Ophellas' soldiers were out of the camp foraging for fodder and food, and since he could see that

Ophellas had no idea of his intentions, he convened an assembly of his own men and accused his newly arrived ally of conspiring against him. As soon as he had aroused his men's ardour he led them, fully armed, against the Cyreneans.

[4] Despite the shock of this sudden attack, Ophellas decided to resist. But he had no time to get ready and the forces that remained available to him were inadequate, so he died in the battle. [5] Agathocles forced the rest of his men to lay down their arms, won their allegiance by means of generous promises, and thus took over Ophellas' entire army. So Ophellas died, a man of high ambition, but too trusting for his own good.

43. In Carthage, Bomilcar was looking for a suitable opportunity to carry his long-held project through to completion and set himself up as tyrant. Circumstances had often created the conditions for him to put his plan into effect, but every time he had let some trivial obstacle get in the way. Anyone who is about to set his hand to an illegal venture of any importance is prone to superstition, so that delay seems preferable to action, procrastination to completion, and that is exactly what happened then in Bomilcar's case. [2] He sent the most eminent of his fellow citizens out on the campaign against the Numidians so that there would be no man of substance to oppose him, but then he was held back by a fit of caution, lost his nerve, and failed to realize his attempt on the tyranny.

[3] When he did finally launch his attempt to seize power, it happened to coincide with Agathocles' attack on Ophellas. Neither side was aware of what the other was doing. [4] Agathocles did not know about Bomilcar's attempt on the tyranny and the chaos in the city, when Carthage might easily have fallen to him. After all, once Bomilcar had been caught red-handed, he would have enlisted Agathocles' help rather than giving his fellow citizens the opportunity to exact their revenge on his body. Nor, for their part, had the Carthaginians heard about Agathocles' attack, and they might easily have overcome him by adding Ophellas' army to their own. [5] It seems to me, however, that in both cases their ignorance was understandable, despite the scale of the events and the fact that the perpetrators of these great ventures were close to each other. [6] Agathocles was about to kill a man who was a friend, so he never turned his mind to what the enemy were up to, and Bomilcar, who was trying to deprive his country of its liberty, was entirely unconcerned about events in the enemy

camp, since what he had in mind at the time was getting the better of his fellow citizens, not the enemy.

[7] Now, there is a sense in which one might find the writing of history deficient, seeing that, although in life many different events go on at the same time, those who write them up are compelled to interrupt their narratives and to separate out simultaneous events in a way that does not correspond to reality.* This means that although the truth of historical events can be captured by experience, it cannot be captured by the written record, which falls far short of displaying the true disposition of the events it reproduces.

44. Be that as it may, after carrying out a review of his troops in New Town, as it is called, which lies a short distance outside Carthage,* Bomilcar dismissed the rest, but <retained>† the five hundred citizens and a thousand or so mercenaries who were in on the attempt, and declared himself tyrant. [2] He divided these men into five battalions and went on the offensive, slaughtering everyone he encountered on his way. The tumult in the city was so extreme that at first the Carthaginians supposed that the city had been betrayed and that the enemy was inside the walls. When they learnt the truth, however, the men of military age quickly assembled, formed themselves into companies, and set out against the tyrant.

[3] Bomilcar made his way rapidly through the streets, killing those he encountered, and entered the agora, where he found a large number of unarmed citizens, whom he cut down. [4] But the Carthaginians occupied the buildings around the agora, which were tall, and since the whole area was within their range, the conspirators soon found themselves being wounded by a hail of missiles. [5] Since they were having a hard time of it, they closed ranks and raced together through the streets into New Town, with missiles pelting down on them constantly from whichever buildings they happened to be close to at any given moment. The rebels occupied a hill, and were blockaded there by the Carthaginians, now that the entire citizen body had assembled under arms. [6] In the end, the Carthaginians sent a delegation of qualified elders as envoys, offered an amnesty, and brought hostilities to an end. They kept to the amnesty where the rest of the rebels were concerned, without blaming them for the danger the city had faced, but in Bomilcar's case they ignored the oaths they had sworn and tortured him horribly to death.

So the Carthaginians recovered their traditional constitution after having faced the gravest danger.* [7] Agathocles, meanwhile, loaded cargo ships with booty, put on board any men who had come from Cyrene but were of no military use to him, and sent them to Syracuse. But storms arose, and only a few of the ships reached Syracuse safely, while some were lost and others were driven on to the Pithecusae islands, off the coast of Italy.*

[8] In Italy, the Roman consuls went to help the Marsi,* who were being attacked by the Samnites; they won the battle and killed the enemy in large numbers. [9] They then marched through Umbria and invaded Etruria, which was enemy territory, and besieged the fortress called Caerium into submission.* When the locals sent envoys to ask for an end to hostilities, the consuls made peace with the people of Tarquinii for forty years, but with all the rest of the Etruscans for only one year.

307/6

45. *At the beginning of the following year, Anaxicrates became Archon in Athens, and in Rome Appius Claudius and Lucius Volumnius were elected consuls. In this year:*

Demetrius, the son of Antigonus, was assigned a powerful army and navy by his father, along with appropriate quantities of artillery and every other kind of siege equipment,* and set sail from Ephesus. His orders were to free all the cities in Greece, starting with Athens, which was garrisoned by Cassander. [2] He landed at Piraeus with his army, launched multiple attacks straight away, and issued a proclamation.* Dionysius, the commander of the Munychia garrison, and Demetrius of Phalerum, Cassander's governor of Athens, who had a large number of soldiers at their disposal, set about resisting his attacks from the walls.

[3] Some of Antigonus' soldiers, however, managed to force their way over the wall at the Piraeus headland, and they admitted more of their comrades as well. This led to the fall of Piraeus, and of the defenders Dionysius, the garrison commander, fled to Munychia* and Demetrius of Phalerum retreated to Athens. [4] The next day, he went as one of a delegation of envoys to Demetrius to discuss the restoration of self-determination to Athens and his own personal

safety. Once he had obtained a guarantee of safe conduct, he gave up his governorship of Athens and fled to Thebes, and later to Ptolemy in Egypt.* [5] So Demetrius was driven from the city of his birth after having governed it for ten years, while the Athenian people, having recovered their freedom, decreed honours for those who had been responsible for the restoration of their autonomy.

Demetrius brought up his siege engines and artillery pieces, including his stone-throwers, and attacked Munychia by both land and sea. [6] The defenders resisted staunchly from the walls, and it turned out that, while Dionysius' position on a hill gave him the advantage of height (since in addition to its natural defences, Munychia had been further strengthened by the construction of fortifications), Demetrius greatly outnumbered his opponents and had a clear advantage in terms of equipment. [7] In the end, after the fortress had been assaulted continually for two days, the soldiers of the garrison found themselves coming off worst, since their ranks were being thinned by the catapults and stone-throwers and they had no reserves to draw on, while Demetrius' men were fighting in relays and were constantly being relieved. Once the wall had been cleared by the stone-throwers, Demetrius' men broke into Munychia, forced the defenders to lay down their arms, and made a prisoner of Dionysius, the garrison commander.

46. These victories took only a few days, and then, once he had demolished the Munychia fortress, Demetrius gave the Athenian people back their freedom and entered into a treaty of friendship and alliance with them. [2] The Athenians voted in favour of a decree proposed by Stratocles to the effect that they should erect, near the statues of Harmodius and Aristogeiton,* gilded statues of Antigonus and Demetrius standing on a chariot; award the two of them crowns worth two hundred talents; found an altar to them and dedicate it to the Saviour Gods;* add two tribes, Demetrias and Antigonis, to the existing ten;* hold games, a parade, and a sacrifice in their honour every year; and embroider their likenesses into Athena's robe.* [3] So fifteen years after the Athenian people had been deprived of power by Antipater as a result of the Lamian War,* they suddenly recovered their ancestral constitution.

Megara had a garrison, but Demetrius besieged it into submission, gave the people back their independence, and was awarded signal honours by them, for the good he had done them. [4] As for Antigonus, when an embassy came to him from Athens, bringing a copy of the decree that pertained to the honours he had been awarded, the ambassadors raised the matters of grain and wood for ship-building, and he gave them 150,000 *medimnoi* of grain and enough timber for a hundred ships. He also withdrew his garrison from Imbros and gave the city back to Athens.* [5] Then he wrote to his son, Demetrius, telling him to form a council of delegates from the allied cities to meet and make policy for the Greeks,* while Demetrius himself sailed with his army to Cyprus and made war on Ptolemy's generals there as soon as possible. [6] Demetrius lost no time in carrying out his father's orders.* He went to Caria and called on the Rhodians to help him in the war against Ptolemy, but they refused, preferring to be on peaceful terms with everyone,* and this refusal was the beginning of the acrimony between the Rhodians and Antigonus.

47. After sailing along the coast to Cilicia, where he gained further ships and soldiers, Demetrius crossed over to Cyprus. He had an army of fifteen thousand foot and four hundred horse, and a navy of more than 110 fast triremes, fifty-three heavier warships used as troop-carriers, and sufficient freighters of various classes to transport the large numbers of cavalrymen and infantrymen. [2] At first, he made camp on the coast near Carpasia, where he beached his ships and strengthened his camp with a palisade and a deep trench. Then he attacked the nearby cities. Urania and Carpasia fell to his assaults, and then, after leaving an adequate guard for his ships, he set out with his army against Salamis.

[3] Menelaus, the man appointed by Ptolemy to govern the island, had withdrawn men from the hill-forts and was waiting in Salamis with the army he had mustered of twelve thousand foot and about eight hundred horse. When the enemy was about forty stades away, he emerged from the city, and battle was joined. It did not take long for Menelaus' men to be overwhelmed and routed, and Demetrius harried them back into the city, taking almost three thousand prisoners and killing about a thousand. [4] At first, after pardoning the prisoners, he distributed them among the units of his own army, but they kept running away to Menelaus because their baggage had been left in Egypt with Ptolemy,* and Demetrius, recognizing that they were intractable, shipped them off to Antigonus in Syria.

[5] At this time, Antigonus was in Upper Syria, seeing to the foundation of a city on the Orontes which was called Antigonea after

him. He was sparing no expense on the project—the city was designed to have a perimeter of seventy stades—because the location was excellent for watching over not only Babylon and the upper satrapies, but also coastal Syria and the satrapies that bordered Egypt. [6] Antigonea did not last long, however, since Seleucus demolished it and moved it to his new foundation, the city that was named Seleucia after him.* But I shall explain all this in detail when we come to the relevant period of time.*

[7] Returning for now to Cyprus, after his defeat Menelaus lined the walls with artillery and counter-siege devices, posted his soldiers on the battlements, and prepared to fight. Since Demetrius was also clearly getting ready for a siege, [8] Menelaus sent messengers to Ptolemy in Egypt to tell him about the defeat and to ask for reinforcements, given that his control of the island was in jeopardy.

48. Seeing that Salamis was no mean city and that there were a great many soldiers inside to defend it, Demetrius decided to build especially large siege towers, catapults of all sizes (both bolt-shooters and stone-throwers), and every other kind of armament that would bring the enemy to their knees. He sent to Asia for craftsmen, iron, a large amount of timber, and suitable building materials for all his equipment. [2] Before long everything was ready, and he constructed a siege tower that was called a 'city-taker'.* Each of its sides was forty-five cubits long, its height was ninety cubits (divided into nine floors), and the whole thing was mounted on solid wheels, each with a diameter of eight cubits. [3] He also had enormous battering rams made and two sheds to convey them. On the lowest floors of the city-taker he had various stone-throwing devices installed, the largest of which were capable of hurling stones that weighed three talents. On the middle floors, he installed his heaviest bolt-shooters, and on the upper floors the lightest catapults and a large number of lighter† stone-throwers. More than two hundred men were stationed in the tower, competent operators of these devices.

[4] Demetrius brought his siege engines up to the city and let loose volley after volley of missiles. He used the stone-throwers to clear the battlements and shook the walls with his rams. [5] But the defenders resisted well and deployed their own contraptions against his. For some days the outcome of the battle was uncertain, since both sides were having a hard time of it and being hit by enemy fire. Eventually, however, the wall collapsed and the city was on the point

of being taken—but just then night fell and the fighting at the wall came to an end.

[6] There was no doubt in Menelaus' mind that the city would fall unless he came up with a fresh initiative. He collected a large amount of dry wood, and in the middle of the night he had his catapults hurl this at the enemy's siege towers, while at the same time all his men shot fire-bearing arrows from the walls.† They succeeded in setting several of the larger siege engines alight, [7] and as the flames suddenly blazed up Demetrius tried to remedy the situation, but it was too late; the towers were burnt to the ground and many of the men who were stationed inside them lost their lives. [8] Despite this setback, however, Demetrius did not give up, but persevered with the siege by land and sea, confident of eventual victory.

49. When Ptolemy received news of the defeat his men had suffered, he sailed from Egypt with a large army and navy. He put in at Paphos on Cyprus, and once further ships had reached him there from the cities he sailed along the coast to Citium, which was two hundred stades distant from Salamis. [2] He had a total of 140 warships, ranging in size from quinqueremes down to quadriremes. These warships were accompanied by more than two hundred troop-carriers, containing at least ten thousand infantrymen.

[3] Ptolemy sent messengers overland to Menelaus, telling him, if he could, to send him the sixty ships he had at Salamis as soon as possible. He did this because he was confident that, with the addition of these ships, he would easily win any battle at sea, since he would be fighting with two hundred ships. [4] But when Demetrius found out what Ptolemy's intentions were, he left a division of his army to see to the siege and manned his entire fleet. He embarked the best of his soldiers, equipped the ships with stone-throwers, and placed on the prows of the ships a good number of heavy bolt-shooters.* [5] Once he had equipped his fleet for battle with a lavish hand, he sailed around Salamis and dropped anchor at the mouth of the harbour, just out of missile range. He spent the night there, preventing Menelaus' ships from joining up with the rest, and at the same time watching out for the arrival of the enemy and maintaining a state of readiness for battle.

[6] The approach of Ptolemy's fleet to Salamis, with the transports following the warships at a distance, was an awesome sight, given the great number of ships involved. 50. When Demetrius learnt that

Ptolemy was on his way, he left his admiral, Antisthenes, with ten ships to prevent Menelaus' ships from leaving and contributing to the battle—only ten ships because the harbour mouth was narrow—and he ordered his cavalry to patrol the shore, so that, if any ship was lost, they could save anyone who swam to land. [2] Then he drew up his ships in battle formation and went to meet the enemy. He had a total of 108 ships,* which included those that had been manned by crews from the places he had captured.* The largest of his ships were septiremes, but most of them were quinqueremes. [3] On his left wing there were seven Phoenician septiremes and thirty Athenian quadriremes, under the command of his admiral Medius. Behind them—because he had decided to strengthen this wing, where he was intending to fight himself—he stationed ten hexaremes and the same number again of quinqueremes. [4] In the middle of the line he posted the lightest of his ships, under the command of Themison of Samos and Marsyas, the author of a history of Macedon.* The right wing was commanded by Hegesippus of Halicarnassus and Pleistias of Cos, who was the helmsman-in-chief of the whole fleet.

[5] Ptolemy at first sailed at speed for Salamis while it was still night, thinking that he could enter the harbour before the enemy was in a position to stop him. But when day broke and the enemy fleet could be seen near by, drawn up for battle, Ptolemy too got ready to fight. [6] He ordered the transport ships to keep their distance, and then he drew up the rest of his fleet in the appropriate battle order. He himself took charge of the left wing, along with the largest of his ships. After he had made his arrangements, both sides prayed to the gods in the customary fashion, with the boatswains* leading and the rest of the crew joining in after them.

51. With their lives at stake and the decisive battle imminent, the two dynasts were extremely anxious. When Demetrius was about three stades away from the enemy, he raised the pre-arranged signal for battle, which was a gilded shield, making it visible to all his men in succession. [2] Once Ptolemy had done likewise as well, the gap between the two fleets rapidly closed. When the trumpets sounded the signal for battle and both sides raised their battle-cries, the ships all bore down on one another in formidable array. At first, they relied on bows, stone-throwers, and volleys of javelins to wound their enemies as they came within range, but then, when the ships were close to one another and the shock of ramming was fast approaching,

the men on the decks crouched down* and, at the urging of their boatswains, the oarsmen fervently increased their efforts.

[3] The force and violence with which the ships collided was such that in some cases they sheared off their opponents' oars, making them incapable of either flight or pursuit, and thwarting the zeal of the marines who were eager to play their part in the fray. In other cases, when ships collided prow to prow with their rams, the marines stationed on the decks set about wounding one another, since their targets were close at hand, as the ships backed water in preparation for another ramming run. In yet other cases, the captains took their opponents in the side and, with the rams stuck fast, men tried to leap aboard the enemy ships, and met or meted out death in terrible forms. [4] Some men, as they grabbed hold of the nearby gunwale of an enemy ship, missed their footing and fell into the sea, where they were immediately stabbed to death by the spears of those who stood over them, while others, who managed to board the enemy ship successfully, either killed their opponents or forced them back along the narrow walkway and toppled them into the sea.

In short, the fighting was varied and full of surprises. Often the weaker side came off best because they had the taller ship, and the stronger side worst because their situation placed them at a disadvantage or because of the unpredictability of this kind of battle. [5] In battles fought on land, there is no mistaking valour because it awards the ability to win, when there are no external, random factors to frustrate it. In sea-battles, however, there are many factors of various kinds that unexpectedly defeat men whose courage should have brought them victory.

52. The most glorious display of martial prowess was put on by Demetrius as he stood at the stern of his septireme. He was attacked by many men at once, who crowded around him, but he either struck them down with his lances or, if they came to close quarters, killed them with his spear. A large number of missiles of all kinds were fired at him, but he dodged those he saw coming and let his defensive armour stop the rest. [2] Of the three men whose job it was to protect him with their shields, one was killed by a lance and the other two fell wounded.

In the end, Demetrius overpowered the ships ranged opposite him, and at the same time as turning Ptolemy's right wing he also forced the next ships in the line to take off as well. [3] But Ptolemy, who had the largest ships and the best men with him, had no difficulty in turning his opponents, and a number of ships were either sunk or captured along with their crews. When he turned back from this victory, he did not expect the rest of Demetrius' fleet to present him with much of a problem, but then he saw that his left wing* had been defeated and that all the next ships in the line had turned to flight, and also that Demetrius was bearing down on him with overwhelming numbers—and at that point he sailed back to Citium. [4] After his victory, Demetrius made Neon and Bourichus responsible for the troop-carriers and told them to go after the men who were swimming in the sea and pick them up. He then adorned his ships with the stemposts of the enemy ships,* took the ships he had captured in tow, and sailed to his camp and the harbour he was using as his base.

[5] While the battle was in progress, Menelaus, the general in Salamis, manned his sixty ships and sent them off, under the command of Menoetius, to help Ptolemy. An engagement took place at the mouth of the harbour with the ships which were guarding the exit and the Salaminian ships forced their way through the blockade. Demetrius' ten ships fled to the army camp, and Menoetius sailed off, but he arrived a little too late and returned to Salamis.

[6] So this was the outcome of the battle. More than a hundred of Ptolemy's transport ships were captured, and they were carrying over eight thousand soldiers.* As for the warships, forty were captured along with their crews and about eighty were disabled and were towed by the victors, full of sea water, to their camp by the city. Twenty of Demetrius' ships were also disabled, but after receiving the proper care they all continued to perform the services for which they were fitted.

53. After the battle, Ptolemy gave up on Cyprus and sailed back to Egypt.* Demetrius took over all the cities on the island along with the soldiers of the garrisons, whom he enrolled in units of his own army. Sixteen thousand infantrymen were enrolled in this way, and about six hundred horse. He lost no time in sending men off on the largest of his ships to his father, to tell him about his success. [2] When Antigonus heard about the victory, he was so exhilarated by the extent to which he outstripped everyone else that he put on a diadem and from then on began to style himself king.* He also let Demetrius have the same title and rank.* [3] Ptolemy's spirits were not crushed by his defeat, however, and he too similarly assumed the diadem and began to refer to himself as 'king' in all his letters.* [4] The other dynasts,

not to be outdone, did the same and also began to call themselves kings—Seleucus, who had recently extended his territory by acquiring the upper satrapies, and Lysimachus and Cassander, who still held the territory they had originally been allotted.*

But I have said enough about these matters, and now I shall move on to what was happening in Libya and Sicily. 54. When Agathocles found out that the dynasts I have just mentioned had assumed the diadem, he awarded himself the title of king. His thinking was that his armed forces were just as strong as theirs, his territory just as extensive, and his achievements just as significant. He decided not to wear a diadem, however, because it was already his constant habit to wear a wreath. He had been wearing a wreath, as a consequence of a priesthood that he held, at the start of his bid for tyranny, and he never took it off throughout the time of his struggle for power. There are, however, some who say that his habit of wearing a wreath came about because he did not have a very good head of hair.

[2] Be that as it may, wanting to do something worthy of the title of king, he marched against the people of Utica, who had defected from his alliance. He launched a surprise attack on the city and captured about three hundred citizens who had been cut off in the countryside. At first, he offered the Uticans a free pardon and demanded that they surrender the city to him. When they turned him down, however, he built a siege tower, hung the prisoners on it, and brought it up to the city walls. [3] The Uticans felt sorry for their wretched comrades, but the freedom of all meant more to them than the lives of those few, so they posted their troops on the walls and bravely awaited the siege.

[4] Agathocles had equipped the tower with catapults, slingers, and bowmen, and in the early stages of the siege he used it to spearhead his assault—and to sear, so to speak, the minds of the defenders. [5] The men stationed on the walls were reluctant at first to fire missiles, since the targets before them were fellow citizens and included some of the leading men of the city. But when the enemy piled on the pressure, the Uticans had no choice but to defend themselves against the attacks of the troops stationed in the tower. [6] What they experienced then was cruel and unusual indeed, and they knew what it was to be treated badly by Fortune, since they were caught in a trap they could not avoid. Given that the Greeks were using the captured Uticans as human shields, the defenders could either spare these men's lives and let their city fall to the enemy, or they could defend

the city by ruthlessly killing a large number of their fellow citizens who had simply been unlucky. [7] And that is exactly what happened. In order to defend themselves against the enemy they relied on missiles of all kinds, and while they shot down the soldiers who were manning the tower, their javelins also struck some of their fellow citizens who were hanging there, and their bolts nailed whichever parts of their bodies they hit to the tower, until they resembled criminals who were being defiled and punished by being crucified. And the chances are that this was being done to them by friends and relatives, since Necessity does not trouble itself with what men call sacred.

55. When Agathocles saw that they had hardened their hearts and were intent on fighting, he posted his men all around the city and managed to force his way inside at a point where the wall had been badly built. [2] The Uticans fled into their houses and sanctuaries, and Agathocles, who was furious with them, set about an orgy of slaughter. Some were killed in combat, anyone who was captured was hanged, and he made sure that those who had sought safety in the sanctuaries and at the altars of the gods were cheated of their hopes. [3] Once he had looted the city of its movable property, he left a guard to look after it and took his army off to the town called Hippou Acra, which was well protected by nature by the marshy lake that lay beside it.* He assaulted the place vigorously and it fell to him once he had defeated the local inhabitants in a battle at sea.

The subjection of these two cities brought him control not only of most of the places on the coast, but also of the peoples who lived inland. The Numidians were the only exception; some of them entered into a pact of friendship with him, but others preferred to wait and see what the final outcome of the war would be. [4] Libya was divided up among four peoples. There were the Phoenicians and the Libyphoenicians; the Phoenicians occupied Carthage in those days, and the Libyphoenicians possessed a large number of coastal towns, intermarried with the Carthaginians, and got their name from their compound ethnicity. Then the most populous of the native peoples, and the oldest, were the Libyans, who loathed the Carthaginians with exceptional bitterness because of the oppressive form of domination under which they suffered. And finally there were the Numidians, who occupied a great deal of Libya, all the way up to the desert.

[5] Agathocles now had the advantage over the Carthaginians thanks to his Libyan allies and the size of his forces, but he was still

very worried about Sicily. He therefore built both undecked galleys and pentaconters, and embarked two thousand of his soldiers. Leaving his son Agatharchus in command in Libya, he put to sea and sailed to Sicily.

56. Meanwhile, Xenodocus, the Acragantine general, who had already freed many of the Sicilian cities and stirred the Siceliots to hope for the restoration of self-determination throughout the island, led his army of more than ten thousand foot and almost a thousand horse against Agathocles' generals. [2] Leptines and Demophilus raised as many men as they could from Syracuse and the hill-forts, and took up a position close to Xenodocus with an army of 8,200 foot and 1,200 horse. A fierce battle took place, in which Xenodocus came off worst. He fled to Acragas and lost at least 1,500 of his soldiers. [3] In view of this disaster, the Acragantines brought their great project* to an end, and with it their allies' hopes of freedom.

Soon after this battle had taken place Agathocles arrived back in Sicily. He sailed into Selinous and forced the people of Heraclea, who had freed their city, to submit to him again. Then he crossed over to the other side of the island, where he won the allegiance of the people of Therma and let the Carthaginians who were garrisoning the city go under a truce.† Then, after besieging Cephaloedium into submission and leaving Leptines there as its governor, he marched through the interior and tried to get into Centuripae under cover of darkness, where some of the citizens were due to admit him. But the plan was discovered, the garrison soldiers came to the rescue, and he was driven out of the town with the loss of more than five hundred men. [4] Next, he went to Apollonia at the invitation of some of the citizens who were promising to betray the city to him, but the traitors had already been found out and punished, so he put the place under siege. On the first day, his assaults were ineffective, but the next day he did succeed in taking the city, although it cost him a great deal of effort and many men. He put most of the people of Apollonia to death and looted their property.

57. While Agathocles was going about all this, Deinocrates, the leader of the exiles, took over the Acragantine policy; he declared himself the champion of liberty for all, and as a result many men flocked to his banner from all over the island. [2] They eagerly placed themselves at his disposal, some moved by the desire for self-determination that is innate in all men, others by fear of Agathocles. Once Deinocrates

had collected an army of over twenty thousand foot and 1,500 horse, all of them men who had been schooled by constant exile and hardship, he camped out in the open countryside, challenging the dynast to battle. [3] And when Agathocles, who was greatly outnumbered, refused the challenge, Deinocrates dogged his heels relentlessly, winning victory by default.

From this moment onwards, there was a downturn in Agathocles' fortunes, in Libya as well as in Sicily. [4] After his father's departure, Archagathus, whom Agathocles had left in command in Libya, got the better of the enemy at first. He sent a division of the army under the command of Eumachus into the interior, and Eumachus captured the sizeable city of Tocae and won the allegiance of many of the Numidians who lived thereabouts. [5] Then he besieged another town, called Phelline, until it surrendered, and compelled the local tribe of pastoralists, who were called the Asphodelodeis and were almost as black as Ethiopians,* to submit to him. [6] The third place he took was Meschelas, a very large and very ancient city, founded by Greeks returning from the Trojan War, as mentioned in my third book.* Then he captured a town called Hippou Acra, which had the same name as one of the towns taken by Agathocles,* and finally he took an independent city called Acris, where he enslaved the population and gave his troops permission to plunder.

58. Once his men were glutted with booty, Eumachus returned to Archagathus. Now that he had a reputation for effectiveness, he campaigned once again in the interior of Libya. He bypassed the cities that had fallen to him on the previous occasion and broke into a city called Miltine, which he took by surprise. [2] But the barbarians united against him and got the better of him in the streets, so that he was unexpectedly driven out of the city, with the loss of many men. After leaving Miltine, he advanced across a high mountain range that was almost two hundred stades in extent. It was filled with cats,* and therefore absolutely no winged creatures made their nests there either in the trees or in fissures in the rocks, because of the aggressiveness of these cats. [3] On the other side of these mountains, he entered a land which teemed with apes and contained three towns called the Ape-towns after these creatures—that is, when the word is translated into Greek.

[4] Many of the customs of these towns were quite different from ours. The apes lived in the same houses as people, for instance; they

were regarded as gods, as dogs are in Egypt, and were allowed to take food whenever they liked from the provisions kept in the storerooms. Parents very commonly gave their children ape-related names, just as we name our children after the gods.* [5] Killing one of these creatures was treated as the worst kind of sacrilege and was punishable by death. This is the origin of the proverbial saying that was current among some of them and was applied to people who are legally killed: 'That's the price of ape's blood.'

[6] Anyway, Eumachus assaulted and took one of these towns and gained the other two by negotiation. But when he found out that the barbarians who lived in the vicinity of these towns were mustering in large numbers against him, he continued on his way with some rapidity, having decided to return to the coast.

59. So far, the Libyan campaign as a whole had gone according to Archagathus' plan, but the next thing that happened was that the Council of Elders in Carthage had a useful meeting about the war at which it was decided to form three armies and send them out of the city, one against the coastal towns, the second into the hinterland, and the third into the interior. [2] The counsellors' thinking was that, in the first place, this would make it easier for the city to endure the siege and would also alleviate the food shortage, seeing that hordes of people from all over the country had taken refuge in Carthage, with the result that they were short of everything, since supplies had already been exhausted. They were in no immediate danger from the siege, however, because the city was unapproachable thanks to its defences—its walls and the sea. [3] In the second place, they thought that their allies would be more likely to persevere if there were a number of armies in the field to come to their aid. But what counted most for them was their hope that the enemy would be forced to divide his forces and withdraw a good distance away from Carthage.

All of these objectives were realized, just as they had planned. [4] Once thirty thousand troops had been sent out of the city, those who remained behind† not only had enough to satisfy their needs, but even had a surplus that enabled them to enjoy plenty of everything, and their allies, who had previously been forced to come to terms with the enemy out of fear, regained their courage and reverted to the friendly relations they had formerly had with Carthage.

60. When Archagathus saw that all Libya was in enemy hands, he too divided his army. He sent one division to the coast, gave a part of

the rest of the army to Aeschrion and sent him on his way, and took command of the other part himself, leaving an adequate garrison in Tunis. [2] With so many armies at large all over the country and with a decisive change expected, everyone was in suspense, waiting to see what the outcome would be.

[3] Hanno, who was in command of the army in the hinterland, laid an ambush for Aeschrion, took him by surprise, and killed more than four thousand infantrymen and about two hundred cavalrymen, including the general himself. Some of the rest were captured, but others made it safely to Archagathus, who was about five hundred stades away.

[4] Himilco, whose job was to campaign in the interior, at first made one of the cities there his base while waiting for Eumachus,† whose army was crawling along, weighed down by all the spoils they had taken from the cities they had captured. [5] Then, when the Greeks drew up their army and challenged him to battle, Himilco left some of his men in the city, armed and ready, with orders to emerge and attack his pursuers when he feigned retreat, while he set out with half of his troops, joined battle a short way in front of the Greek camp, and immediately turned to flight as though overcome by terror. [6] Eumachus' men, exulting in their victory, gave chase with no thought for their formation, and in considerable disorder set about harrying the retreating enemy. But then suddenly the troops poured out from another part of the city as arranged, and when this considerable body of men cried out all at once in response to a single command, Eumachus' men were stricken by panic. [7] Since the men the barbarians attacked were therefore out of order and frightened by the unexpected turn of events, it did not take long for the Greeks to be routed. The Carthaginians had cut off the enemy's line of retreat back to their camp, so Eumachus and his men were forced to flee to the nearby hill, which was short of water. [8] When the Phoenicians besieged the place, the Greeks, who were both weakened by thirst and were no match for the enemy, were almost all killed. In fact, of eight thousand infantrymen there were only thirty survivors, and of eight hundred cavalrymen only forty escaped from the battle.

61. After meeting with such an overwhelming catastrophe, Archagathus returned to Tunis. He rounded up the remnants of his expeditionary forces wherever they were to be found, and sent messengers to Sicily to tell his father what had happened and to convey his urgent request for help. [2] Then the Greeks suffered another setback on top

of the defeats they had already experienced: all but a few of their allies defected from them, and the united enemy forces encamped near by and were awaiting their opportunity. [3] Himilco occupied the defiles and denied his opponents, who were about a hundred stades away, access to the passes from the countryside, while on the other side Atarbas made camp forty stades from Tunis. [4] Since the enemy therefore controlled both sea and land, the Greeks began to suffer from shortage of provisions and faced danger from every quarter.

[5] The general feeling among the Greeks was that their position was hopeless, but when Agathocles heard about the setbacks in Libya, he made seventeen warships ready, with the intention of going to help Archagathus. Although his affairs in Sicily had taken a turn for the worse because of the increase in the number of the exiles who had joined Deinocrates, he entrusted the war on the island to the general-ship of Leptines, while he manned the ships and waited for an oppor-tunity to set sail, given that the Carthaginians had thirty ships blockading the harbour.

[6] Just then eighteen ships arrived from Etruria as reinforcements. They sailed into the harbour under cover of darkness without being spotted by the Carthaginians, and the acquisition of this extra capability enabled Agathocles to defeat the enemy by means of a stratagem.* He ordered the auxiliaries to remain in the harbour until he had sailed out and drawn the Carthaginians into pursuing him, and then he put his plan into effect by setting out from the harbour at speed with his fleet of seventeen ships. [7] The Carthaginian picket ships gave chase, and when Agathocles saw that the Etruscans were emerging from the harbour, he suddenly turned his ships, took up a position for ramming, and engaged the barbarians. This was not what they had been expecting, and with their triremes caught between enemy squadrons the terri-fied Carthaginians turned tail. [8] Then the Greeks captured five ships with their crews, and the Carthaginian general, seeing that his command ship was on the point of being captured, committed sui-cide, preferring death to the captivity he foresaw. But in fact this turned out to have been a poor decision, because his ship caught a favourable wind, and when the emergency sail was hoisted it escaped from the battle.

62. So Agathocles, who had never expected to get the better of the Carthaginians at sea, unexpectedly defeated them, and from then on

remained dominant at sea and was able to protect his merchant shipping. Supplies now began to reach the Syracusans from everywhere, and they soon replaced their shortages with plenty of everything. [2] Agathocles was delighted by his success and sent Leptines to plunder enemy farmland. His orders were to focus on Acragas, because Xenodocus was being maligned by his political opponents and there was factional strife between him and them. [3] Agathocles ordered Leptines, then, to try to tempt Xenodocus to give battle—a battle he would easily win, because Xenodocus' forces would be riven by factionalism and had already known defeat.

[4] And that is precisely what happened. Leptines invaded Acragantine territory and set about laying it waste, and at first Xenodocus did nothing, judging his forces no match for the enemy, but then, when he was rebuked by his fellow citizens for cowardice, he led his army out against the enemy. In terms of numbers, he fell only a little short of his opponents, but he was very inferior in terms of battlefield skills because his army consisted of citizens who had been born to a sedentary life of ease, whereas the enemy army had been trained by service in the field and by constant campaigning. [5] So, when battle was joined, Leptines soon routed the Acragantines and harried them back to the city, and the defeated side lost about five hundred foot and over fifty horse in the course of the battle. Then the people of Acragas, who were angered by their defeats, brought charges against Xenodocus, on the grounds that the two defeats had been his fault. Xenodocus, however, fearing the impending scrutiny and trial, withdrew to Gela.

63. Within just a few days Agathocles had defeated his enemies on land and sea, and he sacrificed to the gods and entertained his friends magnificently. In symposia, he used to shed the lofty demeanour of a tyrant and make himself out to be lower than any of the ordinary citizens of Syracuse. This was a measure he used as a way of seeking the favour of the common people, and since he also allowed men to speak out against him while they were drunk, he learnt exactly what each of them was thinking, since the truth is brought to light in an unvarnished form by wine. [2] He was also naturally given to buffoonery and mimicry, and in fact even in assemblies he used to permit himself to mock the company and imitate some of them, with the result that the masses often broke out in laughter as though they were watching an actor or a showman. [3] Since the masses acted as his bodyguard, he used to enter assemblies unattended—unlike the tyrant Dionysius, who trusted everyone so little that he usually had long hair and a bushy beard, in order to avoid having to bring the most vital parts of his body near a barber's blade, and if he ever needed to have short hair, he used to singe it off, declaring that the only safe course for a tyrant was mistrust.

[4] Anyway, in the course of the symposium Agathocles took the great drinking-cup made of gold, and said that he had not given up working as a potter until in his practice of the craft he had made this fine a cup.* He did not conceal the fact that he had practised the profession, but on the contrary used to boast of it, in the sense that he used to say that it was through his own abilities that he had exchanged the humblest of lives for the highest rank in society. [5] Once, when he was besieging a rather illustrious city and people from the wall were shouting 'Potter! Kiln-operator!* When will you pay your troops?', he replied: 'When I've taken this city.'

[6] Be that as it may, once people's unguarded talk at symposia had enabled him to identify which of his fellow drinkers were hostile to his tyranny, he gave them a personal invitation later to another banquet, along with any other Syracusans who were particularly self-assertive. The total number came to five hundred men, and he surrounded them with those of his mercenaries who were fit for the work and slaughtered them all. [7] He wanted to be good and sure that, while he was absent in Libya, they did not put an end to his tyranny and recall Deinocrates and the exiles. So once he had secured his rule in this way he put to sea and left Syracuse.

64. When he reached Libya, he found the army disheartened and very short of provisions. Under the circumstances, he decided that his best course of action was to fight. He aroused his men's martial ardour and advanced in battle order, challenging the barbarians to combat. [2] His army consisted of all the surviving Greeks, six thousand in number, at least the same number of Celts, Samnites, and Etruscans, and not far short of ten thousand Libyans—though in the event they waited on the sidelines, ready as usual to change sides if the situation changed. [3] In addition to these infantrymen, the army included 1,500 cavalrymen and more than six thousand Libyan war chariots.

The Carthaginians, however, whose camp occupied high and inaccessible ground, chose not to fight men who had nothing to lose. Their hope was that, if they stayed in their camp and remained well supplied with everything, hunger and the passage of time would enable them to defeat their opponents. [4] But the situation left Agathocles no choice except a bold and risky venture, and since it was impossible to draw the barbarians down on to the plain, he led his army against their encampment. The Carthaginians therefore sallied forth, and even though they greatly outnumbered him and had the advantage of the difficult terrain, Agathocles held out for a while, though he was hard pressed on every side. But then his mercenaries and the rest of his men began to give ground, and he was forced to retreat to his camp. [5] The barbarians pursued them closely. They ignored the Libyans and gave them no trouble in order to win their allegiance, but they could tell the Greeks and mercenaries by their weaponry, and they continued to slaughter them until they had driven them into their camp. About three thousand of Agathocles' men lost their lives on this occasion.

On the night following the battle, it so happened that both armies were visited with disaster of an unusual and totally unexpected kind. **65.** After their victory, the Carthaginians were sacrificing at night the best of the prisoners they had taken, as offerings in gratitude to the gods. A great fire was consuming the men who were being burnt as sacrificial victims when suddenly the wind got up and caused the sacred tent, which was near the altar, to catch alight—and then the fire spread to the general's tent and the officers' tents that were next to it, to the considerable dismay and terror of the entire army. Some men were caught by the flames as they were trying to put out the fire, or as they were fetching their panoplies and the most valuable pieces of equipment from their tents. The tents were made of reeds and grass, and the fire was fanned into a furious blaze by the wind, so that it spread more quickly than the soldiers could bring help. [2] The upshot was that before long the entire camp was in flames. Many men were burnt alive, trapped in the narrow corridors of the camp, and paid an instant penalty for their cruel treatment of the prisoners, in a punishment that fitted their crime. As for those who made their way out of the camp amid all the confusion and din, an even greater danger awaited them.

66. This is what happened. About five thousand of the Libyans who had been in Agathocles' army had deserted from the Greeks and were making their way over to the barbarians under cover of darkness. When the outlying pickets saw these men approaching the Carthaginian camp, they thought that the whole Greek army was advancing, armed and ready, and before long they had warned the soldiers about the approaching threat. [2] By the time the message had reached everyone, there was considerable tumult and an attack by the enemy was expected any moment. To a man, they placed their hopes of safety in flight, but since no order had been given by the generals and no one was in formation, the fugitives kept running into one another. Because of the darkness and their terror, they failed to recognize their comrades and fought them on the assumption that they were enemies. [3] There was great loss of life. Given their prevailing disorientation, either men died fighting, or, if they had burst out of the camp unarmed, they fled over rugged terrain, terrified out of their wits by the sudden danger, and fell over cliffs.

In the end, more than five thousand men died, but the rest of the army made it safely to Carthage. [4] Those in the city, however, wrongly believed the report they received from their men, and thought that they had been defeated in a battle and that most of their troops had lost their lives. They were therefore extremely anxious as they opened the city gates and let the soldiers in, amid confusion and agitation, because they were afraid that they were letting the enemy into the city along with the tail-enders. It was only when it was light that they learnt the truth and were at last relieved from their expectation of disaster.

67. But at the same time Agathocles met with a similar disaster, also caused by mistaken beliefs and expectations. After the burning of the Carthaginian camp and the ensuing maelstrom, the Libyans who had deserted did not dare to carry on. They turned back again, and some Greeks who saw them approaching thought it was the Carthaginian army that was coming and told Agathocles that the enemy army was near by. [2] The dynast gave the call to arms and his troops rushed out of the camp in considerable confusion. At the same time, the fire in the Carthaginian camp blazed up high and the din from there became audible, and the Greeks became absolutely certain that the barbarians were advancing towards them in full force. [3] Terror made it impossible for them to think rationally about what to do, panic seized hold of the army, and they all turned to flight. Then, when they met up with the Libyans, and given that the darkness was working to increase their disorientation, they began to fight those they encountered on the assumption that they were enemies. [4] All night long they

scattered all over the countryside in a state of panicked confusion, and in the end more than four thousand were killed. When the truth at last became known, the survivors returned to their camp. So catastrophe struck both armies, because they were deceived, as the saying goes, by the needless alarms of war.

68. After this disaster, all the Libyans defected from his alliance, and since his remaining forces lacked the strength to tackle the Carthaginians, Agathocles decided to leave Libya. However, he did not think it would be possible for him to take his troops back because he had not built any transport ships and because the Carthaginians would never allow it as long as they had control of the sea. [2] Nor did he think that the barbarians would agree to a truce, because they greatly outnumbered him and were determined to discourage future attacks on Libya by annihilating its first invaders. [3] He therefore decided to put to sea in secret with just a few companions, one of whom was to be his younger son Heracleides. He was wary of Archagathus, who he thought might at some point form a conspiracy against him, given his affair with his stepmother* and his impetuous nature.

But Archagathus suspected his father of some such plan and was watching for signs of an impending voyage; his intention was to inform a number of the leading men and get them to stop Agathocles leaving. Archagathus was furious at the prospect of being abandoned and left at the mercy of the enemy. Why should he be the only one to be denied safety, when he had played an active role in the battles, fighting for his father's and brother's interests? [4] He therefore told some of the senior officers that Agathocles was planning to sail away secretly by night, and they met and not only stopped Agathocles, but also told the ordinary soldiers about his deception. This made the soldiers furious, and they arrested the dynast, bound him, and put him under guard.

69. Without leadership, there was confusion and turmoil in the camp, and that night the rumour arose that the enemy were approaching. The men were seized by alarm and terror, and to a man they armed themselves and made their way out of the camp, although no order to that effect had been given. [2] At the same time, the men who were guarding the dynast, who were just as terrified as the rest, thought that some people were calling for them and made haste to bring Agathocles out of his cell, bound in fetters. [3] When the rank-and-file soldiers saw him, they were moved by pity and with one voice

they called out for him to be released. As soon as he had been freed, he embarked on the packet boat with a few companions and stealthily sailed away, even though it was the time of the setting of the Pleiades.*

Thinking only of his own safety, then, Agathocles abandoned his sons, who were murdered by the soldiers* as soon as they learnt of Agathocles' escape. The troops then chose generals from among their own ranks and made peace with the Carthaginians. By the terms of the agreement, the Greeks were to surrender the cities they held on receipt of three hundred talents, and those who elected to serve with the Carthaginians would be paid at the going rate, while the rest, once they had sailed over to Sicily, were to be given Solous to live in.* [4] In general, the soldiers abided by the terms of the agreement and received what was due to them, but those who were occupying the cities clung to their hope of being relieved by Agathocles and their cities were taken by storm. [5] The leaders were crucified by the Carthaginians, while the rest were bound in fetters and forced to bring back into cultivation by their own labour the land they had made barren during the war.

So the Carthaginians recovered their freedom in the fourth year of the war. 70. But, where Agathocles' expedition to Libya is concerned, it is worth remarking on its unusual features and the way in which his sons were punished as if by divine providence. Although he had been defeated in Sicily, with the loss of most of his army, in Libya he got the better of those who had previously defeated him with just a fraction of his forces. [2] He lost all the Sicilian cities and was put under siege in Syracuse, but in Libya he gained all the other cities, pinned the Carthaginians inside their city, and put it under siege. It was as though Fortune were making a deliberate display of her power in hopeless cases. [3] After he had reached the peak of his power and had killed Ophellas, who was a familiar and a guest-friend of his,* the gods clearly indicated that what happened to him later was repayment for his lawless treatment of this man.† For it was on the very same day of the very same month in which he killed Ophellas and took over his forces that he in his turn brought about his sons' deaths and lost his army. [4] And the most interesting thing of all is that, like a good law-giver, the god imposed double the penalty on him. After wrongfully killing *one* friend, he lost *two* sons when the young men fell into the hands of those who had served with Ophellas. Anyway, this is all I want to say in response to those who scorn such matters.

71. Agathocles crossed swiftly from Libya to Sicily, rounded up some of his army, and went to Egesta, an allied city with a population at the time of about ten thousand. Since he was short of money, he set about forcing the wealthy to contribute the bulk of their property. [2] There was widespread anger at this and people began to band together, so Agathocles accused the Egestans of conspiring against him and made the city suffer terribly. He brought the poorest members of society out of the city and slaughtered them by the river Scamander, while those who were allegedly better off were tortured until they revealed how rich they actually were. Some were broken on the wheel;* some were tied on to catapult frames and had arrows fired at them; some were flogged brutally with knotted whips which caused excruciating pain.

[3] He also invented another form of punishment, which was similar to Phalaris' bull;* he constructed a bed of bronze in the shape of a human body, with bars regularly spaced all around it, slotted his victims into it, and lit a fire under it while they were still alive. Compared with the bull, this contraption was superior in that those who were being killed by this form of torture were visible. [4] He maimed the wives of the rich either by crushing their ankles with iron pincers or by cutting off their breasts, and if any of them were pregnant he piled bricks on the small of her back until the weight squeezed out the foetus.

Fear stalked the streets of the city while the tyrant was employing this method of ferreting out wealth. Some people burnt themselves to death along with their houses, while others let the noose end their lives. [5] It took just one calamitous day for Egesta to suffer the loss of all its adult citizens. The girls and boys Agathocles sent over to Italy, where he sold them to the Bruttii. He did not even leave the city its name, but changed it to Dicaeopolis and gave it to the soldiers who had deserted to him, for them to live in.*

72. When Agathocles heard about the killing of his sons, all the men who had been left behind in Libya became objects of his hatred, and he sent some of his friends to his brother Antander in Syracuse, telling him to slaughter all the relatives of those who had taken part in the Carthaginian expedition. [2] Antander lost no time in carrying out his orders, and there followed the widest-ranging massacre the world had ever seen. Not only did he consign to death those who were in the prime of life—brothers, fathers, or sons—but even grandfathers and possibly even great-grandfathers, if they were still alive, men of extreme old age who had already been entirely deprived of their senses by the passage of time, and infants, too young to walk or have any sense of their impending doom. Women too were seized, if they were related by blood or marriage, as, in short, was anyone whose suffering would hurt those who had been left behind in Libya.

[3] A large and motley crowd was taken to the coast for execution. When their killers took up their posts, the mingled sound arose of tears and prayers and lamentation, not just from those who were being callously murdered, but also from those who were stunned by the misfortunes of their neighbours and who, in anticipation of what was about to happen, were just as affected as those who were actually being killed. [4] The hardest thing of all was that, following all the killing, when the bodies of the dead were littering the shoreline, no relative or friend dared to bury them, because they were afraid that it might be interpreted as a confession that they were related to them. [5] So many people were killed beside the sea that a wide expanse of water was stained red with blood and left people far off in no doubt about the terrible savagery of what had happened.

306/5

73. *At the beginning of the following year, Coroebus became Archon in Athens, and in Rome Quintus Marcius and Publius Cornelius obtained the consulate. In this year:*

Phoenix,* the younger son of King Antigonus, died and, after giving him a royal funeral, Antigonus sent for Demetrius from Cyprus and collected his forces at Antigonea. He had decided to march against Egypt. [2] He took command of the land army himself and advanced through Coele Syria with more than eighty thousand foot, about eight thousand horse, and eighty-three elephants. He entrusted the fleet to Demetrius and told him to coast along beside the army as it made its way south. In all, 150 warships had been made ready, along with a hundred transport vessels, which were carrying a great quantity of ordnance.

[3] The helmsmen thought Antigonus should bear in mind† the setting of the Pleiades,* which was expected in eight days' time, but he reproached them with cowardice. He was in camp at Gaza, and

since he was keen to forestall Ptolemy's preparations, he ordered his men to provide themselves with ten days' worth of supplies, and he loaded the camels (which had been collected for him by the Arabs) with 130,000 *medimnoi* of grain and a large quantity of fodder for the animals. With carts conveying his artillery, he proceeded through the desert; it was hard going because there was a great deal of marshland, especially near the so-called Pits.*

74. Demetrius put to sea from Gaza in the middle of the night. At first, since the weather was fine, for several days he had his faster ships tow the transport vessels, but then, given that it was the time of year for the Pleiades to set, a northerly wind arose. Many of his quadriremes were perilously driven by the storm back to Raphia, where there are shoals and the anchorage is poor. [2] As for the ships carrying the artillery, some were sunk by the storm and lost, while others ran back to Gaza. But Demetrius persevered and made it through to Casius with the best of his ships.

[3] This place is situated quite close to the Nile, but it lacks a harbour and in wintry conditions it is impossible to land there. This meant that they had to drop anchor and ride the swell at a distance of about two stades from land, which was extremely hazardous. The waves were choppy and rougher than usual, so that there was a danger of the ships sinking with all hands. Since the land was unsuitable for beaching and was enemy territory, ships could not safely sail up to it nor could men swim there. The worst thing of all was that they had run out of drinking water, and their need was so desperate that if the storm had continued for just one more day they would all have died of thirst. [4] The situation seemed hopeless and death was expected at any moment, when the wind dropped and Antigonus' army arrived and made camp near the fleet. [5] Demetrius and his men therefore disembarked and recovered in the camp while waiting for the ships that had been scattered. The storm claimed three quinqueremes, but some of the men managed to swim to land. Then Antigonus led his forces close to the Nile and made camp two stades away from the river.

75. Ptolemy, who had already occupied and secured the most critical places with guards, dispatched some men in wherries. Their job was to sail up close to where the enemy were disembarking and announce that Ptolemy was prepared to pay men to desert from Antigonus, at a rate of two mnas for every ordinary soldier and a talent for every officer. [2] The proclamation of this offer aroused in Antigonus'

mercenaries the desire to change sides, and even quite a few of the mercenary officers inclined† for one reason or another to find desertion an attractive option. [3] But as his men were starting to desert to Ptolemy in large numbers, Antigonus posted archers, slingers, and a great many bolt-shooters on the river bank and repulsed the men who were trying to draw near in the wherries. Some of the deserters fell into his hands and he tortured them horribly, as a way of intimidating others who were entertaining the same idea.

[4] Once he had been joined by the ships that had been delayed, he sailed to a place called Pseudostomon,* hoping that it would be possible for some of his troops to disembark there. But he found a strong guard there, who kept him at bay with bolt-shooters and various other kinds of artillery, so he sailed away as night was falling. [5] Next, he told the helmsmen to follow the command ship by keeping his lantern in sight, and he sailed to Phatniticum, as this mouth of the Nile is called. But at daybreak he found that many of his ships had strayed off course, and he was forced to wait for them and to send the fastest of the ships that had kept up with him to look for them.

76. All this took quite a bit of time, so when Ptolemy found out where the enemy had landed he raced there with an army to confront them and, when everything was ready, took up a position along the shoreline. But since he failed to disembark his men at this point as well, and since he had been told that the adjacent coastline had natural defences in the form of marshes and lagoons, Demetrius set out back with his whole fleet the way he had come. [2] But then a fierce northerly wind struck and the waves began to run high, and three of his quadriremes and some† of his transport vessels as well were driven violently ashore by the waves and fell into Ptolemy's hands. The rest of his ships, however, were kept from grounding by the efforts of the crews and reached Antigonus' camp safely.

[3] Since Ptolemy had occupied every landing-point on the river and they were well guarded, and since he had a large number of river boats, all laden with various kinds of artillery pieces and with men to operate them, Antigonus found himself in all kinds of trouble. [4] His fleet was useless because the Pelusiac mouth of the river was in enemy hands,* and his land army was prevented from advancing and achieving anything because it was checked by the width of the river, but the most important factor was that, since the expedition had already been going on for many days, he was beginning to run out of food for the

men and fodder for the animals. [5] All these factors meant that morale in the army was low. Antigonus therefore called a meeting† of the officers and men with the agenda of deciding whether it was better to stay and fight, or to return for the present to Syria and then later, when they were better prepared, to launch another expedition at a time when they could expect the Nile to be at its lowest. [6] Everyone inclined to the view that they should leave at the earliest possible opportunity, and so he told his men to break camp and he quickly returned to Syria, with the whole fleet also coasting along beside him.

Ptolemy was extremely pleased at the departure of the enemy.* He expressed his gratitude to the gods with sacrifices and feasted his friends in lavish style. [7] He also wrote to Seleucus, Lysimachus, and Cassander to inform them of his success and to boast about how many men had deserted over to his side. He had successfully defended Egypt for a second time and he now regarded the country as spear-won territory.* And so he returned to Alexandria.

77. Meanwhile, Dionysius, the tyrant of Heraclea Pontica, died after a reign of thirty-two years, and his sons, Oxathras and Clearchus, inherited the reins of power and ruled for seventeen years.

In Sicily, Agathocles went the rounds of the cities that were subject to him, securing them with garrisons and exacting money from them. He did this because he was extremely concerned about the possibility that the Siceliots might take advantage of the setbacks he had suffered to make a bid for independence. [2] In fact, this was when one of his generals, Pasiphilus, in response to the news of the killing of Agathocles' sons and of his losses in Libya, judged the dynast to be no threat and went over to Deinocrates' side. Pasiphilus entered into a pact of friendship with Deinocrates, tightened his hold on the cities which had been entrusted to him, and undermined his men's loyalty towards Agathocles by tempting them with hopes for the future. [3] With his hopes being whittled away on all sides, Agathocles was so depressed that he made contact with Deinocrates and suggested that they make a treaty on the following terms: that Agathocles should resign his tyranny and restore Syracuse to its citizens, that Deinocrates' exile should be brought to an end, and that Agathocles should be given two designated fortresses, Therma and Cephaloedium,* along with their farmland.

78. One might reasonably wonder in all this why Agathocles, who had resolutely endured every other situation and had never lost confidence in himself even when things were at their most desperate,

should at this point have turned coward and ceded to his enemies, without a fight, the tyranny for which he had previously fought so many major battles. The most perplexing thing of all was that, although he was master of Syracuse and other cities, and although he had ships, money, and a fair-sized army, his power of reasoning was blunted and he failed to bear in mind the history of the tyrant Dionysius.

[2] Dionysius was once caught up in a situation that was evidently hopeless. The extent of the danger he was facing made him despair of retaining his tyranny, and he was on the point of leaving Syracuse by horse and going into voluntary exile, when Heloris, the eldest of his Friends, checked him and said: 'Dionysius, tyranny makes a fine shroud.'* [3] Similarly, Dionysius' brother-in-law, Megacles, told him that in his opinion a man who was being expelled from a tyranny should be dragged away by the leg, rather than leave of his own accord. With his spirits raised by these expressions of encouragement, Dionysius endured whatever he was faced with, however frightening it appeared, and not only increased his empire, but, after he had grown old enjoying its benefits, he bequeathed to his sons the greatest realm in Europe.

79. In Agathocles' case, however, since his gloom was not relieved by any such considerations, and because he failed to test his fallible expectations against past experience, he entered into an agreement that required him to give up his great empire. In actual fact, however, the agreement was never put into effect; it was validated by the choices Agathocles made, but Deinocrates' ambition prevented his acceptance of it. [2] Deinocrates wanted sole rule, and he was therefore not in sympathy with the democracy in Syracuse, and was perfectly happy with the supremacy he had at the time. He had at his command more than twenty thousand foot and three thousand horse, and many great cities as well, so that although he was called the general of the exiles, in actual fact he was as dominant as a king, since his power was absolute. [3] But if he returned to Syracuse, he would inevitably be an ordinary citizen, just one among many, since a self-governing city is naturally egalitarian, and in the elections he would be worsted by anyone, however undistinguished, who appealed to the people, since the masses are opposed to the supremacy of men who speak their minds.*

It follows that, while it would be perfectly fair to accuse Agathocles of having deserted his post as tyrant, it would also be fair to hold

Deinocrates responsible for the dynast's subsequent successes. [4] For Agathocles sent embassy after embassy to Deinocrates to discuss the terms of their agreement and to ask him to allow him the two fortresses to live in, but Deinocrates always came up with specious pretexts by means of which he thwarted Agathocles' hopes of an agreement. On one occasion, for instance, he insisted that Agathocles should leave Sicily, while on another he demanded his children as hostages.

[5] When Agathocles realized what Deinocrates was up to, he wrote to the exiles, accusing him of preventing them from gaining their independence, and he sent envoys to the Carthaginians and made peace with them. By the terms of the treaty the Phoenicians would regain all the cities which had formerly been subject to them, and in compensation Agathocles would receive from the Carthaginians gold to the value of three hundred talents of silver (or, as Timaeus says, 150 talents),* and 200,000 *medimnoi* of grain. That was how things stood in Sicily.

80. In Italy, the Samnites took the towns of Sora and Calatia,* which were Roman allies, and sold the populations into slavery, and the consuls invaded Iapygia in strength and encamped near the town of Silvium.* [2] Since this town had a Samnite garrison, they began a siege which lasted quite a few days. Eventually, the town fell to them and they gained more than five thousand prisoners and a good quantity of other kinds of booty. [3] When they had finished with this, they invaded Samnite territory, where they ravaged fruit-bearing trees and wrought destruction wherever they went. The Romans had been fighting the Samnites for many years over the issue of supremacy in Italy, and they hoped that depriving them of their rural properties would force the enemy to submit to their superior strength. [4] They therefore spent five months on the devastation of enemy territory; they put almost all the farm buildings to the torch and made the land barren by destroying everything that was capable of producing a cultivated crop. Then they declared war on the people of Anagnia in response to their infractions, besieged Frusino into submission, and sold their farmland.*

81. *At the beginning of the following year, Euxenippus became Archon in Athens, and Lucius Postumius and Tiberius Minucius were the consuls in Rome. In this year:*

War broke out between the Rhodians and Antigonus, under the following circumstances. [2] The city of Rhodes had a powerful navy and there was no better governed city in Greece; these factors made it an object of rivalry among the dynasts and kings, each of whom wanted to win it over to his friendship. Being far-sighted about where its interests lay, it made separate pacts of friendship with each of them and played no part in the wars they fought against one another. [3] It therefore came to be honoured with kingly gifts by each of the dynasts, and since it remained for many years untroubled by war, it progressed by leaps and bounds. Its power became so great, in fact, that it made itself responsible, on behalf of the Greeks, for the war against the pirates and cleared the sea of those criminals. The most powerful man in history, Alexander, valued Rhodes above all other cities; it was there that he deposited his will regarding the overall disposition of his kingdom,* and there were other ways in which he expressed his admiration for it and helped it to grow in power. [4] So, by entering into pacts of friendship with all the dynasts, the Rhodians carefully avoided giving anyone grounds for complaint, but it was Egypt above all that they inclined to favour with their loyalty, because most of their revenues were due to trade with Egypt and in general the city was maintained by that kingdom.

82. Antigonus was aware of all this and wanted to detach the Rhodians from their association with Ptolemy. His first move—this was when he was at war with Ptolemy over Cyprus—was to send envoys to convey his request for an alliance and to ask them to provide ships to join Demetrius' fleet.* [2] When they refused, he sent one of his generals with a fleet, whose job was to detain any ships sailing from Rhodes to Egypt and to confiscate their cargoes. When this general was repulsed by the Rhodians, Antigonus treated this as an act of war, unjustly initiated by them, and threatened to attack the city in strength and put it under siege.* In response, the Rhodians initially decreed major honours for him and sent envoys to ask him not to force the city to get involved in a war with Ptolemy which would infringe their treaty with him. [3] The king gave them a harsh reply, however, and dispatched his son Demetrius with an army and siege engines. The Rhodians, intimidated by the king's overwhelming power, at first got in touch with Demetrius and promised to support Antigonus in his war against Ptolemy. But when Demetrius demanded a hundred of their most eminent citizens as hostages and ordered

them to admit his fleet into their harbours, they concluded that he had designs on the city and they got ready for war.

[4] Demetrius made the harbour of Loryma* the mustering point for all his forces and prepared his fleet for the attack on Rhodes. He had two hundred warships of various classes and more than 170 transports for conveying his infantry, who numbered not far short of forty thousand, along with the cavalry and the pirates who were his allies. He also had a great deal of ordnance of various kinds, and he had equipped himself massively with everything he might need for a siege. [5] In addition, the army was accompanied by almost a thousand freighters, privately owned by those whose profession was trade. Rhodian farmland had remained unplundered for many years, and large numbers of men had gathered from all quarters—the kind of men who regard the misfortunes of the victims of war as a way to enrich themselves.

83. Demetrius drew up his fleet in a formidable array, as though for a set-piece sea-battle, and advanced his warships, which were equipped on their prows with heavy bolt-shooters. The troop-carriers and horse-transports followed, towed by oar-propelled ships, and then the rear was taken by the pirates' freighters and those of the traders and merchants, who constituted a vast horde, as I have already said. The whole stretch of sea between the island and the opposite shoreline seemed to be covered with ships, and the people watching from the city were struck with fear and terror. [2] The Rhodian soldiers who had been stationed on the walls and were awaiting the approach of the enemy fleet, and the old men and the women who were watching from their houses (which was made possible by the fact that the city is shaped like a theatre)*—all of them were terrified by the size of the fleet and the gleam of weaponry in the sunlight, and were in an agony of uncertainty about the final outcome.

[3] Then Demetrius reached the island. He disembarked his forces and encamped close to the city,* beyond the range of missiles. The very next thing he did was send out suitable men, both pirates and others, to ravage the island by land and sea. [4] He also cut down the trees in the nearby countryside and demolished the farm buildings, using the materials to strengthen his camp. In fact, he surrounded it with a triple palisade and with long stakes closely packed together, so that the enemy's losses were his men's gain, in terms of safety. Then he put all his men to work, including the crews of the ships, and in

a few days he had built a mole between the city and his landing-point, so that he had a harbour large enough for his ships.

84. At first, the Rhodians sent envoys, asking Demetrius to refrain from doing any irremediable harm to the city. Their pleas fell on deaf ears, however, so they gave up trying to find a peaceful solution and sent envoys to Ptolemy, Lysimachus, and Cassander, asking for help on the grounds that the city was fighting the war as their proxy. [2] They offered the foreigners who were living in the city, whether they were residents or temporary visitors,* the chance to fight alongside them if they wanted, and sent those who refused out of the city as useless. This served two purposes: first, they were looking ahead to the possibility that the city might become short of food, and, second, they were guarding against treachery from anyone who was unsatisfied with the situation. When they counted those who were capable of fighting, they found that they had about six thousand citizens and about a thousand foreigners, both residents and visitors. [3] They also voted to purchase from their masters any male slaves who were effective in battle, and to emancipate them and give them citizenship. And they drafted another decree to the effect that the bodies of those who died in the war were to be buried at public expense, and that their parents and children were to be maintained by grants from the public treasury, that their daughters were to be given their dowries at public expense, and that when their sons came of age they were to be honoured in the theatre at the Dionysia with a panoply.*

[4] These measures made everyone determined to endure the coming danger bravely, and the Rhodians also did all they could to prepare in other respects. The entire population was in accord, so the rich paid money into the public treasury, the craftsmen put their expertise towards the making of weapons, and everyone went about their tasks energetically, eager to prove themselves more public-spirited than their neighbours. [5] People were busy with the bolt-shooters and stone-throwers, or with the construction of other artillery pieces, or with repairing damaged sections of wall, and a great many men were carrying stones to the walls and piling them up. They even sent three of their fastest ships out against the enemy and the freighters that were bringing their supplies. [6] They took the enemy by surprise, sank a number of ships belonging to traders whose purpose in sailing was to plunder the land for profit, and even managed to haul quite a few ships on to the shore and burn them. Any prisoners they

captured who were able to provide a ransom were taken back to the
city, because the Rhodians had an agreement with Demetrius whereby
they would give each other a thousand drachmas to ransom a free
man, and five hundred for a slave.*

85. Demetrius had a plentiful supply of everything he might need
for the installation of his siege engines, and he began to build two sheds,
one each for the stone-throwers and the bolt-shooters. Each of these
sheds was mounted on two freighters that had been joined together.†
He also set about building two towers which, at four storeys high, were
taller than the towers of the harbour wall; each of the towers was
mounted on two identical ships† and fastened in place in such a way
that, as they were being advanced, each structure bore down equally on
both of its sides and remained in balance. [2] He also built a floating
palisade that was nailed on to squared logs, which was to act as a forward defence and prevent the enemy from sailing up and ramming the
ships that bore the siege engines. [3] While these were being finished,
he collected the sturdiest of the *lemboi*,* provided each of them with
a protective wall of planks with closable windows, and mounted on
them those of his heavy bolt-shooters that had the longest range. He
put on board competent operators of these catapults and Cretan
archers, and he had the boats approach to within missile range and
shoot down those who were increasing the height of the harbour walls.

[4] When the Rhodians saw that Demetrius was concentrating his
attack entirely on the harbour, they too set to work, to make it safe.
They placed two sheds on the mole and three more on freighters near
the boom of the small harbour; in these sheds they put a large number
of bolt-shooters and stone-throwers of all sizes, so that, if the enemy
disembarked soldiers on the mole or brought his siege engines up
closer, this artillery would thwart their designs. They also placed on
the freighters that were anchored in the harbour platforms suitable
for the catapults that were to be mounted on them.

86. Once both sides had completed the preparations I have been
describing, Demetrius first attempted to bring his siege engines to
bear against the harbours,* but was prevented from doing so by rough
sea. Later, however, when he met with favourable weather at night, he
quietly sailed up and seized the end of the mole of the Great Harbour.
He immediately fortified this beachhead with a barricade of planks
and stones, and put four hundred soldiers ashore there and a number
of artillery pieces of various kinds, since the area he had seized was

only five plethra away from the walls. [2] Then, at daybreak he brought his siege engines into the harbour, accompanied by the blare of trumpets and the cries of his men, and he used his lighter bolt-shooters, which had a long range, to drive off the men who were work-ing on the harbour wall, and his stone-throwers to damage or destroy not only the enemy's sheds, but also the wall across the mole, which was insubstantial and low at this time. [3] The Rhodians put up a strong resistance, however, and the whole of that day passed with both sides inflicting and suffering heavy losses.

After dark Demetrius had tugs pull his siege engines back out of range, but the Rhodians filled some skiffs with dry wood and flammable pine, and put braziers on board. At first, they set out in pursuit of the enemy's engines, and when they were close they set light to the wood, but then they were foiled by the floating palisade and Demetrius' artillery, and were forced to withdraw. [4] As the fire took hold, a few of them managed to put the flames out and return with their boats, but most of them swam ashore as their skiffs were consumed. The next day, Demetrius repeated the same attacking manoeuvres by sea, and he also ordered his men to assault the city by land from all direc-tions, shouting out their battle-cries and sounding their trumpets as they did so. The idea of all this was to make the Rhodians uneasy and frightened, since their attention was being pulled in many different directions at once.

87. After assaulting the city in this way for eight days, Demetrius had obliterated the siege engines which had been placed on the mole with his heavy stone-throwers and damaged not just the curtain wall between the towers, but the towers themselves. Some of his soldiers also occupied a section of the cross-wall by the harbour, but the Rhodians formed themselves up and joined battle. They had the advantage of numbers, and they killed some of Demetrius' men and repulsed the rest. The Rhodians were helped by the roughness of the shoreline beside the wall, because there was a continuous jumble of large boulders outside the wall and right next to it, [2] and quite a few of the ships which were carrying these soldiers were wrecked because they did not know about this hazard.† After quickly detaching the stemposts from the wrecks,* the Rhodians threw dry wood and flammable pine into them, and burnt them up.

While the Rhodians were occupied with this, Demetrius' troops sailed all around the city, brought scaling ladders up to the walls, and launched a robust assault, and their comrades on land joined in by attacking from every direction and chimed in with their battle-cry as well. [3] Men were now recklessly risking their lives and many had reached the top of the walls, so the fighting was fierce, with those on the outside trying to force their way in and the Rhodians running up in large numbers to defend their city. In the end, as a result of some fervent fighting by the Rhodians, those who had mounted the walls were either thrown down or wounded and captured. The prisoners included some of the most senior officers. [4] After the besiegers suffered such a resounding defeat, Demetrius had his siege engines retire back to his own harbour and repaired any vessels and contraptions that had been damaged, while the Rhodians buried their dead fellow citizens, dedicated the enemy's weapons and stemposts to the gods, and rebuilt the stretches of wall that had been brought down by the stone-throwers.

88. Demetrius spent seven days repairing his siege engines and his ships, and once he had everything ready for the siege he again sent the ships to attack the harbour. Its capture was the sole purpose of his efforts, because it would deny the people in the city access to their grain supply. [2] When his ships were within range, he attacked the Rhodian ships that were riding at anchor in the harbour with his fire-throwing artillery, while with his stone-throwers he shook the walls and with his bolt-shooters he shot down any men who showed themselves. [3] The attack was relentless and terrifying, but the Rhodian shipowners, desperately concerned for their vessels, managed to extinguish the fire-bearing missiles, while the Prytanes,* seeing that the harbour was in danger of being taken, called on the highest-ranking members of Rhodian society to endure the danger of battle before all was lost.*

[4] The response to their appeal was ample and enthusiastic, and the Rhodians manned their three strongest ships with picked men. Their orders were to try to ram and sink the ships that were carrying the enemy's siege engines, and they drove forward through a hail of missiles. [5] They did well at first: they broke through the iron-plated palisade,* and then, by repeatedly ramming the ships, they filled two of them with sea-water and overturned the towers, but when the third contraption* was towed back by Demetrius' men, the Rhodians, encouraged by their success, pressed on into battle with inappropriate boldness. [6] The consequence was that they became surrounded

by many large ships and their hulls were shattered in many places by rams. The admiral, Execestus, was wounded and captured, as were the captain of his ship and a few others, although everyone else jumped overboard and swam over to their comrades. One of the ships fell into Demetrius' hands, but the other two escaped.

[7] After the battle, Demetrius built another tower three times as large as its predecessor in height and breadth, but as he was bringing it up to the harbour a southerly gale sprang up which swamped the ships that were lying at anchor and overturned the tower. Just then the Rhodians, cleverly taking advantage of the favourable opportunity, opened a gate and attacked the men who had established the beachhead on the mole. [8] A prolonged and fierce battle took place, and since Demetrius was unable to send reinforcements because of the storm, while the Rhodians were fighting in relays, the king's men, numbering almost four hundred, had no choice but to lay down their arms and surrender. [9] After this victory of theirs, the Rhodians were joined by some allies: 150 men arrived from Cnossus and more than five hundred from Ptolemy. Some of the men supplied by Ptolemy were Rhodians who were in service to the king as mercenaries. That was how things stood in Rhodes.

89. In Sicily, Agathocles had failed to make peace with Deinocrates and the exiles, so he marched out against them with the forces he had at his disposal. His thinking was that the only option left to him was to risk fighting a decisive battle. He had with him no more than five thousand foot and about eight hundred horse. [2] When Deinocrates and the exiles saw this bold move by the enemy, they jubilantly came out to do battle with Agathocles, since, with more than twenty-five thousand foot and at least three thousand horse, they greatly outnumbered him. The two armies halted close to each other at a place called Torgium and then formed up for battle. The fighting was fierce for a short while, given the determination displayed by both sides, but then some of the exiles who were at variance with Deinocrates—there were more than two thousand of them—went over to the tyrant and thereby became responsible for the exiles' defeat. [3] Morale was greatly boosted on Agathocles' side, while Deinocrates' soldiers panicked and turned to flight, because they overestimated the number of the deserters.

Agathocles pursued them for a while, without allowing a massacre to take place, and then he sent envoys to the exiles, asking them to end

404 THE LIBRARY BOOK 20 305/4

their hostility and return to their native cities. After all, he said, they now knew by personal experience that they would never be able to get the better of him on the battlefield, since they were beaten even on this occasion, when they greatly outnumbered him. [4] On the exiles' side, all the cavalrymen survived the flight and made it safely to a village called Ambicae, and some of the infantry escaped after nightfall, but most of them halted on a hill and came to terms with Agathocles. They no longer had any hope of winning a battle and every man longed for his family and friends, his homeland and its amenities. [5] Agathocles gave pledges to guarantee their safety and they left the relative security of their hill. When they had come down, Agathocles disarmed them, surrounded them with his army, and massacred them to a man. Timaeus says that there were six thousand of them, others that there were about four thousand. [6] Agathocles always held pledges and oaths in contempt, and his strength came not from his own resources but from keeping his subjects weak, since he was more afraid of his allies than his enemies.

90. Having wiped out the enemy army in this way, Agathocles took in the surviving exiles and became reconciled with Deinocrates; in fact, he gave him the command of a division of his army and constantly trusted him with crucial business. One might wonder at this point why it was only with Deinocrates that Agathocles, who was otherwise suspicious of everyone, remained on good terms all his life. [2] But, now that he had betrayed his allies, Deinocrates seized Pasiphilus in Gela, killed him, and turned the fortresses and towns over to Agathocles. It took him two years to hand the enemy's possessions over† to the tyrant.

[3] In Italy, the Romans defeated the Paeligni,* took their land for themselves, and granted citizenship to those few who were held to be Roman sympathizers. Then, since the Samnites were ravaging the Falernian Fields,* the consuls marched against them, and a battle took place which the Romans won. [4] They captured twenty standards and more than two thousand of the enemy soldiers. The consuls then immediately took the town of Bola, but Gaius Gellius,* the Samnite commander, appeared with an army of six thousand. A close-fought battle took place, and Gellius himself was made prisoner, while most of the Samnites were cut down, although some were taken alive. The consuls took advantage of their thorough victory and recovered Sora, Arpinum, and Serennia,* the allied towns which had fallen to the enemy.

304/3

91. *At the beginning of the following year, Pherecles became Archon in Athens, in Rome Publius Sempronius and Publius Sulpicius were the next to be appointed to the consulate, and in Elis the 119th Olympic festival was celebrated, with Andromenes of Corinth the victor in the stade race. In this year:*

Demetrius was besieging Rhodes, and since he was having no luck with sea-borne assaults, he decided to attack from the land. [2] He got hold of a great quantity of various materials and built a siege tower called a 'city-taker',* which was far larger than any of its predecessors. Each side of its square base platform, which was made out of squared timbers joined by iron plates, was almost fifty cubits long. The space between the platform and the ground had rows of beams set about a cubit apart from one another, as stations for the men who were to push the tower forward. [3] Despite its weight, the whole thing was movable, since it was mounted on eight large, solid wheels, the rims of which were two cubits wide and plated with strong iron. In order to allow it to move sideways, swivels were devised, by means of which the whole contraption could easily move in any direction.

[4] From the corners there arose pillars, equal in length and just short of a hundred cubits long, which inclined towards one another in such a way that the first floor of the whole structure, which was nine storeys high, had an area of forty-three hundred square feet and the topmost storey nine hundred square feet. [5] He covered the outside of the three exposed sides of the contraption with iron plates, to protect it from fire-throwing artillery. Each floor had windows on the front, the sizes and shapes of which suited the kinds of missile that were going to be fired from them. [6] These windows had shutters, which were raised by a device and were designed to provide the men on each floor with protection as they went about the business of firing their missiles, because they were made out of hides which had been stitched together and filled with wool so that they would reduce the impact of the boulders fired by the stone-throwers.*

[7] Each of the floors had two wide stairways, one of which they used for climbing up with whatever they needed, while the other was used for descending, so that everything could be managed without confusion. The machine was to be moved by 3,400 men who had been

selected from the entire army for their exceptional strength. [8] Some of them were shut up inside and pushed it forward from there, while the rest were stationed behind; the mobility of the contraption was greatly helped by its skilful design.

Demetrius also built sheds, some to protect the work of filling in the moat, others to carry rams, and galleries through which men could safely reach their place of work and return from it. He got the crews of the ships to clear an area four stades wide (which is to say that the work zone covered the length of six curtain walls and seven towers), over which he intended to bring the siege engines up to the city, once they were built. The number of craftsmen and labourers that he assembled was not far short of thirty thousand.

92. Thanks to his large workforce, everything was completed sooner than expected. Demetrius now posed a real threat to the Rhodians. It was not only the size of his siege engines and the large number of troops he had assembled that terrified them, but also the forcefulness and ingenuity that he brought to sieges. [2] He had an extremely good technical mind and it was because he invented many devices that went beyond the skill of the professional engineers that he was called Poliorcetes, 'the besieger of cities'. And when it came to assaulting a city, he had such technical superiority, and brought so much forceful energy to bear, that it seemed that no wall was strong enough to afford the besieged protection from him.

[3] Besides, he was so tall and handsome that he seemed to have the stature of a hero. The sight of his good looks, enhanced by the air of superiority natural to a king, astounded even visiting foreigners, and they joined his train, as he went about, just to keep him in view. [4] Moreover, he was temperamentally aloof and haughty, and treated not only the common people with contempt, but even potentates. But his most distinctive feature was that although at times of peace he spent his time drinking and frequented symposia with their dancing and carousing—although, in short, he imitated the behaviour the mythologers attribute to Dionysus when he was on earth—yet in his wars he was so energetic and sober that both physically and mentally he was more ready for battle than any other practitioner of warcraft. [5] It was, after all, in his time that the greatest artillery pieces were perfected, and engines of all kinds that far surpassed those that had existed earlier; and after this siege and his father's death he launched some truly enormous ships.*

93. When the Rhodians saw how well the enemy's engineering projects were progressing, they built a second wall inside the city, parallel to the one that was likely to be damaged in the course of the assaults. The stones they used were gained by demolishing the outer wall of the theatre and the nearby houses, and even some of the temples, while promising the gods that they would build them more beautiful ones once the city had been saved.

[2] They also sent out nine ships and ordered the commanders to sail far and wide; they were to launch surprise attacks, and to either sink the ships they captured or bring them back to the city. Once these ships had taken to the sea, they separated into three squadrons. Damophilus, who was in command of ships that the Rhodians call 'guards', sailed to Carpathos and found many of Demetrius' ships there. Some he sank by holing them with his rams, some he beached and burnt (while picking out the most useful members of their crews), and he brought back to Rhodes from the island quite a few ships which had cargoes of grain.

[3] Menedemus, who was in charge of three *triēmioliae*,* sailed to Patara in Lycia, where he found a ship whose crew had gone ashore and left it riding at anchor. He put this ship to the torch, and captured many others that were bringing supplies to Demetrius' army and sent them off to Rhodes. [4] He also captured a quadrireme that was sailing from Cilicia, which had on board kingly robes and the rest of the effects that Phila, Demetrius' wife, had devotedly got ready and sent off to her husband. Menedemus sent the clothing off to Egypt, since the robes were dyed with purple and were apparel fit for a king, but he hauled the quadrireme on to land and sold both its crew and the crews from the other ships he had captured.

[5] The remaining three ships were under the command of Amyntas. He sailed to the islands,* where he found many ships that were bringing the enemy materials for their siege engines. He sank some of them and brought others back to Rhodes, and among the prisoners on these ships were engineers who were famous for their artillery and eleven artillerymen of exceptional skill.†

[6] The next thing that happened was that the Rhodian assembly met and some men spoke in favour of tearing down the statues of Antigonus and Demetrius, arguing that it was dreadful to allow their besiegers the same honours as their benefactors. But the people did not approve of the suggestion; they censured the speakers for impropriety and made

no change to any of the honours that Antigonus had been awarded. This was a wise decision, where both the city's reputation and its best interests were concerned, [7] because the high-mindedness and constancy of such a decision by a democracy* not only won the Rhodians praise from the world at large, but also caused their besiegers some remorse. After all, they were liberating cities in Greece which had never responded to their benefactions with loyalty, while they were plainly trying to enslave a city which had proved itself to be perfectly constant in repaying favours. The decision also protected the Rhodians against the vicissitudes of Fortune, in the sense that, if it so happened that the city fell, the memory that they had upheld their friendship would persist as a way for them to plead for mercy. So this was a wise decision by the Rhodians.

94. When Demetrius' sappers had undermined the wall, a deserter told the besieged Rhodians that the men working in the underground tunnels would soon be inside the city. [2] The Rhodians therefore dug a deep trench, parallel to the stretch of wall that was expected to collapse, and before long their own mining work had brought them into contact underground with their opponents and they had stopped them advancing further. [3] Both sides posted sentinels to watch over the mines, and some of Demetrius' men tried to bribe the officer whom the Rhodians had put in charge of the guard. His name was Athenagoras, and he was a Milesian by birth, but he had been dispatched to Rhodes by Ptolemy as the captain of the mercenaries.* [4] He promised to turn traitor and named a day when Demetrius should send one of his senior officers to come up into the city through the tunnel under cover of darkness, so that he could see the place where the soldiers would arrive. [5] But after raising Demetrius' hopes so greatly, Athenagoras informed the Rhodian council, and when Demetrius sent one of his Friends, a Macedonian called Alexander, the Rhodians seized him after he had climbed up into the city through the mine. They awarded Athenagoras a golden crown and presented him with five talents of silver, because they wanted to encourage loyalty towards the people in the rest of the mercenaries and foreign troops.

95. Once all his siege engines had been completed and the space leading up to the wall had been entirely cleared, Demetrius stationed the city-taker in the centre and deployed the sheds which were to protect the work of filling in the moat. There were eight of these and he

stationed four on either side of the tower, and joined a gallery on to each of them to make it possible for the men to come and go, and do their work in safety. He also deployed two huge ram-bearing sheds, each of which had a ram† 120 cubits long, reinforced with iron* and capable of delivering a blow similar to that of a ship's ram. It was not difficult to get the ram moving forward, because it was on wheels and energy was imparted to it in battle by a crew of at least a thousand men.

[2] Just prior to moving the contraptions up to the city walls, he placed the appropriate stone-throwers and bolt-shooters side by side on each floor of the city-taker, [3] sent his ships against the harbours and the areas adjacent to the harbours, and distributed his infantry wherever the remaining stretches of wall could be attacked. [4] Then all his men raised the battle-cry at once in response to a single command and signal, and he set about attacking the city from every side. But as he was battering the walls with his rams and stone-throwers, envoys arrived from Cnidus, who asked him to hold off and promised to persuade the Rhodians to accept the most feasible of his demands. [5] The king broke off the attack and the envoys went back and forth, busy about their negotiations, but in the end they were unable to forge an agreement and the siege started up again. Demetrius caused the collapse of the strongest of the city's towers, which was made out of square-cut blocks of stone, and weakened an entire curtain wall, so that the defenders were no longer able to gain access to the battlements at that point.

96. Around this time King Ptolemy sent a large number of supply ships to Rhodes, carrying three hundred thousand *artabas* of grain* and pulses as well. [2] As they were approaching the city, Demetrius sent ships to try to bring them to land at his camp, but a wind sprang up that favoured the Egyptians and they swept along under full sail and docked in the proper harbours, while the ships sent by Demetrius returned empty-handed. [3] Cassander too sent the Rhodians ten thousand *medimnoi* of barley, and Lysimachus gave them forty thousand *medimnoi* of wheat and the same amount of barley. Now that the Rhodians had such large stocks of supplies, their morale rose—the siege had by then ground them down mentally—and they decided that their best course of action was to attack the enemy's siege engines. They made a large number of fire-throwing devices ready, stationed all their stone-throwers and bolt-shooters on the wall, [4] and that night, at about the second watch, they began without warning to

bombard the city-taker with fire-bearing missiles. All their other kinds of missiles were used to shoot down the men who were congregating there.

[5] The unexpectedness of the attack made Demetrius concerned for the safety of the devices he had built, and he ran to the rescue. [6] It was a moonless night, and the fire-bearing missiles glowed as they hurtled through the air, but the missiles fired by the bolt-shooters and stone-throwers were invisible, and a lot of men died because they were unable to see what was coming at them. [7] Some of the plates on the city-taker happened to have fallen off, leaving an area unclad, and the fire-bearing missiles were striking the exposed wood of the structure. Demetrius was worried, therefore, that the fire would spread and that in the end the entire tower would be ruined, so he lost no time in coming to the rescue. He tried to extinguish the spreading fire with water that had been stored on every floor of the tower, and eventually he used the trumpet to round up the men whose job it was to move the contraptions and they pulled them back out of range of the Rhodians' missiles.

97. Then, the next day, he ordered the camp followers to collect the missiles that had been fired by the Rhodians, because he wanted to use them to calculate how much ordnance they had in the city. [2] His orders were soon carried out, and more than eight hundred fire-bearing missiles were found of various sizes and at least 1,500 catapult bolts. That was a great many missiles to have been fired, at night, in a short space of time, and Demetrius was impressed by the resources the Rhodians possessed and by their prodigal use of them.

[3] Next he repaired the damaged devices and saw to the burial of the dead and the treatment of the wounded. [4] Meanwhile, the Rhodians used the respite they had gained from assaults by the siege engines to build a third wall. This one was crescent-shaped and included within its arc every stretch of wall that was at risk. Despite this, they also dug a deep trench to protect the part of the wall that had collapsed, to make it difficult for the king to launch a sudden assault on the city and break his way in. [5] They also sent out the best sailers of their navy, with Amyntas in command, and he sailed over to their Peraia in Asia* and took by surprise some pirates who had been sent there by Demetrius. They had three undecked galleys and the reputation of being the best men in the king's army. A brief battle took place, in which the Rhodians overpowered the pirates and captured the ships along with their crews, including the pirates'

leader, Timocles. [6] They also attacked some merchantmen, seized quite a few galleys which were fully laden with grain, and brought both them and the pirate ships back to Rhodes under cover of darkness, without being spotted by the enemy.

[7] Once Demetrius had repaired his damaged towers, he brought them up to the wall. He drove back the men who were stationed on the battlements with a relentless barrage of missiles from all his artillery pieces, while with his rams he battered the adjacent area and brought down two curtain walls. The Rhodians, however, were determined to save the tower in between these walls, and fierce and continuous conflicts broke out, one after another, with the result that even their general, Ananias, died fighting fervently, and many ordinary soldiers also lost their lives.

98. Meanwhile, King Ptolemy sent the Rhodians at least the same amount of grain and other supplies as he had sent before, along with 1,500 soldiers under the command of a Macedonian called Antigonus. [2] At the same time, envoys came to Demetrius from Athens and other Greek cities. There were more than fifty of them, and with one voice they asked the king to make peace with the Rhodians. [3] A truce was accordingly arranged, and many arguments of various kinds were presented to the Rhodian assembly and Demetrius; but they found it impossible to reach agreement, and the envoys therefore returned without having accomplished their mission.

[4] Demetrius decided to launch a night attack on the city at the point where the wall had been brought down, and he selected the most suitable men from the army, including his best fighters. This task force consisted of about 1,500 men, [5] and their orders were to approach the wall silently at about the second watch of the night. He also deployed men on either side of the city and it was their job to raise the battle-cry at his signal and attack from both land and sea. [6] His orders were duly carried out, and the force that made for the breach in the wall cut down the pickets at the trench, burst into the city, and occupied the area by the theatre. [7] When the Rhodian Prytanes learnt what had happened and saw that the entire city was in turmoil, they ordered the troops who were stationed at the harbour and on the walls to remain at their posts and to keep those on the outside at bay, in the event of an attack, while they took the elite battalion and the soldiers who had recently arrived from Alexandria and set out against those who had forced their way inside the wall.

[8] When daylight returned and Demetrius raised the standard, the men who had been designated to attack the harbour and those who had taken up positions all around the wall shouted out their battle-cry to encourage their comrades who had occupied part of the theatre district, while the massed women and children in Rhodes gave way to fear and tears in the belief that their city was being taken by storm. [9] Nevertheless, a battle took place between the Rhodians and those who had forced their way into the city, with heavy losses on both sides. For a while, neither side broke formation, but Rhodian numbers were constantly increasing and they had no hesitation about facing danger, since they were fighting for their homeland and all that they held most dear. The king's men found themselves hard pressed, and in the end Alcimus and Mantias, the senior officers, died from the many wounds they had received and most of the other soldiers of the task force either died fighting or were captured, though a few fled and made it safely back to the king. Many of the Rhodians lost their lives as well, including Damoteles, one of the Prytanes, a man who had been famous for his valour.

99. It seemed to Demetrius that it was only bad luck that had denied him the capture of the city when it had appeared to be within his grasp, and he got ready to resume the siege. But then his father wrote and told him to make peace with the Rhodians on the best terms he could, and Demetrius began to wait for the perfect opportunity, one that would give him a plausible reason for coming to terms. [2] Since Ptolemy had written to the Rhodians, saying, in the first instance, that he would be sending them a great quantity of grain and three thousand soldiers, but then later advising them to make peace on reasonable terms with Antigonus, if they could, everyone was inclining towards peace. [3] Just then envoys arrived from the Aetolian Confederacy to argue for peace, and the Rhodians made peace with Demetrius on the following terms: the city was to be self-governing and ungarrisoned; it would keep its revenues;* the Rhodians would fight for Antigonus as his allies, except if he went to war with Ptolemy; and they would give as hostages a hundred of their citizens, who would be chosen by Demetrius, with city officials exempt.

100. So this was how the Rhodians brought the war to an end after the siege had gone on a year.* They honoured with the appropriate rewards men who had fought bravely in battle and granted freedom and citizenship to slaves who had proved their courage. [2] They also

erected statues of King Cassander and King Lysimachus—not that they took first prize, in their opinion, but they had still contributed significantly towards keeping the city safe. [3] But in Ptolemy's case they wanted to repay his favour with an even greater one, and they sent sacred ambassadors* to Libya, to ask the oracle of Ammon whether he advised them to honour Ptolemy as a god.* [4] The oracle gave its approval, and they consecrated a square precinct in the city, which they called the Ptolemaeum, and built on each of its sides a stade-long stoa. They also rebuilt the theatre, the collapsed stretches of wall, and the parts of other districts that had been destroyed, all far more beautifully than before.

[5] Now that Demetrius had made peace with the Rhodians as his father had wanted,* he sailed away with his entire army and, after skirting the islands, he put in at Aulis in Boeotia. [6] Cassander and Polyperchon had enjoyed impunity in the recent past and were ravaging most of Greece, so Demetrius planned to free the Greeks. He first liberated Chalcis, which had been garrisoned by the Boeotians, and the Boeotians were so terrified that they felt compelled to abandon their friendship with Cassander.* Then he entered into an alliance with the Aetolians* and set about getting ready for war with Polyperchon and Cassander.

[7] Meanwhile, Eumelus, the king of Bosporus, died in the sixth year of his reign, and his son, Spartacus,* succeeded to the throne and reigned for twenty years.

101. Now that I have elucidated developments in Greece and Asia, I shall move on to other parts of the world. In Sicily, Agathocles launched a surprise attack on the people of Lipara, even though they were not at war with him, and exacted fifty talents of silver from them—from people who had done him no prior harm at all. [2] Now, many people agree that the facts I am about to recount reveal the activity of the gods, in that his lawless behaviour earned the attention of the divine. This is what happened. Although the Liparaeans asked him for more time to come up with the full amount, since there was a shortfall, and said that they had never misused their sacred dedications, Agathocles insisted that they give him the dedications from the town hall, some of which had inscriptions to Aeolus, others to Hephaestus. As soon as he had been given them he sailed away—and eleven of the ships that were carrying the money were wrecked in a gale. [3] And so it occurred to many people that the god who was

said in those parts to be the master of the winds* had punished
Agathocles straight away, as soon as he set sail, and that it was
Hephaestus' turn at the end, when he came up with a punishment for
the tyrant in his homeland that fitted his crime, by burning him alive
on hot coals, as you would expect from a being named Hephaestus.*
After all, it takes the same moral code and sense of justice to refrain
from harming those who were saving their parents at Etna* and to
deliberately hunt down those who commit sacrilege against the divine.

[4] However, as far as Agathocles' death is concerned, when we
come to its proper place in the narrative the facts will confirm the
truth of what I have just said, but I must turn now to events in nearby
Italy. [5] Embassies came and went between the Romans and the
Samnites, and they made peace with each other,* after having been at
war for twenty-two years and six months. One of the consuls, Publius
Sempronius, invaded the territory of the Aecli* and it took him fifty
days in all to capture forty towns. He compelled the entire people to
submit to Rome, and then returned home and celebrated a famous
triumph. The Roman people entered into an alliance with the Marsi,
the Paeligni, and the Marrucini.*

102. *At the beginning of the following year, Leostratus became Archon in
Athens, and Servius Cornelius and Lucius Genucius were the consuls in
Rome. In this year:*

Demetrius undertook to carry on fighting Cassander and liberating
the Greeks, but his first project was to settle Greek affairs. His thinking was not just that allowing the Greeks their independence would
earn him great glory, but also that, before proceeding against Cassander
in person, he should first eliminate Prepelaus and the rest of Cassander's
generals, and only then attack Macedon itself.†

[2] He launched a surprise attack by night on the city of Sicyon,
which was garrisoned by Ptolemaic troops* under the command of
Philip, a very illustrious general, and broke into the city. The garrison
then retreated to the acropolis and Demetrius made himself the master of the lower town and occupied the area between the residential
district and the citadel. He was about to bring up his siege engines
when the terrified soldiers surrendered the acropolis on terms and

sailed off to Egypt. Demetrius rehoused the Sicyonians on the acropolis and demolished the part of the city next to the harbour, on the grounds that it was completely indefensible. He helped the citizens with the building work and restored their freedom, and for the favour he had shown them he was awarded godlike honours by the Sicyonians. [3] They named the city Demetrias and voted to perform sacrifices, celebrate festivals, and hold games in his honour every year, and to grant him all the other honours that are proper for the founder of a city.*

Time with its periodic alteration of conditions has eliminated these honours by now, but, seeing that the site to which they moved was a vast improvement, the Sicyonians have continued to live there right down to our own day. [4] The area enclosed by the acropolis wall is level, spacious, and surrounded on all sides by sheer cliffs which leave no point where siege engines can be brought close. There is plenty of water there, which has enabled them to create luxuriant gardens. In short, it looks as though the king was exercising sound foresight when he came up with his plan, in terms of both peacetime amenities and wartime safety.

103. After putting Sicyonian affairs in order, Demetrius set out at full strength to Corinth, where Cassander's general Prepelaus was in charge of the garrison. He was let inside through a postern gate at night by some of the citizens, and immediately took control of the city and its harbours.* [2] The garrison soldiers withdrew either to the so-named Sisypheium or to the Acrocorinth,* but Demetrius brought siege engines up to the fortifications and took the Sisypheium by storm, although he suffered serious losses in doing so. Then, when the soldiers from there fled to those who had occupied the Acrocorinth, he intimidated them too into surrendering the citadel. [3] This king had such a good technical mind when it came to building siege engines that he was extremely difficult to resist when he was assaulting a place. After the liberation of Corinth he installed a guard on the Acrocorinth,* because the Corinthians wanted the city to be protected by the king until the war against Cassander came to an end.

[4] Following his ignominious ejection from Corinth, Prepelaus retreated to Cassander, while Demetrius went to Achaea. He took Bura by storm and gave the citizens back their independence, and then he captured Scyrus*—it took only a few days—and expelled the garrison. [5] Then he marched against Orchomenus in Arcadia

and ordered Strombichus, the commander of the garrison, to surrender the town to him. Strombichus refused and even heaped foul abuse on Demetrius from the city wall, so the king brought up siege engines, brought down the wall, and took the city by storm. [6] He crucified Strombichus, who had been appointed by Polyperchon to command the garrison, in front of the town along with about eighty others who were hostile to him, and he incorporated into his own forces the approximately two thousand mercenaries whom he captured.

[7] After the fall of Orchomenus, the commanders of the nearby hill-forts, realizing that it would be impossible for them to avoid being overwhelmed by the king, surrendered their strongholds to him. Likewise, since Cassander, Prepelaus, and Polyperchon were not coming to help them, and since Demetrius was approaching with a large army and the best siege engines, the commanders of the garrisons in towns also voluntarily withdrew their forces. That was how things stood with Demetrius.*

104. In Italy, the Tarentines, who were at war with the Lucanians and the Romans, sent envoys to Sparta, asking for reinforcements and for Cleonymus as general.* [2] The Lacedaemonians had no hesitation about sending them the leader they were asking for, and when the Tarentines sent money and ships, Cleonymus recruited five thousand soldiers at Taenarum in Laconia* and before long he had put in at Tarentum. He recruited there at least the same number again of mercenaries, and from the citizen body he enrolled more than twenty thousand foot and two thousand horse. He also won the support of both the majority of the Italian Greeks and the Messapians.* [3] His forces were so strong now that the terrified Lucanians entered into a pact of friendship with the Tarentines, and when the people of Metapontum refused to submit to him he persuaded the Lucanians to invade their territory and seized the opportunity to cow the Metapontines into submission.

Entering the city as a friend, he exacted more than six hundred talents of silver from them and took two hundred unmarried girls from the highest-ranking families as hostages—not so much to secure the city's fidelity as to satisfy his own lust. [4] For, once he had put off Spartan clothing, he lived a life of luxury and treated those who had trusted him as his slaves. Despite the strength of his army and his abundant supplies, he did nothing worthy of Sparta. He contemplated a campaign in Sicily, to put an end to Agathocles' tyranny and give the Siceliots back their independence, but then he postponed this expedition for the time being and sailed to Corcyra, where he gained control of the city, exacted a great deal of money, and installed a garrison, since he intended to make the place his headquarters while waiting for developments in Greece.

105. And indeed, before very much time had passed envoys came to him from both Demetrius Poliorcetes and Cassander to ask for alliances, but he joined neither of them. Instead, when he found out that the Tarentines and some of the others had risen up against him, he left an adequate guard in Corcyra and quickly sailed with the rest of his forces to Italy, to bring the rebels to heel. He came to land in territory that was defended by the barbarians, captured their town,* enslaved the population, and plundered the farmland. [2] He also besieged and took a town called Triopium and gained about three thousand prisoners. But then the barbarians from the countryside banded together and attacked his camp at night. In the battle, they killed more than two hundred of Cleonymus' men and took about a thousand prisoners. [3] Moreover, a storm arose during this battle and destroyed twenty of his ships that were lying at anchor near the camp. After these two serious setbacks, Cleonymus sailed back to Corcyra with his forces.*

106. *At the beginning of the following year, Nicocles became Archon in Athens, and in Rome Marcus Livius and Marcus Aemilius were the next to be appointed to the consulate. In this year:*

Cassander, the king of Macedon, seeing that the Greeks were getting stronger* and that the conquest of Macedon was the sole objective of the war, became very alarmed about what the future might hold for him. [2] He therefore sent envoys to Antigonus in Asia, asking for a peace treaty with him. But Antigonus replied that he recognized only one basis for a settlement and that was if Cassander were to give up his possessions. This frightened Cassander and he asked Lysimachus to come from Thrace so that they could make common cause in the supreme struggle. [3] It was Cassander's invariable practice, when he was faced with the greatest danger, to get help from Lysimachus, not just because of the Thracian king's abilities, but also because his kingdom bordered Macedon.

After the kings had met and discussed what was the most advantageous course of action for both of them, they sent envoys to Ptolemy, the king of Egypt, and to Seleucus, the master of the upper satrapies, stressing the arrogance of Antigonus' reply and explaining that the war posed a threat for all of them together, [4] because if Antigonus gained control of Macedon, it would take him little time to deprive the others of their kingdoms as well. After all, they pointed out, Antigonus had often given them proof of his ambition and had demonstrated that he kept all power for himself and shared it with no one. They argued that it would be in all of their best interests to work together and make war against Antigonus their common project. [5] Ptolemy and Seleucus agreed; they were not slow in giving their consent, and they undertook to come in strength to one another's assistance.

107. Cassander, however, chose not to wait for the enemy to attack, but to march against them first and seize the advantage. He therefore gave Lysimachus part of his army and sent a general along with it, while he went with the rest of his forces to Thessaly, where he intended to fight Demetrius and the Greeks. [2] Lysimachus crossed over from Europe to Asia with his army. Lampsacus and Parium voluntarily gave him their allegiance, so he left them free, but since he had to besiege Sigeum into submission he installed a garrison there.* Then he gave his general, Prepelaus,* six thousand foot and a thousand horse, and sent him off to win over the cities in Aeolis and Ionia, while he set about besieging Abydus and equipping himself with artillery, siege engines, and so on. [3] After a while, however, a large body of soldiers sailed in, sent by Demetrius to help the besieged people of Abydus, and since there were enough of these men to make the city safe, Lysimachus gave up this attempt. Instead he won over Hellespontine Phrygia and besieged the town of Synnada, where a large amount of the king's possessions were kept. [4] At this juncture he persuaded Antigonus' general, Docimus, to come over to his side,* and with his help he took Synnada and some of the fortresses where the king's valuables were stored.

In the course of his march, Prepelaus, the general who had been sent by Lysimachus to Aeolis and Ionia, gained Adramyttium, and then, when he put Ephesus under siege, the terrified inhabitants surrendered the city to him. He repatriated the hundred Rhodian hostages* who were being held there and left the Ephesians free,† but because the enemy had control of the sea—and because the final outcome of the war was uncertain—he burnt all the ships he found in the harbour. [5] Then he won over Teus and Colophon. He was unable to take Erythrae and Clazomenae because help arrived by sea, but he ravaged their farmland before setting off for Sardis. There, once he had persuaded Antigonus' general, Phoenix, to break with the king, he gained the city, but not the citadel, because Philip, one of Antigonus' Friends, was defending it and remained loyal to the man who had entrusted it to him. That was how things stood with Lysimachus.

108. Antigonus had decided to hold a major festival in Antigonea, involving athletic and other contests, and by offering generous prizes and fees he had assembled the most famous athletes and artists from all over the world. But when he heard about Lysimachus' arrival in Asia and the defection of his generals, he cancelled the festival and paid off the athletes and artists, at a cost of at least two hundred talents. [2] Then he gathered his army and set out by forced marches from Syria to confront the enemy. When he reached Tarsus in Cilicia, he gave his men their wages for three months, using money that he had brought down from Cynda. [3] In addition to this money, he was also carrying three thousand talents with the army, to draw on for his expenses.

After Tarsus, he crossed the Taurus and headed for Cappadocia. Then he attacked those who had deserted his cause in upper Phrygia and Lycaonia and brought them back into his alliance. [4] Just at this time, Lysimachus, responding to the news of the enemy's arrival, held a meeting of his council to decide what to do in the face of this threat. [5] They decided not to engage Antigonus in battle until Seleucus had arrived from the upper satrapies,* but to occupy a defensible location, secure their camp with a palisade and trench, and wait for the enemy's approach. These measures were rapidly put into effect.

When Antigonus was near the enemy's position, he drew up his forces and issued a challenge to battle. [6] No one ventured to come out against him, so he occupied certain places through which his opponents' supplies were bound to have to pass. Lysimachus was worried that, if their food supply was cut off, they would be at the mercy of the enemy, so he broke camp at night, marched for four hundred stades, and halted at Dorylaeum, [7] which had plenty of grain and other supplies, and lay on the banks of a river that could afford protection to an army that was encamped there. So he pitched camp and fortified it with a deep trench and a triple palisade.

109. As soon as Antigonus found out about the enemy's with-drawal, he set out after them. He halted near their camp and, since they refused battle, he began to surround their encampment with a trench, and he sent for catapults and artillery, because he intended to assault their position. There were some clashes between light-armed troops at the trench, as Lysimachus tried to drive off the men working on it, but Antigonus always came off best. [2] Time passed and the trench was nearing completion, and then, since the besieged were becoming short of food, Lysimachus waited for a stormy night, broke camp, and retreated over the hills to winter quarters.*

At daybreak, when Antigonus saw that the enemy had left, he had his men shadow them on the plains. [3] The rain poured down, and since the land had deep, clayey soil, many pack animals and a few men were lost, and in general everyone in the army found the going very tough. [4] Wanting to let his men recover from their ordeal, and also because he could see that winter was drawing in, the king gave up the pursuit, chose the best spots for winter quarters, and divided his army up. [5] However, when he found out that Seleucus was on his way from the upper satrapies with a large army, he sent some of his friends to Demetrius in Greece, ordering him to join him with his army at the earliest possible opportunity. He wanted to be absolutely certain that he was not forced to decide the outcome of the war on the battlefield, with all the kings united against him, before his European forces had arrived.

[6] Lysimachus did much the same: he too divided his army up for wintering, in the plain called Salonia. He was plentifully supplied from Heraclea, because he had made a marriage alliance with the city [7] by taking as his wife Amastris, who was the daughter of Oxyartes, niece of King Darius, and former wife of Craterus (in a marriage arranged by Alexander), and was now the ruler of the city.* That was how things stood in Asia.

110. In Greece, Demetrius, who was in Athens, wanted to be initi-ated into the Mysteries and to experience the rite at Eleusis. There was still some time to go before the official day on which the Athenians normally celebrated the rites, but he persuaded the Assembly to repay him for his benefactions by altering the way things were traditionally done. So he presented himself in civilian clothes to the priests and was initiated before the appointed day.*

He then left Athens, [2] and his first stop was Chalcis in Euboea, where he had his fleet and land army congregate. But then he found out that Cassander had already occupied the pass;* realizing that it would not be possible for him to reach Thessaly by land, he transported his army by sea and put in at the harbour of Larisa.* No sooner had he disembarked his troops than the town surrendered, and, once he had taken the acropolis, he bound the garrison troops in fetters and placed them under guard. Then he gave the people of Larisa back their independence. [3] Next he won over Antrones and Pteleum, and thereby made it impossible for Cassander, who was in the process of moving the peoples of Dium and Orchomenus to Thebes,* to complete the relocation.

When Cassander saw how well everything was going for Demetrius, he increased the strength of the garrisons guarding Pherae and Thebes, and, once he had united all his forces, he made camp in close proximity to Demetrius. [4] He had in all about 29,000 foot and 2,000 horse, while Demetrius' army consisted of 1,500 horse, at least 8,000 Macedonian infantrymen, about 15,000 mercenaries, 25,000 soldiers from the Greek cities, and at least 8,000 light-armed troops, including all the various kinds of pillagers who gather for wars and opportunities for plunder. In other words, the total number of his foot soldiers was about 56,000.

[5] The two armies confronted each other for many days. Both sides drew up their forces, but neither of them chose to provoke battle, since they were both waiting for the outcome of the decisive battle in Asia. [6] But when the people of Pherae appealed to him, Demetrius forced his way into the city with a division of his army and besieged the citadel into submission. He let Cassander's soldiers leave under a truce and gave the Pheraeans back their liberty.

111. That was the situation in Thessaly when the men sent by Antigonus reached Demetrius. They made his father's wishes quite clear and told him to take his army over to Asia as soon as possible. [2] Realizing that he had no choice but to obey his father, the king made peace with Cassander on the understanding that their pact would be valid only if it was acceptable to his father. In actual fact, he knew perfectly well that Antigonus would not approve the agreement, since he had firmly decided to bring the present war to an end by force of arms, but Demetrius wanted to give his withdrawal from Greece a respectable veneer and to make it look less like flight. By the same token, one of the conditions included in the agreement was that the Greek cities, whether in Greece or in Asia, were to be free.

[3] Demetrius next equipped himself with transport vessels to convey his men and matériel, and put to sea with his entire fleet. He sailed past the islands and put in at Ephesus, where he disembarked his forces and made camp near the city walls. He forced the city to revert to its former alignment* and let the soldiers of the garrison (which had been installed by Prepelaus, Lysimachus' general) leave under a truce. Once he had established his own guard in the citadel, he went to the Hellespont and recovered Lampsacus, Parium, and a few other towns that had gone over to the other side. Then he went to the entrance to the Black Sea, where he built a camp by the Sanctuary of the Chalcedonians* and left three thousand foot and thirty warships to guard the place. Then he divided the rest of his forces up and sent them to this town or that for the winter.

[4] Another event of this year was that Mithridates, who owed allegiance to Antigonus but was widely believed to be abandoning him in favour of Cassander, was killed at Cius in Mysia,* after having ruled Cius and [...]* for thirty five years. His heir, Mithridates, acquired many new subjects, and ruled over Cappadocia and Paphlagonia for thirty-six years.*

112. Around this time, after the departure of Demetrius, Cassander regained the cities of Thessaly and sent Pleistarchus to Asia with an army of twelve thousand foot and five hundred horse to help Lysimachus. [2] But when Pleistarchus reached the entrance to the Black Sea and found that the region was already in enemy hands, he gave up the idea of crossing over to Asia there, and instead went to Odessus, which lies between Apollonia and Callatis, facing Heraclea on the Asian coastline, where some of Lysimachus' forces were. [3] Since he did not have enough transports to take all his men across at once, he divided them into three. The first division to be dispatched crossed safely to Heraclea, but the second was captured by the ships that were guarding the entrance to the Black Sea. Pleistarchus himself was crossing with the third division when a storm arose of such ferocity that most of the ships and men were lost. [4] In fact, the hexareme which had the general on board sank and there were only thirty-three survivors out of the five hundred men, at least, who were sailing in her. But one of the survivors was Pleistarchus, who had grabbed hold of a piece of wreckage and was cast ashore half dead. He was taken to Heraclea, and after he had recovered from the disaster he went to join Lysimachus in winter quarters, having lost most of his forces.

113. Another thing that happened around this time was that King Ptolemy set out from Egypt with a substantial army and gained the submission of all the cities of Coele Syria.* But, while he was besieging Sidon, some men came to him with a false report. They said that the kings had fought a battle, that Lysimachus and Seleucus had been beaten and had retreated to Heraclea, and that the victorious Antigonus was now on his way to Syria with an army. [2] Ptolemy was taken in by them and, believing the report to be true, he made a truce of four months with the Sidonians, secured with garrisons the cities that had fallen to him, and withdrew back to Egypt with his army.

[3] Meanwhile, some of Lysimachus' soldiers—two thousand Autariatae and about eight hundred Lycians and Pamphylians— deserted from their winter quarters and went over to Antigonus.† Antigonus made them welcome, paid them the wages they said they were owed by Lysimachus, and honoured them with gifts. [4] Just then Seleucus arrived as well; from the upper satrapies he had crossed the mountains into Cappadocia with a large army, where he had wintered, with his men in huts that he had had them make. He had about twenty thousand foot, about twelve thousand horse (including mounted archers), 480 elephants, and more than a hundred scythed chariots.

[5] So the kings' forces were assembling, since they were all determined to decide the war on the battlefield in the coming summer. But, in keeping with the plan announced at the beginning of this book, I shall make the war that these kings fought against one another for supremacy the starting point of the next book.*

EXPLANATORY NOTES

ABBREVIATIONS

FGrH F. Jacoby, *Die Fragmente der griechischen Historiker* (Leiden: Weidmann/Brill, 1923–).

Harding P. Harding, *From the End of the Peloponnesian War to the Battle of Ipsus*. Translated Documents of Greece and Rome 2 (Cambridge: Cambridge University Press, 1985).

Rhodes/Osborne P. Rhodes and R. Osborne, *Greek Historical Inscriptions 404–323 BC* (Oxford: Oxford University Press, 2007).

BOOK 16

1.2 *this principle*: what Diodorus seems to mean (as the following sentence makes clearer, and compare 5.1.4) is that, in Philip's case, he will not only cover his career from start to finish, but be able to do so within a single book, because it all happened so fast. The whole idea, which seems trivial, makes more sense if one remembers that a 'book' was a papyrus roll, and therefore it was convenient to have all the information about one king within a single roll. The roll could then be clearly marked 'Diodorus of Sicily on Philip of Macedon', for easy identification on the shelf. It is one of Diodorus' regular claims for his history that it is designed to be useful and convenient for the reader, and this is one aspect of it. But, in fact, it was only for Books 16 and 17 that Diodorus was able to adopt this biographical approach, and in Book 18 he reverts to his more usual kind of preface, in which he states how many years the book will cover, and what its main theme will be. He also often includes in his prefaces an idea of the contents of the book, and of the previous book, which was an important aid to readers in the age of papyrus rolls. One had only to pull a roll off the shelf and read the first paragraph to find whether one needed that roll or another one.

1.3 *this one book*: the earliest historians, such as Herodotus and Thucydides, did not divide their work into books; the division was imposed on their work by later editors. It was Ephorus of Cyme in the fourth century who introduced the fashion of choosing his own book divisions and writing a preface for each book, as Diodorus does.

1.4 *willingly submitted to him*: actually, he finally gained the hegemony of the Greeks by defeating them at the battle of Chaeronea, as Diodorus well knew (16.84–7). He is being deliberately provocative at the start of a book, to draw readers in.

1.5 *Scythians*: in what follows, Diodorus omits Philip's Scythian campaign of 339.

1.5 *further reinforcements*: not true: Alexander was sent fresh forces from Macedon from time to time (as Diodorus knew: e.g. 17.49.1, 17.65.1, 17.95.4), took over the Greek mercenaries of those he defeated (e.g. 17.76.2), gained allies along his way east, and trained up native troops (17.108.1).

1.6 *achieve all this*: the relative powers of Fortune or human ability were a long-standing debating topic, but given Diodorus' stress on Fortune throughout *The Library* (Introduction, pp. xxv–xxvi), his denial here that Fortune was a factor in Philip's life is remarkable. In Book 17, for example, Alexander is constantly subject to Fortune.

1.6 *brilliant strategist and outstandingly brave*: Philip may well have had both these qualities, but this is one of Diodorus' formulae for military leaders, applied, for example, to Antiphilus at 18.13.6, a general who was certainly not of Philip's stature. There is another assessment of Philip, in similar terms, at 32.4.1–3.

2.1 *360/59*: since the Athenian year started in late June or early July, at the first new moon after the summer solstice, an Athenian year, when referred to as a whole, has to be written like this—that is, from July 360 to July 359, in our terms.

2.1 *stade race*: this was a sprint, over a distance of almost 200 metres at Olympia. The practice of naming the Olympiad after the winner of this race was long established.

2.1 *Aemilius*: full names of Roman consuls mentioned by Diodorus, and corrections to his versions of their names, can be found in Appendix 2 (pp. 543–9).

2.3 *Epaminondas' foster-brother*: this is wrong: Epaminondas was considerably older than Philip, and Plutarch tells us that Pammenes, not Epaminondas' father, was responsible for Philip in Thebes (*Pelopidas* 26). Philip's sojourn in Thebes probably started about ten or twelve years later, and was not instigated by the Illyrians: Diodorus gets it right at 15.67.4. The name of Epaminondas' tutor was Lysis (10.11.2), who came from Tarentum, southern Italy being the principal homeland of Pythagoreanism at the time. At 15.39.2–3, Diodorus again attributes Epaminondas' calibre to his Pythagorean background. Hostages were, of course, guarantees of good behaviour.

2.3 *no less than that of Epaminondas*: comparison of great leaders was a common trope, taken to great lengths by Plutarch with his series of parallel biographies.

2.4 *Philip...took over the kingdom*: the heir to the throne, Perdiccas' son Amyntas, was still an infant. Philip, his uncle, might have been expected to become regent, but given the current crisis and the need for a strong hand at the helm, the Macedonians tolerated his bid for kingship. Amyntas remained alive, but never became king; when Alexander the Great came to the throne, he murdered the young man, his cousin, as a potential rival.

2.6 *a campaign against Macedon*: it is not clear why the Illyrian king, Bardylis, did not press home his advantage. He waited a year, and was then

defeated by Philip (16.4). One of Philip's wives was Illyrian, so possibly
Philip negotiated a truce, leaving upper Macedon in Illyrian hands, and
took this wife at this time to gain him the respite he needed.

2.6 *to see to his restoration*: we know too little about Pausanias and Argaeus to
assess the validity of their claims to the throne.

3.2 *heroes at Troy*: Homer, *Iliad* 13.131–4.

3.2 *his creation*: these sentences give a poor idea of the extent and importance
of Philip's military reforms, on which see e.g. King, *Ancient Macedonia*,
107–14. But Diodorus is right that Philip formed the Macedonian phalanx
or heavy infantry; previously, Macedonian infantry had been few and
light. It is not clear that Philip would have had time to turn to military
reform *before* dealing with all the various threats facing Macedon. He
initiated them, perhaps, and did so quickly enough to be able to defeat
his enemies, but it took quite a few years for them to be complete.

3.3 *the recovery of Amphipolis*: Amphipolis in Thrace commanded the local
trade routes for timber and precious metals. Colonized by the Athenians
in 437, it became independent in 424 and was never recovered, despite
frequent attempts.

3.4 *to see to his restoration*: this probably means that he bribed the Thracian
king to murder Pausanias. The king was probably Berisades, who held
western Thrace while his two brothers had divided the rest on the death
earlier this year of their father Cotys.

3.5 *Mantias…with the mercenaries*: Mantias must have set off from Athens
before Philip became reconciled with the Athenians by withdrawing his
troops from Amphipolis. Aegae was the earliest capital of Macedon, pre-
dating Pella, and was still the centre for many religious and ceremonial
activities.

3.6 *surrendered the exiles to him*: i.e. Argaeus and his friends, who were
undoubtedly put to death.

3.7 *Crenides*: Crenides was a refoundation rather than an original settlement. Its previous name was Datus.

3.8 *of which five are lost*: all are lost now, but we have over two hundred
fragments.

4.1 *no longer claiming Amphipolis for himself*: this was a trick, and Diodorus
records Philip's seizure of Amphipolis under the following year.

4.2 *made them subjects of Macedon*: it is to Agis' credit that for the first time
he united the Paeonians sufficiently to be a threat, but after his death the
temporary unity fell apart and the Paeonians became vulnerable to
Philip. His victory was easy, and good training for his new army.
However, the next time we meet the Paeonians, only a few years later
(16.22.3), they are again hostile to Macedon. They were more fully subjected, perhaps, by Alexander (17.8.1), and thereafter, although Paeonia
retained its own kings, we find them as allies of Macedon—and a useful

buffer zone between Macedon and the Danube tribes. Paeonia is roughly equivalent to the country currently known as the Republic of North Macedonia (the former FYROM).

4.7 *buried his dead*: battlefield dead were generally cremated, and the bones and ashes were buried.

4.7 *this battle*: it would be hard to overestimate the importance of this battle, which freed the Macedonians after decades of domination by the Illyrians, and enabled the further expansion of Macedon under Philip.

5.1 *his father*: Dionysius I (reigned 405–367).

5.2 *peace treaty*: the Carthaginians occupied the west of Sicily, as the Greeks did the east, so that they were constantly at each other's throats.

5.4 *secured by adamantine bonds*: it was a famous saying: as well as 16.70.2 below, see Plutarch, *Dion* 7 and 10, and Aelian, *Historical Miscellany* 6.12.

6.1 *Dion…fled from Sicily*: actually, Dion had left, with Dionysius' connivance, some years earlier, and had spent some time in Greece, especially Athens, before going to Corinth.

6.3 *brother of this second wife*: he was also married to Dionysius' daughter.

6.3 *an advanced philosopher*: and, famously, a student of Plato: ps.-Plato, *Seventh Letter*, 326e–327b.

6.5 *sailed into Corinth*: Corinth was the mother city of Syracuse, founded by Corinthian settlers in 733 BCE.

7.1 *the historian Timaeus*: for Timaeus, see p. 541.

7.1 *'stay on Taurus'*: Diodorus has the etymology of Tauromenium coming from the name of the hill plus the root *-men-*, to do with 'staying'. See also 14.59. Tauromenium had certainly existed prior to this episode, so perhaps Andromachus was resettling the site. Naxos was the earliest Greek settlement on Sicily; it never fully recovered from its destruction by Dionysius I in 403.

7.1 *Caesar*: that is, Caesar Augustus, the first emperor. The sentence is an important clue to Diodorus' dates: see Introduction, p. x.

7.3 *their alliance*: the Second Athenian League (so called to distinguish it from the Delian League of the fifth century) lasted from 379 until 338, and at its peak had about sixty members. Athens lost this Social War ('war of the allies'), but retained a few members of its alliance. Other former members sought stronger partners, such as Mausolus of Caria. At 16.22.2 Diodorus says that the war lasted for four years, whereas he rightly says 'three' here.

8.1 *a major battle*: see 16.4.

8.1 *his subjects*: that is, Philip incorporated into Macedon the tribal states of Upper Macedon and Orestis.

8.2 *Next*: Diodorus omits Philip's securing of his southern border with Thessaly, despite saying correctly in 16.14.2 that Philip 'returned' to

Thessaly in that year. See Buckler, *Philip II and the Sacred War*, 59–62. Diodorus also omits Philip's marriage to Olympias, which helped keep the Epirotes on good terms.

8.2   *in considerable force*: the Amphipolitans had asked the Athenians for help, but the Athenians believed Philip's promise that he had no designs on Amphipolis (16.4.3) and ignored their pleas.

8.2   *banished his enemies*: an inscription exists listing some of the Amphipolitan exiles: Harding, no. 63.

8.3   *wanted for their own*: the terms of the alliance survive on a mutilated inscription: Harding, no. 67. Diodorus omits the fact that the Athenians declared war on Philip over his seizure of Amphipolis and Pydna, but they waged the war in a desultory fashion, arriving too late to save Potidaea, for instance. The reason for their apathy was probably the looming Social War, which demanded their attention: see 16.21–2.

8.5   *importance and standing*: Diodorus, or his strongly pro-Philip source, is being a bit naive. This was part of Philip's basic approach to Athens, which was to keep them guessing whether he was a friend or enemy.

8.6   *Crenides*: he relieved Crenides from an attack by Cetriporis of Thrace, who had succeeded his father Berisades. Crenides had only been refounded a couple of years previously (16.3.7), and was probably more a collection of mining settlements than a town. His takeover of Crenides in due course allowed the further expansion of Macedon to the east.

8.6   *Philippi after himself*: he was able to increase its population because he drained the local marshes for farmland. Philippi was heavily fortified, to protect this vital resource.

8.7   '*Philips*': gold coinage was an innovation in the Greek world. Philip probably did not begin to mint gold coins until the 340s.

9.2   *grain*: but it appears from 16.13.3 that Dionysius was short of grain.

9.2   *unassailable citadels*: Syracuse had two citadels, one on Ortygia (which Diodorus just calls the Island), and the other in Epipolae, a plateau west of the city. Both acropolises had been heavily fortified by Dionysius I.

9.4   *an account of the particular events*: for the Dion narrative that follows, compare Plutarch's *Dion*, written early in the second century CE.

9.4   *Cocalus, the king of the Sicanians*: Daedalus, the legendary craftsman, and his son Icarus, were imprisoned by Minos on Crete, but famously escaped by flying to Sicily on wings secured with wax, leading to Icarus' death when he flew too close to the sun and melted the wax.

9.5   *Sicanians and Sicels from the interior*: the Sicels and Sicanians were the two main non-Greek peoples on the island, with the Sicels to the east of the Halycus river and the Sicanians to the west. The Halycus flows down from the central highlands of Sicily, south and then south-west, to join the sea at Heraclea Minoa.

10.2 *recently founded*: see 16.5.3.

10.4 *Achradina*: a western suburb of Syracuse that extended into the plateau of Epipolae.

10.5 *banished to the Peloponnese*: a thousand Syracusans had been banished along with Dion.

11.3 *Caulonia in Italy*: Caulonia is on the Ionian Sea, in south-east Italy, but at 16.10.2 Dionysius was on the Adriatic.

11.3 *Philistus*: also a historian, but only fragments of his work survive.

11.3 *later than Dion*: Dion had not taken Ortygia, the Island, which was strongly fortified, virtually impregnable, and remained in the hands of Dionysius' troops, affording him a base when he arrived even though Dion had the mainland city.

13.1 *citadels*: the plural is puzzling, since by now Dion certainly held the Epipolae acropolis. Perhaps Diodorus was thinking of the garrison Dionysius had at Rhegium, just across the water on the toe of Italy.

14.1 *bribing of the mercenaries*: Diodorus means no more than that they offered to pay them well, to win their personal loyalty.

14.2 *their noble lineage*: they were the aristocratic family that ruled Larisa.

14.3 *Among the historians*: Diodorus scatters similar references to historians (and occasionally other writers) throughout his work, creating a kind of historiographical timeline alongside the historical narrative. These writers' histories come and go, and Diodorus means to give us the impression that his work encompassed all of their work and more besides. His interest was not just in the writers themselves, but also in the key events at which they chose to start or finish their histories. The start of the Third Sacred War was one of the stepping-stones of history, as far as Diodorus was concerned—a fixed point to which other events could be related.

14.3 *his father had failed to cover*: i.e. Ephorus' Book 30 (his final book: see 16.76.5), on the Sacred War, was actually written or completed by Demophilus. On Ephorus, see pp. 539–40.

14.3 *eleven years of warfare*: Diodorus gives the length of the war as ten years at 16.59.1, but here he is counting not to the end of the war, but to the elimination of the wrongdoers, which happened after the end of the war (16.61–4). More puzzling is why he mentions Demophilus' account of the Sacred War under this year, when he thought that it started two years later, as he says clearly at 16.23.1. It may be that the Phocians seized Delphi in this year—that is the event with which Demophilus' book started—but that the Amphictyonic Council did not declare war until later.

14.4 *history of Greece in ten books*: on Callisthenes, see p. 538.

14.5 *Diyllus of Athens*: on Diyllus, see 16.76.6 and p. 539.

15.1 *Porus of Malis*: this is probably the same Porus who won the race at the previous Olympics (16.2.1). He was perhaps born in Cyrene and moved to Malis.

15.2 *runaway slaves*: there is no way of knowing whether Diodorus' deriv-
ation of 'Bruttii', perhaps from Oscan, is correct, but the Bruttii had
existed under that name before this occasion. The location of Terina is
uncertain.

17.4 *circumstances left him no choice*: the circumstances were that the Syracusans
had grown suspicious of his motives and tired of his harsh measures.

18.1 *Locri*: currently part of the Syracusan empire, along with much of
southern Italy, and Dionysius' preferred place of residence.

18.3 *the Arethusa spring*: the famous spring on the island of Ortygia, the site
of the original foundation of Syracuse.

20.2 *Hexapylon*: a northern entrance to the suburbs of Syracuse.

20.6 *his worship as a hero*: according to Plutarch (*Dion* 46), he was worshipped
as a god, not just as a hero, and in fact that is more plausible, since
no one could be a hero until after his death, but a man could be an
embodied god.

21.1 *Chares … with sixty ships*: 16.7.3.

21.4 *an enormous sum of money*: probably only Timotheus was fined, with
Iphicrates acquitted.

22.1 *his entire army*: Athenian finances were so unstable in the early and middle fourth century that generals often had to find creative ways to raise
money.

22.3 *the Thracian king, the Paeonian king, and the Illyrian king*: respectively,
Cetriporis, Lyppeius (a.k.a. Lycceius), and Grabus. They had an alliance with the Athenians, who were too busy with the Social War to help.
It should be noted that, whenever Diodorus (and other Greek historians)
speak of 'the Illyrians' or 'the Paeonians', as though they were unified
peoples, it is possible that only some, or the majority, of the tribes making
up the Illyrians (etc.) were involved.

23.1 *nine years*: eleven years in 16.14.3 (but see the note on that passage), nine
here, and ten, correctly, at 16.59.1. The nine-year count here may be due
to his counting from the actual declaration of war by the Amphictyonic
Council, rather than the occupation of Delphi by the Phocians.

23.1 *This is how it happened*: much of what follows is repeated in 16.29, under
the following year.

23.2 *the Leuctran War against the Boeotians*: the war is more usually known
today as the Boeotian War (378–371). It ended with the decisive defeat
of Sparta by the Thebans at Leuctra in Boeotia.

23.2 *the Cadmea*: this incident (repeated with a bit more detail at 16.29.2) took
place in 382; the Cadmea, the Theban acropolis, remained illegally or at
least unjustifiably occupied by Spartan troops for over three years. It is not
clear why the Thebans waited so long to bring charges against Sparta.

23.3 *Cirrhaean sacred land*: land that had once belonged to Crisa, but which
was declared sacred after the First Sacred War early in the sixth century.

The land in question was what tourists nowadays describe as the 'sea of olives' below Delphi.

23.3 *failed to pay what they owed*: that is, the first tranche. They were eventually forced to pay, as we shall see—and a fragmentary inscription survives, recording the first five payments: Rhodes/Osborne, no. 67.

23.3 *the delegates*: there were two from each state represented on the Council.

23.3 *stealing from the god*: their land, once consecrated to the god, would become unavailable for any other use than grazing the herds and flocks from which those consulting the oracle had to buy animals, to perform the required sacrifices. 'The god' is Apollo, the main god of Delphi.

23.4 *the Greeks*: that is, the delegates of the Amphictyonic Council.

23.5 *lines that read*: Homer, *Iliad* 2.517 and 519; the omitted line just gives the parentage of the named leaders. This was not the first time the Phocians had laid claim to Delphi; the Athenians had supported them in a failed attempt in 449.

23.5 *Pytho*: the ancient name of Delphi. Cyparissus was a nearby town.

24.1 *General Plenipotentiary*: for what little we know of the Phocian constitution, see the relevant chapter in H. Beck and P. Funke (eds), *Federalism in Greek Antiquity* (Cambridge: Cambridge University Press, 2015).

24.1 *the Lacedaemonian king*: until the third quarter of the third century, Sparta had two concurrent kings from different houses. Archidamus III was the Eurypontid king, and Cleomenes II was his Agiad colleague.

24.4 *the letters*: inscriptions were written with no separation between words, so where we would say they obliterated 'words', the Greeks said 'letters'. Philomelus annulled in this way not only the decree against the Phocians, but also that against the Spartans, now his allies.

25.1 *sent troops into the field*: we hear no more of these soldiers.

25.1 *one and a half times the usual rate*: he may have had to pay them well to compensate them for taking part in the sacrilegious occupation of Delphi. This was by far the largest recruitment of mercenaries in Greek history, and from now on the hiring of mercenaries in large numbers became standard procedure.

25.2 *permission to collect them*: this was normal procedure; the Locrian response was unusual, but they wanted to make a point.

26.1 *goats for consultations of the oracle*: a goat was sprinkled with cold water; if it shivered, consultation of the oracle was allowed to go ahead.

26.2 *'inaccessible'*: the *adyton*, or inaccessible area, was the innermost part of a temple. It was not open to the general public, and often housed the cult image of the deity. In the temple of Apollo at Delphi, it was where the Pythia (the prophesying priestess) did her business.

26.4 *those who sought answers*: this story of the Pythia inhaling toxic fumes is still told to tourists today, but it is false. There is no fissure, and even if there were, the building of the temple would have covered it up. In any case, the temple authorities would not have relied on such an unreliable source, and any vapours would have dispersed in the open air. All over the Mediterranean, prophesying priestesses simply went into a self-induced trance and spoke what came to them. But the story recurs in Plutarch (*On the Decline of Oracles* 42 = *Moralia* 433c–d), Pausanias (*Description of Greece* 10.5.3), and in Pompeius Trogus (Justin, *Epitome of the Philippic History of Pompeius Trogus* 24.6); and the fissure or chasm is mentioned by several other writers.

26.6 *Artemis*: the virgin goddess par excellence.

27.1 *the oracle that suited him*: there is a very similar story about Alexander the Great and the Delphic oracle at Plutarch, *Alexander* 14.4 (alluded to by Diodorus at 17.93.4).

27.3 *Athens, Sparta, and Thebes*: these were the three great Greek powers at the time on the mainland.

28.3 *the Phaedriades*: the great south-facing cliffs just to the east of Delphi, called 'gleaming' because they used to reflect the sun more than usual. It is commonly believed that this is the same battle that has already been mentioned in 16.24.4, under the previous year, but there may have been another Locrian attack.

29.1 *confederacies and cities*: the two most common forms of political organization in Greece at the time. See Waterfield, *Creators, Conquerors, and Citizens*, 37–41.

29.1 *joined the Phocians*: this was basically northern and central Greece versus southern Greece.

29.2 *the Leuctran War*: see the first note to 16.23.2.

30.1 *the oracular shrine*: see also 16.14.3 for the claim that Philomelus plundered the sanctuary; perhaps more plausibly, however, Diodorus denies it at 16.28.2 and 16.56.5. It was his successors who did so.

30.1 *high wages*: see 16.25.1, of which this is a doublet.

31.1 *the town*: it is not clear where this action took place, or what its relation is with the preceding paragraph. The town may be Tithorea.

31.6 *Pagae*: there is no such place known in northern Greece and the name may be corrupt. Editors tend to correct to 'Pagasae', the port of Pherae, but this is unlikely. Philip did take Pagasae, but in 352: see the second note to 16.35.5.

31.6 *Spartacus*: more usually spelled 'Spartocus'. These are the kings of the Cimmerian Bosporus.

31.7 *Falisci*: an Italic people, occupying part of Etruria. For the war, see Livy, *History of Rome* 7.16.

31.7 *Callippus*: an Athenian, and a former student of Plato's Academy in Athens, who had accompanied Dion on his return from Greece in 357/6.

32.1 *Eudemus*: this should be Thoudemus.

32.1 *returned home*: a curious decision, since the Thebans (commanded by Pammenes) could have taken advantage of their defeat of the Phocians to liberate Delphi.

33.1 *great growth and glory*: just as Philomelus also misunderstood the gods at 16.27.

33.3 *the Thessalians to remain neutral*: Thessalian neutrality was a result not so much of Phocian bribery as their own internal troubles: 16.35.

33.3 *Thronium*: a strategic town. The Phocians were on their way to creating a Greater Phocis in central Greece.

34.1 *Artabazus*: the Persian satrap of Hellespontine Phrygia.

34.1 *after Chares had left*: see 16.22.2.

34.3 *returned to Sparta*: the episode is repeated in 16.39.4, under the following year. Orneae was a dependency of Argos.

34.3 *slavery*: the importance of Sestus (located on the north shore of the Hellespont, directly north of Abydus) was not just that it commanded the shipping route from the Black Sea, but also, and more immediately, that the Athenian fleet there trapped Pammenes and his men in the Propontis.

34.4 *Cardia*: which was not Cersobleptes' to give away.

34.4 *cleruchs*: a cleruchy was an overseas settlement on land confiscated by the Athenians, where the emigrant cleruchs ('allotment owners') lost neither the privileges nor the obligations of Athenian citizenship. Cleruchies often served as garrisons for restive or economically important states in the Athenian alliance.

34.4 *to the cities*: unmentioned by Diodorus is the important fact that Olynthus and the Chalcidian Confederacy, previously on good terms with Philip (16.8.3–4), asked for an alliance with Athens. It was refused—but the Olynthians' treachery explains Philip's hostility towards the town (16.52–3).

34.4 *under siege*: the siege of Methone was also mentioned under the previous year, at 16.31.6; see Introduction, p. xxxvi. Methone was the last of the several former Athenian possessions in this area of the northern Aegean; the unspecified 'enemies' were presumably Athenian troops. The Athenians sent a relieving force, but it arrived too late. Once Philip had Methone, he had the entire Macedonian coastline, which had formerly been largely in Greek hands.

34.5 *a single item of clothing each*: citizens are specified because resident foreigners would simply be expelled and slaves would be taken and resold.

35.1 *Pherae*: Pherae was in Thesssaly too: 'the Thessalians' means a coalition of other Thessalian states, chiefly Larisa, Crannon, and Pharsalus.

35.2 *defeated them twice*: these were the worst, and almost the only, defeats of Philip's career. There is an account of the first battle in Polyaenus, *Stratagems in War* 2.38.2. Philip's life and his position on the throne were briefly under threat. It is not impossible that these defeats prompted a change of policy. Philip now realized that he had to go on winning in order to secure the loyalty of the Macedonians, and so turned his thoughts to further conquest—even of Asia Minor.

35.5 *Thessalian cavalry*: the affair is known as the battle of the Crocus Field.

35.5 *happened to be sailing by*: Chares had been sent by the Athenians to protect the port of Pagasae, but it fell to Philip before he arrived.

35.6 *as temple-robbers*: these gruesome actions were supposed to impress the Greeks with Philip's pious defence of Delphi, and so earn him goodwill. Temple-robbers were to be denied proper burial (so that their souls would never settle in Hades) and so drowning was a suitable punishment. This was the largest mass drowning in Greek history, and the battle was one of the bloodiest in Greek history.

36.1 *double the usual rate of pay*: following the massacre and mass drowning, it must have been difficult to recruit further mercenaries, hence the double pay.

36.2 *sister and wife*: sibling marriage was very unusual indeed, and shocking to the Greeks. Carians were culturally but not ethnically Greek. The tradition started by Mausolus continued among Carian dynasts. It was supposed to (a) guarantee the purity of the dynastic bloodline; (b) reduce the number of cousins (by turning some of them into brothers and sisters) who might be rivals for the throne at the death of a ruler; (c) advertise the superiority of the royal family to conventional morality.

36.3 *fifteen years*: other sources say that Clearchus' brother Satyrus took over.

36.4 *the river Tiber*: the river on which Rome was situated. This war between Rome and a coalition of three important Etruscan towns lasted from 357 to 349. Diodorus' account is far from complete, and should be supplemented by the (also patchy) account in Livy, *History of Rome* 7.

36.5 *sailed into Syracuse*: if Polyaenus is right, however (*Stratagems in War* 5.4), Hipparinus was based in Leontini, and would therefore have travelled overland to Syracuse, not by boat.

36.5 *Callippus...from the city*: he seems to have withdrawn to Catane and made himself tyrant there.

37.3 *Nausicles*: these Phocian allies were probably united by suspicion or hatred of Thebes. Phocis was their preferred power in central Greece.

38.1 *the reorganization of Thessaly*: which included his appointment as lifelong Archon of Thessaly, the first time a non-Thessalian had been so privileged. The annexation of Thessaly gave him men and resources equal to those of Macedon. He had already more than doubled his kingdom by incorporating upper Macedon and parts of Thrace; now he doubled it again. He also increased the population of Macedon (and therefore the manpower available for military service) by settling thousands of Thracians, Scythians, and Illyrians, usually former prisoners of war, within the borders of Macedon.

38.2 *the pass*: Thermopylae was the best way into Greece from the north for a land army, and was therefore the site of many battles and confrontations. In those days, it was a very narrow pass. The Athenians helped the Phocians not so much out of sympathy with their cause, as out of fear about what Philip's intentions were for Greece south of Thermopylae. They were proud of this gesture of defiance; Demosthenes, for instance, mentions it several times in his political speeches (e.g. 4.17, 18.32). The Athenian troops were those commanded by Nausicles: 16.37.3.

38.2 *returned to Macedon*: Diodorus omits Philip's campaigning this year in Thrace and elsewhere.

38.3 *Epicnemidian Locris, as it is called*: that is, the western part of Locris (named after the dominant tribe), while the eastern part, centred on the city of Opous, was called Opountian Locris. Locrians also lived on the north coast of the Corinthian Gulf, between Aetolia and Phocis; they were called Ozolian Locrians, after the dominant tribe there.

38.4 *Abae*: the Phocian town of Abae, north of Lake Copais, was famous as the location of an oracle of Apollo.

38.6 *a wasting disease*: perhaps tuberculosis, or some form of cancer.

38.6 *ignited the Sacred War*: at 16.23.1 it is Philomelus who ignited the war.

39.1 *racked by disturbances and upheavals*: there were four main centres of power in the Peloponnese at this time: the old cities Sparta and Argos, and the new cities Messene and Megalopolis. Despite its weakness (witness the fact that it needed allies for this campaign), Sparta continued to try to re-establish its former hegemony.

39.1 *King Archidamus*: the Spartans' reason for this campaign was to try to restore territory lost to the Megalopolitans when Megalopolis had been founded in 371.

39.1 *their allies*: in Athens, this was the occasion of Demosthenes' Speech 16, *For the Megalopolitans*.

39.3 *the sources of the Alpheius river*: in the highlands of Arcadia, roughly halfway between Megalopolis and Tegea. At 110 kilometres, the Alpheius is the longest river in the Peloponnese, flowing through Arcadia and Elis, where it passes by the sacred site of Olympia.

39.5 *Helissus*: also known as Helisson, a small town west of Mantinea.

39.6 *Some time later*: in the following year, in fact. The campaign took place in Arcadia.

39.6 *Telphousa*: the place is more usually called Thelpousa.

40.1 *Thessalus*: this name should be Theëllus.

40.3 *Cyprus*: Egypt had been in revolt since 404. Diodorus has made a mistake: this expedition belongs to 346/5, and led to the recovery of Egypt two or three years later. Artaxerxes may have campaigned in Egypt in 351/0 and the following years, but he did not recover it at this time.

40.6 *to transport supplies*: these figures are, of course, exaggerations. The resources of the Persian empire were so great that the Greeks were prone to such exaggerations.

41.1 *and Tyrians*: Arados, Sidon, and Tyre being major Phoenician cities in their own right. Tripolis was formed, perhaps in the fifth century, by resettling people from all three cities. In what immediately follows, Diodorus slides from talking about the Sidonian quarter of Tripolis to talking about Sidon itself.

41.1 *issues of major concern*: the 'Phoenician council' perhaps consisted of local satraps and governors. A 'Phoenician assembly' is mentioned at 16.45.1, making it sound as though the council had the function of preparing the agenda for a larger assembly.

41.3 *preparing for war*: numismatic evidence—an interruption of the regular issue of Sidonian coins by Mazaeus—suggests that this insurrection should be dated a few years later, to 347–346.

42.4 *nine important cities*: Salamis, Citium, Paphos, Curium, Amathus, Marium, Soli, Lapithus, and Ceryneia.

42.6 *recently acceded to the position*: he was the successor of Artemisia: see 16.36.2 and 16.45.7.

42.7 *Phocion of Athens*: Athenian generals hired themselves out as mercenary commanders, just as Spartan kings did in this period (e.g. 16.63.1).

43.2 *Thessalion*: slave names often indicated the country of their origin.

43.3 *hand-token*: by Persian custom, model hands took the place of handshakes for parties wanting to make pledges without being in each other's presence.

45.3 *to him and the king*: the implication that this was his first approach to the mercenaries must be wrong. We were told earlier that Tennes had already suborned Mentor and others inside the city, and Tennes would not have risked making promises to the Persian king if he was not yet certain of entry.

45.4 *before the king reached them*: this must have been a major blow for the king, since he had been planning to use the fleet to reconquer Egypt.

45.5 *the entire city*: this must be an exaggeration (it is a common one in the Greek historians), since the city was flourishing again a dozen or so years later.

45.8 *Praeneste*: this was the end of the hostilities between the Latin town of Praeneste (modern Palestrina) and the Romans. From now on, Praeneste remained loyal to Rome.

45.8 *the Samnites*: this is the first time the Samnites appear in history. They were a league of Oscan-speaking peoples, claiming kinship and occupying the south-central Apennines. The treaty made with Rome in this year was probably an agreement to share the task of repelling common enemies such as the Celts, but it also served to delay the outbreak of warfare between them and the Romans; both peoples were aggressively expanding their territories, so that a clash was inevitable. The Samnite wars began in 343, and their eventual defeat in those wars was a crucial stage in the Roman takeover of Italy.

45.8 *Tarquinii*: an important Etruscan town. Livy (*History of Rome* 7.19.2–3) gives the number of slaughtered Etruscans as 358, and provides context: earlier, roughly the same number of Roman prisoners of war had been slaughtered by the Etruscans.

45.9 *Syracusan power-possessors*: they may have been Syracusan power-possessors (though actually Callippus was Athenian), but Diodorus is misleading in implying that they possessed Syracuse itself. At 16.36.5 Callippus was expelled from Syracuse and Hipparinus took over. Callippus made himself tyrant of Catane, and Leptines held Apollonia.

46.1 *Protagoras*: this should be Pnytagoras.

46.2 *in Asia*: numismatic evidence suggests that he became the king of Sidon for a few years.

46.3 *as it was felt he deserved*: a euphemism for death, presumably.

46.5 *in my first book*: Diodorus' first book was devoted to Egyptian antiquities; here he refers to 1.30. As described there, the Pits ('Perdition' would be another possible translation) sound like quicksands.

47.2 *the Magi*: at *Histories* 3.76–9, Herodotus told how seven noble Persians overthrew the regime of the Magi, an action which soon led to the seizure of the throne by Darius the Great in 522. Rhosaces (or Rhoesaces) therefore belonged to one of the great families of the Persian empire.

47.6 *Warriors, as these Egyptians are called there*: Herodotus, *Histories* 2.164–6, described them as a caste of Egyptian society, but they were more like the citizens of semi-independent enclaves within Egypt, sometimes of Libyan origin, who owed military service to the Egyptian crown (as payback for the fact that they were granted land by the pharaoh), but were also free to sell their services to others. They often formed the backbone of the Egyptian armed forces, but much about them is obscure.

48.7 *Memphis*: the main city of Egypt, before Alexandria was built. Even then, it remained the centre for Egyptian religion and ceremony.

49.4 *Bagoas*: in the next chapter, we find that Bagoas was busy at Bubastis. It was probably Rhosaces who was engaged at Pelusium. For Bagoas' career, see E. Badian, 'The Eunuch Bagoas', in id., *Collected Papers on Alexander the Great* (London: Routledge, 2012), 20–35.

50.8 *master of the kingdom*: in 343 he became chiliarch, second only to the king.

50.8 *in the appropriate years*: there is more about Bagoas in 17.5.3–6, but this promise is not really fulfilled.

51.2 *all Egypt*: all of northern Egypt, anyway; his hold over southern Egypt was not yet secure. Nectanebo's 'flight' to Ethiopia (i.e. Nubia) was probably a tactical retreat, and he was hoping to return via southern Egypt and retake the north.

51.3 *Pherendates as satrap of Egypt*: it is possible that Diodorus has made a mistake, since a Pherendates was the satrap of Egypt in the early fifth century. At 17.34.5 the name of the Egyptian satrap is given as Tasiaces.

52.2 *the prize for valour*: an occasional post-battle or post-campaign award—but the recipients tended to be officers or cavalrymen rather than rank-and-file soldiers.

52.2 *valuable artefacts*: stolen from Egypt.

52.3 *Memnon*: Memnon was Mentor's brother, and their sister was Artabazus' wife.

52.4 *the number of Artabazus' children*: especially unusual at a time of high infant mortality.

52.5 *first campaign this year*: see the note to 16.40.3: the expedition against Hermias took place probably in the late 340s.

52.6 *had him arrested*: and subsequently killed. In the epigram the philosopher Aristotle wrote for Hermias' gravestone (Aristotle was Hermias' son-in-law), he stressed the treachery.

52.8 *the Persians*: we hear nothing more about Mentor, and it is likely that he died quite soon after this episode. He passed both his wife Barsine (his niece, the daughter of Artabazus) and his command on to his brother, Memnon (17.23.6).

52.9 *Zereia*: the location of Zereia is unknown, and since the text is corrupt at this point, the name may not even be correct.

52.9 *Peitholaus, the dynast of the city*: at 16.37.3 and 16.38.1, Peitholaus has already been expelled from Pherae. Perhaps he returned in the meantime, or perhaps this is another of Diodorus' doublets (but his doublets are usually only a year apart, not several years).

52.10 *the king of Pontus*: careless: they were kings of the Cimmerian Bosporus, as Diodorus knew perfectly well; see 16.31.6, 20.22.1, and 20.100.7. Pontus had not yet become an independent kingdom, though it would be Spartocus' descendants who would rule it. Spartocus (the more correct spelling of the name) actually died in 342, after sharing the throne with Parysades (whose name is spelled 'Pairisades' in Rhodes/Osborne, no. 64).

53.2 *in that part of the world*: Chalcidice, which is nowhere near the Hellespont, but Philip presumably did not want to leave the powerful Olynthians in his rear. Moreover, they were harbouring two pretenders to the Macedonian throne, and had drawn close to Athens. That was Philip's excuse: they were not behaving like allies, despite their treaty with him. Mecyberna was the port of Olynthus. Unmentioned by Diodorus, Philip also campaigned in Thrace, impinging on Athenian interests in the Thracian Chersonese. He then turned back against Olynthus, and after Olynthus he had some troubles on his northern and western borders to settle.

53.2 *to take the city*: compare the account in Demosthenes 19.194–8 and
      305–10 (*On the Dishonest Embassy*). Lasthenes and Euthycrates became
      infamous examples of traitors: Demosthenes 8.40 (*On the Situation in
      the Chersonese*), 19.265 (*On the Dishonest Embassy*). The Athenians sent
      a force to relieve Olynthus, but it was ineffective, and Philip captured
      a number of Athenians in Olynthus and took them as hostages to Pella.
      Part of the reason for the Athenians' ineffectiveness was that they were
      involved in trying, not very successfully, to stop the island of Euboea
      falling into the hands of a tyrant who was a friend of Philip's.

54.2 *a crop of traitors, so to speak*: the metaphor is Demosthenes': 18.61 (*On
      the Crown*).

54.4 *guest-friends and familiars*: another echo of Demosthenes' famous speech
      On the Crown: 18.46–52, 109, 284. 'Guest-friends' is the traditional, some-
      what awkward translation of the Greek *xenoi*. Guest-friendship was a for-
      mal kind of friendship between members of the elite from different states,
      entered into and maintained by oaths and the ritual exchange of gifts.

54.4 *pernicious form of diplomacy*: under the influence of Demosthenes in this
      passage, Diodorus is portraying Philip as a villain, not as the hero of
      much of the rest of the book. But the basic point is correct: Philip assidu-
      ously cultivated friendships in the Greek cities as a way of weakening
      their opposition to him.

55.1 *Olympia*: a festival of Zeus held at Dium in Macedon, under Mount
      Olympus.

55.2 *during the symposium*: after eating, the guests settled down to a sympo-
      sium, in which hard drinking was accompanied by elegant conversation
      and contests of wit.

55.3 *the actor Satyrus*: this story was first told by Demosthenes, at 19.192–5
      (*On the Dishonest Embassy*).

56.1 *Hya*: more commonly called Hyampolis, the town lay to the north of
      Lake Copais, close to the border with Boeotia.

56.2 *towns in Boeotia*: Orchomenus, Coronea, and Corsiae, as we learn from
      16.58.1.

56.2 *on their way back home*: these two Boeotian invasions of Phocis belong to
      different years, the first to the campaigning season of 349 and the second
      to that of 348, with the Phocian capture of the three towns in between.
      See also Demosthenes 19.148 (*On the Dishonest Embassy*).

56.3 *relieved of his post*: the faction that had always been opposed to the seizure
      of Delphi had gained the upper hand in Phocis.

56.3 *three generals*: it is not impossible that three generals was the Phocian
      norm, and that single Generals Plenipotentiary, such as Phalaecus, were
      elected only at times of crisis.

56.5 *the brother of Philomelus*: Diodorus has not mentioned this relationship
      before; he repeats it in 16.61.2, but it is almost certainly wrong.

56.6 *a lion and a woman*: possibly Cybele (the Great Mother) with her sacred lion.

56.6 *thirty talents*: on Croesus' dedications, see Herodotus, *Histories* 1.50–1.

56.6 *its equivalent in silver*: the gold–silver ratio was about 15:1 at the time, before Alexander the Great released huge amounts of gold, stolen from the Achaemenid treasuries. There were 60 mnas in a talent.

56.7 *the Persian treasuries*: actually, Alexander took at least 180,000 talents of bullion and coined money, and then other valuables such as statues and textiles.

56.7 *which read*: Homer, *Iliad* 9.40–5. Pytho was an old name for Delphi.

57.3 *to wish you well*: this was the standard way to start a letter, much as we write 'Dear so-and-so'.

57.4 *their ancestral deity and their forebear*: the entire Ionian sub-ethnicity of the Greeks, of which the Athenians sometimes claimed to be the leader, looked to Apollo as their forebear and presiding deity.

57.4 *their universally admired constitution*: the Spartans believed that their constitution had been invented at a stroke by an eighth-century lawgiver called Lycurgus, who was either galvanized to do so by the Delphic oracle, or even had the whole thing dictated to him by the oracle: Herodotus, *Histories* 1.65–6.

58.3 *to curb their post-Leuctra pride*: see the first note to 16.23.2.

59.1 *gave King Archidamus the command*: the Phocians also approached the Athenians, who sent a sizeable force. The object was to block Thermopylae, as they had earlier (16.38.1–2), but the Phocians' surrender allowed Philip through the pass and made the enterprise futile. Diodorus has seriously downplayed Athens' role in these years, and has even omitted the peace treaty between Athens and Philip—the Peace of Philocrates, made in 346 and prompted by the Phocian surrender, which left the Athenians little choice but to make peace. Nor did the Peace of Philocrates settle Athenian relations with Philip; intense diplomacy, omitted by Diodorus, continued after it, Philocrates was sent into exile in 343, and relations between the two states ultimately broke down altogether.

60.2 *at the time of the robbery*: an inscription exists (Harding, no. 88), detailing the payment of a second tranche of thirty talents in 343 or 342. By then, the Phocian towns had been rebuilt and repopulated, so that they could afford to manage their debt better.

60.2 *the Pythian games*: since these international games were held at Delphi once every four years, the festival had not been celebrated for the duration of the Phocian occupation of Delphi.

60.2 *religious crimes*: this is obscure, because the Corinthians had nothing to do with the organization of the Pythian games, nor is it clear how they were implicated in the Phocians' crimes. Perhaps some text has dropped out, saying that the Corinthians (and others similarly implicated) were excluded from the games, and explaining why.

60.3 *sell their horses*: weaponry was expensive, but the Phocians' weapons had been used for sacrilegious purposes and therefore had to be utterly destroyed.

61.4 *four hēmioliae*: a *hēmiolia*, 'one-and-a-half', was a kind of light galley, a ship with one complete and another incomplete bank of oars.

62.3 *first assault*: Lyctus was a neighbour of Cnossus and a frequent rival.

62.4 *from whom they were descended*: Tarentum was founded in the late eighth century BCE by Spartan settlers.

62.4 *to prioritize their case*: the Lyctians too claimed kinship with the Lacedaemonians.

63.2 *reigned for fifteen years*: Agis ruled for seven or eight years: 338–331. Diodorus is closer to the truth at 16.88.4 and 17.63.4, where he assigns him a nine-year rule. His mistake is thinking that Archidamus died soon after arriving in Italy, when he actually died there six years later, in 338.

63.4 *Elean exiles*: there were two main factions in Elis, those in favour of cooperation with Sparta, and those in favour of cooperation with Macedon. The pro-Spartans had the upper hand and had expelled the pro-Macedonians.

64.1 *their freedom*: Sparta was defeated by Antipater in 331, Athens in 322.

64.2 *a fit of madness*: Helen is Helen of Troy. Eriphyle's legendary necklace was cursed, and caused a lot of trouble in its multi-generational history before being purified by dedication in Delphi.

65.1 *various tyrannies*: this sentence is a very condensed summary of years of chaos in Syracuse, and severe disruption elsewhere, until the east of the island was depopulated and impoverished.

65.1 *envoys to Corinth*: see the note to 16.6.5.

65.2 *Timaenetus*: or possibly Timodemus. The Timoleon narrative that follows sporadically down to 16.90 should be compared with Plutarch's *Timoleon*. Corinth had never before interfered in the domestic politics of Syracuse, originally founded by Corinthians, and it is unclear why the weakened city would do so now.

65.3 *acting like a tyrant*: a bodyguard was a traditional sign of a tyrant.

65.5 *commending the man as a tyrant-slayer*: Athens, for a while, had a law making it no crime to kill a tyrant or would-be tyrant; perhaps Corinth did too.

65.7 *A verdict had not yet been reached*: actually, Timoleon's murder of his brother, or connivance at his murder, occurred many years earlier, and Timoleon had been in retirement since then.

66.1 *Marcus Fabius and Servius Sulpicius*: these consuls belong three years later. See p. 545 with the footnote.

66.3 *all the way to Italy*: comparison with Plutarch's account (*Timoleon* 8) suggests that this phenomenon was actually the Lyrid meteor shower of late March 344.

66.4 *their sacred island*: Sicily had a lot of good agricultural land, so worship of the cereal goddesses was central there.

67.1 *Hicetas, the ruler of Syracuse*: actually, as the next chapter makes clear, Hicetas was not yet the master of Syracuse, but took control with Carthaginian help. See also Plutarch, *Timoleon* 7.3–7, 9.2–7. Hicetas was currently the master of Leontini.

67.2 *pairs of horses for the chariots*: it was standard practice to take spare teams of trained horses, because they were very vulnerable on the battlefield. There is no mention of cavalry in this list: something like the 'two thousand horse' I have supplied has dropped out of the text.

67.4 *on the basis of their kinship*: these Campanians, originally mercenaries of Dionysius I, had been settled in these Sicilian cities as a reward for their service. Entella was a town in west-central Sicily, south-east of Egesta. The location of Galeria (or, more properly, Galaria, as we know from coin finds) is unknown.

68.1 *Dionysius was master of Syracuse*: Diodorus failed to mention Dionysius II's return in 346. He had been biding his time in Locri, the southern Italian town which his father had especially favoured. On his departure, the Locrians, who had hated his rule, tortured the members of his family to death.

68.1 *the Olympieium*: a sanctuary of Zeus not far from the shore of the Great Harbour of Syracuse.

68.5 *twenty triremes*: the Carthaginians were supporting Hicetas' takeover of Syracuse, and trying to prevent Timoleon's arrival there. They argued that since Hicetas already had all Syracuse except Ortygia, held by Dionysius, there was no need for Timoleon.

68.9 *Adranum*: a small town near Centuripae, in the foothills of Mount Etna.

69.1 *treaty of friendship*: actually, it was the second treaty: Polybius, *Histories* 3.22–7. Friendship was conditional on neither side's trespassing on the other's zones of interest, which were stipulated in the treaty.

69.2 *his sister–wife Ada*: see the note to 16.36.2.

69.3 *encamped on the shore*: thus exposing Hicetas as nothing more than a Carthaginian-backed tyrant.

69.4 *Marcus*: this may be a mistake for the name Mamercus (Plutarch, *Timoleon* 13.1), or it may be that Mamercus' first name was Marcus. The alliance did not last long, once Mamercus realized that Timoleon's intention was to stamp out tyrannies such as his. Mamercus had replaced Callippus as tyrant of Catane.

69.4 *dispatched them to Syracuse*: this was probably a response to the arrival of Dionysius in Corinth (mentioned by Diodorus at the beginning of the next chapter), which acted as proof of Timoleon's success.

69.5 *for no good reason*: Plutarch supplies some reasons: Timoleon had induced Hicetas' mercenaries to desert (*Timoleon* 20). Probably Mago, the Carthaginian commander, and Hicetas had fallen out as well.

69.7 *invaded Illyris in force*: it is not certain which Illyrians he went against—either the Ardiaei or the Dardanians.

69.8 *expelled the tyrants from their cities*: Larisa had recently fallen under a tyrant, and so, it seems, had other cities.

69.8 *the Thessalians' gratitude and loyalty*: Philip also undertook further reorganization of Thessaly at this point. After this, Thessaly was more or less a satellite of Macedon.

70.2 *adamantine bonds*: see 16.5.4.

70.2 *in reduced circumstances in Corinth*: the expression 'Dionysius in Corinth' became proverbial for an uncrowned king.

70.5 *democratic laws*: actually, and even though Plutarch agrees with Diodorus on this, Timoleon probably replaced his tyranny with an oligarchy. See Talbert, *Timoleon*, 130–43.

70.6 *the Romans granted citizenship to the Siceliots*: see Introduction, p. xv, n. 13.

71.2 *curbed their aggressiveness*: these garrison towns were created not just to police the local inhabitants, but also to develop local farmland. The most important of them was Philippopolis, modern Plovdiv in Bulgaria. This was a long campaign, lasting up to 340, and while Philip was away Antipater acted as his viceroy in Macedon.

71.3 *the expulsion of Dionysius the Younger*: if the figure of fifty years is correct, Theopompus did not start at the start of Dionysius I's tyranny, because that would make sixty-one years until the expulsion of Dionysius II: 405/4–344/3. On Theopompus, see p. 541.

72.1 *Arymbas... reign of ten years*: Arymbas ('Arybbas' is the better spelling) did not die, but was banished; and he had reigned for more than ten years, since he came to the throne in 357. The Molossians were one of the major tribes of Epirus; Philip was in the process of reducing them to vassal status.

72.5 *just as he had with Engyum*: Timoleon gave the Sicilian cities back self-governance, but usually under an oligarchy, not a democracy. He left some tyrants in place as well. His overall intention was to create a league of allies, with Syracuse at the helm; he may even have given Syracusan citizenship to at least some of his allies: 16.82.4. Apollonia lay a little inland from the north coast, halfway between Himera and Messana. Engyum lay north of Centuripae.

73.2 *Entella*: Entella must have fallen to the Carthaginians as a result of the action mentioned in 16.67.3–4.

73.3 *Iberian, Celtic, and Ligurian mercenaries*: central Mediterranean states commonly recruited mercenaries from these three peoples in the Hellenistic and Roman periods.

74.1 *Cleitarchus...put in place by Philip*: Philip installed several tyrants in Euboean towns in these years, not just Cleitarchus. Before long, the Athenians threw them out and installed Callias of Chalcis instead as the head of the Euboean Confederacy.

74.2 *Perinthus...favoured the Athenians*: Demosthenes had visited the area and brought Perinthus, an ally of Philip, over to the Athenian side, giving Philip the pretext he needed for attack. His attack on Athenian friends in the Thracian Chersonese was the logical continuation of the eastward offensive of 16.71, but it would inevitably cause open warfare between himself and the Athenians, who had vital interests in the region. Philip probably had already decided to invade Asia Minor, so he needed a peacable Chersonese. In order to delay the Athenian response, Philip wrote them a letter, which exists as item 12 in the Demosthenic corpus.

76.2 *the appearance of a theatre*: ancient Greek theatres were steeply banked.

76.3 *Philip divided his forces into two*: this seems a strange move, since if Philip could not take Perinthus with the complete army, how could he hope to take Byzantium with only half of it? He was perhaps trying to provoke the Athenians into rash action. It was at the siege of Byzantium that torsion artillery, newly developed by Philip's engineers, was used for the first time.

76.5 *the return of the Heraclidae*: in legend, the descendants of Heracles were expelled from the Peloponnese, only to return at the head of a Dorian army and establish themselves there.

77.2 *the peace that they had concluded with him*: the Peace of Philocrates, made in 346, but omitted by Diodorus. In actual fact, Philip had probably already declared war on Athens.

77.3 *made peace with the Athenians and the other Greeks*: no peace was made. Philip's actions in the Sea of Marmara led to war not peace, when the Athenians repudiated the Peace of Philocrates. Still, it is not clear how Philip extricated himself from the Sea of Marmara, so perhaps a temporary truce was made. After his failures on the Chersonese, Philip campaigned with more success against the Scythians.

77.5 *just a few men*: on Timoleon's troop numbers, see Talbert, *Timoleon*, 55–69.

77.5 *added Hicetas' men to his own*: it seems odd that Hicetas would have chosen to help Timoleon, given their enmity. He probably realized that, divided, the two of them would never be able to repel the Carthaginian invasion. After the defeat of the Carthaginians, according to Plutarch, Hicetas then sided with them again against Timoleon; hence, at 16.82.4, Timoleon finally does away with Hicetas.

78.3 *hot-head called Thrasius*: 'hot-head' (*thrasys*) puns on Thrasius' name.

78.4 *I described a short while earlier*: especially 16.61–4.

79.2 *Gelon's victory*: at the battle of Himera in 480, Gelon, the tyrant of Syracuse, had inflicted a memorable defeat on the Carthaginians.

79.4 *wove the celery into crowns*: wild celery is thin and stringy, and can be bent without breaking.

79.5 *the river*: the Crimisus, a river in the far north-west of the island.

82.3 *the Lycus river*: this should probably be the Halycus river (the modern Platani), but Plutarch has 'Lycus' as well. Perhaps it was an alternative name for the river.

82.6 *drawn up by Diocles*: Diocles' democratic revision of the Syracusan constitution had taken place towards the end of the fifth century: see 13.33–5 and Aristotle, *Politics* 1304a27–8. But see the note to 16.70.5.

83.2 *'the Hall of Sixty Couches'*: presumably a venue for grand public dining.

83.2 *made out of different kinds of stones*: like mosaics.

83.3 *Agyrium*: picked out by Diodorus for mention because it was his home town. It lay west of Centuripae.

84.2 *committed himself to war with Athens*: all this seems rather abrupt, because Diodorus has omitted the build-up. The Amphictyonic Council responsible for Delphi (but now more or less Philip's puppet) declared a sacred war against the Locrians of Amphissa and invited Philip to take charge of the war—invited him, that is, to enter central Greece with an army. But when Philip moved south, he ignored the Locrians and seized Elatea instead, in Phocis and on the road to Athens.

84.2 *peace... between them and Philip*: this is the peace of 16.77.3—but see the note on that passage.

84.3 *the entire population converged on the theatre*: the Theatre of Dionysus on the south-eastern slopes of the Acropolis was regularly used for meetings in Diodorus' day, but in fact this meeting was held as usual on the Pnyx hill, which was capable of holding about six thousand people.

84.3 *proclamation by the Archons*: this may conceivably have been the practice in Athens in Diodorus' day, but at the time he is writing about the Athenian Assembly was convened by the praesidium of the Council, or by the generals, not by the Archons.

84.4 *not a single speaker came forward*: all this is heavily dependent on a famous passage of Demosthenes: 18.169–79 (*On the Crown*).

84.5 *kept looking towards Demosthenes*: because for some years he had been the most outspoken advocate of war with Philip.

84.5 *join them in the struggle for freedom*: the Thebans and Athenians had long been on bad terms, and the Thebans were terrified of Philip, so gaining an alliance with the Thebans was both a bold move for Athens, and a major coup for Demosthenes.

84.5 *in two days' time*: actually, though Philip may have been only two days' march away, he waited several months before advancing. In the meantime, he tried to recruit allies and sent Parmenion to deal with Amphissa.

85.1 *the allegiance of the Thebans*: the cost was high, however: Athens was to recognize Theban mastery of the Boeotian towns and pay most of the expenses of the war.

85.2 *Chaeronea in Boeotia*: actually, Chaeronea was the second position taken up by the allied forces, after Philip threatened to come at their previous position from the rear.

85.4 *but I stood firm*: this is from Demosthenes 18.136 (*On the Crown*), referring to a visit by Python to Athens in 343, not to the Boeotian debate.

86.2 *taking command of the other themselves*: Diodorus glosses over the fact that neither Philip nor the Athenian–Theban alliance was able to secure many more Greek allies.

86.3 *Alexander... a breach in the enemy lines*: he was up against the renowned Theban Sacred Band, 300 strong, which was annihilated. The famous statue known as the Lion of Chaeronea was erected as their communal grave marker.

86.4 *even to Alexander*: rivalry between Philip and Alexander is a constant theme of the Alexander historians.

87.1 *unmixed wine*: the Greeks generally drank their wine heavily diluted with water, and considered it barbaric to drink it neat. The story derives from the Greek tradition that painted Philip as a heavy drinker. A more creditable story has him bursting into tears on the battlefield at the sight of the dead of the Theban Sacred Band. This is a striking example of a common Greek historiographical practice—a snapshot of the victor after his victory.

87.2 *Thersites*: Agamemnon was the leader of the Greeks at the Trojan War, Thersites from a lower rank. This is a typical Greek wandering story, which was attributed also to the Cynic Diogenes of Sinope.

87.2 *part and parcel of a revel*: such as masks for the participants and outsized model phalluses. The *kōmos*, or revel, was a ritualized, if riotous, affair, requiring such paraphernalia.

88.1 *twelve years as manager of the exchequer*: actually, Lycurgus' twelve-year stint did not end until 327/6.

88.3 *the battle*: this battle, Archidamus' death, and Agis' ascension have already been mentioned at 16.63.1.

89.1 *the most notable Greek cities*: Sparta would usually have made up a third with Athens and Thebes, but it was still in a post-Leuctra slump—with its kings, as we have just seen, taking service abroad in order to make money. Following the battle, Philip imposed settlements and garrisons on the Greek cities that had opposed him. Athens was treated leniently, Thebes harshly.

89.2 *crimes against Greek sanctuaries*: during the Persian invasion of 480–479, many Greek temples had been burnt and ransacked. Despite the fact that this occurred almost 150 years earlier, revenge against the Persians was still a live issue—or was kept alive by ambitious politicians and kings. Philip's other aim in invading Asia Minor was to liberate Greek cities from Persian control. It is not clear that he wanted to damage Persian interests further—as, of course, his son would—but he does seem to have been motivated by the desire to make himself the greatest leader in the known world.

89.3   *General Plenipotentiary of Greece*: they first formed the League of Corinth, a common alliance among almost all the Greek states, and then the league formally elected Philip General Plenipotentiary (or whatever his official title was, perhaps 'Leader'). Some of the oath the Greeks were required to swear has survived: Rhodes/Osborne, no. 76. From now on until 1832 CE, the Greeks were subject to imperial masters. For Philip's other arrangements for Greece, see Ellis, *Philip II*, 201–4.

90.2   *Ariobarzanes ... Mithridates*: kings of the Anatolian city of Cius, Ariobarzanes II and his younger brother Mithridates II.

90.2   *confiscated a portion of the enemy's land*: such confiscations were typical of the Roman imperialist process in Italy. The land was given to colonists or was made the property of Rome. These two sentences are all that Diodorus gives us about the Latin War of 340–338, in which the Romans were allied with the Samnites.

91.1   *Pythodorus*: this should be Pythodelus.

91.2   *free the Greek cities*: they achieved only limited success. The Greeks of Asia Minor seized the opportunity to throw out their Persian-installed garrisons, but they saw the Macedonians as just the next in a succession of masters.

91.4   *Olympias' full brother*: there had been trouble in the Macedonian court. Olympias and Alexander felt themselves sidelined by Philip's new closeness to his generals and recent marriage to the niece of one of them, Attalus (Philip's first non-foreign bride), and had taken themselves off to Epirus while things cooled down. The marriage between Cleopatra and Alexander of Epirus was meant to soothe the Epirote king, who had been offended by Philip's treatment of his elder sister. The breach between Philip and his son was less easily mended.

92.1   *golden crowns*: the gift of golden crowns (of varying weights and values) was at the time a common way to honour someone.

92.3   *the following lines*: from a lost tragedy by an unknown author. The text is somewhat uncertain.

92.3   *Hades, source of much grief*: Hades was the god of the underworld, and hence Death personified.

92.4   *oracle ... at Delphi*: 16.91.2.

92.5   *the twelve gods*: the usual list is: Zeus, Poseidon, Hades, Hera, Hestia, Apollo, Artemis, Athena, Hephaestus, Demeter, Ares, and Aphrodite, but Dionysus sometimes took the place of Hestia.

93.1 *himation*: a *himation* was the standard item of Greek outer clothing. It was simply an oblong of cloth, about 2.5 metres by 1.8 metres in size, that was draped around the body and pinned in place.

93.8 *denounced Attalus to the king*: the veracity of this ugly story is confirmed by the contemporary evidence of Aristotle, *Politics* 1311b.

93.9 *nephew*: in fact, he was Cleopatra's uncle.

94.1 *also be mentioned*: this is another floating story, attributed by Plutarch (*Alexander* 55) to an interchange between Callisthenes and Hermolaus.

94.4 *Attalus*: this is a different Attalus, not the general who was already in Asia Minor with Parmenion (16.91.2) and was hostile towards Alexander. This Attalus was a friend of Alexander, and played a notable part in the months immediately following his death.

94.4 *stabbed him to death*: thus leaving it for ever unclear whether Pausanias acted alone, or was the front man of a wider conspiracy—possibly even instigated by Olympias and Alexander (see Justin, *Epitome of the Philippic History of Pompeius Trogus* 9.7).

95.5 *in a single book*: see 16.1 for Diodorus' 'original plan' and the importance to him of encompassing a single king's exploits within a single book. Book 17 is incomplete, however (pp. 148–9), and if complete it would have been very long for a single book. Even as it stands, it seems not to have made a single 'book' (roll of papyrus). At the end of 17.63 there is a note in the text: 'The end of the first part of Book 17.' So it looks as though, at some point in its life, Book 17 (like the long Book 1 as well) was divided between two papyrus rolls after all, and Diodorus' design was thwarted.

BOOK 17

1.2 *as well as contemporary events elsewhere in the known parts of the world*: actually, this book entirely omits events in Sicily and Italy in order to focus on Alexander.

1.2 *ends joined to their beginnings*: see also Diodorus' remarks at the beginning of Book 16. Both these two prefaces follow the same pattern of methodological reflections followed by a eulogy of the central character of the book.

1.4 *much of Europe*: much of the Balkans, anyway.

1.5 *Aeacidae*: the kings of Epirus, who in their turn claimed descent from Achilles.

1.5 *the years that belong in the book*: Diodorus' Alexander narrative contains many gaps—of course, since he was planning to fit it all into a single book. Other historians should be consulted to supplement him: Arrian (Lucius Flavius Arrianus), *The Expedition of Alexander* (2nd century CE); Quintus Curtius Rufus, *History of Alexander* (first century CE); Plutarch, *Alexander* (late first / early second century CE); and Justin, *Epitome of the*

Philippic History of Pompeius Trogus (a second-century-CE epitome of a first-century-BCE work). Diodorus' account is closer to those of Curtius and Justin than those of Arrian and Plutarch.

2.1 *Manius*: full names of Roman consuls mentioned by Diodorus, and corrections to his versions of their names, can be found in Appendix 2 (pp. 543–9).

2.1 *as they deserved*: that is, he seized the opportunity to do away with potential rivals; Pausanias was the only known murderer.

2.3 *brother of . . . Cleopatra*: see the note to 16.93.9.

2.3 *a child*: the sources are divided over whether this was a girl or (more threatening to the throne) a boy.

3.4 *the Cadmea*: the acropolis of Thebes; the garrison had been installed after the battle of Chaeronea.

3.4 *Arcadians . . . never acknowledged Philip's leadership*: not true. If this was true of any Peloponnesian state, it was Sparta.

3.5 *the Argives . . . had set their sights on independence*: the inclusion of the Argives in this list is interesting because Argos was usually pro-Macedonian. Presumably an anti-Macedonian faction was temporarily in power.

3.6 *though barely an adult*: he was 20 years old.

4.1 *the Thessalians*: urged on by the Athenians, the Thessalians had blocked the pass at Tempe, which would normally have been Alexander's route south. But he cut a steep path down the side of Mount Ossa and entered Thessaly without using the pass at Tempe.

4.1 *from his father*: like his father, he was made lifelong Archon of Thessaly.

4.7 *Cithaeron*: a mountain range on the border of Attica and Boeotia.

4.8 *a crook*: this is taken from Aeschines 3.173 (*Against Ctesiphon*), but with the words in a slightly different order.

4.9 *crimes against the Greeks*: see the note to 16.89.2.

5.1 *from Demosthenes*: 'Demosthenes wrote letters to the generals in Asia, trying to arrange an attack from there on Alexander' (Plutarch, *Demosthenes* 23.2).

5.2 *as ordered by the king*: Attalus' wife and children were also killed in Macedon.

5.3 *Ochus . . . Arses*: Ochus was Artaxerxes III (reigned 358–338); Arses was Artaxerxes IV (338–336).

5.4 *in the third year of his reign*: Diodorus gets this right (Artaxerxes IV did die in the course of his third regnal year), but a Babylonian document (*BM* 71537) implies that he died of natural causes.

5.5 *helped him gain the kingdom*: Darius III (reigned 336–330).

5.5 *a former Persian king*: Artaxerxes II Mnemon (reigned 405–358).

6.1 *Cadusians*: they lived around the south-western coastline of the Caspian Sea.

7.4 *the daughter of Melisseus*: Melisseus' two daughters, Ida and Adrasteia, looked after the infant Zeus on Mount Ida—but usually the Ida on Crete, not this one in north-west Asia Minor.

7.4 *Alexander*: this Alexander is Paris, prince of Troy, who judged the mythical beauty contest between Hera, Athena, and Aphrodite, winning Helen as his prize and causing the Trojan War.

7.5 *Dactyls*: often conceived of as dwarfs, the Dactyls were associates of the Mother of the Gods, and, in their capacity as metal-workers, of Hephaestus.

7.6 *the rising of the Dog Star*: mid-July at the time; the Dog Star is Sirius.

7.8 *very nearly took it*: he disguised his men as Macedonians: Polyaenus, *Stratagems in War* 5.44.5. The Cyzicenes' crime was to have entered into an alliance with Macedon.

7.9 *Pitane under siege*: so Parmenion was campaigning on the coast of Aeolis.

7.10 *the Troad*: the district around Troy/Ilium. Rhoeteum was a small town between Ilium and Abydus.

8.1 *the neighbouring regions*: Diodorus and other writers in the same tradition omit Alexander's campaign against the Triballians, which was presumably not covered in their sources. The Triballians were a Thracian tribe, occupying land that today straddles the border between Serbia and Bulgaria.

8.3 *Alexander suddenly appeared*: this was a famous forced march; Alexander reached Thebes with astonishing rapidity in order to prevent the rebellion spreading to the Spartans and Aetolians (Arrian, *The Expedition of Alexander* 1.7.4).

8.5 *paid for out of his own pocket*: not quite: he was using money given him by the Persians.

9.5 *to join the Great King*: the Persian king was subsidizing the Theban rebellion.

10.2 *as big as a himation*: this was a large cobweb; see the note to 16.93.1. But the story is plausible: in Greece, spiders from the Tetragnatha species construct webs several square metres in size during the mating season.

10.3 *the national oracle of Thebes*: the presiding deity was Apollo Ismenius.

10.4 *the marsh at Onchestus*: better known as Lake Copais. The pseudo-Aristotelian work *Problems* devotes a paragraph (25.2) to explaining bellowing marshes.

10.5 *temple... built with Phocian spoils*: this description is hard to decipher. As far as we know, the Thebans never founded a temple in Delphi and we cannot contextualize the reference to Phocian spoils. There was a Theban treasury at Delphi, but it was built after the defeat of the Spartans at Leuctra.

10.5 *the gods were departing from the city*: it is not clear how they arrived at this interpretation, but Aelian (second/third century CE) says that the likeness of Demeter was seen in the web: *Historical Miscellany* 12.57.

10.6 *Leuctra... by their valour*: the unexpected defeat of Sparta at Leuctra in Boeotia in 371 brought Spartan supremacy to an end and initiated the slow decline of Sparta as a Greek superpower. The next nine years constitute the period of Theban supremacy in Greece.

11.5 *Mantinea*: the Theban victory at Mantinea in 362 was, however, qualified by the death in the battle of Epaminondas, their extremely talented general and statesman. The battle effectively brought to an end the period of Theban hegemony in Greece. On Leuctra, see the first note to 16.23.2.

13.2 *grasping the knees of the victors*: a traditional gesture of supplication.

13.5 *enemies of the Thebans*: these enemies were chiefly other cities in Boeotia. Throughout the long history of the Boeotian Confederacy, Thebes was invariably dominant, and its rule was resented by the others. They saw their chance now: the destruction of Thebes would mean that its farmland would be divided up among them.

13.6 *the same language spoken*: this is Diodorus' first-century perspective. In the fourth century, Greeks had fewer qualms about killing one another.

14.1 *the common council of the Greeks*: the council of the League of Corinth.

14.2 *at the time of Xerxes' invasion*: King Xerxes led the Persian invasion of Greece in 480–479.

14.4 *in accordance with the will of the council*: if this was an attempt to deflect responsibility, it failed: moral responsibility for the destruction of Thebes lies squarely with Alexander. Only the temples and the house of the poet Pindar were spared.

15.2 *go to their deaths willingly*: in legend, the Lacedaemonian Hyacinthus moved to Athens and sacrificed his four daughters in order to save the city from being taken by King Minos of Crete.

15.3 *to help him make up his mind*: Demades was not normally a political ally of Demosthenes: see 16.87 for his closeness to Philip.

16.2 *argued against them*: the first hint of the constant tension between Alexander and the 'old guard' of those who had served his father. Diodorus repeats the story here, even though Parmenion was in Asia Minor and not in Macedon. Alexander's failure to produce an heir resulted in the chaos narrated by Diodorus in Books 18–20.

16.3 *Archelaus*: king of Macedon 413–399.

17.2 *sailed... to the Troad*: the rest of the fleet of 180 or so ships remained at Abydus.

17.3 *a precise count of the army that had accompanied him*: he must have returned to Abydus for this exercise. Diodorus makes it sound as though he were still at Ilium.

17.4 *Agrianes*: the Agrianes were from Paeonia, the Odrysians and Triballians were the two main Thracian peoples. They were all light-armed troops.

17.4 *Erigyius*: actually, Erigyius gained his first cavalry command later. It was probably Alexander the Lyncestian who had this command at this time.

17.4 *Cassander*: this should be 'Asander'. As we shall see, this is a recurrent error in Diodorus' work, but probably stemming from the scribal tradition rather than Diodorus himself.

17.4 *4,500*: a careless mistake in Diodorus' addition: the total is 5,100. Generally speaking, however, the numbers given by Diodorus for Alexander's initial forces are held to be more accurate than those found in other writers.

17.6 *the sanctuary of Athena*: a famous sanctuary at Troy (Ilium). See also 18.4.5.

17.6 *in front of the temple*: presumably the statue had been toppled after Ariobarzanes (this is Ariobarzanes I of Cius) had joined the Satraps' Revolt and been crucified for his pains in the late 360s.

18.4 *greatly outnumbered the Macedonians*: actually, they may have had a smaller army than Alexander for this battle, but it is automatic in most Greek historians to assume that the Persians always had vast armies.

19.3 *ready for battle*: Diodorus' account of the battle is irreconcilable with that of Arrian (*The Expedition of Alexander* 1.13), who has the attack take place in the afternoon, but there are difficulties with Arrian's account as well. It may be that Diodorus is to be preferred here. The fact that the Persians did not contest the river crossing dooms Diodorus' account for some scholars, but it might only mean that the Persian cavalry lines were quite far from the river, so that it took time for them to get there.

19.4 *with the Hyrcanian cavalry*: satrapal armies were usually recruited locally, so it would be unusual for the 'satrap of Ionia' to have cavalry from Hyrcania under his command, but there was an expatriate Hyrcanian community in Lydia (Strabo, *Geography* 13.4.3), and it must have been them who supplied this cavalry contingent.

20.2 *Kinsmen*: see Glossary.

20.3 *pierced his breastplate*: just the joint of the breastplate, according to Plutarch (*Alexander* 16), which is the shoulder strap. But there is some doubt whether Alexander would have been carrying a shield, since his hands were occupied with riding and with wielding his lance and sword.

22.5 *treated the Milesians generously*: equally generous treatment had already gained Alexander Ephesus, Magnesia, and Tralles.

22.5 *disbanded it*: Alexander disbanded the Greek fleet because he did not trust the Greeks. He was right not to trust them: when Memnon made Samos his naval base, the Athenians living on the island cooperated with him. But the disbanding of the fleet was a huge tactical error, and allowed Memnon to make a nuisance of himself in the Aegean as Alexander marched east: see 17.29.1–4. Despite the defensive work of the Macedonian fleet, Miletus, for instance, was back in Persian hands by 333. Alexander's intention was to make the Persian fleet redundant by conquering the Persian empire, rather than risk a sea-battle, but if Memnon had not died, the plan might have been a great failure. Even so, Alexander had to admit his mistake by commissioning (in 333) another fleet for the Aegean, but by then the Persian fleet had been weakened by Darius' recall of troops from the west to bulk up his army for what he hoped would be a decisive land battle in the eastern Mediterranean. After Alexander's victory at Issus, the remainder of the Persian fleet fell apart.

23.3 *Agathocles...defeated...tens of thousands*: see 20.7.

23.5 *Memnon sent his wife*: she was called Barsine. She was captured at Damascus after the battle of Issus, became Alexander's mistress, and bore him a son, Heracles, who made an ill-starred bid for the Macedonian throne and was murdered in 309 (20.20.1, 20.28.1–2). Barsine and Alexander may have been childhood acquaintances.

24.2 *Ada...asked for his help*: see 16.69.2 and 16.74.2 for Ada's earlier deposition.

24.2 *the rulership of Caria*: once Alexander had taken Halicarnassus he made Ada satrap of Caria, but he left a Macedonian in charge of the garrison.

25.5 *Neoptolemus*: Arrian (*The Expedition of Alexander* 1.20.10) says that this Neoptolemus deserted to the Persian side. It is not certain whether Arrian or Diodorus is to be preferred.

27.6 *considerable size*: in effect, then, the siege of Halicarnassus was a defeat for Alexander, or at least indecisive. It was still held against him, the enemy fleet was still intact, now based on the island of Cos, and he had to leave larger numbers of troops there than he would have wanted. The enemy troops on the acropolis (actually, the city had two citadels, one of which was on an island) could be supplied by sea. It took Alexander's troops several more months to complete the seizure of the city.

27.7 *coastline up to Cilicia*: in making it sound as though Alexander followed the coastline, Diodorus omits several inland campaigns and the famous story of his diversion inland to Phrygia and the cutting of the Gordian knot. See e.g. Arrian, *The Expedition of Alexander* 2.3, Plutarch, *Alexander* 18. While Alexander was on this campaign, Parmenion was mopping up resistance in Lydia; the divided army met again at Gordium.

28.1 *the Marmares*: Diodorus is our only authority for this story, but he may be a bit muddled. The ancient name of the place was Physkos, which is today known as Marmaris because of the rich marble deposits of the district. Perhaps Diodorus confused the name of the place with the name of the people.

30.1 *Memnon's death*: in his essay *On the Fortune of Alexander*, Plutarch makes Memnon's death a prime example of Alexander's good luck.

30.2 *Charidemus... his chief counsellor*: this is a real muddle. Charidemus was a freelance commander who spent much of his life fighting Philip, and never worked for him. Nor was he, strictly, an Athenian. He had been given Athenian citizenship as an honour, but he was from Oreus in Euboea. The king Charidemus mostly worked for was Cersobleptes, the

Odrysian. The simplest solution may be to delete 'Philip' as an ignorant scribal addition, so that the text reads only that Charidemus 'fought alongside the king'—i.e. the king of Persia.

30.4 *the Persian method of arrest*: see also Xenophon, *The Expedition of Cyrus* 1.6.10.

31.1 *from all quarters*: not from the upper satrapies, apparently: see 17.39.3.

31.2 *his wife and children*: more accurately one of his two wives, and three of his five children.

31.6 *one of his most trusted friends*: Diodorus omits the famous story in which he trusted Philip and drank the medicine despite having been warned that it was in fact a poison: Arrian, *The Expedition of Alexander* 2.4.7–11.

32.2 *awaited his trial in prison*: he is finally killed at 17.80.2. He was one of Alexander's closest rivals for the throne. His two brothers had already been killed in the course of the purge immediately following Alexander's accession, and Alexander had been spared only because he was quick to acknowledge his namesake's kingship.

33.1 *a single battle*: for a good account of Issus that depends on sources other than Diodorus, see Hammond, *Alexander the Great*, 95–110.

34.5 *Atizyes*: the satrap of Phrygia did die in this battle, but not at the Granicus river, as in 17.21.3.

34.5 *Tasiaces*: his name was more properly Sauaces or Sabaces.

34.6 *attempted to shake off their bits*: perhaps what Diodorus is trying to describe here is the way a frightened horse shakes its head and tries to grab the bit with its teeth so that it can bolt.

35.3 *accompanied the army*: they had been left at Damascus (17.32.3).

35.5 *tearing at their clothes*: a conventional response in the ancient world to grief or other profound emotions.

36.5 *the Royal Pages*: see Glossary.

37.6 *He is Alexander too*: an anecdote indicating how close Alexander and Hephaestion were. In all probability, they were lovers.

37.6 *his second mother*: actually, his third, because (in addition to his natural mother Olympias), in an incident omitted by Diodorus but belonging in 17.24, Alexander was adopted by Ada of Caria.

38.1 *show him royal honour*: in seeing to the children's future, in addition to calling her 'mother', Alexander was acting like her eldest son, now her guardian since she was deprived of Darius. If this traditional story of Alexander's generous treatment of the royal Persian women is true, his reasons were strategic: to make noble Persians doubt the wisdom of resisting him, and to hold the best possible hostages.

38.2 *her former happy state*: it is not certain that this particular promise was fulfilled. Darius' wife, Stateira, seems to have died in childbirth more than nine months after her capture.

39.2 *the tone of which suited him better*: that is, because it was more insulting. Diodorus is the only one of our sources to suggest that any of Darius' letters to Alexander were forgeries.

39.3 *the speed of the previous campaign*: is this plausible? The Persian empire was vast, but eighteen months elapsed between the Granicus river and Issus.

40.1 *the victor*: in the stade race, that is. The man's name, however, might be Eurylas, not Grylus, and the Athenian Archon's name should be Nicetes.

40.2 *he advanced towards Egypt*: Alexander chose to go to Egypt rather than pursue Darius because he could not leave the Phoenician ports and Egyptian garrisons intact in his rear.

40.2 *prevented him from entering the city*: the 'Tyrian Heracles' is Melqart, the main deity of Tyre. The Tyrians had submitted to Alexander, as had all the coastal towns further north, but they (correctly) read Alexander's request to enter the island city, accompanied by soldiers, as a request for unconditional surrender, and refused him entry.

40.4 *treated with contempt by a single, unexceptional city*: this, of course, is not a good reason to spend a great deal of time and money over a siege that cost him a lot of lives. The real reason was probably that Alexander felt that Tyre could act as a base for the Persian fleet.

40.5 *Old Tyre*: which was on the mainland.

41.1 *Poseidon*: the god of the sea.

41.1 *Carthage*: Carthage had originally been founded by settlers from Tyre.

41.5 *an incredibly large sea-creature*: perhaps a whale. The two largest species of whale in the Mediterranean are the Fin whale (*Balaenoptera physalus*) and the Sperm whale (*Physeter macrocephalus*).

42.2 *no way to protect themselves*: clearly, the Tyrians controlled the sea at this stage of the siege.

42.4 *their harbours*: Tyre had two harbours, one on the north and one on the south of the island. Diodorus veers between talking of one or two harbours.

44.4 *crows*: a kind of grappling hook.

45.3 *ineffective when they struck*: this is a more detailed doublet of 17.43.1. So is the sentence that follows.

45.7 *committed himself again to the siege*: the support of the inner circle of Friends was crucial for a king, and he would usually follow their advice. Alexander is shown to be exceptional, in this as in so many other ways.

46.4 *a great many people ... to Carthage*: this contradicts 17.41.2, unless there had been further voyages to Carthage during the siege.

47.1 *Straton*: according to Curtius (*History of Alexander* 4.1.15–26), Straton was the king of Sidon, not Tyre. According to Arrian (*The Expedition of Alexander* 2.13.7), Straton was the king or prince of Arados, and the king of Tyre during the siege, who was deposed by Alexander at the end of it, was called Azelmicus (Arrian, *The Expedition of Alexander* 2.15.7, 2.24.5).

48.2 *Amyntas…fought for the Persians in Cilicia*: he was the overall commander of the Greek mercenaries. He had fled from Macedon shortly after the death of Philip II and had joined the Persians shortly before Issus.

48.6 *whatever services were appropriate for the situation*: most importantly, this Persian counter-offensive regained them Cappadocia and Paphlagonia, Miletus, and some of the Aegean islands. Antigonus Monophthalmus (of whom much more in Books 18–20), left behind in Asia Minor by Alexander for this purpose, played an important part in checking the counter-offensive.

48.6 *the delegates of the Greek states*: that is, the council of what is nowadays called the League of Corinth: see the end of 17.4.9.

49.1 *fit for service*: Amyntas returned with fifteen thousand fresh troops shortly after Gaugamela.

49.2 *the temple of Ammon*: a famous oracular shrine, well known even among the Greeks. Ammon (the name of the god as well as the place) was considered the equivalent of the Greek Zeus. The place is nowadays called the Siwa Oasis.

50.2 *Danaus of Egypt*: in Greek legend, in order to avoid his fifty daughters having to marry the fifty sons of his brother Aegyptus, Danaus and his daughters fled from Egypt and settled in Argos in Greece. Aegyptus and his sons followed them there, and the marriage went ahead, but Danaus instructed his daughters to kill their husbands on the wedding night. Forty-nine of them did so.

50.2 *consecrated to the god*: so that the temple received all the profits from working the land.

50.4 *in a paradoxical fashion*: the original Greek source of this story is Herodotus, *Histories* 4.181. The pool, later known as Cleopatra's Bath, can still be visited. There is nothing abnormal about its changes of temperature, however.

50.6 *inclination of the god's head*: I imagine that the courtyard of the precinct acted like a giant ouija board, with areas, for instance, that indicated future happiness or future sorrow. The god somehow indicated with his head where to go, and the prophet adapted the results to the question that had been asked. Elsewhere, we are told that a forward motion of the cult statue meant 'yes' and a backward motion 'no': see P. Goukowsky, *Diodore de Sicile, Bibliothèque Historique, Livre XVII*, 205. The number eighty for the priests is surely a great exaggeration.

51.2 *I shall be called your son*: Alexander speaks to the priest as if he were speaking directly to the god, and in a moment, when the priest speaks, the god speaks through him.

51.3 *The one who begot him*: so Alexander set out on the path of deification while still alive. See also the second note to 20.46.2.

52.1 *a great city in Egypt*: Diodorus and the vulgate tradition place the foundation of Alexandria after the visit to Siwa, but Arrian and Plutarch place it before. Perhaps he made the first decision as to its location before, and then started work after. Not the least importance of Alexandria was that it provided a good harbour on the notoriously inhospitable Egyptian coast. The lake in question is Lake Mareotis, which formed the southern border of Alexandria.

52.2 *the layout of the streets*: Alexandria was built on a grid plan, so what Alexander did was divide the city into quarters.

52.2 *called Alexandria after him*: the first of a dozen or so foundations named after him. In naming cities this way he was imitating both Persian and his father's practice (Crenides became Philippi, for instance).

52.2 *the etesian winds*: the fierce northerly winds of the summer months, known as the *meltemi* in modern Greece.

52.3 *a military cloak*: a rough rectangle.

52.5 *the greatest in the world*: by Diodorus' time, Alexandria was the second city of the Mediterranean, after Rome. When he says that it is the largest and most populous city, he probably means the largest *Greek* city—unless he is subtly putting Rome down (see Introduction, pp. 14–15).

52.7 *the reorganization of Egypt*: some details in Arrian, *The Expedition of Alexander* 3.5.2–7.

53.2 *three spans long*: about 66.5 cms, or 26 ins.

53.4 *Nineveh*: the famous Assyrian city, sacked in the seventh century BCE, located on the Tigris by modern Mosul.

53.4 *a village called Arbela*: Arbela was a town rather than a village (see 17.64.3); the nearby village was called Gaugamela, and the battle is usually called the battle of Gaugamela, but Diodorus is following a different tradition. This battle is one of Arrian's great set-pieces: *The Expedition of Alexander* 3.7–15.

54.1 *silver as well*: see 17.39.1.

54.5 *if I were Parmenion*: there is a recurrent theme in the Alexander historians (though less prominent in Diodorus) of tension between Alexander and Parmenion, who was his leading general as he had been his father's before. The theme is perhaps meant to explain or even justify Alexander's eventual elimination of Parmenion.

54.6 *the power to do so*: the king of Persia was known as the King of Kings. Many kings and chieftains were his vassals, and his satraps were the equivalent of kings in their provinces. Alexander is saying that Darius was welcome to have them as his subordinates, as long as he was Alexander's subordinate himself. Since it was clear that Darius would never accept this option, Alexander was provoking the king to battle, even without the sneering tone of his message.

54.7 *Darius' wife died*: see the note to 17.38.2.

55.2 *he did not bother to guard it*: was this negligence, or has Diodorus' source misunderstood the Persian strategy? Darius might have wanted Alexander to cross the river, so that battle could be joined on terrain that favoured the Persian forces.

57.1 *Cleitus 'the Black'*: so called to distinguish him from another prominent Cleitus, 'the White'.

57.1 *the rest of his Friends*: they formed what is usually known as the Companion Cavalry. Diodorus has already used the term at 17.37.2.

54.1 *the other seven cavalry units*: that is, the other seven units of the Companion Cavalry, which was divided into eight squadrons—seven plus the Royal Squadron (Arrian, *The Expedition of Alexander* 3.11.8). But if the unit of 'Friends' also refers to the Companion Cavalry (previous note), then there is a muddle here, since the Companion Cavalry will have been mentioned twice.

54.2 *the Silver Shields*: this regiment will play a considerable part in the wars that followed Alexander's death. It was an elite infantry unit formed by Alexander probably in 326 from the pick of his hypaspists.

57.2 *the Elimiote Battalion, as it is called*: Elimiotis was one of the cantons of Upper Macedon (along with Orestis, Lyncestis, and Tymphaea/ Stymphaea) that had been incorporated into the state by Philip II.

57.4 *Achaean mercenaries*: Achaea, being poor, was (along with Arcadia) one of the regular sources of Greek mercenaries.

57.5 *slantwise*: that is, forming an oblique backward angle, necessarily *en échelon*, to increase coverage of the flank and prevent encirclement.

57.6 *without endangering the Macedonians*: this was standard practice: compare Xenophon, *The Expedition of Cyrus* 1.8.20, and Cassius Dio, *Roman History* 40.2.4. For an analysis of the use of scythed chariots in this battle, see W. Heckel, C. Willekes, and G. Wrightson, 'Scythed Chariots at Gaugamela: A Case Study', in E. Carney and D. Ogden (eds), *Philip II and Alexander the Great: Father and Son, Lives and Afterlives* (Oxford: Oxford University Press, 2010), 103–9.

57.6 *responsible for the decisive victory*: the right wing was very often under the command of the general-in-chief of an army, which gave it prestige, but also the necessity of proving itself more valiant than the other units.

59.3 *Apple-bearers*: named for the butt-spikes of their spears, which were golden and shaped like apples, they formed a prestigious regiment of five hundred and acted as the foot guards of the king.

59.3 *Mardians and Cossaeans*: Mardian homeland was south of the Caspian Sea, while the Cossaeans lived in the Zagros mountains. The Cossaeans would later make trouble for Alexander (17.111.4–6) and worse trouble for Antigonus Monophthalmus (19.19.2–7).

59.5 *take the baggage*: the baggage train contained not just the army's equipment and the men's personal belongings and accumulated booty, but even (see 19.43.7) their families and womenfolk, so it was a not uncommon tactic to try to capture it, as a powerful bargaining counter. Alexander's army was effectively an entire city on the move.

60.3 *Darius... turned to flight*: interestingly, Babylonian documents (*BM* 36761 and 36390) suggest that the Persian troops abandoned the king, not the other way around.

60.4 *the continuous cracking of whips*: the Persians were said to use whips to lash cowards back on to the battlefield.

60.7 *in his pursuit of the enemy*: other historians say that Alexander had to break off his pursuit in order to help Parmenion, whose situation was critical.

61.3 *more than ninety thousand men*: certainly a huge exaggeration, though Persian losses were undoubtedly enormous. But all the figures of Persian troop numbers in these battles—the Granicus, Issus, and Gaugamela—are hugely exaggerated. For Gaugamela, Diodorus assures us that Darius had an army of a million men (17.53.3)!

61.3 *Hephaestion, the commander of the bodyguards*: Hephaestion was Alexander's chiliarch, the commander of his personal bodyguard.

62.1 *while the Persian empire still remained*: the battle that Diodorus is about to describe took place in 331, before the battle of Gaugamela, and so was not triggered by the news of Gaugamela, as Diodorus has it. This is the start of some slippage in Diodorus' dating of Alexander's expedition. Diodorus' dating of the events of these years should be compared with a reliable, detailed chronology of Alexander's expedition, such as that on pp. xv–xxii of P. Cartledge, *Alexander the Great: The Hunt for a New Past* (London: Macmillan, 2004).

62.5 *Memnon... persuaded the Thracians to rise up against Alexander*: since Memnon still held high rank later, this is probably wrong. Perhaps the Thracians rose up in revolt, but not at Memnon's instigation.

62.7 *more than any other Greek state*: see 17.15.5. But the Athenian decision was not as easy as Diodorus makes it sound. There was considerable debate in Athens as to whether or not to support Agis.

63.1 *from his Greek allies*: he had to do this, because he had recently sent fifteen thousand Macedonian troops off to join Alexander (see the note to 17.49.1).

64.4 *more than thirty days*: Babylon was surrendered to Alexander by Mazaeus, the high-ranking Persian who had been prominent in Diodorus' account of the battle of Gaugamela. In return, Alexander appointed him satrap of Babylonia, the first but not the last time he appointed a native. He did this partly because he had no choice—there were not enough

Macedonians to fill all the senior posts—but also as a matter of policy, to blend Macedonian and Iranian rule, and to win over to his side the supporters of Mazaeus and the other appointees. Diodorus tells us little about the administration of Alexander's empire; the gap can be filled by reference to Anson, *Alexander the Great*, 121–79, and Bosworth, *Conquest and Empire*, 229–58.

64.5 *the Babylonian acropolis*: actually, Babylon had two acropolises, one on either side of the Euphrates.

65.1 *Trallians*: a Thracian tribe.

65.1 *bodyguards*: as Royal Pages, presumably.

65.3 *strong ties of affection*: command had traditionally been based on ethnic factors: a general recruited and commanded the fighting men from his canton of Macedon. So, for instance, at 17.57.2, we find Polyperchon in command of the Stymphaeans. Alexander's innovation was to promote men on the basis of their military service, which served to weaken the feudal hold of the generals over their men and bind them more closely to himself.

65.4 *to increase their effectiveness*: this is very vague; Curtius, *History of Alexander* 5.2, is clearer. See also Arrian, *The Expedition of Alexander* 3.16.11.

66.2 *darics*: a daric was a standard Persian gold coin, named after Darius I the Great (reigned 522–486), who introduced it. It bore the image of the king kneeling, as an archer. One daric was worth 35 drachmas in Greek monetary terms.

67.1 *the Tigris river*: the Pasitigris, actually—the Karun, nowadays. The mistake is common in ancient authors.

67.2 *the mountains inhabited by the Uxians*: the Zagros mountains.

67.3 *the Tigris*: here Diodorus does seem to be talking about the Tigris rather than the less navigable Pasitigris.

67.4 *Madetes, a Kinsman of Darius*: Madetes (or Madates) was not just a Kinsman in the honorary sense, but was married to the daughter of the sister of Darius' mother.

68.1 *destination . . . Persis*: he had divided the army. While he took the lighter troops through the mountains, Parmenion led the main army and the baggage train by the more direct route to Persis along the Royal Road.

68.4 *pulled back three hundred stades*: a much smaller figure is needed; Diodorus' figure places the camp about 50 kilometres away from the pass. Curtius' figure of 30 stades is more likely (*History of Alexander* 5.3.23).

68.4 *admission of defeat*: by the conventions of Greek warfare, asking an enemy for permission to collect your dead was formal acknowledgement of defeat.

69.1 *responsible for the city*: and in particular for the rich royal treasuries of Persepolis.

69.3 *resettled*: for a list of known Greek deportations, see P. Goukowsky, *Diodore de Sicile, Bibliothèque Historique, Livre XVII*, 268. Since these unfortunates cannot be identified with any known deportation, the whole episode may be fictional. It does sound rather implausible.

69.8 *fifty medimnoi of wheat*: one *medimnos* was equivalent to about 40 kg (88 lbs)—i.e. a large sack of grain.

70.1 *the capital of the Persian empire*: actually, the Achaemenid kings had several 'capital' cities (e.g. Sardis, Celaenae, Ecbatana, Susa), and travelled around from one to the other, depending on the season and their need to be seen somewhere. On Persepolis, see A. Mousavi, *Persepolis: Discovery and Afterlife of a World Wonder* (Berlin: de Gruyter, 2012).

70.3 *purple*: purple dye from the murex shellfish was so laborious to collect and extract in quantity that it was very expensive, and throughout the Mediterranean purple-dyed textiles were a sign of rank and wealth.

71.1 *the gold-to-silver ratio*: the value of gold in relation to silver at this time, before Alexander released so much on to the market, stood at about 15:1.

71.3 *to destroy Persepolis utterly*: actually, Persepolis survived and continued as the capital city of Persis (19.21–2, 19.46.6).

71.4 *Three circuit walls*: archaeology has not confirmed the existence of three walls. Could Diodorus be taking the tall platform on which the palaces were built to be a wall?

71.7 *Four plethra away*: away from what? Perhaps the palace. Four plethra is about 120 metres or 400 feet.

72.2 *Thais, an Athenian by birth*: Thais was later married to Ptolemy, the future king of Egypt, but it is not clear whose companion she was at this time—perhaps Alexander's.

72.2 *a revel*: usually, at a symposium, the guests did not get so drunk that things got out of hand, but if they did, they might take to the streets in a revel (*kōmos*). See also the second note to 16.87.2.

72.3 *crimes against Greek temples*: see the note to 16.89.2.

72.6 *for fun*: archaeology has uncovered the layer of ash from Alexander's burning of the palace, revealing it to have been probably a premeditated act, not a piece of drunken foolishness. For one thing, the palace had been carefully cleared of valuables before it was burnt. It looks as though Alexander focused on destroying buildings associated with Xerxes, the invader of Greece; he was being true to his mission of avenging the Persian invasion of 480.

73.2 *Bactra*: the chief city of Bactria, modern Balkh in northern Afghanistan.

73.5 *a major battle*: the battle of Megalopolis, covered in 17.63.

73.5 *the common council of the Greeks*: that is, the body we call the League of Corinth.

73.5 *for him to resolve*: Alexander was unexpectedly merciful: the Lacedaemonians were required only to pay a small indemnity to Megalopolis, which they had attacked.

74.1 *Nabarzanes and Barxaes*: Nabarzanes was Darius' chiliarch (second-in-command) and Barxaes (better known as Barsaentes) was the satrap of Arachosia.

74.2 *king*: not just king of Bactria, but of the whole empire, with the royal name of Artaxerxes V. This was a setback for Alexander, who was trying to present himself as the legitimate successor of the Achaemenids, by having conquered the empire and by having gained the acceptance of as much of the Iranian nobility as he had already won over. It is more likely that Bessus proclaimed himself king immediately on the death of Darius, rather than waiting until he was safe in Bactria.

74.3 *army assembly*: this is the first recorded army assembly. Over the years, the infantry troops, both Macedonians and mercenaries, assembled more and more often, and sometimes not when convened by one of their leaders—which is to say that over the years they took more power on to themselves, especially under the Successors.

75.1 *Hecatontapylus*: more usually 'Hecatompylus', but the meaning is the same: the city of a hundred gates. It was later the capital city of the Arsacid dynasty of Parthia.

75.2 *once more into the open air*: this is apparently a fair description of the spring called Cheshmeh-Ali ('Fountain of Ali') in northern Iran.

75.4 *more productive than anywhere else*: the marvels that follow are not untypical of the edges of the earth in the Greek imagination. A *metrētēs* was about 40 litres (somewhat over 10 liquid gallons US, 8.5 liquid gallons UK). The average yield of a vine in reality is about 4.5 litres of wine. For modern equivalents of a *medimnos*, see the note to 17.69.8.

75.6 *extremely pleasant*: some species of fig, tamarisk, and oak produce a sweet resin.

75.7 *in our part of the world*: see I. Beavis, *Insects and Other Invertebrates in Classical Antiquity* (Exeter: University of Exeter Press, 1988). Some aphids and scale insects secrete a sugar-rich liquid, called 'honeydew', as they feed on plant sap, but this *anthrēdōn* is probably a kind of wasp.

76.3 *the Mardians*: this was an unprovoked attack, but the burning of the farmland suggests that Alexander thought it could have supplied an enemy army.

76.6 *Demaratus of Corinth*: the famous alternative story of how Alexander acquired Bucephalas by taming him is well told by Plutarch, *Alexander* 6.

77.1 *paid him a visit*: it is of course troubling to have fiction like this story included in the history. How many of the other stories about Alexander are fictional? Arrian makes no mention of the Amazon queen, but the story recurs in all our other sources, though Plutarch mentions it only to reject it as fictional. On the Amazons, see A. Mayor, *The Amazons: Lives and*

Legends of Warrior Women across the Ancient World (Princeton: Princeton University Press, 2014).

77.1 *her domain*: the south-eastern coastline of the Black Sea. Diodorus' major description of the Amazons can be found at 2.44–6.

77.4 *ushers of eastern origin*: their job was to control access to the king—that is, to make the king more aloof and remote, a distinct break from Macedonian tradition.

77.5 *Persian diadem*: a diadem was a Persian sign of high rank, but it was no more than a simple fillet or headband, knotted in a bow at the back of the head. Kings wore a tall tiara, bound to their head with a diadem. Alexander's innovation was to wear the diadem by itself as a sign of royalty. On the delicate balance of East and West in Alexander's style of kingship, see E. Fredricksmeyer, 'Alexander the Great and the Kingdom of Asia', in A. B. Bosworth and E. Baynham (eds), *Alexander the Great in Fact and Fiction* (Oxford: Oxford University Press, 2000), 136–66. Alexander had to adopt features of eastern kingship to make himself acceptable to the Iranians, just as the Achaemenids before him had learnt aspects of their courtly behaviour from those they conquered.

77.5 *kandys*: a sleeved coat fastened at the neck like a cloak.

78.1 *marched against him*: Satibarzanes had formally submitted to Alexander, so this was sheer treachery.

78.1 *Chortacana*: more usually called 'Artacoana', the capital of Areia.

79.1 *some of what the king was doing*: this is very vague, but probably means that he disapproved of Alexander's increasing orientalism.

79.2 *very young*: typically a 'boyfriend' (*erōmenos*) would be aged between 14 and 18, while the lover (*erōn*) would be in his 20s.

80.1 *the foremost of Alexander's Friends*: Parmenion was just about the last of the 'old guard'—those who had risen to prominence under Philip rather than Alexander. His and Philotas' removal left room for men of Alexander's own generation to be promoted.

80.2 *the Macedonian manner*: by being stoned or lanced to death.

80.2 *three years*: he was arrested in 17.32.2, in the year 333/2.

80.2 *Antigonus*: this should be 'Antipater', whose son-in-law he was.

80.3 *dromedaries*: the word 'dromedary' literally means 'racing camel', as opposed to the slower, two-humped Bactrian camel.

80.4 *the bluntness with which they spoke*: this paragraph seems to be based on a source hostile to Alexander—especially with its implication that he was reading his men's letters home—unlike Diodorus' usual glorifications. Alexander also comes off less than gloriously in 17.5.1–2 (where Attalus is killed despite proving loyal), in 17.39.1–2 (where Alexander undermines peace negotiations by forging a letter), in 17.70.1–3 (where he allows Persepolis to be sacked), in 17.77.4–78.1 (where he adopts outrageous 'oriental' habits and bribes dissenters into quiescence), and in

17.84 (where he massacres some mercenaries, contrary to his promise to them).

81.2 *appropriate gifts*: he made them responsible for a larger amount of territory, though they were still answerable to one of his satraps.

81.3 *rebellion*: this was one division of a more concerted rebellion in the north-eastern satrapies, which was being set in motion by Bessus. Satibarzanes was quickly dealt with, but settling the entire rebellion took many months.

81.3 *only a few days*: the speed of this conquest (and others in the eastern satrapies) was due to the fact that these provinces were relatively uninhabited, so that the conquest of one or two main towns constituted the conquest of the entire province. Arachosia was what is now southern Afghanistan.

82.1 *In this year*: see the note to 62.1. This march through the Hindu Kush took place in the winter of 330/29, not in 328/7.

82.2 *under the Greater and Lesser Bear constellations*: this phrase usually means 'in the far north', but this is hard to square with the location of the Paropanisadae in the Hindu Kush. Diodorus must be using it to refer to anywhere really cold.

82.3 *closed on all sides*: that is, they had no central courtyard, as Greek houses typically did.

82.5 *inhospitable and inaccessible*: this is something of an exaggeration: not all the country was a wilderness. The Paropanisadae were an important link in the commercial routes between India and the Near East.

82.7 *reflected light*: if they had read their Xenophon, they would have known what to do to counteract the glare: *The Expedition of Cyrus* 4.5.12–13.

83.1 *made camp*: this is not the same Caucasus as the range between the Black and Caspian Seas; this Caucasus is what we call the Hindu Kush, which the Greeks thought was a continuation of the true Caucasus, which, in turn, was a continuation of the Taurus mountains of south-east Asia Minor: see 18.5.2.

83.1 *Alexandria*: since almost all of Alexander's eastern foundations were called Alexandria, this one is distinguished by being called Alexandria of the Caucasus, or Alexandria in Paropanisadae. See Fraser, *Cities*, 140–51.

83.1 *marks of the chains*: Prometheus was the fundamental Greek culture hero. In order to preserve the human race and allow it to develop, he stole fire for them from the gods, and for this he was punished by being chained to a rock (in a cave, on this version of the story); every day an eagle came and pecked out his liver, and every night he healed again in anticipation of the next day's torture.

83.2 *other towns as well*: perhaps outlying fortresses to protect Alexandria.

83.7 *got into an argument*: we learn elsewhere that Bagodaras advised Bessus to surrender to Alexander: Curtius, *History of Alexander* 7.4.8–19 (where he is called Cobares).

83.9 *punishment*: the brother of Darius is presumably Oxathres: 17.77.4.

84.1 *the queen*: Queen Cleophis of the Assacei: Curtius, *History of Alexander* 8.10.22–36. Her kingdom was in the Lower Swat Valley, in what is now Pakistan. The notes of P. Goukowsky, *Diodore de Sicile, Bibliothèque Historique, Livre XVII* (in French), and Stronk, *Semiramis' Legacy*, are particularly useful for the Indian campaign. See also A. B. Bosworth, *Alexander and the East: The Tragedy of Triumph* (Oxford: Oxford University Press, 1996).

84.1 *the city*: Mazagae or Massaga. By the terms of the truce, these Indian mercenaries were to be incorporated into Alexander's army.

84.2 *slaughter them*: at several points in the Indian campaign (including some episodes lost in the great gap that precedes 17.84) Alexander's savagery was on display. Once he found out how enormous the country was, he was in a hurry to get on, and he used terror tactics to cow peoples into submission, so that he would not be held up by the necessity of fighting them.

85.2 *Heracles*: the Indian 'Heracles' was either Indra or Krishna. For the identification of Aornus and other places in Pakistan, the fundamental work remains A. Stein, *On Alexander's Track to the Indus* (London: Macmillan, 1929). Aornus is probably Mount Pir Sar.

86.2 *fifteen elephants*: this is the first mention of war elephants, but in fact Alexander first encountered them in the Persian army at Gaugamela. On their use, see C. Epplett, 'War Elephants in the Hellenistic World', in W. Heckel, L. Tritle, and P. Wheatley (eds), *Alexander's Empire: Formulation to Decay* (Claremont, CA: Regina, 2007), 209–32.

86.7 *Taxiles*: since Taxiles was clearly the local king name, 'the king of Taxila', this is to say that Alexander recognized his kingship. Mophis is elsewhere called 'Omphis'. Taxila was the country around Rawalpindi.

87.3 *the Indians*: Diodorus' account of Alexander's clash with Porus is brief and should be supplemented by Arrian, *The Expedition of Alexander* 5.8–19. Porus was the king of Pauravas, an ancient kingdom to the north-east of Mathura. Its exact location is unknown, however, because the rivers of the Punjab have altered their courses over the centuries.

89.5 *the Ocean*: the legendary river that surrounded all the land-masses of the earth. Here it presumably refers to what we call the Bay of Bengal.

90.1 *exceptionally long*: probably pythons.

90.2 *this is what the hunters do*: on these imitative apes, see also Aelian, *On Animals* 17.25.

90.4 *Sasibisares*: this 'Sasibisares' is the 'Embisarus' of 17.87.2. In fact, as we know from elsewhere, the man's name was Abisares. Either Diodorus has made two mistakes, or the text has become corrupt in both places, and Diodorus did originally write 'Abisares'. He was the king of what is now western Kashmir.

90.5 *overshadowed three plethra of ground*: this is perhaps a reference to the banyan tree, famous for its shade. See Theophrastus, *Enquiry into Plants* 4.4.4.

90.7 *antidote*: perhaps the root of *Hemidesmus indicus*, which clinical tests have shown to significantly reduce the effects of snake bites on rats.

91.1 *the Gandaridae*: Porus fled because Alexander supported one of his rivals, but he had already surrendered to Alexander, so Alexander treated his flight as defection. The Gandaridae (or 'Gangaridae') lived to the south: 17.93.2–4.

91.2 *the Cathaeans*: they probably lived around modern Sialkot. It is not clear who the Adrestae were, but they were presumably neighbours of the Cathaeans.

91.3 *poisoned her husband*: the practice of *sati* (or *suttee*) of course became very widespread in India, until being outlawed in 1987. See also 19.33.3 on *sati*.

91.7 *received it back again*: as a vassal king, clearly—and possibly even a vassal to the friendly Porus, who along with Taxiles would emerge as Alexander's chief proxies in India. It is not clear who Sopeithes is or quite where his kingdom was.

93.1 *the Hyphasis river*: the five rivers of the Punjab (which means 'land of five rivers') are the Chenab, the Jhelum, the Ravi, the Sutlej, and the Beas—respectively, to the Greeks, the Acesines, the Hydaspes, the Hydraotes, the Zadadrus, and the Hyphasis. As Alexander retraces his steps from the Hyphasis, Diodorus mentions only the Acesines and the Hydaspes.

93.2 *a desert*: the Thar desert. Phegeus is otherwise unknown.

93.2 *the Gandaridae*: their exact location is unknown, as is that of the Tabraesi.

93.4 *dominion over the whole world*: Ammon had also called him invincible (17.51.3). The story about the Pythia is not in Diodorus, but can be found in Plutarch, *Alexander* 14.4.

94.2 *worn thin by non-stop travel*: it is not clear when and where horseshoes were invented, but the Greeks did not have them yet.

94.3 *storms for seventy days*: it was the monsoon season.

94.5 *he abandoned the plan*: other Alexander historians make much more of this, with a full-scale mutiny by the troops, and Alexander trying to win them over and failing. See Arrian, *The Expedition of Alexander* 5.25–9; Curtius, *History of Alexander* 9.2–3.19; Plutarch, *Alexander* 62. It makes a great deal of difference: were the troops Alexander's passive tools, or were they a force to be reckoned with in the army? See Roisman, *Alexander's Veterans*, 31–40.

95.1 *the twelve gods*: see the note to 16.92.5.

95.5 *in the battle with Porus*: according to Plutarch (*Alexander* 61, though he seems rather hesitant about the story), Alexander also named a city after

his favourite hound. Nicaea and Bucephala are the two cities also mentioned at 17.89.6, but there they were said to be founded by a different
river, the Hydaspes.

96.1 *the southern Ocean*: the Arabian Gulf.

96.1 *led by Craterus and Hephaestion*: Alexander's two most senior officers
had fallen out, and they marched on opposite sides of the river.

96.2 *the rock*: see 17.85 for the Rock of Aornus and Heracles' expedition. The
name 'Sibi' might be related to the god Siva. See the *Barrington Atlas of
the Greek and Roman World* (Princeton: Princeton University Press,
2000), 6, for the rough location of these and the other peoples mentioned by Diodorus.

96.2 *as kin*: the Argeads, the ruling house of Macedon, claimed descent from
Heracles.

97.1 *the Indus*: actually, the confluence with the Indus is much further south;
this was just the confluence of the Acesines and the Hydaspes, as Arrian
says (*The Expedition of Alexander* 6.4.4).

97.2 *danger of capsizing*: Plutarch agrees that Alexander could not swim
(*Alexander* 58.4).

97.3 *just as Achilles had*: *Iliad* 21.212–382 is an account of a monumental battle between Achilles and the river Scamander.

99.4 *Alexander was saved*: this famous story attracted many falsifications
which Arrian (*The Expedition of Alexander* 6.11) set out to correct.

99.6 *after Alexander's death*: Diodorus here conflates two Bactrian rebellions.
The three thousand may have got safely home—Curtius suggests they
did: *History of Alexander* 9.7.11—and the later rebellion after Alexander's
death, involving twenty thousand, was the one that was massacred: 18.4.8,
18.7.1–9.

100.2 *the most notable games*: the four 'crown games' (where crowns and prestige were won, not cash prizes) were the Olympic, Pythian, Isthmian,
and Nemean games. Dioxippus was a boxer and pancratiast, and in what
follows uses his skill at pancration (similar to today's Mixed Martial
Arts) to defeat his opponent.

100.4 *the Greeks were on Dioxippus' side*: this incident should not be generalized
into evidence of deep-seated hostility within Alexander's army between
Macedonians and Greeks. They naturally supported their own men in
this contest, and Alexander's subsequent hostility towards Dioxippus
probably had much more to do with the fact that he had shamed
a Macedonian in front of Indian and Iranian dignitaries. On the Greek–
Macedonian dynamic within the army, see Anson, *Eumenes of Cardia*.

102.2 *democracies*: this probably means no more than that they had no king.

102.4 *worship as a hero*: in Greek culture, no one could be worshipped as
a hero until after his death. Diodorus is presumably trying to say that
they worshipped him as more than human—as a *deva* perhaps.

102.4 *the Sodrae*: neither the Sodrae nor the Massani can be further identified.

102.4 *settlers ... to inhabit it*: the settlers were probably a mixture of native Indians and a few of Alexander's soldiers.

102.7 *Brahmans*: the word is reminiscent of the Brahmins, the highest, priestly caste of Hindu society. As for Sambus, *Sambhu* is one of the titles of the god Siva.

103.1 *Harmatelia*: the identification of this town is uncertain. But see P. Eggermont, *Alexander's Campaigns in Sind and Baluchistan, and the Siege of the Brahmin Town of Harmatelia* (Leuven: Peeters, 1975).

103.6 *a great favourite of Alexander's*: Diodorus is clearly drawing here on an account favourable to Ptolemy, perhaps the future king's own history of the expedition and his part in it. In fact, Ptolemy was not yet that prominent in the expedition. It was only about now, and especially in India, that Alexander began to entrust him with major commands.

103.8 *ground it up*: a very similar story was told of the fifth-century Athenian statesman Pericles: see Plutarch, *Pericles* 13.8.

104.1 *two islands that he found there*: the two islands were probably Cilluta and Aban Shah.

104.1 *to Tethys and to Ocean*: in mythology, Tethys and Ocean were Titans, sister and brother, and also wife and husband.

104.1 *Patala*: the town is probably modern Thatta.

104.3 *take note of everything they saw*: exploration, and scientific and anthropological research, were always two of Alexander's goals, and intellectuals of all stripes accompanied the expedition. Nearchus wrote an account of his voyage, which is lost, but Arrian drew on it for his *Indica*.

104.4 *Abritae*: that is, the Arabitae, living on the east bank of the Arabis river (the modern Hab), while the Oreitae lived on its west bank.

104.8 *Alexandria*: on this city, see Fraser, *Cities*, 164–8. It was not by the sea, as Diodorus has it; the coastal foundation was no more than a depot.

105.5 *the creatures' scales*: if these 'monstrous sea-creatures' are whales, as seems likely, whales do not have scales. Perhaps they used sections of whale skin. Shark scales are small.

105.7 *laden with food and other supplies*: an implausible story (though repeated by others, with the exception of Arrian), because he needed food immediately, not in the future, and Parthyaea, Drangiana, and Areia are a long way from Carmania.

106.1 *celebrations*: Arrian dismissed this story (*The Expedition of Alexander* 6.28), but it is probably largely true.

106.4 *Salmous*: better known as Harmozia (modern Hormuz).

106.6 *sizeable islands*: mud banks or sand banks, presumably, and perhaps colonized by mangroves, as is common along this coastline.

106.6 *a large number of unbelievably enormous sea-creatures*: probably a large school of whales.

107.1 *Caranus*: the other Alexander historians call him Calanus, and that is perhaps what we should read here.

107.6 *Hephaestion's wife*: fulfilling the promise of 17.38.1.

107.6 *Persian women from the most noble families*: this was a famous occasion. About ninety of Alexander's senior staff took eastern wives, and Alexander took two further wives. In addition to Stateira, he also married Parysatis, a daughter of Artaxerxes III. The intention was to signal the end of warfare and the start of peace, but also perhaps to create a future mixed-blood master race to rule the empire. Many of the Macedonians resented this forced marriage and, subsequently, the only truly multicultural court was that of the Seleucids.

108.3 *the Ganges river*: Diodorus means the Hyphasis: 17.83–4.

108.3 *counterweight to the Macedonian phalanx*: there was at least one other reason: the young men were hostages for their fathers' good behaviour.

108.4 *the Red Sea*: to the Greeks, this meant either what we still call the Red Sea, or what we call the Persian or Arabian Gulf.

108.5 *tomb for her in Attica*: on the tomb, see Plutarch, *Phocion* 22.

108.6 *a bolt-hole there*: he was awarded honorary Athenian citizenship for his benefactions to the city.

108.6 *left Asia*: this was not the first time Harpalus had fled. In 333 he had absconded with some money, but he was pardoned by Alexander and reinstated as Imperial Treasurer in 331.

108.7 *Cape Taenarum in Laconia*: Taenarum in these years was a huge mercenary camp, under the authority of Sparta, and a place where recruiters were certain to find large numbers of professional soldiers.

108.7 *Olympias demanded his extradition*: this is an important indication that Olympias, despite being a woman, was able to play a part in international politics. Royal Macedonian women with enough spirit could break out of their confining moulds to a certain extent. See Carney, *Women and Monarchy* (on royal women in general) and *Olympias* (on Olympias in particular).

109.1 *When the Olympic festival was held*: this is the Olympic festival of 324, mentioned now because Diodorus is giving the context of the proclamation Alexander ordered to be read out then—the context being Harpalus' removal of six thousand mercenaries to a footloose existence in Greece, as mentioned in the previous chapter (17.108.7), and the general alteration of the ethnic make-up of Alexander's forces, which involved the dismissal of his mercenaries as well (17.106.3, 17.111.1). For more on the Exiles Decree and its importance, see 18.8.

110.2 *twenty thousand Persian archers and slingers*: Peucestas had been rewarded for saving Alexander's life (17.99.4) by being made satrap of Persis.

110.2 *the kind of integrated army that he aimed to have*: army units were usually segregated along ethnic lines.

110.3 *left Susa*: Diodorus (and Curtius) have Alexander still in Susa for the 'mutiny' of the end of 17.109, but Arrian places it in Opis, near Babylon, a few weeks later.

110.3 *the Carian Villages*: actually, the Carian Villages (mentioned also at 19.12.1) were located to the east of the Tigris, not the west. They were probably named after a population that had been removed by some Persian king from Caria to Babylonia, perhaps the Milesians mentioned by Herodotus at *Histories* 6.20.

110.4 *uprooted during Xerxes' expedition to Greece*: in 480–479. These are presumably the Eretrians mentioned by Herodotus, *Histories* 6.119. See also the note to 17.69.3.

110.5 *Bagistana*: south-west of Ecbatana, Bagistana is better known as Behistun (or Bisutun), famous for the giant inscription and carvings commissioned by Darius I around 500 BCE, celebrating his victories and warning against future rebellions in the empire. The inscription overlooked one of the main caravan routes, so it was widely seen and known.

110.7 *sixty thousand*: these were the famous Nysaean horses of Media, which were generally the largest and strongest breed in the known world at the time.

111.1 *the so-called Lamian War*: for Diodorus' narrative of the war, see 18.9–18.

111.1 *Cape Taenarum in Laconia*: see the first note to 17.108.7.

111.3 *the Aetolians ... were no friends of Alexander*: largely because of the Exiles Decree, which was also the chief cause of Athenian alarm. The Aetolians had taken over the Acarnanian port of Oeniadae, and by the terms of the decree they would lose it. The Athenians had occupied the island of Samos for decades, and the prospect of the eviction of their citizens from the island by the returning Samian exiles—let alone the loss of this strategic and fertile island—was what drove them to war.

111.4 *mountains of Media*: modern Khuzestan.

112.2 *observation of the stars*: Diodorus has a nice digression on the Chaldaeans at 2.29–31.

112.3 *the tomb of Bel*: Bel, 'Lord', was a title of the god Marduk, the guardian deity of Babylon. Arrian (*The Expedition of Alexander* 3.16.4) has Alexander rebuilding the temple during his first visit to Babylon (17.63–5).

112.3 *Belephantes*: 'he who speaks for Bel'.

112.5 *arguments drawn from philosophical texts*: the gist of the arguments were 'what was subject to fate was beyond the knowledge of mortals, and what was due to nature could not be changed' (Justin, *Epitome of the Philippic History of Pompeius Trogus* 12.13.5).

112.6 *the words of the philosophers*: Diodorus forcefully presents Greek philo-sophical rationalism as superior to Babylonian superstition, despite the fact that in this case the Greeks were wrong and the Babylonians right. Alexander changes his mind back again at 17.116.4.

113.1 *Agesias*: more properly, Hegesias.

113.2 *the Libyphoenicians*: see 20.55.4.

113.2 *the Pillars of Heracles*: the Straits of Gibraltar.

113.2 *the first time that Greeks had ever come across Celts*: several Celtic tribes lived around the Danube, and were therefore neighbours of the Thracians, and the Greeks had certainly come across them before. The Celts they had no experience of were those from Gaul. But would the Gallic Celts have sent ambassadors to Alexander? It seems unlikely. At *The Expedition of Alexander* 17.15.4–6 Arrian reports that the Etruscans sent an embassy to Alexander—and, though he doubts the story, the Romans.

113.3 *protesting the return of the exiles*: see the notes to 17.109.1, 17.111.3, and 18.8.2.

113.4 *according to the importance of the sanctuary*: the sanctuaries were, in order: Olympia, which was managed by the Eleans; the Ammon oracular shrine; Delphi; the sanctuary of Poseidon on the isthmus of Corinth; and the sanctuary of Asclepius at Epidaurus.

114.1 *preferred him to all his other Friends*: for some years before his death, Hephaestion had been Alexander's chiliarch, the second-in-command of the kingdom. Perdiccas now succeeded to this post.

114.2 *He is Alexander too*: the story is repeated from 17.37.5–6, perhaps because to identify Hephaestion and Alexander at this point makes Hephaestion's death and funeral a foretaste of what was about to happen to Alexander.

114.3 *no one greater than Alexander*: meaning, I suppose, that Olympias' enmity would always be outweighed by the fact that Alexander loved him. The use of the royal or authorial 'we' in the letter is odd; the letter is almost certainly spurious, although some kind of rivalry between Olympias and Hephaestion is plausible within the rivalrous court of Alexander.

115.1 *tore down a ten-stade stretch of the city wall*: it seems unlikely that he actually demolished a stretch of wall. He probably just removed the brick facing, for reuse as the foundation of the pyre. Remnants of this foundation, consisting of bricks piled up to more than seven metres, have been discovered by archaeologists. For help with understanding Diodorus' description of the pyre, see P. McKechnie, 'Diodorus Siculus and Hephaestion's Pyre', *Classical Quarterly* 45 (1995), 418–32.

115.4 *a centauromachy rendered in gold*: the battle between humans and cen-taurs was commonly used to symbolize the war between Greeks/Macedonians and Persians, suitable for Hephaestion's pyre. For the relevance of each level of ornamentation to Hephaestion, see O. Palagia, 'Hephaestion's Pyre and the Royal Hunt of Alexander', in A. B. Bosworth and E. Baynham (eds), *Alexander the Great in Fact and Fiction* (Oxford: Oxford University Press, 2000), 167–206.

115.6 *an adjunct deity*: adjunct to Alexander, presumably.

115.6 *as a god*: as a hero, according to Arrian, *The Expedition of Alexander* 7.23.6, which sounds more plausible. See also Plutarch, *Alexander* 72.3.

116.4 *that is what Alexander did*: if we ignore the element of the man's miraculous escape from prison, this is close to being a story of the sacrifice of a scapegoat, killed in order to avert danger from the king. Scapegoats were often drawn from condemned criminals.

117.4 *his foremost Friends*: see also 18.1.4. These 'games' are the wars that the Successors fought among themselves for the right to possess at least some of Alexander's empire. They are the subject of Books 18–20. But the tale of Alexander's last words is fiction; one of the main symptoms of his ailment was that he could not speak. He may have died from a ruptured oesophagus (Boerhaave's Syndrome), which can follow heavy drinking.

118.1 *fallen out with Olympias*: the precise reasons are not known. As a native Epirote, Olympias returned to Epirus (18.49.4).

118.1 *obedient to the gods' commandments*: the Greeks believed that care and respect for one's parents were religious duties.

118.1 *the king's cup-bearer*: the son's name was Iollas (or Iolaus). In Athens, the rumour of poisoning was taken seriously, and it was proposed that Iollas should be honoured for having killed the king. And later Olympias disturbed Iollas' tomb, in alleged revenge for the poisoning (19.11.8). However, the rumour is unlikely to be true, because if there had been a plot to murder Alexander, the killers would have been more organized. The chaos that followed Alexander's death suggests that no such plot existed.

118.2 *murdered Olympias...refounded Thebes*: respectively 19.51 and 19.53.2.

BOOK 18

1.2 *telling Achilles about his impending death*: Homer, *Iliad* 22.355–60.

1.4 *a memorable contest among my Friends*: see also 17.117.4.

2.1 *Decius Junius*: full names of Roman consuls mentioned by Diodorus, and corrections to his versions of their names, can be found in Appendix 2 (pp. 543–9).

2.1 *a major bone of contention*: Diodorus omits much of the negotiation and conflict that followed Alexander's death. See Bosworth, *Legacy*, 29–63; Meeus, 'Power Struggle'; Roisman, *Alexander's Veterans*, 61–86.

2.2 *Arrhidaeus...to become king*: it is impossible to be certain what was wrong with Arrhidaeus, Alexander's older half-brother. He could function fairly well, but was liable to embarrassing displays of emotion in public (e.g. Plutarch, *Phocion* 33). Might he have been autistic?

2.2 *Bodyguards*: there were seven Bodyguards and they were all in Babylon: Aristonous, Leonnatus, Lysimachus, Pithon, Perdiccas, Peucestas, and Ptolemy.

2.4 *men of noble principles present*: the most prominent was Eumenes of Cardia (Plutarch, *Eumenes* 3).

2.4 *under the name of Philip*: he became, in our terms, Philip III of Macedon. It is a powerful testament to the hold the Argead house had on the hearts and minds of Macedonians that they would choose Argead kings even when they were not fully competent.

2.4 *Perdiccas...seal ring*: 17.117.3.

2.4 *custodian of the kingdom*: Diodorus' wording is vague, and the word translated 'kingdom' can equally mean 'kingship'. Perdiccas became the guardian or curator or custodian or manager of the kings, with the right to take decisions in their names and to command the royal army. It is not clear whether this was an official title—Custodian of the Kings—or whether Diodorus is using the words more loosely. He fails to mention the birth of Alexander IV to Rhoxane a few months later, and also makes no mention at this point of Alexander's son Heracles, by his mistress Barsine.

3.1 *no opportunity to invade them*: actually, the Paphlagonian tribes had submitted to Alexander, but they had soon rebelled.

3.1 *Asander*: the manuscripts have 'Cassander' here and on every other occasion when it should be 'Asander' (18.39.6, 19.62.2, 19.62.5, 19.68.5, and 19.75.1). In fact, Diodorus probably originally wrote 'Asander' (see the seventh note to 18.39.6, and the note to 19.68.5), which would make 'Cassander' in all these places a scribal error. It is an error that occurs in other historians as well (e.g. Justin, *Epitome of the Philippic History of Pompeius Trogus* 13.4.15).

3.1 *Menander*: Diodorus or a scribe mistakenly wrote 'Meleager'.

3.2 *Lysimachus...Black Sea coast*: there is little about Lysimachus in the surviving portions of Diodorus' history. In general, Lysimachus and Ptolemy appear in the narrative only when their history coincides with that of Eumenes, Antigonus, or Demetrius (who were the chief focuses of Diodorus' source, Hieronymus of Cardia). In the years immediately following Alexander's death, Lysimachus was trying to pacify his satrapy, and tended to stay aloof from the earlier wars of the Successors which drew historians' attention.

3.3 *Pithon*: see 18.39.1–2: this Pithon, the satrap of India, was the son of Agenor; he is not Pithon the son of Cratevas and satrap of Media.

3.3 *the Caucasus*: see the first note to 17.83.1.

3.3 *Media to Atropates*: Atropates received the north-western portion of Media, known as Lesser Media, which soon became independent and was ruled by his descendants for a long time (and hence became known as Media Atropatene). The rest of Media, Greater Media, was given to Pithon, the son of Cratevas.

3.3 *Arrhidaeus*: a different Arrhidaeus, not the one who has just become King Philip III. On the city of Ammon, and its temple, see 17.49–51. On Arrhidaeus' bier, see 18.26–8.

4.1 *discharged soldiers*: see 17.109.1.

4.4 *as follows*: not every scholar accepts the authenticity of these famous Last Plans of Alexander, for which Diodorus is our main source. They are of course astonishing—especially the dream of a Mediterranean empire—but Alexander never did things by halves.

4.4 *the Pillars of Heracles*: the Straits of Gibraltar.

4.5 *Delos, Delphi, and Dodona*: the three most sacred sites of Greece; the first two were sacred to Apollo, the third to Zeus.

4.5 *the Seven Wonders of the World*: the ancient list varied somewhat, but a common version was: the hanging gardens of Babylon, the lighthouse of Alexandria, the Colossus of Rhodes, Pheidias' statue of Zeus in Olympia, the Great Pyramid of Giza in Egypt, the Mausoleum of Halicarnassus, and the temple of Artemis at Ephesus.

4.7 *Meleager on the charge of having plotted against him*: the elimination of Meleager must surely have taken place before the assignment of satrapies, as all our other sources have it.

4.8 *put them down by force*: see 17.99.5–6, with the note.

5.2 *one continuous range of mountains*: the 'Caucasus' here is the Hindu Kush.

5.3 *Red Sea*: as often, this must be the Persian Gulf. Diodorus' description of the other seas is hardly clear, but he must mean respectively the Arabian Gulf and the Bay of Bengal (which has also just been called simply 'the eastern Ocean'), where the Ocean is apparently conceived of as running directly alongside the coast. Diodorus gives a description of the geography of India, as he understands it, at 2.35–7.

5.4 *those that face south*: see Map F for the satrapies of the former Persian empire.

5.4 *Tanais river*: the Tanais is what we call the Don, but the Greeks often confused the Oxus and even the Jaxartes rivers with the Don; here the Oxus is meant.

5.4 *a distinct body of water*: that is, it is an inland sea, according to Diodorus, not an inlet of the Ocean, as some geographers thought. Hyrcania was wrapped around the south-eastern coastline of the Caspian Sea.

6.1 *the great many war elephants they had*: four thousand, according to 17.93.2. See also 2.37.

6.2 *five rivers*: Diodorus is talking about the Punjab, which means 'five rivers'.

6.3 *two rivers… which have given the satrapy its name*: 'Mesopotamia' means 'the land between the rivers'.

6.3 *Coele Syria, which includes Phoenicia*: 'Coele Syria' is a slightly vague term in the Greek writers. To Diodorus, it seems to mean much of

Lebanon, while the northern part, around the mouth and lower reaches of the Orontes, he calls Upper Syria.

7.5 *the spoils among his men*: this twist to the tale is deeply suspect. If Perdiccas knew that Pithon was planning to set himself up as king of the upper satrapies, he would have killed him, or at least not trusted him with this mission. Pithon must in fact have acted as a loyal satrap on this occasion, and the story of his ambitions became grafted on at a later date, after he had indeed tried to make himself master of the upper satrapies in 319 (on which see 19.14.1–4).

8.1 *the Rhodians*: they had submitted to Alexander in 332. For Rhodes in the Early Hellenistic period, see R. Berthold, *Rhodes in the Hellenistic Age* (Ithaca: Cornell University Press, 1984).

8.2 *restored to their homelands*: on the notorious Exiles Decree, see Bosworth, *Conquest and Empire*, 220–8. The Exiles Decree was notorious because Alexander did not have the right just to issue a fiat about such a matter, without going through the League of Corinth. It was bound to cause states a great deal of political and economic turmoil, because many of the exiles had been banished for political reasons, and their land had been confiscated and resold. Their return would raise the whole question of the legality of their banishment in the first place. Could Alexander conceivably have been trying to stir up trouble in Greece, to give himself an excuse for interference and the imposition of direct rule? A long inscription survives from Tegea (Rhodes/Osborne, no. 101; Harding, no. 122) that shows the kinds of moves states had to make to re-incorporate their exiles.

8.3 *the victorious herald*: the ancient Olympic games always included more than athletic contests. One competition pitted heralds or town-criers against one another, to see who had the loudest and clearest voice. The winner was used to make announcements at the festival. Nicanor's visit took place during the Olympics of 324. Nicanor may be the nephew of the philosopher Aristotle, who (unmentioned by Diodorus) was the tutor of Alexander the Great.

8.7 *cleruchy*: see the second note to 16.34.4.

9.1 *in the previous book*: see 17.108.4–8.

9.1 *Cape Taenarum in the Peloponnese*: see 17.106.3 and 17.111.1–2.

9.2 *Leosthenes would not appear . . . to constitute any kind of threat*: presumably, then, Leosthenes was not yet an official Athenian general, though he was appointed in time for the war.

10.2 *the other three tribes*: for administrative and military purposes, all Athenian citizens were divided up among ten tribes.

10.3 *the common homeland of the Greeks*: this sounds obvious to the modern ear, but in fact 'Greece' was made up of hundreds of individual states, great and small, who, so far from treating one another as kin, were often at war. The idea that all Greece was the homeland of the Greeks (rather than, say, Athens being the homeland of the Athenians, Corinth of the Corinthians, and so on) was scarcely possible in the fourth century, and was the view of only a few statesmen and thinkers.

10.3 *the barbarians*: a reference to the Persian invasion of 480–479.

10.4 *Theban catastrophe*: see 17.8–14.

10.5 *confederacy... individual city-states*: see the first note to 16.29.1.

11.1 *Arhyptaeus*: this should probably be Arybbas, the uncle of Olympias—the same man as the 'Arymbas' of 16.72.1. He had been in exile, but had returned and reclaimed the throne. He was soon to die, however, and was succeeded by Aeacides, who is king by the time we reach 19.11.2.

11.2 *the Headland*: the eastern peninsula of Argolis was commonly referred to as just 'the Headland'. It turned out that most of the Peloponnesian contingents were unable to reach the battlefield because of the strong Macedonian garrison in Corinth.

11.3 *had to pass through Boeotia*: because, as we find out shortly, Leosthenes was at Thermopylae, where he planned to meet the Macedonian army.

12.1 *Philotas*: this is a mistake for 'Leonnatus'.

12.1 *one of his daughters in marriage*: this form of 'bedroom diplomacy' was widely practised by the Successors, in their desperate search for alliances that would give them an edge over their rivals.

12.4 *Lamia*: Antipater may have retreated to Lamia for safety, but his possession of the town also prevented Leosthenes from leaving Antipater's forces in his rear and launching a direct assault on Macedon itself.

13.2 *some internal business*: we have no idea what this 'internal business' was: an invasion by the Acarnanians, who were often enemies of the Aetolians? Their annual assembly and elections? In any case, as light-armed troops, the Aetolians were less necessary for a siege.

13.5 *the funeral eulogy*: the speech survives, even if not in its entirety, and is traditionally numbered the sixth of Hypereides' extant speeches.

13.6 *Demosthenes... was in exile at the time*: see 17.108.8.

14.1 *In Asia... Egypt*: Egypt was considered part of Asia by some geographers, part of Africa by others.

14.1 *he inherited*: the money had been raised by Cleomenes, a high official in Alexander's Egypt. Ptolemy's killing of Cleomenes was one of the things that had irritated Perdiccas. It casts doubt on Diodorus' assertion that Ptolemy took over Egypt 'without any trouble'.

14.4 *the final struggle*: we hear no more of this, and rather than fighting, Seuthes and Lysimachus seem to have reached a modus vivendi (sealed by Lysimachus' marriage to an Odrysian princess), since archaeological evidence shows that Seuthes' main town, Seuthopolis, flourished despite Lysimachus' presence.

14.4 *Hecataeus*: the tyrant of Cardia.

14.5 *Macedonians in large numbers for his army*: this is a bit surprising, given that we were told in 18.12.2 that Macedon was short of men of military age. More likely, most of Leonnatus' troops were those assigned him by Perdiccas for the purpose of installing Eumenes in Cappadocia (an order which is not mentioned by Diodorus). But instead of using them for this purpose, Leonnatus took them to Greece. Antigonus too was supposed to help Eumenes, but refused, leading to a total rift between him and Perdiccas (18.23.4). On the draining of the Macedonian population of men of military age, see (controversially) Bosworth, *Legacy*, 64–97.

15.1 *Meliteia*: a town north of Lamia, in Achaea Phthiotis.

15.3 *back to the baggage train*: so Leonnatus' great hopes came to nothing. Olympias had offered him her daughter Cleopatra as his wife, which would have been a route to the Macedonian throne. He was related to the royal house anyway, and had long affected a number of mannerisms and extravagances that spoke of royal pretensions.

15.9 *the Echinades*: these islands are off Acarnania, and near Oeniadae, which may well have been a scene of conflict (18.8.6). But is Diodorus talking about two engagements, both near the Echinades, in which Athenian losses were heavy, or three engagements, two elsewhere (presumably in the Aegean) and one off the Echinades? Discussion by A. B. Bosworth, 'Why Did Athens Lose the Lamian War?', in O. Palagia and S. Tracy (eds), *The Macedonians in Athens, 322–229 BC* (Oxford: Oxbow, 2003), 14–22, and by G. Wrightson, 'The Naval Battles of 322 BCE', in Hauben and Meeus (eds), *The Age of the Successors*, 517–35. Diodorus' focus on the land war has caused him to neglect the war at sea, which was arguably decisive.

16.2 *met in battle*: it took two battles for Perdiccas to defeat Ariarathes (Arrian, *After Alexander* F 1.11 Roos/Wirth).

16.3 *impaled*: in Achaemenid times, this had been the usual penalty for rebels against the Persian throne, so Perdiccas was taking a leaf from the Persian book. But at 31.19 Diodorus says that Ariarathes died in battle.

16.3 *Eumenes of Cardia, to whom it had originally been assigned*: Eumenes clearly did not have enough forces of his own to secure his satrapy, so Perdiccas had to help. Originally, Antigonus and Leonnatus had been supposed to help install Eumenes (see the note to 18.14.5). After the battle of Ipsus in 301, Ariarathes' son, Ariarathes II, recovered his kingdom with the help of the Armenian king. He later became a vassal king of Seleucus, a position he passed on to his successors.

16.4 *crossed from Europe into Asia*: he had ten thousand or so with him in Cilicia (17.109.1, 18.4.1), so, in a change of plan, he left four thousand of these veterans behind. They included the 3,000 Silver Shields, whom we will meet in 18.58–63. The 'four thousand added in the course of the march' were mercenaries.

16.5 *by the river Peneus*: near the town of Crannon, after which the following battle is usually named.

18.1 *against Athens*: Demosthenes and other anti-Macedonian politicians left the city, but they were hunted down. Demosthenes committed suicide.

18.1 *sue for peace*: on Demades' usefulness as an ambassador to Macedon, see 16.87 and 17.15.3–5.

18.4 *he changed the constitution from democracy*: the democracy was renewed later, more than once, though in somewhat diluted forms, but essentially this was the end of the great Athenian experiment in democracy, initiated by Cleisthenes almost two hundred years earlier.

18.4 *disruptive and hawkish*: see 18.10.1 for this political division in Athens between rich and poor.

18.5 *more than twenty-two thousand*: some editors emend the text to 'twelve thousand', to bring it into line with Plutarch, *Phocion* 28.7, but the Athenian democratic system could scarcely have functioned with a citizen population of only 21,000 (12,000 plus the 9,000 who remained as citizens), so the higher figure (making a citizen population of 31,000) is more likely to be correct.

18.5 *the laws of Solon*: Solon was popularly regarded as one of the founders of the Athenian democracy, but he actually put in place (this was early in the sixth century) a wealth oligarchy, so the comparison of Athens' new constitution with his is apt.

18.5 *to prevent any sedition*: the garrison was installed on the Munychia hill of Piraeus.

18.6 *the kings*: this is Diodorus' first use of the plural 'kings'—an acknowledgement that Alexander IV had been born and was now joint king with Philip III, both under Perdiccas' guardianship. On Samos, see 18.8.7. The Athenians appealed to Antipater to reverse the Exiles Decree in their case, but the decision was now referred to the kings—that is, to Perdiccas (18.18.9).

18.7 *return to Asia*: Antipater's helping Craterus was an aggressive move against Perdiccas. Unmentioned by Diodorus, Perdiccas had made Craterus joint General in Europe with Antipater, but Craterus was refusing to be confined to Europe, and wanted to return to Asia to make a bid for real power. This decision is firmed up in 18.25.4. For a character sketch of Phila, see 19.59.4–5.

18.8 *good constitutions in place*: Diodorus was writing at a time when the Roman empire depended on the cooperation of the landowning class in all the provinces. So a constitution that favoured landowners was a 'good' one.

18.8 *awarded crowns*: Diodorus makes it sound as though the Lamian War was entirely over, but the Aetolians never surrendered, and were soon to suffer an invasion by Antipater and Craterus: 18.24–5. For the gift of crowns, see the second note to 16.92.1.

19.1 *in their proper sequential order as much as possible*: Diodorus implies that some of the preceding material has been presented out of order. He is probably thinking of the Bactrian rebellion. For this suggestion, and an analysis of Diodorus' reason for not following a strict sequence (because he wanted the Bactrian rebellion to serve as a 'literary overture' to the Lamian War), see Walsh, 'Historical Method'.

19.2   *as I explained in the previous book*: at 17.108.4–8, though there Harpalus was said to have brought six thousand mercenaries with him, not seven thousand.

19.3   *this venture*: in theory, Thibron, a Spartan adventurer, was supposed to be restoring these exiles to Cyrene. In practice, he was intending to make himself master of the city. Since Cyrene was one of the largest and most prosperous Greek cities of the Mediterranean, this was a bold plan.

19.4   *the port*: Cyrene's port was called Apollonia.

21.1   *Cape Taenarum*: see 17.108.7 and 17.111.1 for Taenarum as a temporary mercenary settlement.

21.9   *King Ptolemy*: this is premature, since Ptolemy did not begin to style himself king until 306 or possibly 304 (20.53.3). But he then back-dated his kingship to 323, when he had taken over Egypt.

21.9   *dependencies of the Ptolemaic kingdom*: Ophellas stayed on as the governor of Cyrenaica, and we will meet him again in 20.40–2. Cyrenaica remained a dependency of Egypt (with occasional interruptions) until 96 BCE, when it was taken over by the Romans. Ptolemy at this time also entered into a series of strategic alliances with the kings of the Cypriot cities. Both this and his takeover of Cyrene will have disturbed Perdiccas.

22.1   *satrap and military governor*: he was satrap and military governor of Cilicia, with responsibility, it appears, for Pisidia as well. The point of mentioning that he was both satrap and military governor is that Alexander often separated these two functions, so that each incumbent would act as a counterweight to the other; Balacrus must have been especially trustworthy. The date of his assassination is uncertain.

23.3   *Antipater's hostility*: Perdiccas' brother Alcetas had been advising him to marry Nicaea, while Eumenes was recommending Cleopatra. Eumenes was close to Olympias, and his objective was invariably to secure the future of her grandson, Alexander IV. At this moment in time, Perdiccas seemed the most promising protector of the child.

23.3   *Antigonus got wind of what Perdiccas was up to*: Antigonus' informant was probably Menander, the satrap of Lydia, where Cleopatra was resident, in Sardis.

23.3   *Perdiccas decided to get rid of him*: the chief reason was Antigonus' refusal to obey Perdiccas' order to help establish Eumenes in Cappadocia: Plutarch, *Eumenes* 3.

23.4   *the Athenian ships*: we do not know what Athenian ships these were, or what they were doing in Asia Minor. Perhaps they were taking Athenian cleruchs off Samos and back to Athens.

23.4   *his son Demetrius*: Demetrius would have been about 14 years old. This was the first time he had set foot in Europe.

25.3 *as soon as Perdiccas had married Cleopatra*: in the event, the marriage to Cleopatra never went ahead (see 20.37.4).

25.4 *but on good terms with them*: like Craterus, Ptolemy became a son-in-law of Antipater. Perdiccas had been alarmed by Ptolemy's takeover of Cyrenaica and other signs of independence, but the last straw was yet to come: the hijacking of Alexander's corpse (18.28.3, with note).

26.1 *In this year*: the next two Archon years, heralded by the usual chronographic indicators, do not occur in our text. Normal service resumes at 18.44. See Introduction, p. xxxvii, for the suggestion that there is a largely unsuspected lacuna in the text. Thanks to the lacuna, the entire First War of the Successors has been compressed, making the dating of events down to the Triparadeisus conference (18.39) difficult. Probably Perdiccas' death is to be dated to the late spring of 320 (Athenian year 321/0) and the conference to the late summer of 320 (Athenian year 320/19).

26.3 *and preserving it*: needless to say, the body had already been embalmed. It had taken Arrhidaeus almost two years to complete the carriage.

26.6 *with Ionic capitals*: so it was like a miniature temple, though with a vaulted roof. See the various reconstructions in S. Miller, 'Alexander's Funeral Cart', *Ancient Macedonia* 4 (1986), 401–11.

27.1 *Persian Apple-bearers*: see the first note to 17.59.3.

27.3 *Persian-style wheels revolved*: Persian wheels apparently tended to be larger in diameter, with more solid rims and a greater number of spokes, than Greek wheels.

27.4 *uneven ground*: without being at all certain, I think this means that the rods simply penetrated the floor of the carriage, into the open space of the vault, so that, with nothing to stop the rods rising and falling, the axle system had play.

28.3 *to meet the catafalque*: in Diodorus' version (which coincides with that of Curtius and Justin), Alexander's body was always due to be buried in Ptolemy's territory, and all Ptolemy did was change the destination from Siwa (Ammon) to Alexandria. Arrian, however, implies that the body was due to be buried in Macedon, and has Ptolemy, with Arrhidaeus' connivance, hijack it to Egypt (*After Alexander* F 1.25 Roos/Wirth).

28.3 *the city founded by Alexander*: Alexandria. Pausanias (*Description of Greece* 1.6.3 (second century CE)) has the corpse interred first in Memphis before being moved later to Alexandria, which would have been a building site at the time of the corpse's arrival in Egypt.

29.2 *his skill as a strategist*: actually, Eumenes was relatively untested as a general. He did brilliantly. Diodorus' account of Eumenes is consistently favourable, and is almost certainly derived from Hieronymus of Cardia, a fellow citizen and probably a relative of Eumenes.

29.4 *brought their forces over from Europe*: Eumenes was unable to stop them because, unmentioned by Diodorus, Perdiccas' admiral, who was patrolling the Hellespont, defected. This was Cleitus 'the White', who would duly be rewarded with a satrapy by Antipater (18.39.6), and then fought for Antipater's successor (18.72).

29.4 *Neoptolemus...secretly got in touch with Antipater*: it was probably Antipater who made the first contact: Arrian, *After Alexander* F 1.26 Roos/Wirth. It was not just jealousy that made Neoptolemus loathe Eumenes; earlier, Perdiccas had sent Eumenes to Armenia, to settle affairs where Neoptolemus had failed.

29.5 *Eumenes won the rest of them over to his side*: according to Plutarch (*Eumenes* 5), Eumenes had captured the enemy baggage train, so that must have helped him to persuade the Macedonians to join him.

30.2 *allow them the whole of the enemy's baggage train to plunder*: that is, without him or his officers taking their shares.

32.2 *once he had taken possession of the bodies of the two enemy generals*: we are not told, but he probably wanted to return them to their families, as a diplomatic gesture.

33.1 *At the news of Eumenes' victory...far more daring*: this is directly contradicted by 18.37.1, where the news of Eumenes' victory arrives too late to help Perdiccas. This latter version is more likely.

33.6 *Hypaspists*: see Glossary.

35.6 *river-dwelling creatures*: crocodiles and hippopotami.

36.5 *the Greek rebellion*: see 18.7.

37.4 *Memphis*: Diodorus omits Attalus' unsuccessful attempt to seize the island of Rhodes: Arrian, *After Alexander* F 1.39 Roos/Wirth.

38.1 *their agreement with Perdiccas*: this is the first we have heard of this agreement, but of course it makes sense that Perdiccas and the Aetolians would unite against the common enemy.

38.2 *Amphissa*: the town had been garrisoned by Antipater and the Aetolians did not want to leave this force in their rear when they invaded Thessaly.

38.6 *Polyperchon won*: Polyperchon was generally a better diplomat than general; it seems likely that he put the Acarnanians up to their invasion, so as to give himself a better chance of winning in Thessaly against the Aetolians' mercenaries.

39.1 *Triparadeisus in inland Syria*: a *paradeisos* was an ornamental park and hunting ground for Persian royals and nobles, so Triparadeisus must have been a good place for a summit meeting, the equivalent of the luxury hotels used by today's leaders. It might be the place that later became Baalbek.

39.2 *Queen Eurydice*: this is abrupt, since Diodorus has omitted her marriage to Philip III in 321 (see the note to 19.52.5). Diodorus is slightly inaccurate in calling her queen. It was not until a few decades later that the wife or wives of kings began to be called queens, or at least 'royal women'. Eurydice (whose birth name was Adea) was the daughter of Amyntas (the infant king whose place on the throne was taken by Philip II) and Cynnane, a daughter of Philip II (called 'Cynna' at 19.52.5).

39.4 *frightened Eurydice into quiescence*: Arrian has more on this: *After Alexander*
F 1.30–3 Roos/Wirth. See also Roisman, *Alexander's Veterans*, 136–44.
Money was at the root of the trouble: the Macedonians had not been paid
for a while; and Pithon and Arrhidaeus had promised to consult Eurydice
before doing anything, but then ignored her. Eurydice was still a teenager,
possibly as young as 17. This was not her last bid for power: see 19.11.

39.5 *impossible to remove him anyway*: Ptolemy was not the only one to be
retained in his satrapy: compare the following list with the one in 18.3.

39.6 *Cilicia to Philoxenus*: actually, Philoxenus was already the satrap of Cilicia,
having been installed by Perdiccas to replace Philotas (18.3.1), who was
a friend of Craterus and was therefore removed. Antipater now confirmed
Philoxenus' appointment, which suggests that he had cooperated with
Antipater and won his favour.

39.6 *Arbelitis*: Upper Mesopotamia, named after the town of Arbela, where
the battle of Gaugamela was fought (17.53.3–61.3).

39.6 *Babylonia to Seleucus*: Diodorus gives no reason for the sudden eleva-
tion of Seleucus, but it is possible that he was one of the assassins of
Perdiccas (Cornelius Nepos, *Eumenes* 5.1).

39.6 *Parthyaea to Philip*: but see 19.14.1, where the satrap of Parthyaea is said
to be Philotas. Philip is probably correct.

39.6 *Bactria and Sogdiana . . . Stasanor of Soli*: we would expect a mention of
the reassignment of Arachosia to Sibyrtius at this point. Perhaps it has
dropped out of the text.

39.6 *the north-facing satrapies*: Diodorus is referring to his classification of
the satrapies in 18.5.

39.6 *Caria to Asander*: see the first note to 18.3.1. The mention of Cassander
a few lines later, and his introduction as Antipater's son, makes it likely
that Diodorus originally wrote 'Asander' here—and if here, then elsewhere as well.

39.7 *without Antipater hearing about it*: this judgement about Cassander's
appointment is probably a later accretion; originally, it would have been
seen as a gesture of friendship for Antipater to assign his son to Antigonus.

40.6 *a plain in Cappadocia*: location uncertain.

40.7 *and thirty elephants*: Antigonus' full forces were much larger (18.45.1,
although by then he had also incorporated many of Eumenes' former
soldiers), but he had to leave troops to guard against an attack by Alcetas
from Pisidia.

40.8 *Eumenes' camp*: Apollonides was later captured by Eumenes and executed
(Plutarch, *Eumenes* 9.3). As well as suborning Apollonides, Antigonus
seems also to have tricked Eumenes by having a fake dust-covered messenger run up and tell him (Antigonus) about the arrival of reinforcements, in the hearing of Eumenes' envoys, so that the news would get
back to Eumenes' camp and undermine morale (Polyaenus, *Stratagems in
War* 4.6.19).

41.1 *called Nora instead*: the precise location of this fortress is unknown; it
was on the border of Lycaonia and Cappadocia (Plutarch, *Eumenes* 10).
It might be the fortress later called Neroassus, at modern Gelin Tepe.

41.6 *subsequently*: the negotiations are repeated in a somewhat different form
under the following year (18.50.4), where they more properly belong.
They are summarized for a third time at 18.53.5.

42.1 *History of the Successors*: this work by Hieronymus of Cardia, which no
longer survives, was almost certainly Diodorus' chief source for the
Successor period. Nothing seems to have come of Hieronymus' mission
to Antipater on Eumenes' behalf.

42.2 *his absolutely steadfast loyalty*: it would be nice to think that this statement is ironic, given that within a very few months Eumenes betrayed
his agreement with Antigonus: 18.58.1–2.

43.2 *a brief and effective campaign*: see Appian, *Syrian History* 52 for more
details. This illegal (or at least highly aggressive) campaign was an early
sign of Ptolemy's ambitions.

44.2 *2,500 stades in seven days*: an astonishing rate of about 65 km (40 miles)
a day, suggesting that only cavalry and light troops were involved.

47.3 *unburied*: in the Greco-Macedonian worldview, an unburied man was
unable to enter the underworld and find peace, so it was a common punishment to leave enemies unburied. Mutilation of a corpse by cutting off its
extremities was supposed to stop the dead man taking revenge on his killer.

47.3 *buried it with full honour*: a rock-cut tomb, plausibly identified as that of
Alcetas, exists near the site of ancient Termessus. An internet search
under 'Alcetas tomb' will bring up some images.

48.1 *old age a factor as well*: he was in his seventies; the average age of death
for men at the time was about 45.

48.1 *remove the garrison from Munychia*: see 18.18.5.

48.2 *attack Antipater*: Demades memorably described Antipater as 'the old
and rotten thread' by which Macedonian and Greek affairs were sus-
pended (Plutarch, *Phocion* 30—a slightly different version of this story).

48.4 *Antipater appointed Polyperchon*: formally, of course, the appointment
would have been made in the name of the kings, not by Antipater of his
own accord.

48.5 *chiliarchy... became a very powerful and highly regarded post*: Alexander's
first chiliarch was Hephaestion, and then Perdiccas. On the chiliarch's
responsibilities, see A. Collins, 'The Office of Chiliarch under Alexander
and the Successors', *Phoenix* 55 (2001), 259–83.

49.4 *the custodianship of Alexander's son*: Polyperchon seems to be suggesting
a division of labour, with him remaining guardian of Philip III (if
Eurydice would let him have any influence there), while Olympias was
guardian of Alexander IV. It is curious that Diodorus rarely names
'Alexander's son', preferring such circumlocutions.

50.1 *a large army*: the Royal Army: 18.39.7.

50.2 *the treasuries*: the main Asian treasuries at this time were at Ecbatana, Susa, and Cyinda (somewhere in Cilicia).

50.4 *the stronghold called Nora*: for Nora, see 18.41.1–3, and 18.42.1 for Hieronymus' presence there and his mission. He seems to have been on his way back from Macedon to Nora when Antigonus intercepted him.

51.1 *to install garrisons in the most important cities*: the Greek cities of Asia Minor, like those of Greece, were theoretically independent—located within satrapies, but not part of them. It was therefore an act of war for Arrhidaeus to use force to impose garrisons on them.

51.1 *siege equipment*: Arrhidaeus had first tried to install a friend of his as tyrant in Cyzicus, and attacked the city when that tactic failed.

51.5 *they had control of the sea*: if this was the case, it is unclear how Arrhidaeus expected to exert enough pressure to impose a garrison on them.

52.4 *gain him as an ally*: we hear nothing more of this. Perhaps Eumenes had already been freed from Nora by the time Arrhidaeus' men arrived.

52.7 *to pay his mercenaries*: this theft must have been the final straw for Polyperchon, and a *casus belli*.

53.7 *in the fortress*: there were six hundred in the fortress according to 18.41.3.

53.7 *the appropriate points of the narrative*: 18.57.3–58.2.

54.2 *hunting expeditions*: all this is repeated from 18.49.

54.3 *straight away*: these are the troops of 18.68.1.

55.4 *The resolution was as follows*: on this resolution, see especially E. Poddighe, 'Propaganda Strategies and Political Documents: Philip III's *Diagramma* and the Greeks in 319 BC', in V. Alonso Troncoso and E. Anson (eds), *After Alexander: The Time of the Diadochi (323–281 BC)* (Oxford: Oxbow, 2013), 225–40. It was in effect an invitation to the Greek cities to rise up against their current masters.

56.1 *our throne ... we*: the royal 'we': the decree was clearly written in the name of Philip III, since he was the only one of the two kings who could speak of 'our father Philip'. His name alone was used, probably because he was more acceptable to the Greeks than the mixed-race Alexander IV.

56.3 *our absence far abroad*: Philip III had been in Babylon at the time.

56.3 *the generals*: Antipater and Craterus.

56.4 *politically inspired antagonism*: a very common occurrence, since many exiles had been banished for political reasons, because they were oligarchs trying to undermine a democracy, or vice versa.

56.5 *exiles from ... Heraclea*: we do not know enough to be sure why all these men were excluded from the amnesty. Best guesses: Poddighe (op. cit. in the note to 18.55.4), 234–5. Pharcadon and Tricca were in Thessaly, but Amphissa was in Ozolian Locris, and of the several towns named Heraclea, probably the one by Mount Oeta in central Greece is meant.

56.5 *the thirtieth of Xanthicus*: the sixth month of the Macedonian year, corresponding to March/April. He means 30 Xanthicus 318.

56.6 *as it is at present*: possession of Oropus, a strategic and sacred town on the border between Attica and Boeotia, was frequently disputed between the two parties. Most recently, it had been assigned to Athens by Philip II; it became independent during the Lamian War.

56.7 *our father Philip did*: this reverses the decision taken by Alexander in the Exiles Decree, and confirmed by Antipater, that Samos was to be removed from the Athenians. The mention of Philip II is due to the fact that Athens was allowed to keep Samos in the settlement that followed Chaeronea.

57.2 *inherited his father's kingdom*: this repeats 18.49.4. The lack of mention of Philip III is somewhat sinister; the kingdom is assumed to be destined for Alexander IV. It looks as though there were effectively two rival courts in Macedon, one for each of the kings. Adea Eurydice was the main player in Philip III's court, and Polyperchon was inviting Olympias to come and challenge Eurydice.

59.3 *declared their loyalty and commitment*: despite this, Eumenes' later troubles came from the leaders of the Silver Shields, who were the cream of Alexander's former army and considered themselves almost an autonomous force. For Eumenes' relations with the Silver Shields, see Roisman, *Alexander's Veterans*, 177–236.

59.4 *their own ruling*: it might not have been an official ruling, but just an outburst of hatred by the Macedonian troops in Egypt after the murder of Perdiccas. See 18.37.1–2.

59.6 *the misery of the unfortunate*: this was a commonplace of Hellenistic historiography: see Introduction, p. xxiv.

60.6 *at the head of his kingdom*: the main point of the last two paragraphs is that Eumenes, anxious about the envy of his immediate subordinates (Antigenes and Teutamus, especially), tried to make out that he was not their superior and that they would all be equal before Alexander's royal throne.

61.1 *diadem, sceptre, and...panoply*: like the throne, these were probably replicas of Alexander's regalia, not the originals. The originals had either been deposited in a treasury or incorporated into Alexander's catafalque.

61.1 *fire altar*: an eastern element to the ritual, reflecting the blending of East and West in Alexander's own monarchical style.

62.1 *unanimously condemned to death by the Macedonians*: see the note to 18.59.4.

62.2 *Cyinda*: the location of the fortress of Cyinda in the mountains of Cilicia is unknown. It had been used as a treasury since Assyrian times in the seventh century, and was one of the main treasuries used by the Successors.

62.4 *Philotas, as his agent*: this is probably the Philotas who had originally been assigned the satrapy of Cilicia (18.3.1), but was then removed from his post (18.39.6).

63.6 *all the cities to send him ships*: Phoenicia and Cilicia together had the largest cluster of ports with ship-building as well as harbour facilities, and, with long traditions of seafaring and wealth, every major city there had a good-sized fleet.

64.1 *Nicanor... asked the Athenians to stay loyal to Cassander*: Nicanor was Cassander's man, not Polyperchon's. Pretty much the first thing Cassander had done as chiliarch of Macedon (18.48.4) was replace Menyllus (18.18.5) with Nicanor.

64.3 *the resolution on Greek independence*: the resolution of 18.55–6.

65.1 *Olympias... ordered him to return Munychia and Piraeus to the Athenians*: so Olympias was now openly working against Cassander.

65.1 *Olympias back to Macedon*: see 18.49.4 and 18.57.2.

66.3 *as they pleased*: Polyperchon did not really make it a free choice. Plutarch reports (*Phocion* 34.3) that he got Philip III to write a letter to the Athenians the gist of which was 'that while he had no doubt of the men's treachery, he left it up to them, as free and autonomous agents, to reach a verdict'. In other words, if they were to please Polyperchon, they had to execute Phocion and the others.

67.6 *the traditional method of execution*: the drinking of hemlock was a common form of execution, used for instance on the philosopher Socrates in Athens in 399; it was not a particularly gruesome way to go, and it was held to absolve the community from the pollution of taking a life because it was self-administered and involved no shedding of blood.

67.6 *thrown out unburied beyond the borders of Attica*: the traditional post-mortem punishment of a traitor, and a universal Greek practice, was to deny his body burial, and especially to deny it burial in its homeland. See also 16.16.4.

67.6 *victims of vilification*: Diodorus' anti-democratic bias is clearly on display. See Introduction, p. xiii.

69.2 *Cassander... sailed back to Piraeus*: Cassander returned to Salamis later and took it.

69.3 *an alliance with him*: this looks like an attempt to form the Peloponnesian cities into some kind of league, under Macedonian domination.

72.1 *more pressing matters*: it would have been nice to have been told what these were. For the suggestion that he led a campaign in Asia Minor, see P. Paschidis, 'Missing Years in the Biography of Polyperchon (318/7 and 308 BC Onwards)', *Tekmeria* 9 (2008), 233–50.

72.2 *an enemy of Antigonus*: see 18.51–2.

72.9 *some of Lysimachus' soldiers*: this presumably happened in Thrace, Lysimachus' satrapy. So Lysimachus was cooperating with Cassander and Antigonus, but if there was a formal treaty of any kind in place we know nothing of it. The defeat of Cleitus gave Antigonus control of the sea. Unmentioned by Diodorus, Nicanor next sailed to Cilicia (Polyaenus, *Stratagems in War* 4.6.8–9) and captured Eumenes' fleet.

73.2 *illegally occupied by Ptolemy*: see 18.43.2.

73.3 *by Seleucus*: at 19.12–13, however, Diodorus correctly locates this incident at the Tigris, not the Euphrates.

74.3 *at least ten mnas*: this needs setting in context. Ten mnas (or 1,000 drachmas) was the minimum qualification for citizenship and voting rights, so Athens became an oligarchy—but the previous phase of oligarchy, under Antipater, had (see 18.18) been twice as stringent, since it set the minimum qualification at 2,000 drachmas. Nevertheless, democracy was once again dissolved.

75.2 *ally themselves with Cassander*: we have already been told about this trend at 18.74.1.

75.3 *my original intention*: see 18.1.6.

BOOK 19

1.3 *ostracism*: under the fifth-century democracy, every year the Athenian Assembly had a chance to send a prominent citizen into exile, if he was felt to be a threat to the democracy. A minimum of 6,000 votes had to be cast, in a secret ballot, and of the several candidates for exile, the one with the most votes was sent away for ten years. Votes were cast by inscribing the candidate's name on a shard of broken pottery (the ancient equivalent of a scrap of paper)—an *ostrakon*, hence the name 'ostracism'. The exiled man was not treated as a criminal—he retained his property and his business interests in Athens—but he could not live in Athens or take part in political life. Diodorus makes it sound as though it was a common event, but although the debate took place every year, ostracism was used only fifteen times between 488/7 and 417/16.

1.4 *the following couplet*: the middle two lines of the six-line F 9 West. The full fragment is quoted at 9.20, along with the longer F 11 West. Solon had probably died before Peisistratus first tried to seize power in 560, so he was not predicting that particular tyranny so much as tyranny in general, and indeed there seem to have been attempts to seize power in the 580s, more immediately after Solon's legislation. Alternatively, if the verses do refer to Peisistratus (and F 11 West also seems to), they were probably retrospectively assigned to Solon. A few scholars, however, believe that Solon's work should be dated to the 570s or 560s, and so that he could have been contemporary with Peisistratus. Peisistratus' tyranny began in 546, though he had attempted to make himself tyrant also in 560 and 556.

1.5 *the Romans gained possession of the island*: the Roman takeover of the island was complete by 210.

1.7 *he worked as a potter*: Agathocles' background is not as certain as Diodorus makes out. One of the men sent into exile by Agathocles was the historian Timaeus of Tauromenium (on whom see p. 541). Timaeus naturally gave Agathocles a very poor write-up in his history of Sicily. An impoverished background was a fairly standard sneer against tyrants, and

Diodorus is following the Timaean tradition at this point. Elsewhere, however, he admits that Timaeus' account of Agathocles was strongly biased (21.17). The sneer 'He worked as a potter' could, from the mouth of a member of the landed elite (or of a satiric poet), easily be a deliberate downgrading of 'He owned a chain of pottery workshops.' From time to time, Diodorus cannot help reflecting a different view of Agathocles' background: he claims that in Sicily his father Carcinus of Rhegium was poor—but also that he was prominent enough to 'instruct' the Carthaginians of Therma, and to be concerned about attracting the hostility of the Carthaginians (19.2.3, 19.2.7); Agathocles held a priesthood (20.54.1), and these posts were generally restricted to the rich. See also the note to 19.2.9.

1.7 *the largest and fairest island in the world*: we now know that Sicily is the forty-fifth largest island in the world.

1.7 *Libya*: that is, all of North Africa west of Cyrenaica.

1.8 *this terrible*: actually, earlier Syracusan tyrants raised the bar for savagery very high.

1.10 *after the fall of Troy*: the Greeks came up with many dates for the start of the legendary Trojan War; for historians, the war served as a baseline chronographic marker, so dating it was important to them. Diodorus follows his primary chronographic source, Apollodorus of Athens, who wrote his *Chronicles* in the second century, and was in his turn following third-century Eratosthenes of Cyrene in choosing 1183 BCE as the date of the start of the Trojan War.

1.10 *seven years*: Diodorus is still keen to have each of his books focus on a single individual whenever possible; see the prefaces to Books 16 and 17, especially the former.

2.1 *Fulvius*: full names of Roman consuls mentioned by Diodorus, and corrections to his versions of their names, can be found in Appendix 2 (pp. 543–9).

2.3 *sacred ambassadors*: theōroi were sent by a state to represent them at international religious festivals such as the Pythia at Delphi. It is interesting that, this early, the Carthaginians were sending representatives to a Greek religious festival, but they had already adopted the worship of Demeter and Korē (the chief deities of Sicily), so it is not implausible that they would have wanted to pay their respects at this important religious centre.

2.4 *make sure it died*: exposure was practised throughout the Greek world. Because it involved no direct bloodletting, it was considered a non-polluting way of getting rid of unwanted children. Some—perhaps quite a lot of—abandoned babies were reared in other households as slaves, and Carcinus' guards must have been ordered to make sure that this did not happen.

2.6 *seven years old*: so this would be in 354.

2.8 *Crimisus river*: see 16.79–80. The battle was fought in 341.

2.9 *a dedication*: in honour of her dead husband. Marble statues were not cheap, so again Diodorus slips if he really wants to portray Agathocles' background as poor.

3.1 *replaced him with Agathocles*: Damas would have become Agathocles' lover when the boy was in his mid-teens, many years before Agathocles would have been made a chiliarch. It was typical of Greek homosexual customs that the boy's older lover would later help him gain a start in public life, even if by then the sexual side of their relationship was over. We know nothing more of this war between Syracuse and Acragas, which must have taken place in the early 320s, and was one of the few disturbances to mar the twenty or so years after Timoleon.

3.3 *Sosistratus*: for almost all occurrences of the name 'Sosistratus', one or more MSS have 'Sostratus'. I have gone with 'Sosistratus' throughout, which is the version of Plutarch (*Pyrrhus* 23).

3.3 *in the previous book*: not so: Sicilian affairs play no part in Book 18 at all. Might there be a gap in the manuscripts for Book 18, as for Book 17? See also the note to 19.10.3.

4.3 *sent into exile*: it was probably Agathocles' defeat of the oligarchs at Rhegium which put an end to their regime in Syracuse. The oligarchy had been in power for some years, but now Syracuse became a democracy, with Agathocles in a position of some authority.

5.1 *Some time later*: in the late 320s.

5.1 *Acestoridas of Corinth . . . General in Syracuse*: Plutarch reports (*Timoleon* 38.4) that in recognition of all the good Timoleon had done them, the Syracusans voted always to have a Corinthian as their General at a time of foreign war—i.e. war with the Carthaginians. Hence Acestoridas quietly drops out of the story at the beginning of the next paragraph, where peace is made with the Carthaginians.

5.4 *the Carthaginians as well*: there is a bit more detail of this phase of Agathocles' life in Justin, *Epitome of the Philippic History of Pompeius Trogus* 22.2.

6.1 *Erbita*: the exact position of this town is unknown.

6.4 *the Timoleontium*: a gymnasium named in honour of Timoleon and built around his tomb. Compare Polyaenus, *Stratagems in War* 5.3.8, on this incident.

7.3 *courtyard doors of houses*: a typical Greek house opened from the street into a courtyard, surrounded by a portico with rooms off it.

7.3 *the temple precincts*: where they should have been safe, since all temple precincts were supposed to be inviolable; but Greek history is littered with breaches of this unwritten law. See e.g. 19.63.5.

8.4 *tragic effects . . . in the historians*: Diodorus obviously found his sources going to town over this episode. On the whole Diodorus does avoid rhetorical excesses, but he does occasionally slip in passages that are supposed to set some moving scene directly before the reader's imagination; see Introduction, p. xxvii.

8.5 *the absolute power of their bitterest enemies*: these atrocities tended to occur at the end of every successful siege, but it is surprisingly rare for ancient historians to highlight such an episode. It was, unfortunately, one of those aspects of warfare that they took for granted.

9.2 *himation*: see the note to 16.93.1.

9.5 *to abolish debts and give land to the poor*: this was the usual revolutionary programme in Hellenistic Greece. Compare, for example, the reforms of Cleomenes III of Sparta in the 220s, as reported by Plutarch in his *Cleomenes*.

9.6 *a completely different kind of person*: Polybius too, citing the historical tradition, attributes this sudden change of character to Agathocles (*Histories* 9.23). It may originally have been a way of reconciling two contrary traditions about Agathocles—the bloodthirsty tyrant and the benevolent king. In any case, as Diodorus' account makes plain, he seems to have remained no less savage towards his enemies than he was before.

9.7 *diadem*: see the note to 17.77.5.

10.1 *as they had been for eight years*: a confession by Diodorus that he has been less than meticulous in his recording of Roman history, although, to be fair, not much happened in the first years of the war beyond some skirmishing. Still, Diodorus' omissions should be made up by consulting Books 7–9 of Livy's *History of Rome*. The First Samnite War lasted only from 343 until 341, and ended with a renewal of the treaty of 350 (16.45.8), but this second one went on from 326 to 304 (albeit with a period of uneasy truce from 320 until 316), and a third one was to follow, from 298 to 290, until Rome was finally victorious. The struggle would decide whether it was the Romans or the Samnites who were supreme in Italy.

10.2 *Canusium*: Canusium was a Hellenized city in Apulia, which was being punished for its alliance with the Samnites. The Daunii lived in northern Apulia, just under the spur of Italy.

10.2 *Falerna and Oufentina*: both these tribes were groupings of enfranchised Campanians.

10.3 *in the previous book*: again (see the second note to 19.3.3), this is not so as Book 18 stands. See Introduction, p. xxxvii.

11.1 *return to Macedon*: she had been living in Epirus for seven years: 18.49.4, 18.57.2, 18.58.3–4.

11.1 *Cassander in the Peloponnese*: where he was trying to undo some of Polyperchon's gains (18.69.3–4). Eurydice had recently prevailed upon her husband, Philip III, to depose Polyperchon from his regency of the kings in favour of Cassander, and the king had written around all the Greek cities to that effect.

11.2 *Evia (a Macedonian town)*: the location of Evia is uncertain; it was perhaps in Orestis.

11.7 *the weight of her misfortunes*: later, Philip III and Eurydice were given a proper royal funeral by Cassander: 19.52.5. The relief sculptures of Eurydice's grave have survived: see O. Palagia, 'The Grave Relief of Adea, Daughter of Cassander and Cynnana', in T. Howe and J. Reames (eds), *Macedonian Legacies: Studies in Ancient Macedonian History and Culture in Honor of Eugene N. Borza* (Claremont, CA: Regina, 2008), 195–214.

11.8 *avenging Alexander's death*: for the idea that Alexander was poisoned by Cassander's brother Iollas, see 17.118.1.

11.9 *at the point of death*: see the preface of Book 18.

12.2 *division of the satrapies at Triparadeisus*: 18.39.6.

12.2 *condemned to death by the Macedonians in assembly*: see the note to 18.59.4.

12.5 *wherries*: I use this word in the British sense of large, light, flat-bottomed vessels. Diodorus' word is literally 'a vessel propelled by a pole', but in midstream the river would have been too deep for poles, so they must have had sails as well.

13.2 *wiped out by the flood*: these events were also mentioned prospectively in 18.73.3, though as happening at the Euphrates, not the Tigris.

13.7 *earlier*: see 18.73.4.

14.1 *General of the Upper Satrapies*: it is not clear whether this was an official appointment, or whether Pithon took the position for himself.

14.1 *Philotas, the incumbent satrap of Parthyaea*: see the fourth note to 18.39.6: we should probably read 'Philip' here.

14.4 *Peucestas…for his courage*: he was made a Bodyguard, as well as a satrap, after saving Alexander's life in India: 17.99.4.

14.6 *Polemon…satrap of Carmania*: 'Polemon' is a mistake for 'Tlepolemus'; see 18.3.3, 18.39.6, and 19.28.3.

14.8 *Eudamus came from India*: this Eudamus is not Pithon's brother, mentioned at the start of this chapter. He became satrap of 'India' after Alexander's first satrap, Philip, was murdered.

15.4 *with a throne in it*: see 18.60.4–61.3 for this ruse of Eumenes'.

16.1 *Attalus…Philotas*: see 18.45.

16.4 *handed over to her bodyguard*: Docimus turns up later working for Antigonus: 19.75.3, 20.107.4.

17.1 *Deinomenes*: other sources call him Demosthenes or Deinosthenes. This last name, supported by an inscription found at Olympia, seems to be the correct one.

17.2 *set out against the enemy*: there is an excellent account of the following monumental clash between Antigonus and Eumenes in Iran in Bosworth, *Legacy*, 98–168.

17.3 *Xenophilus…Susa acropolis*: Xenophilus had been appointed by Alexander.

17.3 *the Tigris*: this should be the Pasitigris; see the note to 17.67.1.

17.3 *the Red Sea*: that is, the Persian Gulf. At 17.67.2 Diodorus said that the non-mountainous stretch of the river was 600 stades long.

17.3 *the rising of the Dog Star*: see the note to 17.7.6. Sharks can still be found in the Karun river, the ancient Pasitigris.

18.4 *forage for food*: they were probably light-armed troops, who were commonly used for foraging.

19.1 *Badace... Eulaeus*: the location of the city is unknown, and the identification of the river uncertain. If the Karun is the Pasitigris and the Dez is the Coprates, then the Eulaeus may be either the Shaur or the Karkheh. The river systems in this part of the world have changed a great deal over the centuries.

19.2 *the Royal Road system*: the famous Persian Royal Road ran from Smyrna in western Asia Minor east, and then south-east to Susa, running alongside the east bank of the Tigris. It was created in the fifth century. There were regular staging posts along the way, where horses could be exchanged and food found, and it was said that a courier could do the whole journey of almost 3,000 kilometres in about nine days. We do not know quite where Calon was, though it was presumably near the Zagros mountains.

19.3 *independent since ancient times*: at 17.111.4–6, however, Diodorus told us that Alexander subdued the Cossaeans. Presumably they regained their independence after his death.

21.1 *inland provinces*: Ecbatana was too far north for Antigonus to be able to stop Eumenes returning west and threatening Babylonia and Syria. That is what Eumenes wanted to do, but it would leave the upper satrapies vulnerable to attack by Antigonus from Media.

21.2 *the so-called Ladder*: a literal description: it was a stair-cut pass through the mountains to Persepolis.

22.2 *four concentric circles*: circular banquets had been a feature of the Achaemenid court.

23.2 *drawing near Cappadocia*: it seems that Eumenes' men knew of Olympias' return to Macedon, but not of Cassander's subsequent success against her. But then Diodorus has not yet told us this part of the story; we have only got as far as Olympias' success (19.11.2–9). The rest comes at 19.35–6 and 19.45–51.

23.3 *written in Syrian*: that is, Aramaic, which had been the official language of the Achaemenid empire.

23.3 *Orontes*: the Orontids were hereditary rulers of Armenia, vassal kings of the Persian and then the Macedonian empire. This is Orontes III, who reigned from 321 until 260.

23.4 *condemned to death by the army assembly*: Sibyrtius supplied some troops (19.14.6) and was in the camp, where he was put on trial and from where he escaped. Why was his baggage not in the camp? Perhaps he had sent it on ahead, intending to follow it himself when he could. He must have known that trouble was in the offing. In fact, however, Eumenes never got around to deposing him: at 19.48.3 he is still the satrap of Arachosia.

26.1 *Gabene*: a district of Susiane, called 'Gabiene' by some of the sources, probably around modern Isfahan.

26.3 *that night*: the use of false deserters to convey misinformation was a common tactic. See, in general, F. Russell, *Information Gathering in Classical Greece* (Ann Arbor: University of Michigan Press, 1999).

27.1 *sixty-five elephants*: when Diodorus enumerates Antigonus' units in 19.29, we find a significant discrepancy in the numbers. The infantry numbers add up, but Diodorus makes no mention of Antigonus' light infantry (see 18.73.1), who by now probably numbered around fifteen thousand. Otherwise, he is vague on the elephant numbers, and enumerates far more cavalry than the 8,500 mentioned here.

27.5 *the military settlements of the upper satrapies*: that is, the garrisoned fortresses established especially by Alexander.

28.3 *a slanting formation, divided into four squadrons*: a slanting formation is necessarily stepped (in an echelon formation); here, then, there were four steps.

28.4 *and 114 elephants*: none of the numbers add up. The infantry numbers are way off, but Diodorus has omitted the light infantry—the irregulars, as it were—in Eumenes' army, as he did for Antigonus (see the note to 19.27.1). There must have been eighteen thousand of them. The cavalry numbers are only two hundred off. Diodorus enumerates 125 elephants (five more than Eudamus brought (19.14.8)), but then claims the total was 114. But other than these problems with the numbers, Diodorus' account of the battle of Paraetacene is the best of his battle narratives. It is undoubtedly based on the eyewitness account of Hieronymus of Cardia, and the generally superior battle narratives of Books 18–20 (with statistics, an understanding of terrain, and the times and distances of marches) may be attributed to Hieronymus. Battle descriptions elsewhere tend to be formulaic.

29.2 *loyal to him*: the name 'Tarentine' means 'from Tarentum', the Greek city of southern Italy. But the name was used for cavalrymen armed with a javelin and employing Tarentine tactics, whether or not they were actually from Tarentum. Tarentine tactics involved wheeling and harrying, just like the other light cavalry listed in this paragraph.

29.2 *'two-horsers'*: the tenth-century Byzantine encyclopedia called the *Suda* claims (s.v. *hippikē*) that these cavalrymen rode into battle with an extra horse trailing the one they were riding, so that they could rely on the second one if the first was disabled.

29.3 *given . . . when he had been made custodian of the kingdom*: see 18.39.7.

29.4 *for the first time*: Demetrius was not yet 20 years old.

30.6 *quite elderly*: at 19.41.2 Diodorus says that none of them was younger than 60, which may not be much of an exaggeration. They had served with Alexander since the beginning of his eastern campaigns and many had served Philip before that.

31.3 *beyond dispute*: by military convention, the army in possession of the battlefield at the end was the victor, and the losers indicated their acceptance of defeat by applying for a truce during which they could collect their dead.

32.1 *the collection of their dead*: Polyaenus, *Stratagems in War* 4.6.10, says that he did this so that the herald would not see that Antigonus' losses were greater than those of Eumenes. It also bought time for the wounded and the heavy baggage to get away.

33.4 *the greatest of honours*: Strabo (*Geography* 15.1.30) gives the same bizarre account of the origin of *sati*.

34.7 *Paraetacene*: a large district straddling the border between Media and Persis.

34.8 *uninhabited and waterless desert*: perhaps the large salt plain known as the Kavir desert.

35.1 *Tegea under siege*: Tegea had remained loyal to Polyperchon.

35.1 *had been treated*: see 19.11.8.

35.2 *on good terms with Olympias and Polyperchon*: the bedrock of Aetolian policy had for some decades been hostility to Macedon; they saw a chance to get on better terms with what might turn out to be the new Macedonian regime.

35.5 *Pyrrhus... who later fought the Romans*: in 280, Pyrrhus (by then king of Epirus) went to help the southern Italian Greek city of Tarentum resist the Romans. He fought well, but ultimately indecisively, against them, and withdrew a few years later (after failing to make himself king of Sicily as well) when it became clear that the Romans could not be beaten.

35.7 *his previous invasion of Macedon*: this expedition is also alluded to at 18.75.1, where it is said that many Macedonians came over to his side. This seems unlikely, since it was a raid rather than a full-fledged invasion.

36.3 *neutralizing Aeacides*: this was a brilliant campaign by Cassander, particularly in his exploitation of the geography of the region: by having Deinias and Atarrhias occupy the passes into Macedon, Olympias was cut off from help by land, while Polyperchon was neutralized in Perrhaebia.

36.3 *Aeacides was desperate to help Olympias*: they were first cousins.

36.4 *Neoptolemus, the son of Achilles*: see Plutarch, *Pyrrhus* 1, for legendary and early Epirote kings.

36.5 *civil and military governor*: the Epirotes did not abolish the monarchy, but they now promoted the other branch of the royal family (Plutarch, *Pyrrhus* 2), and Cassander sent Lyciscus to support the new young king, Neoptolemus II.

37.1 *Gadamela*: this is presumably the same place as the Gamarga of 19.32.2, or perhaps one was part of the other, but neither name is otherwise attested.

40.1   *22,000 foot*: as with the figures for the battle of Paraetacene, Diodorus omits the numbers of light infantry.

40.1   *the extra troops raised in Media*: see 19.20.2–3.

40.2   *the Magus, Smerdis*: see the note to 16.47.2. This Mithridates is Mithridates II of Cius.

42.1   *the majority of the cavalry*: that is, the cavalry on Antigonus' right wing, commanded by Demetrius, and the cavalry on Eumenes' left wing, commanded by Eumenes.

43.1   *greatly outnumbered*: it is unlikely that the 3,000 Silver Shields routed so many thousands of Antigonus' men; they must have been working in conjunction with the rest of Eumenes' infantry.

43.2   *gain the enemy's as well*: this echoes the famous saying of Alexander the Great at Gaugamela, when he learnt that his baggage train was captured, that 'the victors will recover their own belongings *and* take those of the enemy' (Curtius, *History of Alexander* 4.15.7).

43.5   *the river*: Diodorus has not told us, but this river must be the rallying point for Eumenes' army, otherwise there would be no one to whom the Silver Shields could denounce Peucestas. However, there is no way of knowing what river this might be, since rivers (and lakes) in this desert are seasonal and temporary.

43.7   *could not live without*: slaves, that is.

43.8   *handed him over*: according to Plutarch (*Eumenes* 16), Antigenes, Teutamus, and the satraps had decided before the battle to kill Eumenes immediately after the battle. But in Diodorus' version of events, Antigenes, at least, is loyal to Eumenes. Since Antigenes was put to death by Antigonus, Diodorus' version seems likely.

43.8   *enrolled in Antigonus' army*: Antigonus, however, still punished them, or some of them, for their long resistance to him: see 19.48.3–4.

44.2   *spared his life at Nora in Phrygia*: see 18.53.5, 18.58.4.

44.2   *the Macedonians . . . see Eumenes punished*: 'the Macedonians' here means those in Antigonus' army who still adhered to the condemnation of Eumenes that had taken place in Egypt after the murder of Perdiccas: 18.37.2.

44.4   *named after a disaster that happened there in the past*: Diodorus (along with other Greek authors) wants 'Rhagae' to derive from the Greek word for 'fracture' or 'cleft', in the sense that the region was broken up by the earthquakes.

45.1   *recently been founded*: Rhodes town was founded in 408.

45.7   *safe and sound*: bricks were made out of sun-dried mud, so they would dissolve in water.

46.5   *the military governor*: in appointing a Greek or Macedonian military governor to act as a counterweight to a native civil governor, Antigonus was taking a leaf out of Alexander the Great's book. But the size of the forces assigned to Hippostratus suggests that he was responsible for keeping the peace throughout the upper satrapies, not just Media.

48.1 *the satrapies*: the upper satrapies, that is, where the rebellion had taken place and satraps needed to be replaced.

48.2 *Evitus to Areia*: Stasander, who had sided with Eumenes, must have fled, or been killed or captured.

48.5 *took him with him*: Peucestas remained in the service of the Antigonids, but never again held high office. The fact that he was not killed by Antigonus after the battle of Gabene suggests that his poor performance there was due to his having been suborned.

48.6 *at Antigonus' disposal*: Antigonus had made Seleucus interim satrap of Susiane, on top of his satrapy of Babylonia: 19.18.1. Now that Eumenes was dead, Xenophilus was prepared to treat with Antigonus.

48.8 *the golden, vine-entwined tree*: first mentioned by Herodotus, *Histories* 7.27.

49.2 *five choenixes of grain*: a *khoinix* was a dry measure of a little over a litre.

49.2 *inside the city*: they were fed on sawdust, presumably.

49.4 *Some barbarians*: all cities had non-native residents; in this case, they were probably Thracians.

50.7 *Bedyndia in Bisaltia*: the location of Bedyndia is unknown.

51.1 *his advancement by Alexander*: at the time of Alexander's death, Aristonous was one of the seven elite Bodyguards: see the second note to 18.2.2.

51.1 *prosecute her*: the charge was presumably regicide.

51.4 *a trial before the assembled Macedonians*: she has already had a trial before the Macedonians, in the previous paragraph, but she was not actually present to plead her case in person. But Diodorus may have mistakenly made two trials out of a single one.

51.6 *Alexander, who campaigned in Italy*: in 334, Alexander I of Molossis responded to a plea for help from the southern Italian Greek city of Tarentum, which was at war with the local native peoples. It was at his marriage to Cleopatra, Alexander the Great's sister, in 336, that Philip was assassinated. For Pyrrhus' Italian campaign, see the note to 19.35.5.

52.1 *Thessalonice, one of Philip's daughters*: her mother was Philip's third wife, Nicesipolis of Pherae. Her name means 'Thessalian victory'.

52.2 *take up residence there as well*: Olynthus had been destroyed by Philip: 16.53. At much the same time, Cassander also founded Thessalonica, named in honour of his wife. Pallene is the most westerly of the three fingers of Chalcidice.

52.4 *to make sure that there was no natural successor to the throne*: it is probably rather too early to attribute this to Cassander, and anyway how would Diodorus or his source know, since Cassander certainly kept it to himself (see e.g. 19.105.1)?

52.4 *in the customary manner*: see the note to 17.36.5.

52.5 *Cynna, whom Alcetas had killed*: it was traditional for the new king to bury
the old king, so in doing this Cassander was claiming the position of king;
compare Ptolemy's hijacking and burial of the corpse of Alexander the
Great. Cynna, or Cynnane, a half-sister of Alexander the Great (her
mother was Philip's first wife, Audata of Illyris), had been killed in 321 by
Perdiccas' brother Alcetas, who was trying to prevent the marriage of her
daughter Adea to Philip III. The marriage went ahead and Adea took the
royal name Eurydice. There are a number of scholars who believe that the
original occupants of Tomb II at Aegeae were not Philip II and one of his
wives, as is commonly believed, but Philip III and Eurydice. 'Aegeae' is
more usually known as 'Aegae' (as, in our manuscripts, at 16.3.5), modern
Vergina, where (among other things) the palace and fabulous, probably
royal tombs have been excavated.

52.6 *Polyperchon... was on good terms with the Aetolians*: so the Aetolian ploy
of 19.35.2 had been successful.

53.1 *from the Peloponnese*: Alexander had taken advantage of Cassander's
absence, as had been feared in 19.35.1.

53.2 *refounding Thebes*: destroyed by Alexander the Great in 335 (17.8–14), so
Cassander was boldly reversing one of the Conqueror's major decisions.

53.4 *come together from various locations*: 'Sparti' could mean 'scattered', but
it is more usually taken to mean 'the sown men' and to refer to the race
that descended from the survivors of the warriors who sprang up from
the ground when Cadmus sowed the teeth of a dragon.

53.5 *driven out of the city*: the Encheleans were an Illyrian people, and they
were associated with Cadmus in legend, but this is the only occasion on
which we are told that they sacked Thebes.

53.5 *the seven-gated city of Thebes*: Homer, *Odyssey* 11.263. Amphion and
Zethus attacked Thebes to seek revenge for the maltreatment of their
mother by the current king and his wife.

53.5 *what had happened to his children*: Amphion's wife, Niobe, boasted of her
large family of seven sons and seven daughters, and claimed to be a better child-bearer than Leto, the mother of Apollo and Artemis. In punishment, her sons were shot down by Apollo and her daughters by
Artemis.

53.6 *rulers of Thebes*: Eteocles and Polyneices, the sons of Oedipus. They had
agreed to share power, but Eteocles refused to stand down to let Polyneices
have his turn, so Polyneices came from Argos with six other heroes—the
Seven against Thebes—but failed to take the city. The Epigoni, shortly to
be mentioned, were the sons and successors of the Seven against Thebes,
and it was they who successfully captured the city.

53.7 *Alalcomenae and Mount Tilphosium*: Alalcomenae lay on the south shore
of Lake Copais in Boeotia, with Tilphosium the nearest high ground.

53.8 *the oracle of the crows*: the exiled Thebans were living in Thessaly, to the
annoyance of the local inhabitants. The Thebans were reassured when

they were told by the Delphic oracle that they would remain there until white crows were seen. Eventually, for a drunken prank, some young men painted crows white, and the Boeotians were expelled and returned to their homeland.

54.2 *the work that needed doing*: a very damaged inscription survives, detailing some of the donations and benefactors: Harding, no. 131.

54.4 *Ithome*: Diodorus retains the old name of Messene, named after the mountain on which it was located.

54.4 *at the Gerania isthmus*: Mount Gerania, between Corinth and Megara, was a formidable barrier for anyone entering central Greece via the isthmus, and relatively easy to defend.

55.3 *during Alexander's lifetime*: in other words, Seleucus was insisting that he was Antigonus' equal, not his subordinate.

55.4 *what had happened to Pithon*: see 19.46.

55.4 *the potential to take power*: it is not clear why Antigonus found Seleucus a threat. Perhaps it was no more than he wanted to be absolutely sure of whoever was responsible for the great wealth of Babylonia.

55.7 *lose his life in battle against him*: the Chaldaeans were a priestly class of astrologers and astronomers; see 17.112, but especially 2.29–31. The talk of Antigonus' death at Seleucus' hands refers to the battle of Ipsus in 301.

55.8 *if he entered Babylon*: 17.112.2.

55.9 *when we come to the relevant period of time*: the account would have been in Book 21, now largely lost. Seleucus seems to have attracted prophecies—or even to have encouraged them for propaganda purposes. See also 19.90, and there are others in other sources (especially Appian, *Syrian History* 9.56). See D. Ogden, *The Legend of Seleucus: Kingship, Narrative and Mythmaking in the Ancient World* (Cambridge: Cambridge University Press, 2017), especially pp. 68–98 on this passage of Diodorus.

57.1 *all Syria to Ptolemy*: Ptolemy already held the southern half, up to the river Eleutherus.

57.4 *sent there by Cassander*: it is not clear what Cassander was up to in Cappadocia, but nothing seems to have come of it. At 19.69.1, Diodorus attributes to Cassander a desire to conquer Asia Minor for himself, but this seems unlikely, and Cappadocia would be an odd place to start.

58.2 *medimnoi of barley*: for modern equivalents of a *medimnos*, see the note to 17.69.8.

59.1 *an alliance with Ptolemy*: the alliance had been in existence since 320. Salamis (of which Nicocreon was king), Soli, and Paphos were the powerful cities Diodorus refers to, but the alliances Agesilaus did manage to arrange were enough to distract Ptolemy's attention so that Antigonus could advance further down the Phoenician coast.

59.2 *Joppa and Gaza*: these were Ptolemy's last outposts, so Antigonus now had all of Phoenicia and Palestine.

59.3 *Old Tyre*: see the note to 17.40.5.

59.6 *the final crisis of Demetrius' reign*: this account would have occurred in one of the lost books of Diodorus' history, and was probably attached to an account of Phila's suicide in 287, when the Antigonid cause seemed lost.

61.1 *visitors*: Macedonian visitors, presumably, since at 19.62.1 the assembly is said to have consisted of Macedonians.

61.2 *destroyed by the Macedonians*: it may have been destroyed by the Macedonians, but, strictly, they were acting on Greek orders: 17.14. Antigonus' attempt to undermine Cassander's marriage to Thessalonice reveals how important an element it was in Cassander's legitimation as king of Macedon.

61.3 *officially appointed general and legitimate custodian of the kingdom*: this was probably true enough, not just an attempt to usurp the position. It is likely that Antipater ceded the guardianship of the kings to Antigonus at the Triparadeisus conference, even though Cassander soon prevailed upon his father to take the kings to Macedon for protection.

62.1 *the freedom of the Greeks*: it was of crucial importance to the Successors that they gained the allegiance of the free Greek cities within their domains, and won friends in the Greek cities in lands they intended to add to their domains. The cities, with their dependent villages, formed the basic infrastructure of the Successor kingdoms; they acted as hubs for the collection of taxes and as sources of manpower and expertise. Hence, apart from anything else, the Successors' many new city foundations and resettlements. The relative urbanization of Asia was one of the main ways in which the Successors changed the face of the world.

62.2 *Asander*: see the first note to 18.3.1.

62.5 *go to Caria to help Asander*: we hear no more of this force of 10,000 mercenaries; given Asander's defeat in Caria, they were clearly ineffective.

62.8 *galleys*: presumably the rest were triremes, left unmentioned because they were still the most common class of warship. For the designs of the various classes of ship, see Murray, *Age of Titans*.

63.4 *Cenchreae*: the southern port of Corinth, on the Saronic Gulf.

64.1 *the city*: Diodorus can say just 'the city', because there was only one in Messenia, Messene (called 'Ithome' at 19.54.4).

64.1 *the Nemean festival*: the Nemean games were held every two years; these are the games of the summer of 315.

64.5 *the Rhodian ships*: presumably the ships of 19.58.5. It seems that they are different from the Rhodian ships commanded by Dioscourides, which was perhaps an existing Rhodian fleet, rather than ships specially built by the Rhodians for Antigonus.

64.8 *Ecregma*: a town roughly halfway between Gaza and Port Said, situated at the point where the marshy Lake Serbonis opens, through a ravine or fissure (that is the meaning of 'Ecregma'), into the Mediterranean. On this meeting, see R. Simpson, 'The Historical Circumstances of the Peace of 311', *Journal of Hellenic Studies* 74 (1954), 25–31.

65.2 *hēmioliae*: see the note to 16.61.4.

65.3 *after a siege*: Mylae was a Messanian possession, nearby on the north coast of Sicily.

65.6 *Abacaenum*: Abacaenum lay a little south of Tyndaris in the north-east of the island.

65.7 *Ferente, a town in Apulia*: there is no known town called Ferente in Apulia, but there is a Forentum (Livy, *History of Rome* 9.20.9).

65.7 *an alliance with the Samnites*: Nuceria Alfaterna rejoined the Roman fold a few years later.

66.1 *for the second time*: actually, both consuls were holding their fourth consulships. Papirius would go on to have a fifth, in two years' time.

66.2 *the Aetolian assembly*: gaining the Aetolians was a major coup; given the weakness of their former ally Polyperchon, they must have leapt at the chance of an alliance with Antigonus. Aristodemus was always a faithful and effective agent for the Antigonids.

66.2 *Cyllene*: this town had formerly been Elis' port, so they must have lost control of it at some point. In 400 the Eleans had been compelled to dismantle Cyllene's fortifications, but the fact that they put it under siege now proves that the fortifications had been rebuilt.

66.3 *as promised in the decree*: the Proclamation of Tyre: 19.61.1–3.

67.1 *pretending to be his friends*: Alexion was acting, wittingly or unwittingly, as an Antigonid agent, punishing Alexander for his defection.

67.1 *Cratesipolis*: her name means 'holder of cities', and is so decidedly unfeminine in a Greek context that it was probably awarded her as a nickname as a result of her successful command of Sicyon and Corinth. But compare Nicesipolis of Pherae, the mother of one of Philip II's wives, whose name means 'victory over cities'.

67.3 *the Campylus river*: location unknown, but presumably in the west of Aetolia, near the border with Acarnania.

67.4 *Agrinium*: nothing more is known of the Derieis, and the location of Sauria is unknown, but it cannot have been too far from Oeniadae. Oeniadae already existed as a strong town in the fifth century; the reason the Acarnanians did not flock there from their villages was presumably that it was currently in Aetolian hands. It was a superb harbour, and its possession was often a bone of contention between the two peoples. Agrinium lay to the south-east of Stratus, and had previously been an Aetolian town. Hence the brutality of the Aetolians when they took it back (19.68.1).

67.6 *the Hebrus river*: no such river is known under this name in Illyris.

67.6 *Glaucias*: Glaucias was king of just one tribe, the Taulantians. The many Illyrian tribes never fully united, but Glaucias' coalition was very strong at the time, and before long Cassander's presence on the Adriatic coast had been more or less eliminated (19.70.7; 19.78.1).

67.7 *returned to Macedon*: as far as we know, neither Apollonia nor Epidamnus owed allegiance to any of Cassander's enemies. The point of this campaign was to secure his western flank against an attempt to invade Macedon from that direction.

68.5 *Asander*: see the first note to 18.3.1. The fact that the true Cassander is mentioned very shortly makes it likely that Diodorus originally wrote 'Asander'.

68.5 *his father's funeral*: his father, Antigonus' brother, was also called Ptolemaeus.

68.5 *Caprima, in Caria*: Caprima is unknown. It must have been in northern Caria.

69.3 *with their crews*: so Cassander's Carian campaign had been a complete disaster, since he lost on both land (19.68.5–7) and sea. The ships from Pydna were in the region probably because they had been used to transport the land army.

70.5 *the battle against Antipater*: 17.62–3. The battle had taken place many years earlier, in 331, but apparently resentment of Acrotatus still lingered.

70.5 *opposed the decree*: by Spartan custom, Spartiates who surrendered (rather than winning or dying on the battlefield) were called 'Tremblers'; they were treated with disdain and lost some citizenship rights. But since Sparta was critically short of citizens, they did not apply the convention in this case, to the dismay of the hardliner Acrotatus.

70.6 *the approval of the Ephors*: five Ephors were chosen each year in Sparta, with wide-ranging powers, especially as regards internal security, foreign policy, and public finance. They also chaired assembly meetings and issued the orders that executed assembly decisions.

70.8 *their kinship*: Tarentum had been founded by Spartans in the eighth century.

71.6 *the Messanians*: the inclusion of the Messanians here is probably a mistake; see 19.102.

71.7 *Heraclea*: this is the town of Heraclea Minoa, which is called just 'Minoa' at 16.9.4.

72.3 *Plestice*: location unknown, and 'Plistica' may be the better spelling. This Samnite offensive was a response to Roman aggression against the Volscians, and marked the resumption of the Second Samnite War after some years of peace. Sora was a Latin town about 100 kilometres east-south-east of Rome.

72.4 *Saticula*: a Samnite town on the border of Campania, east of Capua.

72.5 *in the vicinity of the Apulian towns*: a very insecure generalization. The war was still being fought all over central Italy.

72.6 *Master of Horse*: that is, Fabius became dictator. The Master of Horse was the traditional second-in-command to a dictator. At this period of Roman history, dictatorship was awarded for an initial period of six months, or until the task (usually military in nature, as here) had been completed. For the duration of the crisis, even consuls were subordinate to the dictator.

72.7 *Laustolae*: or 'Lautulae', a small Latin town near Tarracina.

72.9 *right up until today*: Luceria was especially important as a base during the Second Punic War against Hannibal (218–201).

73.1 *a town on the left coast of the Black Sea*: that is, on the left as one enters the Black Sea from the Bosporus, on the Bulgarian coastline known as the Dobrudja.

73.3 *through Thrace*: he was probably based on the Thracian Chersonese, the modern Gallipoli peninsula. At any rate, that was where, starting in 309, he built his new capital, Lysimachea, on the site of former Cardia.

73.6 *Hieron*: presumably the so-named place on the north-east coastline of the Bosporus, though that was some distance from the towns threatened by Lysimachus.

73.7 *unsettled Lysimachus*: Antigonus was perhaps intending to defeat Lysimachus, take over his satrapy, and come at Cassander in Macedon from Thrace. We hear no more of Lycon and his fleet, however.

74.1 *Telesphorus*: a nephew of Antigonus, the son of an unknown sibling.

74.2 *Polyperchon's headquarters*: Sicyon and Corinth were currently ruled by Cratesipolis (19.67.1), but she had obviously remained on good terms with her father-in-law.

74.3 *to take command of the war against the Aetolians*: Cassander's general on the west coast of Greece was basically Lyciscus (19.36.5, 19.67.5), so Philip's appointment was presumably temporary, while Lyciscus was ill or otherwise engaged. Lyciscus reappears at 19.88.2.

74.3 *Aeacides of Epirus had returned to his kingdom*: see 19.36.4 for his exile in 317.

74.4 *engaged them straight away*: the battle took place at Oeniadae.

75.6 *an alliance with them*: ratifying the alliance with the Aetolians arranged by Aristodemus at 19.66.2. The Aetolians and Boeotians were at least cooperating, if not actually in alliance.

75.6 *no common ground at all*: Antigonus was trying to split up the enemy alliance by coming to terms with them separately; he had already tried this with Ptolemy at 19.64.8. In the famous Letter to Scepsis (Harding, no. 132), Antigonus puts the blame for the failure of the negotiations squarely on Cassander.

76.2 *Cinna*: Cinna is not otherwise known. Perhaps we should read 'Pinna' or 'Tarracina'.

76.2 *more than ten thousand lives…for a long time*: it was during the pursuit that a vanquished army was at its most vulnerable. An extended pursuit such as this one was unusual, since even the victors needed not to stray too far from the battlefield in case the enemy rallied. It implies that the defeat of the Samnites was so thorough that there was no chance of their recovering.

76.3 *Master of Horse*: neither of these names is quite right: the dictator was Gaius Maenius, and the Master of Horse was Marcus Folius, according to Livy (*History of Rome* 9.26.7).

77.1 *Parmenion of Mytilene*: the Eusebian list of Olympic victors gives this man's name as Parmenides.

77.2 *to free the Greeks*: Antigonus' commitment to the freedom policy announced in the Proclamation of Tyre is impressive. Of course, it was also good propaganda, but it would be a mistake to think that it was entirely cynical.

77.4 *Salganeus*: a small town on the east coast of Boeotia, north-west of Chalcis.

77.6 *Pleistarchus*: Cassander's brother.

78.2 *supremacy in Greece*: a later Macedonian king, Philip V (reigned 221–179), named Chalcis one of the three 'fetters of Greece', along with Demetrias and Corinth: Polybius, *Histories* 18.11.5; Livy, *History of Rome* 32.37.3.

78.4 *with a view to making an alliance*: although Demetrius was nominally the sole ruler of Athens, and whittled away at democratic institutions, it appears that he could still be forced to go along with the Assembly's wishes. The Athenians who were in secret contact with Antigonus must have been an unofficial group, because Demetrius would never have allowed such contact to be official.

78.5 *After Attica*: despite his intense programme of liberating cities, Ptolemaeus left Cassander's garrison on the Munychia acropolis of Piraeus in place, presumably because he lacked the strength to evict it.

78.5 *continuous assaults*: in short order, Ptolemaeus brought almost all of central Greece into alliance with Antigonus.

79.4 *Pygmalion*: Pygmalion was the king of Citium. The last we heard of Citium (19.62.6), it was under siege. Pygmalion probably surrendered and was allowed to stay on as king.

79.4 *Stasioecus, the ruler of Marion*: when we last met Stasioecus, at 19.62.6, he was on Ptolemy's side.

79.6 *Potami Caron*: this place, 'Carian Rivers', is not otherwise known. It must have been near Posideium. These were not major towns. Ptolemy's gains were slight in military terms, but had considerable propaganda value. If he could persuade others in the Antigonid realm that Antigonus was incapable of protecting them, he could encourage secession.

80.2 *twenty-four stages*: a 'stage' was not a determinate distance, but simply the distance between staging posts on a route.

81.3 *his father was elderly*: Antigonus was born *c*.382.

81.4 *exceptionally handsome and tall*: his father was so large that in addition to his nickname 'Monophthalmus', the one-eyed, he was also known as 'Cyclops', the one-eyed giant from Homer's *Odyssey*.

82.2 *a hundred Tarentines*: for Tarentines, see the first note to 19.29.2.

83.2 *stop the creatures moving forward*: I suppose this to resemble the medieval *cheval de frise*, which was portable and easy to plant firmly on the ground. Some scholars think that Diodorus is talking not about pointed stakes (i.e. a palisade), but about a long chain of iron (not 'iron-clad') spikes—a kind of series of connected caltrops. But it is hard to get this sense from the Greek. Besides, why would one connect caltrops together? The first elephant to tread on them would drag them away from the others.

84.7 *without their armour*: this is all we hear about the heavy infantry. Did they even engage in the battle? See the next note.

85.3 *more than five hundred men*: five thousand, according to Plutarch, *Demetrius* 5.2. If this figure is right, the heavy infantry must have engaged. The eight thousand who surrendered were presumably the mercenaries. The death of Pithon, son of Agenor, left Babylonia without a satrap, and therefore paved the way for Seleucus' return.

85.4 *the nomes*: a nome was an administrative unit—a 'county', perhaps—in ancient Egypt. The number of nomes varied, but ultimately there were forty-two of them. It was standard practice for a victorious Successor to incorporate his enemy's mercenaries into his own army. Ptolemy also gave his mercenaries land in Egypt, so that more land would be farmed and brought within the taxation system, and so that soldiers would be easily available for call-up.

86.3 *desire his friendship*: these sentiments are clearly taken from a pro-Ptolemy source, as are the assessments of his character in 18.28–36.

87.2 *reduced the population to slavery*: this is a typically Greek way of saying that he set himself up as sole ruler.

87.2 *the sanctuary at Olympia*: which was under Elean protection.

87.3 *the god's property*: the god of Olympia was Zeus.

87.3 *gave it back to the Eleans*: Diodorus tells us no more of Telesphorus, but he seems to have remained loyal to the Antigonids after this brief defection.

88.1 *on the death of their king, Aeacides*: killed by Cassander's general Philip at 19.74.3–5.

88.1 *Arymbas*: more usually 'Arybbas'; see also the notes to 16.72.1 and 18.11.1. Alcetas was Aeacides' brother. The Epirotes 'gave' the kingship to Alcetas, just as in 19.36.4 they banished Aeacides (if that was indeed pan-Epirote action, rather than just Molossian), because they had formed themselves into a confederacy, constitutionally powerful, but still ruled by a king.

88.4 *Eurymenae, a town in Epirus*: the location of Eurymenae is not absolutely certain, but it probably lay south of Lake Pamvotis, the lake on which the modern city of Ioannina is situated.

89.1 *gone over to the Illyrians*: see 19.70.7 and 19.78.1.

90.4 *the god had addressed him as 'King Seleucus'*: 'Branchidae' is another name for Didyma, near Miletus, where there was a famous oracle of Apollo managed by a priestly family or group of families called the Branchidae. Seleucus' consultation took place after Ptolemaeus had chased him away from Erythrae (19.60.4).

91.1 *Macedonians who had been settled in Carrhae*: they were probably former mercenaries of Antigonus.

91.5 *recovering Babylonia by these means*: cuneiform evidence allows us to date Seleucus' return to May 311.

92.3 *the Royal Road*: see the note to 19.19.2.

92.4 *Evagrus*: possibly the same man as the Evagoras of 19.48.2.

92.5 *some of the neighbouring territories*: presumably Persis, Areia, and Parthyaea. Diodorus' account is very compressed, since the process took Seleucus at least a couple of years. As he extended into the upper satrapies, it is not known in detail what administrative measures he put in place or took over. Most likely, he copied Alexander's triad of satrap, general, and finance minister. To supplement his meagre forces, he seems to have recruited the mountain-dwelling Cossaeans, who had been enemies of both Alexander and Antigonus. Trouble from India was averted in 303 by ceding much of the frontier satrapies of southern Afghanistan, Pakistan, and southern Iran to the emperor Chandragupta Maurya, in exchange for several hundred war elephants.

93.1 *a major battle*: the battle of Gaza: 19.81–4.

93.2 *Myous*: this is the only occasion on which we hear of a town in Syria with such a name.

93.5 *as earlier he had fought Perdiccas*: Perdiccas' invasion of Egypt and its consequences are the topic of 18.33–6.

93.6 *the natural defences of the region*: Egypt's natural defences were chiefly two: that a land army had to cross a desert to get there, and that there were few good harbours for ships.

94.1 *the Nabataeans*: this is the Nabataeans' first appearance in history. Any visitor to the rock cities of Petra in Jordan and Al-Hijr in Saudi Arabia knows some of their later history.

94.5 *Arabia Felix, as it is called*: Arabia Felix (Fertile Arabia) refers to the south-western part of the peninsula, modern Yemen.

94.10 *wild honey*: see also 17.75.6–7.

95.1 *at a certain rock*: probably the place later known as Petra; 'rock' is *petra* in Greek.

95.2 *2,200 stades*: the figure clashes badly with that of 19.98.1.

96.1 *written in Syrian*: see the first note to 19.23.3.

97.1 *only a single, man-made way up to it*: continuing with the assumption that the 'rock' being talked about is in fact Petra, this path must be the winding flight of stone-cut steps that leads up to the fortified summit of the tallest of the towering cliffs of Petra.

98.1 *the Asphalt Lake*: the Dead Sea, as we call it, which regularly sends up asphalt from its depths, though today not in such large quantities as Diodorus describes.

98.1 *the satrapy of Idumaea*: what follows (down to 'palm trees') is taken almost verbatim from 2.47.7–9.

98.1 *loses its characteristic colouring*: asphalt commonly contains sulphur (hence, in part, the foul smell that Diodorus is talking about), and although nothing tarnishes gold, sulphur tarnishes the base metals, of which there are traces in gold. The same goes for silver, and bronze tarnishes anyway.

99.2 *stays afloat just as a swimmer would*: this phenomenon is a result of the extreme saltiness of the Dead Sea. It is still a popular tourist attraction.

99.3 *the preservation of the corpse can be permanent*: this is probably not true. Asphalt (bitumen) was more likely used in the mummification process to coat the bandaged body. Its biocidal properties were known, since it was used, for instance, to protect vulnerable plants against pests, so the mummifiers probably appreciated that about it too. It might also or alternatively have been used to blacken the skin of the mummy. Diodorus has a fuller account of embalming at 1.91, and along with Herodotus, *Histories* 2.86–8, it is the most important account. No Egyptian description survives, and, as far as literary sources are concerned, we rely largely on these two Greeks. The recent discovery of an ancient embalming workshop at the Saqqara necropolis in Egypt should cast more light. Asphalt was also used to waterproof boats, and as a builder's mortar.

100.4 *return promptly to the coast*: it is not clear why Antigonus insisted on Demetrius' prompt return.

100.5 *the Red Sea*: the Persian Gulf. Euteles was presumably Seleucus' governor of the region.

100.6 *to keep an eye on the enemy*: and to interrupt their supplies. Patrocles was conducting a kind of guerrilla warfare, which was not at all common in the ancient world.

100.7 *due back as ordered*: the information in this chapter on the Antigonids' Babylonian war against Seleucus is precious; the war is otherwise little known. It seems to have gone on for two years (311–309), with a second major invasion, by Antigonus, in 310–309 (once the Peace of the Dynasts had freed him up), and to have finally been settled to Seleucus' advantage by treaty. See Wheatley, 'Antigonus Monophthalmus in Babylonia'; van der Spek, 'Seleukos'; and Vădan, 'Inception'.

101.3 *Fregellae*: the colonization of this town in Samnite territory by the Romans in 328 was the catalyst for the Second Samnite War. It was surrendered to the Samnites in 320, after the Roman defeat at the battle of the Caudine Forks in 321 (unmentioned by Diodorus). After being taken back by the Romans in 313, it remained within the ambit of Rome.

101.3   *the citadel of Nola*: Nola lay south-east of Capua in Campania; 'Calatia' is a correction of a garbled text, and so the name is not absolutely certain. The nearby town of Caiatia would fit the bill as well.

101.3   *the island known as Pontia*: off the south-west coast of Italy, directly west of Cumae.

102.2   *instructions, privately delivered*: presumably because the exiles in Messana had sympathizers in Syracuse who would leak the information to them if they had the opportunity.

103.4   *cut off the hands of the crews*: where was the Syracusan fleet? Why were there only two ships in the harbour?

103.5   *and the Phoenicians*: Carthage had been founded, perhaps late in the ninth century, by settlers from Phoenicia (from Tyre, to be precise); hence Diodorus occasionally substitutes 'Phoenicians' for 'Carthaginians'.

105.1   *concluded a treaty with him*: the treaty that brought the Third War of the Successors to an end is commonly called the Peace of the Dynasts.

105.1   *cities in Libya and Arabia*: in other words, these three dynasts gained little or nothing, and certainly nothing like what they had demanded in 19.57.1. The war was pretty futile, and therefore a victory for Antigonus. But by granting all Asia to Antigonus, they left Seleucus, with territory in Asia, as a prominent loose end and guaranteed that there would be further fighting between him and the Antigonids. Seleucus was excluded from the treaty because it was a treaty for peace, and he was still at war. Besides, he had just declared himself 'General of Asia'—the title once claimed by Antigonus—and that might have made the others suspicious of his intentions. But it is still puzzling why Ptolemy, say, did not come to Seleucus' assistance against Antigonus and Demetrius. The bargain must have been that Ptolemy's help came to an end with his gift of men to help Seleucus return to Babylon; see the use of the word 'until' at the end of 19.86.5.

105.1   *the Greeks should be autonomous*: in the Letter to Scepsis (Harding, no. 132), Antigonus claims that this clause was his doing and, given his crusade to free the Greek cities, the claim is plausible.

105.2   *completely secret*: as a consequence of this tactic, no one is quite sure when the murders took place; 308 is perhaps a better bet than 311/10, the year we are currently in.

105.4   *Asia, Europe, Greece, and Macedon*: from this point onwards our knowledge of the doings of the Successors decreases in line with Diodorus' increasing interest in events in his native Sicily. But since the accounts of the Successors in these years are also patchy in Plutarch and Justin, it is not impossible that they all found less material in their sources.

105.5   *Marrucini*: an Italic tribe with territory on the east coast of south-central Italy. They were allies of the Samnites. Pollitium is unknown.

105.5 *the place known as Interamna*: the purpose of the colony was probably to protect the local farmland from Samnite raids. 'Interamna' means 'between the rivers'. Of the several towns with this name in Italy, this one is Interamna Lirenas (on the Liris), south-east of Fregellae. As well as this colony, and those at Luceria (19.72.8) and on Pontia (19.101.3), they also in these years (314–312) founded colonies at Suessa and Saticula, effectively ring-fencing the Samnites with Roman allies. From now on, the writing was on the wall for the Samnites.

106.2 *chariot-riders*: it is not clear what the unique Greek word *zeugippai* means. If my translation is correct, perhaps they fought from a light chariot. Alternatively, if *zeug-* means 'pair' rather than 'yoke', perhaps they rode a pair of horses into battle, like the 'two-horsers' (*amphippoi*) of 19.29.2.

107.2 *at the strait*: the Strait of Messina, between Sicily and the toe of Italy.

108.1 *called Ecnomus . . . unfortunate victims*: 'Ecnomus' could be taken to mean 'lawless'.

108.6 *Carthaginians of the highest rank*: there would not be very many such men. I suppose their presence was a tactical factor because each of them would have been accompanied by a sizeable personal cavalry guard.

109.4 *the season of the Dog Star*: see the note to 17.7.6.

109.4 *salt water*: the river's modern name is the Salso, the salt river. It runs from north to south, joining the sea between Gela and Acragas.

110.4 *the first to transfer their allegiance to Hamilcar*: Syracuse was left effectively isolated, prompting Agathocles to make the bold move of taking the war to North Africa.

BOOK 20

1.1 *oratory*: this was an extremely common Greek historiographical practice. Diodorus was perhaps thinking in particular of Theopompus of Chios, who worked as a speech-writer as well as a historian and relished speeches in his historical writing, or of Timaeus of Tauromenium, who was well known for inserting lengthy speeches into his history. Diodorus was not the only historian to have cut down on speeches; he may have borrowed the idea from Cratippus of Athens, a fourth-century historian (see *FGrH* 64, F 1), and Pompeius Trogus seems also to have felt that speeches interrupt the narrative (Justin, *Epitome of the Philippic History of Pompeius Trogus* 38.3.11). There are also echoes of Polybius' words at *Histories* 36.1.1–7.

1.1 *keen to acquire a knowledge of history*: this was a historian's cardinal sin, as far as Diodorus was concerned: see also the preface to Book 16.

1.2 *praise or find fault with their subjects*: that is, epideictic rhetoric, speeches written for display, as distinct from the political oratory implied by 'politicians and ambassadors'. The third branch of rhetoric identified by Aristotle in *The Art of Rhetoric* was forensic, speeches written for the law courts. But Diodorus despised this branch of rhetoric: 1.76.1–2.

1.3   *proportionality*: see Introduction, p. xxviii.

2.2   *make use of speeches*: in the extant books of Diodorus, extended speeches
are very rare. There are none in the books translated in this volume.
They occur only at 8.12, 10.34, 13.20–32, 13.52–3, 14.65–9, 21.21,
27.13–18, and 31.3. However, he is happy to give us short bursts of
direct speech (in our books: 16.43.4; 16.87.2; 17.54.4–5; 17.66.5; 18.60.6;
19.97.3–5).

2.3   *883 years after the sack of Troy*: compare 19.1.10: Diodorus should have
written '873' here.

3.1   *Aemilius*: full names of Roman consuls mentioned by Diodorus, and
corrections to his versions of their names, can be found in Appendix 2
(pp. 543–9).

3.3   *men who had been schooled by danger*: the Carthaginians had of course been
fighting for a long time in Sicily, but Diodorus means (a) that Carthage
itself had not been a theatre of war, and (b) that the Carthaginians themselves were no fighters; they largely employed mercenaries, especially
from North Africa. Hence the importance of detaching the 'Libyan
auxiliaries'.

4.5   *seized some of the dedications that had been given to the temples*: under
normal circumstances, this would have been sacrilege, since dedications
were the gods' property, but in an emergency temples might make some
of their wealth available.

4.8   *freedom*: not just to bulk up his numbers, but also to ensure a loyal
militia.

5.5   *stars visible all over the heavens*: the eclipse was that of 15 August 310 BCE.

7.1   *Demeter and Korē*: Korē, 'the Maiden', is a common Greek name for
Demeter's daughter Persephone.

7.2   *magnificent himation*: see the note to 16.93.1 on the *himation*. The garland was traditional headgear for a sacrifice.

7.2   *a burnt offering to them of the entire fleet*: that is, he had vowed to do so, or
was pretending to have vowed to do so, if they were saved. Demeter and
Korē, goddesses of cereal crops, were the protectors of Sicily because of
its fertility.

7.3   *the sacrificial victims*: that is, something about the entrails and especially
the liver of the sacrificed animal or animals indicated victory.

7.4   *stood by the stern*: ships were beached with their prows towards the sea,
for rapid departure if needed.

7.5   *in danger*: see 17.23.1–3.

8.1   *Agathocles' sorcery*: the idea that rhetoric is a kind of sorcery is as old as
Gorgias of Leontini (fifth to fourth century), one of its earliest practi-
tioners, who said as much in his *In Praise of Helen*.

8.4   *make them pleasing*: passages such as this suggest that Diodorus' source
for Agathocles' African campaigns had visited Carthage.

8.7   *White Tunis*: this was probably on the site of modern Tunis (though this makes nonsense of Diodorus' idea that it was 2,000 stades distant from Carthage; the distance is more like 100 stades). The site of Megalopolis is unknown.

9.1   *the city of Carthage as a whole*: see also 19.106.4 on the draping of the city walls with black sackcloth at a time of public mourning.

9.2   *stowed them in their own vessels*: the sheaths that went over the ramming timbers were made of flawless bronze and were therefore very valuable as booty; they might also be used to decorate a monument commemorating naval victory.

10.2 *the safety of the city as a whole*: presumably because Hanno would see that Bomilcar's tyrannnical ambitions were thwarted.

10.4 *I shall come back to him later*: see 20.12.5–6, 20.43–4.

10.5 *and the allied cities*: the 'troops from the countryside' would be largely Libyans, and the 'allies' Libyphoenicians.

10.5 *two thousand war chariots*: if these figures are right, almost all male Carthaginians of military age must have been called up for service.

10.6 *the Sacred Battalion*: see 16.80.4.

11.1 *his son, Archagathus*: Diodorus varies between the form 'Archagathus' (which is also found at Justin, *Epitome of the Philippic History of Pompeius Trogus* 22.5) and, less commonly, 'Agatharchus' (as at 20.55.5 and at Polybius, *Histories* 7.2.4).

11.2 *shield covers*: shields were covered with cloth or leather during transport, to keep them safe and shiny.

11.4 *Athena*: one of Athena's most prevalent functions was as a goddess of war.

11.5 *responsible for significant victories*: Diodorus may be thinking of the celery episode of 16.79.3–4.

12.1 *pass through their lines*: see also 17.57.6.

14.1 *the god of their founders*: Heracles was the Greek equivalent of Phoenician Melqart. The worship of Melqart was central to every colony founded by Tyre.

14.3 *temples, simulacra and all*: these were small model temples offered as dedications in Melqart's sanctuary. The simulacra were miniature statuettes of the god.

14.4 *Cronus...as well*: Cronus was the Greek equivalent of Phoenician Baal Hammon.

14.6 *fiery pit*: this is clearly fanciful. It is more likely that the children were first burnt and then their remains were thrown into the pit—that is, *if* the Carthaginians really did practise child sacrifice, which is not certain. The fanciful nature of Diodorus' account (as well as contradictions in other sources), combined with the commonplace topic of Carthaginian cruelty, should make one pause before attributing child sacrifice to them.

At the most, it was an occasional, emergency practice, not as regular as Diodorus implies.

14.6 *sacred fire within*: Euripides, *Iphigeneia in Tauris* 625–6. The words 'and she replies' have dropped out of the transmitted text and I have restored them. In our MSS of Euripides, the second line has 'a great pit of stone'.

14.7 *Cronus did away with his children*: Cronus knew that his children would depose him from his position as chief deity, so every time a child was born he swallowed it. But when Zeus was born, Cronus' wife, Rhea, gave him a stone to swallow instead of the child, and arranged for Zeus to be brought up. And in due course he took over his father's position as chief deity.

15.1 *completely wiped out*: this stratagem would of course be exposed as soon as he sent the reinforcements to Carthage, but he was hoping to force the Syracusans to surrender before that.

15.3 *opposed to what they were doing*: they could not afford any dissent in the city, since they intended to continue resisting the siege and to wait for Agathocles to return.

16.1 *weak man*: 'weak man' translates the Greek *anandros*, while Antander's name is *Antandros*—a rare Diodoran pun.

16.1 *Erymnon of Aetolia*: presumably the commander of the mercenaries, and therefore on the war council.

17.1 *Neapolis*: the city was destroyed by earthquake and tsunami in the fourth century CE, and has only recently been rediscovered by underwater archaeologists.

17.1 *Hadrumetum*: an important Phoenician colony, pre-dating the foundation of Carthage, on the coast south of Carthage.

17.5 *the stratagem*: compare Eumenes' tactics at 19.38.3.

19.1 *the Autariatae*: a powerful Illyrian tribe.

19.3 *the mutual agreement entered into by the dynasts*: see 19.105.1.

19.3 *garrisoning the cities*: despite the basic Antigonid policy of Greek freedom, it was always hard for the Successors to keep a promise to leave cities ungarrisoned. They might avoid installing a permanent garrison, but if the city was close to a war zone it might well have one temporarily.

19.4 *the growth of Antigonus' power*: these moves by Ptolemy were a response to Seleucus' success in the East. He could now (only six months after the peace) provoke Antigonus, knowing that he would have a powerful ally in Seleucus. Ptolemaeus' rebellion, just mentioned, was also a response to relative Antigonid weakness.

20.1 *grudge against Cassander*: the grievance dated originally from Cassander's resentment of Polyperchon's regency and attempts to depose him: 18.49, 18.54, etc.

20.1 *summoned Heracles, the son of Barsine, from Pergamum*: this must have happened with Antigonus' approval, since Pergamum was under his control.

He had been hoarding Heracles, so to speak, in order to use him some time against Cassander. Now that Heracles was almost of an age to be king, he put the plan into motion. Clearly by now the killing of Alexander IV (19.105.2–3) was no longer a secret.

20.3 *the Aetolians... his wishes*: they were still on good terms with Polyperchon (19.52.6), as long as he was not working with Cassander.

21.1 *Nicocles, the king of Paphos*: many scholars believe that the king so cruelly murdered by Ptolemy was not Nicocles of Paphos, but Nicocreon of Salamis, who was being punished by Ptolemy for treachery, since he had been Ptolemy's viceroy of Cyprus (19.79.5).

21.3 *this tragic fashion*: Diodorus means this literally, not metaphorically: it was like the plot of the kind of Greek tragedy in which calamity falls unexpectedly on a household.

22.1 *the Cimmerian Bosporus*: this Bosporus has nothing to do with the well-known strait by Byzantium. The Bosporan Kingdom occupied the east of the Crimean peninsula and the Taman peninsula opposite.

22.3 *the river Thates*: the river flowed into the Sea of Azov (Lake Maeotis to the Greeks), but its precise location is unknown, and so therefore is the territory occupied by the Siraces.

24.3 *Agarus, the king of the Scythians*: Agarus appears to have been king of a Scythian people living to the north of the Sea of Azov.

24.4 *the ancestral political system*: it is not clear what Diodorus means by this, since what follows does not add up to a 'political system'. The Spartocid dynasty, of which Eumelus was a member, had ruled Panticapaeum for over a hundred years, and before that the city had been ruled by tyrants. Perhaps an emergency constitution had been in place for the duration of the war.

24.4 *no more wealth taxes at all*: the *eisphora* (literally, 'paying in') was an occasional tax on the rich to raise money in an emergency, usually for war.

24.5 *ruled as Archon*: a Spartocid king's fullest title was 'Archon of Bosporus and Theodosia and King of the Sindoi, Toretae, Dandarioi, and Psessoi'.

25.2 *Callatis under siege*: see 19.73. Either the siege went on for a number of years, or this indicates a separate uprising by Callatis. In either case, we do not know the outcome.

25.2 *Heniochians... Taurians... Achaeans*: peoples living here and there on the coastlines of the northern Black Sea.

25.4 *Sindice*: a district within the Bosporan kingdom.

26.1 *'mouse'*: 'mouse', *mys* in Greek, was also the word for 'muscle' in general and for the biceps in particular.

26.4 *Cataracta and Ceraunilia*: if Ceraunilia is modern Cerignola in Apulia, presumably Cataracta (the name implies a waterfall or rapids) was nearby. Talium is equally unknown. Diodorus' account of Roman activity against the Samnites in this year is completely different from that of others (Livy, *History of Rome* 9.31; Zonaras, *Extracts of History* 8.1). It may be that Diodorus is to be preferred here.

27.1 *Demetrius of Phalerum*: Demetrius was of course also the dictator of Athens (18.74.3). Since it is unlikely that he would have entrusted his gaining the Archonship to a lottery, which had been the way Archons had been chosen (from a list of volunteers) in Athens since 487, this is good evidence that he substituted election for sortition, probably as soon as he gained power in 317. In fact, it is likely that all the Archons Diodorus lists for the ten years of Demetrius' regime were close associates of the dictator. He probably wanted the Archonship in this year because it was a year in which the Great Panathenaea was celebrated, which it was the Archon's job to organize—a chance to shine and win popular favour. He would also have presided over Athens' other major festival, the City Dionysia.

27.1 *King Ptolemy*: see the first note to 18.21.9.

27.3 *After that*: Ptolemy undoubtedly took over more cities than those mentioned (e.g. Myndus: 20.37.1). The Ptolemies held this vital corner of Asia Minor for decades.

27.3 *his uncle*: see 20.19.2.

27.3 *to cooperate with Ptolemy*: Ptolemaeus, with his possessions in mainland Greece, would make a very useful ally for Ptolemy, who was planning to invade Greece (20.37).

27.3 *drink hemlock*: we know from an inscription (*I.Iasos* 2) that before his death Ptolemaeus had done valuable work for Ptolemy, bringing the town of Iasus (which he had earlier won for Antigonus: 19.75.5) over to his side as part of his takeover of the region.

28.1 *Stymphaea*: Stymphaea, or Tymphaea, was the region of Macedon from which Polyperchon originally came.

28.1 *fickleness...go over to Heracles*: the fickleness of the Macedonian troops was perhaps not a factor so much as their fierce loyalty towards the Argead house, given that (a) Cassander had murdered the last legitimate king, Alexander IV, and (b) Heracles was therefore the last surviving male member of the house. Even so, Diodorus is premature in calling Heracles 'king', since he did not yet have possession of his kingdom; but perhaps Polyperchon had arranged for him to be publicly acclaimed king in Stymphaea.

28.2 *General of the Peloponnese*: in other words, he would have the same position under Cassander that he had under Antigonus, whom he was now betraying.

28.3 *done away with the young man*: this despicable act became a paradigm of the evil consequences of moral weakness: Plutarch, *On Spinelessness* 4 = *Moralia* 530d.

28.4 *Boeotians and Peloponnesians*: we would like to know more about this. Who were these pro-Antigonid 'Boeotians and Peloponnesians'?

29.1 *sixty years and ten months*: at 15.60 the text, clearly corrupt, has 34 years for Cleomenes' reign. Despite his longevity, Cleomenes appears to have been a rather ineffectual king.

29.3 *the Olympieium*: see the note to 16.68.1.

29.4 *Euryelus*: high ground opposite the high ground of the Olympieium, with the Anapus river valley between them.

31.3 *the liberation of the Greek cities*: which had been garrisoned by either the Syracusans or the Carthaginians as they swept across the island after the battle of the Himeras river.

31.4 *Xenodicus*: he is called Xenodocus below, in 20.56.1–2 and 20.62.2–5.

31.5 *Herbessus*: a town overlooked by Mount Heraea, west of Morgantina and north of Gela.

32.1 *Echetla*: the location of Echetla is unknown.

32.2 *Megara*: commonly known as Megara Hyblaea, with the eponym referring to a Sicel king called Hyblon, who gave the Megarians land to settle in.

34.1 *undertake to bring their forces over to them*: it should be remembered that the majority of Agathocles' forces were mercenaries rather than native Syracusans. They were usually led by a professional mercenary captain and recruiter, who, like his men, owed allegiance above all to a reliable paymaster and would be prepared to desert for a better offer.

35.1 *Sutrium*: the Etruscans, Rome's ancient enemy, had decided to intervene in the war between the Romans and Samnites, in favour of the Samnites. Sutrium, east of Tarquinii, occupied an important position on the main route between Rome and Etruria, and had long been in Roman hands.

35.2 *Iapygian communities which were loyal to Rome*: the Iapyges occupied southern Apulia.

35.2 *Allifae*: a Campanian town north of Capua. But Allifae was back in Samnite hands only three years later. Perhaps Marcius assaulted the town but failed to take it.

35.5 *Arretium, Cortona, and Perusia*: Etruscan towns. It seems likely that only inland Etruscan towns were involved in this offensive, not the coastal towns.

35.5 *Castola*: Castola is unknown.

36.1 *censors were elected*: two censors were elected, under normal circumstances, every five years for a term of eighteen months, to conduct a census, promote or downgrade people from one census class to another, according to their stated income, contract out public works, and, as guardians of Rome's morals, decide on entry to and expulsion from the Senate. This 312 censorship is the first we know of where the censors had this full range of powers.

36.1 *Lucius Plautius*: Plautius' first name should be Gaius. It appears from Livy, *History of Rome* 9.29, that Plautius resigned in protest at his colleague's popularism, and that from then on Claudius acted as sole censor.

36.1 *eighty stades*: the *Aqua Appia* ran for about 16.5 km (10 miles) east of
Rome. Much of it was underground, for security, and it has been esti-
mated that it delivered about 73,000 cubic metres of water to the city
every day.

36.2 *expended the entire revenue of the state*: this is not as wilful as it sounds,
because he himself was responsible for increasing Rome's revenues by
his successful military campaigns. The Appian Way was intended, in the
first instance, for military use, to enable Roman armies to move quickly
and safely against the Samnites.

36.4 *census classes of their choice*: by these measures, Claudius made it possible
for freedmen, and poor and landless men, who had previously almost
entirely lacked political influence, to make their voices heard. Many freedmen were rich, but not in landed property, and by custom landless men
voted last, by which stage of the process a majority had invariably been
reached, so that their vote was ineffective. Claudius made it possible for
their wealth to be assessed by their movable property, so that they could
be assigned to the class to which their wealth entitled them. Likewise,
he effectively enfranchised the poor by distributing them among all
the tribes, rather than the four to which they had been restricted before,
whose voices were rarely heard.

36.5 *deprived none of them of his horse*: Knights (*Equites*) were given not just
a horse by the State, but also money for its upkeep (and for that of their
mounted batman). So if a censor refused a man his horse, it was a sym-
bolic way of denying him entry into that census class, and if a man
was already registered as a Knight, to deprive him of his horse was to
downgrade him.

36.5 *he expelled none of them as unworthy*: see the first note to 36.1.

36.5 *the consuls*: that is, the consuls for the following year.

36.6 *the most prestigious of the aedileships*: at this stage of Roman history, there
were four aediles, responsible especially for the maintenance of public
buildings and public order, and for overseeing public festivals and mar-
kets. They also had some judicial functions. The four formed two pairs:
one pair (plebeian aediles), elected by the people, were the original two;
the other (curule aediles), introduced in 367, were elected by the tribal
assembly. It is not clear what Diodorus means by calling one aedileship
more prestigious, seeing that the functions of both pairs were very similar,
but since the plebeian aediles were not elected by the entire people of
Rome, he was perhaps not counting it as a proper political office at all,
leaving just the pair of curule aediles.

36.6 *pretended to be blind and stayed at home*: this was how Claudius gained
his *agnomen* Caecus, 'the blind'. He stayed at home because if he had
emerged he would have faced reprisals from the Senate.

37.1 *Apollonides of Tegea*: the Eusebian Olympic victor list has Andromenes
of Corinth here, but since he was also the winner in the subsequent

Olympics, perhaps his name was miscopied for this festival too, in which case Diodorus' version is to be preferred.

37.1 *liberated Andros and installed a garrison*: the island of Andros had also been garrisoned by Antigonus. It was a member of the Confederacy of (mainly Cycladic) Islanders, the protection of which Ptolemy would soon take over.

37.1 *in the previous book*: see 19.67.1–2. We hear no more of Cratesipolis. We do not know what happened to her, or whether the cession of her realm to Ptolemy was coerced or voluntary.

37.2 *greatly increase his power*: Ptolemy is often portrayed by modern scholars as cautiously pursuing a policy of securing his core territory, Egypt, and being little interested in emulating Antigonus and others in their attempts to take over the entirety of Alexander's empire. But this expedition, in combination with the prospect of marriage to Cleopatra, Alexander's sister (next paragraph), was Ptolemy's great bid for power. It came to nothing, but that should not alter our assessment of his ambitions. Talk of 'liberating' the cities probably means that he wanted to form them into a league, along the lines of the League of Corinth founded by Philip II. See especially the papers by Hauben, Meeus, and Strootman in Hauben and Meeus (eds), *The Age of the Successors*.

37.2 *sailed back to Egypt*: he retained the two cities for several years, until Demetrius, son of Antigonus, took them from him (20.102.2–3). His departure from Greece was perhaps prompted by news of Cleopatra's death, which thwarted his bid for rulership of Macedon. Ptolemy was also claiming to be an illegitimate son of Philip II, but that was not enough on its own to legitimate rulership of Macedon.

37.3 *the Alexander who campaigned in Italy*: that is, Alexander I of Epirus, who died in Italy in 331. See the note to 19.51.6. For Cleopatra's role in these years, see A. Meeus, 'Kleopatra and the Diadochoi', in P. van Nuffelen (ed.), *Faces of Hellenism: Studies in the History of the Eastern Mediterranean (4th Century BC–5th Century AD)* (Leuven: Peeters, 2009), 63–92.

38.1 *the Numidians*: the same noun means both 'Numidians' and 'Nomads', because that is how the Numidians lived in those days; but within a century they had begun to urbanize and were moving in the direction of statehood, though nomadism remained a central aspect of the economy.

40.1 *Ophellas in Cyrene*: Ophellas was Ptolemy's governor of Cyrenaica; see 18.21.7–9.

40.5 *Marathon*: the battle of Marathon fought in 490 BCE.

40.6 *joining the expedition*: as mercenaries, that is. This was not an official Athenian force.

41.2 *straight up to a peak*: as far as I am aware, no such cave has been discovered west of Automalax, but Diodorus' description might fit the Slontha cave temple in Cyrenaica, at the modern village of Aslanta Lasamisis, where there are relief carvings representing Lamia.

41.3 *after all the children born to her had died*: Zeus was the father, and out of jealousy his wife Hera killed the children.

41.4 *her name still terrifies them*: in some versions of the myth, she became a child-devouring monster.

41.5 *measure*: we still occasionally use 'basket' as a measure, as in 'a punnet of strawberries' or 'a quarter cran of herring'.

41.6 *he says*: the lines are from an unknown play of Euripides, perhaps the *Busiris*. A better version has Lamia speaking the lines herself: 'Is there anyone on earth who does not know my name, a name to horrify mortal men, the name of Libyan-born Lamia?'

42.2 *the Syrtis*: the great gulf (the modern Gulf of Sidra) on the North African coast.

42.2 *similar in colour to the ground on which they lay*: perhaps the Saharan sand viper.

43.7 *does not correspond to reality*: at any rate, this is a limitation of Diodorus' annalistic method of writing, whereby events that take several years are necessarily broken up as many times as there are years. But Diodorus occasionally circumvents this limitation by giving an extended history of a place, as of Thebes at 19.53.3–8.

44.1 *a short distance outside Carthage*: it was a suburb of Carthage, as New Town, Leontini, was of Leontini, and likewise for New Town, Syracuse.

44.6 *the gravest danger*: Bomilcar's failed coup was the last attempt we know of by any single individual to make himself king. Absolute kingship had given way to a monarchy tempered by the aristocratic Council of Elders in about 480 BCE, but from now on Carthage was a republic.

44.7 *off the coast of Italy*: Pithecusae is today called Ischia; it lies off the Bay of Naples.

44.8 *the Marsi*: an Italic people of central Italy.

44.9 *Caerium into submission*: Caerium is unknown. It was probably a fortress near Caere, an important Etruscan town, as in Greece Ambracus was a fortress near Ambracia.

45.1 *siege equipment*: he also had a purse of 5,000 talents.

45.2 *issued a proclamation*: the proclamation would have focused on what he had come for: to free Athens and then the other Greek cities, in accordance with the promise made by Antigonus at the Proclamation of Tyre (19.61.1–3). Perhaps he would also have mentioned the league his father wanted him to create (see 20.46.5).

45.3 *Munychia*: the Piraeus acropolis.

45.4 *to Ptolemy in Egypt*: where he became Ptolemy's chief adviser for the creation of the library within the Museum. It was modelled on Aristotle's library, which Demetrius knew well, as a member of Aristotle's school.

46.2 *Harmodius and Aristogeiton*: by assassinating the brother of the tyrant Hippias in 514, these two were considered to have established democracy in the city and were venerated as its saviours. This was the most prestigious position imaginable for statues of Antigonus and Demetrius. Plutarch (*Demetrius* 10) lists more honours than those mentioned by Diodorus. Stratocles was the most prominent politician in the years of Antigonid supremacy in Athens, with over twenty-five surviving decrees in his name, and many more undoubtedly lost.

46.2 *Saviour Gods*: it was possible within Greek religion for living men to be regarded as gods, as long as they had godlike achievements to their name. Demetrius and Antigonus had saved Athens from starvation and tyranny, and held out the prospect of renewed glory in the future, so they were Saviour Gods.

46.2 *Demetrias and Antigonis, to the existing ten*: these new tribes were made up of demes removed from the other ten tribes. The council of five hundred necessarily became a council of six hundred, with each tribe still supplying fifty councillors each year. Before long, the rule that no one could be a councillor more than twice in a lifetime had to be given up, because the pool of citizens was not large enough for the rule to be retained with the two extra tribes.

46.2 *Athena's robe*: the robe was presented to Athena with great ceremony each year. The gods showed their displeasure with this obsequious move by having a storm rip the robe as it was being escorted to the Acropolis (Plutarch, *Demetrius* 12).

46.3 *the Lamian War*: for the Lamian War, see 18.12–13, 16–17, and for Antipater's dissolution of the democracy, 18.18.4.

46.4 *gave the city back to Athens*: like most islands, Imbros had only the one city, so to possess the city was to possess the island. Imbros was usually occupied by Athenian cleruchs, whose job was to send grain back to Athens, and was considered therefore an overseas extension of Athenian territory, along with other islands, including Lemnos, which, unmentioned by Diodorus, was also returned to Athens at this time.

46.5 *make policy for the Greeks*: in other words, Demetrius formed the Greek cities and confederacies (or at least those that were Antigonid allies) into a league, a revival of Philip II's League of Corinth. Harding, no. 138, is a copy of the charter of the league. Its first task was to decide how to respond to Cassander's inevitable counter-attack.

46.6 *his father's orders*: but were the orders a mistake? Demetrius was very close to securing Greece for the Antigonid cause, but his efforts would start to unravel without his presence, until eventually he had to return urgently (20.100.5).

46.6 *peaceful terms with everyone*: the Rhodians were prosperous traders and preferred peace to war for that reason. They had particularly strong commercial links with Egypt, and served in effect as brokers for Egyptian grain throughout the Aegean.

47.4 *baggage...left in Egypt with Ptolemy*: presumably as a way of ensuring the loyalty of these mercenaries.

47.6 *named Seleucia after him*: Seleucus did indeed build several cities called 'Seleucia' (the two most important were Seleucia Pieria, the port of Antioch, and Seleucia-on-the-Tigris, not far north of Babylon); but the one that replaced Antigonea was Antioch, or Antiocheia-on-the-Orontes, to give it its full name.

47.6 *when we come to the relevant period of time*: this account must have occurred in the lost books. Seleucus' main building years were the 290s.

48.2 *he constructed...a 'city-taker'*: along with all other Greek historians, Diodorus has the habit of saying that a king 'did' something when in reality he 'saw that it was done'. But in this instance the active tense is right, because Demetrius' hobby was engineering.

49.4 *heavy bolt-shooters*: literally, 'catapults capable of firing bolts three spans in length'. The word occurs only twice more (20.83.1, 20.85.3), and has on each occasion been translated 'heavy bolt-shooter'. Three spans is about 66.5 cms, or 26 ins.

50.2 *108 ships*: this seems too low, and emendations have been suggested (see H. Hauben in *Chiron* 6 (1976), 1–5) that would make the figure either 180 or 190, aligning it more closely with the figures of 20.47.1 and with other sources.

50.2 *crews from the places he had captured*: whose loyalty might therefore be suspect.

50.4 *Marsyas, the author of a history of Macedon*: on Marsyas, see p. 540.

50.6 *the boatswains*: 'boatswain' translates *keleustēs* or 'orderer'. He was originally the man who beat the time for the rowers to follow, but by now he had long had others to do the physical work for him, while he was a senior officer, responsible, among other things, for the oarsmen and for transmitting the captain's orders to them.

51.2 *the men on the decks crouched down*: to keep their balance and make themselves small targets.

52.3 *left wing*: Diodorus meant to write 'right wing'.

52.4 *adorned his ships with the stemposts of the enemy ships*: as trophies of victory.

52.6 *over eight thousand soldiers*: as mercenaries, these men were promptly incorporated in the Antigonid army.

53.1 *sailed back to Egypt*: the loss of Cyprus was bad enough for Ptolemy, but he also lost control of the sea, which remained Antigonid for many years.

53.2 *to style himself king*: on the diadem as a sign of kingship, see the note to 17.77.5.

53.2 *the same title and rank*: joint kingship with the favoured son became a common tactic in the early Hellenistic kingdoms. It was a way of trying to ensure a smooth succession, as well as a practical way of managing such vast and complex kingdoms.

53.3 *in all his letters*: he was also the first to style himself king on his coinage.

53.4 *the territory they had originally been allotted*: this is true of Lysimachus, but not of Cassander, who was not involved in either of the two major allotments of territory—at Babylon in 323 (18.3), and at Triparadeisus in 320 (18.39)—and who gained his territory by conquest.

55.3 *lake that lay beside it*: this Hippou Acra is the same as Hippo Diarrhytus, which lay on the coast north-west of Carthage, beyond Utica.

56.3 *their great project*: the liberation of the Greek cities: 20.31.2–5.

57.5 *almost as black as Ethiopians*: to Diodorus 'Ethiopia' means, geographically speaking, the huge desert area south and west of Ammon (17.50.2). He probably thought of it as extending far in both directions, because 'Ethiopian' in Greek just means 'black' (literally 'burnt face'), so Ethiopia was wherever black-skinned people lived.

57.6 *as mentioned in my third book*: there is nothing about this in Book 3 as it stands. This is yet another sign that Diodorus did not revise the final text of the *Library*. Book 7 would be a more natural home for material following the Trojan War, so perhaps the material was in the lost Book 7, in which case Diodorus' only mistake was to have written 'Book 3' instead of 'Book 7'.

57.6 *the same name as one of the towns taken by Agathocles*: see 20.55.3. There was also a third Hippou Acra further east along the coast. The word is Phoenician, although in Greek it could mean 'horse headland'.

58.2 *filled with cats*: the African wildcat, presumably—*Felis silvestris libyca*.

58.4 *we name our children after the gods*: for instance, our very own Diodorus, the 'gift of Zeus'.

61.6 *by means of a stratagem*: as a result of this success, Agathocles postponed his voyage to North Africa.

63.4 *made this fine a cup*: for Agathocles as a potter, see 19.2.7.

63.5 *Potter! Kiln-operator!*: Diodorus' original readers would have immediately caught the snobbery implicit in these words. The 'rather illustrious city' is steeped in upper-class disdain of those who had to work for others, and especially to work indoors by a fire, ruining their bodies by doubling the noonday heat. See, for instance, Xenophon, *On Estate-management* 4.2–3.

68.3 *his affair with his stepmother*: see also 20.33.5.

69.3 *the setting of the Pleiades*: the setting of the Pleiades in November was traditionally taken to be the end of the sailing season (as their rising in spring was its start) and the onset of wintry weather. See also 20.73.3 and 20.74.1.

69.3 *murdered by the soldiers*: ordinary soldiers may have been involved in the murders, but it appears from Polybius, *Histories* 7.2.4 that certain high-ranking individuals were the ringleaders.

69.3 *given Solous to live in*: Solous was a town in Carthaginian-controlled territory in north-west Sicily.

70.3 *a guest-friend of his*: see the note to 16.54.4.

71.2 *broken on the wheel*: the victims were tied to large cartwheels and then beaten with clubs, the gaps between the spokes of the wheel guaranteeing that their bones would be broken.

71.3 *Phalaris' bull*: see 19.108.1. There is a fuller description at Polybius, *Histories* 12.25.

71.5 *soldiers who had deserted to him...to live in*: it is not clear who these deserters were. Perhaps some of the garrison of Egesta had deserted to him. Egesta (or Segesta) soon recovered its original name.

73.1 *Phoenix*: this should be 'Philip'.

73.3 *the setting of the Pleiades*: see the note to 20.69.3. But Antigonus felt he had to persevere, in order to take advantage of Ptolemy's relative weakness after Demetrius' great victory at Salamis.

73.3 *the so-called Pits*: see 16.46.6. The desert is the Sinai desert.

75.4 *Pseudostomon*: the word means 'false mouth', so perhaps the town was founded on a mouth of the Nile delta that had become silted up. Note that although Antigonus is the subject of this sentence, it was Demetrius who was in fact in charge of the fleet. As often with kings, generals, and other potentates, 'He sailed' means 'He had his men sail'.

76.4 *the Pelusiac mouth of the river was in enemy hands*: Antigonus' strategy had been designed to get around this difficulty. Demetrius had been supposed to land beyond Pelusium, thereby forcing Ptolemy to weaken his defences there by withdrawing men to face Demetrius.

76.6 *Ptolemy was extremely pleased at the departure of the enemy*: it is not impossible that it was at this point that Ptolemy began to call himself king, as mentioned by Diodorus at 20.53.3.

76.7 *spear-won territory*: as at 18.43.1. The first invasion was that of Perdiccas, at 18.33–6.

77.3 *Therma and Cephaloedium*: on the north coast of central Sicily.

78.2 *tyranny makes a fine shroud*: the story is repeated by Diodorus from 14.8 and is commonly referred to by other writers. The meaning of the saying is that, since one is going to die anyway, one might as well die as a tyrant.

79.3 *men who speak their minds*: it was a common criticism of democracy that one had to dissemble before the people, because to speak one's mind would get one into trouble.

79.5 *150 talents*: the gold–silver ratio at the time was about 10:1.

80.1 *Sora and Calatia*: this represents an unexpected Samnite irruption into Campania.

80.1 *Silvium*: the town had been captured by the Samnites a couple of years earlier.

80.4 *their farmland*: Anagnia and Frusino were towns of the Hernici, southeast of Rome. Their 'infractions' were to have succumbed to Samnite pressure and taken up arms against Rome. Anagnia lay less than 65 km (40 miles) from Rome.

81.3 *his will regarding the overall disposition of his kingdom*: this contradicts Diodorus' narrative at the start of Book 18, where he assumes that Alexander left no will, and that the Successors had to decide things for themselves. Almost certainly, Alexander left no will, at Rhodes or anywhere else. See A. B. Bosworth, 'Ptolemy and the Will of Alexander', in A. B. Bosworth and E. Baynham (eds), *Alexander the Great in Fact and Fiction* (Oxford: Oxford University Press, 2000), 207–41.

82.1 *ships to join Demetrius' fleet*: this is probably the episode mentioned in 20.46.6.

82.2 *put it under siege*: Rhodes had entered into an alliance with Antigonus in 312 (see 19.77.3). We do not know the terms of the alliance, but it is possible that the Rhodians were infringing it by refusing to help the Antigonid cause and therefore that Antigonus was justified in threatening them. But the problem they faced (as emerges from Diodorus' next sentence) was that they also had an alliance with Ptolemy, which Antigonus was asking them to infringe. On the other hand, Diodorus has just said that Antigonus approached the Rhodians for an alliance now, in 306, so perhaps the 312 alliance had lapsed, having been only a temporary measure.

82.4 *Loryma*: in Caria, on the Anatolian mainland across from Rhodes, and one of the island's mainland possessions. See the note to 20.97.5.

83.2 *shaped like a theatre*: see 19.45.3.

83.3 *close to the city*: to the south of the city, where there was space for a camp.

84.2 *residents or temporary visitors*: in Classical Athens, foreigners were allowed to stay in the city for a month before they were required to register as 'metics' (resident aliens, but literally 'immigrants'). Perhaps the time allowed in Rhodes was longer, so that even temporary foreigners might want to stay and fight.

84.3 *honoured in the theatre at the Dionysia with a panoply*: these and other similar provisions for the treatment of war dead and their families are known from other Greek states, such as Athens and Thasos. The Dionysia, the festival of Dionysus, was used for such purposes in Athens as well, displaying the might and magnanimity of the state.

84.6 *five hundred for a slave*: does this make sense? First, rather large sums of money are involved. Second, why bother with the money? Why not just exchange prisoners? Third, the alleged arrangement would strongly favour the Rhodians, by keeping the number of defenders up, so it is unlikely that Demetrius would have agreed to it.

85.3 *the sturdiest of the lemboi*: a *lembos* was a small, fast galley, usually undecked, with oars at one or two levels.

86.1 *the harbours*: Rhodes had two harbours, the Great Harbour and a smaller one, adjacent to each other on the north-east side of the city. Diodorus does not always make clear which harbour he is talking about.

87.2 *detached the stemposts from the wrecks*: tokens of victory to be dedicated to the gods.

88.3 *the Prytanes*: five Prytanes were elected every six months in Rhodes, to oversee the Council (the members of which were also elected for six months), whose job was to prepare business for the popular assembly and to preside at assembly meetings.

88.3 *before all was lost*: it is puzzling that the rich were not already involved. The Prytanes can only have been asking them for money (to pay, in this instance, for the crews of ships), but Diodorus' account makes it sound as though they crewed some ships themselves. There were not enough of them to do that. It looks as though Diodorus has misunderstood his sources or conflated two episodes.

88.5 *the iron-plated palisade*: this is another way to describe the 'floating palisade' of 20.85.2 and 20.86.3. 'We should probably envision a long boom made of squared logs held together with iron nails and reinforcement plates at the joins between the logs' (Murray, *Age of Titans*, 115).

88.5 *the third contraption*: Diodorus' language implies that there were only three siege engines mounted on ships, but in 20.85.1 there were four, two sheds and two towers. Perhaps there were only three left by now.

90.3 *the Paeligni*: an Italic tribe, and staunch allies of the Samnites. Their neighbours were the Marrucini (19.105.5) to the east, and the Marsi (20.44.8) and Aecli (20.101.5) to the west.

90.3 *the Falernian Fields*: the *Ager Falernus* in northern Campania, exceptionally fertile land.

90.4 *Gaius Gellius*: at *History of Rome* 9.44.13, Livy calls him Statius Gellius. In general, Livy's account of the events of this year is somewhat different from that of Diodorus. Bola is unknown.

90.4 *Serennia*: a mistake for 'Cesennia' (Livy, *History of Rome* 9.44.16), but the town is in any case unidentifiable.

91.2 *a 'city-taker'*: he built a city-taker also for the siege of Salamis (20.48.1–3). There is another description of the current monster in Plutarch, *Demetrius* 21.

91.6 *reduce the impact of the boulders fired by the stone-throwers*: compare the similar devices made by the Tyrians at 17.45.3–4.

92.5 *some truly enormous ships*: we hear of his commissioning 'thirteens', 'fifteens', and 'sixteens' (Plutarch, *Demetrius* 32 and 43). For the designs of the various classes of ship, see Murray, *Age of Titans*.

93.3 *triēmioliae*: see the note to 16.61.4, though these ships are called *triēmioliae*, not just *hēmioliae*. They seem to have had a third half-bank of oars for extra speed.

93.5 *the islands*: the Cyclades, presumably.

93.7 *such a decision by a democracy*: democracies were often charged by their opponents with narrow-minded self-interest and fickleness.

94.3 *captain of the mercenaries*: these are presumably the mercenaries we heard of at 20.88.9.

95.1 *reinforced with iron*: probably in order to stop such a long ram buckling.

96.1 *three hundred thousand artabas of grain*: an *artaba* was an Egyptian dry measure, approximately equal to a *medimnos* (see the note to 17.69.8).

97.5 *their Peraia in Asia*: the Rhodian 'Peraia' (the 'land on the other side') consisted of the towns, villages, and farmland possessed by the Rhodians on the nearby mainland of Asia Minor. Many islands close to coastlines had such a Peraia.

99.3 *keep its revenues*: I take this vague phrase to mean both that they would continue to be allowed to do business even with Antigonid enemies, as they had before, and that they would be untaxed by Antigonus.

100.1 *after the siege had gone on a year*: it may not seem that Diodorus' narrative covers a whole year (and he has no doubt omitted some details he found in his sources), but there were long periods of stalemate, while, for instance, Demetrius built the city-taker, or repaired his machines.

100.3 *sacred ambassadors*: see the note to 19.2.3.

100.3 *honour Ptolemy as a god*: it might have been at this time that Ptolemy took the divine eponym *Sotēr*, Saviour.

100.5 *as his father had wanted*: Antigonus was presumably motivated by the news that the situation in Greece was critical and demanded Demetrius' attention.

100.6 *abandon their friendship with Cassander*: the last time we met the Boeotians, in 20.28.4, they were still honouring the treaty they had made with Antigonus in 19.75.6. Cassander had won them over in the interim, while Demetrius was absent from Greece.

100.6 *an alliance with the Aetolians*: the Antigonids had entered into an alliance with the Aetolians at 19.75.6. Either Diodorus has forgotten this, or the alliance had lapsed in the interim.

100.7 *Spartacus*: more usually spelled 'Spartocus'.

101.3 *the master of the winds*: Aeolus; see especially Homer, *Odyssey* 10. Lipara was the largest of the so-called Aeolian Islands, north of Sicily.

101.3 *a being named Hephaestus*: the name of the god of fire, 'Hephaestus', was often used as a synonym for fire. Agathocles' death is recounted by Diodorus at 21.16.4–6. He was poisoned and then placed on his funeral pyre while still alive.

101.3 *saving their parents at Etna*: in legend, Amphinomus and Anapia were rescuing their parents from an eruption of volcanic Etna, and Hephaestus, whose workshop was said to be inside the mountain, parted the lava flow and allowed them to pass. The spot where this happened was known as 'the Place of the Pious'.

101.5 *peace with each other*: the peace probably left both sides with what they currently possessed—in other words, major gains for the Romans, and major losses for the Samnites.

101.5 *the Aecli*: otherwise known as the Aequi, they occupied a substantial part of the mountains east of Rome. They had been restive for a while, and had inclined to support the Samnites in the war. The Roman campaign against them was particularly brutal, and was certainly a factor in persuading nearby peoples to end the war against Rome; see the next note.

101.5 *an alliance with... and the Marrucini*: a single alliance, because these neighbouring peoples of the Abruzzi region of Italy formed a confederacy.

102.2 *garrisoned by Ptolemaic troops*: see 20.37.1–2.

102.3 *the founder of a city*: it was universal practice for founders of cities to be venerated as heroes—more than human, but less than gods. Within a couple of years, the city had reverted to its original name.

103.1 *its harbours*: Corinth had two harbours: a northern one on the Corinthian Gulf called Lechaeum, and a southern one on the Saronic Gulf called Cenchreae. Cenchreae fell to Cassander at 19.63.4, but it seems that his occupation was only temporary.

103.2 *the Acrocorinth*: the massive acropolis of Corinth; the shrine of Sisyphus, a legendary king of Corinth, was probably situated somewhere on its northern slope, overlooking the town.

103.3 *a guard on the Acrocorinth*: this Antigonid garrison remained for sixty years, until 243.

103.4 *Scyrus*: location unknown.

103.7 *how things stood with Demetrius*: he was close to eliminating Cassander from southern Greece. The roll call of places that fell to him is incomplete in Diodorus; from elsewhere, we can add or infer Argos, much of Argolis, and possibly Elis too.

104.1 *Cleonymus as general*: in an earlier war, the Tarentines had also received help from Sparta: 16.62.4. Tarentum was originally founded by Spartans. It is not clear that the Tarentines were already at war with Rome, or whether they first clashed some years later. Certainly Diodorus does not mention the Romans again in this stretch of narrative. He might have been confused by the fact that after the end of the conflict with the Lucanians, the Tarentines entered into a formal treaty with the Romans, who were allies of the Lucanians. Or he might have been confused by the fact that Cleonymus, at any rate, does seem to have clashed briefly with the Romans, according to Livy (*History of Rome* 10.2).

104.2 *Taenarum in Laconia*: see the first note to 17.108.7.

104.2 *the Messapians*: the Messapians occupied much of the heel of Italy; the Lucanians, who were immediate neighbours of the Tarentines, some of the toe.

105.1 *captured their town*: we do not know what Lucanian town Diodorus means. The location of Triopium is unknown.

105.3 *Cleonymus sailed back to Corcyra with his forces*: Cleonymus continued his career as a cross between a mercenary commander and a brigand for a while before being accepted back in Sparta; in 272 he died in the course of, or as a consequence of, an unsuccessful bid for the Agiad throne which he had launched with the help of Pyrrhus of Epirus. He had expected to gain the throne originally on the death of his father, Cleomenes II, in 309 or 308, but he was a second son, and the Spartans instead chose Areus, the son of Cleomenes' dead eldest son.

106.1 *the Greeks were getting stronger*: as a result of the ejection of his and Polyperchon's garrisons, covered by Diodorus in 20.102–3.

107.2 *he installed a garrison there*: Sigeum was on the coast near Troy, Lampsacus and Parium on the Hellespont.

107.2 *his general, Prepelaus*: since Prepelaus was primarily Cassander's general, it is quite possible that his name has dropped out of the text and should be restored a couple of sentences earlier: Cassander 'sent Prepelaus as general' along with the forces he gave Lysimachus, who was clearly the commander-in-chief of the anti-Antigonid forces.

107.4 *come over to his side*: this was not Docimus' first act of treachery: see 19.16.3–4. There was a town in Phrygia, not far north of Synnada, called Docimeum, which was presumably his headquarters.

107.4 *repatriated the hundred Rhodian hostages*: see 20.99.3.

108.5 *Seleucus...from the upper satrapies*: Seleucus was bringing not just troops, but hundreds of war elephants—well worth waiting for.

109.2 *to winter quarters*: in the section of his *Stratagems* called 'On Escaping from Difficult Situations', Frontinus says (1.5.11) that Lysimachus' men filled in sections of the trench with rubble to aid their escape.

109.7 *Amastris...the ruler of the city*: the Persian princess Amastris became Craterus' wife at the Susa mass wedding (see 17.107.6). Then she married Dionysius, tyrant of Heraclea Pontica, and when he died (see 20.77.1), she acted as regent for her underage sons. Before Lysimachus' marriage to Amastris, the powerful city had been aligned with Antigonus, so this was a major coup.

110.1 *initiated before the appointed day*: for the Eleusinian Mysteries, see H. Bowden, *Mystery Cults of the Ancient World* (Princeton: Princeton University Press, 2010). Diodorus' account of this episode is vague. Demetrius' chief Athenian flatterer, Stratocles (20.46.2), arranged for the three-stage initiation to happen all at once by dint of renaming the current month twice. Bizarre though this may sound, it should at least be noted that renaming months was not uncommon in cultures that had a 360-day year, where extra months had to be added every few years.

110.2 *occupied the pass*: at Thermopylae.

110.2 *the harbour of Larisa*: this is not the famous Thessalian Larisa, but Larisa Cremaste, on the mainland just north of the north-western tip of Euboea, in Achaea Phthiotis.

110.3 *Thebes*: again, this is not the famous Thebes—Demetrius was not in Boeotia—but Phthiotic Thebes, and the other places mentioned are all in Achaea Phthiotis. Dium and Orchomenus are not otherwise known, but they were villages or small towns, and we do not know the names of every village or small town in ancient Greece, so it is better not to emend the text. Cassander was trying to strengthen Phthiotic Thebes by incorporating more of its outlying villages. It was far from unknown for recent Macedonian kings, since the time of Philip II, to merge towns, moving populations around. For the topic in general, see Boehm, *City and Empire*.

111.3 *revert to its former alignment*: that is, to resume membership of the Antigonid empire.

111.3 *Sanctuary of the Chalcedonians*: probably the same place as Hieron at 19.73.6 (though see the note there); *hieron* means 'sanctuary'.

111.4 *Mithridates... was killed at Cius in Mysia*: presumably by Antigonid agents. For Mithridates II of Cius, see also 16.90.2, with the note.

111.4 *Cius and [. . .]*: the transmitted text has 'Arrine', but there is no such place in or near Mysia, and no emendation is very plausible. We have to accept that we do not know the name of the other town.

111.4 *ruled over Cappadocia and Paphlagonia for thirty-six years*: Mithridates III of Cius, probably the son of Mithridates II (some sources say his father was Ariobarzanes), was probably a member of the Iranian noble family that had ruled Cappadocia for quite a while, and so came to inherit the throne of Cappadocia-cum-Paphlagonia as well. He used this as a foundation for carving out a new kingdom, that of Pontus, so he is known not just as Mithridates III of Cius, but as Mithridates I Ctistes (the Founder) of Pontus.

113.1 *all the cities of Coele Syria*: Ptolemy was helping his allies—and helping himself, since he always wanted to possess Phoenicia and Coele Syria—by attacking Antigonid interests in the Near East.

113.5 *the next book*: very little of the final twenty books of Diodorus' history survives. We have only excerpts preserved by other authors and an occasional longer paraphrase.

TEXTUAL NOTES

NOTED here are the places where I have adopted a different reading from the Teubner text. They are marked in the translation by an obelus (†).

16.10.2   The words added by Fischer do not seem strictly necessary.

16.10.5   Reading Συρακοσίων with Reiske.

16.13.3   Reading οὐ πολλὰς with the best MSS.

16.14.2   Retaining ἐπανελθὼν with the MSS.

16.21.4   There is no need to change the text from τοῖς στρατιώταις to τοὺς στρατιώτας.

16.26.5   Reading πάντας (Capps) for παντός.

16.27.1   I suggest ἀπανηναμένης (from ἀπαναίνομαι), and then omit ὅτι ταῦτά ἐστι τα πάτρια, which must have been added when ἀπανηναμένης became corrupted to ἀποκριναμένης, which demanded a ὅτι clause.

16.33.1   Reading ἀναθεῖναι after ζημιώματος (Post), with a comma, making what follows a genitive absolute clause.

16.35.4   Reading σπουδῇ πάσῃ (Capps).

16.45.9   Reading ἐξεπολιόρκησαν (Dindorf).

16.46.8   Reading τοῦ Σπαρτιάτου (Hertlein).

16.52.9   Reading Ζερείαν (Meritt/Wade-Gery/McGregor).

16.56.6   Adding φασὶ with Fischer.

16.59.2   Adding ἱκανὸν with Fischer.

16.60.1   Reading εἴκοσι τριῶν with Stroth. Demosthenes 19.123 (*On the Dishonest Embassy*) makes it twenty-two, and Pausanias twenty-one (*Description of Greece* 10.3).

16.61.4   Reading ὁμολογίας (Sherman).

16.65.5   There is no real need for Fischer's added δεῖν.

16.67.2   There is no mention of cavalry in this list: something like the 'two thousand horse' I have supplied has dropped out of the text.

16.76.1   Omitting αὐχένος with Fischer and other editors.

16.79.2   Omitting τὴν with Fischer.

16.84.1   Diodorus or his source (or a scribe) wrote 'Charondas' by mistake.

16.90.1   Deleting τοὺς τυράννους καταλύσας καὶ, which is not found in the best MSS.

16.92.3   Reading θεῶν (Schmidt).

17.4.9   I suggest εἰωθότως.

17.7.6   Reading συνεστραμμένον with Hertlein.

17.17.4 Adding καὶ with Milns (*JHS* 1966).

17.17.6 Reading Ἀρίστανδρος with Freinsheim.

17.20.6 I suggest ξίφος instead of ξυστόν. Alexander's lance is already
         broken (and he would not have carried two). Plutarch
         (*Alexander* 16.8) says that by this stage Alexander had drawn his
         sword.

17.27.1 Reading ῥοπὴν with Madvig.

17.32.2 Omitting Fischer's added Κιλικίας. The pass was most com-
         monly known simply as the Gates.

17.36.1 Reading μεγαλεῖα with Goukowsky.

17.36.1 Reading παρώρμηντο with Goukowsky. Then there is no need for
         Fischer's apparent lacuna.

17.49.5 Reading διεξεπέρασαν with Post.

17.50.3 I read στρατιωτῶν for the nonsensical τόπων.

17.51.2 Deleting τῆς φωνῆς with Goukowsky.

17.53.2 The words συνήρμοστο . . . δρέπανα add nothing and are simply
         confusing; they are best omitted, I believe, as a later gloss that
         has crept into the text.

17.60.3 Retaining the MSS position for αἰεί.

17.61.1 Reading Μαζαῖος for Δαρεῖος, with Goukowsky; the mistake
         might be Diodorus', however.

17.65.3 Reading ἀρίστων with RX.

17.65.3 Reading μείονος with Reiske.

17.75.7 Reading ἐμφέρειαν with Richards.

17.78.2 It is pointless to try to guess the missing name, as Fischer and
         others have done.

17.78.4 Reading Ἀρείας with Goukowsky.

17.81.1 Reading Ἀριάσπους with Goukowsky.

17.82.1 It seems a bit cavalier, given the variety of ways in which
         Diodorus introduces the successive years, and his general incon-
         sistency, to add the details of the stade winner (Cleiton of
         Macedon), as Fischer does.

17.82.3 Reading συνηγμένην (Hertlein).

17.83.2 Reading ἄλλην πόλιν . . . ἀπέχουσαν with F.

17.85.7 The received text has 'abandoned', which makes little sense:
         we want a word for 'withdrew' or 'recalled'. 'Abandoned' has
         somehow bled up the text from its use a couple of lines later.
         This is probably a scribal fault, not Diodorus', so I have
         corrected it.

17.94.4 Reading παραποταμίαν with F.

17.97.3 Reading νεόντων (Post).

17.105.7 Reading φορείων with Goukowsky.
17.114.1 Reading μάλιστα instead of ταῖς, with Reiske.
18.3.3 Reading Πίθωνι δὲ instead of τούτων δὲ, after Madvig.
18.3.3 I read ἔταξεν.
18.4.5 Reading Κύρρῳ with Gronovius.
18.4.7 Reading ἐπιλαβόμενος . . . διαβολῆς with Stephanus.
18.6.2 Reading πέντε ποταμῶν with Goukowsky.
18.7.5 There seems no particularly good reason to change 'Lipodorus' to 'Letodorus'.
18.10.1 There appears to be a lacuna, though it is anybody's guess what it contained.
18.12.2 Adding πεζοὺς with Goukowsky.
18.13.2 Transposing this sentence, with Goukowsky, from its place in the MSS a few lines later (before 'But just when Antipater . . .').
18.17.2 Reading πολλῶν with Post.
18.17.8 Reading μετὰ τὴν τῶν ἰδίων στρατιωτῶν ἐπάνοδον with Goukowsky.
18.18.5: Retaining the MSS' δισμυρίων.
18.21.2 Reading πρὸ δὲ τῆς τούτων παρουσίας with Rhodomann.
18.26.3 The sense is plain, but the word for 'chest' or 'container' has dropped out, and the word order suggested by Fischer in his apparatus criticus is preferable. Possibly, however, the word ἁρμόζον is a corruption of whatever neuter word is needed for 'chest' or 'container'.
18.26.5 Reading θρᾶνος with Ussing.
18.35.1 Reading τοῦ πόρου with Wurm.
18.35.1 Reading ἐκδεχομένους . . . καὶ πραΰνοντας (Rhodomann, Goukowsky).
18.41.7 Reading περιγενομένους with Richards.
18.43.1 Reading γῆν instead of τινα, with Goukowsky.
18.46.5 I read μεθ' ἡμέρας τινὰς.
18.52.4 I read παρασκευάσασθαι for the MSS πειρᾶσθαι.
18.52.8 Reading Κύμην πολιορκήσας (Madvig).
18.65.2 Reading <συμφερ>όντως, as suggested by Fischer.
18.71.4 Reading ἀνακαθήραντος with F.
18.75.2 A scribe—or perhaps Diodorus himself—carelessly wrote 'Antipater' here.
19.6.3 Adding τῆς with Dindorf.
19.15.3 Retaining ἵστατο with the MSS.
19.19.2 Reading Κάλωνος with MS F, to bring the text into line with Polybius' and Strabo's 'Cal[l]onitis'.
19.22.2 I suggest κλισίας instead of θυσίας.
19.27.2 Reading πλῆθος (Post) for the certainly erroneous βάθος.

19.29.2   I suggest πτέρυγος—an easy enough emendation, but a *hapax* in this sense, as far as I am aware.

19.29.5   Reading, with Bizière, ὑπῆρχον τούτοις ἴσαι καὶ παράλληλοι.

19.29.6   Retaining περὶ with the MSS.

19.30.8   Reading ἐγγυτέρας with MS F.

19.38.6   Reading ἐπ' ἀκέραια with Fischer (in the apparatus).

19.41.3   Reading δι' οὖ with Wesseling.

19.46.5   Reading ἱππεῖς δὲ πεντακοσίους with Dindorf.

19.58.2   There is a short gap in the text, which would have included the amount of barley.

19.58.3   I have transposed the last two sentences.

19.71.4   Reading πολυτελευόμενος with MS R.

19.74.1   Reading τιτρώσκειν with Reiske.

19.79.4   Some name seems to have dropped out of the text.

19.79.4   Reading καὶ Στασίοικον τὸν τῶν Μαριέων with Rhodomann.

19.94.7   Reading ἀργιλλώδους with MS F.

19.95.3   Omitting Kallenberg's added ἐωθινῆς.

19.103.4   Reading ἐξ Ἀθηνῶν, τὰ μὲν with Geer.

19.106.2   I read κατήρτισαν.

20.4.6   Reading ὑπομενεῖν with Dindorf.

20.11.1   How ἡμίσους got into the text is puzzling, but we must read some word for 'left' or 'the other'.

20.11.3   Adding πεζῆς with Dindorf.

20.11.5   Reading τοιαῦτα with Hertlein.

20.23.3   I read διάσπασας.

20.26.3   Reading πολεμίαν with Burger.

20.29.1   The text is corrupt and lacunose, but must originally have been something like what I have translated, following a suggestion by Post.

20.44.1   The verb is missing from the transmitted Greek text.

20.48.3   Adding ἐλαττόνων with Fischer.

20.48.6   Reading, with Fischer, πάντες οἰστοὺς πυρσοφόρους.

20.56.3   Reading τῶν Καρχηδονίων τοὺς φρουροῦντας with Reiske.

20.59.4   Reading ἐν τῇ πόλει with Dindorf.

20.60.4   Reading ἐφήδρευε ἔν τινι (Holm) πόλει προσδεχόμενος (Reiske).

20.70.3   The meaning of this sentence is clear, but the text is corrupt.

20.73.3   Retaining ἀπιδεῖν with the MSS.

20.75.2   Reading ῥέπειν instead of εἶναι, with Capps.

20.76.2   Reading τινὰ instead of ἅμα, with Rhodomann.

20.76.5   Reading παρακαλῶν with Capps.

20.85.1   Reading διαβεβηκυίας κατεζευγμένων with Geer.

20.85.1   Retaining ἴσων with the MSS.

20.87.2   Reading ἄγνοιαν with Geer.

20.90.2   Reading παράδοσιν with Rhodomann.

20.93.5   Reading τεχνῖται τῶν ἀξιολόγων πρὸς βέλη καὶ καταπελταφέται τῶν ἐμπειρίᾳ διαφερόντων ἕνδεκα with F.

20.95.1   Reading εἶχε γὰρ ἑκατέρα δοκὸν with Reiske.

20.102.1 Transferring ἢ ἐπ' αὐτὸν πορεύοιτο τὸν Κάσανδρον, with Madvig, and then reading Μακεδονίαν instead of ἡγεμονίαν, with Reiske. These seem the minimal changes to get a comprehensible sentence.

20.107.4 Reading ἐλευθέρους with Reiske.

20.113.3 Reading ἔνιοι (Capps) τῶν παρὰ Λυσιμάχῳ στρατιωτῶν αὐτομολήσαντες ἦλθον (Rhodomann).

GLOSSARY

Acropolis or 'citadel'. The high point of a city, used especially for defence and worship.

Agora the civic centre, marketplace, and administrative heart of an ancient Greek town.

Amphictyonic Council the council formed of *amphiktyones*, 'neighbouring states', with the job of looking after the interests of the sanctuary of Apollo at Delphi. As a league of states, its decisions often had political weight.

Archon literally 'ruler' or 'leader'. The title was used for senior officials of many states. In Archaic and Classical Athens, nine Archons were chosen each year, and the 'Eponymous Archon' gave his name to the year for dating purposes. Diodorus drew on a list of these Athenian Archons to structure his work.

Assembly the chief executive organ of democratic Athens and other democracies, with lesser powers under oligarchies and monarchies.

Attica the hinterland of the city of Athens.

Barbarian the word often means little more than 'non-Greek', but the Greeks did also attribute savagery and lack of culture to such people, even to the highly civilized Persians and Carthaginians, so that they were 'barbarians' in our sense of the word as well.

Bodyguard apart from its obvious meaning, Alexander formed an elite group of seven Bodyguards, who were the senior marshals of the empire.

Cadmea, the the acropolis of Thebes, named after the city's legendary founder, Cadmus of Phoenicia.

Chiliarch literally, 'commander of a thousand'. In the Achaemenid empire the chiliarch was the commander of the Apple-bearers, the royal bodyguard. Alexander adopted this system, appointing Hephaestion his chiliarch, and the last chiliarch we hear of is Cassander, appointed chiliarch to Polyperchon. The office then fell into disuse. See Diodorus' remarks at the end of 18.48.

Consul two consuls were elected in Republican Rome every year as its leaders, with both military and domestic political responsibilities.

Cubit a cubit (the distance from the elbow to the tip of the middle finger) was considered to be 1.5 feet, or about 44.5 cm (17.5 inches) in our terms.

Dedication everyone from kings to poor people gave things to sanctuaries, in thanks, out of sheer devotion, to celebrate a victory in war or sport, or to fulfil a vow. The best of these dedications were extremely valuable, and this is the main way in which sanctuaries—especially international ones, such as Delphi and Olympia—became very wealthy.

Drachma *see* **Talent**

Dynast any sole ruler, but the word is chiefly used of baronial rulers of fiefdoms rather than kingdoms.

Forum the Roman equivalent of an agora.

Friend (with a capital F) a formal title for those closest to the king in the Persian court or the courts of the Hellenistic kings and tyrants. It should be noted, however, that in ancient Greek 'friend' and 'Friend' are identical, so that it is a matter of guesswork for a translator to decide when to use an initial capital. I have erred on the side of caution.

Hegemony literally 'leadership', but used especially where one state subordinates its allies to itself by political and economic means, and by the real or implied threat of military intervention, while allowing them formally to retain their autonomy.

Hoplite a heavy-armed Greek foot soldier, typically armed with a thrusting spear and a short sword, and protected by various pieces of armour and, above all, a large shield.

Hypaspist the Hypaspists were an elite infantry unit, armed more like Greek hoplites than Macedonian phalangites. However, Diodorus also uses the word for a 'foot guard' (17.99) and for a member of the Household Guard (17.110; 20.34). By the time of the Successors they were known as the Silver Shields regiment.

Kinsmen the so-called Kinsmen of the Persian court were not always relatives by blood or marriage of the King; it was also an honorary post, and they formed an elite regiment. The honorary title of 'Kinsman' was later perpetuated in both the Seleucid and Ptolemaic courts.

Lacedaemonians inhabitants of Lacedaemon, otherwise known as Laconia, the territory that included Sparta, where the Spartiates, the full citizens, lived, but also all the other towns and villages inhabited by the so-called *Perioikoi* ('those who live around us'), who had lesser rights than Spartiates. The political entity constituted by 'the Lacedaemonians' (as 'the Athenians' constituted Athens) is also referred to as 'Sparta' or 'the Spartans'.

Libya the Greek name for the North African coastline as a whole, other than Egypt; not the modern country of Libya.

Mna *see* **Talent**

Paean a solemn hymn in praise of a god, or a song of triumph.

Peltast a foot soldier with lighter arms and armour than a hoplite (q.v.), originally named after his crescent-shaped shield, a *pelta*, but also referring to variously armed, sub-hoplite soldiers. The Antigonids had an elite corps of 'peltasts', numbering three thousand (19.19.4).

Phalanx a rectangular formation, usually with a much greater front than depth, of closely packed infantry troops. Diodorus also sometimes uses 'the phalanx' to mean 'the infantry' or 'the heavy infantry'.

Plenipotentiary someone—a diplomat, general, or politician—is plenipotentiary if he is answerable to no one but himself, not even to the political authorities back home.

Plethron *see* **Stade**

Royal Pages it was a custom of the Macedonian court, learnt from the Persians, that the sons of high-ranking Macedonians joined the royal court in Pella during their teenage years, to serve as the king's attendants, and to be the friends and future Friends of the heir apparent, who was educated with them.

Satrap a governor of a province (a satrapy) of the Persian empire. The word is derived from the Old Persian *khshathrapavan*, 'Protector of the Kingdom'.

Siceliot a Sicilian Greek.

Spartiate a full Spartan citizen, a member of the Spartan landowning elite.

Stade 1 stade = 6 plethra = 600 feet (a Greek foot was much the same length as ours). In our terms, 1 plethron = *c*.30 metres (32.5 yards); 1 stade = *c*.177.5 metres (194 yards). So 10 stades = *c*.1.75 km (a little over a mile); 50 stades = *c*.8.75 km (*c*.5.5 miles); 100 stades = *c*.17.5 km (*c*.10.8 miles).

Symposium a highly ritualized drinking party for the elite, generally taking place after a banquet or to celebrate a special occasion.

Talent Greek coinage was not on the whole fiduciary, but was worth its weight. Hence measures of weight are at the same time monetary measures. 1 talent = 60 mnas = 6,000 drachmas = 36,000 obols. A talent weighed almost 26 kg (*c*.57.25 lbs), and a mna weighed over 430 grams (over 15 oz), so these were measures of value, but were too heavy to be coined weights. A drachma weighed over 4.25 grams (*c*.0.15 oz). Wages are extremely difficult to estimate, but a labourer might count himself lucky if he made 2 or 3 drachmas a day, and a man was considered very well-off if he was worth 4 or 5 talents.

Trireme from the end of the sixth century, the most common type of ancient Greek warship. Light and manoeuvrable, and propelled by three banks of oarsmen on either side, it was used largely as a guided missile to ram and disable enemy ships.

Triumph in Rome, a magnificent parade in honour of a significant military victory, in which prominent captives and booty were displayed before being dedicated in temples or handed over to the state. It was considered one of the high points of a Roman military career.

Trophy a token of victory, set up on the battlefield at the point where the enemy turned to flight. The Greek word for 'trophy' is cognate with the word for 'turn'. A trophy was often a stake of wood hung with weaponry taken from the enemy and made to look vaguely humanoid. This was a Greek practice, but not a Macedonian one.

Upper satrapies in the empires of the Persians, Alexander, and his Successors, the far eastern satrapies, such as Bactria, were called the 'upper' satrapies. They were 'upper' because they were inland, and for the Greeks one always travelled 'up' from the coast.

Watch it appears from 19.38.3 that the Macedonians were using a three-watch system, so, however many hours of darkness there were (which of course varied according to the time of year) were divided into three.

APPENDIX 1

DIODORUS' SOURCES FOR BOOKS 16–20

SINCE Diodorus was a compiler rather than much of an original writer, it would be good to know which earlier historians were his sources for Books 16–20. In these books Diodorus was writing about events that took place around 250 years earlier than his lifetime. Under these circumstances, a historian is only as good as his sources—or as his discriminating use of those sources.

The following historians are the most likely sources followed by Diodorus in Books 16–20. I should stress that these are mostly scholarly guesses, since in our books Diodorus rarely names his sources, and at the same time we hardly ever have a fragment of the original sources that corresponds to Diodorus' text and so can act as a control. I should also stress that there may be a number of lesser sources that we simply cannot identify. What follows should be regarded as a list of Diodorus' main sources for Books 16–20, with the work of several others lurking untraceably below the surface.

Furthermore, we cannot always be sure whether Diodorus read every one of these historians himself, or whether in some cases their views came to him with another of his predecessors as intermediary. So he may not have read Ptolemy's own account of Alexander's eastern expedition, rather than Cleitarchus' or Diyllus' paraphrase of Ptolemy. This less thorough approach was typical of the Greek historians. As for Diodorus' chronographic indicators—Olympiads, Athenian Archons, and Roman consuls—it is likely that he found all of these together in a single chronographic source, based ultimately on the work of Apollodorus of Athens (see 1.5.1), and that this source was a little-known writer called Castor of Rhodes, an older contemporary of Diodorus. Castor or a similar writer is probably also the source of a lot of Diodorus' more incidental information: notices about the reigns of monarchs, the beginnings and endings of wars, and the foundation of cities.

AGATHARCHIDES OF CNIDUS (second century). Very little survives of Agatharchides' historical work (as distinct from his account of an expedition to explore the Red Sea, of which more has survived), but he wrote a universal history covering both European and Asian affairs, with a strong geographical and ethnographical bent that would have attracted Diodorus. We know that Diodorus consulted him for Book 3 (see 3.11.2), and he very likely lies behind some stretches of other books as well, including Books 16–20.

ANAXIMENES OF LAMPSACUS (fourth century) wrote extensively on
   Greek and Macedonian history. His mention at 15.89.3 makes it likely
   that he was one of Diodorus' sources. He started his histories in mythological time, but he was not a universal historian in geographical terms;
   he was interested only in Greek history.

ATHANIS (OR ATHANAS) OF SYRACUSE (fourth century), an almost
   unknown historian to us, was the continuator of the Sicilian history of
   Philistus (below). His mention at 15.94.4 suggests that he was consulted
   by Diodorus for Sicilian history.

CALLISTHENES OF OLYNTHUS (died 327). The nephew of the philosopher Aristotle, Callisthenes accompanied Alexander the Great on his
   expedition, until he was executed for treason. He wrote not just about
   Alexander (whom he greatly admired—until they fell out), but also
   a monograph on the Third Sacred War and a ten-book *History of the
   Greeks* down to 356 BCE. Diodorus' direct use of him was probably
   largely limited to the Sacred War (16.23–40, 16.56–64).

CLEITARCHUS OF ALEXANDRIA (probably mid-third century). The
   so-called 'vulgate' tradition on Alexander the Great's eastern expedition,
   consisting of Diodorus, Curtius, the Metz Epitome, and Justin, is held
   to have largely followed Cleitarchus.[1] His twelve-book history was
   extremely popular, and was probably largely based on information
   acquired by autopsy and interview, leavened by Cleitarchus' love of
   a good story. He did not personally accompany Alexander on his eastern
   expedition, but he drew on several historians who did.[2] Very few fragments remain, but he was very likely Diodorus' major source for the
   eastern expedition in Book 17, and therefore the nature of his work can
   be glimpsed through Diodorus' reworking.

DEMODAMAS OF MILETUS (third/second century). Demodamas is little
   more than a name to us, but he was a close associate of Seleucus, and some
   of the pro-Seleucid material of Book 19 may derive ultimately from him.

DEMOPHILUS OF CYME (later fourth century). Very little is known about
   this historian, the son of a more famous father, Ephorus. Diodorus tells
   us (16.14.3) that he completed his father's history of Greece by writing
   or finishing the final, thirtieth book on the Third Sacred War, so it seems
   likely that Diodorus consulted him for this war.

[1] See V. Parker, 'Source-critical Reflections on Cleitarchus' Work', in P. Wheatley and
R. Hannah (eds), *Alexander and His Successors: Essays from the Antipodes* (Claremont,
CA: Regina, 2009), 28–55.
[2] Certainly Callisthenes, Onesicritus, and Nearchus; possibly Aristobulus and Megasthenes
too. The question is whether Diodorus consulted any of these authors directly, or only via
Cleitarchus.

DEMOSTHENES OF ATHENS (384–322). Some of Demosthenes' work clearly lies behind the account of the weeks before the battle of Chaeronea (17.84–5), but this was probably already paraphrased in one of Diodorus' main sources, perhaps Diyllus.

DINON OF COLOPHON (early fourth century). Dinon was the father of Cleitarchus, and wrote, apparently in a romantic vein, a three-part account of Persian history. His work may underlie some of Diodorus' history of the Persians, especially as filtered through Cleitarchus. Ctesias of Cnidus and Heracleides of Cyme also wrote *Persica* in the fourth century, but Diodorus, or rather Cleitarchus, does not seem to have made use of them.

DIYLLUS OF ATHENS (early third century). Diyllus wrote a universal history (including the western Greeks) starting with the Third Sacred War in 357 and ending with the death of Cassander in 297 (16.14.5)—that is, he deliberately started where Ephorus' history ended (16.76.6). He may have been Diodorus' main source for Philip's and Alexander's dealings with the Greeks, and an additional source for Sicilian history as well.

DURIS OF SAMOS (*c*.340–*c*.260). Duris was the tyrant of Samos (succeeding to his father's position), but also found time to write a history of Macedon in about twenty-three books, a favourable biography of Agathocles of Syracuse (Duris may have been born in exile on Sicily), and a history of the island Samos. He has a reputation for having focused on sensational events, but that is probably an accidental result of his fragments having been preserved by authors who were attracted to sensationalism. It is unclear whether Diodorus used him directly, but his work may lie behind some of the Macedonian history that Diodorus recounts, the account of Alexander's dealings with the Greeks in Book 17, and the account of Agathocles' career in Books 19 and 20. He was a moralizing historian, emphasizing especially the deleterious effects of luxury and all forms of immoderation.

EPHORUS OF CYME (*c*.400–330). Ephorus was Diodorus' main source for much of *The Library*, for all of early Greek history until early in Book 16. Polybius calls him the first universal historian (*Histories* 5.33.1), though Diodorus criticizes him for having omitted the mythological period (4.1.2–3; see also 1.3.2–3). He started with the return of the Heraclidae (supposedly the first properly historical event) and at the time of his death had brought his history down to 357, with drafts of some future sections completed as well, down to 340. His son Demophilus (see above) completed the work by covering the Third Sacred War, which Ephorus had not yet written up. Despite being a universal historian, Ephorus did not make use of chronographic indicators such as Athenian

Archons or Roman consuls, but divided time up by generations, and structured his work by alleged synchronicities between events of one part of the world and another. He had access to sound primary sources and approached them with a good, critical eye. He was the first to divide his own work into books (rather than leaving that to later editors) and to write a separate preface for each book, a practice followed by Diodorus. Ephorus' presence is slight in Books 16–20, except for some of the material on Philip II's early life and career, the material on Dion of Syracuse, and perhaps some Persian history.

HIERONYMUS OF CARDIA (354–250). Hieronymus first served Eumenes (who was a fellow citizen and probably a relative), and then, after Eumenes' death, the Antigonids: Antigonus Monophthalmus (for whom, *inter alia*, he supervised the extraction of asphalt from the Dead Sea), Demetrius Poliorcetes (for whom, *inter alia*, he governed the Greek city of Thebes), and Antigonus Gonatas, the first king of a stable Macedon. The unique and often eyewitness perspective he gained thereby makes the loss of his *History of the Successors* particularly painful. His history started with the death of Alexander the Great in 323 and went up to the death of Pyrrhus in 272. Diodorus relied primarily on him for his account of the Successors in Books 18–20, and the quality of that account is generally held to be due to the superior quality of Hieronymus' work. He seems to have been a sound and entertaining historian, a good writer and a good researcher. He emphasized the personal motives underlying historical events, but his moralizing was low-key compared with other historians.

MARSYAS OF PELLA (fourth century). The mention of Marsyas at 20.50.4 makes it likely that his *History of Macedon* was a source for Diodorus, but too little remains of the work for us to be sure.

PHILISTUS OF SYRACUSE (*c*.430–356). Philistus' *History of Sicily* covered the island's mythical origins and took the history down to the reign of Dionysius II, so he may well have been one of Diodorus' sources for Sicilian history.

PTOLEMY OF EGYPT (367–282). The first Macedonian ruler of Egypt and founder of the Ptolemaic dynasty wrote his own account of Alexander's eastern campaigns, in which he played up his part in them. The passages in Diodorus' work which eulogize Ptolemy's character (17.103.6–8; 18.14.1; 18.28.3–6; 18.33.3–4; 18.34.4; 18.86.3; 19.55.5–56.1; 19.86.3–5) depend ultimately on Ptolemy's own work, but probably as filtered to Diodorus through another historian, and Cleitarchus is the best candidate, since he was patronized by Ptolemy.

ROMAN HISTORIANS. In our books, Diodorus' accounts of Roman history are usually no more than brief notices of the kind he would have found in his annalistic source or sources (e.g. 16.31.7; 16.36.4; 16.45.8; 19.10.1; 19.105.5). Sometimes, they are more thorough, however (19.72.3–9; 19.76; 19.101; 20.35–6; 20.80; 20.90.3–4), and the question is from where Diodorus got his information. But early Roman historians tend to be little more than names to us, and it is impossible to tell exactly who Diodorus' source or sources might have been. The chief possibilities are: Quintus Fabius Pictor (late third century), Lucius Cincius Alimentus (early second century), Gaius Acilius (mid second century), Aulus Postumius Albinus (mid second century), Gnaeus Gellius (late second century), and Lucius Cassius Hemina (late second century).

THEOPOMPUS OF CHIOS (378–320). Among other works, he wrote a twelve-book *Greek History*, which was a continuation of the *History* of Thucydides down to 394, and a fifty-eight-book *History of Philip*, which, despite its title, set out to be a universal history with Philip II as its core. He was given to Herodotean digressions on topics such as ethnography and geography, and wrote in a studied, rhetorical style, which was very popular in its day. He was known for exploring the psychology and motivations of his protagonists. He was a moralizing historian, who expressly vilified statesmen and generals for their wrongdoing. Since his *History of Philip* is mentioned at 16.3.7, Diodorus probably made use of him for his account of Philip's career, especially for negative stories such as 16.87.1, since Theopompus seems to have played up Philip's flaws. Diodorus may have used him also for Sicilian affairs in Book 16 (see 16.71.3). He also wrote a monograph on the Third Sacred War—*On the Funds Stolen from Delphi*—and may have influenced Diodorus' account of the war.

TIMAEUS OF TAUROMENIUM (*c*.350–*c*.260). Timaeus was exiled by Agathocles from his native city (which his father had refounded: 16.7.1) and spent much of his life in Athens, researching and writing. He paid close attention to chronology, and tried to reconcile the lists of Olympiads with those of Ephors and kings of Sparta, priestesses of Hera at Argos, and Athenian Archons. His major work was a *History of Sicily* in thirty-eight books, up to the year 264. In this book, he also covered Carthaginian affairs and gave a potted history of early Rome, whose rise to power he was one of the earliest historians to note. The *History of Sicily* became the standard work in the ancient world on the history of the western Greeks. He was the first explicitly to assess the worth of his predecessors' efforts as historians. His work is referred to twice by Diodorus in our books (20.79.5; 20.89.5), making it clear that he was one of Diodorus' sources for Sicilian history; in particular, Diodorus probably combined Duris' favourable account of Agathocles with Timaeus' hostile version. Timaeus was a moralizing historian, who used a full palette of techniques to get his points across.

ZENO OF RHODES (late third/early second centuries). Zeno is an obscure historian to us, but some of his work is commonly thought to lie behind Diodorus' account of the siege of Rhodes (20.82–8; 20.91–100).

I should repeat that this is all speculation. Since the work of these historians survives only in fragments, and sometimes in very few fragments, we cannot be absolutely sure that or to what extent Diodorus drew on them. Nevertheless, scholarly consensus has settled on them as Diodorus' likely sources for Books 16–20. The cases for Cleitarchus, Timaeus, and Hieronymus are pretty solid, but identifying the other sources involves a greater or lesser degree of guesswork. But even with these identifications, the difficulty is in deciding how much belongs to the original and how much to Diodorus.

APPENDIX 2

ROMAN CONSULS OF BOOKS 16–20

HERE I compare the names given by Diodorus with those in the definitive list of Roman magistrates: T. R. S. Broughton, *The Magistrates of the Roman Republic*, vol. 1 (New York: American Philological Association, 1951). Broughton's list was drawn up from a variety of sources, both literary and inscriptional, including Diodorus. But Broughton followed the dating system invented by M. Terentius Varro, a contemporary of Diodorus, whereas (for the books translated in this volume, at any rate) Diodorus followed a different system, the origin of which is unknown. Diodorus is several years ahead of Varro (a varying number of years at different points), so that, for example, his 356/5 is Broughton's 359.

Diodorus	Broughton
360/59	
Cn. Genucius &	Cn. Genucius Aventinensis &
L. Aemilius	L. Aemilius Mamercinus
359/8	
Q. Servilius &	Q. Servilius Ahala &
Q. Genucius	L. Genucius Aventinensis
358/7	
C. Licinius &	C. Licinius Calvus &
C. Sulpicius	C. Sulpicius Peticus
357/6	
M. Fabius &	M. Fabius Ambustus &
C. Publius	C. Poetelius Libo Visolus
356/5	
M. Publius Laenates &	M. Popillius Laenas &
Cn. Maemilius	Cn. Manlius Capitolinus
Imperiosus	Imperiosus

Diodorus	Broughton
355/4	
M. Fabius &	C. Fabius Ambustus &
C. Plautius	C. Plautius Proculus
354/3	
C. Marcius &	C. Marcius Rutilus &
Cn. Manlius	Cn. Manlius Capitolinus
	Imperiosus
353/2	
M. Publius &	M. Popillius Laenas &
M. Fabius	M. Fabius Ambustus
352/1	
C. Sulpicius &	C. Sulpicius Peticus &
M. Valerius	M. Valerius Poplicola
351/0	
M. Fabius &	M. Fabius Ambustus &
T. Quinctius	T. Quinctius Poenus Capitolinus
	Crispinus
350/49	
M. Valerius &	M. Valerius Poplicola &
C. Sulpicius	C. Sulpicius Peticus
349/8	
M. Gaius &	C. Marcius Rutilus &
P. Valerius	P. Valerius Poplicola
348/7	
C. Sulpicius &	C. Sulpicius Peticus &
C. Quinctius	T. Quinctius Poenus Capitolinus
	Crispinus
347/6	
C. Cornelius &	L. Cornelius Scipio &
M. Popilius	M. Popillius Laenas
346/5	
M. Aemilius &	L. Furius Camillus &
T. Quinctius	Ap. Claudius Crassus Inregillensis

Diodorus	Broughton
345/4	
M. Fabius &	M. Valerius Corvus &
Ser. Sulpicius[1]	M. Popillius Laenas
344/3	
M. Valerius &	C. Plautius Venno &
M. Popilius	T. Manlius Imperiosus Torquatus
343/2	
C. Plautius &	M. Valerius Corvus &
T. Manlius	C. Poetilius Libo Visolus
342/1	
M. Valerius &	M. Fabius Dorsuo &
Cn. Publius	Ser. Sulpicius Camerinus Rufus
341/0	
C. Marcius &	C. Marcius Rutilus &
T. Manlius Torquatus	T. Manlius Imperiosus Torquatus
340/39	
M. Valerius &	M. Valerius Corvus &
A. Cornelius	A. Cornelius Cossus Arvina
339/8	
Q. Servilius &	Q. Servilius Ahala &
M. Rutilius	C. Marcius Rutilus
338/7	
L. Aemilius &	L. Aemilius Mamercinus Privernas &
C. Plautius	C. Plautius Venno
337/6	
T. Manlius Torquatus &	T. Manlius Imperiosus Torquatus &
P. Decius	P. Decius Mus
336/5	
Q. Publius &	Q. Publilius Philo &
Ti. Aemilius Mamercus	Ti. Aemilius Mamercinus

---

[1] These two consuls belong three years later, under 342/1. If they are placed there, and each of the next three Diodorus entries is moved up one year, correspondence with Broughton is restored.

Diodorus	Broughton
335/4	
L. Furius &	L. Furius Camillus &
C. Manius	C. Maenius
334/3	
C. Sulpicius &	C. Sulpicius Longus &
L. Papirius[2]	P. Aelius Paetus
333/2	
K. Valerius &	K. Duillius &
L. Papirius	L. Papirius Crassus
332/1	
M. Atilius &	M. Atilius Regulus Calenus &
M. Valerius	M. Valerius Corvus
331/0	
S. Postumius &	S. Postumius Albinus &
T. Veturius	T. Veturius Calvinus
330/29	
C. Domitius &	Cn. Domitius Calvinus &
A. Cornelius	A. Cornelius Cossus Arvina
329/8	
C. Valerius &	C. Valerius Potitus &
M. Claudius	M. Claudius Marcellus
328/7	
L. Platius &	L. Plautius Venno &
L. Papirius	L. Papirius Crassus
327/6	
missing	L. Aemilius Mamercinus Privernas &
	C. Plautius Decianus

---

[2] L. Papirius was one of the consuls for the following year, not this one.

Diodorus	Broughton
326/5	
P. Cornelius &	P. Cornelius Scapula &
A. Postumius	P. Plautius Proculus[3]
325/4	
L. Cornelius &	L. Cornelius Lentulus &
Q. Popillius	Q. Publilius Philo
324/3	
C. Publius &	C. Poetelius Libi Visolus &
Papirius	L. Papirius Cursor
323/2	
L. Frurius &	L. Furius Camillus &
D. Junius	D. Junius Brutus Scaeva
322/1	
C. Sulpicius &	C. Sulpicius Longus &
C. Aelius	Q. Aulius Cerretanus
321/0	
missing	Q. Fabius Maximus Rullianus &
	L. Fulvius Curvus
320/19	
missing	T. Veturius Calvinus &
	S. Postumius Albinus
319/18	
Q. Popillius &	L. Papirius Cursor &
Q. Publilius	Q. Publilius Philo
318/17	
Q. Aelius &	Q. Aulius Cerretanus &
L. Papirius	L. Papirius Cursor
317/16	
L. Plautius &	L. Plautius Venno &
M'. Fulvius	M'. Folius Flaccinator

[3] The consul names for this year are not absolutely certain, but even so Diodorus' 'A. Postumius' seems out of place.

Diodorus	Broughton
316/15	
C. Junius &	C. Junius Bubulcus Brutus &
Q. Aemilius	Q. Aemilius Barbula
315/14	
S. Nautius &	S. Nautius Rutilus &
M. Popillius	M. Popillius Laenas
314/13	
L. Papirius &	L. Papirius Cursor &
Q. Publius	Q. Publilius Philo
313/12	
M. Publius &	M. Poetelius Libo &
C. Sulpicius	C. Sulpicius Longus
312/11	
L. Papirius &	L. Papirius Cursor &
C. Junius	C. Junius Bubulcus Brutus
311/10	
M. Valerius &	M. Valerius Maximus &
P. Decius	P. Decius Mus
310/9	
C. Julius &	C. Junius Bubulcus Brutus &
Q. Aemilius	Q. Aemilius Barbula
309/8	
Q. Fabius &	Q. Fabius Maximus Rullianus &
C. Marcius	C. Marcius Rutilus
308/7	
P. Decius &	P. Decius Mus &
Q. Fabius	Q. Fabius Maximus Rullianus
307/6	
Ap. Claudius &	Ap. Claudius Caecus &
L. Volumnius	L. Volumnius Flamma Violens
306/5	
Q. Marcius &	Q. Marcius Tremulus &
P. Cornelius	P. Cornelius Arvina

Diodorus	Broughton
305/4	
L. Postumius &	L. Postumius Megellus &
Ti. Minucius	Ti. Minucius Augurinus
304/3	
P. Sempronius &	P. Sempronius Sophus &
P. Sulpicius	P. Sulpicius Saverrio
303/2	
Ser. Cornelius &	Ser. Cornelius Lentulus &
L. Genucius	L. Genucius Aventinensis
302/1	
M. Livius &	M. Livius Denter &
M. Aemilius	M. Aemilius Paullus

INDEX OF PROPER NAMES

A **bold** letter by a place name indicates that it has an entry on one of the maps on pp. xlv–l. Square brackets around a page number indicate that the relevant name belongs there, but Diodorus' text erroneously has a different name. I have omitted from this index names which are merely addenda to a main personal name, such as insignificant patronymics and place names used merely for identification ('Menes of Pella'). Nor does the index include the names of the Athenian Archons, Roman consuls, and Olympic victors by which Diodorus marks each year.

Cyrene, Cyrenaica, F, 121, 195–7, 308,
    364–7, 369
Cyrrhus, B, 181
Cyrus the Great of Persia, 138, 146
Cyzicus, Cyzicenes, D, 86, 219–20

Dactyls, 86
Daedalus (legendary artisan), 11
Damas, 242–3
Damascus, E, 106, 324
Damis, 236, 294
Damophilus, 407
Damoteles, 412
Danaus, 122
Darius III of Persia, 85, 96, 97, 98, 99,
    103–13, 119–20, 124–34, 136,
    139–43, 148, 168, 174, 178, 180,
    192, 420
Daunia, 248
Deidameia, 271
Deinias, 270, 315
Deinocrates (Phocian), 49
Deinocrates (Syracusan), 247, 326–7,
    355–7, 379–80, 383, 385, 394–6,
    403–4
Delos (island), A, 181
Delphi, -ians, A, B, 3, 15, 21–6, 29, 50–1,
    55–6, 67, 78, 88–9, 174, 181, 241
Demades, 74, 93, 193–4, 217
Demaratus, 142
Demeas, 217
Demeter (goddess), 58, 88, 245, 337
Demetrias (Sicyon), 415
Demetrius (herald), 76
Demetrius of Phalerum, 239, 298, 308,
    353, 369–70
Demetrius Poliorcetes, 199, 265, 275,
    291, 299, 309–13, 315, 318, 321–5,
    348, 369–76, 391–3, 397–403,
    405–18, 420–2
Demophilus of Cyme (historian), 15
Demophilus (general), 327, 379
Demophon, 159
Demosthenes, 48, 72–3, 82, 83–4, 87,
    92–3, 169, 190
Derieis, 298
Deucalion, 285
Dicaeopolis (Egesta), 390
Dimnus, 144–5
Diocles (Syracusan law-maker), 70
Diocles (Syracusan oligarch), 245

Dion of Syracuse, 8, 10–14, 16–20, 29, 33
Dionysia (festival), 32, 399
Dionysius (garrison commander), 298,
    369–70
Dionysius of Heraclea Pontica, 75, 394
Dionysius I of Syracuse, 8, 33, 50–1, 62,
    385, 395
Dionysius II of Syracuse, 7–8, 10–15,
    16–18, 40, 59–62
Dionysus (god), 139, 167, 279, 406
Diophantus, 42
Dioscourides, 293, 299
Dioxippus, 161–2
Diphilus, 317
Dirce (spring), 89
Dium (Achaea Phthiotis), 421
Dium (Macedon), B, 93, 181
Diyllus of Athens (historian), 15, 65–6
Docimus, 215, 254–5, 305, 418
Dodona, B, 181
Dolopians, B, 27, 187
Doris, Dorians, B, 27, 30, 187
Dorylaeum, D, 419
Drangiane, F, 144, 146, 166, 180, 211,
    253
Drypetis, 168
Dyme, -aeans, A, 297

Ecbatana, F, 132, 145, 171, 257, 278, 280
Echecrates, 25
Echetla, 357
Echinades (islands), 191
Ecnomus (hill), 327, 330
Ecregma, 295
Egesta, -ans, C, 390
Egypt, -ians, E, F, 36–46, 107, 112, 118,
    120, 121–4, 180, 181, 183, 190,
    196–7, 200, 202, 203, 206–9, 211,
    214, 223, 287, 288, 290, 299, 308,
    309, 313, 317, 318, 323–4, 328,
    348, 353, 362, 370, 371, 372–3,
    376, 381, 391–4, 397, 407, 409,
    415, 418, 423
Elatea, B, 71–2
Eleusis, A, 420
Elis, Eleans, A, C, 55, 83, 87, 174, 188,
    296, 314
Embisarus/Sasibisares, 152, 154
Encheleans, 286
Engyum, 62–3
Enna, C, 357

The Oxford World's Classics Website

www.worldsclassics.co.uk

- Browse the full range of Oxford World's Classics online
- Sign up for our monthly e-alert to receive information on new titles
- Read extracts from the Introductions
- Listen to our editors and translators talk about the world's greatest literature with our Oxford World's Classics audio guides
- Join the conversation, follow us on Twitter at OWC_Oxford
- Teachers and lecturers can order inspection copies quickly and simply via our website

www.worldsclassics.co.uk

American Literature

British and Irish Literature

Children's Literature

Classics and Ancient Literature

Colonial Literature

Eastern Literature

European Literature

Gothic Literature

History

Medieval Literature

Oxford English Drama

Philosophy

Poetry

Politics

Religion

The Oxford Shakespeare

A complete list of Oxford World's Classics, including Authors in Context, Oxford English Drama, and the Oxford Shakespeare, is available in the UK from the Marketing Services Department, Oxford University Press, Great Clarendon Street, Oxford OX2 6DP, or visit the website at www.oup.com/uk/worldsclassics.

In the USA, visit www.oup.com/us/owc for a complete title list.

Oxford World's Classics are available from all good bookshops. In case of difficulty, customers in the UK should contact Oxford University Press Bookshop, 116 High Street, Oxford OX1 4BR.